# PRAISE FOR *AN UN-AMERICAN LIFE*

"A thrilling cloak and dagger story of espionage, stolen secrets, dual identities, smuggled messages, treachery and murder. A psychological drama of the anguish of a man who felt that love of his country was a higher moral duty than fidelity to his friends. This definitive biography by Sam Tanenhaus is a fast narrative, a moving portrayal of spiritual suffering, and has a moral for our time: honour those who speak unpopular truths."

**Tina Brown, former editor of *Vanity Fair* and *The New Yorker***

"A sensitive biography of a complicated man in a troubled time. Much more than the life story of Whittaker Chambers, Sam Tanenhaus's book is a major contribution both to the history of the Cold War in America and to the history of intellectuals and political engagement in the twentieth century."

**Tony Judt, author of *Postwar: A History of Europe Since 1945***

"Tanenhaus has dissolved many myths and made Whittaker Chambers a necessary journey for his once cocksure accusers."

**Alistair Cooke**

"Sam Tanenhaus has convincingly closed the case of Whittaker Chambers and Alger Hiss, and thus put to rest one of the most persistent (and repellent) myths of the fellow-travelling Left."

**Christopher Hitchens**

"Remarkable... the kind of writing that can keep you propped up against your pillow late at night."

**Richard Bernstein,** *The New York Times*


"Magisterial... An epic tale, rich in pity and terror, with a great theme: the human cost of political morality.... Here is biography at its best."

**Steven Koch,** *Wall Street Journal*


"Marvellous... One of the best books ever written about the Communist experience... As compelling as a good novel."

**Hilton Kramer,** *The New Criterion*


"Riveting... As compelling to read as any espionage thriller... The result is a monumental work of scholarship which benefits from a vast amount of new documentation."

**Mark Falcoff,** *Commentary*


"One of the most dazzling biographies in recent history"

*USA TODAY*


"Clear, trenchant and well paced... Mr Tanenhaus's admirable biography goes as far as one can reasonably expect in unravelling the puzzle... A serious and absorbing work."

**Arthur Schlesinger Jr,** *The New York Times Book Review*


"The story is told as imaginatively as a novelist might tell it, though the restraints of history are scrupulously observed... Tanenhaus is masterful at compressed eloquence."

**William F Buckley Jr,** *First Things*

Also by Sam Tanenhaus

*Literature Unbound: A Guide for the Common Reader*

# An Un-American Life:
## The Case of Whittaker Chambers

# AN UN-AMERICAN LIFE

*THE CASE OF WHITTAKER CHAMBERS*

# *SAM TANENHAUS*

OLD STREET PUBLISHING
LONDON

Copyright © 1997 by Sam Tanenhaus

First published in the United Kingdom in 2007 by
Old Street Publishing Ltd
14 Bowling Green Lane, London EC1R 0BD
ISBN13: 978-1-905847-07-5

Printed by Creative Print and Design, Wales

First published in the United States with the title WHITTAKER CHAMBERS:
A BIOGRAPHY by Random House, Inc., New York,
and simultaneously in Canada by Random House of Canada Limited, Toronto.

Except where marked otherwise, all images are reproduced by kind permission of
*The New York Times.*

*Book design by Bernard Klein*

*Title page photo*: Whittaker Chambers testifies before HUAC on August 25
1948 - "Confrontation Day" - while Alger Hiss looks on  (far left).

*To the memory of*
*Joseph Tanenhaus*
*(1924–1980)*
*and to*
*Kathy and Lydia*

*"An intellectual hatred is the worst."*

. . . he went his way,
Down among the Lost People like Dante, down
　　To the stinking fosse where the injured
　　Lead the ugly life of the rejected.

And showed us what evil is: not as we thought
Deeds that must be punished, but our lack of faith,
　　Our dishonest mood of denial,
　　The concupiscence of the oppressor.

And if something of the autocratic pose,
The paternal strictness he distrusted, still
　　Clung to his utterance and features,
　　It was a protective imitation

For one who lived among enemies so long:
If often he was wrong and at times absurd,
　　To us he is no more a person
　　Now but a whole climate of opinion. . . .

—W. H. Auden, "In Memory of Sigmund Freud"[1]

# CONTENTS

# INTRODUCTION

The idea for this book came to me in late 1988, a time when the cold war had reached its ceremonial endgame: Mikhail Gorbachev acknowledging the autonomy of peoples long after they had liberated themselves, valiant students halting tank columns in Tiananmen Square.

It made for impressive, if occasionally hollow, spectacle, and it inspired a chorus of sweeping pronouncements in the United States. "'Peace' seems to be breaking out in many regions of the world," Francis Fukuyama exulted in "The End of History," the period's signature manifesto, published in the summer of 1989, six months before the Berlin Wall came down. At the time it was still possible to think that "the developed world," having writhed through a century-long "paroxysm of ideological violence, as liberalism contended first with the remnants of absolutism, then bolshevism and fascism, and finally an updated Marxism that threatened to lead to the ultimate apocalypse of nuclear war," had suddenly achieved "an unabashed victory of economic and political liberalism."

It didn't take long for the gyre to wobble back onto its dependably blood-soaked course, pushed along by fresh gusts of ideological violence and absolutism. But for a brief period it really did seem that history, if it had not actually ended, had at least momentarily stopped, particularly for baby boomers like Fukuyama (and me), born in the 1950s. The cold war was the only geopolitical reality we knew—or could seriously contemplate—raised as we were on the eschatology of the nuclear "option," as the experts called it, the same experts who drew up mathematical formulas to explain how many cities we could afford to have vaporized, and which ones, in the event of a "showdown."

Every child knew the "ultimate apocalypse" was eminently thinkable. We all had watched footage of blossoming mushroom clouds and fictive images of a finger pushing a button. It was thinkable for a more literal reason: it had already happened, twice, in Hiroshima and Nagasaki. And we knew who had dropped the bombs. It is not a coincidence that in the blackest of black cold war comedies, *Dr. Strangelove*, it is a homespun American general, not a sinister Russian, who strikes the nuclear match.

In such a climate, politics unfolded as constant low-grade emergency, with occasional oscillations and pulse-quickening alarms: the Bay of Pigs, the Cuban Missile Crisis, the planes shot out of the sky. We were calmly assured, after each bleak episode, that all was being efficiently managed. And perhaps it was. But the stresses showed, most obviously in the near normalization of violence in the 1960s, much of it televised: racial battles in city after city, armed militants storming campus buildings. The first presidential election I followed closely, in 1968, when I was twelve, included two assassinations and a police riot in Chicago.

This was the steep cost of "the twilight struggle," in John. F. Kennedy's lugubrious phrase, the contest between the planet's only remaining great powers, the United States and the Soviet Union, lethally well-matched colossi, each geographically vast, each primed, after many years on the sidelines, to dominate the global game. Each also espoused a purifying doctrine, the Soviets' derived from Marx by way of Lenin, the Americans' derived from . . . what exactly? Here was the trouble. A nation so new and so devout in its pluralism could offer no theology but itself, the miracle of its existence, in all its superabundance, the same theology our leaders offer today. In those days too our presidents, each in his turn the "leader of the free world," told us that we were innocent of imperial ambition and desired only that other peoples be free—free, that is, to become like us; this applied not only to the "captive nations" behind the Iron Curtain, but also to the left-leaning social democracies of corrupt Europe. The battle was moral, for "hearts and minds." Of course this was what the Soviets, though the vocabulary was different, claimed about *their* utopian project.

So in 1988, my question was not why there had been a cold war, but rather how it had come to assume its curious shape. These thoughts led me to George Orwell, the truest prophet of the "twilight struggle," whose *Nineteen Eighty-Four*, published in the incubatory stage of the cold war, had foretold much of what was to come: the all-seeing television eye, the creepy language (Orwell could easily have coined "balance of terror," "limited nuclear war," "Mutually Assured Destruction"), the proxy wars staged in distant regions of the globe (Vietnam, Afghanistan, the Congo—*the Congo?*), the orchestrated paranoia. It was all the more impressive because Orwell's strength, as everyone knows, was his literalism, his English "common sense." He was not an especially imaginative writer. Yet he had seen with matchless clarity where things were headed, and this in turn suggested his novel had been as much a feat of reportorial study as of invention: his starting point had been a concrete set of facts. But which facts? I grew obsessed with the idea of rewriting *Nineteen Eighty-Four*, in reverse. Like Orwell I would begin with the year 1948 (a simple transposition of digits had yielded his hypothetical future date) but my account would be factual. It would describe what had actually happened that year. There was no shortage of events to choose from: the Berlin blockade, the Communist coup in Czechoslovakia, the advances of Mao's Red Army, the formation of Korea's "Democratic Republic," the disintegration of governments in Greece and Belgium, and all the rest.

Except my history had to take place in America, where the cold war—one side of it anyway—had sprung into being. Also I preferred an event or sequence of events that could be related narratively and on a human scale. And so I found myself examining the case of Alger Hiss, the senior diplomat who in the summer of 1948 had been accused on the floor of Congress, more specifically by the House Committee on Un-American Activities (HUAC) of being a Soviet agent and then had stood trial (twice) for lying about it. From the opening days of congressional testimony up through Hiss's perjury conviction, in January 1950, the event had attained the scope of a great political trial. There had been a clash of ideas and worldviews, moments of genuine surprise and reversal. And there had been serious consequences. The case had initiated the Red hunts (or "witch hunts") of the early 1950s, which themselves mirrored postwar purges in Czechoslovakia and Hungary, though of course the outcome in America had been much milder. Political figures like Rudolf Slánský and László Rajk were branded Titoist "spies" when they dared resist Stalin's clenching grip and then were rushed through mock trials and summarily executed.

In the U.S. the purge had been bloodless. Well, almost. The "atom spies," Julius and Ethel Rosenberg, were killed—an appalling and unwarranted fate, to be sure, but one the defendants consciously chose, when plea-bargains were available. Even so the scent of blood had hung in the air. But not in the Hiss trials. There was much posturing, along with naked displays of opportunism, during the congressional hearings,

but the trials were models of restraint. Even Hiss's sentence was surpass-
ingly mild: five years for perjury in a minimum-security prison in Pennsylvania. He was released sixteen months ahead of schedule, a better man
for the experience by his own account, and he lived to the age of 92.
The very ordinariness of this outcome—and Hiss's continued presence
as a hero-victim of the left—felt right for the story I wanted to tell. It
suggested that the case had been absorbed into the larger narrative of
cold-war America.

But there were complications. For one, there was strong evidence that
Hiss, unlike Slánský and Rajk, really had been a spy (though I was prepared to conclude otherwise, once I began my own in-depth examination of the case). This didn't bother me terribly much. What, exactly,
did guilt mean in the first years of the cold war? Besides, a guilty man is
often more interesting than an innocent one. There was also the sugges-
tive arc of Hiss's public life, the familiar tale of a rapid upward climb—
triumph at Johns Hopkins University, then at Harvard Law, secretary to
Supreme Court giant Oliver Wendell Holmes, State Department man-
darin, president of the Carnegie Endowment for International Peace at
age 42—followed by a terrible fall. And his private life was rich in misery and shame. He had grown up in Baltimore in conditions of shabby
gentility, his family well established but in decline. There were two brutal suicides (Hiss's father and sister) plus alcoholism (in the Prohibition
period, when liquor could kill). Hiss, the survivor, had borne this suffering stoically, but the wounds were deep. Though a gentle man, he
now and then revealed his contempt for the bluestockings among whom
he had been reared, the "horrible old women of Baltimore." More
telling, at the peak of the Moscow trials he had observed, admiringly, of
Stalin, "he plays for keeps." His most impressive trait, the one outward
clue to the Bolshevik within, was his discipline. It had seen him through
much.

Yet this same discipline made Hiss, finally, uninteresting, as was glar-
ingly evident during the HUAC hearings. One could understand why
he tenaciously maintained his innocence and wriggled out, insofar as he
could, from under the mounting evidence. What rankled was his refusal
to bring even a hint of imagination to his role. In the tensest moments
of the hearings—moments that came as close as any such ritualized event
ever can to offering authentic revelation—Hiss refused, time and again,
to declare himself, to say who he was and what he really stood for.
Instead, retreating behind the boyish grin and well-tailored suits, he took
refuge in hedged lawyerly answers, in hair-splitting qualifications, and

murky evasions. He was a "flat" rather than "round" character, whose single idea of how to meet the signal crisis in his life was to pose as a Gilbert and Sullivan parody of the civil servant, in almost comical defiance of the truth, for it was well known that Hiss had belonged to the most radical faction of the New Deal in its most experimental phase, when it had included burgeoning leftists enrolled in Communist "study groups" or "cells." So common was this knowledge that when Hiss was girding for his first HUAC appearance, John Foster Dulles, his sponsor at the Carnegie Endowment and the most conservative of men (later Secretary of State under President Eisenhower), counseled Hiss to admit he'd flirted with radicalism in his youth, like so many others, but had since outgrown it. Hiss, rejecting this advice, instead feigned wide-eyed innocence, testifying not only that he had not been a Communist but, absurdly—with no trace of irony— that he'd not *known* any Communists. This was not simply the overstatement of a "guilty" man. It was a reverse instance of the abject confessions made by Bolsheviks who had wilted before Stalin a decade before. As they had owned up to crimes they had never dreamed of, so Hiss prostrated himself before his inquisitors, falsifying his past and disguising his actual beliefs. It was impossible not to see in this performance the careerism that had served him so well in his "other" life.

If there was a British equivalent to Hiss it was the Cambridge spies. Like him they were at once audacious and craven, and their radicalism, like his, was bound up with the resentments and antagonisms not of the proletariat but of the social-climbing middle class. The parallels were clear enough to one of the Cambridge Five, Donald Maclean, who reportedly confessed to Cyril Connolly, "I am the English Hiss." Orwell, again, had grasped this phenomenon at its root. "It was only *after* the Soviet regime became unmistakably totalitarian that English intellectuals, in large numbers, began to show an interest in it," he had written in the mid 1940s. And, he was certain, they were impelled by a "secret wish: the wish to destroy the old, equalitarian version of Socialism and usher in a hierarchical society where the intellectual can at last get his hands on the whip." The romance of the proletariat, in other words, faded before ambitions fed by the private history of hidden injuries and accumulated abasements. And it is no less true today: The intellectual left still nurtures the dream of the whip handle, just as the educated right dreams of the day when the intelligentsia will be the first to feel the lash.

But if Hiss disappointed, his accuser, Whittaker Chambers, did not. To reread transcripts of the hearings and the trials—as well as contemporary reportage, including Alistair Cooke's tour de force, *A Generation on Trial*—is to be startled by the almost mesmeric force Chambers exerted in his role of reluctant informer. This was partly because, in addition to being the prosecution's chief, and on key matters, its sole witness, Chambers was also, in the language of the day, a "self-confessed Communist," a courier for the Soviet spy network who still seemed morally trapped within the nimbus of his crimes. That such a man existed in the flesh and, what was more, had come tumbling into view from the gilded pinnacle of the Time-Life Building in Rockefeller Center, was itself a remarkable fact at a time when the home-grown "Communist menace" still consisted, in the public mind, of immigrant Jews or shadowy figures like the Comintern official Gerhart Eisler, who had sneaked out of the country, aboard a liner headed for Poland, while awaiting trial in New York. Whittaker Chambers was one of the few American Communists his countrymen had laid eyes on, and a curious specimen he was, with his risibly WASPY name, the toad-like somnolence of his physical being, the cadaverous-looking dark suit too long in the sleeves, the wry half-smile, verging at times on a smirk, hinting at arcane, hideous truths available to him alone.

Strange that such a man had been a Communist spy, stranger still that he was an "old-stock" American and also an intellectual—indeed much more of one in the traditional humanistic sense than Hiss. A gifted literary man and largely self-taught linguist, Chambers had been a published poet in his twenties, had translated Heinrich Mann and Franz Werfel from the German and mastered French sufficiently well to have been commissioned to translate the last volume of Proust. When FBI interrogators showed him the final report they had written after grilling him for many months, Chambers had scrawled on the last of its many pages the concluding line of *The Inferno* (*E quindi uscimmo a riveder le stelle*). "He spoke Gipsy!" his long-time friend Meyer Schapiro, the great art historian, told me in 1990, the astonishment still fresh.

Not that this earned Chambers much respect. It is almost impossible to convey the robustness of Chambers-hatred when I began writing this book, nearly thirty years after his death and forty years after the Hiss verdict. Though few remembered the details of the great case, many still had a vivid picture of Chambers, the turncoat and snitch. They blamed him for the rise of Richard Nixon, who as a thirty-five-year-old "freshman" congressman ingeniously stage-managed the HUAC hearings, and also of Senator Joseph McCarthy, whose first carnal bleats—"I have here in my hand a list of 205," etc — came fifteen days after Hiss's sentencing in the winter of 1950.

I had doubts about Whittaker Chambers, too. I was aware of him chiefly because of my longstanding interest in the intellectual world of the 1930s-50s. Many of the period's best writers had known him, but few had anything good to say about him. Saul Bellow once wittily remarked that Chambers had done more public harm as the culture editor of *Time* than as the accuser of Alger Hiss—a judgment colored, no doubt, by Chambers's having rather hilariously dismissed him one or two days into a film reviewing stint at *Time* magazine in 1943 when Bellow was a postulant freelancer, recommended for the job by their common friend James Agee. (In later years Bellow often related this incident, with retrospective delight, and a version of it appears, in veiled form, in his novel *The Victim.)*

Chambers's relationship with another major figure, Lionel Trilling, was more complicated and ambiguous. The two had a history dating back many years, beginning with their days together at Columbia University in the 1920s when both were undergraduate contributors to the campus literary magazine. Chambers was the more mature writer (as Trilling readily conceded; the mentor they shared, the poet Mark Van Doren, agreed). But he also burned with extra-literary hungers. He was, Trilling later recalled, "the first person I ever knew whose commitment to radical politics was meant to be definitive of his whole moral being, the controlling element of his existence." And there was a shocking physical emblem of his Otherness, his gruesomely decayed teeth (not fixed till he got to *Time;* they would provide a source of absurdist byplay during the Hiss confrontation). "That desolated mouth was the perfect insigne of Chambers's moral authority," Trilling wrote. "It annihilated the hygienic American present—only a serf could have such a mouth, or some student in a visored cap who sat in his Moscow garret and thought of nothing save the moment when he would toss the fatal canister into the barouche of the Grand Duke."

The two reconnected in the 1930s when Chambers, after some years in the "open" Communist Party, joined its conspiratorial underground, and was doing industrial espionage, while Trilling, safely nestled in the outer orbit of fellow-travelers, observed Chambers's revolutionary escapades with mingled amusement and awe. *The Middle of the Journey* *(*1947), Trilling's penetrating novel about the 1930s Left, includes a character modeled on Chambers— a Communist defector shunned in New York intellectual circles by his former acquaintances when he reemerges from the Soviet underground, precisely as Chambers had been shunned when he quit the Party in 1938. A decade later, when the Hiss case went to trial, one of Hiss's lawyers, scouring literary Manhattan for witnesses who might impugn Chambers's character, approached Trilling but was sent away with the words, "Whittaker Chambers is a man of honor." In his last years Trilling seemed embarrassed by this remark and studiously put distance between himself and Chambers, explaining that, yes, he had known Chambers for many years, and yes, he believed he had told the truth about Hiss, but Trilling and Chambers, of course, had not ever been "friends." In fact, the two had been close enough for Chambers to sound out Trilling's wife, Diana, herself a formidable writer and critic, for "secret work" in 1933. "I knew that I was not going to do what he asked of me," Diana Trilling later wrote. "Yet I was enormously flattered that he thought me capable of such an assignment and I was ashamed to refuse him. . . . I felt greatly complimented."

Here then was the truth about the intellectuals and Chambers. They admired him even as they recoiled from him. They were *engagé*; he was thoroughly enrolled in the revolution—and preparing for the moment when he would be summoned forth to play a historic role, the role, as it happened, of witness, or scourge. It was one for which he was superbly cast, with his gravid air of fatalism, of persecution and guilt, of tormented secrecy and penitential disclosure. Even so the charges he made against Hiss (and others) came forth reluctantly. And, more remarkable still, he perjured himself repeatedly on Hiss's behalf, until Hiss, in a ghastly miscalculation, dared him to produce evidence that would substantiate his charges.

That Chambers's disclosures were truthful we now know with certainty, confirmed as they were by documents released from Soviet and American intelligence archives in the 1990s, cited in this book. And very few now seriously argue that Chambers's testimony was inaccurate in any meaningful way.

Today Chambers compels new interest, because of his second historic role, as a principal founder of modern American conservatism. In fact there were hints of it in his *Time* period, for example in his historical fable, "The Ghosts on the Roof," published in March 1945, a month after the Yalta summit. At the time the Big Three accord was almost universally praised, and an enfeebled Roosevelt (weeks away from death) had gone before Congress to summarize all that had been won. But the clear victor, plainly, was Stalin, still a wartime ally and a hero to many. In Chambers's analysis, whimsically put in the mouths of the murdered

royal "ghosts" of the 1917 revolution, Stalin was the latest and most audacious of Russian czars, "greater than Rurik! greater than Peter! For
Peter conquered only in the name of a limited class. But Stalin embodies the international social revolution. That is the mighty new device of
power politics which he has developed for blowing up other countries
from within."

Chambers the Cassandra could be heard also at key moments in the
Hiss case—most memorably when he and Hiss were at last brought
together publicly, and Chambers was asked (by Nixon) about rumors
that his accusations arose from some obscure personal animus (involving,
it was speculated, both mental illness and homosexuality). Rather than
attack his attackers, Chambers accepted the burden of moral guilt and
recast it in the rhetoric of high sacrifice: "The story has spread that in
testifying against Mr. Hiss I am working out some old grudge, or
motives of revenge or hatred. I do not hate Mr. Hiss. We were close
friends, but we are caught in a tragedy of history. Mr. Hiss represents the
concealed enemy against which we all are fighting, and I am fighting. I
have testified against him with remorse and pity, but in a moment of historic jeopardy in which this nation now stands, so help me God I could
not do otherwise."

It was classic Chambers down to the echo of Martin Luther ("*ich kann
nicht anders*"), fraught with suppressed melodrama. In one sense he was
not an intellectual at all. He was not a systematic thinker, in contrast with
his friend James Burnham, the ex-Trotskyist reborn as right-wing sage
whose analysis of modern bureaucracy, *The Managerial Revolution,* was a
source text for Orwell, and whose aggressive "rollback" doctrine provided the theoretical basis for today's preemptive "war on terror." What
Chambers had was imagination. No one ever spun cold war poetry as he
did, reams of it, first in *Time* and then in his memoir, *Witness.* He was the
first great technician of the new era's magnificent cant. At the time very
few saw this. Rather, they noticed the cant, but not the magnificence,
partly because Chambers's tone was distinctly old-fashioned. Though
steeped in the Modernists, he was untouched by them. His models were
St. Augustine, Victor Hugo, above all Dostoevsky. And his preferred
contemporaries were the ideologues-philosophes Koestler (a reciprocal
admirer), Malraux (ditto), and Camus. When I began serious work on
this book and sent letters to writers who might have known him, the
most telling reply came from Czeslaw Milosz, who as it happened, had
not met Chambers. Still, he wrote, "I have always felt great sympathy for
him and thought about his tragic life. He suffered much . . . and was

excluded from the circle of people worthy of having their hands shaken." The only full acknowledgment Chambers received in his life-time came in the spring of 1959, two years before his death. In the sum-mer he traveled to Europe at the urging of Koestler, who arranged for him to meet Manès Sperber, the great Galician novelist (and ex-Com-munist) and introduced him to Margarete Buber-Neumann, the daugh-ter-in-law of Martin Buber and friend of Milena Jesenská, beloved of Kafka (the two women had been together at the Nazi death camp in Ravensbrück). "So there we sat and talked," Chambers wrote in a let-ter to a friend. "Then, we realized that, of our particular breed, the old activists, we are almost the only survivors." It is fitting that of all Cham-bers's English contemporaries it should have been Rebecca West, herself driven by ideological furies, who deemed *Witness*, published in 1952, one of the great modern autobiographies, "so just and so massive in its resuscitation of the past."

Written in the immediate aftermath of the Hiss case at the urging of James Agee, *Witness* is indeed a towering memoir, but it is more urgently a spiritual manifesto and a call to moral arms. Chambers had completed the arc of disenchantment—his last shreds of patience with the left destroyed by the Hiss case—and now stood defiantly on the right. He was all for America now, but betrayed himself in his prose, which as Arthur Schlesinger, Jr. noted in a review, exuded "an un-American . . . or at least un-Anglo-Saxon intensity." This did not lessen its impact on postwar conservatism—among the movement's writers but also among its political figures, keenly responsive to Chambers's distillations of large ideas into quotable oratory and to his oddly sonorous invocations of the apocalypse. The Second World War, he wrote, "simplified the balance of forces in the world by reducing them to two." This was more or less what most Americans, including American intellectuals, believed in 1952. But Chambers typically went further, embracing a Manichean dualism, though even this had its Marxist angle. As a practiced revolutionary he knew—as did Lenin and Trotsky, for all their fealty to "historical materialism"— that political movements rise to power not on the wings of theory but through the politics of irreducible choice.

American conservatives, in their prolonged moment of ascendancy, which looks now to be ending, excelled at the politics of stark polariz-ing choice, beginning with the presidential election in 1968 of Alger Hiss's prosecutor, Richard Nixon, who in the years following the case remained Chambers's friend and in some sense his disciple. It was Nixon who shattered the "consensus" politics that had prevailed during the first twenty-odd years of the cold war and contrived a strategy of divisiveness in which the "silent majority" of God-fearing, law-abiding citizens seized the whip from the unbelieving elite—the people who (in Nixon's view, not entirely wrong) had never forgiven him for exposing Hiss. Another Chambers disciple, Ronald Reagan, posthumously awarded Chambers the Medal of Freedom (the nation's highest civilian honor) and more than once startled aides by reciting passages of *Witness* from memory. Its tonalities are audible in the scripts Reagan wrote for his popular radio addresses in the 1970s, when he was mounting his run at the presidency, and also in his notorious formulation "the evil empire," derived from Chambers's description of Communism as "the focus of the concentrated evil of our time."

The epithet "evil empire" sent shudders through much of the civilized world when Reagan first uttered it in 1983. But he was speaking in terms the Soviets themselves understood; he gave voice to the binary theology that joined the two great powers in their elaborate death-struggle. Schlesinger, no admirer of Reagan, writing in 1985, pointed out that the Soviets too saw "the enemy as unchanging and unchange-able, a permanently evil empire . . . Each regime, reading its adversary ideologically rather than historically, deduces motive from imputed essence and attributes purpose, premeditation and plan where less besot-ted analysis would raise a hand for improvisation, accident, chance, igno-rance, negligence and even sheer stupidity . . . Moreover, ideology, if pursued to the end, excludes coexistence. How can we compromise with evil without losing our immortal soul? Ideology summons the true believer to a *jihad,* a crusade of extermination against the infidel."

The danger too was in overestimating the adversary. In the 1980s, when Chambersian absolutism was very much in vogue, the official view of the Reagan White House was that the USSR was not only "perma-nently evil" but indestructible, growing in ambition and in charismatic might even as the evidence oppositely pointed to a dysfunctional econo-my, a political spoils system rotten with corruption, republics seething with ethnic hatreds, satellite countries in rebellion. But when the col-lapse came the Manichean belief that America had singly "won" the cold war seemed vindicated. *Our* theology had triumphed. Even so forceful a thinker as Francis Fukuyama, updating the dialectic, though along Hegelian rather than Marxian lines, credited the triumph to "the realm of consciousness or ideas, since consciousness will ultimately remake the material world in its image." Since then Fukuyama has acknowledged he and his fellow neoconservatives were wrong, with terrible consequences. For the fiction persuaded them to inaugurate a new cold war, even though no suitable adversary, and no empire at all, exists for America to struggle against.

Chambers, unburdened by intellectual discipline, also came to recognize the folly of the dualism he had espoused so vividly. He was in fact among the first on the right to interpret the death of Stalin, in 1953, and the rise of Khrushchev, as signaling a new phase in the "twilight struggle." In yet another of his volte-faces, the most unexpected of all, Chambers refashioned himself into a liberal in his last years. He became a defender of civil liberties (including Hiss's when he was denied a passport) and of the Keynesian policies promoted by John Kenneth Galbraith. He ardently opposed the arms race, which struck him as an exercise in madness. And he came to see that the theology of Americanism was empty. Nations must scrub themselves before they seek to cleanse the souls of their enemies. "It is idle to talk about preventing the wreck of Western civilization," he wrote his friend William F. Buckley Jr., the young intellectual leader of the nascent postwar conservatism movement, in 1954. "It is already a wreck from within. That is why we can hope to do little more now than to snatch a fingernail of a saint from the rack or a handful of ashes from the faggots, and bury them secretly in a flower pot against the day, ages hence, when a few men begin again to dare to believe that there was once something else, that something else is thinkable . . . that there were those who, at the great nightfall, took loving thought to preserve the tokens of hope and truth."

Meanwhile, the Manichean Chambers remains a towering presence on the right. In July 2001, the Bush White House, eager to polish its ideological credentials, paid homage to Chambers by holding an event in commemoration of his hundredth birthday. The speakers included William Buckley and Robert Novak, the syndicated columnist best known today for his subsequent role in the Valerie Plame affair, which led to the indictment of Vice President Cheney's top assistant I. Lewis Libby. The president did not attend, but two of his speech writers, Michael Gerson and David Frum, did, a fact that resonated some months later when, following al Qaeda's attacks on New York and Washington on September 11, Gerson and Frum composed the phrase "axis of evil," ushering in the new counter-jihad.

By then it was plain that "the war on terror" would be fought in precisely the terms Chambers had spelled out in his bleakest phase, the lonely period following the Hiss case; his heirs had settled on an immovably absolutist course. Chambers had furnished the text for this too, in

*Witness*: "In this century, within the next decades, will be decided for generations whether all mankind is to become Communist, whether the whole world is to become free, or whether, in the struggle, civilization as we know it is to be completely destroyed or completely changed. It is our fate to live upon that turning point in history."

Substitute "Islamo-fascist" for "Communist" and it is distressingly clear how little has changed. The worldview Whittaker Chambers outgrew is, alas, the one that guides us today. It is a punishing irony, and one can imagine all too easily how he would have greeted it: with the sly half-smile of one who knows better.

*Sam Tanenhaus*
*New York, November 2006*

# OUTCAST

## (1901–1925)

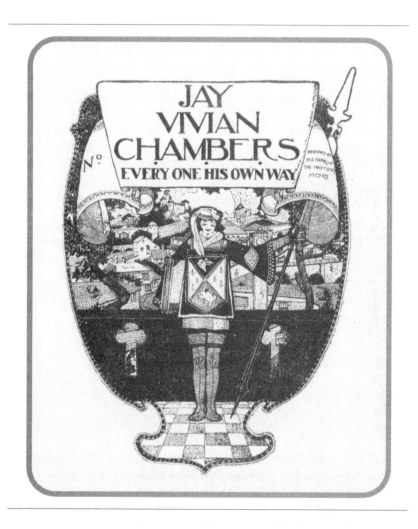

*Bookplate designed for the infant Jay Vivian Chambers by his father, Jay, in 1902.*

# 1

# *Vivian*

Jay Vivian Chambers was born on April 1, 1901—April Fool's Day, as he liked to point out. He was named for his father, Jay Chambers, a graphic artist at the *New York World*. The boy's middle name, chosen by his mother, Laha, dismayed her husband and also its bearer, called Vivian all through childhood. Jay, however, refused to utter the hated syllables and so inflicted on his son the nickname Beadle, evidently a comment on his demeanor, watchful, grave, and severe.[1]

In 1903, after a second son, Richard, was born, Laha decided the young family should move from their apartment, near Prospect Park, Brooklyn, and resettle in the suburbs. She loathed New York City and missed the open spaces she had known in her own childhood, spent in Wisconsin.[2]

Jay resisted the move. A city boy from Philadelphia, he enjoyed Brooklyn, its brownstones and tree-lined pavements. He liked too the easy access, by elevated subway, to his Manhattan office and the theaters and galleries he frequented. Also, he had recently lost his job at the *World* to a news camera, and although he soon found new employment—with a design studio on Union Square that did book covers and magazine illustrations—the venture was in its infancy and its prospects uncertain.[3]

But Laha, insistent and strong-willed, prevailed over Jay, who was passive and retiring, and in 1904 the family moved to Lynbrook, a pretty coastal village on Long Island's South Shore, twenty miles east of Manhattan, with a population of less than two thousand. The year the Chamberses moved there, Lynbrook got its first water mains and its first brick building, M. L. Levinson's Hardware Store.

The family took up residence on Earle Avenue, an unpaved street lined with silver maples.[4] The house, formerly a postal coach stop, was a sturdy clapboard structure, two stories plus a slope-ceilinged attic. It sat back from the street on a swatch of lawn. Though in need of repair, 228 Earle Avenue gave every appearance of being a suitable place for the young family to achieve stability and for Laha to regain the "paradise" of upper-middle-class respectability she had known in childhood.[5]

Laha's father, Charles Whittaker, a Scottish immigrant born in 1840, had immigrated to Milwaukee in 1845, with his parents and twelve siblings.[6] In 1869, a language teacher and principal in Milwaukee's public schools,[7] he married Mary Blanchard, a fetching sixteen-year-old with wide-set eyes and a broad forehead. She came from Wauwatosa, a grouping of frame houses set among oak and maple groves, near the banks of the Menomonee River. The descendant of Huguenots, Mary spoke fluent French. Many years later she taught Vivian the language, using a convent primer.[8]

Even as he advanced his pedagogical career, Charles pursued other interests. He was the founding publisher of Milwaukee's first city magazine and registered several patents.[9] But he suffered stinging reversals. In 1878, when Laha was seven, her father was forced to auction off the substantial house he had built only two years before near Milwaukee's exclusive "Yankee Hill," overlooking Lake Michigan.[10] In 1880 Charles and Mary Whittaker departed Milwaukee, tracing the southern sweep of the Great Lake to Chicago. Laha, their only child, stayed behind at the Home School, a private academy in Racine.[11] In Chicago Charles manufactured and sold brass castings[12]—and again went bankrupt, losing everything just in time to foreclose on Laha's long-held dream of attending an elite college in the East.[13]

She went instead on the stage, touring the Midwest and Far West with stock companies.[14] After six or seven hard years she gave it up and joined her parents, who had moved again, this time to New York. They were now operating a lunch counter on West Twenty-third Street, in Manhattan, and living above it in tiny, cramped rooms.[15] Laha came to cook and waitress and help care for her father, afflicted with cancer of the tongue. Charles Whittaker died in 1899, at age fifty-nine. He left his widow and daughter a twelve-dollar-a-month Civil War pension, fifty dollars' worth of kitchen utensils, and a couple of hundred books.[16]

By then Laha had met Jay Chambers,[17] a customer at the eatery. He was short, dark, plump, and boyish—and five years Laha's junior. A recent graduate of Philadelphia's Drexel Institute of Art, Science, and Industry, he had come up to New York to work as an illustrator at the *World,* a job he obtained through his father, James Chambers, a well-known journalist.[18] After a two-year courtship Jay and Laha were married in January 1900 over the strenuous objections of the groom's mother, Dora, who judged Laha unworthy of her only son.[19] In her indignation Laha taught her sons that their father came from inferior stock, deficient in "breeding." The truth was that Jay had reached below his station to rescue her, a penniless waitress nearing thirty with a history on the provincial stage.[20]

These distinctions meant little to Jay. He cared only for art. A product of the 1890s, the mauve decade, he quietly deplored middle-class standards of respectability. While Laha strove to establish the family in Lynbrook, Jay stood to the side, mocking. He regarded the suburbs and their inhabitants with droll disdain. He once bet a friend he could walk to Lynbrook's center, the "Five Corners," clad only in his pajamas and not attract a single comment from his complacent neighbors. He won the bet. At home he raised the gaudy pennant of aestheticism. He wore a linen "samurai robe," planted a large replica of the Venus de Milo on the living room floor, and mounted on its walls a permanent exhibition of his bookplates (prized by collectors) and whimsical Christmas cards (prized by his friends).[21]

It amused Jay to adorn the house, but he steadfastly refused to fix it, despite its poor condition. The yellow exterior coat had been bleached of color by the salty ocean winds. The shutters, a sickly green, nagged at their rotted hinges. The interior was even worse. One day a portion of the dining room ceiling dropped. Laha covered the hole with cheesecloth. Vivian and Richard watched transfixed as mice nested in its bulges, their scampering feet leaving "twinkling" impressions. Another project was the wallpaper, aged and blistered. Jay would not replace it. Laha wrapped up her few valuables and took them to Manhattan pawnbrokers, returning with enough cash to hire a team of workmen. When the job was finished, Jay said nothing. Laha's sobs "were dreadful to hear."[22]

But she was not deterred. With or without Jay's encouragement, she was determined to carry her mission forward, to conquer Lynbrook in the name of her sons, anchoring them in the community. She was elected president of the local mothers' club and was on the committee that founded and staffed the village's first library. She also secured entrance into the "exclusive" Friday club, limited to thirty-five women, most of them "wives of leading figures," with newcomers drawn from a waiting list. Laha's dramatic "monologues" and "readings" were a staple of the club's afternoon entertainments.[23]

Yet the Chamberses never quite blended in. Neighbors found them "clever" and "brilliant" but faintly disreputable. The house, cluttered with Jay's artwork and the mismatching "antiques" Laha rummaged up, had the appearance of a seedy museum. And its curators were themselves odd: the plump, aloof artist who rode the commuter train in virtual silence; the actressy wife with her stagey voice and florid gestures, her talk of important "friends" in the theater. Locally, they were referred to as "the French Family."[24]

Vivian early realized his family was "peculiar." More painful still, he watched his parents' marriage crumble. Laha craved affection from all those around her. Jay would not—or could not—give it. The couple enacted rituals of devotion, but the children were not fooled. Each evening Laha ceremonially positioned Vivian and Richard in the front hallway so they could plant a kiss on their father's cheek when he returned from work. Jay, stooping to receive his welcome, wore a farcical smile. At the dinner table, lavishly spread with "high sauces and cheeses, lobsters, oysters and hot curries," Jay ate in greedy silence, speaking only to reprove his sons when an elbow sneaked indecorously onto the table. Supper concluded, Jay slipped upstairs to his room, donned his robe, and busied himself with his many hobbies—his bookplates, his elaborate puppet theater, the tiny matchbox houses he built, precise in every detail, and his vast collection of "penny toys." His sons, forbidden to touch their father's baubles, grew to loathe them. "An artist must be pampered or he would not be an artist," says a character in one of Vivian Chambers's first short stories, written when he was seventeen.[25]

With Jay in retreat, mother and sons gathered in the parlor. Cradling Richard in her arms, Laha rocked in a Windsor chair and sang lullabies. Vivian, creeping amid the shadows cast by the oil lamps, shrank from the desperate melancholia in his mother's voice, meant, it seemed, for some unseen audience.[26]

Soon Jay was delaying his nightly return from the city. Laha and the boys waited at the table, weakly reassuring one another he would be on the next train, while the sumptuous sauces congealed. Late at night Vivian sat up in his cot listening for his father's return—the sound of the front door opening and then the tread of feet mounting the stairs. Hours passed in which he heard only Richard's breathing in the cot beside him and the lisp of "the surf pouring without pause on the beaches." The Atlantic felt especially near on winter nights "when the cold air brought it in clearly. I was frightened, for it seemed about to pound away the land. It was the sound of inhuman force—the first I knew." When at last the knob turned downstairs, often past midnight, the boy surrendered himself to sleep, except on those nights when his parents' voices erupted in fierce quarrels. In the morning, with Jay again out of the house, Laha assailed him in monologues, while she paced the living room floor. Vivian and Richard listened raptly, though ordered to stay in the kitchen, the warmest room in the house, heated by a "big, black, nickel-trimmed coal range." Once, when Laha emerged, Vivian noticed "black and red marks on her throat."[27]

Then one evening, probably in 1908, Jay did not return. He had moved back to Brooklyn and its bachelor pleasures. He remained in hiding for at least a year. His sons did not see him. Laha "never attacked my father to us children but she was able to convey to us that we shouldn't like him."[28]

It was many years before Vivian realized the origins of her frustration and rage. Jay Chambers was bisexual. But even as a child Vivian had grasped that his father's life was divided into "separate compartments." So would the son's be, with far greater complexity.[29]

Jay's departure brought a measure of relief to Laha and the boys, reifying an absence long felt. They became "a tightly knit unit," bound together by the effort to maintain the household on the exiguous sum Jay sent them—eight dollars a week, by Vivian's recollection. Laha earned a few dollars more through her own industry. In her, as in Jay and her elder son, fanciful flights coincided with practical skills. She raised chickens, tended a vegetable garden, and, a skilled baker, filled cake orders from neighbors. Vivian made deliveries door to door and "developed a small route in the town." For fuel, mother and sons raided nearby construction sites and filled burlap bags with scraps of lumber. Vivian and Dickie harvested lumps of coal from the railroad tracks, not electrified until 1910.[30]

Laha bathed their privations in the glow of frontier romance. Here she was in step with the times, with the national yearning for the vanished glories of pioneer hardships. Laha, a daughter of the "Northwest," excited her sons with talk of an impending adventure in Idaho or Montana, states she had toured in stock. She also talked of a return to the stage. Not yet forty, she had a natural vivacity and still had her trim figure and "lustrous" brown hair. Most thrilling to her sons was her talk of buying a farm. They all paged excitedly through catalogs she sent for, "but when spring came we never went." Vivian finally realized this dream in 1940, when he bought a hundred acres of cropland in rural Maryland.[31]

At night mother and sons retired to her room, where the boys' cots now stood alongside Laha's joyless marriage bed. Laha bolted the door and jammed a bureau against it. Deep into the night she roused her sons with a sharp whisper to sudden noises, the shiftings and creakings of the old house, the fumblings of prowlers, she was sure. She kept an ax in the bedroom closet in the event an intruder penetrated their defenses. "A woman with an axe is a match for any man," she explained. When an actual thief was nabbed in the neighborhood, Laha placed the weapon under her bed.[32]

In truth the danger to the household came not from lawless outsiders but from the upstanding citizens of Lynbrook. The unraveled marriage had not long remained a secret, nor had the genteel poverty that had overtaken 228 Earle Avenue. The most voluble source of gossip was local merchants, whose patience frayed as Laha overextended her lines of credit. "Tell your mother, no more credit till the bill is paid," one shopkeeper told Vivian. Another was blunter, leaning on the counter to sneer, "Your mother is a broken-down stagecoach." The family had begun to slide—Laha's worst fear. Valiantly she kept up appearances, though it was difficult when Vivian, dressed in Eton collar and floppy bow tie, came knocking on neighbors' doors bearing their orders of eggs and cakes.[33]

In 1907 Vivian began his formal education at the Union Avenue grammar school, a frame building some blocks south of Earle Avenue, across the railroad tracks—the wrong side of the tracks. He entered first grade as a boy shorter than usual, plumpened by starchy meals. He was blond—with his mother's light blue eyes and round, gentle face—and not always well scrubbed. His teeth too were in poor shape. Laha never sent her sons to the dentist.[34]

In some respects Vivian was ahead of his classmates. Laha had already taught him to read. At an early age he and Dickie were fans of the children's magazine *St. Nicholas,* a favorite among the cultured middle class.* Contemptuous of public schools, Laha sometimes kept the boys home "for her and their amusement." Nonetheless Vivian was listed on the honor roll in the sixth and seventh grades.[36]

But his true education came in the schoolyard. In his first years Vivian had not been allowed to play with neighborhood children. He was seen on the street only in his mother's company. Now he was thrust in among the sons and daughters of Lynbrook's merchants, farmers, and the area's hardy "baymen," who harvested shellfish in the tidal creeks and marshes or combed the ocean shallows in trawlers. It was rough company for a pudgy "butterball" dressed like Lord Fauntleroy and ever mindful of the fine points of etiquette drummed into him by his mother. Vivian inevitably became the "butt of the school." A teacher remembered the boy "standing always at the side of the school playground, silent and observant, but never taking part," imagining other worlds.[37]

* Another avid reader of *St. Nicholas* in these same years was Chambers's future employer and ally Henry R. Luce.[35]

## 2

# *Distant Horizons*

In about 1910 Jay, who had been spending Sundays at Lynbrook, resumed his full-time obligations as husband and father. As before, he retreated to his aerie, but for longer periods. He ceased even to dine with
his family. Vivian carried in his father's supper. Jay made "a great show
of clearing the heap of artist's materials from his table so that the messenger from afar could set down the tray of food." Downstairs Laha and
the boys lowered their voices when they sensed Jay was near. *He* had become the intruder, pressing against the bolted door.[1]

Yet to the outside world Jay and Laha seemed reborn as a couple. They
inaugurated a new public phase as emissaries of culture, performing together in skits and "dialogues" and in full-dress plays staged in the parish
halls, libraries, and auditoriums of Lynbrook and adjacent South Shore
towns. Jay also mounted tableaux vivants, or "living pictures," a holdover
fad from the nineties. His favorite text was the *Rubaiyat*. Jay and other ac-
tors, elaborately costumed, stood frozen in assigned poses while Laha recited the corresponding verses from FitzGerald's poem. Vivian and
Richard were also dragooned into performing. Richard was young
enough not to mind. But Vivian never forgot the shame of being perched
wobbily atop a wooden globe, a piece of cloth draped skimpily across his
stomach. Laha intoned the purplish text:

> *I sent my Soul through the Invisible,*
> *One letter of that Afterlife to spell:*
> *And by and by my Soul returned to me,*
> *And answered "I Myself am Heav'n and Hell."*[2]

Meanwhile, Laha pursued her mission, determined as ever "to live entirely for her children"—that is, to burden them with her ambitions. Through her many civic activities she met faculty at South Side High School, much superior to Lynbrook High, located in the neighboring town of Rockville Centre. For a small fee Vivian was permitted to enroll.[3]

It did not seem to him a favor. "Lives in Lynbrook (nuff sed)" is the "misdemeanor" attributed to Chambers in "The Class of 1919's Criminal Record," a facetious profile of the senior class assembled by the students in lieu of a yearbook. With brutal candor the "Criminal Record" clarifies Chambers's standing among the twenty-two "convicts" his year. His "alias" is not "Duke" or "Zeke," but "Girlie." His favorite occupation is not "fooling with his flivver" or "sleeping in civics." It is "talking to himself"—the watchful reserve already a pronounced, even defiant trait.[4] His appearance invited further ridicule. Rather than buy his son long pants, Jay fobbed his own discarded clothes on the boy. Vivian wore them "as a badge of shame." He accentuated the effect by letting his hair grow until it straggled over his collar and by going days without bathing. To "Girlie" were added the epithets "Stinky" and "Mr. Chamber Pot."[5]

Chambers could easily have redeemed himself in the classroom but chose not to. "One of the most avidly intellectual men of the century," as John Kenneth Galbraith was to call him,[6] made only spotty appearances on South Side's honor roll and was not among the eight seniors who graduated with honors. He excelled only in English and languages, subjects in which his large aptitude overcame his indifference.[7]

The trouble was not laziness. Chambers had wide and varied interests and pursued them with disciplined passion. Growing up in a house "full of books," he early was awakened to the joys of literature and languages, stirred by the example of his grandfather Whittaker, whose legacy of books, cached in barrels in the Earle Avenue attic, included novels by George Eliot and Thackeray as well as biographies of American statesmen—Hamilton, Lincoln, and Henry Clay.[8]

One book, Victor Hugo's *Les Misérables,* captured Vivian's interest above all others. He first read the novel at age eight or nine and returned to it many times, he reports in his own masterpiece, *Witness.* Like other writers of his generation (André Malraux and Henry Roth, to name two), Chambers was enthralled by Hugo's massive social panorama, a "full-length picture of the modern world—a vast, complex, scarcely human structure, built over a social abyss of which the sewers of Paris was [*sic*] the symbol, and resting with crushing weight upon the wretched of the earth." In *Les Misérables*'s wrenching drama of suffering and self-sacrifice, Vivian discovered "the play of forces that carried me into the Communist Party, and [later] carried me out."[9]

Charles Whittaker's library also included several grammars. Vivian became their proud custodian. In his teens he embarked on a private course of language study and eventually acquainted himself with German, French, Italian, Spanish, and more exotic tongues—"Arabic, Persian, Hindustani, and the Assyrian of the cuneiform inscriptions." At age sixteen he visited Gypsy camps on Long Island and sent lists of the words he overheard to George Fraser Black, a linguist then compiling a Romany lexicon.[10] The language he became most proficient in was German. His fluency was to aid him greatly during his Communist years, when German remained the first language of the revolution.

Chambers received assistance in his study of it from a remarkable woman he met in Lynbrook, Dorothea Ellen, the wife of a local Realtor. She had briefly been music tutor at Theodore Roosevelt's compound in Oyster Bay, Long Island. In about 1915, Chambers became a regular guest at the Ellen home. Of German descent, Mrs. Ellen played Beethoven sonatas on the piano, read Goethe with Vivian, and tutored him in German. "Insofar as my mind is civilized at all, she chiefly civilized it," Chambers later remarked. Mrs. Ellen offered something more solid than the "artiness" of Jay and Laha: a picture of "the old European tradition of culture as a continuing process." It was a rare gift to bestow on an American adolescent in the 1910s, a time when the word *intellectual* had barely entered the national idiom. Mrs. Ellen was the first adult to nourish Chambers's adolescent "yearning for horizons" that stretched beyond the confines of Lynbrook. She also treated the boy to his first adult lunches in New York, at Lüchow's and the Waldorf.[11]

A devout Christian Scientist, Mrs. Ellen tried to convert Chambers to that faith. She took him to services, presented him with his first Bible, and loaned him German translations of Mary Baker Eddy's tracts. It all had some effect. In 1920 Chambers scrawled "Christian Science" under "religion" on his application to Columbia University.[12]

Mrs. Ellen's other passion was European politics. Mentor and pupil secured their friendship during the peak of the Sinn Fein movement in Ireland; both were anti-British.[13] Vivian was roused more deeply by World War I. Like his parents, he was a Francophile, for whom Paris was the "capital of Light." He charted early campaigns by sticking colored pins in a wall-size military map and was overjoyed by the victory at the Marne. He dreamed of fighting in the trenches of France.[14]

The war is the subject of Chambers's first-known short story, published in the "Liberty Loan Number" of South Side High's literary magazine, the *Breeze,* in May 1918, a month after the author's seventeenth birthday. "Kedding Zee Kaiser"—that is, "kidding the Kaiser"—deals with sabotage, a subject much on the minds of Long Islanders because of munitions explosions on the Delaware and New Jersey coasts. The villain, Karl Heine Schlange, a German American millionaire (his fortune was made on Wall Street), suddenly undergoes "a revolution in his manner of looking at things," coming "to see in war a legitimate means of German expansion." He donates vast funds to seditious socialists and then, anticipating his seventeen-year-old author, becomes a spy, or tries to; the "wireless" he installs on his roof to transmit "rare news bits to Berlin" mainly captures fatuous radio commercials. In the end Schlange is outwitted by a trio of stalwarts who include an American counterintelligence agent, an Alsatian spy, and a crafty Wall Street banker. Chambers sides with the Allies, but his imagination goes out to the saboteur.[15]

Another important influence on the young Chambers was Jay's father, James Chambers, an editor at the *Philadelphia Public Ledger.* Jim Chambers was in every way the opposite of his mild, aesthetic son.[16] Said to resemble Ulysses Grant, with his reddish beard and piercing blue eyes, the elder Chambers was gruff and ill-tempered, a tyrant in the newsroom best known for having mercilessly taunted and then fired a dilettantish cub reporter, Richard Harding Davis, who, properly chastened, eventually became the most admired journalist of his day.[17]

Age and success mellowed Jim Chambers, "Uncle Jim," as a new generation of reporters called him.[18] Vivian knew him as an overweight, bald, and earthy man, noisily profane, who lavished unrestrained love on his grandsons. Jim Chambers's annual visits to Lynbrook, dreaded by Laha, were much anticipated by Vivian and Richard. Over Laha's bitter protests, Grandfather Chambers insisted his two "jack rabbits" accompany him on a tour of the local taprooms. These expeditions usually concluded with them all in a tavern in Brooklyn or Queens, Jim soused, his grandsons bloated with root beer and bar food. On the way home Vivian and Dickie clutched the hands of their doddering grandfather as he staggered on and off the train and trolley.

There was more to these rounds than gluttony. There was also talk about politics. As a reporter Jim Chambers had covered the national, state, and city beats. A staunch Republican, he remained on a first-name basis with Philadelphia's bosses and pols. He was delighted by Vivian's interest in history and encouraged the boy to express his views. The two exchanged letters on the Russo-Japanese War, the decline of the great European empires, on the Great War. Under his grandfather's tutelage, Vivian learned that politics was "the present tense of history."[19]

By the time Chambers reached enlistment age, on April 1, 1919, the war was over. The missed opportunity haunted him for years to come. As late as 1924 he was still writing stories and poems about World War I.[20]

He paid less attention to the war's most dramatic subplot, Russia's revolution of October 1917, the "ten days that shook the world." Vladimir Lenin's seizure of power interested Chambers "only as it affected Allied strategy." Soon, however, he came to see the 1917 revolution as "undifferentiated savagery," as did many Americans of the time. He was amused when Laha suggested he study Russian in preparation for a career in "military intelligence." He did indeed memorize some vocabulary, purely for the novelty, not thinking he would achieve a career that reversed the one Laha envisioned.[21]

In June 1919 Chambers finished his four unhappy years at South Side High School. In recognition of his literary abilities, his classmates elected him class prophet, charged with composing a "prophecy" to be read aloud on class day, the event preceding the graduation ceremony. His remarks, submitted in advance to the principal, were deemed "cynical and materialistic . . . the product of a more mature mind." He was told to revise them and did. But on the appointed day Chambers read from his original unedited text, which foretold, among other future events, a career in prostitution for one of his classmates. Chambers was denied his diploma until Laha appeared in the principal's office, pleading that her son's artistic temperament deserved indulgence. The commotion satisfied J.V.W. Chambers, as he was listed on the class roll. It was no small accomplishment to be a prophet without honor at age eighteen.[22]

In keeping with her grand plans, Laha hoped her elder son would attend a prestigious college and join the ranks of his true equals, the "scions" of the upper middle class. But Jay emerged from hiding long enough to recommend Vivian set aside all thoughts of college and go to work. The boy agreed. He had had his fill of formal education. He wanted to be out in the world, following the distant curve of his "horizons." But where could he go and what could he do? Competition for jobs was high in the summer of 1919. Three and a half million young men were out of uniform, or soon to be, many headed straight for "the white-collar world" where Jay and Laha thought their son belonged. For the time being Laha got her son a job clerking at the Lynbrook National Bank, where the family's small savings were deposited.[23]

Ready for something bolder, Chambers discussed his plight with a friend, Anthony Muller, who had gone overseas during the war and was back in Lynbrook, restless. Together the two "cooked it up to run away from home." They were not exactly runaways. Muller was a veteran, and Chambers was three months past his eighteenth birthday. But their departure was clandestine, and Chambers thought of it as a flight.[24]

The pair left Lynbrook one Saturday morning in July with a vague idea of reaching Mexico. They rode the Long Island Rail Road to Penn Station and there bought tickets for a southbound train—to Baltimore, as far as they could afford. Chambers was left with ten dollars in his pocket, enough to share a room in a flophouse.

On Monday morning, after Chambers had tasted his first sips of coffee, the two friends consulted want ads and went to a downtown storefront where a construction company, Engel & Hevenor, was hiring laborers to lay rails in Washington. The boys from Lynbrook joined a block-long line of men and filed past the shrewd gaze of the hiring boss, who inspected their hands for calluses. Muller's were acceptably hardened. Chambers's were not. His clothing too was suspect. Here was one occasion when his usual dishevelment was called for, but he was neatly turned out in his blue serge graduation suit. Dismissed by the straw boss, he slumped off dejectedly. But other applicants, taking pity, pulled Chambers aside, yanked off his jacket and tie, stuffed his hat into his pocket, mussed his hair, and sent him once more through the line. This time he made it.[25]

Since childhood Chambers had been waiting to shed his embarrassing given name. He now had the opportunity and also the need. His parents' alarms might soon reach the local police. Chambers chose the alias

Charles Adams in honor of his grandfather and also of Henry Adams, whose *Education* had been published posthumously in 1918.[26]

Engel & Hevenor had been contracted to replace railroad tracks within blocks of the Capitol. This meant ripping out the existing track and breaking up concrete slabs with a pneumatic drill. It was risky work; if the driller nicked the third rail, the shock could hurl him through the air. Chambers was assigned a less dangerous task, cracking bolts with a sledgehammer and chisel. Even this required know-how he conspicuously lacked. He gripped his instruments too tightly, and by afternoon his hands were scraped raw. That night, when he joined the other workers in a boardinghouse, near the Capitol, he held out his wounded hands while another man poured iodine over them.

He had left Lynbrook in search of the wider world, and at his first stop he found it—in the men with whom he worked, dined, and bunked. They were the wretched of the earth, massed at the base of the social heap. There was a Russian, a Pole, a Belgian, and numerous Latin Americans. With his quick ear, Chambers managed to communicate with them all and to learn something of their Hugolian misfortunes. On Saturday nights he and a Venezuelan coworker strolled along Pennsylvania Avenue and debated the merits of the League of Nations—Manuel convinced "it was the hope of mankind," while Chambers scoffed "in a kind of pidgin Spanish." It was the same debate going on just a few blocks distant, where the U.S. Senate was in the process of rejecting the League's Covenant and of spurning the one-world vision of President Wilson.[27]

Even as he guarded his identity, Chambers boasted of his adventures in letters to schoolmates, colorfully dilating on his experiences. He also wrote to Laha, disclosing that he was in Washington, a clue she passed along to Jim Chambers, who notified the police. But local law enforcement officials were occupied with matters more pressing than hunting down a high school graduate who dutifully sent letters home to his mother. Chambers and Tony Muller lasted on the job, unharassed, until it ended in September.[28]

They had spent little of their wages and so were able to prolong their adventure, proceeding by the Southern Railroad to New Orleans, where they took a room in a hotel near the depot. New Orleans had been a major naval station during the war, and in these peak months of demobilization the streets teemed with jobless veterans. Tony Muller fell in with the horde, and Chambers hocked his graduation suit and bought a cast-off army uniform so he too would fit in.

Work was not as easy to find as it had been in Washington. The two friends haunted the docks, but hundreds of others, better experienced, were hired ahead of them. There were stymied too by the hiring codes of the segregated South. Chambers tried to earn a few dollars by joining a crew he saw unloading a banana boat berthed at the Canal Street wharf, but the boss, a white man, told him to move along; the job was "nigger work." Chambers next tried getting a job on ship, but that required union papers, and he was underage and underfunded.

Within a few days the runaways moved to a seedy rooming house on Bienville Street in the French Quarter. Traffic passed steadily between the house and its twin across the alley, a brothel operated by Glenn Evans, a well-known madam. Chambers and Muller's narrow second-floor room opened on to a railed porch—or gallery, in New Orleans parlance.

Their landlords were a quarrelsome couple, George ("the Greek") Nicholas, a peanut vendor, and his bibulous Irish wife, Jane. She was arrested on at least one occasion for disturbing the peace, probably after one of her many iron-lunged orations on the "vices and professions of her tenants." Jane's sister also lived in the building. She was in an advanced stage of tuberculosis. Chambers knew her only as "a dry cough" rasping behind a closed door. He saw more of the couple upstairs, a prostitute, known simply as One-Eyed Annie, and her pimp and lover, Sam Monti. The couple befriended Chambers and invited him to their room, although their sudden violent embraces sent the eighteen-year-old virgin fleeing in embarrassment.

By day Annie hustled on riverboats that steamed a few miles up the Mississippi and back, to the ragged strains of Dixieland, the music then being perfected by the teenage Louis Armstrong. In Annie's absence Sam glided down to Chambers's room and, like a prototype of Tennessee Williams's Stanley Kowalski, impatiently stalked the tiny quarters in an undershirt, baring the luxuriant tattoos on his powerful shoulders as he held forth, in a voice of "caressing softness," on the "wisdom of the deep slums—a jungle theory of individualism, in which a man was merely a phallic symbol, as strong as his power to attract women, or pull a knife or a gun on the rest of life which was natural prey." At twilight, however, Sam stationed himself at a window, staring past the rooftops and listening for the whistle that meant the *Sidney*, with Annie aboard, was returning to port.

Chambers had discovered life as Hugo described it, a kind of prison, harsh and cruel, but lit from within by tender sentiment and from without by sudden shafts of illumination. Borrowing a volume of Shakespeare from a neighbor, a widow who sometimes invited him in for coffee, Chambers opened the book to *Antony and Cleopatra* and read all day in bed, "stunned by the opulence of violence and language."

> *Let Rome in Tiber melt, and the wide arch*
> *Of the ranged empire fall! Here is my space.*
> *Kingdoms are clay: our dungy earth alike*
> *Feeds beast as man. . . .*[29]

His savings nearly exhausted, Chambers tried the shipyards again, with no luck, and next asked his landlady to pose as his mother and sign papers authorizing him to get a job on a cargo ship. But drunk as usual, Mrs. Nicholas bungled the facts her "son" had told her to recite, and the two were laughed out of the shipping office.[30]

Chambers scarcely minded. He loved New Orleans, more beautiful than he had thought it "possible for a city to be." But after two months he was "going downhill rapidly" and wired home for money. When it came—from grandfather Chambers—the runaway gave some dollars to Tony Muller, who had decided to enlist in the marines, and with the rest bought his passage back to New York. Laha and Richard met him at Penn Station.[31]

It was November 1919. Four months had passed. The soft adolescent, first hardened by manual labor and then emaciated by want, had touched the bottom of the "social abyss." Beginning as a sympathetic observer of the wretched of the earth, he had become, he believed, one of their number. It was a progression he was to follow all his life. His was to be a witness offered up from the depths of experience. His parents treated him gingerly. Laha no longer tried to smother him or plumb his secrets; there was a large accumulation better left unexplored. Jay "had the good sense to ask me nothing at all. He was gracious. He seemed to recognize that something had happened."[32]

Chambers too had conceded something. He had, after all, come home. Provisionally willing to resume his place in the family, he agreed to enter college the following fall and until then clerk at Frank Seaman Inc., a midtown advertising agency where Jay had recently become art director.

As they rode together to work on the morning of Vivian's first day, Jay instructed his son to use an alias at the office, a precaution against potential charges of nepotism. As an explanation it was transparently weak: What but nepotism had gotten Vivian the job in the first place? Chambers suspected another reason: Jay's fear that "I might not do a good job."[33]

But Jay had still another motive. He wanted to preserve the compartments he had constructed so painstakingly over the years. The chief pleasure he took in the new job—perhaps the only one—was in the escape it afforded him from his family. At the office he was able to shut out their intrusive claims[34]—but not with his elder son underfoot. Stung by this most blatant rejection yet—a literal denial of filiation—Chambers chose the alias Charles Whittaker, a declaration of his own loyalties to Laha's family.[35]

But the job brought father and son closer together. Each day the two rode in side by side on the train, walked the few blocks to Seaman's offices, and repeated the journey at day's end. Peering into the closed compartment of Jay's work life, Vivian glimpsed a different man, much liked by his colleagues, witty and gentle and "bubbling over with appreciation of the humorous and ridiculous." Vivian realized his father was not simply the villain of 228 Earle Avenue but in some way its victim. His too was "a human case."[36]

After six months in the mailroom, college no longer seemed so dismal an option. Chambers's first choice was Columbia; its urbanity and size were attractive. Also, since the university was within commuting distance of Lynbrook, Jay would be spared the cost of board.

But Laha objected. Columbia might be one of the nation's great universities, but it was not what she had in mind. It was too large, with too many Jews. A junior copywriter at Seaman's recommended his own alma mater, Williams. This was more like it. Williams was refined, genteel, exclusive.[37] Laha firmly overrode Jay's objections to the expense, and in August Chambers visited the bucolic campus, in Williamstown, Massachusetts, and sat for a pre-entrance exam in German. The next month he arrived as a member of the freshman class but felt instantly out of place, repelled by the postcard-pretty campus. Lost amid the mass of "young collegiate faces," he shunned all the orientation events. Skipping a freshman dinner, he stayed behind to read the Bible. When his roommate returned, Chambers announced that "a great light had come to him." After three days at Williams, he took the night train to New York—and Columbia University.[38]

# 3

# *A Serious Man*

A change in Columbia's admissions policy, instituted during the war, permitted applicants from New York State to waive general entrance exams and instead sit for an "intelligence test."[1] Whittaker Chambers, as he now called himself (paying equal tribute to his two grandfathers), passed without difficulty and was admitted as a member of the class of 1924, a self-described political conservative and Christian Scientist who hoped to "make of myself a good man, a fine gentleman, and American patriot."[2]

Local freshmen unable to meet housing and board expenses—a minimum of $400 on top of the $256 tuition—were allowed to live at home and commute to the campus, in uptown Manhattan.[3] Chambers economized further by taking in a bag lunch. On mild days he ate outdoors on a bench and on inclement ones in the locker room or on the gym floor alongside several dozen other students as tightly budgeted as he.[4] At day's end he made the roughly hourlong trip home to Lynbrook, via the subway and the Long Island Rail Road.

Physically Columbia was much more to Chambers's liking than Williams, a distinctively urban campus with tall peaked-roofed buildings linked by crowded walks. There were pastoral spaces as well, with statuary and plantings, and a great stretch of lawn where student soldiers had drilled in formation in 1917–1918.[5] Beyond the borders of the terraced campus were the diverse attractions of Manhattan's Upper West Side, the busy commercial streets, including Broadway with its many shops and cheap restaurants. To the west ran Riverside Drive, where grand apartment houses, some of them modeled on Tuscan villas, jutted out from bluffs overlooking the Hudson River; to the east was Morningside Park, a high ridge that rose up steeply from the valley of Harlem.

The 1920s were a glorious decade for Columbia. Long a prestigious local institution, it had recently become, under President Nicholas Murray Butler, the model of a twentieth-century urban university. Its faculty included such giants as John Dewey and Franz Boas, leaders in their disciplines and also in the larger world of thought.[6] Columbia's undergraduates, from all over the country, were housed in spanking-new high-rise dormitories and were instructed not in remote lecture halls but in the intimate setting of seminar rooms, where their professors encouraged them to think for themselves, rather than simply absorb facts in the Victorian tradition that still dominated higher learning in American universities.[7]

Many took up the challenge—brilliantly. Chambers's undergraduate contemporaries included Meyer Schapiro, Lionel Trilling, Louis Zukofsky, Mortimer J. Adler, Clifton Fadiman. Chambers knew them all and others nearly as gifted. Some became his trusted friends. Most were Jewish. Laha's suspicions were exaggerated but not wholly misguided. While only a handful of Jews won appointment to the Columbia faculty, they composed roughly 20 percent of the undergraduate population—much less than at City College (80 percent) or at New York University (50 percent), but decidedly more than at Williams and similarly elite schools.[8]

Chambers, who knew few Jews in Lynbrook, was fascinated to find himself, for the first time, in the presence of minds like his own, though the product of vastly different circumstances. Raised in immigrant homes and sprung from the busy hatcheries of the New York City public school system, some of these youths were prodigies of erudition who had skipped a year or even two of school and then won citywide scholarship competitions. Chambers listened, awestruck, as they ranged easily over whole areas of knowledge. Though by no means solemn—Chambers strained to decipher the earthy jokes they traded in Yiddish—this "dingy proletariat" presented a collective vision of invincible seriousness, moral and intellectual. Much later Chambers referred to them by a German phrase he picked up in the Communist underground. They were *ernste Menschen* (serious men).

It was the *ernste Menschen* who shaped Chambers's idea, never altered, of the intellectual life. Mrs. Ellen had taught him reverence for art, for its monumentality. His new friends introduced him to what was pulsingly alive—subversive, dangerous, intoxicating—in literature and ideas. Under their influence he read the modern masters of Central and Eastern Europe: Tolstoy, Dostoevsky, Ibsen, Chekhov, Strindberg, Hauptmann, and others—great artists and also unsparing anatomists of an expiring culture, who expanded the Hugolian vision, lifted it onto a modern plane.

The *ernste Menschen* also gave him his first coherent understanding of bolshevism, locating the events of 1917 within a radical tradition that traced back to the theories of Marx and Engels, through the exploits of Bakunin and Nechaev, the writings of Prince Kropotkin, and the agitations of the *Narodniki,* who had been the first to organize uprisings among Russian peasants.[9]

Chambers did not submit passively to this vision of history. He argued fiercely with his friends. When Kip Fadiman urged him to read the *Communist Manifesto,* Chambers mocked its "horrible rhetoric." When others expounded views they picked up at the Young People's Socialist League, Chambers countered by upholding what he called "aristocratic anarchism."[10]

As these new friends were Chambers's "first" Jews, so he was their first WASP, one of the few really gifted ones they had known, and easily the most exotic. Older than these city boys, he had traveled, lived on his own, been out in the world in a way unthinkable to them. He could fake his way through half a dozen tongues. "He spoke Gypsy!" remembered an amazed Meyer Schapiro, himself an intellectual prodigy at sixteen. Strange that this blond blue-eyed Gentile raised in a white-collar suburb, a resort town by the sea, was a veteran of the third rail, the waterfront, and the flophouse, with stories to tell (and embellish) of One-Eyed Annie and Sam Monti, the jungle theorist. Strange too that a boy with such refined eating habits should, upon opening his mouth, reveal "a devastation of empty sockets and blackened stumps," the consequence of years of neglect.[11]

More striking still was Chambers's confident expectation that a momentous future beckoned him. This did not emerge in boasts or fervent declarations. On the contrary, though Chambers "could on occasion speak eloquently and cogently," recalled Lionel Trilling, who observed Chambers from a critical distance, he normally confined himself to "gnomic, often cryptic" remarks or said nothing at all, lapsing into long, studied silences.[12] These only magnified his aura. "In a penetratingly quiet way he called attention to himself as a man of destiny," remembered Chambers's friend John Gassner, a tiny Hungarian immigrant, later Sterling professor of drama at Yale. "He dressed like a derelict but carried himself like a king."[13]

Chambers and his new friends flocked to a charismatic young English instructor, Mark Van Doren, hired in the spring of 1920—just in time to teach Chambers's freshman composition class. Rare for an English professor of his day, Van Doren was a practicing writer, a fine lyric poet influenced by Robert Frost. Today, a quarter century after his death, he is revered as the greatest teacher in Columbia's long history. While older professors lectured grandly on literary history and themes, Van Doren, only twenty-six—handsome, slim, unfailingly courteous—approached his subject with "heroic humility," in the words of Thomas Merton, one of his many protégés. As Van Doren went through a poem, line by line, asking simple but pointed questions, he seemed to be composing the work himself. The effect was to exalt the poet and at the same time bring his creations down to earth.[14]

Like so many others, Chambers was intoxicated. He decided "the literary life is best in the world and that to be a poet is among the highest callings known to man." He wrote his first poems and shyly submitted them to his teacher's judgment. Van Doren was deeply impressed. Chambers combined sensitive lyricism with a mature economy of expression. Van Doren encouraged the freshman to write more and bestowed on him the highest possible praise. He allowed Chambers to believe "I was to be a poet."[15]

Chambers's prose was equally good,* though he chose surprising topics, for instance, bolshevism. He railed against its evils, citing scripture and sprinkling in stately quotations from *Have Faith in Massachusetts*, the collected speeches of Calvin Coolidge.[17]

Van Doren discovered that Chambers meant what he wrote. In midterm November Chambers missed a few assignments. Van Doren called him in to warn him he was in danger of not receiving full credit for the course.

"I'm so busy with politics that I can't keep up with my work," Chambers explained.

---

* Van Doren later rated Chambers the "best" of all the undergraduates he knew in the 1920s, surpassing Clifton Fadiman, John Gassner, Meyer Schapiro, the journalist Herbert Solow, Lionel Trilling, and Louis Zukofsky.[16]

Van Doren was startled. "Politics? What are you doing?"

"I'm distributing handbills for Calvin Coolidge for Vice-President."

"Why Coolidge?" Van Doren wondered. Chambers then "asked me in turn if I had not heard about that great man's action in settling the Boston police strike." Van Doren, a contributor to *The Nation,* the liberal weekly, refrained from expressing his own opinion of the "great man."[18]

Chambers's politics might be conventional. His vehemence was not. In 1920 few undergraduates were paying any attention to the upcoming election. But Chambers pitched himself into it headlong. He began a one-man mass mailing campaign, sending pro-Coolidge letters to newspaper editors across the land. When Coolidge spoke at a rally at Madison Square Garden, Chambers, arriving after the doors had closed, climbed a fire escape in order to hear him.[19]

It was remarkable conduct for one otherwise preoccupied with "poetry, philosophy, and all manner of abstract things," as Van Doren recalled. The teacher did not criticize his pupil or his beliefs. "His politics were not my business, and anyway he was so passionate a Republican that he would not have listened to anybody."[20]

After a year Chambers was happy enough at Columbia to take up residence on campus, an expense his parents were prepared to meet since Laha had begun a job as a caseworker with a Queens unit of the New York City Bureau of Child Welfare.[21]

He moved into Hartley Hall, a new elevator building ten stories high. Its three hundred rooms, singles and suites, each had a nine-foot-high ceiling, heavy oak furniture, and an "enameled basin with hot and cold water." There were four bathrooms, with showers and tubs, spaced along the hall. Students congregated in a sixty-foot "assembly room" with a large open hearth.[22]

Chambers's roommate was Edward Lewis, a math major from Baldwin, a town near Lynbrook. As a freshman Chambers had spent many weekends at Lewis's house, bicycling the four miles from Earle Avenue. Lewis's father, a Methodist minister, was moved by Chambers's religious struggles, and both father and son tried to convert him to their faith, with little success, though he regularly attended services at Reverend Lewis's church. On campus Chambers was tenderly protective of Edward, a cripple, helping him around the dorm and pushing his wheelchair along the walkways of Morningside Heights.[23]

As a boarder Chambers plunged into Columbia's busy literary activity. He joined the staff of *Varsity,* an undergraduate magazine, and belonged to Boar's Head, a Conversazione Society (named for the Falstaffian tavern in *Henry IV, Part One*) founded by English Professor John Erskine.[24] As Van Doren gave inspiration and encouragement to campus writers, so Erskine organized forums for them. In addition to Boar's Head, he sponsored the revival of a defunct literary magazine, *The Morningside,* in 1920. In its pages the sophomore Chambers first made a reputation as Columbia's most daring and original writer.

His debut came in the issue of March 1922. Chambers contributed a long story, "The Damn Fool," which occupied the first twenty-one pages, or two thirds, of the magazine. It was the first important autobiographical prose Chambers published. In it may be found the germ of his later important writings—and actions.

Narratively the story is heavily indebted to Joseph Conrad, the first modern novelist Chambers read, and then at the zenith of his renown. The story opens with two world-weary men seated in a harbor café. Their meal finished, they light up cigarettes and survey the placid scene.

> The chimes in the little church on the hill struck as the sunset gun fired. A line, flying the yellow flag, swung sluggishly at anchor outside Quarantine. Soon lanterns flickered from masts and sterns. Out of the dusk, on one of those ships, a guitar twanged and a voice, a tenor, struck up a minor dirge in a Slavic dialect. From regarding the hushed traffic of the lower bay, McDowell turned his eyes on his companion. The odd, estimating twinkle sparkled there.
> "Do you remember Everett Holmes?" he asked slowly.
> Burton laughed. "Yes," he drawled, "Holmes, who ——?"
> "Exactly. The damn fool. You do remember him."[25]

The remainder of the story is an account, narrated by McDowell, of Everett Holmes's improbable adventures. Initially he cuts a shabby figure. He is "the sort of a fellow who never has good tools—doesn't brush his coat, or if he does, is immaculate except his shoes. They're never shined." His conduct veers erratically from the ridiculous to the lofty. "He was capable of the damndest stunts and then—he'd defend himself sublimely. . . . [H]e was really brave. He might meet a crisis and take high ground."

Fired from an office job, Holmes thoroughly reinvents himself. He changes his name, shedding the genteel Everett for the more manly Edward. Then he sets off to find high adventure and a noble cause, fighting the Bolsheviks. He lands a berth on a ship to Constantinople and then steals through the Turkish countryside. "In his filthy rags and with a crucifix he'd bought somewhere, or made, he was not unlike those crazy fanatic monks who run all over the Greek Orthodox countries." When accosted, he pretends he is deaf and mute.

By the time he reaches the port of Varna, on the Black Sea, Holmes has fallen ill but has also acquired an aura of divinity. He finds another ship. The crew eyes him suspiciously. But when he fishes a sailor out of the ocean, "they let him stay from superstition—bad luck, they said, to put off a saint—he took courage in place of strength."

In Russia Holmes becomes a latter-day St. Joan, guiding men into battle with his upraised crucifix. The troops "fought behind me with faith in that cross," he writes in a letter to his mother. "That cross is a power." Wounded in battle, "the dumb, mad priest" is transformed from religious to secular "crusader." He discards his crucifix and dons a uniform.

The front, when he reaches it, is a mass of carnage. The enemy forces are overwhelming. Doomed to die, Holmes sends home his last message, "a strange letter, like the others, but more so. He talks about the righteousness of wars, strangely personal and general." He cannot wait to fling himself suicidally into battle. "This is a magnificent hara-kiri," Holmes exults. "A chance to die with honor when you can no longer live with honor."[26]

In his last hours Holmes rediscovers religion. "To win we must have Faith," he declares, citing examples of soldiers past. "Cromwell's invincibility was simply the consequence of his absolute faith in God. His Iron-clads charged into battle singing the psalms of David. His battle-cry was The Lord of Hosts. And what is more sublime in history than Washington praying in the winter woods?"

Like Conrad's Kurtz in *Heart of Darkness,* Holmes meets a grisly and humiliating end. He is killed, and his corpse is mutilated. The story concludes with McDowell and Burton in the café, pensively reflecting on the hero's strange journey.

The lights twinkled red, white and green and trembled in long liquid rays on the black waters. The chimes in the belfry struck another hour and a ship's bell clanged across the Bay. After a long silence Burton laid his cigarette on the table.

"He was a damn fool, you see that[,] don't you, Mack?" he asked.
McDowell started to object.

"What he did gives weakness a false appearance of glory. He wasn't
glorious. How many weary miles did he tramp to escape himself?"

"He gained some things, though, I think. I did not say he was glorious. He was a strange chap."

"The Damn Fool" was greatly admired at Columbia, as was the fiction that followed. Chambers seemed to have the makings of a poet or
novelist—possibly a major one. "We were convinced he would leap into
fame," recalled historian Jacques Barzun, an undergraduate acquaintance
from this period.[27]

What dazzled everyone was Chambers's prose, its "elegant austerity,"
in Lionel Trilling's phrase.[28] At twenty-one Chambers had bypassed the
normal phase of self-conscious writerliness and achieved a striking maturity of expression. This seemed precocious, and was.

But few saw that "The Damn Fool" was less a work of imagination
than of projection. The story has an unacknowledged source text, "The
Soldier's Faith," the famous 1895 Harvard commencement address of
Oliver Wendell Holmes (hence the protagonist's name), much admired
by Theodore Roosevelt, President Grover Cleveland, and other advocates of the "strenuous life." Holmes, then a judge on the Massachusetts
Supreme Court, had extolled war as a theater for secular martyrdom in
which the most ordinary soldier will "throw away his life in obedience
to a blindly accepted duty." By his faith, said Holmes, the soldier proves
each "has in him that unspeakable somewhat which makes him capable
of miracle, able to lift himself by the might of his own soul, unaided, able
to face annihilation for a blind belief."[29]

Chambers too seeks a "blind belief," a totalizing mission to which he
can abandon himself unrestrainedly. In him, as in Everett Holmes, what
seems vanity is in reality the deepest humility. He is prepared to kill for his
cause and also to suffer ostracism and death. All must be sacrificed to it.

For Chambers the college sophomore, language is purely instrumental, as it is for prophets and propagandists. The beauty of words stirs him
less than his need to declare himself and his destiny.

Chambers's sophomore year was productive and pleasurable. He was
troubled by the tensions in Lynbrook but on furlough, at least, from the

house itself. He was growing to love the Columbia campus. He haunted the many college libraries and reading rooms, especially College Study, in Hamilton Hall, with its five thousand volumes, and was an energetic salesman of *The Morningside*.[30]

In the evenings he spent hilarious hours with his friends. *Morningside* editor Charlie Wagner, a prizewinning campus poet, remembered one night when a group all had been drinking mildly alcoholic Prohibition beer. "[Chambers] was in the middle of one of [his] spoofs when the glare of a street lamp began to bother him. [He] shouted, 'Let's put that thing out!' and through the open window reached out into space. . . . I made a dive for him and caught his feet . . . when he was halfway out."[31]

But Chambers was also an *ernste Mensch*. "He thought hard, he studied hard, he was curious about everything," recalled John Gassner. "He was impatient with sloth and he scorned mediocrity in any form."[32]

By nature an autodidact, Chambers organized his own schedule of study, guided by his many interests. He spent long hours in his room working on stories and poems and exploring the literature of several languages. He also tutored foreign students in English several nights a week. And he developed a strict physical regimen, doggedly training alongside the varsity wrestling team—he was not good enough to make the squad—and toning up with laps in Riverside Park and feverish games of handball.[33]

But he was finding it difficult to "pull in harness." His grades were good, especially in literature and language courses. But poor attendance cost him requisite "points," and he received warnings from the undergraduate dean, Herbert Hawkes.[34]

Chambers did not try to explain what the problem was: that he was searching for something his professors could not or would not give him. Columbia's expansive curriculum—the panoramic survey courses, the piles of great books—seemed feckless to him. He detected a vacuum in the catholicity of texts and in his instructors' dexterous glide from one system of ideas to the next. They offered a "higher hodgepodge" of worldviews. He craved the one right answer to which he could dedicate himself.[35]

So insulated did his preceptors seem that Chambers was bestirred to disorient them. On one occasion he phoned the Columbia philosopher Irwin Edman at his home.

"Hello, Irwin," said Chambers. "Are you there?"

"Where are you?" the professor asked.

"In time and space."

"How did you get there?" Edman asked

"On Kantian lines" was Chambers's enigmatic reply.[36]

But sometimes he went further, indulging his taste for the "damndest stunts." One time he accosted Raymond Weaver, a distinguished member of the English Department, and nonplussed the professor with a fabricated account of his escapades in a Harlem brothel, capping the performance by flourishing the results of a syphilis test.

Chambers also subjected friends to hamfisted pranks. Two involved David Zablodowsky, a member of the literary crowd who wrestled on the varsity team, to Chambers's envy. Once when Zablodowsky was innocently eating a sandwich at the "Q and D" (Quick and Dirty), an off-campus hangout, Chambers suddenly materialized and flung the contents of a ketchup bottle on Zablodowsky's suit. Chambers quickly apologized and handed the victim, more stunned than angry, a dollar to have his suit cleaned.

Another time Chambers paid a call on the parents of Zablodowsky's roommate, Jack Schultz, who lived just outside New York. Taking with him Meyer Schapiro, Schultz's other roommate, Chambers posed as Zablodowsky and plied the Schultzes with intimate questions about their son. They answered readily but were annoyed when they discovered the true identity of their questioner.

Some found these pranks amusing. Others did not. "His extramural activities frightened me," recalled Lionel Trilling. "I did my best to stay away from him."[37]

At the end of Chambers's sophomore year the editors of *The Morningside* elected him editor in chief for the following year, succeeding Charlie Wagner. That summer, back at Lynbrook, Chambers prepared the fall edition of the magazine, the first to come out under his editorship. It was also the last.

The year 1922 was an *annus mirabilis* in modern literature. James Joyce's *Ulysses* was published, in Paris, to mingled fanfare and outrage. The U.S. Post Office set fire to copies of the novel smuggled through the mails. Chambers read another new masterpiece, T. S. Eliot's "The Waste Land," in *The Dial*.[38]

Excited by these insurgent energies, Chambers and his fellow editors agreed the fall number of *The Morningside* must make a bold statement.

It must exhibit "more cynicism and get away from more lyrical characters in the magazine."[39] Thus was born the "profanist" issue of *The
Morningside*. In an editorial note Chambers explained: "Profanism, its ad-
herents tell us, derives from the Latin 'pro fano,' outside the temple. . . .
[T]he Profanist dares to look at life unhesitatingly and dares to represent
it without the veils. . . . Profanism is the healthiest sign of the determination of Columbia men to wipe away the lactic droolings of the late
century and accept something more nearly approaching reality than the
ethical, religious and materialistic hypocrisy of modern life."[40]

The number came out in October. Reviewing it in Columbia's student newspaper, *The Spectator*, Mark Van Doren warmly recommended
its entire contents and especially its "brilliant" lead piece, " 'A Play for
Puppets,' by John Kelly (whoever he is), conceived in the purest profanism and dedicated to the Antichrist." John Kelly was Chambers, as
Van Doren well knew. Fearing the playlet might offend college authorities, Chambers had shown the original manuscript to his mentor, who
assured him it was publishable.[41]

"A Play for Puppets"—the title may have been suggested by Jay
Chambers's miniature theater—opens with two centurions standing before Christ's tomb:

> YOUNG C: This Jesus in here was a poor fellow.
> OLD C: He was obstinate and proud.
> YOUNG C: They say he never lay with a woman.
> OLD C: I wouldn't blame no man for that. Women are wicked snares
> to the young. But he tried to keep others from it. That's where he went
> wrong. Now, Mark Anthony was a man! He could sack a city, a wine jug
> or a woman to beat any man in the Roman armies.[42]

There follows ribald bantering, mostly on the topic of women's
breasts. Then Christ ("dressed in grey kimono, long red hair covers
bowed head, hands folded in front of Him") speaks wearily from the
tomb to abjure his impending resurrection. "Roll back the stone," he
languidly tells the centurions, "and go thy way. It is very quiet in the
earth and I will sleep." When an angel bids Christ to rise, he does so reluctantly and exits the stage, murmuring weakly, "I am the truth, the
way and the light."

Read today, the four pages seem innocent enough, if rather less
brilliant than Van Doren claimed. But "A Play for Puppets"—and the

author's provocative Irish Catholic alias—achieved the intended furor, and then some. "That issue of the magazine sold out in about two hours," Chambers later said, with an editor's pride.[43] Outraged faculty called for the immediate expulsion of John Kelly, whose true identity did not long remain a secret.[44] A student delegation, denouncing the play as "filthy, sacrilegious, and profane," complained to President Butler.[45] Dean Hawkes ordered the author to retrieve all the copies of *The Morningside.* Chambers refused. He and Charlie Wagner repaired to a Chinese restaurant to discuss the crisis, rather to joke about it. "Whittaker was never happier," Wagner recalled. "Something ha[d] been released in him."[46]

Hawkes and Erskine hastily convened a meeting of the student committee on publications, which then drafted a letter to *The Morningside*'s editors demanding Chambers's immediate resignation and threatening suspension of the magazine "upon the reappearance of any material similar to the play by John Kelly."[47]

Within days the controversy had spread beyond the campus. "Columbia University, battle ground for many causes and movements, is torn today between a small group calling themselves 'profanists' and the rest of the student body," the *Evening Post* reported. *The New York Times* and the *Tribune* also covered the incident.[48] Nothing was said about Van Doren's endorsement of Chambers's play. And no one at Columbia seemed to remember that only a few months before, the rebel playwright had been a dedicated Christian, far more serious about religion than most of his classmates. No one saw the complete picture: that Chambers was less a blasphemer than a tormented doubter, hungry for a sustaining faith.

Unprepared for such censure, Chambers sank into despondency. He stopped going to classes and "filled up my room with books and began to read all day." A friend came by Chambers's room at Hartley Hall with a bottle of bootleg whiskey, potent beyond anything Chambers had tasted. After a few drinks he lost control and "tore the place apart." There were more binges in the following weeks.[49]

By January, drained of recrimination, Chambers decided it was he, after all, who had been at fault. In a poem he reflected that "no word or act that any one has said or done" was responsible for his state of mind. He had been spoiling for a fight, and Columbia had complied. He felt nothing now but "simple regret for a ruined thing."[50]

A college education could serve no useful purpose. In January, he wrote to Dean Hawkes informing him he had left the College and would not return for at least a year, if at all.[51]

Hawkes did not try to dissuade Chambers. But he did ask Van Doren for an explanation.[52]

Chambers "is very impulsive, and takes things seriously," Van Doren replied. "He took conservatism seriously as a freshman, and he took radicalism seriously as a junior. Just now he doesn't know quite how to take an institution that taught him to think and then forbade his saying what he thought in the way he liked. He has an idea that he will come back in a year or two and be able to make a better adjustment. I am confident he will take good care of himself. I still consider him a valuable man."[53]

Meanwhile what should he do with himself? Van Doren suggested going to Russia—not to fight the Bolsheviks but to help them. Famine had struck the Soviet Union. Many charity organizations were sending over relief expeditions. Van Doren had contacts at the American Friends Service Committee.[54]

In late January Chambers went to Philadelphia for an interview with AFSC officials. He stayed with his grandparents, who had moved to the Germantown home of their daughter Helen and her husband, a banker. One night, while Whittaker was visiting, Grandfather Chambers was late returning from the *Public Ledger*. The police phoned to say he had died in the arms of his mistress, at age sixty-nine. The next day Chambers helped the city editor of the *Public Ledger* concoct an explanation for the old man's death. He was reported as having "dropped dead of heart disease on the street . . . while on his way to his home" after a strenuous day at the office.[55]

The Quakers rejected Chambers's application. He suspected "A Play for Puppets" was the cause.[56] For the time being he was too confused to plot an alternative course, though he wished to avoid Lynbrook. A reproachful Laha was unbearable. There was also a new and malign presence in the house, Laha's mother, Mary. Footloose since the death of her husband, in 1899, she had begun to decline and now was forced on the charity of her daughter. Mary sealed herself in an upstairs room on Earle Avenue from which mysterious odors had begun to waft. One day Chambers rammed open the door with his shoulder and stumbled into the room. His grandmother showed him her "little contrivance"—"a tiny oven made of a tomato can with the top cut out" and a flame burning beneath.[57]

The Grand Guignol was further enriched by the arrival of a second boarder, the widowed Dora Chambers. The two grandmothers did not get along, and soon Dora moved out of the house and into a nearby apartment, where she remained until her death in 1931.[58]

For Whittaker, there was only one escape. He went back to Columbia, camping in the rooms of friends who sneaked him cafeteria food. Unfettered by course work, he resumed the existence he had begun after the "Puppets" scandal. He played handball and wrestled in the Columbia gym and spent long hours reading and writing, gathering up volumes by the dozen at College Study.[59]

On visits to Lynbrook, Chambers went off by himself on long, solitary rambles. As an adolescent, when the pressures of Earle Avenue had become too great, he often had arisen at dawn, while his family slept, and spent the day exploring the woods and the Atlantic beaches. Now, at odds once more with the human world, he consulted the harbors, the tide, and the star-filled sky, seeking "some meaning to the life we live."[60] His gaze also traveled outward, to the sea and beyond. The distant horizons renewed their call along with the obscure tidal message of "inhuman force." Chambers wanted to go abroad. Laha tried to discourage him, fearing a repetition of his first escape. But much to Whittaker's surprise, Jay agreed to let him buy a boat ticket to Europe.[61]

# Signing On

Meyer Schapiro decided to go too. So did another friend, Henry Zolinsky,* a student poet at CCNY and editor of its literary magazine, *Lavender*. The trip was to be a culture binge. The friends would work on languages, haunt museums, and savor the Continental atmosphere of boulevards and cafés. It cost very little to travel in postwar Europe, especially for Americans.[1]

Schapiro and Zolinsky departed first, in early June, working their way over as second-class stewards on a Holland-America liner. They landed in Rotterdam and proceeded to the German border, where they met trouble. Dutch guards would not accept seamen's passes, the only documents the travelers had. Rather than turn back, the pair tried to sneak across. Zolinsky made it. Schapiro was nabbed and locked up in a cell with smugglers. He won his release by drawing flattering sketches of the jailer's son and soon caught up with Zolinsky for the train ride to Berlin.[2]

In Lynbrook, Chambers shook Richard's hand and kissed Laha goodbye—both pleaded with him not to leave[3]—and sailed on the *Seydlitz*, which departed for Bremerhaven on June 20.[4] On board he met his first Germans, tourists trimmed out in garish caps and plus fours. Chambers socialized with them, polishing his German. At mealtimes they urged pickled herring on the young American as a preventative against seasickness, though he was not so afflicted.

---

* In 1942, Zolinsky changed his surname to Zolan.

Chambers, the author of fictive sea adventures, was primed to savor every romantic frisson of this real voyage. He roused himself before day-break to stand shivering at the deck rail as the first rays of sunlight tinted the English Channel, "coldly peaceful in the dawn," and the cliffs of Calais and Dover "waking/In early morning from the mist." He pre-served these moments in poems he transcribed onto the blank pages of a bound travel diary, *Places I Have Visited*.[5]

At Bremerhaven, on the North Sea, Chambers took the night express, third class, to Berlin, speeding through the medieval towns and industrial fortresses of Saxony and the forests and lakes of Brandenburg. In Berlin he joined Schapiro and Zolinsky in the room they had rented in the house of one Frau Haupt, whose spotless kitchen was hung with an em-broidered motto: *Immer rein und fein/Müss mein Flettbrett sein* (Always clean and nice/Must my kitchen board be).

By law Frau Haupt was required to register her guests with the police. But since Schapiro and Zolinsky lacked the proper papers, they faced eviction and their landlady the loss of their dollars—this during the peak moment of Weimar Germany's mad postwar inflation. So Frau Haupt did not report her guests, guarding their secret as they did hers: The re-spectable landlady was "living flagrantly" with a policeman who lounged around the house all day.[6]

The travelers could not have picked a more volatile time to visit Ger-many. The year 1923 would be long remembered as a fateful one in the country's history, "a crazy time, a bad time," as one historian has written. In January, French troops had occupied the Ruhr, Germany's industrial heartland, sealing off the steel factories and coal mines responsible for 80 percent of the stricken country's production. Later that year the fanatical nationalist Adolf Hitler, an ex-corporal in the kaiser's army, staged a clumsy "beer hall" putsch against the republican government of Bavaria.[7]

Yet Berlin in 1923, though gripped by "an epidemic of fear [and] naked need," was one of the world's most exciting cities, the capital of Prussia and of the empire, and a cultural mecca as well. On the Kurfürs-tendamm, packed with bars and dance halls, three Americans could dally over a meal at a sidewalk restaurant and take in the displays, voluptuary and dangerous: respectable burghers panting after "made-up boys with artificial waistlines," purse snatchers darting into the throng of strollers, noticed but ignored. Chambers long remembered the sight of a woman, "handsomely dressed, extremely dignified," with tears "streaming down her face; tears which she made no effort to conceal, which did not even distort her features. She simply walked slowly past, proudly erect, unconcerned about any spectacle she made. And this was the terrifying part: nobody paid the slightest attention to her."[8]

There was something else, as new to Chambers and as stirring, "little knots of furtive figures selling newspapers at some of the street corners." The paper was *Die Rote Fahne* (The Red Flag), the outlawed publication of the Communist Party. Early one morning Chambers was awakened in his room to the sounds of marching Communists, their voices soaring in unison as they sang an anthem he was later to learn by heart:

> Schmier die Guillotine, schmier die Guillotine, schmier die
>   Guillotine
> Mit Tyrannenfett.
> Blut müss fliessen, Blut müss fliessen, Blut, Blut, Blut.
> *(Grease the guillotine . . . with the fat of tyrants. Blood*
> *must flow . . . blood, blood, blood.)*[9]

After several weeks Frau Haupt notified her renters she had no choice but to register them. The authorities were growing suspicious. More than once Schapiro and Zolinsky had been trailed home from sightseeing tours by police. It was time to move on.

At the American Embassy the tourists were told the only country they could enter legally was Belgium. But at the railroad station they were denied tickets so far west. They traveled instead to the industrial city of Hamm, in Westphalia, and then, at dawn, bought new tickets, south to Cologne, and then to Liège, and finally to Brussels.[10]

In Brussels the American Student Exchange helped the tourists find lodgings on the Rue de l'Union. Chambers and his companions "read and thought, wrote, painted and sketched in the moments when we were not picture-gallerying," and made side trips to Antwerp and Liège. Schapiro sketched portraits of himself and his companions. Chambers sports a mustache in his.[11]

Chambers, with his acceptable documents, took the train alone to Paris. In northern France he saw "heaped wreckage and broken walls" and the "still-raw battle lines of the old Western front." At one point passengers crowded against the window to glimpse the remnants of the church of St.-Quentin, shelled during the war.[12]

Chambers stayed a week in Paris, which was fast becoming the citadel of expatriate America, its bars and bistros soon to be celebrated in Hemingway's *The Sun Also Rises*. Unaware of these excitements, Chambers explored more conventional pathways. He visited the Louvre, tramped in Montmartre, loitered along the Seine, and distilled these pleasures into a long narrative poem in couplets. But even as he soaked up the ambient glow of the "Capital of Light" he felt himself recoil from "the sickening apotheosis and striving after *ART*" so common "among our American generation."[13] Though he did not yet realize it, he much preferred the Berlin Communists he had glimpsed as they fled with copies of their outlawed newspaper.

In mid-September the three tourists sailed home. Schapiro and Zolinsky toiled again on the *Rotterdam* (Schapiro, an indifferent steward, was banished to the scullery). Chambers sailed on the *Belganland*, which departed from Antwerp.[14]

Days after his return Chambers heard from Charlie Wagner about a job opening at the New York Public Library, the massive main building on Fifth Avenue and Forty-second Street. The job required him to sit at a desk in the newspaper room and retrieve papers for patrons as they filed requests. The hours were 5:00–10:00 P.M. Monday through Friday, with a longer shift on Sunday. Wagner, enrolled at the Columbia Journalism School, had turned the job down. But Chambers grabbed it and its monthly wage of $67.50.[15] It seemed the ideal situation. At night the patrons were few, and Chambers had ample time to read and write at his desk.

With savings from his new income, Chambers moved out of Earle Avenue and covered half the rent in a room he shared in uptown Manhattan, near City College, with Henry Bang, a fellow Columbia dropout who had found a job with a utility company. The two had met during freshman hazing. Bang came from East Rockaway, only a mile and a half from Lynbrook, and had often commuted with Chambers to Morningside Heights. The two had also spent many hours together on Long Island, camping on the beaches and touring the shore by bicycle.[16]

When their room caught fire that summer, the pair moved to Long Island, pitching a tent in the dunes on Atlantic Beach. It was an enchanted spot, and they were joined by other friends—Wagner, Zukofsky, Zolinsky, Kip Fadiman—and by Henry's teenage brother Frank, called Bub.

(The Bangs called Chambers Charlie.) "On the Beach," a playlet Chambers published in 1926, captures the languid pleasures of that summer: the suppers of clams steamed over driftwood fires at twilight while gulls skimmed the breakers, the sunsets reddening the harbor sky, the mysterious moonlight, the turbulent surge of the surf.[17]

By this time Chambers had conceived a far more ambitious literary project, a sequence of lyrics on the vanishing joys of the South Shore. The landscape of his childhood was undergoing a rapid change, as Henry Ford's mass-produced Model T brought more and more city dwellers out to Long Island, crowding the beaches and meadows, and as developers began to parcel up the farms.[18]

Dismayed by this blighting of his beloved countryside, Chambers also began a strenuous reading program, his main texts socialist treatises, economic and philosophical. He dutifully plowed through the Fabians— Beatrice and Sidney Webb, G.D.H. Cole, R. H. Tawney—but was more stimulated by Georges Sorel's *Reflections on Violence,* the classic defense of the syndicalist movement and of the general strike as a revolutionary tactic. In the quasi-mystical Sorel, who died in 1922 at age seventy-five, Chambers found a kindred spirit, half revolutionist, half reactionary, who favored monarchy over parliamentary democracy and fervently extolled the military virtues.[19]

But Chambers was not yet sold on political action. In Europe he had been impressed by the reactionary French novelist and critic Paul Bourget, a convert to Roman Catholicism and royalism, at war with modernity. He also imbibed the gloomy prophecies of Oswald Spengler's *The Decline of the West* and was moved by Leo Tolstoy's pacifist tract *The Kingdom of God Is Within You,* in which the great novelist implored Christians to shun all political and economic programs and deliver themselves over to the Gospels, which alone could end the world's violence and establish "the unity of mankind."[20]

The summer of 1924 was important for another reason. Chambers had his first love affair, with a woman whom he later referred to as Mrs. Mainland. Married and a mother, she lived on Long Island's North Shore in a house overlooking the beach. Her husband was not much in evidence. Chambers spent languorous afternoons lounging on the porch in a deck chair, watching Mrs. Mainland's two children splash in the surf at high tide. To Meyer Schapiro, his confidant in these matters, Chambers proclaimed his great happiness.[21]

Yet he was in a confused state and receptive to Mrs. Mainland's suggestion that he try college again. In July he wrote to Dean Hawkes and humbly asked if he could return to Columbia since he had matured during his months away. Hawkes replied generously. "I am very glad to hear from you and to know that you wish to take up your collegiate work again." If Chambers really wished to continue his education, "I see no reason on earth why you should not do so."[22]

In September Chambers wrote to Van Doren and announced he was returning to Columbia. Showing his rebel streak, he bragged to Van Doren of having lied to Dean Hawkes, telling him his goal was to teach history when his actual goal was to placate Mrs. Mainland.[23]

Within weeks of enrolling, he had lapsed into the old habits. He missed classes and skipped exams.[24] But in General Honors, an advanced seminar for upperclassmen, he dazzled his oral examiners—among them the young Mortimer J. Adler—who greeted his performance with spontaneous applause. "Chambers was simply brilliant," Adler recalled.[25]

Meanwhile his personal life had turned chaotic. Late in 1924 Chambers drunkenly confided to Meyer Schapiro that an unnamed mistress, evidently not Mrs. Mainland, had borne him a son. Henry Zolinsky also remembered hearing of this incident, from Louis Zukofsky. But nothing further is known about this child.[26]

Chambers's sexuality had become a new and troubling question for him. He seems to have begun his affairs with women as a means of overcoming an attraction to men. He confided his secret to Zolinsky, who was surprised. In Brussels the two had shared a bed without incident. Later, however, Chambers reproached Zolinsky: "You kept me at arm's length." Many years passed before Zolinsky understood what Chambers meant.[27]

Chambers himself barely understood it. He was shocked when he heard friends whispering about his "homosexual relationship" with Henry Bang's younger brother, Bub, seven years Chambers's junior. Bub often camped with his brother and Chambers on Atlantic Beach and had begun to visit during the day as well. The two swam, canoed, fished, and talked. Rather Chambers talked and Bub listened, trying to follow his learned friend, though "half the time I didn't know what he was talking about."[28]

The two remained in touch for many years, even after both were married with children. Like Chambers, Bub long insisted the relationship was chaste, its intimacy "psychological" rather than sexual. But many years later Bub concluded: "I think he [Chambers] was probably bisexual."[29]

Chambers's confusion was heightened by the enigma of Jay. By this time Whittaker had discovered his father's secret. In 1915 Jay had taken an apartment in Manhattan with a man and been reduced to tears when his roommate broke up the arrangement to get married.[30]

"The Damn Fool" includes an oblique reference to Jay's homosexuality.* And in another story, Whittaker's sexual dilemma emerges more starkly. "In Memory of R.G.," published in *The Morningside* in December 1924, includes the following physical description:

> What a splendid thing he was. And he stood not quite six foot with one hand on the railing. He was stripped but for short black tights about the groin. His legs were firm and columnar. His knees were small, the muscle not yet completely developed. His thighs lean with a perpendicular fluting. His stomach was perfectly flat, not a crease over the navel. And his chest that heaved dangled such arms, long, sinewed, brown, joined to the shoulder with plates of ligament. His jaw was heavy but gentle. His mouth large but curved downward. His nose straight, his eyes deep and brown, his hair black. He was still struggling for quiet breath and the sweat lay over his limbs in a thin lacquer.[31]

The hungrily observant eyes are a mother's, fastened on her son. But Chambers, it is evident, had studied male physiques with ardent attentiveness.

Similar imagery courses through Chambers's poetry. In "Lothrop, Montana," published in *The Nation* in 1926, he likens cottonwood saplings to "boy-trees" whose "clean, green, central bodies" stand close together but apart. Only their roots, hidden from view,

> *Wrap one about another, interstruggle and knot;*
> *the vital filaments*
> *Writhing in struggle.*[32]

He also wrote an explicitly homosexual poem, "Tandaradei," published in June 1926 in *Two Worlds,* a journal edited by the pornographer

---

* "After the husband, you know that story. And what the revulsion must have been!" (p. 94).

and "booklegger" Samuel Roth, notorious for his pirating of Joyce's *Ulysses,* a portion of which ran in the same issue as Chambers's steamy verses. Once again Chambers summons the image of trees:

> *As your sap drains out into me in excess,*
> *Like the sap from the stems of a tree that they lop.*[33]

Meanwhile Chambers's family was disintegrating. Grandmother Whittaker was now erupting in violent denunciation of Jews, John D. Rockefeller, and, most often, Jay and his "depravities." She sometimes wandered the house in ghostly silence, clutching a kitchen knife and sometimes scissors. It was Whittaker's task to disarm her. There was usually a "sharp scuffle," and he was left with lifelong scars on his fingers.[34]

But Whittaker's chief worry was his brother. Superficially Richard seemed Whittaker's opposite in every way, a good-natured, uncomplicated, and attractive youth. Though less brilliant than Whittaker, Richard had varied abilities. "He could sketch. He could compose verses. He was excellent in mathematics. He was also a good mechanic." He lettered in several sports and was popular with classmates and teachers alike. Yet beneath his sunny exterior, Richard was troubled. He seemed to lack an identity of his own and was unable to contest Laha's imperious will. Her control over him was total. She had delayed Richard's entry into grammar school and then kept him home so often he needed an extra year to complete his grammar school education. She also kept him out of high school at her whim—Richard needed five years to graduate. He was twenty when he received his diploma, in June 1924.[35]

In September, at the same time Chambers resumed his studies at Columbia, Richard began his freshman year at Colgate University, in upstate New York. His troubles started immediately, when he was snubbed by a fraternity that had rushed some of his friends. Stricken, Richard fled, going as far as Buffalo. It was his first rebellion, and he boasted of it in a rare letter to his brother, with whom he now felt in league, as a profanist. After a few days Richard limped back to Colgate and finished out the term.

In Lynbrook at Christmas, Richard drunkenly spouted nihilist sentiments. "Look around you," he told his brother, "look at people. Every one of them is a hypocrite. Look at the world. It is hopeless. Look at religion. Nobody really believes that stuff, even the people who pretend to. Look at marriage. Look at Mother and Jay. What a fraud! Look at the family. Look at ours! It's a crime to have children. . . . We're hopeless people," Richard declared. "We can't cope with the world. We're too gentle."[36]

Chambers's career at Columbia ended quietly. The long-running protest petered out. By December he had stopped going to class altogether. He had found a new intellectual passion, bolshevism. At one of the many secondhand bookshops on Fourth Avenue, in lower Manhattan, he had come upon a fifty-cent edition of a speech Vladimir Lenin made to his Soviet colleagues in April 1918, five months after their coup. Titled *The Soviets at Work,* the speech was one of the first inside reports on the most successful political uprising since the French Revolution.

Lenin's remarks set forth no facet of socialist theory Chambers could not have found elsewhere. What made *The Soviets at Work* exciting was that it went far beyond mere theory. Lenin was not a dreamer. He was a world leader at the zenith of his power. He had toppled a government, installed another in its place, and promised still-greater things to come, an international revolution. "This was not theory or statistics," Chambers later wrote of Lenin's pamphlet. "This was the thing itself."[37]

The ex-radical Max Eastman, writing in 1955, remembered being "enraptured" by his first reading of *The Soviets at Work:* "The monumental practicality, the resolute factualness, of Lenin's mind, combined as almost never before with a glowing regard for poor and oppressed people, anxiety over their freedom, devotion to the idea of their entrance into power, swept me off my feet. I still think it one of the noblest—and now saddest—of political documents."[38]

What Chambers does not say (nor does Max Eastman) is that *The Soviets at Work* is written in a prose of almost unrelieved brutality, a combination of insults ("Let the poodles of bourgeois society scream and bark") and threats ("everyone who violates the labor discipline in any enterprise and in any business . . . should be discovered, tried and punished without mercy").[39] Lenin's analogies are drawn almost exclusively from the battlefield. He is thrilled by the spectacle of violence. His favorite adjective is "merciless." Nor does Lenin conceal the authoritarian character of the government he is assembling. Democracy in the new world can be achieved, he explains, only "by subjecting the will of thousands to the will of one." Lenin admits "no contradiction in principle between the Soviet (Socialist) democracy and the use of dictatorial power [by] individuals."

Humane revolutionists, such as Prince Kropotkin, Rosa Luxemburg, and Emma Goldman, had warned against the incipient tyranny of the emerging Bolshevist state.[40] But Lenin's authoritarianism is precisely what attracts Chambers. Like Everett Holmes, the Bolshevik Lenin is a puritan. Like Oliver Wendell Holmes's faithful soldier, he exhibits fanatic dedication to his cause. With Sorel, he declares that "middle courses are impossible." Above all, he is a moral reactionary who inveighs against the bourgeoisie, a depraved and fallen race, greedy, lazy, aimless. Lenin disdains the "anarchy" of capitalism and hails a new order ruled by "an iron hand," an "organization of strict and universal accounting and control." At the same time he lauds the "self-discipline of the workers" and goads them to a "merciless struggle against chaos and disorganization." For Chambers, Lenin's vision gave new clarity to the "undifferentiated savagery" of 1917, transformed it into the "tremendous imagery" of a world surging toward futurity. At a time when all other statesmen seemed to be groping in confusion, Lenin alone was "knowingly engaged in bringing to birth, in bringing to reality, a new age of history."[41]

Studied under the lamp of Leninism, things at last fitted into place. Chambers could examine himself, Jay, Laha, Richard and see their failures not as aberrations but as symptoms of a wider malady. What was the "French family" if not a textbook example of the eclipsed middle class, of families that had lost their way in the twentieth century? The threads of decline had been spun on the loom of generations: the ruinous schemes of Charles Whittaker, the fleshly corruptions of James Chambers, the frail posturings of Jay and Laha, the confusions of their troubled sons. Far from being too gentle for the world, they were all too much *of* that world, formed in its "tiny image." With its cracks and fissures 228 Earle Avenue was the heartbreak house of a doomed world. Aflame with this new knowledge, Chambers alternated between exaltation and despair. At night, back from the library, unable to sleep, he tramped for miles, "brooding over my family, which seemed to represent in miniature the whole crisis of the middle class."[42]

In 1925 the crisis still hovered out of view, occluded by the vision of hope. "The Communists have found a way out," Chambers told his brother. Richard laughed.[43] It would not do for him. But it would for

Whittaker. One chill winter evening he sat in his overcoat on a concrete bench at Columbia, near the statue of Alexander Hamilton, one of his early heroes. A few steps away Dean Hawkes worked behind his open door, and next to it stood Hartley Hall, where Chambers had draped himself in scandal. Columbia could do him one last favor. He searched out Sender Garlin, a red-haired radical from Glens Falls, New York, and asked him where he could find the Communist Party and how he could join. Garlin explained no such party existed. The Palmer raids had dispersed the membership and driven the remnants underground. They had resurfaced as the Workers Party of America. Garlin would see if Chambers could be put in touch with it.[44]

Several weeks later a short, stocky young man, Sam Krieger,[45] appeared in the newspaper room of the public library and asked Chambers if he was the one who "wanted to join." Chambers said he was, and one night Krieger escorted Chambers to a loft on the West Side of Manhattan, near the Hudson River, where some forty or fifty men and women, most of them shabbily clad, drank glasses of hot tea as they conversed in a babble of languages—until the meeting came to order, when everyone shifted laboriously into English, though a version unlike any Chambers had heard, thickly accented and clotted with Bolshevik jargon. Eyeing his "future comrades," Chambers was dismayed to see what looked "less like the praetorian guard of the world revolution than a rather undisciplined group of small delicatessen keepers."[46]

His new comrades were as dubious about him, with his cultivated diction and polite middle-class manners. It was not easy to efface the bourgeois birthright, the fatal signs of privilege,[47] though Chambers tried strenuously to do so. But if his demeanor was suspect, his ardor was not. He was quickly approved for membership. On February 17, 1925,[48] a year and a month after Lenin's death, Chambers was given a red Party book, with his membership number, stamped with the Party seal and signed by Bert Miller, the Party's organization secretary for the New York district. Chambers later knew Miller at the *Daily Worker,* and they met again under very different circumstances.[49] Spurning the advice of his new comrades, Chambers signed the card under his own name rather than take an alias.[50] The card was inscribed with these words: "The undersigned, after having read the constitution and program of the Communist Party, declares his adherence to the principles and tactics of the

party and the Communist International: agrees to submit to the discipline of the party as stated in its constitution and pledges to engage actively in its work."[51]

Thus Chambers joined a movement that in 1925 included at most sixteen thousand other Americans.[52] So much the better. He was used to
being outnumbered. He had at last found his church.

# BOLSHEVIK

## (1925–1932)

# His Brother's Keeper

Becoming a Communist in 1925 did not mean simply accepting a creed and its vision of history. "It meant a conversion, a complete dedication," Ignazio Silone was to write. "The Party became family, school, church, barracks; the world that lay beyond was to be destroyed and built anew."[1]

Sam Krieger found Chambers his first "Jimmie Higgins work," or gofer job. It was for the *Daily Worker*, the Communist paper published in Chicago. Chambers was assigned to make newsstand collections for the circulation office in New York. He rode the subway to remote precincts in Brooklyn and the Bronx and lugged back a bulging suitcase stuffed with unsold copies of the Party's "central organ." It was a dreary, nonpaying task, but Chambers did not object. The cause demanded small sacrifices as well as great.[2]

New recruits were also expected to begin a course of study. Chambers received private tutelage from Krieger "in the ways and the habits" of the Party. Two years Chambers's junior, Krieger was a seasoned radical. As a teenager he had been a delegate of the militant Industrial Workers of the World—the "Wobblies"—before the glorious events of 1917 won him over to communism. In sessions at the Yonkers apartment he shared with his common-law wife, the daughter of a cafeteria magnate, Krieger competently led Chambers and other "cell" members in discussions of the primary Communist texts.[3]

Along with the others, Chambers enrolled in a seminar at the Rand School of Social Science, "the intellectual center of socialism in New

York," on Union Square. His teacher was the economist Scott Nearing, a celebrity of the American left. Handsome and lean, a crowd-pleasing chautauqua orator and energetic pamphleteer, Nearing was less revolutionist than nonconformist. His passions included health food and organic farming. He was not yet a member of the Communist Party, though he became one in 1927, recruited by Chambers's future colleague Harold Ware.[4]

The goal of Nearing's seminar was to produce a book on "the law of social revolution," with each student writing a chapter. Chambers was assigned the Hungarian uprising of 1919. He read up on it at his desk at the library, his main text *Class Struggles and the Dictatorship of the Proletariat in Hungary* by the Hungarian Communist Béla Szántó. Chambers read the book in German. This caught the attention of a library patron, a small dark man of middle age, neatly dressed. Upon discovering Chambers was *ein Kommunist,* the man invited him home one evening to hear "the whole story." Home was an unheated room in a walkup near Penn Station furnished with a bed, table, and chair. This asceticism impressed Chambers. It was "a monk's room—that is to say, in the 20th century, a Communist's room."[5] Chambers returned for follow-up discussions. The Hungarian, speaking in clipped, precise German, explained basic organizational matters, new to Chambers, though he later found most of them set forth in *What Is to Be Done?,* Lenin's early primer on the Bolshevist movement. Long after these sessions ended—with Chambers's chapter on Hungary left unfinished[6]—the image of his quiet, forceful tutor lingered in Chambers's mind. The Hungarian seemed the ideal revolutionist, wholly merged with his cause, "the most thoroughly integrated human being I had ever met, and the one most responsible for turning me into a real Bolshevik."[7]

Chambers's friends puzzled over his new identity as a Communist. Some, like Kip Fadiman, thought the very idea absurd. "Do you drill in a cellar with machine guns?" he asked. Others decided it was another of Chambers's histrionic displays, one more "mystification." To Mark Van Doren, Chambers's latest enthusiasm "had an abstract sound, and I could not take it seriously." On one occasion, when Chambers was visiting his mentor's apartment, Van Doren's wife, Dorothy, remarked that Chambers's teeth needed fixing. The newborn Communist grinned, baring his broken upper incisors, and explained they made him look "like one of the people."

But others could see he was in earnest. To Lionel Trilling it seemed Chambers's "commitment to radical politics was meant to be definitive of his whole moral being, the controlling element of his existence," down to his broken teeth, "the perfect insigne of Chambers's moral authority."[8]

But not even communism could spare Chambers the fatiguing drama of Earle Avenue. Grandmother Whittaker, a permanent lodger, could be heard upstairs inveighing against her invisible enemies or seen lurking in the kitchen brandishing a knife. She also became familiar to the citizens of Lynbrook, who encountered the old lady on the street wrapped in the full-length sealskin coat she wore even on blistering days, a tattered souvenir of past prosperity. Sometimes she carried "trinkets" or a container of the "curative" ointment—its ingredients included cat urine—that she manufactured in her upstairs room and hawked to passersby. On the first day of each month Mary paced the sidewalk in front of the house, impatiently awaiting the arrival of the mailman with her Civil War widow's pension check, as if afraid someone else in the family would beat her to it. Jay was, as ever, the focus of her rage. "Oh, that *depraved* face," she cried as soon as he stepped inside the door, home from his day at Seaman's and, she supposed, a Sodomic tryst.[9]

On one of his brooding evening rambles Chambers chanced upon his grandmother some miles from Lynbrook. A voice, she explained, had summoned her to Brooklyn. Ignoring Whittaker's pleas, the old lady boarded a trolley and ended up in Jersey City, where she rented a room at the YWCA from which she charged into the street, clad only in her nightgown, raving that "those old Jews" had bored a hole in her ceiling and begun to pump gas into it. Local police deposited her in the mental ward of a nearby hospital and then notified Lynbrook authorities. Laha went to Jersey City to retrieve her mother. "You will have to stay up tonight," Laha told Whittaker. "She may try to kill us all."[10]

Richard too was in a bad way. At the same time Whittaker joined the Communist Party, his brother dropped out of Colgate and came home. He moped around in a garish costume—"vivid plaid pullover, violent checkerboard knickerbockers and green or red golf stockings"—and at night traced a great circle route of the local bars, following the example of Grandfather Chambers; only the taprooms had become speakeasies, seedier than before and even more numerous, the local resort hotels having deteriorated into roadhouses and gambling halls.[11] The alcohol they served could be lethal. Richard did not mind. He had begun to talk of suicide.[12]

He seemed to find a partial cure in an ambitious project, remodeling the family house. Its initial disrepair had worsened, after twenty years, into dilapidation. Richard built a new bathroom, shored up the ceilings on the main floor, and placed wood panels above the fireplaces. Jay descended from his hermitage to decorate them in his best pre-Raphaelite manner. With steady labor Richard brought the house closer to the ideal Laha had envisioned so long before.

Laha paid Richard for his labors, and with his earnings he built himself a toolshed behind the house, piping in gas from the main structure. He added a fireplace and hauled in a couch, on which he slept. This lodging enabled him to keep irregular hours. He was often away till dawn and sometimes brought back "fast" local girls; the twenties roared for at least one of the Chambers brothers. But not happily. One day Richard, his face "pinched and white," asked Whittaker to join him in a suicide pact. Whittaker refused. "You're a coward, Bro," Richard taunted.[13]

No matter how far Richard strayed, he was still tethered to Laha. This worried Chambers. "She knew how and where he spent his nights, the names of his friends and that girls were involved. She knew the details of his most intimate life. I was horrified that she should have to hear such things and shocked that he should dream of telling them to her. I saw that he was a man in his actions, but a child in his relations with his mother."[14]

Laha appointed Chambers his brother's keeper. At night, back from the library, he accompanied Richard on his drunken rounds. Neither brother handled alcohol well. Richard launched into boozy ravings, angry and maudlin, about Jay and Laha's many sins against their sons, while Whittaker defended the family honor. After one outburst Whittaker dashed whiskey in his brother's face. The two fought, grappling on the barroom floor, and had to be pulled apart.

Thereafter Whittaker began to skip his brother's nights out. One time, overhearing a commotion downstairs in the kitchen, Whittaker burst in and found Jay pummeling Richard, too drunk to ward off his father's fists. Whittaker struck Jay a blow that sent him to the floor. Then, one night, Whittaker came home and discovered Dickie "slumped across a chair" in the kitchen amid a heavy odor of gas. He had tried to kill himself. Whittaker revived him. "You're a bastard, Bro," said Richard. "You stopped me this time, but I'll do it yet."[15]

Chambers once again was appointed to watch over his brother. He no longer tried to chaperon Richard but sat up late many nights awaiting his return. Sometimes the living room door opened, and Grandmother Whittaker appeared, spectral and silent. Chambers wished "the house would burn down with all its horrors."[16]

In July he briefly escaped, quitting his library job for a monthlong tour of the Far West. He traveled as a hobo, by thumb and rail, his clothes stuffed in a backpack borrowed from Henry Zolinsky. In Seattle he joined the Wobblies on the advice of a hobo who told him boxcars were "ruled" by IWW men. He wrote some poems and sent them to Mark Van Doren, now literary editor of *The Nation*. In December, Van Doren had published Chambers's lyric "Quag-Hole," later included in an annual of American poetry published in 1925. Of the new batch, Van Doren accepted "Lothrop, Montana," which appeared in *The Nation* in June 1926.[17]

Then it was back to the nightmare of Earle Avenue. Richard had taken up with an eighteen-year-old Lynbrook girl, Dorothy Miller. Laha tried to break up the relationship. With funds from her Welfare Department job, she bought Richard a used Ford roadster in the hope it would keep her mechanically minded son "busy and out of mischief."[18] It did not. Richard had promised Dorothy he would marry her, and under pressure from her family he did so on May 29, 1926, at a tavern near Lynbrook. The witnesses were some of Dickie's drinking pals. Chambers, who thought the bride "a terrible specimen," was not present at the ceremony. No family members were. Laha refused to let the couple live in her house, so they rented three rooms in Rockville Centre. Richard found a job as a file clerk in the Nassau County surveyor's office. Thereafter Whittaker paid scant attention to Dickie and his woes.[19]

In the spring of 1926 Chambers made fresh plans to go on the road. He applied for a three-week vacation from the library, effective July 1, and then secured a leave of absence, extending his furlough through August.[20]

He had in mind another trip West, like the one he had taken the summer before. He had saved enough, living at home, to buy a secondhand car. He did not have a driver's license. But Bub Bang did. He had just graduated from high school and was eager to go along. Bub's parents opposed the trip, but he defied them, and in early July the pair set off. After four or five weeks they ran out of funds and turned back.[21] Not expected back at the library until September, Chambers had a month of free time. He and Bub camped, boated, rode horses, and made excursions in Chambers's car. On September 4 Chambers returned to his desk in the newspaper room.[22]

All the while he had been ignoring Richard, whose troubles had multiplied. Dorothy was unable to curb her husband's drinking, and the marriage was collapsing. Richard started coming around, alone, to Earle Avenue. In early September Dorothy fled the apartment, going first to Buffalo and then to Fire Island, to join her parents, who were vacationing there.

For solace Richard drove his roadster each night to the Lynbrook train station and waited for Whittaker to return from his job in the city. The brothers then went to a bar or simply sat in the car at a wharf. Dickie, lighting up cigarette after cigarette, stared desolately across the miles of black ocean to Fire Island and its gleam of lighted cottages.

They met in this way for three or four nights, but not on September 8, a Wednesday. Richard drove to the station with a friend but the train, when it pulled in, did not discharge Whittaker. Nor did the next train or several after that. Dickie finally gave up and went home.

The following morning Whittaker was asleep in his room when Laha picked up the ringing phone and let out a shriek. She rushed over to Rockville Centre with Whittaker and Jay. According to the police report, Richard "was lying on two chairs, face upward with his head resting on a pillow in the oven of a small gas range in the kitchen. His lifeless form was cold" and fully dressed. Richard had died in the middle of the night. "That he had carefully planned his death was indicated from his position at the gas stove," the *Nassau Daily Review* reported. The paper did not mention, nor did the police record, that a quart of whiskey stood empty on the floor. "The boy was normal in every respect," Jay told local reporters. "I am up against a stone wall." The couple's neighbors had noticed nothing, of course, only two young lovers, "perfectly devoted to each other," who never quarreled.

It fell to Chambers to "supervise the barbaric rites of a modern funeral," held in the living room Richard had lovingly restored. The widow, back from Fire Island, attended the service, welcome at last in

Laha's home. The next day, under a warm late-summer sun, Richard Chambers was buried, without a headstone, in the Rockville Cemetery, fifteen days before his twenty-third birthday, the latest casualty of the "middle-class family," failed by them all, including his brother.[23]

In the fall and winter, consumed by grief and guilt, Chambers haunted the cemetery and eulogized his brother in poems. One, "September 8, 1926," is at once an apology to Richard and also a statement of Chambers's faith in communism. He extols the "masses," subtly playing on the word's many meanings and elaborating on the Marxian parallel between natural and social forces:

> Only the moving masses of cloud have any meaning
> Of this tortured world now. Only the motionlessness
> As of these cars, in beings or things,
> Remain undemeaning.
>
> Only the momentum of the movement of masses,
> Beings or substance, has any meaning;
> Or their cessation upon the perfect turn
> Of the experience motion amasses.
> . . . . . . . . . . . . . . . . . . . . . .
> You know it is the perfection of the motion in me
>    I am waiting,
> Not lack of love, or love of the motion of beings,
> Or things, or the sun's generation, that keeps me,
> But my perfection for death I am waiting.*

"This was the point at which I became a thorough Communist," Chambers later said of Richard's suicide. "I felt that any society which could result in the death of a boy like my brother was wrong and I was at war with it. This was the beginning of my fanaticism."[25]

---

* In February 1931 the poem—retitled "October 21st, 1926," and with the last stanza subtly altered—was published in the famous "objectivist" issue of Poetry guest-edited by Louis Zukofsky. Zukofsky composed his own elegy to Richard, included in his magnum opus, "A."[24]

# 6

# *Upheavals*

On April 13, 1927, Chambers's coat locker at the public library was opened by his supervisor with a master key. Inside were found several books missing from the open stacks. Chambers had "induced a page boy" to procure the volumes for him. He also had "smuggled" books from various divisions throughout the library. He was dismissed after "an informal hearing." Jay, known to library officials through exhibitions of his work at various branches, made an appeal on his son's behalf, to no avail.

Next a "special investigator" from the library's circulation department knocked on the door of 228 Earle Avenue in search of more books. He confiscated fifty-six. None came from the public library. All had been removed some years before from Columbia—"forty-two came from College Study, the rest from various libraries and reading rooms." Chambers had "at least tried to destroy the identification marks" from many of the books. The college took no action except to bar him permanently—and belatedly—from future enrollment.[1] Chambers enjoyed the commotion. "Radical books & handbills discovered," he wrote to Schapiro on April 24, in his best Bolshevist tone.[2]

Toppled from his comfortable perch, Chambers found another, the Greenwich Village bookstore owned by Louis Zukofsky's brother, Morris. Chambers and Louis were supposed to help customers at noon, when the regular staff broke for lunch, but were indifferent, sometimes negligent booksellers, seldom stirring from their seats. Henry Zolinsky, a frequent visitor, once put them to a test, asking for a volume. When

Chambers and Zukofsky assured him it was not to be found, Zolinsky walked over to the shelves and pulled down the book himself.[3]

Chambers also was writing. He contributed book reviews on political and economic theory to *The Literary Review,* a new Saturday book supplement published by the *Evening Post.* Various members of the old *Morningside* crowd—Fadiman, Trilling, Schapiro, Mortimer Adler, and Herbert Solow—published in it as well.[4]

But most of his writing now was for the *Daily Worker.* In January 1927 the propaganda sheet moved its editorial offices from Chicago back to New York, "the home city of the imperialist oppressors," and published its first edition in time for the annual Lenin Memorial Demonstration held in Madison Square Garden.[5] At the urging of two Communist friends, Sender Garlin and Harry Freeman, who were writing for the paper, Chambers contributed to it too. His first signed work was a poem, "March for the Red Dead," a didactic explanation of May Day. It ends with a lugubrious incantation: "For the dead, the dead, the dead, we march, comrades, workers." Chambers published more such verse (commemorating "the clubbed, the maimed, the shot, the prison-penned") and also did some translating for the paper. Soon he was spending a lot of time at the *Daily*'s offices, at 30 Union Square.[6] In August 1927 he wrote his first news articles, on the Nicaraguan rebel General Augusto Sandino, who had stood off a U.S. Marine detachment. Though the story bore a Managua dateline, Chambers lifted the facts from *New York Times* reports and then "class-angled" them to fit the Party line.[7]

Before long Chambers was the *Daily*'s regular "reporter" of foreign news. When Harry Freeman moved over to the copy desk and eventually to the New York office of Tass, Chambers was easily grooved into the vacated slot. It helped that he could make his way through several languages. The paper often published translations from the overseas press.[8]

Chambers also contributed to other Communist publications. He did translations for the *Labor Defender,* sponsored by the International Labor Defense, one of the Party's most active fronts, closely involved with the Gastonia strike, among other causes. He also appeared occasionally in *The New Masses,* the radical monthly, soon to become the Party's chief literary publication.[9]

Chambers's conception of the newsman's life had been formed by the example of Grandfather Chambers, with contacts all over Philadelphia and his finger on the pulse of the nation's political life. No such dynamism was evident at Union Square. The *Daily Worker* resembled few other newspapers. Chambers's first boss, J. Louis Engdahl, a veteran radical journalist, was thoroughly jaded and lived off the scraps thrown by his superiors. Glumly positioned at the head of the newsroom, his lantern face turned blankly toward the window, Engdahl seemed to be measuring the distance to Moscow, or at least to Party headquarters, which in the fall moved from Union Square all the way uptown to 125th Street, so as to escape the milling crowds of Party members and hangers-on. Chambers could not remember hearing the editor "utter five coherent sentences."[10]

The rest of the staff was equally lethargic. A job on the "central organ" was the end of the line for older Party hands. The sediment of failure seemed to weight them to their desks. They were roused to enthusiasm only when there was gossip to spread or when young women from the business office came to the editorial office and, much to their dread, had to squeeze past its gauntlet of crowded desks. Yet Chambers did not question his colleagues' commitment or resolve. "There was not one of them who did not hold his convictions with a fanatical faith; and there was scarcely any one of them who was not prepared to die, at need, for them."[11]

Dismal as the *Daily Worker*'s offices were, the quality of the publication itself was worse. Despite heavy cash infusions from the Comintern and the move to New York, the paper's circulation was stuck at about twenty thousand.[12] Engdahl's stewardship was so poor that the staff petitioned for his removal, a rare act of defiance to which Party chiefs at last acceded, sending the editor to Moscow as the American representative to the Comintern, where he busied himself chasing skirts instead of keeping his supervisors briefed on Party doings.[13]

Engdahl's replacement on the *Daily Worker* was Robert Minor, a superb political cartoonist and sometime editor of *The Masses,* the vivacious socialist weekly that had flourished before the war. Some greeted the appointment dourly. Minor, who often remarked the resemblance between his bald dome and Lenin's, had recently "been bitten by the bug of political ambition," in the words of an adversary, and was obviously intent on making himself a force in the Party. His tenuous grasp of Communist doctrine led to much foolishness—for instance, a front-page banner headline declaring THERE IS NO GOD[14]—but at least he took his job seriously. He nominally professionalized the *Daily Worker,* going so far as to dole out salaries on occasion. He also set up a copy desk and, better yet, imported new staff, younger and more enthusiastic.[15]

Chambers became friendly with two, in particular. Jacob Burck, a bricklayer's son born in Poland, was a gifted cartoonist and muralist. In 1941 he was awarded a Pulitzer Prize and still later, during the Red hunts of the 1950s, was threatened with deportation.[16] Another new arrival was a young labor writer, Michael Intrator, an acutely intelligent "child of the slums." He had studied Marxian economics at the Workers School under Bertram D. Wolfe, a top Party ideologue and later an eminent anti-Communist.[17]

Still the level of journalism in the *Daily Worker* did not rise perceptibly. Chambers the radical newsman was rarely sent to "cover a story" in the usual sense. Instead he picked up facts from the regular press and squeezed them into the familiar boilerplate.

But on his own initiative he found useful work. Lenin was an advocate of "worker correspondence"—letters that "simple workers in the shops, or soldiers and sailors in the services, or peasants, voluntarily wrote to the party." During its term in Chicago the *Worker* had kept up reasonably well with the influx of submissions, awarding prizes to the best. In New York the letters poured in but lay unread in thick piles. No one objected when Chambers volunteered to sift through the heap and edit some letters for publication. It was an engrossing task. Mixed in among the aimless and incoherent ramblings were authentic messages congruent with Chambers's own romantic Communist vision. He published a reminiscence of the Russian Civil War written by a soldier who had gone over with one of the American regiments sent to aid the White Russians but been converted to the cause of the Bolsheviks. He also published a testimonial by a "Seaman Correspondent" fresh from "a year or so of slavery on various tramp ships operated by the Dollar Line of New York."[18] It was as if Chambers had rediscovered the voice of Everett Holmes.

He stayed on the *Daily Worker* through the fall of 1929 and also contributed the occasional poem and book review to *The New Masses*.[19] He was known as a useful "literate," cautious about thrusting himself into the political fray. "He was shy and stayed away from unit meetings," recalled Bert Wolfe.[20] Indeed he skipped so many such meetings that his former tutor Sam Krieger was sure Chambers had been "dropped from the party in 1927 for refusing to reregister when the party structure changed from foreign-language speaking and street branches to industrial units." He did, however, teach a course in "Labor Journalism" at the Workers School.[21]

Chambers had enrolled in the Party at precisely the time when its "inner life was particularly ugly and unprincipled," as one history of the movement puts it. His position at the *Daily Worker* afforded him an unimpeded view of the Party's destructive intrigues. The troubles originated in Moscow, where an internal power struggle was in its final phase. Lenin, who died in January 1924, at age fifty-three, had not designated a clear successor. His closest associate had been Trotsky. But a second Lenin protégé, the Georgian Joseph Stalin, the Party secretary, had also emerged as a leading contender. Though he lacked Trotsky's intellectual heft and visionary strength, Stalin was an administrative genius, particularly skilled at internal maneuver. By 1927 he had secured his authority, crushing all opposition and expelling Trotsky from the Party. In 1929 Trotsky was deported and began the final phase of his life as an exile and a hunted émigré, disowned by the cause he had helped create and pursued by the secret police he had been instrumental in making a permanent fixture of the regime. Meanwhile Stalin completed the Soviet Union's transition from a one-party to a one-man dictatorship.[22]

These events were closely followed by the American Party, which charted its course on cue from Moscow. After Trotsky's defeat American Communists, led by Jay Lovestone, rushed to denounce him in terms of escalating scorn. The leaders of the Trotskyist opposition, James P. Cannon and Max Shachtman, were swiftly read out of the Party, and Cannon's Manhattan apartment was burgled by "Lovestoneites," who filched correspondence and then published it in the *Daily Worker* as proof that Cannon was locked in a conspiracy with Trotsky and Trotsky's American translator, Max Eastman, to "lead a world-wide counter-revolutionary campaign against the Soviet Union."[23]

Chambers voiced no public protest, but privately he deplored this program of "calculated degradation by lies and slander."[24] Learning of these sentiments, Max Shachtman approached Chambers, known for his skill at translation, and showed him an important document, Trotsky's appeal to the Sixth Congress of the Comintern, written in German. Chambers offered to translate it for *The Militant,* the Trotskyist weekly. What happened next left Shachtman's colleague James Cannon bitter for twenty years:

"Shachtman gave him the copy, the only copy we had, and that's the last we ever saw of it. We waited impatiently for the translation to be completed, but heard nothing from Chambers. Finally Shachtman called him up and asked when the translation would be ready. Chambers answered that he had turned it over to the Central Committee of the CP," betraying unaccountably the man he considered, "after Lenin, the Communist Party's best brain, and one of the outstanding political minds of the age."[25]

Chambers's clumsy attempt at intrigue harmed rather than enhanced his standing. Party chieftains knew Shachtman would not have approached Chambers unless he was fairly confident Chambers was an ally. Indeed, rumors of closet Trotskyism were to dog Chambers during his entire thirteen years in the Party.[26] In *Witness* he enigmatically insists, in ironic echo of hearing room disclaimers, "I was not then and never have been a Trotskyist."[27]

In June 1927 Gertrude Hutchinson, the wife of a Columbia friend of Chambers's, separated from her husband and invited Chambers to live with her in a tiny house she had rented in Whitestone, Queens. Chambers stayed for about a year. It was his first "party marriage," an extramarital arrangement condoned by the movement since it represented yet another blow against the weakening walls of the bourgeois state. This was all the excuse Communist bosses needed to change wives as often "as one does an overcoat," in the words of the ex-Communist Benjamin Gitlow.[28]

Chambers insisted Bub Bang move in as well. Not long after Dickie Chambers's suicide Bub's mother had died. The two friends had grown even closer of late. The quarters were close—two rooms plus kitchen— and stimulating, at least for Chambers, who ruled this tight roost. He proposed that Bub acquire sexual experience by sharing the favors of Hutchinson, who consented reluctantly, no doubt aware her body had become the means by which her two roommates consummated their passion for each other. The situation grew "rather intolerable and tense," and Chambers finally ended it and the "marriage" in 1929.[29]

By this time he had begun a second relationship, with Ida Dailes, a red-haired divorcée employed as a stenographer by the Workers International Relief, a Communist agency in Manhattan. She also taught a course, "Fundamentals of Communism," at the Workers School, where Chambers taught journalism. Like Chambers, Dailes was born in 1901 (her parents were Russian immigrants), and like him too, she had joined the Party in 1925. She was well known in Party circles for her tough hide and sharp tongue. Once, having been propositioned by a comrade, she snapped, "I refuse to be used as a Party toilet!"—a remark much repeated on the left.[30]

In the summer of 1929 Dailes left her apartment on Nineteenth Street and moved in with Chambers. First they shared an apartment east of Greenwich Village and then, in the fall, leased an off-season cottage in East Rockaway near the beaches Chambers loved and near, once more, to Lynbrook. The family had always tormented one another most effectively from close range: Jay punished Laha by locking himself in "the best room in the house"; Dickie had humiliated his parents from the tool-shed, a few steps from the kitchen door. Now their surviving son had installed his Party "wife," the common-law "Mrs. Chambers," in a house two miles from Lynbrook. Laha, in her shame, avoided the couple—until one morning in late October, when she appeared at the door of her son's cottage with the news that Jay had died. "You will have to come home and move his body," she told Whittaker.

Jay had been in the bathroom shaving before the mirror when he collapsed. Chambers found him in his robe, lying on "the sea-blue tiles" Richard had laid. Laha helped her son lift Jay onto the bed. The cause of death, liver disease, had first been diagnosed in January 1929. Jay had since been under a physician's care until "la grippe" and "exhaustion" finished the patient off, twelve days past his fifty-third birthday and a day after he had completed the final touches on a last bookplate.[31]

Jay was buried in Rockville Centre, alongside Richard, the son he had outlived by three years. Dickie's suicide had affected Jay powerfully. He read in it a summary judgment of his shirkings and escapes, "the failure of his whole life." In atonement Jay had reached a hand toward Whittaker, and the two occasionally met for lunch—in Manhattan, out from under the shadow of Earle Avenue.[32]

Much as he had hated all his jobs, Jay had been dependably employed until the end. Most of what he made he kept to himself. His one extravagance had been meals. Visitors at Earle Avenue were surprised, after Chambers's reports of poverty, at the lavish supper table Laha set.[33] But Jay had not withheld much. He left behind not quite five thousand dollars after expenses were met. Two thirds went to Whittaker—the final coin of reconcilement—and the rest to Laha, who also came into ownership of the house. The estate, like all Jay's creations, was small. But it was more solid than many built by his more grandiose contemporaries. The same day Jay slumped to the bathroom floor, the stock market, after some weeks of mad fluctuation, finally crashed. As the colossal paper fortunes dissolved into nullity, Jay Chambers's Bolshevik son came into a cash inheritance.[34]

The house on Earle Avenue now stood emptier than ever. Only Laha and Mary, age seventy-seven, remained amid the ghosts. Longing for human, not spectral, company, Laha humbly beseeched Whittaker to come home—with Ida Dailes if she must come too. The couple moved in that November. The arrangement was short-lived. Ida did not conceal her marriage plans. A visitor to 228 Earle remembered her casting appraising looks at the house and its furnishings, Laha's "antiques." But a divorced Jewish Communist, Ida was Laha's nightmare vision of a daughter-in-law. An immediate and mutual antipathy sprang up between the women, and a new tenseness settled over the house.[35]

Ida could hold her own with Laha. It was Bub who worried her. He was enrolled now at New York University, his tuition covered by Chambers, who dipped into his inheritance from Jay. Bub, living at home, often came to Lynbrook, though Ida tried to chase him away.[36] Chambers had other friends over too: Mike Intrator, Jacob Burck, *Daily Worker* staffer Abe Magill, and a strikingly handsome Communist from Ireland, Kevin O'Malley, the "Romeo of the Tenements," who entertained the household by playing the zither.[37]

Chambers also brought a young family into the house. Henry Zolinsky, now married and the father of an infant daughter, hoped to become a schoolteacher, teaching French, but, like so many others, was jobless in the last months of 1929. He gratefully accepted Chambers's offer of room and board in Lynbrook. Husband, wife, and baby all crowded into Jay's room. Mary Zolinsky nursed the baby, Nancy, while Henry nursed his poems and the occasional translation assignment. More than once he was startled to see a pair of eyes glinting through the open door. It was Grandmother Whittaker sizing up the strangers before shuffling down the hall to her own room, where she could be heard muttering and on occasion emitting "shrieks."[38]

After a quarter century the homestead Laha had purchased so hopefully now resembled a seedy rooming house. The boarders all survived on Jay's dwindling patrimony and on such dollars as they themselves contributed, with the exception of Grandmother Whittaker, who hoarded the pension checks that arrived each month until her death in December 1931, at age seventy-nine.[39]

Before long Ida Dailes announced she was pregnant. She quit her stenographer's job and stayed at home, strengthening her territorial claim and assuming, grudgingly, some household obligations, such as preparing lunch. "She starved me," Henry Zolinsky grumbled sixty years later, still tasting the watered-down soup. To Laha, Ida's pregnancy was an added affront. Their quarrels worsened, and after an especially fierce one, in January or February 1930, Ida stalked heavily out of the house and in the direction of the train station.[40]

Laha's victory was brief. Chambers soon followed Ida out of Lynbrook. The couple leased a flat in Manhattan and then returned to East Rockaway, living above a store opposite the railroad station, and remained there through the summer of 1930, when they moved yet again, this time to uptown Manhattan, near Riverside Drive.[41]

It was the last address they shared. Chambers had begun another relationship, with Esther Shemitz, a young artist he had met in 1926 at the Passaic textile strike, the first important labor action managed by the Communist Party. Esther had braved the raised billy clubs of policemen. "Get that bitch in the brown beret," a cop had shouted as he advanced toward her menacingly. She wore her bruises proudly on the train back to Manhattan. Chambers sat beside the young woman, attracted to her quiet courage and dark looks.[42]

After the Passaic incident Chambers saw Esther casually. She was among a group that camped on Atlantic Beach. She was usually there in the company of her roommate, Grace Lumpkin, a pretty blond Southerner who had come north with dreams of a literary career. Both women worked on the staff of *The World Tomorrow,* a pacifist magazine. The jobs helped subsidize the women's more serious pursuits. Since 1927 Esther had been taking courses in drawing, painting, and sculpture at the Art Students League.[43] Grace, who came from a venerable Old South family—her brother was a U.S. senator and later a federal judge—had come north in 1924 to be a writer. The two shared an apartment east of Greenwich Village.[44]

Though more interested in art than revolution, Esther had a history of political engagement. Russian-born—her family had immigrated when she was a small child—she had studied at the Rand School, on a scholarship, had been a bookkeeper at the International Ladies Garment Workers Union, had traveled to Boston to protest the execution of Sacco and Vanzetti, had briefly been enrolled in the Socialist Party. She and Grace, both "warm fellow travelers," frequented the Communist Party bookstore, on Union Square. Their apartment, in a pretty brick house behind a tenement, was a gathering place for young radicals aflame with visions of "the perfect world we were going to make," Grace later recalled. The "most admired" of the visitors was Chambers, who "knew everything about art, music, books. He was witty and charming."[45]

Chambers also saw Esther at the John Reed Club, founded by the Party in 1929 to encourage working-class artists. Esther was one of fifty charter members.[46] Grace, a gifted writer, was headed for JRC stardom. Chambers and Esther met on occasion at the JRC clubhouse, on Fifteenth Street, and he helped her hang pictures at a JRC exhibition in the Bronx.[47]

Soon Mike Intrator was involved with Grace Lumpkin, and Chambers began to court Esther Shemitz. She resisted at first. She had seen Ida Dailes on the Long Island beaches and at Communist functions and knew her as Chambers's Party "wife." Chambers swore the affair was over. He was searching for a way to leave Ida "without hurting her feelings too much."[48] In fact he first pressured Ida into getting an abortion and then abruptly dropped her, a humiliation she remembered for many years.[49] Gradually Esther overcame her distrust, and the relationship flowered. Chambers recognized in Esther someone more "integrated" than he, comfortable in the worlds of art and politics but consumed by neither. Her salient quality was radiant selflessness. Rebecca West, taken to meet strikers in Passaic by the young Esther Shemitz, recalled forty years later "something about her which was not of this world."[50]

Chambers moved into Esther's apartment, adjoining the place she had shared with Grace—it now housed Grace and Intrator. The two couples lived as a foursome, separated by a thin partition. There was only one bathroom, so Intrator and Chambers cut out a doorway, uniting the apartments. With rumors already engulfing the two couples, this domestic arrangement had the appearance of a ménage, similar to Chambers's Whitestone adventure, though with increased combinative possibilities. "You are living in a sea of shit," Jacob Burck sternly told Chambers, echoing the sentiment of other acquaintances, some of whom suspected all four friends were homosexual.*[51]

---

* In fact Intrator was an energetic womanizer. He and Lumpkin were divorced in 1941.[52]

But in early 1931 Lumpkin and Intrator were married, and on April 15 Chambers and Shemitz were too.* There was no ceremony. The couple exchanged vows at the Manhattan Municipal Building. The witnesses were Grace Hutchins and Anna Rochester, Communist bluestockings and also patrons of the proletarian arts.[54]

Chambers found domestic stability at the same time that his political life suffered another convulsion. The troubles traced, once more, to Moscow. Stalin, having dispensed with Trotsky, was worried about a new rival, the amiable Nikolai Bukharin, an outstanding theorist whose influence had mounted even as Stalin consolidated his power. In 1929 Stalin declared Bukharin persona non grata—for opposing economic policies less coercive than the general secretary's own—and then ejected him from an important post in the Politburo. (He was executed in 1938.)[55]

This time there was a fight. Some of Bukharin's strongest support was in the Communist Party of the USA (CPUSA), as the organization was renamed in 1929. Jay Lovestone, by then CPUSA chief, was outspokenly loyal to Bukharin and so was summarily ordered to Moscow for prolonged browbeating. Bert Wolfe and other Lovestoneites went too. At one session the dictator himself addressed the heretics. "Who do you think you are? Trotsky defied me. Where is he? . . . Bukharin defied me. Where is he? And you? When you get back to America, nobody will stay with you except your wives." For Lovestone and his ilk, Stalin promised, "there is plenty of room in our cemeteries." Lovestone and company were detained briefly in Moscow and then expelled—or in some instances, "suspended"—from the Party.

In America Communists scurried to enact the ritual farce of dissociation, betrayal, and atonement. The spectacle was even bleaker than after Trotsky's expulsion because Lovestone, as the leader of the CPUSA, enjoyed the support of 90 percent of the rank and file, an unheard-of majority in a movement notorious for factional turf wars. Loyal Communists found themselves branded "renegades" and "deviationists," often by those who had been devoted Lovestoneites only weeks or even days before.[56] By 1930, despite the addition of 6,000 new members, the

---

* Three weeks after the marriage Chambers's last remaining grandparent, Dora Chambers, died in her rented room in Lynbrook. She was seventy-four.[53]

total number of pledged Communists had dwindled to 7,545.[57] Their new chief was Earl Browder, who outlasted all his predecessors and was not himself deposed until 1945.

At the *Daily Worker*, Chambers comforted a Lovestoneite staffer, John Sherman, who sat sobbing at his typewriter on the day of his dismissal. Another colleague, Harrison George, confided to Chambers that the Stalinists were looking for an opportunity to depose Robert Minor "if it would not give ammunition to the opposition." After warning Minor— "They've got the knife out for you, Bob"—Chambers confessed his own desire to "take some time off to think over the changed situation." Minor brushed aside this request and demanded the name of Chambers's source. Chambers demurred. No matter. Minor had learned enough to better his own standing. He reported Chambers to Charles Dirba, chairman of the Party's Central Control Commission, who ordered Chambers to Communist headquarters, on Union Square, where Dirba and other national leaders had offices on the fabled "Ninth Floor." Ignoring the summons, Chambers visited Mike Intrator, an early casualty of the purge, who was in Chicago licking his wounds. Chambers stayed on for two or three weeks and then went back to New York and resigned from the *Daily Worker*. He too had become a "renegade."[58]

# The Hottest
# Literary Bolshevik

Chambers's withdrawal coincided with his sudden return to the world of bourgeois letters, courtesy of Kip Fadiman, now an editor at a new firm, Simon and Schuster, and "something of a *Wunderkind* in the publishing world."[1] In the winter of 1928 Fadiman hired Chambers to translate a children's novel, *Bambi*, by Austrian novelist Felix Salten.[2] The book had been widely acclaimed on the Continent. Chambers's rendering, for which he was paid either $500 or $250,[3] left the editors confident enough to gamble on an enormous first printing, seventy-five thousand copies. *Bambi* was also picked up by a new mail-order retailer, the Book-of-the-Month Club, which cosponsored advertising for the book. Released in July, with a prefatory blurb by the novelist John Galsworthy, *Bambi* proved as popular in the United States as it had been abroad. Critics praised Chambers's translation, putting him in demand.[4] In the next few years he translated a dozen books: three more of Salten's novels, plus other children's fiction, along with serious novels from the German by Heinrich Mann and Franz Werfel, and some tepid erotica.[5]

By 1932 Chambers's reputation was such[6] that he was one of several candidates approached by the firm of A. & C. Boni to translate the final volume of Proust's *À la Recherche du temps perdu,* completing the massive enterprise left unfinished by C. K. Scott Moncrieff. Barrows Mussey, a translator and publisher, interviewed the candidates:

Chambers, an early choice, appeared in the office with a cloth cap such as burglars wear in cartoons. I seem to remember a gap in his front teeth, and his suit and shoes stamped on a lifelong impression that all eminent translators are tatterdemalions. . . . Chambers seized upon the French volume of Proust, and departed, promising to submit a sample chapter forthwith from some telephoneless hideout on Long Island. It was then that I began hearing about him around the office. They said he was a good translator, only the Party would keep ordering him to organize trouble in the West Virginia coal fields, and you never got your manuscript.

The sample chapter came in all right. We heaved a sigh of relief. The last of Proust had already been dangling for a couple of years, but here was the end in view.

It was not. Chambers rejected the standard fee of $5 per thousand words and held out for $7.50. The publisher agreed, by telegram, but then heard nothing from Chambers, who at last "sent back the book with a letter saying he could not do the job if he was to be hounded."[7]

Though outside the Party, and at odds with its tactics, Chambers clung to the revolutionary program, styling himself "an independent Communist oppositionist." But this was an untenable position. Even though "I considered myself a better Communist than the Stalinists," he needed to belong to a movement, to subordinate himself to an organization, even one whose methods appalled him.[8] By 1931 he was ready to rejoin the Party, if it would have him, and was casting about for ways to make himself useful. He had, as he knew, only one distinct talent. He could write. Literature became the vehicle of his rehabilitation.

Chambers found inspiration under his own roof. Esther was deeply immersed in the radical art movement. In autumn 1930 she had begun studying at the Art Students League under the painter Thomas Hart Benton, and she remained active in the John Reed Club. Some of her work had been exhibited at the Workers Cooperative Apartments in the Bronx. She had also illustrated a Communist pamphlet with line drawings and in May 1931 published her first cartoon, of evicted tenants, in *The New Masses.*[9] And nearby Grace Lumpkin, subsidized by a fifteen-hundred-dollar loan from Anna Rochester, was finishing up a novel, *To Make My Bread,* based on the Gastonia textile strike. It would win the Maxim Gorky Award as "the best proletarian novel of the year," beating out John Dos Passos's *1919,* and was adapted for the Broadway stage, as *Let Freedom Ring.* It ran for six months in 1935.[10]

The times were catching up with Chambers, who had early grasped the possibilities of proletarian literature, in poems he published in *The New Masses* in the mid-1920s, poems that, like his eulogy to Richard, combined a tender feeling for nature with revolutionary themes.[11] Many thought his poetry superior to his fiction, but he had since decided his true métier was prose,[12] and in the first days of 1931 he began to write the fiction that clinched his reputation on the literary left and smoothed his reentry into the Party.

He wrote, in all, four short stories. The first of them remains a pinnacle of American Communist fiction. It is based on an actual event. On January 3, 1931, five hundred Arkansas farmers, whose cotton crops had failed in a drought, stormed the town of England, crying, "We want food!" "We are not going to let our children starve!"[13]

Many heard in those cries the mounting desperation brought on by the Depression. But Chambers detected something else, the seeds of the "spontaneous upsurge" advocated by Lenin as the most authentic form of proletarian revolt.[14] Expertly building on the skeletal facts, Chambers placed at the story's center a homespun Bolshevik, Wardell, who unassumingly, and with quiet force, guides his fellow farmers toward an organized protest but is himself jailed, a martyr to the revolution. A parallel climax occurs when Wardell's wife strangles her starving infant rather than stand by helplessly while the baby is "tortured to death by inches."[15]

Working in the flat on Avenue B, Chambers wrote the story in a single night, finishing at dawn. "All that I wanted to say fell into place at one stroke in my mind." The obvious place to publish the story was *The New Masses,* now overtly tied to the Party. Chambers knew the magazine's managing editor, Walt Carmon, a *Daily Worker* alumnus. Carmon was out of the office when Chambers submitted his pages, but his assistant, the poet Norman Macleod, read the story, accepted it, and titled it "Can You Make Out Their Voices?," taken from the manuscript's last line.[16] It ran in the issue of March 1931.

The opening scene made it clear this was no ordinary exercise in agitprop:

> You could see the bottom of the wind-mill shaft, though it stood surrounded by aspens at the back of the farm-house: the leaves were thinned out as it were autumn. And as less and less water was pumped up, it was cloudier and cloudier and tasted sickeningly of alkali. The poor farmer, Wardell, his wife and two boys, began to envy the aspen roots that went

down and sucked up whatever water there was: they ended by hating them.

Animals overcame their fear to seek water near the houses. The Wardell boys found a gopher, a pair of jackrabbits, dead. A red-headed woodpecker lay on the front path, its wings spread out. The boys took it into the house. In the shade it revived. They gave it a drop of their water; it uttered its single sharp scream; batting itself against the windows that were always shut now, to keep out the wind that blew the length of the prairie, and dried the saliva out of your mouth.

Unlike so much "workers' art," this had the ring of authenticity. "I had been brought up in a country village close to the land," Chambers later explained. "I thought that I knew exactly what had happened."[17] He recast the characters as dirt farmers, drawing on his memories of Laha's vegetable garden, the chickens she incubated in the attic, and the Interior Department publications that had awakened both Whittaker and Richard to hopeful visions of farm life.

Chambers's second strength was his familiarity with Communist doctrine. He had been in the movement since 1925. He had read Marx and Lenin, had soaked up the lectures of the ascetic Hungarian Communist and the reminiscences of Sam Krieger and other working revolutionists. He combined all this into a convincing literary vision.

A friend of Chambers's from this period, the novelist Robert Cantwell, once remarked Chambers's knack "for picking out of the social air phrases of common speech that sounded like Tolstoy, perhaps a line spoken by a hitchhiker he had picked up on the road, or the waitress in a restaurant where he ate alone."[18] "Voices" too is an exercise in sacral mimicry. Chambers seeks to ennoble the idiom, roughhewn yet also poetic, of simple heroes risen from the soil. He presents Wardell and his neighbors as a kind of chorus, the collective voice of the proletariat—the technique later employed by Ignazio Silone in *Fontamara* and John Steinbeck in *The Grapes of Wrath*. Like those works, Chambers's, on its smaller scale, translates political message into moral fable. Years later esteemed veterans of the literary left, such as the novelist Albert Halper and the critic Granville Hicks, still rated Chambers's story among the best to come out of the Communist movement.[19]

In 1932 the reaction was instantaneous. Letters flooded into *The New Masses* from excited readers all over the country. Overnight Chambers had become the "hottest literary Bolshevik" in New York.[20]

Among the many messages *The New Masses* received was an inquiry from the stage director Hallie Flanagan, then heading the Experimental Theatre at Vassar College and later famous as the director of the New Deal's Federal Theatre Project. Flanagan was eager to stage a production of "one of the great American short stories," less a work of propaganda, in her view, than of social realism. "The drought-stricken farmers, their hunger and desperate need, Hilda's strangling of the baby she could not feed, the raid on the food store, the arrest of the leader, Wardell—all this was drama out of everyday life in our own age and country."[21]

Working quickly, Flanagan and her collaborator, Margaret Clifford, had a stage version ready in less than a month. They created the simplest production possible—it required only one set—so workers' groups could duplicate it themselves. They also softened the revolutionary message by adding a subplot centered on the daughter of a wealthy congressman who amid the frivolities of her coming-out party suffers the birth pangs of social conscience and organizes a charity drive.

Some objected to this ideological impurity, but *The New Masses* deemed *Can You Hear Their Voices?,* as it was retitled, "the best play of revolutionary interest produced in this country." It soon became a staple of the radical repertory, staged throughout America and worldwide—in Greece, China, Hungary, Finland, Denmark, France, Russia, Spain, and Australia. There was even a Yiddish version.[22]

Chambers never bothered to attend a stage performance of *Can You Hear Their Voices?* He had written it for a political, not literary, purpose, achieved soon enough when official praise came—from Moscow and from no less an authority than Anna Elistratova, the rising star of the Soviet literary-critical establishment. Writing in the January 1932 issue of the Comintern's *International Literature,* Elistratova singled out "Can You Make Out Their Voices?" as the only existing work of American fiction that "gives a revolutionary exposition of the problem of the agricultural crisis and correctly raises the question of the leading role of the Communist Party in the revolutionary farmers' movement."[23]

Chambers published three more stories* in *The New Masses,* all well received, each about the martyrdom of proletarians—a Chinese peasant,

---

* "You Have Seen the Heads" (April 1931); "Our Comrade Munn" (October 1931); "The Death of the Communists" (December 1931).[24]

a union organizer, strikers executed in a prison—who fling themselves on the altar of the revolution. One of them, either "Our Comrade Munn" or "The Death of the Communists," had a powerful impact on Lincoln Steffens, elderly dean of the muckrakers, who wrote to Chambers on June 18, 1933:

> My dear Whittaker Chambers:
>
> My hat came off while I was reading today a story of yours. How you can write! And your stuff—
>
> Whenever I hear people talking about "Proletarian art and literature," I'm going to ask them to shut their minds and look at you. I hope you are very young, though I don't see how you can be. I hope, too, that you are daring, that you have no respect for the writers of my generation and that you know as well as I do that you can do it. Now I'll put on my hat again.[25]

His period of disfavor had ended. He was added to *The New Masses'* contributors' board, and his photograph was featured in the magazine. It showed him in a suit and tie, grimly unexpressive. The caption was touched up to give the ideal image of the "worker-writer": "Boyhood in eastern United States. Youth as periodically vagrant laborer in deep South, Plains, Northwest. Brief Columbia college experience, ending with atheist publication. Formerly member Industrial Union, 310 I.W.W. Joined revolutionary movement 1925."[26]

His rebirth as a Communist writer came at an opportune moment. The Depression, by creating a plausible vision of capitalist ruin, had made prophets of revolutionists dismissed as crackpots only a few years before. Soon "enormous prestige" accrued to card-carrying Communists. Many outstanding intellectuals either joined the Party or loaned their talents to it, jumping aboard with a naïveté Chambers had long since outgrown.

As a refulgent star of the movement—as indeed "the purest Bolshevik writer ever to function in the United States"—Chambers involved himself in various projects. In the fall of 1931 he joined Jacob Burck, Langston Hughes (an acquaintance from Columbia and the John Reed Club), and playwright Paul Peters to form the New York Suitcase Theater, with the idea of creating "a repertory of working class plays to be given before labor organizations." Chambers completed a play, never staged, about the coal miners' strike in Harlan, Kentucky.[27]

Chambers was also made a contributing editor of the *Labor Defender*[28] and placed on the national advisory board of the Comintern-organized Workers' Film and Photo League. He teamed up with five other writers to script *Winter 1931,* an ambitious documentary meant to publicize the stark Depression images Hollywood resolutely ignored: "the flop houses, the tattered clothes, the bread lines, the lonely men freezing to death, spontaneous strikes, suicides, the more and more insistent demands of the starving millions, their hunger marches and demonstrations." Filming was under way when the project was scrapped for lack of funds.[29] In March Chambers was appointed to the Sponsoring Committee for Production of a Soviet Film on Negro Life along with Hughes, Malcolm Cowley, Floyd Dell, and others.[30]

The Communist work that had isolated Chambers in the 1920s now, in the 1930s, led him to the center of New York literary life. A community of radical intellectuals flourished in the restaurants and cafés of downtown Manhattan. There was drinking at John's Restaurant, on East Twelfth Street, where Mike Gold, Carlo Tresca, and lesser-known figures might meet: Communists, socialists, anarchists. The poet Harry Roskolensko recollected leisurely evenings with Chambers in which the two conversed about "poetry, the class struggle, aspects of humanity that did not entail Marxism" and talked yearningly about "the frontier or what was left of it—the world outside the cities, about farming." Chambers had a "great range of feelings" and was not shy about exhibiting them, for this was a time, short-lived, when "it was possible . . . to be political and still be civil in regard to the politics of others."[31]

In the spring of 1932 Chambers and Esther moved to a farm in rural New Jersey, near the town of Glen Gardner. The property was owned by Franklin Spier and his wife, Della Day, well-known figures in the bohemian community to which Chambers now prominently belonged. (Della Day, Esther's good friend, was the sister of Dorothy Day, the Catholic activist.) It was the Chamberses' first experiment in rural living, amid a valley nestled against the flank of "a densely wooded mountainside," alive with the song of thrushes and the burbling of a nearby brook. Their quarters, in a barn, were barely habitable, with neither heat nor electricity. But Esther loved the "enormous garden" whose abundant produce kept the couple nourished. They began to remodel the place,[32] though soon had only weekends free for this task.

In the spring Mike Gold, *The New Masses'* ideological czar, offered Chambers editorship of the monthly, at fifteen dollars per week.[33] It was an important job. Some of America's best writers were now appearing in the magazine: Katherine Anne Porter, John Dos Passos, Edmund Wilson, Langston Hughes, among others. Moscow wanted to ensure that their work, prized though it was, did not dilute the magazine's political message.[34] Flattered by the appointment, Chambers quickly ironed out his differences with Charles Dirba and in March assumed his first editorial duties.[35] In April he supplanted Walt Carmon, who was vacationing in Florida and did not learn he had been ousted until his return.[36] The next month, at the first national conference of the John Reed Clubs, Chambers was elected to the organization's eleven-man board. He had joined the elite councils of the proletarian literary movement.[37]

It had been a rapid climb but not a smooth one. In the two and a half years since Chambers had quit the *Daily Worker,* he had seen loyal Communists read out of the movement and the finest Soviet minds defamed as "counterrevolutionists." He had discovered that the dictatorship of the proletariat was in fact the tyranny of a single man, Stalin. He had been divested of all his illusions save one. He still was certain communism, for all its faults, possessed the will and the means to destroy the existing world and make possible a new and better one.

Thus reconciled to the Party, Chambers did not hesitate to enforce its policies. Enthroned in a "little dark office" in *The New Masses'* tiny quarters on Fifteenth Street, he became a literary commissar, "a fiercely orthodox Marxist critic to whom everything not on the party line was outside the pale," recalled Robert Cantwell. Chambers put it more succinctly: "I edited as a Communist"—that is, as a Stalinist. He weeded out contributors he suspected of heresy or deviationism and delivered edicts to others on the imperatives of "Bolshevik self-criticism."[38]

In the very first number of *The New Masses* he edited, in May 1932, Chambers sent a message "To All Intellectuals":

> You are either pioneers and builders of civilization, or you are nothing. You will either aid in moulding history, or history will mould you, and in the case of the latter, you can rest assured that you will be indescribably crushed and maimed in the process. And the end will be total destruction. History is not a blind goddess, and does not pardon the blindness of others. In history, defeat is the penalty of blindness or apathy—and sometimes annihilation.[39]

When the poet Horace Gregory, one of many impressed by Chambers's nature lyrics, tried to engage Chambers in a discussion of them, the single-minded editor cut him off, saying literature no longer interested him. The days of expansive talk were over. All that mattered was the revolution, which meant serving the Soviet Union. He had rededicated himself with a soldier's faith to "the advance guard, the hope of progress and civilization."[40]

# *S*PY

*(1932–1938)*

*The "hottest literary Bolshevik" in 1931, a year before he went underground.*

# 8

# *Going Underground*

Chambers had edited three issues of *The New Masses* when he received a summons to the office of Max Bedacht,[1] a top Party official. In his seven years as a Communist, Chambers had never met Bedacht, though he knew of him and of his celebrated instinct for survival. A dedicated Lovestoneite, Bedacht had not only weathered the purge but prospered by it. In 1929, as the defiant Lovestone fell, Bedacht bowed to Moscow's dictates and was rewarded with national secretaryship of the CPUSA, though he remained in the post only a year before he was supplanted by Earl Browder, who shunted Bedacht to the International Workers Order, the Party's fraternal insurance organization. Bedacht loyally built it "into the party's largest and most prosperous auxiliary."[2]

Seated in Bedacht's office at the Workers Center, on Seventeenth Street, Chambers faced an unassuming little man of fifty, with a round face, rimless glasses, and a trim mustache, who looked every inch the barber he had been in his native Germany before he discovered Marx.[3] Speaking in softly accented English, Bedacht informed Chambers he had been selected for one of the Party's "special institutions."[4] Chambers had scarcely been aware such institutions existed,[5] let alone that the self-effacing Bedacht was "liaison officer" between the American Communist Party and the Obyeddinenoye Gosudarstvennoye Politicheskoye Upravlenie—better known as the OGPU.[6] Literally the initials translated blandly as the Unified State Political Directorate. In reality the OGPU was the central agency of Soviet intelligence, domestic and foreign.

In Russia agents spied for the government and stamped out all signs of "counterrevolutionary" activity. Outside Russia OGPU agents spied against enemy governments and their political institutions. OGPU agents also worked in conjunction with operatives employed by another secret branch of the Soviet government, Glavnoye Razvedyvatelnoye Upravlenie—the GRU, the Red Army's Fourth Department, in charge of all-important military intelligence.[7] Eventually Chambers was to be placed under Russian GRU agents and assist them in industrial and military espionage. There was in addition an underground branch of the CPUSA, supervised by the Comintern through Moscow-trained leaders posted from Europe.[8] The relationship among these groups was more rivalrous than collegial, as Chambers soon discovered.

On the face of it, Chambers was an anomalous choice for "underground" work. He was a suspected heretic, not to mention a leading Communist writer whose sudden disappearance from the "open Party"—that is, from the realm of public Communists—was sure to arouse suspicion and gossip. But he also had distinct qualifications. First, at a time when the rank-and-file membership was predominantly immigrant, Chambers was a rarity, an Ivy League–educated WASP well connected to the world of respectable intellectuals. He would find it far easier to infiltrate American institutions than would many others. Next, he was an adept linguist, with idiomatic German—still communism's lingua franca—and so could easily communicate with agents sent from overseas. Finally, Chambers possessed impressive personal characteristics: courage, strength, and guile. During the Lovestone purge, while others all around him fell apart, fleeing the Party or rushing to denounce their comrades, Chambers had stood his ground and then made peace with higher-ups on his own terms. He had shown the same quiet resolve in guiding *The New Masses* along the newly prescribed Stalinist line. Such a man was probably up to the rigors of "special" work.

As for his ideological blemishes, Moscow was not much concerned. Hardly a Communist alive had avoided getting his feet tangled in the ever-changing Party line. And Lovestoneites—real or imagined—made especially good candidates: first, because U.S. government authorities assumed they were completely out of the movement; second, because many Lovestoneites were eager to be reinstated in the Party's good graces and so volunteered for risky jobs.

"What does underground work mean?" Chambers asked Bedacht. The OGPU's liaison man confessed he did not know. "*They* will tell you," he said.

Chambers asked for time to think the proposition over. He was inclined to accept. To enter the illegal underground was to join the ranks
of the true revolutionists. He felt "a quiet elation at the knowledge that
there was one efficient party organization and that it had selected me to
work with it."[9] Discussing Bedacht's proposition with Mike Intrator, still
his confidant, Chambers said he planned to accept the new assignment.[10]

But the decision involved more than Chambers himself. There was
also Esther to think of. Her political passion, always mild, had been diluted further by a year of marriage. She was thinking of starting a family.
Special work, whatever it meant, was probably dangerous. The United
States was by no means czarist Russia, with its secret police and its vast
invisible army of informers. But even if American authorities were not
paying attention, Comintern watchdogs would be. Esther, after hearing
her husband out, pleaded with him to turn it down.[11]

At his next meeting with Bedacht, Chambers reported the disappointing news—and was told in return it was too late. The proposition
was an order. He was to go underground. To Chambers, this made sense.
He already knew too much. He knew there was an underground, knew
Bedacht was somehow involved. His options were to obey, quit the Party
altogether, or vanish—perhaps be sent to Moscow.[12]

The discussion over, Chambers followed Bedacht out of his office and
over to the BMT subway station on Fourteenth Street. Someone was
waiting for them: John Sherman, the *Daily Worker* staffer whom Chambers had last seen during the Lovestone purge, his egg-bald head bent
sobbing over his typewriter. Bedacht, calling Sherman Don, an underground alias, left the two men alone. They strolled, talking. Sherman deflected Chambers's questions about his whereabouts and activities since
1929. "You're in the underground now," Sherman said gaily, "where I
ask questions, but don't answer them, and you answer questions, but
don't ask them." He seemed thoroughly reborn, flushed with the importance of his new work. After a few minutes Sherman sent Chambers
away with instructions to meet him again that evening.[13]

At six o'clock Chambers walked over to 14th Street and waited for the
uptown IRT. He had just seated himself in the car when Sherman materialized beside him. Getting off a stop early, at 110th Street, so as to elude
possible surveillance, the pair climbed up to the street and walked, in the
soft evening light, to the long, narrow limb of Riverside Park, where

Chambers had jogged in his collegiate days. They reached Grant's Tomb, at 123d Street, above the banks of the Hudson, facing the Jersey shore.

A car waited at the curb. The two men entered, and a driver guided the vehicle along Riverside Drive. Sherman addressed the man as Karl. Chambers came to know him by that name but more commonly called him by another, Herbert. A tank officer in Leningrad, Herbert was tall and ruggedly built with a military bearing and "a round, firm, commanding face" topped by "amber-colored" hair.[14]

Herbert dominated the conversation, questioning Chambers, in a thick Russian accent, on his break in 1929 and on his current "ideological position." Chambers explained he was once more fully within the fold and ready to accept Party discipline. The Russian, evidently satisfied, gave Chambers an alias, Bob, which suited the new recruit's bland, WASPish looks.[15]

He also gave Chambers his first order. He was to quit the editorship of *The New Masses*. His new employer was the underground. He would receive $100 a month, paid in cash by Sherman. In time this monthly stipend grew to $165, and he received expenses of up to $200 a month for telephone, rent, medical bills, travel, and food. Chambers submitted regular reports.[16]

Observing Chambers's sloppy attire, Herbert, natty himself in a suit and fedora, peeled fifty dollars from a roll of bills and told the new agent to buy himself a decent suit. The meeting concluded with Bob and Don arranging their next appointment.[17]

Over the next few weeks Chambers laid the groundwork for his departure from *The New Masses*. "I have asked for and been granted a release," he explained to Nathan Adler, a young writer he'd been bringing along. Quietly Chambers's name was dropped from *The New Masses*' masthead.[18]

In subsequent meetings with Sherman, Chambers learned more about his new role. He was to serve initially as the link between Bedacht and the CPUSA underground—the Party used a German term, *Verbindungsmensch* (contact man)—ferrying messages back and forth. Sherman also taught him basic underground procedures. Chambers was never to travel directly to an appointment but always to take a circuitous route, using subways and buses. Rendezvous were preferably held in deserted parks, empty movie houses, drab eateries, usually in Brooklyn or another outer borough.[19]

As Chambers soon discovered, these precautions were not only wearisome but unnecessary. In the early 1930s American counterintelligence scarcely existed. There was virtually no surveillance of known or suspected Communists. "If you wore a sign saying, 'I am a spy,' you might still not get arrested," remembered one of Chambers's Soviet accomplices.[20] Underground agents led a free and easy existence and a privileged one. Sherman took Chambers to the "gallery," a popular gathering place for underground workers in a handsome brownstone just off Fifth Avenue, with a uniformed doorman stationed in front. The apartment, large, oak-paneled, and lavishly furnished, was loaned to the apparatus by Harry and Paula Levine, well-heeled fellow travelers later arrested in Paris as part of a Communist spy ring, headed by Moishe Stern, the top GRU officer in the United States.[21]

On one visit to the gallery[22] Sherman introduced Chambers to a new GRU agent, Aleksandr Ulanovsky, who had arrived in New York in 1931. For the duration of the collaboration Chambers knew him as Ulrich. Of his several Soviet overseers, Chambers remembered this first one the most fondly. A thirty-six-year-old Jew from the Crimea, Ulrich looked nearer fifty, with his lined features. He was short and wiry, with a bright, bold stare and "something monkeylike in his loose posture, in the droop of his arms and the roll of his walk." He had been a revolutionist since his teens, arrested many times. Once, in Siberia, Ulrich had stolen a fur coat belonging to another political prisoner, Joseph Stalin.[23] After the revolution Ulrich, not a Communist, also spent time in Soviet prisons before being rehabilitated and recruited for military intelligence. His latest assignment had been in Shanghai, under Mikhail Borodin, "Stalin's Man in China," who helped lead the Chinese revolution of the 1920s. In November 1930 Shanghai police had moved in on Ulrich's operation. He fled and was posted to the United States, sailing first class with his twenty-eight-year-old wife, the dark and dramatically attractive Nadya. She was also a Soviet agent. Chambers knew her as Elaine.[24]

The Ulanovskys had dreaded coming to America, a demotion. The choice assignments were in Central Europe and Asia, where the Communist Party was better developed and the tasks more important. In addition, the Ulanovskys, conditioned by Soviet propaganda, assumed the United States was a primitive, barbaric wasteland, straight out of the pages of Upton Sinclair's The Jungle. To their surprise, they found a country whose material bounty, even during the Great Depression, seemed limitless. The couple grew used to a standard of living and to personal freedoms unthinkable back home.[25]

This knowledge made for sometimes awkward relations with their American comrades, full of romantic misconceptions about the Communist homeland. Even Chambers, "far advanced in comparison to other American associates," seemed deluded about conditions in Russia. But the truth might not have mattered, so intense was his quarrel with America. Once, when Nadya and Chambers were traveling together on Party business, the colleagues stood at a bus stop and examined the skyline of the small city they were in. "Lucky Americans!" Nadya remembered thinking. "Look, how beautifully they live! A small town like this looks like New York. It even has its own little skyscraper. It has all the conveniences of the city but is an easier place to live." Suddenly Chambers's voice broke in, harshly. "It's awful to live in a town like this. Everyone has the same furniture, everything is the same and interchangeable. No individuality, terrible conventionality." Nadya was taken aback by Chambers's vehemence, so unusual in one who was otherwise "very kind and gentle, incapable of inflicting pain on any living creature."[26] But then Ulanovskaya knew nothing about Chambers's Lynbrook days.

Indeed Chambers presented many contradictions to the Ulanovskys. It mystified the couple that Chambers, with no hint of regret, had given up the editorship of *The New Masses* and the pleasures of the literary life to perform the trivial assignments Ulrich gave him. Yet "Bob" remained, with all, a literary man, "amazingly sensitive" in his judgments, impressively versed in Russian and German literature, a subject he and the Ulanovskys, themselves deeply cultured, often discussed. Chambers even maintained his slackly bohemian appearance, violating underground discipline. He was shabbily outfitted in a poorly cut suit, with wrinkled trousers, and he refused to fix his teeth. "Nobody could do anything" for him, Nadya recalled. When Nadya paid a visit to the Chamberses' quarters in Glen Gardner, she was astonished to find the couple inhabiting "an incredible hut," lit only by a kerosene lamp. Esther too was a curious specimen, clad in sacklike peasant dresses "of unbleached cloth." Her one indulgence was the expensive gloves she bought at fancy shops. It was as if "Bob" had willed himself into an American Siberia.[27]

.  .  .

One day Elaine took Chambers to Gay Street, a charming little street in Greenwich Village. They entered Number 17 and climbed a flight of "dark, narrow, creaking, carpeted stairs" to a floor-through apartment where Ulrich and a Russian American, Leon Minster ("Charlie"), a technical worker, were studying secret messages sent from the Comintern in Germany.[28] The Gay Street apartment, Chambers gradually learned, was "the base of operations for a communications system between the underground in the United States and Europe."[29]

When a ship docked in New York, a member of Ulrich's operation, known to Chambers as Henry, met the courier, who handed him a thin envelope and a dime-store pocket mirror, which Henry delivered to Charlie, who then took a rambling route to 17 Gay Street. The envelope contained a single page of typed German, innocuous remarks on conditions in Weimar Germany. This message concealed a second written in invisible ink. Charlie (and later Chambers, when he was taught how) plunged the letter into a solution of potassium crystals, and Russian script appeared. Ulrich or Elaine studied the letter and then burned it in the fireplace. The second item, the pocket mirror, also contained a message, in the form of a few developed frames of microfilm wrapped in tissue paper and squeezed in between the tiny piece of glass and its cardboard backing. The result, when enlarged, was a message several pages long, containing instructions from Ulrich's GRU superiors, relayed via German Communists.[30]

While the Gay Street team was assigned to overseas communications, other GRU operatives in America concentrated on military and industrial espionage. (Moishe Stern boasted, improbably, of having procured a tank from the U.S. Army, which he dismantled piece by piece and shipped in crates back to Moscow.)[31]

Ulrich's crew also did military espionage, but on a small scale. Sometimes Chambers and Charlie filled a crate with copies of technical periodicals and pamphlets from the U.S. Patent Office and then mailed the box to Moscow. Material of this kind, legally shipped overseas, was valued by the Soviets, who had belatedly developed an interest in American technology.[32]

Chambers was also assigned to more ambitious schemes, all failures. Several times he was sent up to New Haven to photograph blueprints of new submarines being built at the Electric Boat Company. The scheme fell through when a contact at the shipyard confessed to the FBI. On another occasion Chambers and some colleagues tried to induce a clerk to steal documents from the Picatinny Arsenal in New Jersey, but the plan folded before it got under way.[33] Yet another time Ulrich had Chambers purchase a "small cheap toy" in which a letter could be concealed. Well versed in the ingenuities of such items, thanks to Jay's collection, Chambers found a miniature soldier with a drum into which a tiny folded letter snugly fitted. Ulrich sent the toy to the Panama Canal Zone. A second "gift," a wristwatch, soon followed. Chambers later surmised, correctly, that the recipient of these messages was Robert Osman, an American serviceman arrested in 1933 as he prepared to send military documents to New York.[34]

Osman's capture endangered the Gay Street operation. So did another development. In the first months of 1933 Adolf Hitler assumed the chancellorship of Germany, aided by German Communists, who had cynically teamed up with the Nazis to ensure the defeat of their enemies on the left, the Social Democrats—"social fascists." With Hitler in power, communications from Germany abruptly stopped, and the Gay Street workshop was dismantled.[35]

Shortly after going underground, Chambers discovered it was inconvenient to be living so far from the city. He and Esther left the "miserable hut" in Glen Gardner and began a series of moves, six in all (they occupied some residences more than once), occurring over a span of eighteen months, with brief stopovers in Lynbrook. Esther set up provisional households in Greenwich Village, on Staten Island, and in Fort Lee, New Jersey.[36]

In February 1933 Esther became pregnant. A baby was out of the question, said Chambers, because of his special work. They must consider too the injustice of raising a child in the horrific twentieth century with its "inevitable revolutions" and "inevitable wars." Chambers was haunted by Richard's bitter cry: "For one of us to have a child would be a crime against nature."[37] Esther must submit to an abortion.

But she wanted children, and in fact so did Chambers. They decided to defy the laws of the revolution, and on October 17, 1933, Esther gave birth to a daughter at the clinic of Booth Memorial Hospital in lower Manhattan.[38] They named her Ellen, perhaps after Chambers's beloved mentor. Chambers entrusted mother and child to Laha's care, in Lynbrook, and then resettled them in an apartment building, The Castle, in

Fort Lee, New Jersey, in the shadow of the newly built George Washington Bridge.

These arrangements highlighted the incongruity of Chambers's position in the world, its odd compound of bourgeois responsibility and revolutionary commitment. But then, under any conditions, being an underground Communist in the early 1930s seemed a futile enterprise: the long, looping travels made to elude nonexistent pursuers, the confusing procession of bosses and handlers, the bungled schemes. It all seemed trivial in the context of the great political events of the day. Abroad there was the rise of nazism and the specter of impending war. At home the New Deal, in its extraordinary first months, had restored hope to a nation gripped in a crisis more profound than any since the Civil War.

Yet Chambers exulted in his new identity. He had abdicated his place in the "dying world" and had discovered a meaningful niche in the world waiting to be born. He flagrantly violated Party discipline by confiding—or bragging—to friends of his new important role in the coming revolution. To Meyer Schapiro it seemed his friend "had found valuable work and had regained a sense of dignity."[39]

Chambers tried to recruit others to help him, including a number of Trotskyists. Among those he approached asking favors of one kind or another were Schapiro; Bub Bang; the journalist Herbert Solow, a Columbia classmate; another classmate, David Zablodowsky, now an editor at Viking Press; Lionel Trilling's wife, Diana; Robert Cantwell; and Walter Goldwater, a Fourth Avenue bookseller whose shop was popular with Communist intellectuals. Several of these acquaintances served as letter drops, receiving or relaying mail for Chambers.[40]

In addition, Chambers cultivated the radical journalist Lincoln Steffens. Actually it was Steffens who initiated a meeting. The aging muckraker, reborn into celebrity with his classic autobiography, published in 1931, which declared his conversion to communism, was now at work on another book, a biography of E. A. Filene, the Boston department store magnate and social reformer. While staying in Manhattan, at the Hotel Commodore, Steffens invited Chambers to lunch and offered him a large sum to research Filene's life and rough out a manuscript draft. "The man is a bore," Steffens said, "but not his life." Chambers, through with literary projects, declined the offer. On parting, Steffens called, "Keep a warm spot in your heart, Whittaker." Soon afterward Chambers put Steffens in touch with Bob Cantwell, who left an editorial job at *The New Republic* and briefly moved into Steffens's California home to work on the manuscript. Chambers also introduced Steffens to Ulrich, who sounded Steffens out for special work, without success.[41]

Unbeknownst to Steffens, Chambers also contacted the journalist's vibrant young Communist wife, "Red" Ella Winter, when she came to New York. For a month Chambers diligently visited her, urging one task on her and then another. She repeatedly turned him down but permitted him to pay court because she found Chambers a fascinating conversationalist. Finally, she broke off the relationship after Chambers asked her to steal documents from the State Department on a visit to Washington.[42]

Although Chambers's new "secret" identity had become common knowledge, the exact nature of his work remained a source of speculation[43] and at times derision. Typically he overdid his role. He went to elaborate lengths to persuade friends he'd gone to Moscow for training at the Lenin School, although he had not been abroad since 1923 and would never set foot in Russia. Both Meyer Schapiro and Jacob Burck received postcards from Moscow written in Chambers's or Esther's hand. The messages originated in New York and were probably return receipts Chambers had included with materials shipped to comrades in Moscow. Chambers also gave Schapiro's young daughter a book of Russian woodcuts. And in a pseudonymous book review for *The New Republic* (he wrote as Hugh Jones, the alias he also used with Lincoln Steffens and Walter Goldwater), Chambers identified himself as "an engineer who recently returned from an extended visit to Russia."*

Underground life was not always a game. Robert Osman's arrest had put the entire ring at jeopardy.[45] So had internecine rivalries within the New

---

* In later years Chambers heatedly denied he had ever been in Russia. But the story has proved remarkably durable. Friends such as Meyer Schapiro remained convinced for many years that Chambers had made the trip. Allen Weinstein also argues, in *Perjury: The Hiss-Chambers Case,* that Chambers went to Russia. But the record does not support this claim. The most persuasive evidence, a postcard sent to Schapiro, includes a handwritten date— "4/22/33." This was only four days before Chambers visited Diana Trilling at her Manhattan apartment, a date she has fixed definitively as being April 26, 1933. That visit, she has written, "was interrupted by a telephone call in which I learned of the suicide of a close friend—this date I have now established from *The New York Times* obituary files." In

York apparatus. In 1933 Ulrich began to farm out his agents to other handlers. Chambers was placed under a new Soviet overseer, "Herman," an
undersize tough in elevator heels and "a tight-fitting, rumpled suit" from
which he removed a fat roll of bills he fondled lubriciously.[46]

Herman was actually Valentine Markin, a protégé of OGPU commissar Vyacheslav Molotov. He had been sent to New York to take over Ulrich's GRU operation. Crude and bumptious, with rigidly vertical hair
and a booming bass voice,[47] Herman alienated Chambers and others,
none of whom mourned when he turned up in a Manhattan hospital
with a fatal skull fracture. He had been beaten to death in a bar. The
identity of his killers was—and remains—a mystery. Some speculated
Markin had fallen afoul of ordinary hoodlums to whom he had indis-
creetly flashed his money roll. Others believed GRU hit men had got
him, on orders from Moscow.[48]

In the spring of 1934 the Ulanovskys, cut out of operations in New
York, were recalled to Moscow, either as punishment for their failures or
as a precaution against arrest. Chambers hopefully entrusted the couple
with a letter requesting royalties for Soviet translations of his *New Masses*
stories.[49]

The Ulanovskys hated to leave. They had fallen in love with America.
Their daughter, Maya, had been born on American soil. Also, they had
grown fond of "Bob" and were worried about his future. If Markin was
an example of the sort of *rezident* Moscow would now be sending over,
the American could be in for a hard time.[50]

---

the days when Americans traveling to the Soviet Union had first to go by boat (to Riga,
Latvia) and then proceed overland by train, it is inconceivable that Chambers could have
made the reverse journey in only four days. It *is* possible Chambers traveled at another
time—either earlier or later—and wrote a fictitious date on the postcard, so as to obscure
the actual date, although his motive for doing so is hard to fathom, since the postcard itself is a virtual advertisement of the journey. It would have made more sense to cover up
the trip altogether. Moreover, visiting Americans almost always spent several months in
Russia, and in 1933 there is no comparable period of unaccounted-for time in Chambers's comings and goings. Herbert Solow recorded seeing Chambers "fairly often" from
October 1932 to March 1933. Chambers's *New Republic* article was published on July 19,
1933. This leaves an opening of three months, a period in which Chambers reported to
the Ulanovskys, who later remembered no visit to Moscow, and in which Esther entered
the second trimester of her pregnancy. In sum, Chambers seems to have fabricated a visit
to the USSR in order to impress his friends, only to find himself, years later, in the embarrassing position of having to deny a rumor whose original source was himself.[44]

So, as it happened, were the Ulanovskys. Alex was arrested in Denmark in 1935 and imprisoned for two years.[51] Things went no better in Russia. In 1948 Nadya, then a translator with many contacts among English-speaking journalists, was arrested after one of them based a character on her in a novel that unflatteringly described his Russian experiences. Nadya, found guilty of divulging "secret information about her spy activity," was sentenced to fifteen years' hard labor. Her husband protested in a letter to Stalin and received a ten-year sentence for "anarchist activity" and fraternizing with foreigners. While in prison, Ulanovsky wrote a letter to Stalin, pleading for leniency. He apologized for having stolen the dictator's coat so many years before.[52]

# *The Ware Cell*

In the summer of 1934 Chambers was given his first really important assignment. It grew out of a meeting with Harold Ware, one of the most effective Communists America ever produced.

The eldest son of the Communist matriarch Ella Reeve ("Mother") Bloor, Hal Ware was "as American as ham and eggs." He was serious but jaunty, with a frank open face and a trim athletic physique; he had captained his high school baseball team. With a degree in agriculture from the Pennsylvania State College and a yearning for adventure, he had gone on the road in the 1920s as a "harvest hand," joining the migratory workers who hoboed from farm to farm, "following the grain harvests in the Dakotas and the Great Plains."[1]

Ware was thirty-three when the terrible famine hit Russia in 1922. Others contributed money or, like the young Chambers, tried to go overseas with one of the many relief efforts. Ware showed more initiative. He handpicked "nine husky 'sod-busters' " from the North Dakota steppe and took them to Russia, along with "twenty carloads of the latest type American farm machinery, a supply of Canadian rye seed, two passenger automobiles, tents and equipment." Like a socialist Lawrence of Arabia, he led this caravan into the rugged country near Perm, his mission not merely to feed the starving locals but to make them self-sufficient and "help the government's program of teaching the Russian peasants modern agriculture."[2]

He was not greeted warmly. Russia's yeoman farmers distrusted outsiders, especially those with high-mindedly coercive plans. One day the

tractor Ware was driving "accidentally" flipped over. He lay supine beneath the overturned vehicle, leg-pressing its tonnage, until help came.
"It was no cinch over there," he later said, in his laconic way. "They've
got a long row to hoe."[3] Unflappable, persistent, and persuasive, Ware
eventually had the kulaks mastering gearshifts and practicing crop rota-
tion. Lenin, writing in *Pravda,* commended Ware's "exceptional" feats.[4]

In 1931 Ware left the Soviet Union and returned to the United States
to organize American farmers and add "an agrarian wing to the proletarian movement." He penetrated the Farmers' Holiday Association, a radical non-Communist group,[5] and then went to Washington, D.C., where
the New Deal portended a thorough revamping of federal government.

Ware had a long-standing connection to the Department of Agriculture (DOA), having been on its list of dollar-a-year consultants all
through the 1920s, when he had furnished statistics on Soviet farm experiments.[6] He decided to renew the connection. First he established a
base, forming a small think tank, Farm Research, Inc., which published
a monthly journal, *Facts for Farmers,* crammed with agricultural statistics.
In those heady first months of the New Deal it won a following in
"left-wing agricultural circles." The journal was "extremely well-
written, . . . and the analysis made sense," recalled Alger Hiss, a young
lawyer then working in the DOA. Discreetly Ware downplayed *Facts for
Farmers*'s Communist backing, though its articles were reissued in the
Party's *Labor Fact Book.*[7]

Ware supplemented this open, educative work with a clandestine program. In 1933 he began canvassing government agencies for Party recruits.[8] The blitz of New Deal programs created many new government
positions, staffed mainly by young policy intellectuals, trained in the law,
economics, the burgeoning fields of social science. Many shared "a common vision of government—a vision of capable, committed administrators who would seize command of state institutions, invigorate them,
expand their powers when necessary, and make them permanent forces
in the workings of the marketplace."[9]

No New Deal agency was more exciting than the Agricultural Adjustment Administration (AAA), a new wing of the DOA, with a staff of
five thousand, formed by FDR to solve the farm crisis. Its chief counsel,
Jerome Frank, had skimmed talent from Wall Street firms and Ivy League
faculties to create "the greatest law firm in the country."[10] Adlai Stevenson, Abe Fortas, Thurman Arnold, Telford Taylor joined Frank at the

dawn of their distinguished careers. So did others as gifted or nearly so: John Abt, Lee Pressman, Nathan Witt, Alger Hiss.[11]

As a group these "New Deal lawyers" knew little, if anything, about farming or farmers. They did not have to. They were brought in as legal technicians, as drafters of bills and writers of memos.[12] Their job was to build the machinery by which the New Deal would hoist the country from the wreckage of the Depression and at the same time repair the structural defects of an economy sorely in need of regulation. The AAA, in the words of its preeminent historian, "ushered in the New Deal."[13]

But from the outset the Triple A was divided into warring factions. One, composed of old-time "farm men," favored policies geared to helping landowners and big growers. The second, the reform wing led by Jerome Frank, wanted to improve the lot of sharecroppers and tenant farmers, among the worst casualties of the Depression. Agriculture Secretary Henry Wallace, a Republican, tried to appease both camps, siding with neither.[14]

The most radical members of Frank's team, repeatedly stymied by the "farm men," grew restless once it became clear the New Deal would do everything "necessary to preserve the social system but would certainly not dismantle it," in the words of the AAA lawyer John Abt.[15] Some of these "young hotheads," it was rumored, had begun referring to Roosevelt derisively as "the 'Kerensky' of the U.S.A.," a liberal figurehead who would be expelled when, not if, the revolution occurred.[16] For the time being, only committed radicals seemed to be offering concrete solutions. As *The New Republic* editorialized, "The only groups in the country that have given serious attention to the plight of the tenant farmer are the Socialists and the Communists."[17]

Enter Hal Ware. Though no longer affiliated with the DOA, he became a familiar figure at the AAA, camped out in the lunchroom, locked in friendly dialogue with the young reformers, persuasively reciting statistics from the latest issue of *Facts for Farmers*. The case he made was reasonable, untouched by fanaticism and enlivened by "a flow of colorful talk and stories."[18] His voice was "always easy sounding, unlike the staccato of most Party men," remembered Hope Hale Davis, a young employee in the AAA's Consumers Council. Davis found something familiar and reassuring in Ware's "tanned lean face, his rolled-up blue shirt sleeves showing the muscles in his forearms," so reminiscent of the Iowa farmers she had grown up among.[19]

By 1934 Ware had assembled a secret Communist network in Washington, a cluster of seven cells or more, each with a leader who also belonged to an elite nucleus.[20] For Washington Communists, the byword was *secrecy,* and not the winking secrecy of the New York underground. There was already muttering that the New Deal was socialism in disguise. The legislation creating the AAA had been denounced on the floor of Congress as "more bolshevistic than any law or regulation existing in Soviet Russia" and been similarly reviled in the conservative press.[21] So popular, FDR himself could laugh this off. But the bright young men of the Ware unit could not. At the first hint of suspicion their careers would be "wrecked," remembered Nathaniel Weyl, a young economist who within a year quit the unit—and left a choice AAA job—when the pressure of secrecy became unendurable.[22]

Protocol was strict. Underground members were instructed to sever all ties to the visible left. "We must keep away from any place where leftists might gather," one member recalled. "We must avoid, as far as possible, associating with radicals, difficult as that might be in Washington. Even liberals . . . were out of bounds." Ware unit members were forbidden to buy *The New Masses* at a newsstand, although copies of the *Daily Worker* were circulated among them for educational purposes. The most exacting discipline was imposed on those in Ware's elite nucleus, who "were expected to have promising careers in the government" and so were "organized completely independently of the rest of the Washington Communists and set up on the basis of the strictest secrecy."[23] The members, simultaneously protecting their careers and their revolutionary work, came to see the two as being threatened interchangeably.[24]

This led to a paranoid atmosphere. Nathaniel Weyl was not the only one unsettled by the pressure. Charles Kramer, the redheaded AAA economist who led Hope Davis's cell, solemnly cautioned members to expect "interrogation, possible torture. Such an idea, he admitted, might seem rather remote in the radical Washington climate, but climates could change fast."[25]

Yet initially the cell's activity was innocent enough. Members discussed Communist texts as well as "our work in the various agencies where we were employed" and analyzed "the drift and policies of the Roosevelt administration." Now and then a unit member might "draft a report to be given to Hal, who presumably passed it on to the national leadership in New York."[26]

But in the high councils of the Party more ambitious plans were being laid. From the beginning there was a recognizable pattern to Ware's operation: the singling out of prospects, followed by recruitment and then a course of study and the imposition of discipline. It was all preliminary to special work.

Ware's operation was being overseen in New York by Josef Peters, the outstanding figure in the Comintern-controlled American underground. A Hungarian who had fought bravely in World War I, J. Peters, as he was commonly called, had joined the Communist Party in 1918, helping organize railmen in his hometown of Cop. In 1924, at age thirty, Peters was sent to the United States to help Communize labor unions in the Midwest. Chambers met him as early as 1927, when Peters was with *Uj Elore,* the Hungarian-language Party publication that shared printing offices with the *Daily Worker.* Since then Peters had twice been sent to Moscow to receive training in secret work. In 1933 he became head of "the entire underground section" of the American Communist Party. Many years later American Communists still spoke fondly of J. Peters or "Pete," short and dapper, with a Groucho Marx mustache, thick eyebrows, and a charming smile. In his eighties, a publishing functionary in Budapest, Peters suavely assured American interviewers he had never participated in secret work or even heard of such a thing. But Soviet archives and Peters's own memoirs, written in his last years for the files of the Hungarian Communist Party, tell a different story—of the various "special tasks" Peters performed, including his supervision of a clandestine "informational" ring that operated in Washington, D.C., secretly gathering government documents and passing them on to Moscow.[27]

Unlike the passive Max Bedacht, Peters was a fertile deviser of plans and strategies with a sound grasp of the strides America was making in areas of technology useful to the Soviets. He also cultivated contacts on Broadway and in Hollywood, rich sources of Party fund-raising. He even claimed to have infiltrated the FBI.[28]

Peters envisioned two important functions for the Ware Group, two lines of work that must be kept from becoming dangerously tangled. One was espionage, the removal of government documents for copying and transmittal to the New York office and ultimately to Moscow. The second aim, potentially of greater impact, was to "influence policy"—and not only in the DOA. It was J. Peters's hope, his "dream," that Ware's New Deal starlets would someday penetrate "old-line agencies" of government—the departments of State, War, Treasury, Interior—and then rise to senior positions.[29] On his frequent visits to Washington, Peters took quiet stock of unit members, sizing up each candidate, evaluating his prospects for advancement and his potential for secret work.

In the summer of 1934, after the Ware Group had been in existence a year, Peters introduced Chambers to Ware at a Manhattan Automat. Chambers sensed right away that he and Ware would make a good team. "We had the same unromantic approach to conspiracy, the same appreciation of the difficulties of organizing intellectuals, and a common interest in farm problems." Afterward Peters told Chambers he was to establish himself in Washington, D.C. His assignment was to "learn the setup" of the Ware Group and then "separate out some members of the group," forming a "parallel apparatus" that would eventually penetrate the upper reaches of government.[30]

He arrived in Washington, by train, in late June or early July 1934[31] and was met by Ware, who had arranged temporary lodgings for the New Yorker at a music studio where Helen Ware, Hal's sister, taught violin. Ware also took Chambers on a round of meetings with the members of the group—Apparatus A, as Chambers came to know it. The original meeting place had been Helen Ware's studio but had since shifted to an apartment on St. Matthew's Court, near Dupont Circle, belonging to Henry Collins, an employee at the National Recovery Administration and a leading member of Ware's elite unit.[32] The apartment, a converted coach house, "was approached by a long narrow passageway [and] seemed almost too well designed as a secret meeting place," Hope Davis remembered. It was plush, with a mirrored bar and three walls massively lined with books.[33]

At his first meeting Chambers, now using the alias Carl, was introduced as a Party courier and was handed a thick envelope by Henry Collins, "a bland-featured" WASP with social connections much prized by the Party. Inside was cash, Party dues. By Communist standards, these were well-paid men, with annual salaries of three to four thousand dollars, and the Party valued the roughly thirty dollars it received monthly from each member. As he got to know the members better, Chambers received dues separately from them. Eventually he graduated to more important tasks, and another operative assumed this function.[34]

As he came to know the Ware members, Chambers began to understand why Peters and Ware had such high hopes for them. To be among them was to discover how far the Party had come since 1925, when Chambers had found himself in a drafty loft amid a babble of foreign accents. He now was surrounded by men who came from a vastly different world. Five had Harvard degrees; another was a Phi Beta Kappa graduate of the University of Chicago with a law degree from that school. Only one was over thirty years of age.* No wonder Chambers had been singled out to be their contact. He was among the few in the underground who could meet them on their own terms. He was himself an Ivy League product, however anomalous, with ties, however tenuous, to the world of liberal intellectuals.

Not that these men resembled the intellectuals he knew in New York. These were a different breed of *ernste Menschen,* not especially bookish or deeply steeped in culture. Some came from good families. Their thinking had been formed not by the literary and artistic ferment of the 1920s but by the devastations of the 1930s. They were hard-minded idealists convinced the revolution was in view. They felt, said one, that "we had the levers of power in our hands."[36] At the same time they were dedicated careerists, eager to make their names within the New Deal.

This was fine with the Party. Times had changed since the 1920s. The implacable bolshevism in which Chambers had been schooled—the so-called Third Period—was about to give way to the Popular Front, a new phase of outward conciliation with the capitalist democracies. To this day the Popular Front remains the high point of American communism—that is, the high point of its influence, when the movement's

---

* The unit included eight members. The five with Harvard degrees were: Henry Collins (born 1905, M.A. in economics), Alger Hiss (b. 1904, law degree), Donald Hiss (b. 1906, law), Lee Pressman (b. 1906, law), Nathan Witt (b. 1903, law).

John Abt (b. 1904) was raised and educated in Chicago. Charles Kramer (b. 1907, as Charles Krivitsky) had a master's degree from New York University. Victor Perlo (b. 1912) studied mathematics at City College. Nathaniel Weyl (b. 1910; Columbia, London School of Economics)—the son of journalist Walter Weyl, a founding editor of *The New Republic*—left the Ware unit only weeks before Chambers was attached to it. He later identified the same members as Chambers except for Donald Hiss, whom Weyl did not know.[35]

stated aims and values, ingeniously revised, merged seamlessly into the prevailing liberalism of the New Deal era.*

Though the Popular Front was not formally inaugurated until 1935, Peters and Ware anticipated its drift. They encouraged unit members to work within existing constraints to ready themselves for the time when the great change came and the need arose for "men who knew government, politics, something about the management of public affairs."[38]

Of course this required powers of dissimulation and self-control. One had to live one's life in "separate compartments."

Chambers took a room at the YMCA in downtown Baltimore under the name Lloyd Cantwell (borrowed from Bob Cantwell).[39] He stayed there a month and, as in New York, commuted to his job by train. It was a precautionary measure: better to be seen as little as possible in the city where he worked. Also, the influx of New Dealers had driven up rents in Washington. But it soon became a matter of preference. Chambers, much as he abhorred cities, was seduced by Baltimore's tranquillity and distinctive air of place—its harbor, its comfortable row houses, its southern tang.[40]

After a month Esther and Ellen came down from New York to share the apartment Chambers found on the third floor of a brownstone at 903 St. Paul Street, on an attractive block of row houses. It was a short walk to Mount Vernon Place Square and the Walters Art Gallery, the municipal museum opened that year to the public. Chambers signed the lease, again, as Lloyd Cantwell. His landlord was the local chapter of the Woman's Christian Temperance Union, which met on the first floor. The organization's leader lived on the second, with her bedridden sister and alcoholic nephew. There could scarcely be a better cover for a Communist agent. The only disturbances came from drunks, who sometimes tossed bricks through the glass window of the WCTU storefront. The Chamberses called no attention to themselves—except when they turned up the volume on their Victrola.[41]

---

* The classic CPUSA Popular Front statement is Earl Browder's, in 1936: "Communism is Twentieth Century Americanism. The Communist Party continues the traditions of 1776, of the birth of our country, of the revolutionary Lincoln, who led the historic struggle that preserved our nation. In the greater crisis of today only the Communist Party shows a way to a better life now, and to the future of peace, freedom, and security for all."[37]

. . .

All this time Chambers also had business in New York. A new Soviet handler had arrived. Chambers knew him as Bill, a tall, affectless Estonian with a lined, lipless face and a nervous habit of squinting one eye. Unlike the Ulanovskys, Bill did not settle into a frivolous existence in New York. His relations with Chambers were formal, in part because Bill, unlike his predecessors, was frightened of American "secret police."[42]

Bill had been given a major long-range assignment. He was to set up an intelligence apparatus in England, and Chambers was to assist him, traveling to London on false papers.[43] Manufacturing false papers—or boots, as they were called—was a primary activity of the underground. Passports were essential for traveling Communist agents, and American passports were preferred above all others because anyone, even non-English speakers, could travel on them without arousing suspicion, thanks to the country's vast polyglot population, with its many immigrants.[44]

The procedure for obtaining false papers was simple but ingenious. Since applicants had only to submit birth certificates as proof of citizenship, J. Peters kept a team of researchers at the New York Public Library combing through back issues of the nation's newspapers, morbidly exhuming obituaries of infants whose birth dates roughly approximated those needed for particular agents. When a name was found, the agent, using the name, wrote to the appropriate state's records department and requested a copy of "his" birth document, which he then submitted to passport authorities as proof of citizenship. In this manner the Soviet underground produced "at least 100 American passports a month," enough to outfit a large proportion of the Comintern's traveling agents.[45]

Once in London, Chambers would need a legitimate cover. Peters brought Chambers together with Maxim Lieber, a Communist literary representative Chambers had previously met at the John Reed Club. With his delicate features, monocle, and trim beard and mustache, Lieber looked like a refugee from a Proustian salon. In fact, he was the son of immigrants and had been raised on the Lower East Side and in the Bronx. As a boy he had once carried Eugene Debs's soapbox. At one time the editor in chief of Brentano's, Lieber had lost his job when the famous bookstore, battered by the Depression, eliminated its publishing operation. He nimbly switched professions, and his stable of authors, most of them radicals, now included Nathanael West, Langston Hughes, and Richard Wright, as well as the novelists Albert Halper, Tess

Slesinger, and Josephine Herbst (all acquaintances of Chambers's). His most lucrative catch was Erskine Caldwell, whose novel *Tobacco Road* had been adapted for the stage in 1933 and was enjoying one of the longest runs in Broadway history. Lieber was eager to build a roster of English clients and deputized Chambers as his London representative.[46]

The English plan developed very slowly, but Chambers continued to visit New York regularly, in connection with it and yet another spy operation, this one slated for Japan, Russia's longtime rival in Asia. By the mid-1930s it looked as if the two nations were headed for war. Since 1933 GRU chief General Jan Berzin had been dispatching agents to Tokyo. The most important was Richard Sorge, who had been Ulrich's assistant in China and was soon to establish himself as one of the twentieth century's master spies. Posing as a Nazi journalist, he acquired top intelligence from both the Japanese and the Germans and in 1941 alerted Stalin that Hitler planned to betray his alliance with the Soviets, news so shocking Stalin initially greeted it as disinformation.

With Sorge making quiet inroads, the Soviets were keen on setting up "parallel apparatuses," each swelling the volume of information coursing from Tokyo to Moscow. In instances of overlap, data could be compared, and the reliability of the rival groups assessed. Sorge's information was measured, for example, against diplomatic messages intercepted by code breakers.[47]

Thus in New York a new Tokyo operation was getting under way. The agent selected to head it was John Sherman, back in the city in May 1934 after training in Moscow and related activities in California. Once J. Peters had procured a passport for Sherman under the name Charles F. Chase, Chambers and Max Lieber helped devise his Tokyo cover, a news agency, called American Feature Writers Syndicate, that would provide articles to American newspapers marketed through Lieber's New York office. Chambers and Lieber filed incorporation papers, and Lieber found an editor at the *New York Post* who agreed to publish Chase's dispatches.[48]

One obstacle remained. Sherman required a Tokyo assistant, an Anglophone Japanese Communist, preferably with access to "high Japanese circles." The resourceful Peters promptly turned up a candidate, Hideo Noda, a young painter and protégé of the great muralist Diego Rivera. Noda had won a Chicago Art Institute prize in 1932 and in 1933 assisted Rivera on the Rockefeller Center painting that had caused an uproar because it included a portrait of Lenin. Born in California, Noda lived in

New York, spoke fluent English, and was a Party member. He also traveled often to Japan, where he was regarded as a leading young painter. Rather than go through Peters, Chambers consulted Meyer Schapiro, a guru to young New York painters, and asked for an introduction. Noda, as it happened, was a favorite of Schapiro's, who had been helping him in his career, even trying to sell some of his works. Schapiro agreed to arrange Chambers's introduction.[49]

Ned, as he was called, turned out to be a spare young man, aged twenty-six, of aristocratic lineage. Chambers was later haunted by the memory of Ned's face, its refinement and luminous intelligence. Devoutly Communist, Noda was flattered by the offer to assist in special work and at a subsequent meeting with John Sherman, the painter agreed to sail to Tokyo. In September, passport in hand, Sherman ("Charles F. Chase") was ready to depart. He went first to San Francisco and then sailed for Tokyo later in the fall. Noda followed in December. In early 1935 the first of Sherman's reports was published in the *Post*.[50]

Chambers's part in the operation was complete save for one last task. In the winter of 1935 Bill gave him a fat wad of cash and instructed him to deliver it to San Francisco. Chambers, making the trip by train, carried the cash in a money belt. In San Francisco he was met by Sherman's fresh-faced assistant William Edward Crane ("Pete"; also "Keith")— Chambers and Crane had spent some evenings together previously in New York—and together the two delivered the cash to Isaac ("Pops") Volkov, a Communist who operated a courier system to Japan.[51]

Then one day, after Sherman had been in Tokyo about eight months, Bill contacted Chambers. Reports from Moscow said Japanese counterintelligence had staged a raid. Sherman had been nabbed. Chambers rushed over to Max Lieber's office on Forty-fifth Street, "very agitated," as Lieber remembered. "You must break up your organization," Chambers ordered. "Get rid of your secretaries." There was no need. The secretaries were legitimate employees, and the office functioned primarily as a literary agency. The only incriminating evidence was unused AFWS stationery and the hand-painted sign on the door. In short order, every hint of the syndicate had been erased from the premises. Together Chambers and Lieber closed out the bank account. A day or two later, when Chambers reported to Bill, the Estonian sheepishly explained it was all a mistake. The overseas cable had been garbled in the decoding. No one had been arrested in Tokyo.[52]

But the apparatus was being dismantled anyway. Moscow had lost patience with Sherman. He had made only one contact, a low-ranking employee at the U.S. Embassy, whose information was worthless. Sherman's most urgent communiqués were requests for handballs. He was working furiously on his game at the Tokyo YMCA.[53]

A month later Sherman was back in New York* defending his management of the Tokyo apparatus as "all a rational person could be expected to do under the circumstances." It was not easy to meet the standard set by Richard Sorge. But Sherman's superiors took a different view. The American had squandered a good deal of money, a sin not lightly forgiven, and had made no effective use of Ned Noda, leaving the young painter idle the entire time. As punishment Sherman was reassigned to Moscow. He dreaded going but saw no alternative except the unthinkable one of breaking with the Party. Chambers commiserated with Sherman in the final days before the disgraced operative sailed to Riga. Not long after Sherman departed, a package from Japan arrived at Lieber's office. It was a trophy. Sherman had won the handball championship at the Tokyo YMCA.[55]

Hideo Noda also drifted back to New York. He escaped censure and was given another assignment, this time to France. Meyer Schapiro pleaded with Chambers to dissuade the painter, so young and so gifted, from accepting it. Chambers took Ned aside and pointed out the hazards of special work. Noda politely heard him out. Then he went to J. Peters and reported Chambers as a Trotskyist. Peters, amused, relayed the accusation to Chambers, who was not.[56]

In 1939 Noda died in Tokyo, at age thirty, reportedly of a brain tumor. Chambers, by then a defector, assumed the painter had been liquidated by Stalinist agents. He regretted his role in Noda's brief underground career, he told Schapiro, but accepted no responsibility for the outcome.[57]

At the same time that the Japanese apparatus came crashing down, Bill revived his London plans. Chambers and Lieber went to work, and in May 1935 a passport—issued to "David Breen"—arrived at Lieber's of-

---

* Before leaving Tokyo, Sherman had turned over the management of AFWS to a young (non-Communist) journalist, Barbara Wertheim, who later achieved renown under her married name, Barbara Tuchman.[54]

fice. The literary agent accompanied Chambers to the British consul general's office in Manhattan, where Lieber certified Breen as his London representative. Chambers grew a mustache for this new adventure.[58]

Chambers, aware the assignment could last many months, insisted Esther and Ellen accompany him to London or join him there. Getting a passport for Esther was routine. Peters's obituary researchers had only to locate a deceased woman of her approximate age and the process could begin. But what to do about Ellen? The child must have papers identifying her specifically as the daughter of David Breen and "Edna Rogers" (the name found for Esther). Peters was unruffled. A contact in the city hall at Atlantic City, New Jersey, had access to state birth records and was able to insert an entry for "Ursula Breen" with all the appropriate birth information.[59]

Chambers had gone so far as to recruit a possible courier for the London apparatus when the plans were finally abandoned. By this time, however, he was involved in other, more important work.[60]

The Ware Group was moving in a new and important direction.

# 10

# *Saving the World*

As early as 1934 Ware unit members had begun stealing government documents and sending them on to Party headquarters in New York. Most of the documents were routine—reports and memorandums, not highly confidential. But they were of interest to the Party, which was closely monitoring the New Deal's farm measures. If the documents were copies, they could be passed along as they were. But originals had to be duplicated, and the most efficient method was to photograph them. The operation was supervised by Hal Ware's assistant, John Herrmann, the husband of novelist Josephine Herbst. Chambers, who had some experience at this, helped too. J. Peters gave him a Leica camera and a folding stand that fitted into a suitcase and could be assembled and taken apart on the spot. Sometimes they used Herrmann's apartment, sometimes Henry Collins's place on St. Matthew's Court.[1]

Then the Ware Group suffered two setbacks. The first came in February 1935, when the steadily widening rift at the AAA reached a climax. At issue was a contract for cotton growers, due for renewal. The expired agreement had guaranteed government payments to large growers who took acres out of production, artificially inflating cotton prices. It was a boon for growers but disastrous for sharecroppers, put out of work by the cutbacks in production and then evicted from the land because their services were no longer required. Growers were supposed to disburse a fair portion of the subsidy to their tenants, but in fact this seldom happened. The new contract's principal author, Alger Hiss, amended the terms to redress this injustice, adding a provision that disbursed payments directly to tenants and sharecroppers.

AAA chief Chester Davis, not consulted during the drafting of the contract, was irate. He complained to Secretary Wallace that the troublemaker Jerome Frank had gone too far, trying to slip through a major policy change that might cause "revolutionary outbreaks in the South." Wallace himself could be heaved out of the Cabinet "within a month," Davis warned.

The next day pink slips littered the desks of AAA staff. The casualties included Lee Pressman, Frank's top assistant and a member of Apparatus A. Curiously, Alger Hiss was spared, leading to speculation within the agency that he had privately cut a deal with Chester Davis, who indeed offered Hiss Frank's position; at Frank's insistence, Hiss declined. It was also the case, however, that Hiss had been detailed months before to a Senate committee; the cotton contract had been an extracurricular assignment. In any event, the AAA "purge" sent a strong message to the Ware Group. If even a "timid liberal" like Jerome Frank was at risk, then Communists must proceed more cautiously than ever.[2]

The Washington underground suffered a greater setback that summer, when Hal Ware crashed his car into a coal truck while speeding on a Pennsylvania highway. He died the next morning, August 14, 1935, five days shy of his forty-sixth birthday. The group fell into confusion. Unit heads suspended meetings. There was to be "no unnecessary contact with other members," remembered Hope Davis. "If we had to communicate, we must use the conspiratorial techniques we had learned, such as pay phones at preplanned hours and intervals."[3]

Chambers's role in both these developments was minimal. At the time of the purge he had been traveling to San Francisco and back.[4] In the spring he was temporarily in Washington, in fact staying at a Georgetown apartment loaned by a contact.* But Ellen, not yet two, fared poorly in the summer of 1935, one of the hottest on record, with temperatures reaching 110. Chambers moved his family to New York, where they briefly subleased Meyer Schapiro's Village apartment. But the heat there also proved oppressive—as did the rent (ninety dollars)— and in July Chambers gratefully accepted an invitation to join Max Lieber for a summer rental in Smithton, Pennsylvania, on the Delaware River. Chambers stayed on through Labor Day and was there when Ware died.[5]

* Alger Hiss. See page 250.

With Ware gone, John Herrmann tried to establish control over the cells but proved weak and indecisive.[6] J. Peters filled the void, stepping up his visits to Washington and officiating at meetings. He also dissolved the inner nucleus of leaders and re-formed it into two new units. These stayed intact through the 1940s.[7]

By the fall of 1935, with the London operation canceled and the Ware Group reassembled, Chambers turned his full attention to developing the "parallel" apparatus in Washington. Peters arranged for him to meet a new set of Washington operatives, who included a number of U.S. Treasury officials and a chemist at the Bureau of Standards. Some had previously been handled by David Carpenter.

Born in Baltimore, Carpenter—the English translation of his surname, Zimmerman—had grown up in the movement. He was most conspicuous as a union activist, heavily involved with the Federation of Architects, Engineers, Chemists, Technicians (FAECT), a Communist front organization tapped by Moscow for espionage activity in the 1930s. So hated was he by capitalist bosses, Carpenter bragged, that the Party had assigned him a bodyguard. This was possibly true, possibly not. With Carpenter one could never be sure. At age twenty-nine, he "glowed with a smoldering fanaticism," said a colleague, and was determined "to wield power within the Party."[8]

Carpenter's prized government contact was a bespectacled Oxford-educated economist, Julian Wadleigh, recently transferred from the Department of Agriculture to the Trade Agreements section of the State Department. Not long after Wadleigh's transfer Carpenter took the economist to Philadelphia to meet Chambers, "a plump little man . . . with an air of great importance and authority." Introducing himself as Carl, Chambers "spoke in a voice so low it was almost impossible to understand him, as if a life-long practice of being on guard against eavesdroppers had become a habit with him."[9]

Though Carpenter showed deference to Carl, he viewed him as an interloper and resented having to share Wadleigh with him.[10] But the economist liked his new handler. The two dined or lunched together in Washington every week. Carl hinted broadly of other contacts at State and seemed to have important friends in Moscow too. His knowledge of international politics was encyclopedic. One evening Carl talked "about the Chinese people and Chinese politics in such intimate detail that I had no doubt he had spent a considerable time there."

He was, by any measure, a mysterious man. Even his accent was enigmatic. Wadleigh, who had spent most of his youth in Europe, prided himself on his skill at placing foreign accents. But Carl's stumped him. Its inflection was Germanic, or was it Slavic? Wadleigh finally surmised that Carl hailed from "one of the Soviet minority nationalities around the shores of the Caspian Sea."

Carl chuckled quietly. "A very ingenious theory, but it doesn't happen to be true."[11]

In the summer of 1936 the Chamberses again vacationed in Pennsylvania. Max Lieber, enchanted by his stay the previous summer, had bought a farm in Ferndale, in upper Bucks County. Chambers located a place in nearby New Hope. For a nominal rent, met by his underground expense account, the "Breen" family occupied a three-room stone house set in an orchard, with commanding views of maples in front and a long stretch of garden in back. The previous summer Chambers had purchased a secondhand car, a tan Ford, and commuted regularly to Washington and New York. Their landlords, the Marshall family, apple growers, liked their summer tenants. Ellen ("Ursula Breen"), now almost three, played with Charlie Marshall, the landlords' son. Esther, "wonderful with the children," led them into the woods "on nature walks and picnics." Mr. Breen too was a pleasant man, though not much in evidence. The Marshalls did not ask what kept David Breen on the road so often and so long. It was none of their business. Besides, he was quiet and unobtrusive, and he "*always* paid his rent in *cash* the first of every month."[12]

In August the Breens went to Manhattan, again subletting the Schapiros' brownstone, conveniently close to Booth Memorial Hospital, while Esther approached term with her second child, a boy, born August 18, 1936. They named him John.[13] The family then returned to New Hope to prolong their country idyll and stayed on through the winter and spring.[14]

Meanwhile Chambers's Soviet handler Bill had suddenly vanished, summoned home to Moscow. He did not warn Chambers he was leaving. The word came from another Soviet operative, the Latvian Arnold Ikal ("Richard"), who handed Chambers a "tiny penciled note" written in Bill's hand and apprising the courier a replacement was on the way. Only later did Chambers grasp that Bill had fallen victim to the great purge initiated by Stalin in a massive campaign to eliminate "the old cadres of the state, the Party and the army—a 'revolution from above' in many ways as complete as has ever been carried out," as the event's leading historian writes. The Great Terror was under way, and Bill himself had been swallowed up.[15]

One autumn afternoon, when Chambers was in Manhattan, J. Peters led him on a stroll up Fifth Avenue to meet Bill's replacement, Boris Bykov, a GRU agent from Odessa with fifteen years of underground work behind him in Europe. He had come to the United States in the summer, with orders to supervise the whole of the country's Soviet military intelligence operations.[16]

Bykov, about forty years old and Chambers's own height, was turned out neatly in a worsted suit. He wore a hat, in part to cover his hair, which was memorably red. He gave in fact an overall impression of redness. His lashes were ginger-colored, his eyes an odd red-brown, and his complexion was ruddy. He had as yet little English and spoke German with a guttural Yiddish inflection that Chambers strained to decipher. More than once, in the months ahead, Chambers's struggle with his new boss's accent sent the Russian into fits of rage.

After briskly introducing Chambers to the new *rezident,* Peters left. The Russian instantly grew panicky. He told Chambers they must get away. The two executed the usual series of tedious maneuvers so as to elude any possible surveillance. Bykov, suspicious even of Chambers, refused to divulge either his phone number or address, though he grudgingly gave out an alias, Peter, by which Chambers knew the Russian for the duration of their uneasy partnership, the most difficult of Chambers's underground career.[17]

Cowardice was only one of Bykov's unpleasant traits. He also was subject to violent mood swings, switching from ferocious tantrums to grating fits of false jollity. And he was habitually distrustful. Time and again he questioned Chambers sharply on his ideological views and about his previous underground activities.[18]

In truth Bykov early had reason to be suspicious of Chambers. One day, in the winter or spring of 1937, on one of his frequent trips to New York, Chambers paid a call on Maxim Lieber at his new Manhattan apartment. A third man was there, John Sherman, freshly returned from Moscow in a state of extreme agitation. He grabbed Chambers and demanded they talk. As soon as they stepped outside, Sherman poured forth a harrowing account of his stay in Moscow.

First he had been "given the silent treatment." Then he discovered an entire community of lost souls like himself, American agents reduced to the status of untouchables, denied decent food and proper medical care. This went on for months. The Americans finally drew up a list of grievances and submitted them to Herbert, the tank commander who had chauffeured Chambers along Riverside Park in 1932. Sherman then was summoned to an office of the NKVD (the new incarnation of the OGPU) and granted an exit from Moscow, provided he undertook an assignment in England.

Sherman had no intention of carrying it out. "I will not work one hour longer for those murderers," he vowed to Chambers. Instead he was planning to break with the underground. He urged Chambers to do the same. Chambers declined but agreed to assist Sherman by acting as go-between with Bykov. Sherman had written a letter to the *rezident* stating his "intention of leaving his work for the Soviets and returning to the American Communist Party in California." Beyond this, Sherman asked that he be allowed to keep as severance the five thousand dollars he had ferried from Moscow to set up the English operation.

Bykov, though angry, took no immediate action. A week later he advised Chambers that Sherman's resignation had been approved in Moscow, along with his request to keep the five thousand dollars. In return Sherman was asked to meet "representatives" of the NKVD.

Chambers relayed this request to Sherman, who became frantic. An appointment with the NKVD, he was sure, meant he would be liquidated. He must flee to California at once. He implored Chambers "as a friend" to give him two days to start making his way to California, ahead of the NKVD. Chambers complied. Bykov flew into a rage, convinced Sherman had contacted American "secret police." The *rezident* insisted on phoning Sherman's hotel. At a sidewalk phone booth, while Chambers dialed the number, Bykov squeezed into the booth and tried to fit his ear against the receiver. The phone rang in Sherman's room, but the agent did not answer. He had already fled. In California, true to his word, he attached himself to the open Party. Bykov assured Chambers the defector was being watched.[19]

Bykov did not punish or threaten Chambers. Indeed, his tirades aside, he treated the courier with grudging deference, owing to Chambers's importance as the contact man to the Washington cells, or *die Quellen* (the sources), as Bykov called them, in his "foul Yiddish German." Much of Chambers's early interaction with Bykov consisted of grueling cross-examinations about the Washington group. "The main theme, repeated in endless variations was always the same: 'Are they secret police agents? How do you know they are not?' Obviously, if I knew, they could no longer be secret police agents. Therefore the question was always unanswerable,"[20] and Bykov and Chambers went around in circles.

In December 1936, at last satisfied, the *rezident* disclosed his plans for the Washington underground. Some of Chambers's contacts were to begin espionage. It would happen in stages. First, said Bykov, the members must be "put in a productive frame of mind" with cash gifts. But these were idealists, Chambers protested, "Communists on principle." They would be shocked at an offer of payment. Bykov was adamant. The handler must always have some kind of material hold over his asset: *"Wer auszählt is der Meister, und der Geld nimmt müss auch etwas geben* [Who pays is the boss, and he who accepts money must give something in return]."

If cash was out of the question, Chambers must ply his contacts with gifts.[21] Christmas was approaching. Chambers would give *die Quellen* handsome holiday presents. Bykov handed him six hundred dollars with which to purchase Bokhara rugs, woven in one of the Asian Soviet republics and coveted by collectors. Chambers, who knew nothing about rugs, appealed to the expertise of Meyer Schapiro, giving the art historian a check for six hundred dollars just before Christmas. Schapiro chose four brightly designed carpets at an Armenian wholesale establishment on lower Fifth Avenue. All four rugs were delivered by the Railway Express Agency to Washington and distributed to the four contacts* singled out for reward by "the grateful Soviet people."[22]

Next, Chambers arranged for the four sources to come to New York for an interview with Bykov, so the *rezident* could make his pitch for espionage. To Chambers's surprise, Bykov rose to the occasion. Appealing to the agents' strong antifascist sentiments, he pleaded the case for aiding the lonely "Socialist Fatherland," faced with "encirclement by the Fascist powers—Germany and Italy in Europe, Japan in the East"—while the capitalist nations and "imperialist powers" (Britain, France, and the United States) stood idly by.[23]

---

* They were Abraham George Silverman (an economist at the Railroad Retirement Board), Alger Hiss, Julian Wadleigh, and Harry Dexter White.

Rhetoric aside, this was a plausible picture of world events, one widely shared on the left, in any case. That was precisely why *die Quellen* needed no pep talk, just as they needed no bribes. But it was gratifying to hear the plea directly from the mouth of a Soviet operative. Each of the sources, like Julian Wadleigh, one of the four Bykov had selected, wanted nothing more than to do "something practical to protect mankind from its worst enemies."[24]

As before, the Soviets hungered for intelligence on developments in Germany and the Far East. The situation had become tenser. The Anti-Comintern Pact signed by Germany, Japan, and Italy in November 1936 presaged the more aggressive alliance to come. Once Japan subdued China, which was still putting up a fight, Russia might be next. Chambers's most important sources, in the State Department, began to furnish a steady supply of cables, memorandums, and political and economic analyses. Many were confidential reports sent to Washington from its foreign offices around the world.*[25]

Chambers's underground work, and his daily routine, now centered on espionage. In the case of each contact he had first to arrange a rendezvous, in rare instances at the contact's house, more commonly at a neutral site (street corner, park, coffee shop) in Washington. On the appointed day Chambers drove down from New Hope (a distance of 110 miles) and was handed a small batch of documents (at most twenty pages), which he slipped into a slim briefcase.

He next went to an apartment in Baltimore loaned to the apparatus by sympathizers. Chambers let himself in with a key, and the tenants vacated the premises. Photographic equipment was already set up in the kitchen: a Leica on a stand, with direct light supplied by gooseneck lamps. Chambers donned gloves—a clumsy but cardinal precaution, lest he leave fingerpints—and photographed the documents. Later that night, while the microfilm hung drying in strips, Chambers returned the originals to his sources and then drove the three hours to New Hope. Two or three days later he went back to Baltimore, retrieved the developed film, and again drove north, this time two hundred miles to New York, where he delivered the microfilm to Bykov, who relayed it to Moscow in any of several ways—by courier, radio, diplomatic pouch, or diplomatic telegram.[26]

---

* See chapter 23.

It was soon apparent to Chambers that the procedure was too laborious and time-consuming. He tried combining photography sessions, but
it was difficult to coordinate meetings with all his sources, each of whom
followed his own schedule. On one occasion Chambers made three separate trips to New York from New Hope in a single day and fell ill from
lack of sleep.[27] The only solution was to move back to Washington or
Baltimore and so eliminate one leg of his travels.

Still attracted to rural living and eager to provide a stable home for Esther and the children, free from the pressures of illegal work, Chambers
pursued an idea that had been with him since the previous spring. A
friend in the Washington underground* had alerted him to inexpensive
properties in rural Maryland, near Westminster, a pretty town thirty
miles north of Baltimore, just below the Pennsylvania border. Identifying himself as a freelance writer, Chambers had asked a Westminster Realtor, Edward Case, to find him a five- or six-room house habitable from
spring through autumn with "pure water (well or pump), and some kind
of outbuilding that can serve as a garage."[28]

Chambers now recontacted Case and in March and April placed de-
posits totaling $325 on the "Shaw property," a small house with ten acres
of farmland and a stand of persimmons. The house stood on a dirt road,
ten miles outside Westminster. Its owner, who had recently died, had let
the place deteriorate. Chambers hoped to fix it up on the weekends.[29]

Meanwhile he rented an apartment in Baltimore, on Auchentorly
Terrace, a middle-class neighborhood, mainly Jewish, in the northern
part of the city, across the street from Druid Hill Park and its observa-
tory.[30] This was Chambers's address during the peak months of his work
as an espionage agent. He had shortened his travels considerably. He had
only an hourlong commute to Washington, which he could make by
train. There was still the drive to New York, time-consuming and tiring.
But it was an improvement.

There was a second problem, however. Too many facets of the operation were concentrated in Chambers himself in his dual functions of
courier and photographer. This was both inefficient and risky. If he were
nabbed, the operation would be stopped. Chambers raised the matter
with Bykov, who assigned a new man to the operation, a Baltimore photographer, Felix Inslerman.

---

\* Alger Hiss. See chapter 21.

In his late twenties, genial and baby-faced, with rimless glasses, Inslerman belonged to a growing caste of underground workers trained in technical fields; later he received a degree in electrical engineering and pursued graduate work at Johns Hopkins in advanced mathematics and in aerodynamics. He had been recruited into the underground by the Estonian GRU handler Bill and first met Chambers (as Bob) as early as 1935. In the interim Inslerman had traveled to Moscow and then done apparatus work in New York. Relocating to Baltimore, Felix (Chambers did not learn his surname) became the main technical cog in Chambers's espionage ring, first using Chambers's Leica and then buying his own, a newer model, plus lenses. He also acquired a collapsible stand that fit into a canvas bag. Felix set up this equipment in a basement sublease near his own apartment on Callow Street.[31] Before long he took over almost all the photographing responsibilities while Chambers acted solely as courier.

A routine was fixed. Chambers received documents and then turned them over to Inslerman at a prearranged meeting place in Washington, usually near Union Station. Later that night the two operatives met again, and Felix returned the originals to Chambers, who then delivered them back to their sources. Some days later Chambers retrieved the developed microfilm from Felix and drove it to New York. Later they introduced a new precaution, leaving the microfilm undeveloped, so that if Chambers were intercepted and forced to relinquish it, the film would be exposed in the instant the canister was opened.[32]

As the volume of documents grew, a second photographer joined the operation: the ambitious David Carpenter, who removed the equipment from the apartment Chambers had been using in Baltimore and set up a new site in a house in Northeast Washington. Carpenter photographed documents supplied by Julian Wadleigh and another source, a chemist at the Bureau of Standards, active in FAECT. A third photographer, John Sherman's former assistant Bill Crane, who had come East again and been assigned to Baltimore by Bykov, also helped out.[33]

Chambers, curious to see what kind of information he was processing, read some of the stolen documents. They did not seem particularly enlightening, though this changed as he acquired newer and better-placed contacts, with access to military secrets. For the time being he concluded "the secrets of foreign offices are notoriously overrated. There was little about political espionage, it seemed to me, that an intelligent man who knew the forces, factors and general direction of history in our time could not arrive at by using political imagination, backed by a careful study of the available legitimate facts."[34]

Bykov, certain he was being cheated, demanded more and better goods. On one occasion in late 1937 the *rezident* had Chambers arrange a meeting with Wadleigh, who had been handing over State Department documents every ten days. Chambers introduced Bykov as Sasha, and the three dined at a restaurant.

It was an awkward occasion. Wadleigh and Bykov came from different ends of the earth. Educated in the lecture halls and libraries of Europe, Wadleigh retained something of the graduate student's painful serious- ness. The first documents he had delivered were rigorous analyses of the world economic situation, written by himself. Gently it was explained to him that the "Party wanted to use me not as an economic analyst, but as a channel for obtaining classified information." Wadleigh was disap- pointed but not shocked. "After all," he later said, stiffly, "spying was then and is [now] a standard practice in international relations." Besides, Wadleigh knew he was not alone. Carl had made it "abundantly clear" he had other, unnamed, sources at State, and the operative appeared to know a good deal of what was going on in Trade Agreements.

Wadleigh was taken aback when Bykov, in his now passable but gut- tural English, accused him of handing Moscow second-rate goods. The economist agreed his material was "spotty," but not because he was holding back. He was doing the best he could. The trouble was the "rather haphazard" flow of documents in the Trade Agreements section.

"You must always be analyzing your defects and criticizing yourself," Bykov reproved, his manner paternal but severe. "A-A-always analyze— a-a-always criticize."

The *rezident* raised another point. Wadleigh should be thinking of ca- reer advancement. A promotion would mean access to better docu- ments. But Wadleigh did not seem slated for higher things at State. He was a superb economist and had, or thought he had, stimulating ideas. But not even four years at Oxford had given him the required polish. His manner was all wrong: his eager, searching gaze, magnified by rimless lenses; his shock of uncombed hair; his wrinkled suit and droopy socks. At social events, he foundered hopelessly at small talk, gauchely steering the conversation toward the arcana of economic theory. Wadleigh, in turn, resented the "socially elite" snobs at State who "regarded me as a queer character" and sentenced him to the research room and the drudgery of drafting technical reports.

He steeled himself to make peace with the higher-ups at State, though it meant "conforming to a pattern set by convention." He "even sported a handkerchief in the breast pocket of my coat." It was a small sacrifice, given the alternative, which was to "fail in my contribution to the saving of the world."[35]

By late 1937 the "sleeper apparatus" was wide-awake and thrumming. Bykov also built up a productive wing of industrial espionage, via Bill Crane, who had cultivated a metallurgist, Morris Asimow, employed at the Carnegie Illinois Steel Company, a Chicago subsidiary of U.S. Steel. Asimow passed along a formula he had helped develop for making steel alloy. He met with Crane as many as a dozen times, flying to New York for weekend trips, always delivering documents. Crane's contacts also included two émigré Russians, both former officers in the prerevolutionary army of the czar.[36]

But this was ancillary to the growing Washington operation. Chambers was finding new sources. The most important was Franklin Victor Reno, a statistician at the Department of Agriculture reassigned in 1937 to the Ballistics Research Laboratory of the Aberdeen Proving Ground, a principal testing site for the U.S. Army. Shortly after his transfer Reno was introduced to Chambers in Philadelphia, Chambers's favorite neutral site. They discussed Reno's new work "and the information that I could furnish to Carl."

So it was to be espionage, said Reno.

"Intelligence would be a nicer word," said Carl.

Thereafter Chambers scheduled rendezvous with Reno in Washington. Some of the appointments were arranged by Reno's brother, Philip, a Communist employed at the National Labor Relations Board, where Nathan Witt had become a powerful figure.

After a month Reno was able to furnish Carl with a report on "the administration and the entire set-up of the Aberdeen Proving Ground's organization staff." Later he gave Carl two firing tables, one on "the 16-inch gun," the other on a "30 or 50 calibre machine gun." He also gave him sketches outlining his own theories, including a diagram that represented his own best surmise of the Norden bombsight, the top secret targeting device being developed for Army Air Corps bombers. Chambers and Reno met, all told, as many as seven times, continuing through the spring of 1938.[37]

Bykov was triumphant. "In your time it was *Kinderspiel*," he soon gloated to the Ulanovskys in Moscow. "We have agents at the very center of government, influencing policy."[38]

Chambers too could take some satisfaction. He had buried the stigma of Party "literate" and achieved a truly meaningful niche within the revolution. His work was indeed "special." It was also monotonous and exhausting: "meetings by day, meetings and transmission of materials by night. Two meetings, with the precaution of long advance rambles to throw off possible surveillance, would occupy an afternoon." Often he was up well past midnight, assisting his photographers or returning original documents.[39]

And there was the continual eruption of small crises Chambers, as "morale officer," was expected to solve. He had to handle difficult contacts, such as Abraham George Silverman, the economist at the Treasury Department, who, appropriately tightfisted, disliked paying Party dues. There was also Silverman's star contact, Treasury official Harry Dexter White, who alternated moods of abrasive hauteur with others of craven fear and was much happier handing over grandiose memorandums on monetary policy (he was a world-class authority in the field) than in furnishing the mundane reports of high-level Treasury discussions preferred by Bykov and his Moscow superiors.[40]

White's anxiety was atypical. Most agents were relatively unconcerned about being found out. Chambers too operated more or less free of fear. Though Washington was teeming with government workers—and, at least in theory, with counterintelligence agents—in reality it seemed a "big and beautiful village,"[41] its boulevards as quiet and empty as country lanes, invitingly open to him and his accomplices. Perhaps because this work was nocturnal, it seemed dreamlike, occurring within the dark interstices of the government's working hours, when all the great gears had fallen silent and those in authority slept undisturbed.

Later it was said the spy rings flourished so profusely because the New Deal had been a fertile ground for conspiracy. Some would say Communist infiltration was the natural outgrowth of the revolutionary Roosevelt program. Roosevelt's defenders oppositely argued FDR had acted to stave off a collapse like that of the *ancien régime,* a birth of true anarchy. This became one of the angriest debates of the cold war.

But in the 1930s there were only whispers. It was common knowledge that some in the government were Communists. There was talk of "Marxist study groups." There was a wide assortment of activist groups on the left, some Party fronts, others loosely tied to it, others independent, others anti-Communist. The New Deal embraced a "cross-fertilization" of ideologies, some radical, some populist, some hard to categorize.

The same was true of the decade itself. In the 1930s the visions of the extreme left often converged with those of the far right. Socialists and isolationists found common enemies among Wall Street financiers and arms manufacturers. The era's two most potent demagogues, the Louisiana senator Huey Long and the Detroit preacher Father Coughlin, began by calling for programs more radical than any proposed by the New Deal but before long were giving voice to nativist resentments that seemed to draw on the same malign energies as the fascist programs of Hitler and Mussolini.

In fact the New Deal *was* ripe for Soviet infiltration, but not because of the domesticated radicalism of FDR's administration. The reason was simpler. There was as yet no vigorous system of security checks in the U.S. government. The trouble was not the New Deal. It was the national temper, willfully unadapted, at this late date, to the wartime footing the rest of the world had already achieved. In America very few grasped, as Chambers was beginning to, "the forces, factors and general direction of history in our time."

But that direction had become disturbing. By 1937 Chambers could no longer avoid certain facts about the regime he was serving. First, the Moscow trials had reached their zenith. One by one the Old Bolsheviks were dragged into interrogation rooms and then forced onto the witness stand to declare their fictive crimes against the revolution. Then they were executed. In 1937–1938, the Great Terror would claim two million fatalities.

Chambers brooded too on the examples of John Sherman and of Bill. What guarantee had Chambers that he himself was safe? In his dozen years as a Communist he had been guilty of more than one ideological misstep. He had nearly been expelled during the Lovestone purge and had not (even at this late date) severed his ties with the renegade Mike Intrator, whom he sometimes visited on his trips to New York. There was also the ever-suspicious Bykov, disturbingly well briefed on Chambers's comings and goings. The *rezident* had even accused him of being a Trotskyist, reviving the old, and deadly, charge.[42]

It had some basis. Chambers was still a friend of Meyer Schapiro, a member of the Commission of Inquiry, headed by philosopher John Dewey, that had been formed to expose the falsehoods of the show trials and to exonerate Trotsky of the ludicrous charge that he was heading up a "counterrevolution." In early 1937 Schapiro had shown Chambers a transcript of the Moscow hearings, and Chambers had been shaken, so transparently rigged were the proceedings. Even Bykov, upon reading a list of Stalin's victims, was taken aback. "*Dieser Chef wird uns einen stark Brei kochen* [This boss is cooking a strong mush]," he muttered. In early 1937 Chambers was ordered to sever all ties with Schapiro.[43]

Then there was Spain. No event of the 1930s had done more to burnish the Soviets' image than their support for the Spanish Republican government. While Nazi Germany and Fascist Italy rushed aid to the rightist general Francisco Franco, only Russia came forward in defense of the republic, lending troops and weapons. Stalin had proved to the world that the rhetoric of the Popular Front was not empty, that the USSR, and it alone, dared meet the threat of international fascism. But then it emerged that the Soviets had carried the purge over to Spain and were thinning Spanish Loyalist ranks of heretics and dissenters, especially members of the Trotskyist Marxist party (POUM). Hit men were on the loose, carrying out contract murders. When General Jan Berzin, chief of Soviet military intelligence, was sent to Spain to coordinate the Republican armies, he found himself at loggerheads with the NKVD. In July 1937 he was summoned to Moscow for "consultation" and summarily executed.[44]

Chambers's fears grew when Bykov, upon learning Chambers had never been in Russia, ordered him to go there at once, a command he repeated several times. The *rezident,* drawing on his coward's fine instinct for measuring fear, was testing Chambers, trying to determine the limits of his loyalty. In the winter of 1937 Bykov urged Chambers to undertake a dangerous assignment. The Spanish freighter *Mar Cantabrico* rested in the Brooklyn harbor being loaded with weapons, two million dollars' worth, including whole airplanes dismantled and packed into crates. The cargo was meant for Spanish Loyalists. Bykov instructed Chambers to join the *Mar Cantabrico*'s crew to ensure the arms were not diverted en route to a port controlled by General Franco.

The plan was nonsensical. How could Chambers thwart the captain and his crew? Besides, the Neutrality Act of 1935 had embargoed all arms shipments to Europe. The Coast Guard was likely to intercept the boat as soon as it left port. Even if they should make it through and reach Spain, Chambers must then maneuver past Franco's Falangists and also, perhaps, the NKVD. From every angle the assignment was extremely risky. Chambers flatly told Bykov he would not go.

In March the vessel slipped from its moorings and reached the Bay of Biscay, where an enemy cruiser lay in ambush. Spies in the United States had fed the Falangists all the vital information: the ship's route, its communications code and the radio wavelength it would be sent on, as well as the new name the ship would be sailing under. The captors steered their "war prize" into a rebel port. Almost all those aboard were executed. Had the Soviets known all along the ship would never complete its voyage? Had Bykov meant for Chambers to be captured? The *rezident* was pointedly ambiguous. "You are a smart boy," he told Chambers, and "the smartest thing you ever did was to refuse to go to Spain."[45]

It was only a first step. Chambers had begun to contemplate his break from communism and his return to the daylight world he had repudiated twelve years before.[46]

# DEFECTOR

## (1938–1939)

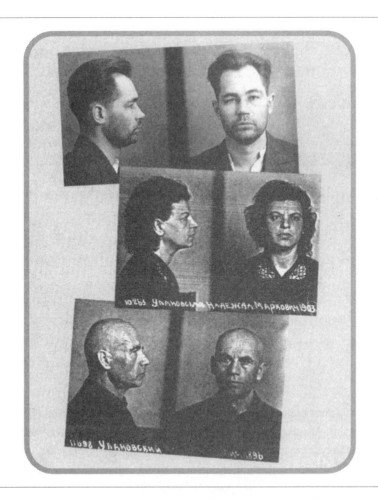

*Victims of Stalin's terror, from the secret files of the KGB: Arnold Ikal, arrested in Moscow, 1937, sent to the gulag, where he perished; Nadezhda Ulanovskaya, arrested 1948, sentenced to fifteen years in the gulag, released 1956; Aleksandr Ulanovsky, arrested 1949, sentenced to ten years in the gulag, released 1956.*

# 11

# *Disappearances*

In the summer of 1937 Chambers's interior struggle had become so great he was ready to quit the underground.[1] He could not simply announce this. The Party would take strong action, as it was doing in the case of other defectors.

In September police found Ignace Reiss, the NKVD *rezident* in Switzerland, sprawled on a highway outside Lausanne, his well-dressed corpse perforated with bullet holes. Reiss had broken with the regime and circulated a letter in which he called Stalin a traitor to the revolution.[2]

In November the world learned of another major defector, Walter Krivitsky, formerly the GRU *rezident* in The Hague. Krivitsky had been ordered to liquidate Reiss, one of his oldest friends, but declined to do so. Disobeying a summons to Moscow, he broke with communism and found asylum in Paris. Like Reiss, he denounced Stalin, but in an open letter published in the European socialist and labor press. The NKVD responded by sending assassins after him. After eluding them in Paris and then in Switzerland, he fled to the United States in December 1937, his path cleared by the U.S. Ambassador to France, William C. Bullitt, bitterly anti-Communist after his diplomatic tour in Moscow.[3]

Grimly assessing these cases—and others[4]—Chambers knew he could not break without retribution. He was less important than the two European *rezidentii,* but not so insignificant as he might wish. He was the linchpin of an efficient espionage apparatus just reaching its maturity, and his knowledge was great. He knew as well as anyone all the ring's players—the active sources in the State and Treasury departments, at the

Aberdeen Proving Ground, at the Bureau of Standards. He could identify photographers, go-betweens, recruits (real and rumored), allies, and
sympathizers, not to mention the Ware Group alumni—some dispersed
into various New Deal agencies, others on the staffs of congressional
committees or in key positions in labor unions. He later estimated he
had knowledge of seventy-five underground Communists in Washington. Chambers's defection would place them all at risk and also expose
the nerve center of the underground, the ninth floor, implicating the
Party's top leadership.

Chambers was frightened not only for himself but for his family.
Stalin's agents were notorious for punishing the spouses, siblings, and
offspring of "counterrevolutionaries." The investigation of Reiss's murder had turned up a box of poisoned chocolates evidently meant for the
victim's children. Trotsky's children would be liquidated for the crime of
belonging to a "clan of enemies."[5]

The logical step for any defector was to seek the protection of authorities by turning himself in and offering to inform. It was an option
Chambers considered. But there were disqualifying factors. He was not
in a foreign land and so would be seeking the protection of the government he had spied against. His revelations would make him subject instantly to arrest and prosecution. Espionage carried a stiff jail sentence,
up to twenty years. Nor did Chambers wish to incriminate others, those
he had groomed for underground work and then encouraged with pep
talks and sermons. He was not looking to be a hero or martyr. He
wanted to make his break, return to the daylight world, and resume the
semblance of a normal existence, doing as little harm as possible to himself and others.[6]

Whittling down his options, he was left with only one: He must escape
the underground and find a place in the outside world where the NKVD
would not dare pursue him. Like a prisoner in his cell, he must dig an invisible tunnel and then one day crawl out to freedom. He must carefully
conceal his activities until the right moment came, keep all his appointments, perform all his routine functions, speak and act as a loyal operative.
He was about to go underground against the underground, to deploy
"against the conspiracy all the conspiratorial method it had taught me."
In the fall and winter of 1937 Chambers dismantled the outward structure of his life, piece by piece, and replaced it with a new one.[7]

.  .  .

First he needed a job, a public context, a place where non-Communists would know him. His present anonymity left him vulnerable. Should he suddenly disappear, no one would notice. In October Chambers arranged through the open Party to get a salaried government position, explaining he needed the job as a cover for his special work. It took less than three weeks for "J. V. David Chambers" to be hired by the WPA as a "Report Editor" on the National Research Project. He was put to work compiling an index of the nation's railroads, at a salary of $166.66 a month.[8]

That done, Chambers took steps to safeguard his family. In October he and Esther enrolled Ellen, who turned four that month, in the Park School, a reputable private day school in Baltimore. Since the tuition was beyond their means, Ellen was granted a partial scholarship, and Esther made up the difference by teaching classes in painting and sculpture.[9]

Chambers's wife and daughter now had public selves. Esther Chambers (not "Edna Rogers" or "Breen" or "Cantwell") was on the part-time faculty of the Park School, and Ellen (not "Ursula") was a full-time pupil. No arrangements were necessary for John ("Patrick Breen"). Only fourteen months old, he was seldom apart from his mother or the maid the family employed at five dollars a week.[10]

Meanwhile Chambers kept up his normal underground routine, meeting at night with his Washington accomplices and traveling on weekends to New York, where he delivered the microfilm to Bykov. In November Chambers casually mentioned to Bykov that he needed a new automobile. His secondhand Ford was buckling under the strain of the Baltimore–New York commute. He asked the *rezident* for five hundred dollars. Bykov failed to come up with it, so Chambers borrowed a smaller sum elsewhere. The spy chief promised to cover the debt and soon produced two thousand dollars. Chambers kept the surplus. "I considered that I was at war with the Communist Party," he explained to the FBI in 1949, "and I confiscated this fund to finance my operations."[11]

On November 23 Esther, who had obtained her driver's license in June, drove the 1934 Ford to a dealership in Randallstown, Maryland, near Baltimore. She traded in the car and paid just under five hundred dollars in cash for a new model. A week later she registered the car in her name. Chambers now had a getaway vehicle that could stand up, if necessary, to a long-distance drive.[12]

Next, in December, he found a new apartment, still in Baltimore, on Mount Royal Terrace,[13] a row of brick twin houses perched on tall stoops atop an embankment. From its steep height the house commanded good views of the street below. Chambers told none of his accomplices he had moved. His plans, so deliberate at the outset, were now speeding up, though not by choice. In 1937 the hand of the purge had reached across to America, leaving two bloody prints in disturbing proximity to Chambers himself.

Chambers's casual acquaintances in New York included a good-natured operative known in the American underground as Richard and to Soviet colleagues as Ewald. His real name, according to a KGB file that came to light in 1992, was Arnold Ikal. Like so many employees in the Fourth Department, including its chief, General Jan Berzin, Ikal was Latvian. Berzin, who was partial to fellow nationals, had done Ikal many favors, the greatest of them in 1932, when Ikal, manufacturing false passports in Berlin, did some sloppy work that exposed a colleague. Valentine Markin, then in the GPU's home office, wanted Ikal disciplined. But Berzin interceded and transferred the Latvian to the United States.[14]

Ikal arrived in New York in May 1932 with orders to procure passports for traveling Comintern agents. He soon linked up with J. Peters.[15] The enterprising Hungarian, with his team of genealogical researchers, could produce documents at a tremendous rate. Peters and Ikal struck a deal. Peters supplied Ikal with passports in bulk, and Ikal overbilled Moscow, pocketing the excess funds. In this way Ikal "annexed the underground Communist Party to the Soviet secret service." He expanded as well into Canada, another polyglot country whose passports cleared customs as readily as American passports did.[16]

Ikal's timing was good. He emerged as an important source of passports at just the moment when Soviet rings were being smashed by raids in Europe and Asia. His factory made it possible for new squads of agents to sally forth, sturdily clad in North American boots, with additional fake documents in reserve. The more passports an agent had, the more fluid were his travels. He could enter a country on one document, exit using a second, cross a new border with a third, erasing his tracks at each stop.

In 1934, as Ikal's operation grew, he eyed the numerous immigrant organizations in the Northeast, a plentiful source of naturalization documents. The key contact was Max Bedacht, head of the International Workers Order. But Bedacht was keeping Ikal at arm's length. Peters asked Chambers to intervene on Ikal's behalf.

Ikal arranged to meet Chambers in Morningside Park. This was a surprise. Soviet agents, with their phobia of the American "secret police," normally favored meetings in deepest Brooklyn. As he came to know Richard better, Chambers was amused to discover that the Latvian had dispensed altogether with the normal precautions and was keeping appointments at a crowded bus stop near Rockefeller Center. This was not bravado or defiance. Richard simply took a tourist's delight in the bustle of midtown Manhattan. Almost every day of the week one could easily spot him on Fifth Avenue, "sauntering with a brief-case under his arm, window-shopping." Bykov, when he arrived on the scene, was appalled. "*Überall nur Geheimpolizei und Ewald!* [Everywhere only secret police and Ewald!]," the *rezident* had fumed after one nerve-racking encounter in midtown Manhattan.[17]

Ikal's American exile was proving a great personal boon. The demands were few, the rewards large. He cheerfully collected his passports, shipped them to Moscow, raked in his profit, and, in the timeworn tradition of business people the world over, socialist and capitalist, padded his earnings by submitting inflated expense reports.[18] He began to think of settling down. In 1933 he met a twenty-five-year-old divorcée, Ruth Braman, née Boerger, at a Communist social. Ikal made a nice impression. In his late twenties, genial and handsome, with brilliantined hair, he resembled the Austrian film actor Oscar Homolka. Ruth was doing secretarial work for the Queens chapter of the Unemployed Council, a Party front. She also taught English to foreign nationals. Ikal signed up for lessons. He introduced himself as Arnold, a publisher. (He had indeed bought part ownership of the Gallian Press, a vanity publisher.) After some months Arnold told her the truth. He was engaged in special work for the international movement, fighting fascism. So were his colleagues. Ruth began helping with passport work. She joined the team at the New York Public Library and was added to her fiancé's payroll at one hundred dollars per month. The following winter Ikal got his naturalization papers and became Arnold Adolph Rubens. In May 1935 he and Ruth were married.[19]

Business was brisk. Between Peters, Alfred Tilton (a top GRU agent), and Sam Carr (a member of the Canadian Party's Central Committee),

Ikal was shipping as many as a hundred passports a month to Moscow. He and Ruth acquired a second apartment—a summer place on Jamaica Bay—and a maid. Then came "two cars, a motor boat at the Oyster Bay Yacht Club," plus membership in a tennis club. It was a steep and giddy climb.[20] In the spring of 1936 the couple briefly visited Moscow, where Arnold basked in the praise of his superiors in the Fourth Department. The couple returned to New York in triumph.[21]

Then, a year later, Ikal learned his mentor, General Berzin, had tangled with the NKVD in Spain and been recalled to Moscow for "consultation." The entire Fourth Department was now vulnerable, above all the Latvians warmly despised by Berzin's enemies. Ikal's summons came that summer. Sensing danger, he delayed his return. Then, to his relief, a message came, signed by "the old man," Berzin himself. The general must be safe. It didn't occur to Ikal, the specialist in forged papers, that the signature might be a fake. In August, unbeknownst to Ikal, Berzin was executed.[22]

One day in October 1937 Chambers, keeping his appointments as he secretly burrowed out from the underground, traveled up to New York and lunched with J. Peters at Zimmerman's Budapest, in midtown Manhattan. Ikal and Ruth were dining at another table. The genial Latvian looked "gray and worried." What was wrong with him? Chambers asked. "You," Peters replied. Ikal suspected Chambers, a fellow operative in the Fourth Department, had been assigned to keep him under surveillance.[23]

On October 16 Ikal and his wife sailed from New York on the Italian liner *Rex,* with two pairs of passports, one pair issued to a Mr. and Mrs. Arnold Rubens, the other to a Mr. and Mrs. Donald L. Robinson. Their eventual destination was Moscow. Ikal had the chilling fatalism of the revolutionary dedicated to the cause even as it threatens to devour him. J. Peters had pleaded with the Latvian to travel alone rather than lead Ruth and her child into the "unstable situation" awaiting them in Moscow. Ikal partly followed this advice, leaving his stepdaughter behind in Philadelphia, with her grandparents.[24] But he took Ruth along, in the hope her American citizenship would protect them both from arrest. A key provision of the recognition treaty of 1933 was that the USSR would detain no American citizens. To date this promise had been kept—at least as far as the U.S. government was concerned. No one tallied up the American Communists who had disappeared in Russia—or even knew of them since they all traveled to Moscow incognito.

On November 5 the couple crossed the Russian border, as Mr. and Mrs. Donald Robinson, and boarded a train to Moscow. They checked in at the National Hotel but did not register next door at the embassy. Soon Ikal took ill and was rushed to a hospital. Days passed, and Ruth heard nothing. The hotel staff would not tell her the hospital's name or address, only that her husband was in an "iron lung" and could receive no visitors.[25]

A frantic Ruth "Robinson" sought out American journalists staying at the Hotel Metropole. They relayed her message to the American Embassy. The next day the American chargé d'affaires, Loy Henderson, inquired at the National Hotel after the missing American citizen named Donald Robinson. The hotel manager said he knew nothing, not even whether Robinson was in a hospital. Henderson tried again the next day, and this time was told Mrs. Robinson too was gone. No one knew where. She had suddenly "departed with her effects in an unidentified automobile." Henderson tried the Soviet Foreign Ministry, again with no luck. Under pressure from American diplomats, Moscow admitted that both Robinsons, husband and wife, were in custody. By this time the story was front-page news in America. Stalin's chief foreign minister, Maksim Litvinov, hinted the couple were not the innocents they seemed. Donald Robinson's journey had originated with a conspiratorial visit to Trotsky, in Mexico.[26] This was a pure fabrication, as was pointed out by John Dewey, spokesman for the Committee for the Defense of Leon Trotsky, an offshoot of the Commission of Inquiry.[27]

Trotskyists or not, these were American citizens, Secretary of State Cordell Hull reminded Litvinov. The Soviets had committed a prima facie violation of the recognition treaty. Privately the Soviet ambassador in Washington, Aleksandr Troyanovsky, urged the State Department to drop its inquiry. The Robinsons were not what they seemed. Had Mrs. Robinson not "waited around the hotel" for nearly a week before reporting her husband's absence and then "kept to herself all facts pertaining both to her husband and herself"?[28]

At the same time Loy Henderson was demanding to see Ruth Robinson. Her family in Philadelphia was frantic. The story, still getting major play in the press, was undermining U.S.-Soviet relations. "I cannot understand why those fools don't let the Americans talk to her," a bewildered Bykov said to Chambers; "she will not dare to tell them anything."[29]

On February 10 Henderson was at last allowed to visit Ruth Robinson in the Butyrka prison. Her color was poor, but she "was neatly dressed and fairly well groomed." She "made no complaint of her treatment" and said she required no assistance from the U.S. Embassy, not even legal advice.[30]

Gradually American officials had begun to unravel the strands of the case: the forged passports; the two names; the accomplices who had helped the couple procure false documents so easily. It was now known that Donald Robinson–Arnold Rubens was not an American but his wife was.[31]

In April 1939 American Embassy officials at last secured the promise of a trial for Ruth Rubens. In June, after eighteen months in jail, she was led, puffy-faced, out of her cell and given her day in court. She spurned a state-appointed advocate, preferring to defend herself. The "trial" lasted forty-five minutes. A two-man tribunal pronounced her guilty "of having entered the Soviet Union illegally with false documents and under an assumed name." She signed a confession of guilt, was given a sentence of eighteen months, retroactive from the day she had been seized, and was released from jail the following day. At the American Embassy she declined an offer of safe passage back to the United States, where she faced possible prosecution under the passport laws: The U.S. attorney in New York had impaneled a grand jury and subpoenaed some of Ikal's accomplices. Also, she wanted to help free her husband. The following October Ruth Rubens became a Soviet citizen and then moved to Kiev. She was never heard from again.[32]

Nor was her husband. At last, in December 1939, a few days after the NKVD had ordered his sister's liquidation in Latvia,[33] Arnold Ikal "confessed" he had been an "agent of Jan Berzin's Latvian national fascist organization" and was sentenced to a labor camp from which he did not emerge.[34] It was one nightmare in the widening fantasia of the Great Terror.

It came as no surprise to Chambers. A State Department contact* had shown him a diplomatic cable discouraging officials from taking any steps on behalf of "Arnold Rubens," now known to be a Soviet agent and not an American citizen.[35] Shortly thereafter the State Department ceased its efforts on his behalf. Later, in his best-selling memoir *Mission*

---

* See chapter 23.

*to Moscow,* Ambassador Joseph Davies recorded that the Rubens case had been "smoothed out" to the satisfaction of all parties.[36]

Simultaneous with the Rubens mystery, there occurred another, no less disturbing, although it took longer to reach the newspapers. In December 1937 the *New York World-Telegram* reported that Juliet Stuart Poyntz had disappeared in June from the apartment hotel in Manhattan where she had been living since the previous February.[37]

Chambers remembered Poyntz from the English-speaking branch of the Communist Party. At the very first meeting he had attended, in the drafty West Side loft, Poyntz, a large-boned daughter of Omaha, Nebraska, had risen from her seat to refute an adversary, placidly remarking, "The comrade is a liar." Poyntz was then forty-two, one of the Party's most visible members and one of its best educated, having studied at Barnard, Oxford, and the London School of Economics and lectured at Columbia. She had been the first director of the Workers School and in 1924 had run for Congress on the Workers' Party ticket.[38]

Reports of Poyntz's unexplained disappearance included the *Daily Worker*'s terse statement that she had "terminat[ed]" her Party membership in late 1934.[39] Insiders knew 1934 was the year she had left the open Party for the underground and begun to recruit female operatives.[40] One of those she approached was Elizabeth Bentley, not yet sufficiently "developed" for such work, though she eventually became a courier with contacts in Washington even more numerous than Chambers's.[41] Poyntz's attorney, Elias Lieberman, convinced his client's disappearance was involuntary, alerted the police and sent an investigator to her room at the American Women's Association Clubhouse, on the Upper West Side. The place looked arranged for its owner's imminent return. Poyntz's shoes were in neat rows; her lingerie was folded in her bureau, her passport tucked in a drawer. Her other possessions were in storage, and her bank account was untouched. Various theories arose, including one that Poyntz, disillusioned by a recent visit to Moscow, intended to expose "the inner workings of the Russian Military Intelligence."[42]

"Where is Juliet Poyntz?" Bykov quizzed Chambers. The *rezident* supplied the answer himself, drawing triumphantly on his growing fund of topical Americana: "Gone with the Wind."[43]

Might the Rubens and Poyntz incidents, separated by almost five thousand miles, be linked? Some close observers thought so. One was the journalist Herbert Solow, Chambers's friend from Columbia. Gloomy, brilliant, with a fierce wit, Solow was probably the most astute political intellectual in New York, a confidant of Trotsky and a leading figure in the small but active circle of liberal anti-Stalinists. For some months Solow had been pursuing his own trail of inquiries into the Communist underground. His remarkably accurate analysis of the Robinson-Rubens case, based on interviews and inspired guesswork, had been published serially in the *New York Sun*. Solow's friend, the antifascist Carlo Tresca, long acquainted with Poyntz, also suspected a connection between the two cases.[44]

Solow's investigation worried Chambers. He had not spoken to Solow since 1935, when they had a falling-out, quarreling angrily over Stalin's cynical policies in Europe, which had helped Hitler to power in 1933. But Solow still considered Chambers a friend and had tried to indicate as much by a pair of articles he published in the socialist *New Leader* under the bylines Walter Hambers and W. C. Hambers.[45] Both articles were on the Rubens mystery. Solow was disappointed that Chambers had not contacted him, directly or through Schapiro, a common friend. In fact Chambers had read the articles and been shaken by them. It was clear Solow had learned a great deal about the underground, possibly enough to cause trouble for Chambers—and at the very moment when he was gathering himself up to defect. What exactly was Solow up to? It was time the two talked.

One winter evening Chambers went to New York and enlisted Mike Intrator to accompany him on a visit to Solow's apartment, a Village sublet on Gay Street, a few steps from the site of Chambers's initiation into espionage. Solow was alone when his bell rang at ten o'clock. He looked out his window to see who had come calling. It was a cold night. Snow fell thickly. Two indistinct figures stood below, their "collars turned up, their hats pulled down."

"Who's there?" Solow shouted.

Chambers's voice rose up. "It's me."

Solow had heard rumors of Chambers's growing doubts about communism.[46] But the journalist was skeptical and refused to let Chambers and Intrator enter the building. Chambers pleaded he had come on "a personal matter." Solow reconsidered. He had known Chambers since 1920. Also, the reporter in Solow was intrigued. Slipping his pipe into his pocket, he "gripped the bowl as though it were the handle of a revolver and set forth. I emerged into the snow, crossed the patio." Surprising himself, Solow declared, "I have you covered. About face and walk through the corridor to the street. Don't look back. When we get to the street light we can stop and talk. One false move and I'll shoot."

"Are you crazy?" Chambers asked.

"Get a move on," said Solow.

The trio trudged off together, Chambers's head turreting nervously in all directions. "Whom did this Stalinist undercover man fear?" Solow wondered. "The police? Which police? The Americans? Or the Stalinist secret police who would not be pleased, perhaps, to see him with such a notorious red-baiter as myself?"

Seated at a nearby coffee shop, Chambers bluntly stated his business. "Are you and Tresca using a rifle or a shotgun?" That is, did the two journalists mean to expose only those directly implicated in the Poyntz story or would they reel off a litany of underground operatives, including Chambers?

Solow replied with a question of his own. "Do you have anything to do with the liquidation of Poyntz?"

"Nothing at all," Chambers said.

Solow noticed Chambers did not flinch at the word *liquidation*. Perhaps Schapiro was right. Solow assured Chambers he had nothing to fear. His name would be kept out of the investigation. It would be limited to the Poyntz and Rubens cases. There the conversation ended. Solow instructed Chambers and Intrator to stay seated until he had gone. He left the restaurant and plunged back into the swirling snow.[47]

All this time Chambers had been keeping up his secret work and the dreaded appointments with Bykov, who piled on new assignments, each a test of the courier's loyalty—and nerve.

At one point an underground contact from the early 1930s, Dr. Philip Rosenbliett, a Russian dentist, reappeared in New York and asked Chambers if he knew an attorney versed in patent law. The Soviets wanted to purchase devices for the automatic loading of machine-gun shells. A few days later Chambers introduced Rosenbliett to Ware Group alumnus Lee Pressman, now chief counsel of the CIO and one of the most important Communists in America. Pressman had done legal work for the Rust brothers, inventors of the mechanical cotton picker that was to make sharecropping obsolete in the South.

An irate Bykov confronted Chambers. "You have seen Dr. Rosen-bliett"—and had better not do so again.[48]

Chambers was stunned. So the dentist too had fallen into disfavor. He did not ask why. However, he ignored Bykov's directive and some days later saw Rosenbliett again. The dentist was now in a panic. Leaving the house of a friend, he had spotted an NKVD agent in the hallway. Since then a cable had come from Moscow summoning him home.

What crimes had Rosenbliett committed? In Moscow he had been the dentist to the legendary Marshal Mikhail Tukhachevsky, the hero of the 1919 Civil War, since executed, one more victim of the purge. Worse, Rosenbliett's wife was the sister of James P. Cannon, the Trotskyist leader—that is, the ringleader of the American chapter of the global counterrevolutionary conspiracy. Arnold Ikal's interrogators eventually extracted the "confession" that Rosenbliett was on the payroll of the "national fascist organization," receiving a lordly $250 per month.[49]

Rosenbliett, for his part, knew his days were numbered. His real purpose in coming to New York was to make a final visit to the grave of his daughter, who had died in childhood. His assignment finished, he meekly traveled home, there to meet his preordained fate and never to be heard from again.[50]

In late January 1938 Chambers received a notice from the U.S. government. Owing to a reduction in work volume, the National Research Project was releasing newer staff. As of February 1, he would be "furloughed without prejudice."[51]

Even without this nudge, Chambers was ready for the final stage of his break. The problem now was money. The WPA job had doubled his income, to more than three hundred dollars a month. Once he made the physical break from the underground, he would have no income at all. He must find a new source, portable work he could do on the run. A literary assignment seemed best, but his connections to the world of letters had dwindled over the years. He appealed to a trusted friend, Meyer Schapiro. In December Chambers had visited Schapiro in New York, breaking a silence that had lasted almost a year, and confided he was planning to quit his underground work. In February he contacted Schapiro again, by phone and letter, asking for help. The art historian promptly found him a translating assignment for the Oxford University Press, in New York.[52] The book was a biography of Jean-Henri Dunant, the founder of the Red Cross, written by a German émigré, Martin Gumpert. A previous translator had been dismissed in early March. It had been five years since Chambers had done such work, but he had kept up his German with Bykov and through his reading. The editor, Paul Willert, agreed to try Chambers out on sample chapters. Schapiro pitched in, polishing pages as Chambers finished them. Chambers submitted the chapters, to Willert's satisfaction, and qualified for $250, one half the total sum, the balance payable upon completion of the job, due May 1.[53]

Chambers set aside the manuscript and turned to another matter, finding temporary safe lodgings for his family. Some of his acquaintances knew he was living at Mount Royal Terrace. He placed an ad for a sub-letter in the *Baltimore Sun* and then "roamed all over the countryside" in search of a hideout, eventually subleasing a single large room in a private home divided into apartments, on Old Court Road in Woodlawn, the rural outskirts of Baltimore. The house stood atop a rise with sweeping views in all directions. The owner, who lived on the premises, kept a police dog.[54]

Here Chambers would gather himself and his family for their flight. He hired a carpenter to seal off the rented room, leaving access only to a tiny upstairs garret where the children would sleep. Every detail must be in order before they left Mount Royal Terrace. The act of moving would be his first decisive step in breaking with the underground.[55]

The next step, on April 1, was for Esther to take the car in for servicing. They were going on the road soon. A day later Esther wrote to the director of the Park School, reminding him that Ellen must abruptly be removed until the fall, when "we look forward to a happy renewal."[56]

Some days later the family quietly moved to Old Court Road. Esther went first with the children, while Chambers stayed behind to supervise the movers, two African Americans—"least likely to be traced if a hunt began and most likely to play dumb with inquisitive white men."[57]

On the first weekend in April the Chambers family went to Lynbrook and on Sunday or Monday returned to Baltimore to await the $250 check from Oxford. Even with all their belongings stacked "from floor to ceiling" on the balcony, quarters in the hideout were close. On Monday, April 11, Esther met with the director of the Park School to discuss plans for Ellen. The next day the check was sent from Oxford—to Mount Royal Terrace, the address Chambers had given Paul Willert. A few days later, possibly on Friday, April 15, Chambers collected his last batch of government documents, handed them over to Felix Inslerman, and returned the originals to their owners, holding on to a small quantity of materials—documents and microfilm—in the event they would prove useful later.[58]

Only then did he deviate outwardly from his carefully established routine. Instead of traveling to New York to meet Bykov, Chambers shepherded his family into the new vehicle Esther had bought for precisely such a journey as this. They drove south, spending the first night in Petersburg, Virginia, the second at Sumter, South Carolina, the third in Jacksonville, Florida.

On the fourth day they reached Daytona Beach, on the Atlantic coast, and drove to the dunes. Atop a sandy crest stood a pair of adjacent weather-beaten bungalows with shallow gabled roofs and a full view of the ocean. One, providentially, had a For Rent sign. The Chamberses took it for the month.

With Esther and the children safe, Chambers settled down to the Oxford assignment. He was behind, and the manuscript was long. During the day he drove inland twenty-five miles to the town of De Land. The junior college there had a decent library.

His most productive hours came late at night, in the bungalow. Seated at the kitchen table, just inside the door, he worked while Esther and the children slept. As the surf pounded out its ominous message, Chambers clumsily thumped the keys of a typewriter, the pages of the manuscript spread out on the kitchen table and a German dictionary open beside it. A revolver, loaned by his neighbor after a rash of break-ins, was also within reach.[59] But Chambers was listening for different prowlers. By now Boris Bykov—and perhaps Moscow too—knew he had defected.

## 12

# "Whose Ghost Are You?"

Bykov had indeed reacted instantly, and with alarm, to Chambers's missed appointment. He reported the incident to J. Peters, and together they called on Maxim Lieber and instructed him to make inquiries in Baltimore. It was a repellent errand but one Lieber had to carry out since the Party, he was certain, would "put a tail on me." In Baltimore Lieber found the Mount Royal Terrace apartment deserted, the furniture cleared out.[1]

Someone else, Paul Willert of the Oxford University Press, was also in pursuit of Chambers. A letter Willert had sent to Mount Royal Terrace had gone unanswered, and a telegram was returned with the notation "Addressee moved—present address unknown." On May 1, when the manuscript was due, Chambers mailed the first hundred pages, all he had translated. As a precaution against being found out by the Party, he advised Willert that all further correspondence should be sent to "General Delivery, St. Augustine, Florida."[2]

Willert was not as baffled as he might have been. A fellow traveler himself, he was aware Chambers had defected from the underground. Still, Chambers's behavior was exasperating. Willert pleaded with him to "remain at your present address or let me know what your movements are." He added that he was expecting the rest of the book by May 14.[3] Chambers nearly made it. He sent the remainder of the manuscript to Oxford in three packages, the first arriving on May 18, the second on May 20, the third on May 22. Willert was relieved when the translated pages proved "excellent."[4]

Three days later Chambers and Esther loaded the children into the car and left Daytona. They sped back north "as if the devil were perched on our tail-light." Outside Baltimore, Chambers bought a double-barreled shotgun and shells at Montgomery Ward's. Then he installed his family once again in the sealed-off apartment on Old Court Road.[5]

It seemed a curious plan: to go back to the city where the Party had last known him to be. But Chambers reasoned that Bykov had by now called off the search in Baltimore and begun to look elsewhere. The family could not stay at Old Court Road; the quarters remained close. Besides, hiding had been a "temporary tactic." Chambers must try to reemerge into daylight. "We knew we just had to establish ourselves on our own, and the sooner the better," Esther recalled in less fearful times. The Shaw property—the rural house and ten acres he had put a deposit on in 1937—was not yet habitable. It would have to be Baltimore again.[6]

In June he and Esther found a house, at 2610 St. Paul Street, near Johns Hopkins University. The house, a spacious two stories, had a small, enclosed backyard where Ellen and John could play. The price was $2,950. Chambers borrowed the $1,000 down payment from Laha, with the rest to be paid like rent, in monthly installments of $40.[7]

Word of Chambers's defection had seeped into the non-Communist world, where he was still known—and the subject of gossip. Chambers confided in only one friend, Meyer Schapiro, who in turn alerted Herb Solow. Only Schapiro, however, knew Chambers's whereabouts.[8]

Then, one day in late July or early August, Chambers phoned Solow in the Village and consented to drop by on the condition the journalist was alone. The estranged friends talked for two hours, and for the first time Solow heard from Chambers himself that he had broken and was in hiding. Solow advised the defector to "decide at once whether he would be 'the American Reiss or the American Krivitsky' "—that is, whether he would try secretly to match wits with the NKVD (as Reiss had done with fatal results) or instead become (like Krivitsky) a public defector, still alive, if not exactly in the clear. Solow sent Chambers off with a book, *The Case of Ignace Reiss,* and also reminded Chambers of his "duty" to make a public statement.[9]

Chambers was skeptical. Going public would mean delivering himself to the U.S. government at a time when it was at last beginning to view the Communist underground as a serious threat. In April indictments had been handed down in the Rubens passport case. The meeting left Chambers uneasy. Solow seemed "chiefly interested in a corpse." This assessment was harsh but just. Solow was keen to break Chambers's story, which he placed accurately in the context of a much larger tale, one that included Reiss and Krivitsky, Poyntz and Rubens, and all the other victims of Stalin's brutal ascendancy. But Chambers was thinking first of survival.[10]

He relied on Schapiro, less educated in these matters than Solow but a devoted friend who made every effort to ease Chambers's worries. He fielded Esther's frantic phone calls, giving comfort and moral support. He also invited the entire family up to his summer house in Londonderry, Vermont, for a few restful days.[11]

In September Chambers faced a new worry. Ellen was about to resume school. Beyond her father's watchful eye the child would be vulnerable to abduction. He had awoken recently from his "first nightmare on this subject." When the term began, Esther drove Ellen over each day and stood guard in the corridor until class ended, all the while clutching the infant John and watching every stranger who entered the schoolhouse.[12]

The invisibility of his pursuers magnified Chambers's fear of them. They could be anywhere at any moment. Desperate to learn what steps the Party was taking, he made an appointment with the one member of the underground he possibly could trust, Maxim Lieber. The risk was obvious: Lieber was in regular contact with Peters. But Chambers hoped the literary representative would place friendship above Party discipline. Lieber agreed, at any rate, to meet for lunch. They met at his Fifth Avenue office and then walked many blocks, losing themselves in the midday crowd. Lieber recounted his mission to Mount Royal Terrace, and Chambers pleaded with him, as he was to do with other accomplices, "Leave the party." Lieber was unwilling. But he did Chambers an important favor: He did not report the conversation to J. Peters.[13]

The defection had already caused repercussions in the underground. In June Peters was demoted from his position atop the Washington operation, and Boris Bykov was to be recalled to Moscow in 1939. When the Ulanovskys bumped into him there, on the street, the *rezident* was a changed man, emptied of bravado. He told the couple he lived in terror of being arrested "any day" for having let the "traitor" Chambers escape. Soon Aleksandr Ulanovsky too was summoned for questioning by NKVD officials and told Chambers's treachery predated the break: He "had been a German agent all along."[14]

Chambers was mulling Solow's advice more seriously. He also confided in the ex-Communist Ludwig Lore. German-born and an early leader of the American Communist movement, Lore had edited its German-language publication, *New Yorker Volkszeitung* (Chambers had been a devoted reader), until forced out of the Party in the 1920s for sundry heresies, not least his long-standing support of Trotsky. He had since become well known for his column in the *New York Post,* "Behind the Cables," wherein he cogently spelled out the dangers posed by Nazi Germany. Short, burly, with a thick bristle of mustache, Lore resembled "a genial Stalin," Chambers later wrote, and was a man of great kindness. His wife, Lillian, was equally kind, and on at least one occasion the couple put up the Chambers family for the night. They all used aliases, even the children. Mrs. Lore had tucked the four-year-old "Ursula" to bed and later recalled how the child, hugging her tightly, had whispered her real name was Ellen, though "her daddy had told her not to tell this to anybody."[15]

Another of Lore's visitors in the fall of 1938 was Herb Solow, who stopped by on other business. The conversation turned to the "mysterious man" who "had broken with the GPU." Chambers was not mentioned by name, but it was obvious to the journalists, as they exchanged notes, that both had spoken with the same man. Solow promptly sent a message, via Schapiro, to Chambers, lest anything get "gummed up between us due to Lore."[16]

Chambers, gaining confidence in Solow, paid another call on him in the last week of October, driving up from Baltimore to Solow's new address, on Joralemon Street in Brooklyn Heights. The two talked until 1:00 A.M. and then were joined by Carlo Tresca. He lived nearby with his mistress, the wealthy widow Margaret De Silver, who had footed some of the bill for the Dewey Commission of Inquiry. Tresca seconded Solow's opinion: Chambers should go to the authorities. Chambers was willing but only if promised immunity. For the first time he began to disclose the outlines of the underground. He divulged no names and discussed no specific activities. But he gave a general picture of the organization and its aims and operations. The conversation lasted until 4:00 A.M.[17]

The next day was October 31. Solow and Tresca had been invited to a Halloween party in Brooklyn that coincided with the publication of *Not Guilty!,* the second volume of the Dewey Commission findings. Solow invited Chambers along. The occasion could be a coming out for the defector and help reestablish his public identity. Besides, John Dewey would be there, and Chambers was eager to secure the philosopher's sponsorship, which might ease the suspicions of government authorities should Chambers decide to inform.

Solow had previously sounded out Dewey's protégé Sidney Hook, the commission's organizer. But Hook was skeptical of Chambers, whom he had met just once, in 1933. The two had been brought together at lunch by Lionel Trilling for the purpose of debating the Communist tactics that had boosted Hitler into power in Germany. It was not much of a debate. Hook, ruthlessly logical, had demolished the Communist theory of "social fascism" while Chambers, not bothering to defend his masters, had sat by imperturbably, "as silent as a little Buddha." Now when Solow explained Chambers's plight and his "hysterical" condition, Hook was unmoved. He suspected Chambers was a double agent scheming to infiltrate the commission. Hook would approach Dewey only if Chambers first established his bona fides by a public denunciation of Stalin's spy apparatus.[18] Chambers was not yet ready for that. He hoped instead for a private audience with Dewey.

That evening Solow, Tresca, De Silver, and Chambers drove together to the party. Chambers waited in the car while the others entered the house, a brownstone in Park Slope. Its basement living room, decorated with Mexican artifacts, and with masks, pumpkins, and skeletons, paid tribute to the holiday and also to the setting of the commission's inquiry, which had been held in Coyoacán, where Trotsky was living as a guest of Diego Rivera.

Solow drew aside one of the hosts, Anita Brenner, an anthropologist and writer, and asked if Chambers could join the festivities. He had broken with the Party, and this was "his first time out." She consented. Solow retrieved Chambers and led him downstairs to the crowded room. The guests included many of Chambers's acquaintances from the 1920s and early 1930s: Schapiro, Hook, the Trillings, Felix Morrow, Philip Rahv (the *Partisan Review* editor whom Chambers had met at the John Reed Club), and novelist James T. Farrell and journalist James Rorty, both *New Masses* contributors in Chambers's day.

Hat lowered over his eyes, coat collar turned up, Chambers made his entrance. A whisper went up: "Whittaker Chambers is here!" He was not warmly received. Most of the guests assumed he was still in the underground. Others had heard of his defection but resented the "libelous fantasy" he was spreading against the Soviet Union. Though Chambers's friends treated him cordially, most of the guests did not. Many turned their back or refused to shake Chambers's hand. Some asked sardonically, "Whose ghost are you?" After half an hour Solow left with Chambers. The ghost departed wearing a "fixed and sickly smile."[19]

Most disappointing of all, Chambers had lost an opportunity to speak with Dewey. The aged philosopher was at the party but in an upstairs room, and Chambers never saw him.[20]

On November 26 Chambers was back in New York, this time at Schapiro's house in the West Village, where he had briefly stayed in the summer of 1935. Herb Solow came over. At 1:00 A.M. Schapiro went to bed, and Chambers and Solow took a taxi to Penn Station. The two then talked at a coffee shop until Chambers's train left for Baltimore, at 3:15. For the first time Solow heard what he had been after since the summer, a thorough rundown of the Communist underground. Chambers named agents: Maxim Lieber, the Ware Group, the government contacts (including at the State Department), and he explained the "Rubens" mystery. Chambers "wants to make a deal with the police," Solow wrote in a memorandum. "If he can't get a promise of executive clemency in advance, he will take his chances with the GPU, figuring that he can keep moving and escape them. In the meantime, he refuses to make any public statement or repudiation of the CP; he claims that will only 'anger' them and speed their work of pursuing him."[21]

A week later Chambers added more pieces to the mosaic and three days hence augmented his story yet further, mentioning details Solow was able to corroborate through other sources—including Walter Krivitsky—though in some instances not for many months.[22]

For the first time Chambers gave serious thought to turning public informer and telling all to Attorney General Francis Biddle. But the conditions must be right. Biddle must be apprised that Chambers "was the head of the institution we mentioned, but broke with them 7 or 8 months ago." Chambers also hoped for "an unconditional pardon for past sins" or, that failing, assurances he could cross the border into Mexico or Canada without fear of extradition or punishment by authorities there. He did not relish informing and the suffering it would cause his former comrades. If he could possibly avoid it, no one would be injured "needlessly."[23]

Shortly after this Chambers visited those he was now considering harming, his former accomplices in the Washington underground. He hoped to break them from the movement. One of his visits was to an idealistic young married couple, Alger and Priscilla Hiss. Chambers reviewed Soviet crimes in Spain. His hosts were not impressed. Chambers's concerns, said Mrs. Hiss, were "mental masturbation."[24]

Chambers also paid a call on Julian Wadleigh, recently back from a nine-month tour in Turkey, and told him he had defected, adding that Moscow suspected him of Trotskyist sympathies. Wadleigh was astonished. Yet, on reflection, there had been telltale signs as early as 1937, when Carl's aplomb had inexplicably vanished, replaced by hesitancy and caution. Wadleigh remembered how Chambers had "brooded over the Spanish tragedy," and once, when Wadleigh had voiced some concern about being detected, Chambers had said, "Why let yourself be worried about a little thing like that? I've had worries that have kept me sitting by my window till the dawn." Now Chambers urged Wadleigh to quit the underground. "I'm going to become a bourgeois," he said on parting, "and you will too."[25]

Chambers had not given up on John Dewey. The most likely go-between remained Sidney Hook, who was furious about Chambers's unannounced appearance at the Halloween party. If word leaked out, the Dewey Commission could be compromised. The conditions for a meeting with Hook remained the same: Chambers must cite chapter and verse on the underground. Solow assured Hook Chambers was coming around and had divulged some important names. One, Laurence Duggan, cured Hook of his doubts. Hook had studied under Duggan's father, Stephen, a political scientist and the founding director of the Institute of International Education, an organization that fostered student exchange programs. Stephen Duggan was "the very model of an Establishment figure," and so was his son, a rising star in the State Department. It was unlikely the "Kremlin would 'blow' a ring so high up in government circles" simply to compromise Dewey. Chambers, then, was in earnest. But when Hook approached Dewey, the philosopher demurred. Though he had nothing against Chambers, whom he still had not met, Dewey feared any dealings with him "would be seized upon by the Kremlin and its agents to discredit the work of the commission." Solow pleaded with Hook to push Dewey harder. Chambers's life was in danger. But Hook thought Dewey's reasoning sound. In his own view, "Stalin had more to fear from the report of the Dewey Commission than from a score of defectors like Chambers."[26]

Chambers meanwhile had taken another precaution. In the summer he had given Ludwig Lore "a package of papers" he had been keeping in Baltimore, probably in a safety-deposit box he had rented in December 1937. On Chambers's instructions Lore had placed the package in a bank vault. Now Chambers wanted the envelope back. He paid a call on his wife's cousin, Nathan Levine, a young attorney who lived with his parents in Brooklyn. Chambers had sometimes stayed with the family on his visits to New York. The defector gave Levine the package with instructions to transfer it to Esther in the event Chambers met a bad end.

And if something happened to *her*?

"You would know what to do with it," Chambers replied.[27]

Money had become a problem. Chambers's earnings were minimal, and his expenses exorbitant: the month in Florida; the many overnight trips to New York; the rental payments on the St. Paul Street house. His only active source of income was a new translation, a novel about the Spanish Civil War by the Austrian Communist Gustav Regler. In the summer Paul Willert had obtained the assignment for Chambers through Oxford's affiliate Longmans Green. Chambers was paid half the commission, $250, up front with the rest due upon completion of the assignment. But he was working slowly, and more pages were expected from Regler, who had yet to finish the novel. The family's finances were so poor that Esther contemplated taking in boarders.[28] There were stretches when the couple subsisted on breakfast cereal, skimping so Ellen and John were fed decently, and more than once Chambers made the rounds of Baltimore pawnbrokers. They had to withdraw Ellen from school because Esther could not afford to put gas in the car. Generous assistance came from friends: handouts from Schapiro, Robert Cantwell, two hundred dollars from Solow, who could barely afford it.

Grace Lumpkin emptied all her meager savings. Laha also helped out on several occasions.[29]

But some seemed unmoved by Chambers's plight. Margaret De Silver turned down Solow's request for a loan. This reinforced Chambers's growing disgust with the community of anti-Stalinists of the left, all of them frightened he might "contaminate them."[30]

Still others ignored his situation or made light of it. Chambers dined one night with Paul Willert at a "fabulously expensive French restaurant" in uptown Manhattan. The Englishman arrived drunk. When Chambers described his troubles, Willert languidly observed that Chambers seemed well set up with translation work. For his part, the editor remarked, "I've never made so much money in my life. Oxford pays me an unheard of salary."[31]

His funds depleted, Chambers went again to Washington. He phoned Julian Wadleigh at the State Department and insisted on seeing him immediately. The man must be crazy, thought Wadleigh. "Appointments with my contacts had never been anywhere near the neighborhood of the [State] department," then in the old Executive Office Building, forty paces from the White House.

"Do you want me to starve?" the defector said, his normally low voice soaring shrilly.

Unnerved, Wadleigh agreed to meet Chambers in Jackson Park, half fearing he was heading into an FBI ambush. He was relieved to find Chambers alone. Without ceremony the defector asked for ten dollars. Wadleigh fished out a twenty, the only bill he had. A "terrifying picture loomed up in my mind of him coming around regularly once a week to me and to each of his other sources. . . . He might even become brazen enough one day to walk straight into my office."[32]

Chambers also called on literary acquaintances. Clifton Fadiman, whose blossoming career had taken him to the book reviewing desk at *The New Yorker,* reacted with disbelief when Chambers came begging for a loan, pleading he was on the run from the NKVD. Mark Van Doren, a literary eminence whose *Collected Poems* would win the Pulitzer Prize in 1940, was at home, entertaining a guest, when Chambers phoned from Penn Station, confiding he was in mortal danger. Arriving at Van Doren's Village apartment, Chambers begged his former mentor to write him a letter "recommending him to literary editors." Generous as ever, Van

Doren wrote the letter on the spot but suspected his former pupil was pulling his leg. He "was so mysterious about all this, and overstated things, I thought, so laughably in the old way."[33]

When not working on his translation, Chambers had been writing short stories. He completed several and submitted one, an allegory about his defection, to *Partisan Review*. It was rejected by Dwight Macdonald, one of the quarterly's editors, who judged the writing "crude" and "obvious."[34] Chambers was also weighing nonfiction ideas. He conferred with Robert Cantwell, who had joined the staff of *Time* magazine in the mid-1930s, after the collaboration with Lincoln Steffens had petered out. Cantwell proposed several projects, including books on the Civil War, on the Ku Klux Klan, on the Nazis and anti-Semitism. None sounded right. He aided Chambers more practically by hiring him to help research articles Cantwell was writing for *Time*.[35]

Chambers's main project, however, was a lengthy article, "The Faking of Americans," on the Soviet passport mill. He typed it on a portable machine Ulrich had given him in 1934. Chambers adopted the alias "Karl" using the German spelling. Should his former comrades seek to discredit him, he added in a note of warning, he would include more damaging information against them and also expose the identities of Max Bedacht and J. Peters, shielded now behind code names. ("Barber" referred to Max Bedacht, the onetime hair cutter; "Sandor" to J. Peters, whose aliases included Ale*xander* Goldberg.)

"The Faking of Americans" has survived, thanks to Herbert Solow, who kept a copy of the manuscript. Its sixty-five typed pages are divided into two parts. The first, the "Soviet Passport Racket," deals with the Robinson-Rubens case. It recounts the incident as outlined in Solow's *Sun* articles but is enlivened by anecdotal glimpses of Rubens, J. Peters, and Bykov. The manuscript also quotes a secret State Department message on the case that Chambers had received from one of his sources. Part II, "Welcome, Soviet Spies!," explains methods employed by the underground to obtain false passports.[36]

Solow, who read the manuscript in December 1938, deemed it unpublishable. "Except for a rehash of the Robinson-Rubens story, the manuscript contained no real names to substantiate its sensational charges." But at Chambers's insistence, he agreed to pass the manuscript on to Isaac Don Levine, an anti-Communist journalist then ghosting the memoirs of Walter Krivitsky, soon to be serialized in *The Saturday Evening Post*. The *Post* was the magazine Chambers had in mind. It had the highest circulation of any existing journal and paid its authors extremely well. A sale might net Chambers several thousand dollars. (Krivitsky's five articles brought in five thousand dollars apiece.) Since Chambers refused to leave the manuscript with Solow, even overnight, Solow took "The Faking of Americans" to Levine, who was intrigued but said the story should be condensed.[37]

Thus encouraged, Chambers delivered a portion of the revised manuscript to Levine, at Levine's apartment, on the Upper East Side of Manhattan. Introducing himself as "Karl," Chambers made his usual disappointing impression. He resembled "a plumber's helper on a repair mission" rather than a spy.

Levine, a Russian Jew, had emigrated from Kiev at age nineteen and still spoke with a faint accent. This made Chambers uneasy. He had developed an aversion to all Russians. The two men were never entirely comfortable in each other's presence, although their association lasted more than a decade.

Levine invited Chambers to lunch in the neighborhood. On Madison Avenue Chambers's head swiveled constantly as he scanned the street for NKVD agents. The restaurant was nearly empty. Chambers surveyed it intently and then "went outside for another look around." Once seated, Chambers mumbled distracted replies to Levine's questions but sketched in the salient facts of his situation: He had defected, he was in hiding, he was broke; at night he slept with a rifle at his side.

Chambers let Levine keep the thirty-odd pages of manuscript and a few days later returned for them and for Levine's verdict. Levine had the same criticism as Solow. Chambers wrote well and had a conspicuous talent for "creating moods." But he had supplied no concrete particulars: "names, dates, places, and documentation." The editors at *The Saturday Evening Post* would raise "a hundred questions," and Chambers obviously was not ready to furnish a hundred answers. Levine advised him to go to the authorities rather than try to write his way to freedom.[38]

Chambers felt the Party closing in. Paul Willert, who had many Communist contacts, relayed unsettling messages. On December 15 the editor contacted Chambers by Western Union: VERY URGENT YOU GET IN TOUCH IMMEDIATELY.

The next day Chambers drove to New York, taking Ellen with him. He left her with Grace Lumpkin and went to the Oxford University Press. Willert looked up from his papers. "Ulrich wants to see you."

"Who is Ulrich?" Chambers asked cautiously, suspecting he knew the answer.

"You know," Willert replied. "Ulrich from Berlin."

Chambers asked for a description of the man. It matched Aleksandr Ulanovsky "and nobody else." To Chambers it meant one thing: His former handler had come on a mission like that of Juliet Poyntz's abductors.[39]

This left Chambers a single option: He must turn informer and seek the protection of his government. Still, he could not bring himself to name accomplices. One comrade in particular was much on his mind, "some agent whom he regards as a sincere and devoted person,"* wrote Herb Solow.[40]

What Chambers really wanted to do was "skip across the border" to Canada or Mexico. But he had no money.[41] There was another option, however: the Westminster property and its ten acres, out of sight behind a dirt road. The house was still a shambles, and the deed had yet to clear. But it would have to do. He and Esther bundled up the children, loaded up the car, and quickly moved into the house. Then, leaving his family there, and the car, he returned to Baltimore. He had work to do, his translation. He roamed the stacks at the Johns Hopkins library, collecting reference books. He also traveled to New York for further discussion with Solow and Schapiro. He visited Esther and the children when he could, once or twice a month, taking the bus to Westminster, getting a lift to the dirt road, and trudging the remaining five miles—in snow, rain, and mud.[42]

Meanwhile he had taken his first bold step against the underground. He wrote a letter, appended to it "photographic copies of handwritten matters," and got it to his onetime photographer, Felix Inslerman, for transmittal to Bykov.

Felix, who knew "Bob" had broken, was himself contemplating a break. Shaken by Chambers's letter, he copied it out by hand before passing it along. Fifteen years later Inslerman showed the letter to a Senate investigating committee.

Chambers had warned: "If you really must continue violent projects against me or my family, you are certainly going to have competition. I do not say you will fail, what I believe is that you will involve yourselves in a major disaster the consequences of which you cannot even begin to

---

* Evidently Alger Hiss.

appraise. . . . In fact, I should guess that the State [Department] is going to be sitting on some very hot coals in the near future."[43]

The one "political" Chambers had stayed in touch with, Maxim Lieber, "was becoming more and more worried about seeing me." Not long after Willert's warning about Ulrich, Lieber had chased Chambers out of his anteroom with the warning, "Katz is in the office."[44]

Chambers fled, though unsure whom he had been warned against. The name Katz meant nothing to him. Curiously he did not connect it with Otto Katz, a renowned Comintern propagandist. A client of Lieber's, Katz was visiting from Paris and staying at Paul Willert's apartment. In fact it was Katz, not Ulanovsky, to whom Willert had been referring as Ulrich, an alias Katz had used in Berlin, where Willert had known him. Katz was not a hit man. But his interest in Chambers meant Comintern officials in Europe knew of Chambers's defection and might be planning action of some kind.[45]

Not long after this Chambers and Lieber met for the last time—in Bucks County, where they had spent many pleasant afternoons. The defector tried one last time to break Lieber from the underground. Again Lieber refused. Chambers was disappointed but deeply grateful to his friend. Lieber "could have betrayed me into the party's hands. He chose not to do so."[46]

The first months of 1939 dragged Chambers to his lowest point. All his literary projects had fallen through. He was separated from his wife and children. He was broke. He had no assurance the NKVD was finished with him. To top it off, there was the Regler manuscript, which was proving difficult to translate, especially as revised chapters came in from the author, throwing him even further behind.[47]

But at least winter was ending. Chambers briefly rejoined his family in the country. He and Esther turned over the first shovelfuls of soil and pruned their fruit trees and rosebushes, and Chambers began laying a rubble driveway. In March came the first good news in many months. An article Bob Cantwell had written for Time on the impending war had been so well received he had been offered a transfer to the Foreign News department. This left a vacancy in Books, and Cantwell had recommended Chambers as his replacement. His journey would go on.[48]

# CRUSADER

## (1939–1948)

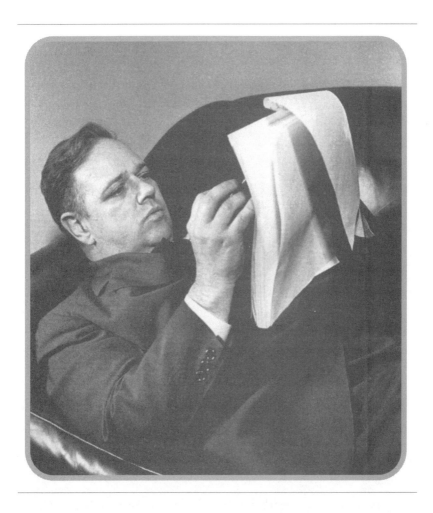

*Editing on the couch installed in his office after his illness in late 1942.*
ALFRED EISENSTAEDT, *LIFE* MAGAZINE, © TIME, INC.

# The Clash of Swords

In 1939 Time Inc. was the largest communications company in the English-speaking world. Its magazines had a net circulation of more than four million and a total readership two or three times as numerous.

Its centerpiece, *Time,* founded in 1923, had prospered so mightily and so rapidly that its cofounder Briton Hadden, who died in 1929, did so in the fulfillment of his dream of becoming a millionaire before his thirtieth birthday. In the decade since, Hadden's partner, Henry R. Luce, had built an empire, creating two sister publications, the photo weekly *Life* and the slick business monthly *Fortune.* By 1939 the forty-one-year-old Luce was the era's greatest press baron, his only rival William Randolph Hearst.[1]

For a magazine that claimed to have its hand on the pulse of world events, *Time*'s environment was curiously insular. In the plush new Rockefeller Center offices, with their glorious views, the atmosphere was at once rarefied and convivial—like a college dormitory, said one writer. "People are always wandering around the halls, dropping into one's office to talk." The "great cosmic weekly almanac," as Luce called *Time,* even ran on its own calendar. The workweek began on Thursday and concluded on Monday evening, when the magazine was sent to press. This schedule imposed a unique rhythm on the staff, its stimulating mix of editors and writers (almost all men) and researchers (women), who moved together in a nebula of deadline frenzy relieved by shared lunches, leisurely dinners, and garrulous late-night drinking bouts.[2]

Into this self-enclosed world slipped David Whittaker Chambers, as he now called himself, late of the Fourth Department of Soviet military intelligence, his wife and children tucked in a safe house in the wilds of Maryland, the NKVD possibly still on his trail. For six years he had gone without a fixed identity, lived at a total of twenty-one different addresses, had signed false names to leases, passports, and checks, had invented aliases for his wife and children, had paid no income tax. His colleagues had included veterans of the Lenin School and of Siberian prisons, with whom he conversed in German or English with Germanic inflections. He seldom ventured into daylight without glancing over his shoulder or searching the faces he met for signs of treachery.

This was the figure who presented himself to one of the gatekeepers to *Time,* associate executive editor Thomas Stanley Matthews—T. S., after his idol, T. S. Eliot, and, like Eliot, called Tom by his friends. Matthews's father was an Episcopal bishop, his mother a Procter & Gamble heiress. The son had glided from the elite St. Paul's School to Princeton and then to Oxford. One of the outstanding editors of the day, he had apprenticed under *The New Republic*'s literary editor, Edmund Wilson, in the 1920s. Since joining *Time* in 1929, Matthews, dubbed "the Grammarian" by Luce, had improved its literary standards, elevating the quirky "Timestyle" into a supple journalistic instrument, sweeping, epigrammatic, glitteringly detailed. And he had made *Time*'s culture pages, the back of the book, the best in the magazine.[3]

He also hired superior writers, such as Bob Cantwell, a friend from Matthews's days at *The New Republic* and now among the most admired writers *Time* had. It had meant something when Cantwell, in making the pitch for Chambers, had pressed on Matthews one of Chambers's *New Masses* stories, likening it to the fiction of André Malraux. "And it *was* something like Malraux," Matthews decided, "shot through with the same murky flashes of rather sinister brilliance."

Tall, lean, lantern-jawed, looking every inch the patrician he was, Matthews appraised the short, dumpy, affectless man seated before him. Spartanly clad in a charcoal suit, white shirt, and black tie, Chambers looked the opposite of brilliant. It was not hard to believe, however, that he was in fear for his life, as Cantwell had told Matthews. Something seemed to haunt this man as he "spoke little, listened with an air of cynical understanding, and sucked a short pipe." He was hired on April 6 on a trial basis, at the considerable salary of one hundred dollars a week, to review books, "the first real job that I had ever held."[4]

The initiation period for new writers was nerve-racking, and Chambers's confidence was not running high. All his recent literary efforts had been duds. Worse, no guidance was forthcoming from his editors. Like every other newcomer, Chambers was simply handed an assignment and shown to a desk where he found a cup full of sharpened pencils, identically shaved to a special Time Inc. size. It was a lonely struggle, and for Chambers a harrowing one, for much depended on his making good. Many times, in his first days, he rose from the books he was thumbing through and the sheets he had covered with spidery copy and anguished erasures and gazed dolefully out his westward-facing window, staring past the piers and the Hudson River, thinking of Esther and the children, alone and unprotected in Westminster. But he passed the test, clinching the job, he was certain, with a book review that began, in cleverly pitched Timestyle, "One bomby Sunday afternoon. . . ."[5]

The review ran on May 1. By this time he was already at work on something far more substantial, the cover story for the May 8 issue, on James Joyce's *Finnegans Wake*. Cover stories—a *Time* invention—were normally entrusted to experienced writers. And this was no ordinary feature. Joyce's six-hundred-page novel, the product of seventeen years' labor, is among the most ambitious experiments in the history of literature, written in an invented polyglot fused of some half dozen tongues, ancient and modern, and meant to approximate the jumbled poetry of dreams. Chambers's job was to make the novel intelligible to *Time*'s mass readership. It was an assignment seasoned journalists might blanch at. To pin it on a novice was an act of folly—in fact of "bad management or bad luck."

Luckily Chambers had linguistic gifts and long experience as a translator, so acquitted himself well, indeed "cleared this first hurdle not only creditably but with extraordinary style," in Matthews's judgment. The article was overlong and had to be cut. Otherwise there was hardly a fault to be found in "Night Thoughts." The highlight of the piece is Chambers's portrait of the artist, a cameo written out of an obvious sense of self-identification with Joyce's marvelous strangeness:

[The novelist] is slight, frail but impressive. He stands five feet ten or eleven, but looks as if a strong wind might blow him down . . . he writes sprawling in bed or on a couch but he does not like it known. He is very formal in public, in restaurants prefers straight-back chairs in which he sits bolt upright.

He dresses with conservative elegance, never goes out without a walking stick, which he manipulates expertly, accenting the delicacy of his
beringed hands. . . .

Joyce's curious glasses give him a somewhat Martian appearance. The
left lens is so thick it is almost a hemisphere, and to focus it is necessary
for him to throw back his head slightly when looking at people.[6]

Like all *Time* articles, this one was unsigned, but in the close, gossipy
atmosphere of *Time,* everyone soon knew who had written the evocative
sentences of "Night Thoughts." Nor was it a secret that he was an unusual man who seldom emerged from behind his closed door and when
he did, to go to the men's room or the elevator, avoided all contact with
his colleagues, meeting even friendly glances with deep-eyed suspicion.

When an amiable young colleague in the book department, Sam
Welles, who shared an office with Chambers, casually suggested lunch,
Chambers put him off repeatedly. At last Welles wore him down, and
Chambers reluctantly agreed. Spurning the many nearby restaurants, he
led Welles on a bewildering expedition. Riding the subway two stops,
they exited at Macy's, traversed the entire length of the ground floor,
which stretched from Sixth Avenue to Seventh, and then repeated this
maneuver on the second, third, and fourth floors, wading through the
midday crush of shoppers. They wound up at the crowded Longchamps
in the Empire State Building. Chambers consumed his meal in almost
total silence, repelling all Welles's overtures at conversation.

Welles waited several days before demanding an explanation. At last
convinced the young man could be trusted, Chambers said he had feared
Welles's offer of lunch might be a pretext for leading him into an NKVD
ambush. The defector then opened his jacket and showed Welles the
holstered pistol he wore these days. Welles, the son of an Episcopal
canon, was flabbergasted. But he saw Chambers was serious, and the two
became good friends.[7]

With his place at *Time* apparently secure, but with Esther and the children still unprotected, Chambers found a subletter for the St. Paul Street
house—to which the family had returned after hiding on the Shaw
farm—and uprooted them once more, this time installing them at Laha's
house, where he himself was staying. Again the citizens of Lynbrook
grew used to the sight of a short, stocky man who slipped out of the
mysterious frame house at 228 Earle Avenue each morning, walked in

the direction of the train station, and briefly reappeared late in the evening—a quiet man, courteous but aloof, his eyes fixed straight ahead.[8]

Chambers remained in limbo. He had yet to follow the example of either Krivitsky or Reiss, yet to confess. Should he now? He had made limited disclosures to his new employers. They knew he was an ex-Communist and had been involved in illegal activity. Of what kind he did not say except to Welles and one or two others. How long could he guard his secret? The question preyed on him. He explored it in the spring and summer of 1939 in discussions with Isaac Don Levine, who had supplanted Herbert Solow as Chambers's confidant. Solow suspected Levine, a rival journalist, had shouldered him out of the picture.[9] This was not the case. It was Chambers who decided to change confidants. He was still uneasy in Levine's company but thought him the more useful ally. Unlike the Trotskyist Solow, Levine was thoroughly anti-Communist, an enemy of the revolution in all its forms, as Chambers had become with growing ferocity. In addition, Levine had high contacts in the Roosevelt administration who could possibly secure a promise of immunity for Chambers and get him a hearing with top officials. Finally Levine was close to Walter Krivitsky, whose case intrigued Chambers. In April the first fruit of Levine's collaboration with the Russian defector had appeared in *The Saturday Evening Post*. Chambers read the memoir closely and was greatly impressed. Levine offered to bring the two ex-agents together, but both resisted. Chambers had not overcome his "organic antipathy" to Russians, while Krivitsky had doubts about Chambers, who had yet to make the public confession that alone would validate his defection.[10]

At last Levine surmounted this mutual suspicion and arranged a meeting one evening at his apartment. Chambers had already arrived when Krivitsky came in, small, slight, neatly dressed, his hair brushed back tautly from his forehead. With his scholar's crinkled face, his eyes almost invisible beneath craggy brows, he looked much older than his forty years. He projected a melancholy fatalism not surprising in one who remained prize game in an NKVD manhunt. He had not allowed *The Saturday Evening Post* to publish his photograph for fear it would aid his assassins. In July the Soviets had begun to lobby for his deportation. He was now living under an assumed name with his wife and young son in rural Carmel, New York.[11]

There was a tense moment as Krivitsky, his gaze fastened on his feet, asked in German, "*Ist die Sowjetregierung eine faschistische Regierung?* [Is the Soviet Government a fascist government?]"

Chambers solemnly answered, *"Ja, die Sowjetregierung ist eine faschistische Regierung."*

And when, asked Krivitsky, had the "turning point" come? He then answered his own question: in 1921, with the uprising at the Kronshtadt naval base, a famous episode in the Russian Civil War. Sailors at Kronshtadt had helped defeat the White Army but then resisted the imposition of Bolshevik rule, for which they were branded counterrevolutionaries. Many were killed or imprisoned. For a host of ex-Communists, down to Boris Yeltsin, Kronshtadt was to stand as the point of no return in the Soviet experiment. It was evidence the revolution had become tyrannous long before Spain and the Moscow trials. Lenin and Trotsky too had innocent blood on their hands. Chambers had come to share this view and with it the conviction that nothing less than counterrevolutionism, the "clash of swords," would suffice in the struggle against communism.[12]

Having broken the ice, the two defectors talked freely and excitedly, exchanging reminiscences. "It was like fitting a jigsaw puzzle together," Levine remembered, "and it was astonishing." Each man held pieces the other had been able only to guess at. Krivitsky filled Chambers in on the histories of Valentine Markin and Boris Bykov, known to Chambers all this time only as Herman and Peter. Chambers summarized the American activities of "Ewald" (Arnold Ikal). At midnight, when Levine went to bed, the ex-agents were still at it, piling cigarette butts in an ashtray. When Levine awoke the next morning, the light was burning in the living room and his guests were talking over coffee. They had stayed up all night.[13]

Chambers and Krivitsky met often in the months ahead. Krivitsky stressed one theme above all others. It was his belief that all defectors were obligated to inform. Others had been telling Chambers this. But Krivitsky, on the run since 1937, spoke from inside the dilemma. He knew firsthand the anguish and the risk and was a target still of NKVD assassins. As recently as March 1939 he had been followed out of a Times Square restaurant by Sergei Basov, a GRU agent. Krivitsky suspected the manhunt was being organized by Bykov, not yet recalled to Moscow for his failure with the "traitor" Chambers.[14]

Krivitsky was also suspicious of the Roosevelt administration, "honeycombed with [Communist] agents." He had met privately with some officials but was convinced everything he told them "had got back to Moscow within 48 hours." The safer course was to testify in a public forum, though that too had its drawbacks. He had appeared before the newly formed House Subcommittee on Un-American Activities (HUAC) but was dismayed by the ignorance of the congressmen who questioned him. They seemed interested only in having him confirm "that the Kremlin ran the Comintern and Stalin ran the Kremlin."[15]

Krivitsky's plight, though more desperate than Chambers's own, mirrored it, and the reflection sharpened Chambers's foreboding as he weighed his options.

Then the "inhuman forces" of history compelled Chambers to act. On Thursday, August 24, 1939, the Soviet Union and Nazi Germany announced they had signed a nonaggression pact. The two totalitarian powers informed the world that over the next ten years neither would "associate itself with any other grouping of powers which directly or indirectly is aimed at the other party."

In practical terms, this meant Hitler could invade Poland without fear of Soviet reprisal while Stalin could annex the Baltic states and launch an assault against Finland. Between them Germany and Russia would divide up much of the Continent. World War II was poised to begin.[16]

The turnabout caught many by surprise. For years Stalin had been the leading proponent of collective security against Hitler, a stance that had won him many admirers in the West. It was not yet known that for years the dictator had quietly been courting Hitler through personal diplomacy and by more elaborate measures. The massive purge of the Red Army had been undertaken, for instance, to rid the military command of those most overtly hostile to a German alliance.[17]

Still, Western leaders had been aware of "the lively exchanges between Moscow and Berlin." The politically educated had also had some inklings. In fact Chambers had foretold the alliance as early as 1938, in "The Faking of Americans," and Walter Krivitsky had also predicted it, in *The Saturday Evening Post*. Yet even to these unsentimental observers, the formal reality of the pact was sobering: communism and fascism made partners at last, their fellowship soon to be sealed with the blood of nations.[18]

Within forty-eight hours Isaac Don Levine appeared at the offices of *Time* fresh from a conference with Krivitsky, who was certain Nazi Germany soon would reap the harvest of the Soviet intelligence-gathering operation Chambers had helped sow in Washington. Chambers agreed this was a real danger. Then, said Levine, the defector had no choice but to meet with "the proper authorities" and divulge the "pertinent details" so the ring could be smashed.

Chambers balked. The U.S. government might well take action against him, a self-confessed spy. "How would *you* like to face a fifteen-to-twenty-year jail sentence if you were in my boots, with a wife and two children, and without any savings?" he asked Levine.

Levine thought a promise of immunity possible. Chambers was all for that—as long as it came directly from President Roosevelt. If an appointment could be arranged with FDR, Chambers would "disclose everything" and back it up with hard evidence. Levine agreed to try. He knew Roosevelt's appointments secretary, Marvin McIntyre, and would set off immediately to see him. Chambers must be on instant call. The defector jotted down Laha's phone number, hitherto "a deep secret," and Levine departed for Washington.[19]

At McIntyre's office, in the White House, Levine reviewed Chambers's story without naming the defector. McIntyre, though interested, ruled out an appointment with the President. Caught unaware by the pact—he had been on a fishing cruise off the coast of Labrador—FDR was in the midst of nonstop briefings and emergency cabinet meetings. But Chambers need not worry. He could meet with Assistant Secretary of State Adolf A. Berle, Jr., the president's intelligence liaison. Levine, acquainted with Berle, went next door to the State Department and conferred with the official, who invited Levine and "the stranger" to dine at his home the following Saturday, September 2.

Back in New York, Levine reported his mixed success. Chambers, though he preferred a meeting with the president, was willing to see Berle, a known anti-Communist and the founder of New York State's Liberal Party. "Berle's word is as good as Roosevelt's," he told Levine.[20]

On Friday, September 1, eight days after the nonaggression pact was announced, World War II began. Three Nazi columns smashed over the Polish border while German aircraft strafed more than twenty Polish cities, an overwhelming show of force—the debut of the blitzkrieg. Hitler declared himself ready for a "ten-year war." The Polish government appealed to Britain and France for help, and the two Western powers responded with one last plea to the Nazis to halt. Evacuations began in London and Paris.[21]

The following evening Chambers flew to Washington. The capital was paralyzed. "The unbelievable has become reality," said *The Washington Post* in a front-page editorial. "Civilization is caught in the current of the maelstrom. The outcome, for much that we take for granted and for everything we hold most dear, is wholly unpredictable."[22]

Chambers met Levine at his hotel, the Hay-Adams, near the White House. They climbed into a taxi and sped north through Rock Creek Park to Woodley Oaks, the house Berle was renting from Henry Stimson, the once and future secretary of war. A Federal-style mansion built in about 1880, Woodley was one of the great private residences in Washington, perched atop one of the highest hills in the capital, near the National Cathedral. In front, towering oaks shaded the wide skirt of lawn. In back, eighteen acres swept down to the Potomac.[23]

It was eight o'clock when Berle arrived. Short and trim at age forty-four, he was a commanding figure in the Roosevelt administration, a member of the original Brain Trust and an architect of the visionary "state capitalism" that underlay so many of the New Deal's innovative reforms.[24] Famous for his mental powers as well as for his hauteur, Berle seemed humble this evening. Since the announcement of the pact he had been putting in twelve- to fifteen-hour days. Over cocktails he spoke grimly of the impending war. At dinner, seated in French chairs below the glassy stare of antlered game, the two guests submitted to the graces of Beatrice Berle, an heiress whose wealth had made possible such comforts as the Woodley rental. After coffee she left the men alone.[25]

They went in back, where lawn chairs were arranged under the leaves of a large tree. Night had fallen, and a refreshing breeze brushed up from the Potomac, channeled through the long sweep of woods. Four presidents had made Woodley their summer residence, fleeing the insect-ridden marshland below for this higher and cooler elevation. In daylight the Washington Monument and the White House were visible from the upper stories of the house. A servant brought drinks. Chambers quickly downed scotch and soda, a tongue loosener. Levine opened the discussion. He reminded Berle that Chambers, an ex-Communist agent, had "special information" to impart. Berle, "extremely agitated," said the United States might be at war within forty-eight hours. Government agencies must be "clean."[26]

It was Chambers's turn. Even with the courage of several drinks, he spoke haltingly, clinging to the shallows of his deep knowledge. He offered general remarks on the Communist conspiracy and the dangers it posed. Berle, sensing Chambers's distress, "slowly manipulated" the defector "to a point where he told some of the ramifications" of the underground activity.[27] Gradually, over the course of two or three hours, Chambers set out the jigsaw puzzle, now and then mislaying a piece that Levine nudged into place. Chambers reviewed the entire underground operation but spoke mainly of the Washington ring. He ran down the roster of government agents. Some of the names were shocking—for instance, State Department officials Laurence Duggan, Alger Hiss, and Donald Hiss, all with sterling reputations, all known personally to Berle; former State Department official Noel Field, now with the League of Nations, in Geneva; economist Lauchlin Currie, a special assistant to FDR. Chambers also mentioned operatives in the Treasury Department and described military espionage, including "plans for two super-battleships" obtained by the ring in 1937 and the sketches of "aerial bomb sight detectors"* passed on by Frank Reno.[29] Several of the names involved were new even to Levine, who jotted them down later that night at the Hay-Adams.

When Chambers was finished, Berle led his guests inside to his study. Seated at a desk below the American flag, he wrote up notes in outline form, captioned "Underground Espionage Agent." They ended with a coda: "*Note*—When Loy Henderson interviewed Mrs. Rubens his report immediately went back to Moscow. Who sent it? Such came from Washington."[30]

It was past midnight. As the visitors prepared to leave, Berle cautioned them not to expect instant results. The matter "required the utmost delicacy" and must be handled secretly. No one wanted a public clamor. It would undermine confidence in the government and inhibit further investigation.[31]

After his guests had departed, Berle made a notation in his diary: "It becomes necessary to take a few simple measures. I expect more of this kind of thing, later." He was not unduly worried. Most of the names Chambers mentioned were familiar. John Abt, Nat Witt. Everyone knew they were Communists. They did not pose much of a threat. As

---

* Krivitsky's fears that spy information would reach the Nazis may have been justified. In 1941 FDR confidant Harold Ickes noted: "Apparently the Norden bombsight for airplanes, which we had been setting great store by and keeping very secret, has been in the hands of the Germans for some time."[28]

for the others, Berle was skeptical. He did not doubt the truth of the overall picture Chambers had given, but he suspected the defector might not be completely reliable on the details. Berle had met ex-Communists. They emerged from the movement still in thrall to "the all-powerful quality of it, probably exaggerating their own experience." Berle would make inquiries.[32]

The informer returned that night to New York plagued by doubts. He respected Berle and President Roosevelt. But Communists remained on the administration's payroll, wielding influence. Despite the promise of immunity, the easiest course for the government was to punish Chambers. So he had withheld something vital, the evidence that substantiated his case, his life preserver. It remained hidden in Brooklyn. Chambers was not ready to hand it over to those who might use it to destroy him.

# "God Bless You, Harry"

Henry Robinson Luce's title, editor in chief of all Time Inc. publications, was no mere honorific. The "cause of Time" was his consuming passion. He came to the office each day with his pockets crammed full of story ideas, some inspired, others daft. The lowliest writer might be summoned to Luce's office to debate for hours the contents of copy Luce found troubling. Editors got used to receiving memos written in "prose hewn by a chilled axe" and sent, as T. S. Matthews once complained, "as if to dogs, not to human beings."[1]

Periodically Luce abandoned his sun-splashed crow's nest at the top of the Time-Life tower for a week of hands-on editing, grabbing the helm of the "great cosmic weekly almanac." He made one such descent in February 1940, when Chambers happened to be working on a review of the film version of Steinbeck's *The Grapes of Wrath*.

The former star of the proletarian movement loathed this most celebrated of proletarian novels, its "exaggerations, propaganda, and phony pathos." But he praised the genius of director John Ford, who had chipped away the encrustation of pieties in Steinbeck's story and found at its center the grand simple "saga of an authentic U.S. farming family who lose their land. They wander, they suffer, but they endure. They are never quite defeated, and their survival is itself a triumph."[2]

"Who reviewed *Grapes of Wrath*?" demanded Luce, domineering a staff meeting with his stammer and beetling brow. "It's the best cinema review ever in Time."[3]

Invited to his first editorial lunch, Chambers soon became one of Luce's informal advisers on world politics and foreign affairs, often accompanying the press baron on coffee breaks at a Rockefeller Center lunch counter.[4]

Luce's own politics were no secret. The son of a famous missionary, Henry Winters Luce, whose chief talent was for fund-raising, Harry Luce worshiped the familiar trinity of Christianity, big business, and the Republican party. To his despair, few on staff shared these ideals. Luce tolerated the collective heresy. He could have hired subordinates whose politics were more to his liking but, as he often groused, "Goddam Republicans can't write."[5]

But in Chambers, Luce recognized a kindred spirit. The two did not agree on everything. Chambers would never abandon, for instance, his bohemian-Bolshevik contempt for businessmen. But as he moved rightward, he increasingly shared Luce's antipathy toward the New Deal. He also found common religious ground with Luce, for Chambers had rediscovered Christianity. In September 1940 he was baptized an Episcopalian at St. John the Divine, the immense cathedral whose dome towered, appropriately, over Morningside Heights, where twenty years before Chambers had undergone the "intellectual pulverization" that had pitched him, so he now believed, into the hell of communism.[6]

Luce later said Chambers was the best writer *Time* ever employed. He meant Chambers uniquely mastered the emerging Luce formula, which consisted of portioning out Big Thoughts, bite-size, to readers in a hurry. Chambers's copy was slick yet had an undertone of moral and intellectual seriousness. Writing draft upon draft, he achieved an enviable "flow," a clever blend of narrative, anecdote, and argument enlivened with colorful phrases and with evocative tag lines from the classics. It helped that Chambers's concept of journalism remained essentially Leninist. He believed, no less fervently than Luce, that a popular magazine could be a powerful vehicle of mass enlightenment.[7]

But if Luce thought Chambers the ideal journalist, others had their doubts, as the defector well knew. From the beginning he had hoped to be moved from Books to Foreign News, following Cantwell. He was given a chance as early as 1939, but the stories he wrote, fiercely anti-Communist, were received poorly. *Time*'s managing editor, Manfred Gottfried, pulled Chambers aside and assured him he need not atone for his past sins in the pages of the magazine. Better to aim "right down the middle," said Gottfried, advocating neither communism nor capitalism. Chambers averted his face, hiding a wry half-smile.[8]

So it was back to Books and Cinema. Chambers did not complain. Instead he fired salvos in his reviews. He was especially hard on former comrades from the early thirties, writers on the left. One he pursued zealously was critic and poet Malcolm Cowley. The longtime literary editor of *The New Republic,* Cowley had made the journal's book pages a platform for pro-Stalinist apologias and defenses of the Moscow trials. Worse, when Walter Krivitsky's memoirs were published in book form, Cowley labeled their author "an opportunist and a coward," a traitor to the revolution. Cowley owned that Krivitsky's book, "for all its dubious passages, belongs to a series of writings and events that have caused me to change my judgment of Soviet Russia." But Krivitsky the man remained "a gangster and traitor," bereft of moral virtue: "Comradeship with those who used to work beside him; love for the heroes of the Russian revolution; reverence for the dead figures of Spain and Germany— everything ends in the embrace of [HUAC Chairman] Martin Dies. Nothing is left him but anguish and hate."[9]

Chambers could not let this go unpunished. In December 1940 he invited Cowley to lunch at a Manhattan hotel, ostensibly to discuss the effect of the Nazi-Soviet Pact on the literary community. Chambers talked at length about himself: his underground experiences; his defection; his newfound anticommunism. Cowley was fascinated but also alarmed. Driven by his hatred of the Party, Chambers sounded paranoid. "He believes that conspiracies, traitors and spies surround us on every side and he is determined to wipe them out," Cowley jotted in his notebook on the train back to Connecticut. "Though he doesn't mention the word capitalism, that is what he is fighting for, quite consciously." Chambers assured Cowley his years as a Communist were not wasted. "He learned the technique of the movement, and now he is going to apply that technique to destroy it. He is fighting now for 'the Christian democratic counter-revolution.' " Chambers paid for the lunch, "nearly $4 worth," Cowley recorded. "It will cost me a great deal more when the article comes out."[10]

It appeared in January 1941, under the title "The Revolt of the Intellectuals." In acid tones Chambers assailed Cowley, John Steinbeck, Archibald MacLeish, Lillian Hellman, Dorothy Parker, and other "literary liberals," all "fellow travelers who wanted to fight fascism. How should they know that Lenin was the first fascist and that they were cooperating with the party from which the Nazis had borrowed all their important methods and ideas?" But then the pact had come, and the literary liberals, hopping off the Red express, "rubbed their bruises" and became "refugees once more in their lonely remodeled farmhouses in Connecticut and the Berkshires. . . . Malcolm Cowley, writing a book 'to clarify my mind,' craved only to be left in peace to lick his spiritual wounds."

Much of this was true. Some was not. What was striking was the lack of humility in one who had toiled impenitently in the Soviet vineyard for six years—and at the height of Stalin's atrocities. Wasn't Chambers guilty of errors more numerous and consequential than those for which he castigated Cowley and company? Hadn't he refused to expose the Communist conspiracy up until the announcement of the Soviet-Nazi Pact, a sweetheart deal he had seen coming as early as 1938? Hadn't Chambers too withdrawn to the rustic sanctuary of *his* farmhouse in the verdant meadows of Maryland?

Of course. But to Chambers this history was his warrant to attack. His grievance against the literary liberals was not their pro-Sovietism but their dilettantism. "Substituting a good deal of intellectual inbreeding for organic contact with U.S. life, they developed a curious cultural provincialism. The Depression came to them as a refreshing change. Fundamentally skeptical, maladjusted, defeatist, the intellectuals felt thoroughly at home in the chaos and misery of the '30s. Fundamentally benevolent and humane, they loved their fellow countrymen in distress far more than they could ever love them in prosperity. And they particularly enjoyed life when applause began to greet their berating of the robber barons, president makers, economic royalists, malefactors of great wealth."[11]

Chambers returned to this theme many times in the years ahead. The fellow traveler—and by extension the modern liberal—plays at politics, toys with history. His commitments, lightly penciled in, are as easily erased. One day he is apolitical, the next pro-Soviet, the next "disillusioned." He slips through the political seasons always in fashion, his hands always clean. From the sanctuary of a magazine he freely mocks the "opportunist" Krivitsky, though Krivitsky is a marked man, willing to die for his cause, whatever that cause happens to be.

Indeed Chambers was by now certain Krivitsky would be liquidated by the NKVD. The first warning had come in the summer, when the most notorious of all "counterrevolutionaries," Trotsky, was murdered by an NKVD agent who smashed the exile's skull with a small pickax.

Felix Morrow, a representative of the Trotsky Defense Committee, had interviewed Chambers at length about the incident. Chambers had predicted, "Krivitsky will be next."[12] It was a reasoned guess. Still in demand as a Soviet expert, the Russian defector was going after his former comrades boldly. In testimony before the Dies Committee, Krivitsky said Russian embassies in Washington and elsewhere were controlled by the NKVD agents and that Soviet agents were "engaged in kidnapping and murder in the United States."

With Trotsky dead, and the danger to his own life mounting, Krivitsky moved his family to Virginia. In October 1940 the Krivitskys became U.S. residents and lived under an assumed name. Not that these precautions would make much difference. "One day," the Russian told his lawyer, Louis Waldman, "you walk along the street and there is a man dead, run over by a car. And you see it is Krivitsky. You say, 'Poor man, he should have been more careful.' You never think it is *they* who killed me so. *They* are too clever!" Krivitsky took out a large life insurance policy.[13]

Still he courted danger. In the fall he traveled to London—by submarine, it was rumored—where he was debriefed for three weeks by British intelligence officials and the Foreign Office. He named nearly a hundred Soviet agents and warned "the Soviet diplomatic bag [was] being put at the disposal of Germany for the despatch of espionage material." Some of the agents, said Krivitsky, were British citizens, although he was able to identify them only by occupation and stray background details. Thus did Donald Maclean, John Cairncross, and possibly Kim Philby all escape detection.[14]

Chambers had been seeing Krivitsky all though this period. The Russian was incurably lonely. The manhunt was still on, he was sure. And he was homesick. He spent hours on the docks of Manhattan, staring at the Russian ships. He found some solace in the company of Chambers, who was also struggling to build a new life. Krivitsky was moved by Chambers's account of his own baptism and, though a Jew (born Samuel Ginsberg), considered converting to Christianity. One evening in the winter of 1941, while tramping the Manhattan streets with the Russian, Chambers promised to introduce him to his minister.[15]

The meeting never took place. Within a few weeks Krivitsky went to Washington to testify again before HUAC. He registered under an alias at a small hotel, the Bellevue, a few blocks from Union Station and the Capitol. The next morning, February 10, at nine-thirty, a maid found Krivitsky's corpse. He had been dead about six hours with a bullet in his temple and a .38 caliber pistol in his hand. J. B. Matthews, HUAC's chief investigator, made the identification at the morgue.

Police and the coroner ruled the death a suicide. The door and window of the hotel room had been locked. The victim's blood had washed the weapon clean of fingerprints. There was also a suicide note written in Krivitsky's hand—three notes in fact. Krivitsky had written in English to Louis Waldman, asking him to help his widow and son. In a letter to his wife, Tonya, Krivitsky wrote, "I want to live very badly. But it is impossible." The third note, in German, was addressed to Suzanne La Follette, the secretary of the Dewey Commission. Krivitsky implored her "to help Tonya and my poor boy."

Waldman suspected the notes were forgeries. So did Matthews. Krivitsky had warned the HUAC investigator he might be murdered. Tonya Krivitsky was certain her husband had not owned a pistol. (In his note to Waldman Krivitsky explained he had purchased the weapon in Virginia.) She also said her husband had not seemed depressed in the days leading up to his death. Nor was he in financial straits. He had earned enough from his *Post* articles to cover his expenses for "at least two to three years." To this day, Krivitsky's death remains unsolved, although there recently has been speculation he was assassinated by a German.[16] Chambers, drawing his own conclusions, was certain Krivitsky "was killed by agents of the Red underground."

Esther and the children had been wintering in New Smyrna, Florida. Hearing the accounts of Krivitsky's death, Esther was "overcome by panic and terror." Unable to reach her husband at *Time,* she "took the children out of school, bundled everything portable into the car," and drove to South Carolina. At last she got through to Chambers, who instructed her it was safer in Florida and told her to return.[17] After Krivitsky's funeral, Chambers put Tonya and Alex Krivitsky on a train to Florida, where they could join Esther. Then he went to Washington and paid a call on Adolf Berle. "I suppose you're here for protection," said Berle. At last the government seemed interested in his case.[18]

In fact Berle had been been looking out for Chambers. As early as March 1940 he had prodded the FBI to follow up on Berle's own inter-

view of September 1939. After Krivitsky's death Berle again had contacted the bureau and offered to share his copious notes. But the FBI,
preoccupied with Nazi spies, was not interested in the Communist underground, and Berle's messages sat unread in its files. It was two years
before FBI agents came to Chambers's office to interview him. To his
surprise, they seemed unaware of the disclosures he had made to Berle.
Chambers phoned Berle on the spot and asked if it was all right for him
to speak to the FBI. Berle assured him it was. But Chambers, his suspicions aroused, proceeded to give so hedged a confession that the bureau
dismissed it all as "history, hypothesis, or deduction."[19]

In the spring Esther returned from Florida with the children and with
Krivitsky's widow and son. They all moved into the small Westminster
farmhouse; Chambers had been fixing it up. Quarters were close, and
Tonya grew lonely in the countryside. When the threat subsided, she and
Alex moved to New York.

But Chambers and Esther had decided rural living was exactly what
they wanted, for themselves and their children. In April, when Chambers got a raise—his second, bringing his salary to seventy-five hundred
dollars—he purchased 115 acres of farmland near the Pipe Creek, adjacent to the ten acres he already owned. The property, which Chambers
named Pipe Creek Farm, included a thirteen-room house. Over time he
installed running water and electricity and provided other comforts. He
also hired a full-time farmhand, Stanley Pennington, who doubled as
watchman, patrolling the grounds. Chambers continued to stay with
Laha four nights a week, but on Monday evening, the beginning of
*Time*'s "weekend," he commuted to Westminster, some three hours by
train and bus, and stayed on through Thursday morning, when he arose
at dawn and made the trip back to Rockefeller Center.[20]

In the next decade Chambers steadily increased his holdings and eventually acquired more than three hundred contiguous acres, most of them
working farmland—three different farms, each with a house. Property
owning became a pillar of his evolving creed. "No man can serve this
country loyally unless he has invested in its soil," he solemnly declared to
his onetime literary comrade Joseph Freeman, upon explaining why
Freeman, who owned no property, was unworthy of employment at
Time Inc.[21]

With remarkable speed Chambers had assembled the new life he had
willed for himself. "Who would dress like that?" wondered *Time*'s the-

ater critic Louis Kronenberger, a friend of Chambers's who enjoyed buoyant literary conversation with him but found his somber Quaker garb off-putting. "A man on call as a pallbearer? an enthusiast of a sternly cheerless sect?"[22] The answer was: Both. Each day, at the office and the farm, Chambers freshly entombed his old self and lived out the new creed he had embraced.

In late 1941, increasingly uncomfortable as an Episcopalian, Chambers discovered a faith closer to his spiritual needs when he read the journal of George Fox, the seventeenth-century founder of Quakerism. The book "summoned me to a direct daily experience of God and told me that His revelation is continuous to those who seek to hear His voice in the silence of all distractions of this world." Chambers initially hesitated to join the Friends because of their pacifism, untenable in a world that demanded the clash of swords. The early saints, after all, were "invariably violent." Even George Fox, though pledged to peace, was "a man of force."

But he overcame his doubts and began to go to the Twentieth Street Meeting House in Manhattan for sessions of silent prayer. These profoundly affected him. So did the Quaker notion of the inner light—each believer's unique intimation of divinity—and the concept of bearing witness. Chambers, Esther, and the children all joined the Pipe Creek Meeting, some twelve miles from the farm, near Union Bridge.[23]

By 1942 Chambers had completely evolved a new religious-political philosophy. Its crux, he explained to Luce, was the "irreconcilable issue" that underlay modern man's spiritual crisis and also defined the struggle against communism:

> Belief in God or Belief in Man. . . . This conflict is not the old conflict between different religions, but the absolutely fundamental struggle between the primacy of God or Man, between God and no God, between soul and no soul. . . . These issues are the real line of cleavage in the modern world between conservative or revolutionary, cutting across all lines of economic class and political party; binding together proletarian and capitalist in a common belief in the primacy of God, just as they inexorably throw together those who believe in the primacy of secular Man no matter what their superficial differences or pseudo-religious trappings.[24]

This is the position Chambers set forth almost a decade later, and in nearly identical terms, in his memoir *Witness,* where it achieved a central place in postwar conservative thought.

In his interview with the Trotsky Defense Committee's Felix Morrow, Chambers had been asked to speculate on the Soviet-Nazi alliance. How secure was the bargain? Very secure, said Chambers, if left up to Stalin alone. "Under no circumstances will Stalin break the pact with Hitler," he predicted. The breach "will come only from Hitler's side."[25]

On June 22, 1941, this prediction came true. Germany invaded the Soviet Union, and the two gangster dictators were restored to their natural condition of enmity, each intent on building an empire in Central and Eastern Europe. The British welcomed the Soviets as allies, and then, in December, when the Japanese attacked Pearl Harbor, the United States found itself leagued with the Soviets. Chambers recognized the necessity of this grand alliance. (He registered with his draft board shortly after Pearl Harbor.)[26] But he remained a vocal opponent of the Soviet Union, convinced Stalin's reversal only magnified the danger of communism.

To many of his colleagues Chambers's obsession no longer seemed eccentric but an insult to the alliance and to the war effort itself. Even the friendly Tom Matthews was alarmed by Chambers's extremism. Whenever he "referred to Stalin or the Soviets, he made them out to be not friendly allies but cynical and treacherous enemies." Matthews did all he could "to keep this bugaboo out of his reach, or at least out of his copy."[27]

But Chambers would not let up. In February 1942 he renewed his assault on Malcolm Cowley, who had left *The New Republic* to take a government job at the Office of Facts and Figures, a new propaganda agency headed by poet Archibald MacLeish. Martin Dies held up Cowley's appointment, citing his long record of Communist front activity. Chambers chimed in with a "review" of Cowley's latest poetry collection, *A Dry Season.* The piece, published in National Affairs, not Books, misleadingly quoted two of Cowley's poems, written years before, as evidence of the poet's ongoing honeymoon with Stalin. In a letter to Luce, MacLeish, a onetime *Fortune* star, complained that Chambers's piece was "outrageous." But it served its purpose. Cowley was forced to submit his resignation and was out of a job. It was an incident he would not forget.[28]

Despite the friendships he made at *Time,* Chambers became more isolated than ever, immured in his mission. He avoided the lunches, the parties, the after-hours carousing. At the end of the workday he rode the train to Lynbrook to spend the night with Laha. At the end of the week he made the long commute to Westminster. When the *Time* week began again, on Thursday morning, Chambers was back at his desk in his dark, wrinkled suit, the cuffs too long, a faint odor of farm manure sometimes wafting from his shoes. In his first two years at *Time,* he even refused summer vacations for fear his adversaries would take advantage of his absence and weaken his standing at the magazine.[29]

Harry Luce admired Chambers's dedication and rewarded him for it with important assignments. In 1941 he asked Chambers to edit one of Time Inc.'s most ambitious undertakings, a series of *Fortune* essays, published in 1942–1944, by prominent philosophers and educators, including Bertrand Russell, John Dewey, Ernst Cassirer, and Reinhold Niebuhr.[30] Then, in the summer of 1942, when Matthews was promoted to managing editor, Luce chose Chambers to succeed him as the editor of the back of the book, with a raise (in July) to ten thousand dollars, double his first salary.[31] It was a big job—there were thirteen departments to oversee—enlarged further by Chambers's determined mission to set off as many anti-Communist detonations as possible, even if it meant, as it often did, writing all the copy himself.

Unable to manage the whole job single-handed, Chambers asked for an assistant, Calvin Fixx. Chambers and Fixx had become friends at Books. Fixx was one of *Time*'s best book reviewers and another of Bob Cantwell's finds. The two, both westerners, had known each other for many years. Fixx had flirted with radicalism in the 1930s without ever abandoning his devout Episcopalianism. Taciturn but enormously sympathetic, he was known as "the chaplain of Time Inc." Chambers found in him a soul mate, who listened without judging.[32] In his new job Fixx became a virtual extension of Chambers. Daily the pair rewrote the back of the book paragraph by paragraph.

Not since the peak of his spying days had Chambers labored with such fanatical dedication. He clocked thirty-six-hour shifts, napping for stretches in his chair or on the office floor. He ballooned to two hundred pounds on meals ordered up and quickly gobbled. Fixx matched him, the two "smoking five or six packs of cigarettes and drinking thirteen or fourteen cups of coffee a day."[33] And Chambers did not let up on the weekend, when he arose at dawn to join Stanley Pennington in the fields. The two "worked many a long hot day," side by side, "from before the sun was up until it was too dark to see."[34]

All this took an obvious toll. After one editorial lunch some expressed concern about Chambers's health. Indignant, he raged to Luce at this "attempted putsch," a transparent ploy to muffle him and his anticommunism. Next would come, no doubt, an assault on the quality of the pages Chambers edited.[35]

Then, one night in October 1942, Calvin Fixx collapsed after a dinner for Time Inc. staff. He had suffered a coronary. He was granted a six-month leave with pay, later extended to a year, and went to Florida to convalesce.[36]

Chambers's new assistant was Wilder Hobson, able and genial, but not a true substitute for the irreplaceable Fixx. Chambers shifted the entire back of the book onto his own shoulders. By November he was suffering chest pains so severe he could barely walk. His Westminster physician, Dr. Elizabeth Wilkens, originally diagnosed angina but later revised it to acute exhaustion. The cure was the same in either case. Chambers was confined to bed indefinitely.

Luce wired an offer of financial assistance, but Chambers refused, though he was relieved when Time Inc. kept him on at full salary, enabling him to pay off his mortgage.[37] Of equal concern was the farm. It needed his attention. Luckily Pennington, Chambers's "sharecropper," was there. Silent and stalwart, he replenished the fallow acres with lime and fertilizer and kept the bins swollen with grain. He also had the gift of foreseeing Chambers's worries. He would see to a task not yet assigned to him and then say to Esther, "Now tell Mr. Chambers he doesn't have to worry about that any more."[38]

There was another daily laborer on the Chambers farm. With her husband away five days out of seven, Esther looked after the livestock, which included a cow, a horse, thirty-four hogs, two hundred chickens, a flock of geese, ducks, and turkeys. She also tended a vegetable garden and stored preserves. In January, when seven large hogs gave birth, the slightly built Esther, all of five foot two, herded them into pens—on the coldest nights of the year. A few weeks later the cow gave birth to a calf unable to take its mother's udder. Esther had to intervene, helping the calf eat and calming the mother. Laha, who turned seventy-one in December, also came down to help.[39]

Meanwhile the patient was ordered flat on his back all day long, remaining as immobile as possible, not even lifting his arms. It was more than he could bear. One day he climbed out of bed to help Laha sand a cabinet—and had another attack that put him flat on his back for another month.[40]

The days passed slowly for Chambers, arduously for Esther and Laha. And it was worse still for the children, now ages nine and six, silently observing their father in his gravely weakened state.[41]

Spring brought relief. Chambers's chest pains subsided. By March he was able to walk. His thoughts roved continually to *Time*. He missed his job badly and kept in touch with Luce by letter. The editor in chief sent on for editing a speech he planned to deliver on the occasion of *Time*'s twentieth anniversary. Chambers barely touched the text, which he found "a simple, authentic testimony of the spirit." He ended his note with a benediction: "God bless you, Harry."[42]

In April a Baltimore heart specialist cleared Chambers's return to full-time work but advised him to get his weight down to 175 pounds, with light exercise—a little walking each day, no straining or lifting. He remained a serious candidate for a heart attack and should always keep a supply of nitroglycerin tablets on hand. "Obviously," the doctor added, "he should have his filthy mouth cleaned up—I suggest 4 or 5 teeth be pulled with novocaine."[43]

Chambers returned to *Time* in June. It had been eight months. His workload was reduced to only two or three of the sections he had handled before his illness. A couch was placed in Chambers's office, and he reclined on it for short periods each day, more often when his chest pains recurred. He also made use of it on Thursday mornings, when the book review staff gathered to discuss the week's assignments. He had under him a talented crew: the novelist Nigel Dennis, poets Weldon Kees and Howard Moss, and Harvey Breit, later an editor at *The New York Times Book Review*.[44]

By fall Chambers had recovered much of his old turf. He divided the back of the book with Wilder Hobson. And the masthead of September 13 listed him for the first time as senior editor, one of only seven on the magazine. In December Matthews nominated Chambers for the elite Senior Group, which met regularly to determine editorial policy. Chambers also was enrolled in Time Inc.'s generous profit-sharing plan. In January 1944 his salary climbed to twelve thousand dollars, this at a time when 90 percent of Americans earned less than five thousand a year. His farm yielded an additional twenty-five hundred dollars. His net worth was thirty thousand dollars. His rehabilitation was almost complete. He even had his teeth fixed.[45]

# 15

## *Ghost on the Roof*

By 1944 Chambers had settled back into the routine he cherished: a week of mental exertion at the office followed by a weekend of strenuous physical labor on the farm. At the same time he succeeded in reducing the demands he placed on himself and adhered, more or less, to his new health regimen. He swore off cigarettes, smoking only a pipe, did without the drink or two he sometimes used to have at lunch, and scaled back his office hours, though not his overall schedule. In fact he began to write book reviews for the *American Mercury,* H. L. Mencken's magazine, reborn as an anti-Communist monthly. Chambers used the pseudonym John Land. The name, he joked to a friend, signaled his return to the "anonymous peasant masses."[1]

These pieces gave him a chance to "let off steam" on forbidden topics, such as the international situation.[2] What intrigued him, and everyone else, was the impending peace. Exactly what shape would it take? Most observers agreed the determining factor was the Soviet Union. Of all the totalitarian powers, Russia alone would emerge from the war newly strengthened. Indeed Stalin stood on the brink of securing an empire. To the Baltic states annexed by means of the 1939 pact, Stalin was now adding all the lands the Red Army occupied as it harried the Nazis back to Berlin. The phrase *World War III* had already entered the language.[3]

There was no escaping that the Soviets had been the Nazis' ally as recently as 1941, that Stalin had switched sides only when attacked and even then retained control of the lands acquired in the secret protocols of the 1939 pact. But what were his intentions now? What did Stalin want? The prevailing forecasts were optimistic. In his best-seller *The Time for Decision,* former Undersecretary of State Sumner Welles argued that the chances of a harmonious postwar era were good since the United States was "the one major power, from Russia's point of view, with whom an enduring friendship should be most easily possible."[4]

Time's foreign correspondents were even sunnier. In July 1944 Foreign News featured a travelogue, "Miracle of the East," filed by Moscow correspondent Richard Lauterbach, giddy after a state-sponsored tour of the Russian hinterlands. What he had seen, Lauterbach reported, was the "vision of a new, raw world." In Omsk "young workers scrubbed clean of factory dirt danced to Russian and U.S. jazz"; in Novosibirsk, "the Chicago of Russia," the local Communist boss "looks and acts like a cross between Jimmy Cagney and a Rotary greeter . . . a sort of Russian Jim Farley [the garrulous crony of FDR], slapping backs, shaking hands."

Lauterbach's account was complemented by Foreign News's vaunting reports on Soviet conduct in Central Europe. *Time's* man in Romania reported that "for all Moscow cares, non-Soviet people have the right to run & ruin their own affairs, strictly without interference." So too in Finland, where "the Russians want an independent Finland with a friendly government." Not one correspondent seemed to doubt that Stalin might have any ambition other than to rid Central Europe of its existing fascist regimes and guide them toward democratic vistas.[5]

Some at Time Inc. thought otherwise. Harry Luce, for one, had been reevaluating his position on the Soviet Union. Though staunchly anti-Communist, Luce had backed Russia, a gallant partner in the war effort. As recently as 1943 Luce had encouraged favorable coverage of the Russians and in early 1944 had rejected a *Life* serialization of Walter Lippmann's *U.S. War Aims*—a rebuttal to Sumner Welles—because Lippmann's realpolitik analysis was too "anti-Russian."[6] But lately Luce had come around to the thinking of Chambers and a few other ex-radicals—such as the *Fortune* editor William Schlamm and the *Life* editor John Chamberlain—who were convinced Stalin was bent on expanding his domain. It was hard to square this view with Foreign News's reports, which seemed meant "to smother honest reporting of Russian policy."[7] By the summer of 1944 Luce had read one too many articles in the Lauterbach mold, and when the sitting Foreign News editor, John Osborne, left for a two-month assignment in Europe, Luce asked Chambers to fill in. It was a bold move. "The man whose prejudice had formerly barred him from so much as reviewing books on Soviet or Communist subjects was now in charge of mighty FN [Foreign News] with its influence over four or five millions of readers in the U.S. and many abroad," as one of Luce's biographers later put it.[8] In Luce's long history of surprising personnel maneuvers, few evoked quite the outrage of this one, and none sowed such discord. Many on staff were convinced Chambers was paranoid, demented, or an outright fascist.[9]

But Luce had his reasons. He had come to know Chambers well. He respected his mental powers and was awed by his grasp of history, "the science of knowing where we have been." In their many talks Chambers presented his views with cogency and point. He believed he knew exactly what course history was taking. He was ready with answers and eager to state them. He also had pronounced gifts. He was a polished writer and an equally good editor. Besides, Tom Matthews, normally so cautious, supported Luce's decision. He too had begun to see that Chambers's view of the Soviet Union might not be "outlandish" after all.[10] Why not give Chambers two months and seven or eight pages of the magazine to make sense of a confusing world?

Chambers was jubilant. This was the job he had coveted since 1939, when he had been removed from FN for failing to "aim down the middle." He had never stopped hoping for a second chance. Granted his opening at last, he wasted no time feeling his way into the job. He was sure "foreign news is going to be the decisive news for the next few decades," and he had little time to chart the coordinates of that future. Osborne was scheduled to return in October.[11]

The first issue Chambers edited, dated August 7, 1944, measured the distance Foreign News was to travel under its new head. He wrote the lead story himself, "Mission to Moscow." The title was a sardonic reference to a sentimental pro-Soviet film of 1943. Chambers's piece, an analysis of Poland's postwar fate, makes plain that the "Committee of Liberation" installed in Poland by the Red Army was not the provisional government the Soviets advertised but a puppet regime slated for permanency. The "hard fact of the Polish question," Chambers wrote a week later, "was that the Kremlin would now dominate Poland," no matter what others, least of all the Polish people, might wish. He predicted further that the harsh fate meted to the Poles was "the Russian blueprint for Eastern Europe above the Carpathians." The Finns too would find "that the hard facts of power politics stared them in the face."[12]

Chambers, again, was right. But there was a problem. *Time* had a talented crew of field correspondents who included Lauterbach, John Hersey, Theodore White, Charles Wertenbaker, and others. All were on the scene, gathering information firsthand, and what they reported home in lengthy cables bore no resemblance to the copy Chambers was running. When they saw the printed editions of the magazine, they were appalled.[13]

It was not only the men in the field who objected. *Life*'s cable editor, Filmore Calhoun, also protested to Luce: "I read the incoming cables, and I am amazed to see how they are either misinterpreted, left unprinted or weaseled around to one man's way of thinking." Stephen Laird, chief of correspondents for both *Time* and *Life,* drew Chambers aside one day and asked him why he was ignoring the cables. Chambers explained his own sources were more reliable. He "made no secret of the fact that everything he received from Hersey or White went right into his wastebasket," a confidant later said. "Half the time he wouldn't even bother to read their dispatches." He substituted his own interpretations, relying mainly on his knowledge of communism, backed up by whatever documentation he could find. Often it did not stand up to *Time*'s rigorous fact-checking system. "Whit would try to build a big story from some squib from some newssheet like the Polish Exile Catholic Society," a colleague recalled. "Such a piece would be impossible to check, and then the tension would rise." The researcher who dared challenge Chambers, citing the news wires, daily press accounts, or cables the editor ignored, was shrugged off or sent away.[14]

On the other hand, Chambers's guesses caught the drift of history far better than the reports he was getting. Much of what he wrote was eerily prescient. He was right about Poland, right about Finland, and right in his overarching view that a crumbling German empire would be supplanted by a more durable Soviet one. Chambers was not reporting. He was explaining, reading political developments through the lens of Leninism. That lens collected its light from a narrow range of the spectrum, but the beam it threw on events was stunning in its clarity. Chambers overstated his case, often seeing dangers where they were not present. And he was not above crimping the evidence to suit his thesis.

Still, he grasped, better than anyone else around him—and as well as any other American of the day—that the postwar world would be formed in the crucible of "power politics."

To make this argument, week after week, was a logistical challenge. He had to turn FN on its head, providing much of the copy himself.[15] But he did not work alone. Before long he won converts among the in-house writers assigned to Foreign News—that is, among those who had not "got themselves transferred elsewhere as fast as they could" when Chambers's appointment was announced. Contributing editor Fred Gruin, on FN a year when Chambers took over, had heard the familiar tales and eyed his new boss with suspicion. Soon he decided Chambers was a "brilliant, innovative, imaginative" editor whose fabled paranoia was in reality a clear-eyed vision of the world born of "his knowledgeable and profound experience and understanding of communism." John Barkham, former chief of the Cairo bureau, also was impressed by Chambers's mastery of world politics. A third FN ally was Craig Thompson, later *Time*'s Moscow bureau chief. These three writers and four researchers—Marjorie ("Mardi") Smith, Blanche Finn, Patricia Divver Roeg, and Yi-Yung Sun—were Chambers's supporters on Foreign News, his anti-Communist "cadre."[16]

Even as tension mounted, day-to-day operations ran smoothly. Each Thursday morning the staff assembled to plot that week's issue in Chambers's office, spacious quarters with sweeping views in two directions, east overlooking Fifth Avenue, south overlooking Forty-eighth Street. Writers and subeditors sat on folding chairs; others squeezed onto Chambers's couch—unless his chest pains were acute, in which case he stretched out on it himself and conducted the meeting supine. Chambers began with a list of story topics gleaned from his own attentive monitoring of global events—the papers and journals he read in several languages. (He could even make his way through *Pravda* and *Izvestia*.) The list was amended as one of the writers read aloud items that had come in over the news wire or through the daily press. Story suggestions were bandied about, and Chambers revised his list, parceling out assignments. Later each writer was paired with a researcher.[17]

The next several days were spent in the feverish activity of putting together the section. The writers first sifted through the often voluminous cables and other sources provided by the researchers. Then they drafted articles, which Chambers edited as they came in. He seldom asked for

rewrites, preferring, like so many *Time* editors, to change the copy himself. Often he revised heavily but sometimes was content merely to insert
a pungent paragraph or sentence. Fred Gruin remembered submitting a
piece on Finland that Chambers left intact but for one change. Gruin had
written, "Over Finland the long darkness of the subarctic winter nights
had begun to close in." Chambers added, "So had the political night." In
another piece, a cover article Gruin wrote on China's Prime Minister
T. V. Soong, Chambers inserted a sentence Gruin was able to recall verbatim forty-five years later: "He [Soong] was determined that his cycle of
Cathay should be a motorcycle."[18]

It was not Chambers's voice alone that rang out from the pages of
Foreign News. The legend that he wantonly ignored overseas cables is
exaggerated. He did not tamper with reports on the liberation of France
or on the Allied debate over the terms of Germany's surrender. He
printed a Soviet correspondent's eyewitness description—one of the first
available—of a Nazi death camp and followed up with a full dispatch
from Richard Lauterbach, the correspondent Chambers trusted least.
Even when the subject turned to communism, Chambers made resourceful use of the cables. He discarded their political observations but
mined them for background material, the "color stuff" Luce prized.[19]

But outside Chambers's tight-knit group, feelings were hardening. In
the space of two months morale had sunk "awfully low." Many looked
forward to October, when Osborne was scheduled to return to New
York and resume charge of FN.[20]

In the fall Luce sounded Chambers out on a possible next assignment.
Only Foreign News would do, Chambers said. "It is my first choice, my
second and my third." He wanted to stay where he was, figuring out history, "for a long time to come." Chambers saw himself not as a temporary substitute but as the department's rightful leader, its Bolingbroke
back from long exile. "I have spent some 15 years of my life actively
preparing for FN," he grandly told Luce. "Some of those years were
spent close to the central dynamo that powers the politics of our time."

The metaphor was borrowed from one of Chambers's literary heroes,
Henry Adams. It also pointedly evoked Luce's most famous utterance,
his 1941 statement (in *Life*) on the "American Century," a plea for the
United States, which had not yet entered the war, to intervene immediately, taking charge of the Allied effort and thereby becoming the
world's next military and economic "powerhouse." Chambers was re-

minding his boss that in the months and years to come the West would be contending with Soviet communism, itself a formidable generator of ideological heat.[21]

Luce did not need much persuading. He liked what Chambers was doing. So did Matthews. Never had Chambers's abilities been shown to finer effect. "Whit puts on the best show in words of any writer we've had," said John Shaw Billings, editorial director of Time-Life. His editorial gifts were as good. "A superb technician, particularly skilled at the mosaic art of putting a *Time* section together," he added depth, texture, and meaning to individual pieces and gave the section as a whole greater heft. His own articles had a distinctive sheen. In October Matthews cabled Osborne to stay on in Europe while Chambers continued to run Foreign News.[22]

But soon a major skirmish broke out, over Asia. Luce, raised in China, had a lifelong passion for the country. That passion was reciprocated, at least by China's ruler, Generalissimo Chiang Kai-shek, who regarded Luce as China's "single most powerful friend in America."[23]

Chambers too had a stake in China. In his proletarian days he had written idealistically, in *The New Masses* and *Labor Defender,* of a Communist victory there. As an anti-Communist he saw the issue in reverse and since 1941 had been denouncing leftist journalists who portrayed Mao Zedong as the leader of a grassroots movement rather than as the Kremlin agent Chambers believed him to be.[24]

But in *Time*'s employ there was someone else whose passion for China was also great and whose knowledge of the country and its people far exceeded both Luce's and Chambers's. He was Chongqing bureau chief Theodore H. White, universally regarded as the most astute foreign journalist in China. In 1939, at age twenty-four, White, then only a stringer, had earned the first byline in *Time*'s history when he risked a journey behind Japanese lines and sent home an eyewitness account of atrocities committed by Japanese troops in Shanshi Province. Soon White was put in charge of *Time*'s China office and became Luce's favorite reporter.[25]

Like Luce, White had long admired Chiang and as recently as May 1944 had extolled the generalissimo (in *Life*) as his nation's indispensable man, gifted with "great intelligence" and a profound understanding of his people. But he had since changed his mind, under the influence of General Joseph Stilwell, the top American soldier in China, sent there to

coordinate Nationalist forces in their fight against Japan. Stilwell was a
Sinophile, fluent in the language and steeped in Chinese history and culture. But his relationship with Chiang was poor from the start. Stilwell
wanted to modernize and humanize the Chinese Army and favored a
truce with Communist guerrillas, effective fighters needed if the invad-
ing Japanese were to be repelled. Chiang resisted this advice and found it
especially galling to have an opinionated outsider thrust on him.[26]

By 1944 the relationship between Chiang and Stilwell had frayed past
mending. They could not coexist. Stilwell petitioned for sole command
of the Chinese Army. FDR complied. Chiang had no choice but to
obey. His government was being kept afloat by vast loans from the U.S.
Treasury. Stilwell himself delivered the communiqué to Chiang. "Beyond turning green and losing the power of speech," the generalissimo
"did not bat an eye." However, he responded with a decree of his own.
Stilwell must be stripped of his command and recalled to the United
States. In mid-October, President Roosevelt "gave 'direct and positive'
orders to remove [Stilwell] from China without delay." The general was
relieved of his post in China and summoned home to Washington.[27]

So close to Stilwell, White had been the first journalist to get the story
of the general's firing, and from Stilwell himself. White wrote up a
"blow-by-blow, fact-by-fact" report and smuggled it aboard the plane
that flew Stilwell and his staff out of China, thus eluding Chiang's vigilant censors and putting *Time* in possession of an exclusive.[28]

The Stilwell dismissal ran as a cover story in *Time*. Titled "Crisis," the
story was drafted by Fred Gruin and "sewn together" by Chambers. The
theme of White's account was that the Stilwell incident was final proof
of Chiang's unfitness to rule. (Stilwell himself likened Chiang to Hitler.)
The Chambers-Gruin account reversed this judgment. It portrayed the
generalissimo as a Lincolnesque figure struggling to keep together a severed nation even as he was undermined by his American allies. Putting
Stilwell in charge of Chiang's army, a "blunder of the first magnitude,"
defied "the traditional path of U.S. policy in the Far East" and weakened
the chance for "a strong, independent, democratic China." Chambers
and Gruin also faulted U.S. leaders who pushed Chiang to accommodate
the Communists in Yan'an, fatally underestimating "the danger to Nationalist China" that any deal with the Communists portended.

The article also castigated American journalists—Edgar Snow, Agnes
Smedley, and others, all "leftists" and "liberals"—who had painted a dis-

honest picture of Chinese Communists, lauding "Yenan's agrarian reforms, labor unions, well-fed troops, efficient guerrilla organization" but ignoring the Party's "rigorous press censorship (much stricter than Chungking's), its iron party discipline, 'traitors' [concentration] camps,' secret police, other totalitarian features." These last details came from Lin Yutang's *The Vigil of a Nation,* which Gruin, an advance reader for the Book-of-the-Month Club, had seen in galleys.

The Chambers and Gruin piece concluded with a dire warning: "If Chiang Kai-shek were compelled to collaborate with Yenan on Yenan's terms or if he were forced to lift his military blockade of the Communist area, a Communist China might soon replace Chungking. And unlike Chungking, a Communist China (with its 450 million people) would turn to Russia (with its 200 million people) rather than to the U.S. (with its 130 million) as an international collaborator."[29]

In Chongqing a stunned Teddy White sent a voluminous *cri de coeur* to Luce, forty-five pages long, listing errors and distortions, large and small. The whole tenor of the published story was wrong. The crux of the China issue, White explained, was that "neither Nationalists nor Communists were democratic in the American sense and that our immediate interest was to support the ones who could help us most against the Japanese."[30]

His faith in Luce shattered, White posted a sign in his office: "Any resemblance to what is written here and what is printed in *Time* magazine is purely coincidental." Soon Luce was to bar him altogether from reporting about politics and order him to submit only "small indigenous colorful yarns." In 1945 White resigned from *Time,* hours before he received word that his book *Thunder Out of China,* co-written with his *Time* colleague Annalee Jacoby, had been purchased by the Book-of-the-Month Club. It sold 450,000 copies and made its authors rich. Eventually he and Luce made up.[31]

White and Chambers remained enemies. White later described Chambers as "a former Communist *apparatchik* of remarkable literary gifts." Chambers told the FBI that White had been part of the "pro-left" contingent at *Time* who had conspired to have him removed from FN.[32]

Each combatant could later claim victory, White in his prediction of civil war in China, Chambers in his prophecy that a Communist China would be totalitarian. But in the end there was no good solution to the Chambers-White debate. It resurfaced in the years ahead, when the question "Who lost China?" became the leading refrain, or taunt, of the cold war.

By this time "office boys, researchers, writers, senior editors and executives" all had chosen sides in what was being called the Chambers War. All Chambers's conspiratorial instincts came to the fore. He might have been back at the *Daily Worker,* where intrigue of this kind was de rigueur. He stymied a head researcher by "giving her deliberately inaccurate lists of scheduled stories so that she wouldn't know what he was up to. He alienated the senior editor in charge of the U.S. at War section by failing to pass along copies of Foreign News stories so that coverage could be coordinated." Staff writers who differed with his figurings out of history often found their stories rewritten top to bottom.[33]

He drew his allies closer, confiding in them about his underground experiences and even divulging the outlines of the Washington spy ring and his role in it. But there were barriers. When Barkham and Gruin kidded Chambers about the precautions he took in restaurants, making sure always to position himself with a clear view of the door, Chambers was not amused. "There was room for humor but not when dealing with the main thrust," Gruin later said. Chambers even disliked the word *Commie* because it lacked seriousness.[34]

To outsiders Chambers's relation with his favored staff had an air of insurgency. They seemed less like subordinates than a coterie—"slaves, who would do anything" for Chambers. His personal authority over his staff was indeed great, and for all the camaraderie that developed out of it, its foundation remained Chambers's missionary aim to transform Foreign News into a pulpit of anticommunism. Even to the sympathetic John Chamberlain of *Life,* himself an ex-radical turned anti-Communist, Chambers's "fear of Stalin seemed a trifle super-heated."[35]

The Chambers War was not wholly an outgrowth of ideological differences. It was rooted as well in *Time*'s still-unformed identity. In its infancy the magazine had not reported the news but packaged it, carving a digestible summary from a mountain of press clippings. Since then the Luce press had developed its own high-powered news-gathering apparatus, with bureaus all over the globe. Yet editorially *Time* had not retooled. Department heads still held sway over the pages assigned to them and were authorized to slant copy as they saw fit, "subject only to the veto of the managing editor," Tom Matthews. And Harry Luce retained a controlling interest, as he periodically reminded intractable staffers: "The chief editorial policymaker for Time Inc. is Henry R. Luce—and that is no secret which we attempt to conceal from the outside world." Even before Chambers took over FN, there had been sharp conflicts between the home office and the field.[36]

By late 1944 the conflict was threatening to sunder Foreign News. "If Whit Chambers continues to ignore the guidance, opinions, and information from our good foreign news men, we could save a lot of money by replacing them with a few good bird dogs a la the Washington bureau," grumbled Allen Grover, Time Inc.'s ombudsman with the U.S. military. "I'm not saying what I think would happen to the magazine if we did."

Luce was not bothered. Nor was T. S. Matthews. "Luce and I were convinced that Chambers knew what he was talking about," Matthews later said. "I had to make a choice: side with Chambers (Communist policy is cynical and sinister) or with his rebellious correspondents (Communist policy is humanitarian and hopeful). My choice was to uphold Chambers."[37]

He did it under trying circumstances. Chambers had whittled his active staff down to a small faction of loyalists (writers and researchers) and all but suspended the overseas information-gathering operation along with the in-house checking system. Luce's own favorite writer, John Hersey, who replaced Lauterbach in Moscow, threatened a work stoppage, withholding copy as long as Chambers continued to "impose a monotone of paranoia" over FN.[38]

At last, fearing a mutiny, Luce instructed John Shaw Billings to poll the correspondents. A questionnaire was sent to all the bureaus overseas. What did the men in the field think of Chambers? The results were tabulated in January 1945. Not one correspondent approved of Chambers's handling of the department. He was guilty of distortions, exaggerations, inaccuracies. His "editorial bias" was "grossly unfair," even "vicious."

Presented with this uniform verdict, Chambers detected a conspiracy. Refusing to believe the evaluations were independent judgments solicited by Luce, he was convinced his adversaries had ganged up to unseat him.

In the end it didn't matter. On January 6 Luce issued his verdict in a memo distributed to all those "concerned with the problem." To no one's surprise, the editor in chief came down squarely on Chambers's side. The correspondents had done a "fine job." But their faith that "the rulers of the world . . . are well-meaning people who are trying to do their best for their own countries and the world" was less persuasive than Chambers's harsher analysis. "Even in that part of the world misnamed the United Nations, things were not going very well," Luce pointed out. In fact "the posture of events in January 1945 seems to have confirmed Editor Chambers about as fully as a news-editor is ever confirmed." Not that the new FN editor was infallible. Chambers portrayed the Soviets as eager for war when, in Luce's view, Russia was, "if anything, over-exploiting her own and the world's desire for peace." Also, he was blind to the crucial distinction between "general revolutionary, leftist or simply chaotic trends" and "the specifically communist politics of various countries." On balance, however, Chambers had provided a vital corrective to many months of naïvely pro-Soviet reports.[39]

Luce's memo dealt a blow to the correspondents, as he had known it would. As a sop, he created a supplement to Foreign News, International, which provided a home for stories Chambers would not print on "the interactions of the Big Powers and the little." FN remained Chambers's preserve, at Luce's insistence. As far as the editor in chief was concerned, the section was week after week "by far the best reading" in *Time*.[40]

Chambers was still in charge in February 1945, when there occurred a signal event, a summit of the Grand Alliance in which Roosevelt, Churchill, and Stalin were to determine the shape of the postwar peace. There was a complete news blackout, for security reasons. Even the site of the conference—the Crimean resort of Yalta—was kept secret.

*Time*'s cover for the week of February 5 was a portrait of Stalin clad in the simple military tunic he favored. The accompanying article, written by Chambers, was a backgrounder to the conference. Much had changed since the Big Three had last met, at Teheran in 1943, when Russia had been buckling under the Nazi assault. Now the Soviet Union had emerged as "Europe's greatest power," poised to "fill the political void left by the crushing of Germany." That prospect, Chambers wrote, was "giving the creeps to practically everybody except professional Communists." The Nazi satellites were fast becoming Soviet ones. Czechoslovakia was feeling the pressure too. The question was, What would ensue? "As lasting a peace as men could contrive" or "the alternative which most Americans preferred not to think of even in the privacy of their own minds—World War III"?

The remaining two pages of the article profiled Stalin, "the most important person in the world last week," and the leader "in whose hands, for good or evil, lay so heavy a responsibility for the world's destiny." Chambers capsuled the nearly twenty years of Stalin's reign. His analysis owed much to James Burnham's "Lenin's Heir," a pathbreaking essay published in *Partisan Review* in the winter of 1945. Burnham, a philosophy professor and until recently America's leading Trotskyist thinker, argued that the prevailing view of Stalin leaned too heavily on Trotsky's contemptuous portrayal of him as "the quintessence of mediocrity, the triumphant Babbitt of the revolution, a suburban Caesar." The events of recent years indicated otherwise. Stalin was, in reality, "a 'great man' in the grand style," a genius whose "creative political imagination" and bold gambling instincts had led him to the verge of gaining domination over Europe and Asia. Stalin had not betrayed the revolution, as Trotsky and his followers bitterly claimed. On the contrary, said Burnham, he had led it to new heights by subsuming rampant nationalist energies into the Marxist-Leninist vision. This did not corrupt the Communist gospel. It expanded it. As a result, Stalin had made possible a truly international revolutionary movement. He was history's great pupil and truly Lenin's heir. "Stalinism is communism," Burnham concluded.

Chambers reiterated this argument in anecdotal terms, writing with the controlled passion of one whose thirteen years as a Communist had coincided with the period of Stalin's ascendancy. Chambers reviewed the enormities of Stalin's rule—the liquidation of the kulaks, the show trials, the purges, the pact with Hitler—and pointed out that each had been carefully undertaken to advance "the world's greatest political revolution," now on the threshhold of global dominion.[41] To the anti-Chambers faction, this was too much. Chambers had ignored the objective requirements of journalism and taken "flight from the realities of the situation" so as to "vent [his] spleen on Russia."[42] And he was not done yet.

On March 1, before a joint session of Congress, a tired President Roosevelt, an apparition of his former self, read aloud a speech summarizing the successes of the Big Three conference, since revealed to have taken place at Yalta. Stalin had cooperated on many pressing issues, said FDR. He had agreed to place no binding figures on the amount of reparations

Germany would be forced to pay. He had accepted without amendment the American "Declaration on Liberated Europe." He had been satisfied with only two extra votes in the United Nations, instead of the sixteen he had originally demanded (one for each Soviet republic).

But on one set of questions the dictator had driven a hard bargain. Stalin had refused to yield the lands—in Poland, East Prussia, Hungary, Czechoslovakia—occupied by Red Army divisions. He also would not give up Yugoslavia, controlled by Marshal Tito's Communist partisans. In Poland, however, Stalin agreed the government should be reorganized through open elections, "the most hopeful agreement possible for a free, independent, and prosperous Polish State."

Public reaction to the speech, and to the accords, was favorable. The Big Three alliance was intact. The Soviets seemed reasonable.[43] But Chambers, eyeing developments from his rampart, had seen something else. Even before the accords were announced, he had begun to write a piece unlike anything else he had done for *Time*—and unlike anything the magazine had ever published. He worked on it secretly and then showed it to Matthews. "As I remember it," Matthews later recalled, "Chambers simply left the piece on my desk, saying that I might like to read it but that it was certainly not for *Time*, and made no attempt to persuade me to run it."

Matthews in turn showed the pages to Luce. "His eyebrows went up. He admitted that it was a forceful piece of journalism and asked me what I intended to do with it. I said I thought of running it in *Time*. The eyebrows went up again; Luce washed his hands of the affair."

Soon Matthews received "an unofficial delegation from the staffs of both *Time* and *Life*, urging me strongly not to print the piece; it would drive a wedge between the Allies, it was biased and bitter, irresponsible journalism"—the work, said one editor, of a "well-poisoner." Matthews momentarily pulled the copy but then changed his mind and sent it to the typesetter.[44]

"The Ghosts on the Roof" was published on March 5, set off in a box that occupied the third and fourth pages of Foreign News. A disclaimer said the unsigned "political fairy tale" did not represent the editorial opinion of the magazine but did not misrepresent it either.

Chambers's piece is written in the form of a historical fable. The ghosts are Russia's last imperial clan, the Romanovs, Czar Nicholas II and his family, executed in 1918 by the Bolsheviks. In Chambers's fable the dead royals invisibly gather, "with the softness of bats," atop the roof of their old home and observe the negotiations taking place within the white granite walls where the Big Three have begun to bargain away the future of Central and Eastern Europe. Czar Nicholas, foreseeing the outcome, can hardly contain his glee. The postwar European map, redrawn with a Soviet pen, fulfills the long-deferred dream, dating back to Peter the Great, of an expanded Russian empire.

Romania and Bulgaria, Yugoslavia and Hungary, Poland and Finland—all have been pulled into the Soviet vortex, with other nations to follow as communism strengthens its grip on Italy, France, Belgium, Germany. "They already control a vast region of China," the czarina delightedly cries. And once the Russians have joined the war against Japan, "we shall take Manchuria, Inner Mongolia, Korea, and settle the old score with Chiang Kai-shek." In due time "we shall sweep through Iran and reach the soft underbelly of Turkey from the south" and then proceed into the Middle East.

The Romanovs marvel at the visionary reach of Stalin, the pockmarked Georgian peasant suddenly metamorphosed into the supreme czar. "There he sits, so small, so sure. He is magnificent. Greater than Rurik, greater than Peter! For Peter conquered only in the name of a limited class. But Stalin embodies the international social revolution. That is the mighty new device of power politics which he has developed for blowing up other countries from within."[45]

In Moscow John Hersey had spent weeks setting up interviews with top Kremlin officials for an article on Yalta. The day "Ghosts" was published, Hersey "got ten phone calls canceling all the appointments." The essay "absolutely destroyed me in Moscow," Hersey later said.[46] The reaction was no warmer at Rockefeller Center. Some, including several of Chambers's adversaries, admired the piece. But most saw it as the culmination of his irrational zeal. No longer content merely to distort the facts, he had resorted to fantasy. Readers too were furious. Chambers had slandered the Russians and endangered the peace. In the Letters column the editors weakly asserted that *Time* "neither said nor thinks that Soviet-U.S. collaboration is 'doomed to failure.' "[47]

Within weeks FDR was complaining to Stalin about "the development of events" since Yalta. Stalin had failed to honor his commitment to free elections in Poland and had barred Western observers. In April an OSS report read by President Roosevelt and then, after FDR's sudden death (on April 12), by President Truman warned that Russia would emerge from the war "strong enough, if the United States should stand aside, to dominate Europe and at the same time to establish her hegemony over Asia."[48]

Like Chambers, Washington policy makers assessed the Soviet danger not in terms of an immediate threat to American security but in the wider terms of geopolitics. This was the consequence of the United States' emergence as the dominant power in the West, supplanting Great Britain, and also of the bitter aftertaste of the war just ending. Stalin's bold aggressiveness, his incursions into Eastern and Central Europe, had an ominously familiar ring. "World War II had been a close enough call," as one historian was to put it. "U.S. leaders dared not stand by and watch another dictator, another potential Hitler, step-by-step expand his realm and base of operations." The next months saw the hardening of U.S-Soviet relations. In February 1946, in a rare public speech, Stalin announced a five-year arms buildup in anticipation of an inevitable military conflict with the West. This was received in the West, even by liberals, as a "declaration of World War III."

The next month at tiny Westminster College, in Fulton, Missouri, Winston Churchill darkly invoked the specter of a Soviet empire, speaking as grimly as he had of the Nazi Wehrmacht. "An iron curtain has descended across the Continent. Behind that line lie all the capitals of the ancient states of Central and Eastern Europe. Warsaw, Berlin, Prague, Vienna, Budapest, Belgrade and Sofia, all these famous cities and the populations around them lie in what I must call the Soviet sphere."

In Moscow diplomat George Kennan composed his famous "long telegram," advising the State Department not to expect an era of "peaceful coexistence" with the Soviets. "We have here a political force committed fanatically to the belief that with the U.S. there can be no modus vivendi." Drawing the same historical parallel as Chambers, Kennan described Stalin as "only the last of a long session of cruel and wasteful Russian rulers who have relentlessly forced their country on to ever new heights of military power in order to guarantee external security for their internally weak regimes."[49]

Asia too was in jeopardy. General George Marshall, sent to China to mediate between Chiang and Mao, returned in failure. The country, he reported, was "lost" to communism, as Chambers had predicted in his "scare" piece on Joseph Stilwell. At the same time the European democracies, depleted by the war and frightened by the enlarging specter of Soviet aggression, turned to the United States for military and economic assistance.[50]

Within a few years the cornerstones of America's postwar foreign policy would be solidly laid: the Marshall Plan, the Truman Doctrine, NATO, the buildup of a nuclear arsenal, all of it premised on the necessity, accepted by liberals and conservatives alike, of standing firm in the face of an expanding Soviet state. It was as if Chambers's presumed paranoia had become the basis of American cold war policy.

In January 1948 *Time* reprinted "The Ghosts on the Roof," this time as political prophecy. After only three years Chambers's outrageous whimsy seemed "a mild and orthodox comment and no eyebrows went up."[51]

# 16

# *Sorrow Songs*

The Chambers War exacted a heavy toll on its protagonist. The vote of confidence from Luce did not lessen the double strain of fending off revolt while piecing together Foreign News more or less by himself. Soon he relapsed into the habits that had immobilized him three years before. He downed coffee by the potful, swelled up again to two hundred pounds, and routinely worked through the night in stretches of up to forty-eight hours. Twice he was laid up with chest pains. One morning in the fall of 1945, commuting from Westminster, Chambers briefly "blacked out" on the train and arrived shaking at Rockefeller Center. It was his worst scare since the winter of 1942–1943.[1]

That memory weighed heavily. Computing the risk, Chambers saw only two options: working himself to death or resigning from *Time*. Tom Matthews suggested a less drastic solution. Chambers could give up Foreign News and go back to Books, writing reviews at home. But Luce, finding the remedy extreme, proposed instead a six-month leave for Chambers, effective immediately.[2]

Foreign News was now without an editor. Matthews offered the post to John Osborne, a curious decision given the direction in which Osborne had led the department. But his views were changing. He was himself beginning to sound like a cold warrior. He had been among the few at *Time* who admired the political acuity of "The Ghosts on the Roof."[3]

But Osborne had not revised his opinion of Chambers's editorial methods and said he would succeed him only if two conditions were met: Chambers must "never again replace me on any job" and not again "be put in a position to misuse and distort the reports of *Time*'s foreign correspondents." Luce agreed. Less optimistic than he had let on, he did not expect Chambers to make a full recovery. Having won these concessions, Osborne promptly relinquished FN and decided to accept an offer from Charles Wertenbaker to head Time Inc.'s London bureau. A new editor, staff writer Max Ways, was installed on a trial basis and was slated to take over the department formally in January.

Then, to everyone's surprise, Chambers made a rapid recovery. His illness had been just another case of exhaustion. After a few restful weeks at Westminster he was ready to resume his job. Ways, never a combatant in the Chambers War, was willing to step aside. But Osborne, less malleable, reminded Matthews of Luce's pact. If Chambers were let back on Foreign News, Osborne would himself resign. Trapped, Matthews had to tell Chambers the change of editorship was a fait accompli.[4]

Chambers had been outmaneuvered. The final battle had gone to his enemies. It was a stinging defeat, all the more painful because it came at a time when his reading of world events was receiving daily vindication. Another man might have resigned. But where else could Chambers go, with his poor health and his checkered history? Where else could he draw a comparable salary? Where could he find a forum equivalent even to *Time*'s back pages? Besides, he had no legitimate grievance. Given the FN job with the understanding it would be temporary, he had wrung an extra ten months from the assignment. Wounded but uncomplaining, he tumbled down "the whole flight of editorial steps" to Books, where he had begun in 1939.[5]

But Luce and Matthews did not intend to banish Chambers or let his talents dry up. Soon they came to him with a proposal. Matthews long had wanted to make room in *Time* for more contemplative stories that required "a particular seriousness and deliberation of treatment not always possible in the hurly-burly of reporting the week's news of the world."[6]

Thus was born a new department, Special Projects, which became the joint preserve of Chambers and one of his closest friends at Time Inc., James Agee. The most gifted writer in *Time*'s history, Agee—"the captive poet," as Tom Matthews called him—was also the most charismatic. "He had about him a quality of voluminous energy, grand imagination, torrential feelings, physical size, almost superhuman generosity and warmth, and kind of a golden heart," a colleague remembered. "Everyone was interested in him." He had come to the magazine from Nashville by way of Harvard, with roots sunk deep in the southern literary tradition. He had begun his Time Inc. career at *Fortune,* where he produced spellbinding drafts that ran as long as thirty thousand words. Luce offered to send him to the Harvard Business School, but Agee was interested in the poor, not in their exploiters. With the photographer Walker Evans he had contrived to visit the Deep South in 1936 for a series on sharecroppers. The result, too disturbing for *Fortune,* was eventually published as the Depression masterpiece *Let Us Now Praise Famous Men.*

Since 1940, when they had shared an office and reviewed books together, Chambers and Agee had been confidants, an oddly compatible pair, the squat, severe ex-Communist glued to his desk and the lanky, feral poet who ambled in long past lunch in dirty tennis shoes and a sweat-stained work shirt. Chambers's inner torment found an answering cry in Agee, whose inner being was a battleground where the poet, the priest, and the sensualist all contested. Agee even had bad teeth.[7]

Reunited at Special Projects, "the two best writers in the shop," as one colleague put it, became a "company within the company" and produced many of *Time*'s cover stories in 1946–1948, some of them high points in the era's journalism.[8] As writers Chambers and Agee had a good deal in common. Both were drawn to the big theme; both had a gnostic appetite for disaster; both were prone to oration, in Chambers's case the blurtings of one normally taciturn, in Agee's the prodigious outpourings of a brilliant monologuist. At times each sounded something like the other. A Chambersian solemnity haunts Agee's famous sentences on Hiroshima, published in *Time* on August 20, 1945: "When the bomb split open the universe and revealed the prospect of the infinitely extraordinary, it also revealed the oldest, simplest, most neglected and most important of facts: that each man is eternally and above all else responsible for his own soul."[9]

And the magical effects of Agee, the southern spellbinder, crept into Chambers's moving tribute to Marian Anderson and the tradition of the Negro spiritual:

> . . . the land in which the slaves found themselves was strange beyond the fact that it was foreign. It was a nocturnal land of vast, shadowy pine woods, vast fields of cotton whose endless rows converged sometimes on

a solitary cabin, vast swamps reptilian and furtive—a land alive with all the elements of lonely beauty, except compassion. In this deep night of land and man, the singers saw visions; grief, like a tuning fork, gave the tone, and the Sorrow songs were uttered.[10]*

The Chambers War had given Chambers the reputation of a one-note writer, obsessed with a single theme. The wide array of subjects he assayed at Special Projects demonstrated the opposite, that he was capable of range and depth and on all subjects wrote from a core of impassioned feeling. For the first time he broke out of *Time*'s "group journalism" and achieved a truly distinctive voice, one to which readers responded. "In Egypt Land," Chambers's piece on Marian Anderson, published in December 1946, brought in a deluge of reader mail. G. Bromley Oxnam, the Methodist bishop of New York, called the essay "the finest statement of the case against racial discrimination that I have read." A Jesuit organization circulated one hundred thousand reprints as part of a campaign to promote racial harmony. After a letter from novelist Marjorie Kinnan Rawlings, who guessed Chambers had written the profile, *Time* parted its Iron Curtain and announced to readers, "Novelist Rawlings guessed right."[12]

Chambers's cover story on Arnold Toynbee's *A Study of History* had an even greater impact. Toynbee's massive work-in-progress offered a Spenglerian panorama of decaying civilizations through the ages, but proposed a triumphal ending: the emergence of a foggily defined universal religion that would arrest the decline and restore the West to spiritual health. When the *Study* appeared in a single-volume condensation, in 1947, Luce decided *Time* should anoint Toynbee, though British, the philosopher-king of the American Century. Chambers, so adept at simplifying complex ideas, was the obvious choice to provide a road map of Toynbee's theory. In "The Challenge," published on March 17, 1947, Chambers, as enraptured as Luce by the *Study,* declared its author had "shattered the frozen patterns of historical determinism and materialism by again asserting God as an active force in history." *A Study of History,* in Chambers's opinion, was nothing less than "the most provocative work of historical theory written in England since Karl Marx's *Capital.*"

* To Agee, "the utmost type of heroism, which alone is worthy of the name, must be described, merely, as complete self-faithfulness: as integrity." Of *Witness,* Agee wrote: "In a sense I even like what I don't particularly like, since it comes out of a degree of faithfulness to one's whole nature, which seems hardly to exist anymore."[11]

*Time* offered reprints, and fourteen thousand requests poured in—from "professors of history, philosophy, and anthropology, from deans of American colleges and universities, heads of public and private schools," as well as "clergymen, congressmen, and the governors of seven states." Toynbee's dense tome became a best-seller, and its author a celebrity.[13]

Next Luce asked Chambers to write a series of essays for *Life* titled, with Lucean bigness, "The History of Western Civilization." The resulting pieces, among the most popular ever published in the Luce press, lavishly exhibited Chambers's feel for history as a live subject. In "The Middle Ages," for example, he offered a shapely vision of the medieval landscape, dominated by three "cathedral spires," each a conjunction of spirituality and intellect: Gothic architecture, with its "prayerful uprush of stone"; the *Summa Theologica* of Aquinas, with its union of Aristotelian logic and Christian mystery; and the *Divine Comedy* of Dante, with its picture of hell "fixed for eternity in the terms of rational Aquinian theology." Chambers wrote seven pieces in all for the series, and in 1951 they were reprinted as the text to an illustrated world history published jointly by Time-Life and Simon and Schuster.[14]

But the piece Chambers was proudest of was the cover he was assigned to write for *Time*'s twenty-fifth anniversary issue, published on March 8, 1948. The story was a profile of theologian Reinhold Niebuhr, titled "Faith for a Lenten Age." Chambers set forth the rudiments of Niebuhr's stringent arguments in terms that reflected his own beliefs: "Under the bland influence of the idea of progress, man, supposing himself more and more to be the measure of all things, achieved a singularly easy conscience and an almost hermetically smug optimism. The idea that man is sinful and needs redemption was subtly changed into the idea that man is by nature good and hence capable of indefinite perfectibility. . . . Man is essentially good, says 20th Century liberalism, because he is rational."[15]

In the first chastening years of the cold war, when pessimism and moral asperity were coming into fashion, such language resonated powerfully. No one, as Murray Kempton later remarked, "could do the drumroll of alarm, of Western civilization come to the brink, like Chambers." Banished from Foreign News at the moment when history seemed to have reached a revolutionary climax, he wrote as if plunged in a perpetual night of despair, convinced he was living in the Communist, not the American, Century.[16]

Chambers's defeat at Foreign News had been alchemized into victory. He had remounted the stairs and established a solid literary reputation. In 1948 he was approached by the English journalist and Labour MP Richard Crossman, who was editing an anthology of personal testaments by ex-Communists and hoped for a statement from Chambers. Not yet ready for a public accounting of this kind, Chambers declined to submit an essay and so did not join André Gide, Arthur Koestler, Ignazio Silone, Stephen Spender, Richard Wright, and Louis Fischer, all contributors to *The God That Failed,* a classic document of the cold war. He was to write his own testament in *Witness* in 1952.[17] But by then he had a much different story to tell.

# WITNESS I:
# THE HEARINGS

## (August–December 1948)

# 17

## *Fetching a Bone*

With the sudden breakdown of the Yalta accords, the U.S. government was at last determined to investigate Communist influence in Washington. The FBI exhumed its wartime dossiers, and ex-Communist informers acquired new status. On March 20, 1945, State Department official Raymond Murphy, who had long been researching Soviet intelligence, questioned Chambers for two hours at Westminster. Chambers retraced some of the ground he had gone over with Adolf Berle in 1939 and then with the FBI, briefly, in 1942. Murphy excitedly wrote up a memo that over the next two years circulated widely through anti-Communist channels in Washington, read by FBI agents, staff members of the House Committee on Un-American Activities, journalists, and sundry investigators.[1]

In May 1945 Chambers was interviewed twice by FBI agents. One session lasted eight hours. He was questioned again in July. For the first time his interrogators seemed well prepared. (In 1943 the bureau had at last obtained Berle's 1939 notes.) Chambers readily named Communists to his new interrogators but kept the most damaging information to himself, especially on the subject of illegal activities. Nothing had come, after all, of his meeting with Berle in 1939.

It was not Berle's fault. The official had taken Chambers's story to the White House, to no effect. And Don Levine had made every effort to reach the president, telling the Chambers story to every contact he knew. One of Levine's recruits, columnist Walter Winchell, had gone directly to FDR but been rebuffed. "I don't want to hear another thing about it!" Roosevelt had said angrily, jabbing a finger at the columnist. "It isn't true."[2]

Meanwhile the Soviets assembled a massive North American espionage network that reached a peak of efficiency during the war, recruiting more than one hundred agents who penetrated the departments of State, War, Treasury, the Office of Strategic Services (the wartime precursor to the CIA), the War Production Board, even the FBI.

Little of this was known in 1945, though evidence had recently been unearthed by cryptanalysts at the U.S. Army's Signal Intelligence Service who had intercepted diplomatic telegrams sent between Moscow and its overseas missions and had begun painstakingly to decipher them. Within a few years code breakers came upon the trail of an atomic spy ring, run by a New York City Communist, Julius Rosenberg, that had infiltrated the Manhattan Project in Los Alamos, New Mexico, where the bomb had been developed. Underground agents there enabled the Soviets to speed up construction on their own weapon by two years. Several hundred more cables, decoded in the years ahead, corroborated Chambers's allegations.

The conspiracy was unraveling, and its outlines were growing clearer. But key facts remained top secret, kept even from leading U.S. officials, including President Truman, and did not reach the public until the 1990s, when documents were declassified in Washington and other archives were opened—briefly—in Moscow and Eastern Europe.

Chambers, observing these matters from afar, saw no reason for hope. His confession of 1939 had resulted in very little detectable action. Some of those he had named remained on the federal payroll all through the war, and a few had risen to disturbing heights. He was not about to try toppling them at the risk of bringing about his own ruin.[3]

His doubts were clinched in the summer of 1945, when the *Amerasia* spy case broke. *Amerasia* was a semischolarly left-wing journal on Pacific affairs. Despite its small circulation, it was a forceful voice in the China debate, strongly anti-Chiang. Its editors had contacts with State Department officials and in some instances with Soviet agents. In June 1945 the FBI raided its offices in New York and seized some eighteen hundred classified government documents. They came from "the War Department, the State Department, the OSS, the Office of Postal and Telegraph Censorship, and the ONI [Office of Naval Intelligence]." Six associates of the journal were arrested and charged with conspiracy to deliver secrets to the Soviet Union. Two pleaded guilty to the lesser charge of unauthorized possession of government papers. A grand jury failed to return indictments against the other four.[4]

As early as 1943 Chambers had paranoically envisioned an American edition of the Moscow trials in which the victims, all ex- and anti-Communists like himself, would be fed to inquisitors to divert the public from the machinations of the important conspirators. The *Amerasia* outcome seemed to bear out his suspicions. It looked as if the Truman administration had placed a higher priority on protecting itself than in rooting out spies.[5]

But the issue of Communist espionage was far from dead. In September 1945 news came from Canada that a major spy ring had been operating in North America. The informer this time was Igor Gouzenko, a Soviet agent employed as a code clerk at the Russian Embassy in Ottawa. Gouzenko had soured on the Soviet Union and then defected with a thick batch of documents. These, and follow-up interviews conducted by Canadian authorities, disclosed a large network centered on atomic espionage, with operatives in Canada and in the United States. FBI Director J. Edgar Hoover dispatched agents to Ottawa to learn more. Under questioning, Gouzenko implicated several high-level American officials, identifying them by position but not by name. Two weeks later the FBI sent a report on Gouzenko's allegations to the State Department. Canada's Prime Minister Mackenzie King then visited President Truman in Washington and showed him Gouzenko's interrogation report.[6]

The hunt for subversives was on. In October Secretary of State James F. Byrnes, distressed by Soviet belligerence at a diplomatic conference in London, began a quiet purge of the State Department. Anyone suspected of being pro-Soviet was either dismissed or demoted. Extra-departmental officers were brought in to "ferret out some of the difficult cases." The FBI also began top secret investigations, discreet inquiries of State Department officials that included background checks, wiretaps, and direct surveillance.[7]

Then, in November, another witness emerged from obscurity to make sensational allegations. Elizabeth Bentley, a thirty-seven-year-old ex-schoolteacher with a degree in languages from Vassar, was a troubled, unhappy woman who had joined the Communist Party in 1935 and gone underground in 1938. She eventually became a courier for the apparatus

Chambers had helped develop in Washington. In 1944 Bentley defected and after some months of lonely anguish confessed to the FBI. The picture she gave of the underground was far more extensive and detailed than anything Chambers had yet disclosed—she implicated more than eighty agents—and was minutely confirmed by later documentation.[8] The FBI matched her allegations against Chambers's and Gouzenko's, and wrote up a seventy-one-page report, "Soviet Espionage in the United States," implicating dozens of government officials. Although Chambers was tipped off about Bentley's revelations by anti-Communist journalists in New York and Washington, he knew few details of her testimony.[9]

As yet most of this counterintelligence activity was being kept secret, partly out of fear the Soviets would learn of it, partly because the Truman administration feared political attack at home. But the issue was taking on a life of its own. In 1946 Republicans, usefully wielding the charge that Truman was soft on communism, had gained control of Congress for the first time since Hoover's presidency. A revitalized HUAC, under its first Republican chairman, J. Parnell Thomas, launched multiple investigations of Communist infiltration—into labor, Hollywood, and the government. One HUAC witness, Soviet defector Victor A. Kravchenko, a former captain in the Red Army, declared that "every responsible representative of the Soviet Union in the United States may be regarded as a possible economic, political or military spy." Hoping to co-opt the issue, President Truman announced his own massive loyalty program, whereby some two million federal employees were subject to background investigations. Truman's attorney general, Tom Clark, issued a list of more than seventy front groups deemed subversive.[10]

As the search for Communists gained momentum, Chambers was pulled deeper into it. In August 1946 Ray Murphy came calling again, this time to discuss J. Peters's plans to "mess up policy" within the "old-line" federal agencies, specifically the State Department. The FBI also followed up, in 1946 and 1947, with a total of five interviews. Chambers was asked about numerous known and suspected Communists, including members of the Ware Group. The White House Loyalty Commission also sent an official to Chambers's office, with questions about Treasury officials, including Harry Dexter White.[11]

Chambers was a cautious informant, still uneasy about betraying onetime accomplices and exposing himself to punishment. He spoke in general terms about the dangers of communism but concealed the most important work he and others had done. Chambers told the FBI he had never "participate[d] in [a] Soviet espionage ring or any branch of Soviet Intelligence." He also claimed to have no "documentary or other proof" of espionage performed by underground Communists in Washington. He was to pay dearly for these lies.[12]

To some, Chambers's secrecy was puzzling—to Don Levine, for one. More actively anti-Communist than ever, Levine had begun to edit an anti-Communist monthly, *Plain Talk,* whose first issue included a sensational report on *Amerasia* and the State Department's "Red lobby." But when shown a copy of the magazine, Chambers "did not warm up to the subject." Nor did he indicate any interest in writing for *Plain Talk,* although many other ex-radicals, including John Dos Passos and John Chamberlain, contributed to it.[13]

Chambers was equally cagey when approached by Harvard historian Arthur Schlesinger, Jr., commissioned by *Life* to write an article on communism in America. Although he sat for an interview, Chambers would not allow himself to be quoted and insisted the names he divulged be kept out of print.[14]

Then, in June 1947, a grand jury was impaneled in New York to hear evidence that the CPUSA was a conspiratorial organization whose purpose was to overthrow the U.S. government. The evidence included testimony on the Washington underground of the 1930s. But when the Justice Department floated his name as a potential witness, prosecutors ruled Chambers out because he had been close-mouthed in the bureau's own interviews, a source only of "negative information."[15]

Don Levine was indignant when Chambers later received credit for being an "anti-Communist crusader." In fact, said Levine, Chambers had gone out of his way *not* to pursue Communists. It was true. At just the moment when the country at large was awakening to the "Red menace," Chambers had lost his zeal for Red hunting. He was willing to state his case in *Time,* keeping the argument on the plane of ideas, but he "had resigned from the Messiah business," recalled Herbert Solow, an occasional confidant in this period.[16]

He had resigned too from the informing business. He had always found it repellent. The informer "risks little," Chambers was to write.

He sits in security and uses his special knowledge to destroy others. He has that special information to give because he knows those others' faces,

voices and lives, because he once lived within their confidence, in a
shared faith, trusted by them as one of themselves, accepting their friendship, feeling their pleasures and griefs, sitting in their houses, eating at
their tables, accepting their kindness, knowing their wives and children. . . . The police protect him. He is their creature. When they whistle, he fetches a soiled bone of information. . . . [T]he informer is a slave.
He is no longer a man.[17]

But anti-Communist journalists had smoked him out. In October
1947 the *Washington Times-Herald* reported evidence of a government cell
headquartered in a "violin studio" on Connecticut Avenue. Harold Ware
was "probably one of the founders." The article included a curious reference to a "hideaway and 'letter drop' in a sleepy little Maryland town less
than 50 miles from the White House." Simultaneously the *New York Sun*
published some of the same facts, again mentioning a small Maryland
town "used as a 'drop' for Communist information."[18] The confusion
originated in Ray Murphy's memo, titled "Westminster, March 20,
1945." Both reporters, the *Times-Herald's* James Walter and the *Sun's* Edward Nellor, had read copies of the memo obtained from the Reverend
John F. Cronin, an official at the National Catholic Welfare Conference
and an energetic anti-Communist.

Nellor had also shown Murphy's memo to Ben Mandel, an ex-
Communist who (as Bert Miller) had signed Chambers's party card in
1925, later helped Don Levine found *Plain Talk,* and was now tracking
down witnesses for HUAC. In March 1948 Mandel paid a call on
Chambers at Rockefeller Center and asked him if he would testify in
upcoming hearings. Chambers said no and pleaded to be spared a summons, though by now he knew one would probably come.[19]

Meanwhile Chambers was having difficulties with his *Life* editor, Joseph
Kastner, and the series consultant, historian Jacques Barzun, a Columbia
acquaintance from the 1920s. Upon reading some changes Kastner and
Barzun had made in his essay on the Protestant Reformation, Chambers
had stormed out of Kastner's office.[20]

The incident underscored Chambers's growing sense of alienation at
Time Inc. His position there had become anomalous. He had attained
new eminence as a writer, had remounted the staircase. But he had lost
his influence as an in-house policy maker. He headed no department and
was less in step than ever with his colleagues. He had also perhaps hung

on too long. Most of the ablest writers of his period had left *Time* or were about to do so. Jim Agee had handed in his resignation in June and was to depart in the summer. Chambers's adversaries John Hersey and Teddy White, both his junior by more than a decade, were already making reputations as independent writers. Chambers's allies too were moving on. Fred Gruin was in Nanking, heading up the China bureau. Calvin Fixx was working in the public relations department, where the stress was lower. A new generation had settled in at Rockefeller Center, young men back from the war, keen on getting ahead, indifferent to ideological wars. *Time* was changing. The magazine Chambers had joined during the Depression was now a venerable institution Luce was guiding into the bland prosperity of the 1950s. Chambers too had entered middle age. Glimpsed in the elevator or at his desk, he seemed less a desperado than a prosperous burgher. Even his funereal uniform invited few comments. Soon much of the staff, and corporate America at large, would be similarly costumed, as the era of the gray flannel suit began.

As a writer Chambers did not feel used up. But he was getting older, and the commute from Westminster was taking its toll. In mid-July 1948 Chambers advised Matthews he wished to resign his staff position as of January 1, 1949, and become a contracted freelancer, supplying essays and editorials to *Life* and occasional covers to *Time*. This would untether him from an office that held no further place for him. He had already begun to write at Westminster several days a week. In a long memo to Luce, dated July 31, Chambers elaborated on his discontentment, citing the enmity many on staff still felt toward him because of ideological differences.[21]

But there was more to Chambers's decision than unhappiness at his job. A spy scandal was brewing. On July 20, 1948, thirteen months after the New York grand jury was impaneled, it returned indictments against twelve members of the National Board of the Communist Party. All were charged under the Alien Registration Act of 1940—better known as the Smith Act—with having conspired to advocate the overthrow of the U.S. government, the conspiracy growing out of their Communist Party membership. The next day the *World-Telegram* reported that the grand jury had not acted on the most important testimony it had heard, from an anonymous witness. A "beautiful blond" ex-Communist had identified many Soviet agents who had been on

the government payroll. The witness was Elizabeth Bentley, the operative who had taken over Chambers's role as courier to the Washington underground. When her name was at last published, reporters and
photographers flocked to the room of the "Red Spy Queen" at the St.
George Hotel in Brooklyn.²²

Congress was after her too. The legislators had been in recess, campaigning for the November election. But President Truman, in a fiery
acceptance speech at the Democratic National Convention, had summoned them back to Washington for a special two-week session to pass
bills stalled during the regular term. House and Senate Republicans retaliated by convening new hearings on government subversion. A Senate subcommittee got to Bentley first. She testified on July 28. Two days
later a *New York Sun* headline declared an unnamed "Editor Supplies
Red Spy Link." "The New York editor," reported Edward Nellor, "was
in at the start of the Red underground in Washington" and later broke
with the Party. He "tried to persuade several other members to make the
break. But he was not successful, and later watched these individuals
climb to positions of power in the New Deal administration."

John Chamberlain was in Chambers's office when Chambers read the
*Sun* article and "turned sort of green around the gills."

"What are you worried about, Whit?" asked Chamberlain. "All you
have to do is go down to Washington and tell what you know."

Chambers cast a glum look in the direction of Tom Matthews's office.
"They don't like informers around here."²³

The next day, July 31, Bentley testified before HUAC. In her dowdy
hat and petal-shaped earrings, she was scarcely the "beautiful blonde" of
the tabloids. But her five-hour testimony was sensational. She said she
had been the courier to a wartime spy ring based in Washington. Her
contacts had been dispersed throughout the government, some in sensitive posts. The names she mentioned included alumni of Apparatus A.
The government had at last found a witness whose trail had crossed
Chambers's own.²⁴ After reading in the paper that Bentley had been
summoned to Washington, Chambers told his wife he expected to be
called too. If so, he would testify.

"What about the children?" asked Esther, fearful of the publicity.

"We must be grateful that we have brought them along so far in happiness and peace," Whittaker replied. It was the couple's first and only
discussion of the subject.²⁵

On August 1, 1948, HUAC's chief investigator, Robert Stripling, announced to a roomful of reporters that Bentley's testimony would soon be backed up. A subpoena had been issued to a new witness, Whittaker Chambers. *Time*'s congressional correspondent, Frank McNaughton, phoned New York to warn Chambers federal marshals were on their way. Chambers already knew this. Hearst reporters had been calling. He was at last to achieve his exemplary role—not as the new age's prophet but as its scourge.[26]

# 18

## *Pure Dynamite*

On Monday, August 2, during a coffee break with Luce, Chambers gloomily confided a subpoena was imminent. He offered to quit on the spot, obviating the plans he had painstakingly spelled out in his memo of July 31.

"Nonsense," Luce said. "Testifying is a simple patriotic duty." Chambers would remain at the magazine.[1]

When he returned to his office, the subpoena had not yet arrived, but a Hearst photographer and reporter were waiting. Chambers sent them both away. The subpoena was served at noon. The committee wanted no delays: Chambers was commanded to appear at a public hearing the next morning, August 3, at eleven. At the suggestion of a colleague Chambers quickly wrote out a brief statement to read aloud to the committee.[2]

Journalists began to call. Chambers told a *Herald Tribune* reporter he did not know Elizabeth Bentley but did know two of those she had accused, Charles Kramer and Victor Perlo. He himself had left the Party in 1937, when "I became convinced that it was evil and a threat to Western civilization."[3]

Monday evening, the final day of *Time*'s five-day production cycle, Chambers boarded his usual train at Penn Station but continued on past Baltimore to Washington. Before leaving, Chambers had spoken with Frank McNaughton, who was putting him up for the night. Chambers had worriedly mentioned Walter Krivitsky and the fate he had met in his hotel room before a scheduled HUAC appearance. McNaughton suggested Chambers jump into a taxi as soon as he reached Union Station and then head straight out to McNaughton's home, a ranch house in suburban Takoma Park, eight miles north of Capitol Hill, where the journalist, who was divorced, lived with his two young sons. Chambers followed this advice, reaching McNaughton's door at 11:30 P.M. He appeared "highly nervous," McNaughton recalled, "in fact somewhat unnerved."

McNaughton knew Chambers fairly well and was familiar with his "broad streak of paranoia." But he had not seen him like this. Chambers paced the living room floor, sucking on an underslung pipe, and kept glancing at the picture window that overlooked the street. He asked McNaughton to close the drapes and then lower the blinds on the other windows. Suddenly Chambers decided he must type the statement he had written. He sat down at McNaughton's typewriter and fumbled with the keys. McNaughton took over and typed out the statement.

He also filled Chambers in on HUAC.[4] McNaughton had been following the committee since its inception in 1938. HUAC's character had been formed in the image of its first chairman, Martin Dies, a flag- and arm-waving Texan, addicted to publicity, who had sat bored through the testimony of Walter Krivitsky but roused himself to denounce the New Deal's sinister cadre of "idealists, dreamers, politicians, professional 'do-gooders,' and just plain job-hunters." Under Dies and his successors, almost all of them southern reactionaries or anti–New Deal Republicans, HUAC's favorite targets seemed to be eastern-educated big-city liberals, who happened, much of the time, to be Jews.

HUAC's current chairman, New Jersey Republican J. Parnell Thomas, lacked Dies's engaging manner and country shrewdness. He had dragged HUAC to its lowest point, in October 1947, when he convened public hearings on "Communist infiltration of the motion-picture industry." These were climaxed by the antics of the "Hollywood Ten"—screenwriters John Howard Lawson, Dalton Trumbo, Ring Lardner, Jr., and others—who noisily defied the committee, making a mockery of the proceedings. All ten had been Communists or still were. But they gained the upper hand by goading Thomas ("Mr. Quisling," as one witness called him) into unseemly high-decibel exchanges. The witnesses, cited for contempt of Congress, went to jail, praised as martyrs to free speech. And HUAC stood tarnished in the eyes of many.[5]

In recent months the Republican-controlled committee had tangled repeatedly with President Truman. This did not sit well with McNaughton.

A Missourian who had been covering Truman since 1936, he was a "poker-playing, Bourbon-drinking friend" of the president, and the author of an admiring account of Truman's first years in the White House. Though on civil terms with the committee, he respected only one member, its youngest, Richard M. Nixon, a thirty-five-year-old freshman Republican from California. Unlike his grandstanding colleagues, Nixon, who had a law degree, stuck soberly to the business at hand, posing "shrewd" questions.[6]

Chambers was less skeptical than McNaughton about HUAC. True, he had been dismayed by the handling of his subpoena, the announcement made to the press before the witness was informed. It seemed to confirm the committee's reputation for "slipshod buffoonery." On the other hand, from his own limited observation over the years, HUAC had been accurate often enough in its choice of targets. As for the committee's history of labeling liberals Communists, to him it was no worse than portraying Stalin as a progressive liberal, as Chambers's *Time* adversaries tended to do.[7]

At 2:00 A.M. McNaughton suggested they go to bed. They had to be at HUAC's offices for a preliminary hearing at 10:00. He showed Chambers to the spare room. After five minutes Chambers reappeared and asked McNaughton to lock all the windows and doors. Alone, Chambers paced and smoked, lighting match after match. Soon he was back in the living room. He couldn't lie down. He must, McNaughton urged. Twenty minutes later Chambers reemerged, talking of Krivitsky and other dead comrades and "laboring under an overwhelming fear."

McNaughton tried to calm him down. "Look, Whit, you're not going to be worth a damn tomorrow, if you can last that long. I've got a 45-caliber revolver here in this desk. It isn't loaded, but to relieve your mind, I'm going to load it and put it right here on the desk. I know how to use it. I can have the police here in less than five minutes. I'm going to sit here at this desk in the front room, and I'll stay awake. You go to bed and get some rest of some kind. Nobody is coming in here, I guarantee you that. Were you followed on the way out here?"

"I don't think so, but I can't be sure," Chambers said.

"I don't think you were," McNaughton replied, "or they'd have tried to kill you before you ever got in the house. Now go to bed."

At five-fifteen, when Chambers reappeared, McNaughton was wide-awake. He fixed breakfast, "bacon and eggs and plenty of coffee." As they ate, Chambers spoke of his early life, "about 'enemies' in Time Inc., about his fears, and his pervading sense of defeat for the U.S. and all its policies and freedoms. He also asked that I stay right with him at the hearings."[8]

McNaughton and Chambers took a cab to Washington shortly before 9:00 A.M. The morning was cloudy and cool. By afternoon the temperature had reached a muggy eighty-six. At 9:15 they mounted the angled flights of the Old House Office Building (now the Cannon Building), a few hundred paces south of the Capitol dome. The press was already gathering. The special session of Congress, convened on July 23, had begun as a curiosity, a small ripple in the sluggish calm that is normally Washington in August. Then Elizabeth Bentley had testified, and a huge story seemed to be taking shape, crowding out all the other business in the capital.[9]

McNaughton steered Chambers down a long marble corridor, past the clump of waiting reporters, who sprang up ("Here comes Chambers")[10] and then fell back, disappointed, as escort and witness marched into HUAC's suite, room 226. Inside, congressmen and staff milled about in preparation for a secret "executive" session, an unscripted audition at which the committee would size Chambers up before putting him on public display.

McNaughton led Chambers to an inner office, adjoining HUAC's hearing room, where the committee's main interrogator, chief investigator Robert Stripling, sat at a large desk. "Strip," as he liked to be called, had been with the committee for the whole of its ten-year history save for a period of military service in 1945–1946, arranged, Stripling was convinced, by his political enemies. This may well have been the case. With Dies's retirement, Stripling, a druggist's son from St. Augustine, Texas, had used his appointed post to become HUAC's dominant figure, a "unique combination of master of ceremonies, chief counsel, main interrogator, and front-running guide through the labyrinths of subversive organizations."

He was superbly fitted for his investigatory role. He had the hallmark attributes of patience and zeal and also a punishing memory. In hearings he seldom consulted files as he fired questions "from the hip" in his East Texas drawl, pursing his thin lips disgustedly while the witness squirmed. Like his mentor Martin Dies, whose district he came from, Stripling was "always alert for the striking and sensational," observed *The New York Times,* and he excelled at getting coverage for his investigations.[11]

At age thirty-eight, Stripling was slightly stooped, with pomaded hair and the sepulchral pallor of one who spent long hours buried in files. The forty pounds he had shed during his involuntary army stint had given him a hollow-eyed, loose-skinned look. But his blue-eyed stare, trained on the witness, was hard. Stripling had not forgotten Chambers's snub in March and had half expected the witness to dodge the August 2 subpoena. Even now he wondered if Chambers secretly planned to subvert the proceedings. The witness's *Time* connection did not bode well. The magazine "never had one kind word to say about anything we had done," Stripling later said.

McNaughton indicated Chambers had brought along a statement. It had better be "pertinent," Stripling warned. Chambers handed over his three pages. Stripling skimmed them and then looked at the witness in surprise. "You want to testify to *this*?" Chambers said he did. Stripling gave the statement to a secretary for copying.[12]

Congressmen, staff, and the witness all adjourned to the sanctum of HUAC's spartan hearing room for a private interview. Stripling swore in the witness, who solemnly identified himself as "David Whittaker Chambers," the baptismal name he had chosen in 1940.* Chambers asked if he could read aloud his statement. It was still being copied, Stripling explained. He could read it later.

Meanwhile there were questions to be asked and answered. The chief investigator plunged directly to the crux of the inquiry. Was Chambers "aware at any time while you were a member of the Communist Party of a so-called espionage ring that was being set up or functioning in Washington?"

"No, I was not." It was a lie, and it was to prove costly. For the moment he tried to mitigate it, saying he had of course known his underground unit "could always be diverted" to espionage and at some point "almost certainly would be."

Did the witness "know whether or not the apparatus was set up with that purpose [espionage] in mind?"

"I would say that was certainly one of the purposes in mind and always is."

---

* All quoted testimony from this preliminary hearing comes from "Testimony of David Whittaker Chambers," August 3, 1948, transcript of the executive session released by the U.S. House Committee on Internal Security in 1974 but never printed. It appears here for the first time.

There was more fencing when Stripling asked, "Who set this apparatus up?"

"We are now talking about a hypothetical apparatus?" Chambers asked in turn.

"Who was the head of that apparatus back in Washington?" cut in John Rankin, a Mississippi Democrat.

"I am trying to establish what apparatus we are talking about," said Chambers. He had come prepared to discuss only one, the Ware Group, "the specific organization I was connected with." Spying had not topped its original agenda.

At Stripling's prompting, Chambers summarized the unit's origins and evolution under the nurturing watch of Harold Ware, whose ambition had been to plant Communists "in key positions" where they could "sway policy, make changes in personnel, or rather, influence personnel in the Government and also, if they deem[ed] fit, [undertake] espionage."

Stripling pounced. So the unit *did* have "the purpose of being available for espionage if necessary."

Not at "the very beginning of this apparatus."

Well, then, what *had* its function been?

Chambers replied with a vaporous lecture on the "theory of underground apparatuses."

His reticence did not alarm his interrogators. "Friendly witnesses" often went to the opposite extreme. Bentley had reeled off thirty-two names, promiscuously lumping together her underground contacts with names she had picked up in casual conversation. On the basis of hearsay alone, she had branded Lauchlin Currie a Communist although she had never met the man, a close aide to FDR, and knew almost nothing about him. Even Congressman Rankin, the antithesis of a civil libertarian, had objected to this smearing of Currie "by remote control."[13]

Against this, Chambers seemed a paragon of restraint. When asked at one point if the New Dealer Aubrey Williams was a Communist, Chambers said he had "no real knowledge" of the man.

But wasn't Williams "friendly with this [the Ware] organization"?

"That is not true," said Chambers. He was simply "regarded as a friend by the Communists."

Chambers did not balk, however, at identifying those he was sure of. Without hesitation, he recited the entire roster of the "top committee" of government Communists organized by Harold Ware. "The head of the committee was Nathan Witt, an attorney with the National Labor Relations Board. Also in that leading group was [*sic*] John Abt, Lee Pressman, Victor Perlo, Alger Hiss, his brother Donald, and Charles Kramer, whose original name was Krevitsky [*sic*], I believe. Also in that group was Henry Collins."

Stripling then brought up another name. "Did you know Harry Dexter White?"

"Yes."

"Was he a member of this group?"

"No."

"Was he a Communist?"

Chambers answered cautiously. "I can't say that I know that he was."

"Was he considered a friend of the Communists?"

Yes, but "not by the members of the group." Only by J. Peters.

"But not to your personal knowledge?" asked Stripling.

"I cannot say he was a Communist," Chambers repeated. "If he was not a Communist, it was a mistake on both sides."

Bentley had identified White, a top Treasury official under both Roosevelt and Truman, as a friend of the underground who had staffed his department with Communists. White had vehemently denied the charge. Chambers had just backed it up. This was the sort of corroboration the committee was after.

Democrat John Wood of Georgia, a once and future HUAC chairman, spoke up. The testimony seemed "relevant," and the witness "conservative and reliable." Wood suggested they open up the session to the press. John McDowell, Republican of Pennsylvania, agreed.

Stripling had another suggestion. A week before, when the special session of Congress was first convened, he had reserved the largest auditorium on Capitol Hill, the Ways and Means Committee hearing room, in the event an appropriate witness emerged from this latest inquiry. Chambers, Stripling believed, was that witness.

There was one dissenting voice. "I move we stay here," said Rankin, wary of Chambers's affiliation with *Time*. Apart from its heretical views on HUAC, the magazine was critical of Jim Crow laws. This was anathema to the sixty-year-old Rankin, as vociferous a racist (and anti-Semite) as could be found in Congress in 1948. The decision was left to Karl Mundt, a South Dakota Republican and HUAC's acting chairman while

Parnell Thomas was at home, bedridden with a bleeding stomach ulcer.[14] Mundt made up his mind quickly. "We will meet in fifteen minutes in the Ways and Means Committee Room."

As usual Stripling had prevailed. And as usual he knew something the others did not. He alone had read Chambers's statement, and it was "pure dynamite."[15]

There was a "buzzing surge" as the committee spilled into the corridor and, trailed by reporters, swept onto the sidewalk and crossed the narrow lane of New Jersey Avenue to the pillared New Office (now the Longworth) Building. Frank McNaughton, waiting outside the HUAC office, fell in beside Chambers. As they walked, Chambers picked out a familiar face in the staring crowd. It belonged to a Communist he had known slightly in the 1930s. Chambers asked McNaughton "to sit between him and that person in the hearing room."

Within minutes the Ways and Means hearing room had filled up as curious legislators, staff, and visitors flocked from all over the Hill. "A great public circus was being rigged, of which I was clearly to be the speaking center," Chambers later recalled.[16]

The ringmaster, portly Karl Mundt, sat flanked by his colleagues at a large curved dais fitted with microphones. Chambers took his place at the witness table amid a starburst of flashbulbs and the blaze of klieg lights. He had had at most three hours' sleep. The next morning's photographs showed a man who looked newly emerged from the sinister depths of the underground, his suit wrinkled, his expression haunted, his eyes averted from the camera as if in guilty flight.

He was sworn in by Mundt, a former elocution teacher who spoke in rounded tones. Then Stripling guided Chambers through preliminary questions—name, date of birth, present occupation. The public-address system was down, and Chambers's voice, trapped in his throat, was inaudible to the journalists straining at their tables. Mundt admonished him twice to speak up. "I will speak as loud as I can," Chambers promised.[17]

His statement was back in his hands. He asked if he could read it. Stripling assured Mundt it was all right: "He has shown it to me." Mundt bade Chambers proceed.

Many auditors on this day, including seasoned journalists, came away with the impression that Chambers's prepared remarks were simple, stark, unembellished. This was true enough of his delivery. His speaking

voice was flat, almost affectless, and he seemed to read "in a rather detached way, as if he had an unpleasant chore to do."[18]

But the words themselves had the heightened tone of Chambers's
*Time* jeremiads. He began by saying the allegations he was about to make
were not new. In 1939—"almost exactly" nine years ago to the day—he
had tried to warn his government of the internal danger it faced from a
Communist conspiracy, a danger magnified and made more immediate
by the Nazi-Soviet Pact. In going to the authorities, Chambers had performed "a simple act of war, like the shooting of an armed enemy in
combat. At that moment in history, I was one of the few men on this
side of the battle who could perform this service."

He then described his own history.

As a young man, Chambers said, he had grown "convinced that the
society in which we live, western civilization, had reached a crisis, of
which the First World War was the military expression, and that it was
doomed to collapse or revert to barbarism." In his despair he had groped
for answers, finding in Marx "the explanation" of the crisis and in Lenin
"the answer to the question, What to do?" But thirteen years in the
Communist Party had taught him that the utopian dream was in reality
a "form of totalitarianism" whose "triumph means slavery to men wherever they fall under its sway, and spiritual night to the human mind and
soul." Finally he had quit the movement, but with a sense of foreboding,
for "so strong is the hold which the insidious evil of communism secures
on its disciples, that I could say to someone [Esther] at the time: 'I know
that I am leaving the winning side for the losing side.' " Still, it was "better to die on the losing side than to live under communism." For a year
he had lived "in hiding, sleeping by day and watching through the night
with gun or revolver within easy reach," afraid the Communists might
try to kill him. "That was what underground communism could do to
one man in the peaceful United States in the year 1938."

His audience primed, Chambers shifted to an account of the Ware
Group, "an underground organization of the United States Communist
Party" from whose ranks "certain members of Miss Bentley's organiza-
tion were apparently recruited." It had four outstanding members.
Nathan Witt initially headed the cell. He was succeeded by John Abt.
"Lee Pressman was also a member of this group, as was Alger Hiss, who,
as a member of the State Department, later organized the conferences at
Dumbarton Oaks, San Francisco, and the United States side of the Yalta
Conference."

Chambers proceeded to reinforce the link with Bentley but at the same time carefully emphasized the difference between his unit and hers.

The purpose of this group at that time was not primarily espionage. Its original purpose was the Communist infiltration of the American government. But espionage was certainly one of its eventual objectives. Let no one be surprised at this statement. Disloyalty is a matter of principle with every member of the Communist Party. The Communist Party exists for the specific purpose of overthrowing the Government, at the opportune time, by any and all means; and each of its members, by the fact that he is a member, is dedicated to this purpose.

The witness concluded on a confessional note. "It is ten years since I broke away from the Communist Party. During that decade I have sought to live an industrious and God-fearing life. At the same time I have fought communism constantly by act and written word. I am proud to appear before this committee."

There was a pause as his voice broke. Then he gathered himself.[19]

The publicity inseparable from such testimony has darkened, and will no doubt continue to darken, my effort to integrate myself into the community of free men. But that is a small price to pay if my testimony helps to make Americans recognize at last that they are at grips with a secret, sinister, and enormously powerful force whose tireless purpose is their enslavement.

At the same time I should like, thus publicly, to call upon all ex-Communists who have not yet declared themselves, and all men within the Communist Party whose better instincts have not yet been corrupted and crushed by it, to aid in this struggle while there is still time to do so.

When he finished, reporters dashed for the corridor—and the telephones.[20]

Questions followed. Stripling patiently extracted all the names of the Ware Group, a total of eight. To the four he had already mentioned, Chambers added Henry Collins, Charles Kramer, Victor Perlo, and Alger Hiss's brother, Donald.

The discussion then ranged over other topics. Chambers gave a capsule review of the Lovestone purge that had stamped out the last vestige of democratic debate within the Party and caused his own brief estrangement in 1929. He gave a bare-bones account of J. Peters's passport operation. He recounted his futile attempts to break some of his accomplices away from the underground after his defection in 1938.

As the session neared its close, Representative Richard Nixon, virtually silent all morning—in the closed session and then in this public one—asked Chambers about the meeting with Adolf Berle and its negligible results. How explicit had Chambers been?

"I named specific names."

Nixon read off the list, one by one. Had Chambers named each?

He could recall omitting only one, Harry Dexter White, "because at that time I thought that I had broken Mr. White away, and it was about four years later that I first told the FBI about Mr. White."

Nixon's point was not lost. The Roosevelt administration had allowed a Communist conspiracy to flourish within its gates at a time "when we could not say by any stretch of the imagination that the Russians were our allies." Next morning's headline in the conservative *Chicago Tribune* read, NEW DEAL COVERUP TOLD.[21]

The most gripping moment of Chambers's testimony came when he described his attempt to break Alger Hiss, a good friend, from the underground in 1938, months after his own defection. Speaking in "almost conversational tones,"[22] Chambers related how he had gone to Hiss's Georgetown home. Hiss was not in, but his wife, Priscilla, "also a Communist," admitted Chambers to the house. When he excused himself momentarily to use the toilet, she had hurried to the telephone. Fearing she was about to contact the underground, Chambers had followed her, and she quickly hung up. When her husband returned, the three dined together, Chambers pleading with Alger Hiss to quit the apparatus. The two debated, wrenchingly. Hiss "absolutely refused to break" and "cried when we separated," Chambers told the committee.

"He cried?" repeated McDowell, who knew Hiss slightly.

"Yes, he did," Chambers replied. "I was very fond of Mr. Hiss."

Karl Mundt, a member of the China Lobby—the loosely organized group bent on propping up the crumbling regime of Chiang Kai-shek—pursued the Hiss connection. "I have had some occasion to check the activities of Alger Hiss while he was in the State Department. There is reason to believe that he organized within that department one of the Communist cells which endeavored to influence our Chinese policy and bring about the condemnation of Chiang Kai-shek." Chambers's allegations matched what Mundt had heard, and Mundt was "quite happy to have it confirmed."

The hearing lasted an hour and a quarter. When it ended, Chambers braced himself for interrogation from the many journalists on hand. But only one approached, with one question. He asked Chambers to spell a German word he had used, *Zersotzuffusteil,* the Communist term for a sabotage unit.[23] The others hurried off to file their stories.

At Chambers's request Frank McNaughton walked directly behind him as they left the hearing room, shielding the witness's back. The two then climbed into a cab, looped the city, and ended up at the National Gallery, where they spent the afternoon. Chambers, his nerves still "spun tight," stayed overnight in Washington, unable to face the trip home to Westminster.[24]

The next day he rode the train to Baltimore. Esther met him at Penn Station. Neighbors had heard radio reports or read news accounts and had been stopping by to give assurances and support. Only Stanley Pennington had seemed distraught. Upon learning of his boss's HUAC testimony, the "sharecropper" abruptly disappeared from the farm. But when Chambers and Esther pulled into the dirt driveway, Pennington was there to greet them. He had "done his thinking" and had concluded that Chambers had shown courage.[25]

After a day on the farm Chambers returned to Manhattan and Time Inc. His job, intolerable only a week before, now seemed a refuge. He immersed himself in background reading for his last *Life* assignment, a centenary essay on the year 1848, the year of European revolution and of *The Communist Manifesto.*[26]

By this time many of the accused had begun to respond. John Abt, general counsel to Henry Wallace's Progressive party, scoffed at Chambers's allegations—"an old and particularly malodorous red herring" that HUAC was trying "to warm up and serve as a substitute for price controls, public housing and civil rights legislation." To Lee Pressman, also attached to the Wallace campaign (and principal author of its pro-Soviet platform), the charges were the "stale and lurid mouthings of a Republican exhibitionist who has been bought by Henry Luce and claims to have met me twelve [*sic*] years ago."

The rhetoric was forceful but vacant; both men conspicuously ignored the substance of the testimony, as they also did on August 20, when they (along with Nathan Witt) appeared before HUAC and refused to answer its questions, citing the constitutional privilege against self-incrimination. Henry Collins, Victor Perlo, and Charles Kramer also pleaded the Fifth Amendment.[27]

But two of the accused reacted differently. Shortly after Chambers left the stand, Alger and Donald Hiss both issued statements. "I flatly deny every statement made by Mr. Chambers with respect to me," said Donald Hiss, an attorney at the prestigious Washington law firm of Covington and Burling. "I am not and never have been a member of the Communist Party or of any formal or informal organizations affiliated with or fronting in any manner whatsoever for the Communist Party."[28]

Alger Hiss, the president of the Carnegie Endowment for International Peace, was equally forthright. "I don't know Chambers," he told reporters who phoned his New York office. "So far as I know I never laid eyes on him. There is no basis for his statements about me."

That afternoon, against the advice of friends—who told him to ignore Chambers's allegations—Hiss repeated this denial in a telegram to Robert Stripling:

> I do not know Mr. Chambers and insofar as I am aware have never laid eyes on him. There is no basis for the statements made about me to your committee. I would appreciate it if you would make this telegram a part of your committee's record, and I would further appreciate the opportunity to appear before your committee to make these statements formally and under oath. I shall be in Washington on Thursday [August 5] and hope that will be a convenient time from the committee's point of view for me to appear.[29]

A session was hastily arranged in the House Caucus Room—in the Old House Building—a shade smaller than the Ways and Means hearing room but equally formidable, with its high coffered ceiling and tall south-facing windows. The capacity audience included a contingent of Alger Hiss's many acquaintances, the fruit of his fourteen years of government service. A Herblock cartoon published that morning in *The Washington Post* depicted an innocent man cornered by a tiger labeled "Smear Statements."[30] The witness was accompanied by his longtime friend William Marbury, a distinguished attorney and member of the five-man Harvard Corporation. Marbury, formerly a War Department official, had offered his legal services after Hiss's first choice, former Undersecretary of State Dean

Acheson, a senior partner at Donald Hiss's firm, declined to appear. (Acheson had helped prepare Hiss's opening remarks, however.) Another attorney, Joseph Johnston, had come up from Alabama for the hearing.

Slim, erect, well tailored, Hiss read his prepared statement "slowly and with emphasis," in the tones of one used to addressing large, attentive audiences. He bluntly met and answered Chambers's allegations. "I am not and never have been a member of the Communist Party. I do not and never have adhered to the tenets of the Communist Party. I am not and never have been a member of any Communist-front organization. I have never followed the Communist Party line, directly or indirectly. To the best of my knowledge, none of my friends is a Communist."[31]

When the witness had finished, Stripling asked him to review his employment history. It was exemplary. First there had been a clerkship under Supreme Court Justice Oliver Wendell Holmes, followed by nearly three years with old-line law firms in Boston and New York. In May 1933, during the first Hundred Days of the New Deal, Hiss had joined the elite corps brought to Washington to serve under Jerome Frank in the AAA. While on its staff, he had been detailed to the Nye Committee, formed to investigate arms manufacturers and their part in leading the nation into World War I. Then came a year in the solicitor general's office, where Hiss had supervised the government's defense, before the Supreme Court, of the AAA as a constitutionally valid agency. He joined the State Department in 1936 and remained there a decade, rising to head the Office of Special Political Affairs—the UN desk—a senior position one rank below assistant secretary. (Hiss's successor, Dean Rusk, had been given the title of assistant secretary shortly after his appointment in 1947.)

The high point of Hiss's career had come in 1945, when as secretary-general of the United Nations Conference on International Organization (UNCIO) he presided over the intricate negotiations, involving delegates from fifty nations, that had resulted in the ratification and signing of the UN Charter. Harry Luce, one of many dazzled by Hiss's performance at San Francisco, had ordered John Osborne to praise it in the pages of *Time.* "In a class by himself was young, handsome Alger Hiss," Osborne had written, "U.S. State Department career man functioning as international secretary general. Relaxed and alert amid innumerable annoyances, Hiss was master of the incredibly complicated conference machinery." His picture ran alongside those of UN advisers Nelson Rockefeller and Senator Tom Connally.

In December 1946 Hiss had resigned from the government to succeed
Nicholas Murray Butler, Columbia University president and onetime
Republican presidential hopeful, as head of the Carnegie Endowment,
an organization closely tied to the UN. Also, though Hiss did not mention it, only days before Chambers testified Secretary of State George
Marshall had named Hiss vice-chairman of the National Citizens Committee for United Nations Day.[32]

It was an impressive, even intimidating résumé—especially the names
Hiss invoked as sponsors. Holmes was a legend. Stanley Reed, FDR's
solicitor general, was a sitting Supreme Court justice. Hiss's first boss in
the State Department, Francis Sayre, was the son-in-law of Woodrow
Wilson and one of the world's most honored diplomats. Jerome Frank
had become a distinguished circuit court judge. At State, Hiss's main
booster had been Edward R. Stettinius, the last secretary of state appointed by FDR.

But of all Hiss's sponsors, the most remarkable, given the partisan climate of the hearings, was John Foster Dulles, the Carnegie Endowment's board chairman and the presumptive secretary of state under
Republican presidential nominee Thomas Dewey, who was leading Truman by a wide margin in polls. The irony of the Dulles-Hiss connection
was not lost on HUAC Democrat Edward Hébert, a former newspaperman from New Orleans who had made his name by attacking in print
the corruptions of Huey Long. Hébert asked Hiss if Dulles had anything
to do with his appointment to the endowment. There were titters when
Hiss replied, "He urged me to take my present position."

Before long a touch of the ludicrous had crept into the hearing. The
witness—so composed, so credentialed, so accommodating—scarcely
resembled the dedicated revolutionary described by Chambers on August 3. The idea of Hiss weeping as he parted with the confessed Communist Chambers seemed an improbable touch in a lurid soap opera.
"Well, he has a vivid imagination anyway," Hiss had dryly remarked to a
reporter upon being told of Chambers's anecdote. "Perhaps he should
be writing mystery stories instead of editing."

Stripling showed Hiss a photograph of Chambers taken at the August
3 hearing. Did the man look familiar? Hiss studied the photo. "If this is
a picture of Mr. Chambers, he is not particularly unusual looking. He
looks like a lot of people. I might even mistake him for the chairman of
this committee"—the moon-faced Mundt, grinning weakly through the

cascading laughter. "I didn't mean to be facetious," Hiss quickly added. "I would like to see him [Chambers] and then I think I would be better able to tell whether I had ever seen him" before.[33]

There was another embarrassment for Mundt when he questioned Hiss about his State Department record. He had already accused Hiss of scheming to bring about the downfall of Chiang Kai-shek. Now Mundt tried to link Hiss, a delegate at Yalta, with the accord that had given the Soviets a voting advantage in the UN General Assembly. "I had nothing to do with the decision," said Hiss. "I opposed [the extra votes]."

"You opposed them?" repeated an astonished Mundt.

It was true. On the day the UN had come up for discussion at Yalta, Hiss had circulated a memorandum titled "Arguments Against the Inclusion of the Soviet Republics Among the Initial Members."[34]

The hearing had reached its denouement. "Do you feel you have had a free and fair and proper hearing this morning?" asked McDowell of Hiss.

The witness gave "the quick sweeping nod and smile" that were to become familiar in the months ahead. He had been superbly controlled throughout. At last he let his anger show. "I am not happy that I didn't have a chance to meet with the committee privately before there was such a great public press display of what I consider completely unfounded charges against me. Denials do not always catch up with charges."

A sheepish McDowell apologized for the damage done to someone whom "many Americans, including members of this committee, hold in high repute."

After Mundt adjourned the hearing, John Rankin stepped down from the podium and led a small procession over to the witness table to shake Hiss's hand. It had been a performance unlike any other in the committee's ten-year history.

Hiss "absolutely took over that hearing," Stripling later said, "took it over immediately."[35]

Meanwhile, at a press conference that morning, President Truman expressed his annoyance that the special session of Congress was being hijacked by partisan Red hunters. A reporter asked if the president considered the issue a "red herring," in John Abt's phrase.

It certainly was, the president snapped. Allegations of communism were old news, which the FBI had investigated and found groundless. A grand jury presented with all the evidence had not indicted a single government employee. And of the roughly forty names dragged out in the new House and Senate hearings, only two still could be found on the federal payroll. All the others had left the government. The Eightieth Congress, said Truman, should be passing legislation, not "slandering a lot of people that don't deserve it."

But others guessed the story could not be brushed aside so easily. Sam Rayburn, the venerable Texas Democrat, spoke off the record to Frank McNaughton. "There is political dynamite in this Communist investigation," Rayburn said. "Don't doubt that."[36]

The committee, huddling at 3:00 P.M. behind closed doors, was "in a virtual state of shock."

"We've been had," Mundt groaned. "We're ruined."

Their only option, said Eddie Hébert, was to wash their hands of the "whole mess" and foist it on the Justice Department.

All the members agreed the committee must find a "collateral issue" to distract the public from this latest fiasco.

A belligerent Mundt emerged from the conference to tell reporters two unnamed witnesses were waiting in the wings; their testimony would break "the whole spy case" open. It was a shopworn ploy—a favorite of HUAC's—but also a dependable one. Next morning conservative dailies, including the *New York Herald Tribune* and *Chicago Tribune,* played up Mundt's promise of "mystery witnesses," neutralizing Hiss's testimony and Truman's press conference.[37]

But on Capitol Hill feeling surged against the committee. The "Red probers" had finally overstepped their bounds. Even HUAC's faithful supporters were disgusted. "This case is going to kill the committee unless you can prove Chambers's story," warned Mary Spargo of *The Washington Post,* a former HUAC staffer turned committee flack. Edwin Lahey of the *Chicago Daily News,* normally sympathetic to HUAC, accosted Richard Nixon and, "shaking with anger," pronounced HUAC "guilty of calumny" for having let Chambers smear Hiss.

House Republicans were equally dubious. "I don't want to prejudge the case," Christian Herter of Massachusetts, a senior House member, told Nixon, "but I'm afraid the committee has been taken in by Chambers." As chairman of the House's Foreign Affairs Committee Herter had numerous contacts in the State Department. All vouched for Hiss's reputation and loyalty.

In its editorial the next morning *The Washington Post* likened Hiss to "an innocent pedestrian, spattered with mud by a passing vehicle."[38]

After a celebratory lunch with friends, Alger Hiss sent a letter to John Foster Dulles, enclosing a copy of the statement he had read to such great effect at the hearing. Dulles, Hiss hoped, would "feel moved" to circulate copies to the twenty-seven other members of the Carnegie board (who included General Dwight Eisenhower and David Rockefeller). A transcript of his testimony would follow as soon as a copy became available. "Your counsel and calm judgment have been invaluable to me," Hiss wrote Dulles, "and I want you to know how deeply I appreciate them." The ordeal behind him, Hiss was experiencing "a very definite sense of relief." He had been dogged for months by "ugly rumors." It was now "clear that they all stem from the same single source."[39]

The "single source" was holed up in the Time-Life Building, reading up for his 1848 essay, when a call came from Robert Stripling's second-in-command, Louis Russell, a former FBI man.

"Are you sure you are right about Alger Hiss?" Russell asked.

"Of course."

But Hiss had "testified just now that he does not know you and never set eyes on you." Could it be a case of mistaken identity? No. Chambers volunteered to go to Washington to testify again. It would not be necessary, said Russell. The committee was coming up to New York that weekend to question him further.

When the calls came from journalists, Chambers was ready with a terse statement. "Mr. Alger Hiss has seen fit to deny under oath the sworn testimony which I gave before the House Committee on Un-American Activities. I have no change to make in my testimony concerning him."[40]

The Hiss case had begun.

# 19

# "I Can Make That Fellow President"

During the August 5 postmortem, when his HUAC colleagues had all wanted to drop the matter, Richard Nixon alone had held out for pursuing it, arguing forcefully that a retreat would only compound the committee's embarrassment. The freshman volunteered to take over the inquiry himself in an attempt to salvage HUAC's honor. Mundt was skeptical. But Stripling sided with Nixon. He told the congressmen he was "vaguely dissatisfied" with some of Hiss's testimony. He also pointed out that the risk of going forward was smaller than it seemed. The committee was tied to neither witness and so could loftily conduct an impartial search for the truth. Reluctantly Mundt acceded to the plan and appointed a subcommittee with Nixon as chairman and Hébert and McDowell added as ballast.[1]

In pushing for the extended inquiry, Nixon and Stripling had withheld something from their colleagues. Both men were confident Hiss, not Chambers, had lied. While many in Washington had professed astonishment at Chambers's charges, those plugged into the busy anti-Communist circuit knew of rumors about Hiss dating back to the early 1930s, when he had been a leader of Jerome Frank's reform group at the AAA.[2]

True, Hiss had terminated his AAA associations by the time he went over to State in 1936. But he remained identified with the New Deal's left wing. And his rather abrupt resignation from State, in late 1946, had come amid speculation he had been forced out. "More than one Congressman, whenever the subject of leftist activity in the State Department was mentioned, pulled out a list of subjects that was invariably headed by Mr. Hiss," *The Christian Science Monitor* had reported at the time. The whispers had trailed Hiss to the Carnegie Endowment. Within weeks of the appointment, John Foster Dulles was fending off complaints from the China Lobby. All this was a matter of record. In fact Hiss himself had freely told HUAC of FBI interrogations he had sat for in 1946 and 1947.[3]

But Nixon and Stripling had further information. Stripling had read Ray Murphy's memo. Hiss was named in it. Separately Murphy had tipped off Stripling some years back that the Communist Hiss was "running the State Department." Still earlier Stripling had been told about the Ware Group by J. B. Matthews, Martin Dies's first investigator.[4]

Richard Nixon also knew a good deal about Hiss, though he was to deny it for the rest of his political career. In his memoir *Six Crises,* Nixon wrote that Chambers's testimony was "the first time I had ever heard of either Alger or Donald Hiss." This was not true. Nixon had known about him for more than a year. His primary source was another Ray Murphy confidant, Rev. John Cronin. Nixon had met the cleric in February 1947, within weeks of his own arrival in Washington, and had read a copy of Cronin's report "The Problem of American Communism in 1945," written for church officials. The report identified Hiss as "the most influential communist" in the State Department. Cronin cited "an affidavit by an editor of a nationally known general magazine"—probably Ray Murphy's memo, though possibly one or another of Chambers's FBI statements. Cronin had access to those as well. Ever alert for potential allies in the Catholic Church, the bureau often leaked files to him. Soon Nixon too was receiving documents straight from the bureau, courtesy of J. Edgar Hoover, an enemy of President Truman's eager for an ally on HUAC.[5]

Nixon, then, knew who Hiss was and knew of the long history of allegations. But he had no proof the man was a Communist. Not even Hoover had turned up a scrap of hard evidence, despite a two-year investigation that included wiretapping, surreptitious study of Hiss's desk calendar, and detailed reports on his comings and goings at home and in the office.[6]

Hiss had also cleared the delicate sensors of other aggressive anti-Communists—John Foster Dulles, for one. Disturbed by the Communist rumors, Dulles had asked a top security officer at State, John

Peurifoy, to examine Hiss's dossier. Peurifoy reported "no evidence of any kind which cast any doubt" on Hiss's loyalty. In fact, said Peurifoy, Hiss had been regarded at State "as rather to the 'right' and [as] more conservative than many in the Department." Hiss was also a vocal supporter of the Marshall Plan, to Dulles's mind an unimpeachable anti-Communist credential.[7]

In sum, there was a history of rumors countered by a history of rebuttals. Yet Nixon went forward confidently. Why? For one thing, he stood to lose little if proved wrong. As a freshman congressman, even one on the rise, he had no reputation to protect. He could afford to be zealous—and mistaken—in a cause his party had embraced. In addition, Nixon had observed Hiss closely on the witness stand. So had Stripling. Both had been listening for false notes. They had heard many. Take Hiss's ringing assertion that he had not known Chambers: "So far as I know I never laid eyes on him." It sounded like a straightforward denial. Yet when Stripling had followed up, asking Hiss if he had ever *seen* Chambers, Hiss had dodged the question, saying, "The *name* means absolutely nothing to me." This left open the possibility that Hiss had known Chambers under a different name—a Communist alias perhaps. Then there was Hiss's intent study of Chambers's photo. To Nixon it had seemed phony, an act. Everyone remembered Hiss's joke about Chambers's facial resemblance to Mundt. But when the laughter died down, Hiss had carefully said, "I would not want to take an oath that I have never seen that man." Once again Hiss had avoided making a flat denial. His testimony throughout had been evasive and legalistic, as though he were carefully laying a defense against some future charge of perjury. He had been "mouthy."[8]

At an early point in the proceedings Nixon had subtly put Hiss to a test. The witness, reciting his résumé, had said some government officials had enticed him out of private practice and to Washington in the early months of the New Deal.

Exactly which officials? Nixon had asked.

Hiss had objected: "There are so many witnesses who use names rather loosely before your committee, and I would rather limit myself."

A rough exchange ensued. "You indicated," said Nixon, "that several government officials requested you to come here [in 1933] and you have issued a categorical denial to certain statements that were made by Mr. Chambers concerning people that you were associated with in Government. I think it would make your case much stronger if you would indicate what Government officials."

Hiss protested. "Mr. Nixon, regardless of whether it strengthens my case or not, I would prefer, unless you insist, not to mention any names in my testimony that I don't feel are absolutely necessary. If you insist on a direct answer to your question, I will comply."

"I would like to have a direct answer," said the congressman.

Hiss at last supplied one name. "Another official of the Government of the United States who strongly urged me to come to Washington . . . was Justice Felix Frankfurter."[9]

Why was Hiss so reluctant to name Frankfurter? For fear, he implied, of sullying the justice's reputation. Why, then, had he blithely run through a long list of eminent sponsors, including Frankfurter's Supreme Court colleague Stanley Reed? Weren't they too in danger of being smeared? But then Frankfurter's reputation differed from the others'. As a Jew, Harvard intellectual, champion of Sacco and Vanzetti, and "socialistic" Svengali to FDR, Frankfurter was warmly hated by the right, attacked many times over the years, most bitterly in 1939, when FDR had nominated him to the Court. During Frankfurter's bruising confirmation hearing, Hiss had been accused of being one of the nominee's obedient followers—"linked frankfurters . . . know[n] as the 'happy hot dogs,' " whose "tails wave madly when they hear the word 'Moscow.' " It was not Frankfurter whom Hiss was looking to protect. It was himself. To Stripling, watching the byplay between Nixon and Hiss, it was clear Nixon had been "angling for Frankfurter's name."[10]

Stripling was right—or half right. Nixon *had* been after Frankfurter's name. This meant he was thoroughly acquainted with Hiss's career—or, more likely, had seen the FBI's interrogation report of 1946, which recorded Hiss as saying two men were responsible for bringing him to Washington. One was Frankfurter. The other was Lee Pressman, widely known to be a Communist. In his questioning Nixon had pointedly reminded Hiss of statements "made by Mr. Chambers concerning people that you were associated with in Government." Those words did not apply to Frankfurter. Chambers had not mentioned the jurist at all. But he *had* mentioned Pressman, the more sensational name. Nixon had not forced Pressman's name out of Hiss. He had not needed to. The struggle to elicit Frankfurter's name was proof enough that Hiss was "following the practice of testifying openly on those matters which he felt the

Committee should know about, and not testifying on those matters which he did not want the Committee to know about."[11]

It was one thing to suspect Hiss was lying. It was quite another to prove he was, or had been, an underground Communist. Hiss had been outwitting Red hunters for years. But none had developed the animus toward Hiss that Nixon had. The two had not met prior to August 5, but the friction between them was immediate and intense. When Hiss had mentioned the names served up "rather loosely" in HUAC hearings, Nixon had turned crimson. The remark implied Nixon was just another witch-hunter, trawling the gutters in the manner of Mundt and Rankin. Hiss, with his Harvard pedigree and diplomat's poise, his cool disdain masked as elaborate courtesy, had "made an ass of" Nixon, in Stripling's assessment.[12]

Henceforth Nixon was to speak angrily of Hiss's demeanor on August 5, of his arrogant, mocking tone. Hiss had been "almost condescending" toward the committee, "insolent" and "insulting in the extreme." He had turned his back on the panel so as to acknowledge his many admirers in the gallery. A quarter century later, brooding on the ruins of his own political career, Nixon would invoke Hiss obsessively, his hatred undimmed, as fresh as it had been on August 5, 1948.

After that first encounter Nixon "set his hat on Hiss," Stripling would remember. "It was a personal thing." He no more cared whether Hiss was a Communist than whether he was a "billy goat."[13]

But it was not that simple. Nixon was motivated by more than dislike of Hiss. He also saw a political opportunity. No stranger to the Communists in government issue, Nixon had ridden it to an upset victory over a popular incumbent, Jerry Voorhis, in 1946 and since his arrival in Washington had been diligently throwing out lines to its dense network of Red hunters. His maiden speech in Congress had been a denunciation of Comintern official Gerhart Eisler, "an arrogant, defiant enemy of our government" and mastermind of "the political and espionage activities" of the CPUSA. He had also been a vocal and visible supporter of the anti-Communist Taft-Hartley bill, which had disempowered labor unions. In the spring Nixon had written a much-discussed bill that required the registration of Communists. It had cleared the House before languishing in the Senate. This zeal impressed Father Cronin, J. Edgar Hoover, and Republican Speaker of the House Joe Martin, who all had tapped Nixon as a comer.

With brilliant clarity Nixon grasped that the emerging Chambers-Hiss mystery could yield great political dividends for the man who solved it. And so he pitched himself into the case with a methodical intensity few in Washington—or anywhere—could match. Nixon would not attempt to "prove" Hiss was a Communist, something no one had yet been able to do, and a nearly impossible assertion to back up in any case, unless a signed registration card suddenly materialized. Instead, following a suggestion by the ex-Communist Ben Mandel, Nixon would establish that Hiss had not been the forthright witness he seemed. He would do this by narrowing his inquiry to a single point. Chambers, if he could be believed, had not only known Hiss but been his friend ("I was very fond of Mr. Hiss"). If this was true, then Hiss's testimony began with a bold lie from which other lies followed.

In the day and a half since gaining control of the probe, Nixon had been working feverishly and in monastic solitude. He stayed deep into night in his office, Suite 528, in the back, or "attic," of the Old House Office Building, combing the transcript of Hiss's testimony, looking for wrinkles on its glassy surface.[14]

On Saturday morning, August 7, Chambers made his way downtown from Rockefeller Center to the thirty-two-story Federal Courthouse on Foley Square, near the Brooklyn Bridge. The committee, or some of it, had gathered in a grim dark-paneled courtroom on the first floor. It was to be another closed hearing. Chairman Thomas was still missing. So were the senior members Mundt and Rankin and Wood, along with J. Hardin Peterson and Richard Vail (who seemed absent even when present). Only Hébert, McDowell, and Nixon had made the trip to New York.

Chambers sat a few feet from his interrogators, a unit diminished in size but not effectiveness. The investigatory staff was well represented: Stripling, and his two top assistants, Louis Russell and Ben Mandel, along with the junior members Donald Appell and Charles McKillips. A stenographer was also present. Normally Stripling handled the questioning of witnesses. Not this time. It was Nixon, a deep-voiced black Irishman, who dominated the proceedings. Chambers was surprised but not distressed. He remembered what Frank McNaughton had said: Nixon was HUAC's best interrogator.

The congressman began by reminding Chambers that Hiss had sworn under oath that "the testimony which had been given by you under oath before this committee was false." They had now convened for the purpose of exploring Chambers's "alleged acquaintanceship" with Hiss so as to "determine what course of action should be followed in this matter."[15]

First Nixon asked Chambers about his name. Hiss had said the name Whittaker Chambers meant nothing to him. Had Chambers gone by another in his Communist days?

Yes. Hiss had known him as Carl, Chambers's Washington alias, for the duration of their relationship, which had lasted roughly from 1935 to 1937. Chambers had used no last name. Nor had Hiss inquired about one. To do so would have been unthinkable for a dedicated Communist like Hiss, a breach of Party discipline.

What made Chambers sure Hiss was a Communist?

J. Peters, chief of the entire underground, had told him so. Also, Chambers had sometimes collected party dues from Hiss, who had been "rather pious" about paying them promptly. Hiss did not have a membership card. No underground Communist did, although Chambers understood "party registration was kept in Moscow and in some secret file in the United States."

Had Chambers any "factual evidence" proving Hiss had been a Communist?

Nothing "beyond the fact that Hiss submitted himself for the 2 or 3 years that I knew him as a dedicated and disciplined Communist."

Nixon was prepared for this. The FBI had asked Chambers for evidence on Hiss in 1946, and he had provided none.[16]

On to the friendship then. How well had Chambers known Hiss? Nixon demanded details. Chambers supplied them, copiously, reaching across a gulch of ten years and more. Alger was about five feet eight or nine, slender, with eyes "wide apart and blue or gray." His wife was a "short, highly nervous, little woman" with "a habit of blushing red when she is excited or angry, fiery red." Alger's nicknames were Hill and Hilly, his wife's Dilly and Pross. The marriage to Hiss was her second. Her first, to Thayer Hobson, a New York publisher, had ended in divorce. When Chambers knew her, Priscilla spoke of Hobson "almost with hatred." However, Hobson paid private school tuition for his and Priscilla's son, Timothy Hobson, called Timmy, a "puny little boy" of about ten when Chambers had known him. The Hiss household also included a cocker spaniel. During the family's summer vacations, on

Maryland's Eastern Shore, the pet boarded in a kennel on Wisconsin Avenue in Washington.

Nixon later credited himself for asking the next question, but it actually came from Ben Mandel. "Did Mr. Hiss have any hobbies?"

Yes. Alger and Priscilla Hiss both were "amateur ornithologists, bird observers." Mornings they often went to the Chesapeake and Ohio Canal and also to Glen Echo. Chambers recalled their excitement one day when they had seen a prothonotary warbler.

"A very rare specimen?" asked McDowell, himself a bird-watcher.

"I never saw one," said Chambers. "I am also fond of birds."

Hiss had not spoken often of his childhood, but Chambers remembered one detail. Hiss had grown up in Baltimore and as a small boy used to "take a little wagon" to Druid Hill Park, "at that time way beyond the civilized center of the city, and fill up bottles with spring water," which he then carted back to his own neighborhood, Bolton Hill, and sold to neighbors.

Chambers had not been intimate with Hiss's brother, Donald. Their relationship was "purely formal." The younger Hiss "was much less intelligent than Alger" and also "much less sensitive." Donald was an opportunist and social climber, "fairly friendly with James Roosevelt," the president's eldest son.*

However, Chambers spoke knowledgeably of Donald Hiss's government career, describing a dispute that had arisen when Donald, then in the Labor Department, was invited to join the newly formed Philippine section of the State Department, under Francis Sayre. Donald wanted to stay where he was and if possible influence the deportation case of Harry Bridges, the Australian-born Communist longshoreman. But J. Peters ordered Donald to accept the transfer, another penetration of an "old-line" agency. There was "a fairly sharp exchange" before Donald "submitted" to Peters's demand and took the new job.[18]

Back to Alger Hiss. Had Chambers been his houseguest? Often. Alger's home had been "a kind of informal headquarters" for Chambers. The witness recalled a sequence of residences Hiss had occupied in the mid-1930s. First, a fourth-floor walk-up on Twenty-eighth Street in one

---

* Alger Hiss later wrote: "At law school I had known [Eleanor Roosevelt's] son James and his future wife Betsy Cushing. My brother Donald and his wife, who were closer friends of the young couple, once dined at the White House."[17]

of two "almost identical" buildings at the dead end of a street "on the right-hand side as you go up." Next, two places in Georgetown, the second on an "up-and-down street" with a basement-level dining room and a small backyard. When Chambers last saw Hiss, on the visit of December 1938, the family had moved across Wisconsin Avenue, to a fourth residence.

None of the homes had been memorably furnished. Each was "kind of pulled together," with "nothing lavish." This was typical of the Hisses. They had few material attachments, and their mode of life was plain. They ate simply ("cared nothing about food"), and Chambers did not remember ever having had a cocktail in their house. Everything about them was modest. Alger "is a man of great simplicity, with a great gentleness and sweetness of character." He had driven a "very dilapidated" car, a Ford roadster. "I remember very clearly that it had hand windshield wipers. I remember that because I drove it one rainy day and had to work those windshield wipers by hand." Later, "it seems to me in 1936," Hiss bought a new car, a Plymouth.

Ben Mandel, the ex-Communist, then asked a second key question. "What did he do with the old car?"

"Against all the rules of underground organization," Hiss had insisted the Ford be "turned over to the open party so it could be of use to some poor organizer in the West or somewhere." Chambers and J. Peters had tried talking him out of it, but Hiss was adamant. At last Peters gave in. He knew of a used-car lot operated by a Communist and had either taken Hiss there or given him the address.

Nixon asked Chambers if he would sit for a lie detector test.

"Yes, if necessary."

"You have that much confidence?"

Chambers gave him a puzzled look. "I am telling the truth."[19]

Back in Washington Stripling assigned a staff member to track down the clues embedded in Chambers's "incredibly detailed account" of his relationship with Hiss: the addresses of the Hisses' homes (and the leases); Timmy Hobson's school records; the Ford; the kennel on Wisconsin Avenue.[20]

That same day the parent HUAC convened in open session in the caucus room, before a full house, and questioned Elizabeth Bentley along with Mundt's "mystery witnesses," Victor Perlo, onetime wunderkind of the Ware cell, and Alexander Koral, an engineer employed by the New York City Board of Education. Bentley reiterated her charges against both men, who declined to answer the committee's questions.[21]

Meanwhile Stripling's researchers had turned up little from Chambers's leads, and Nixon's subcommittee colleagues Hébert and McDowell remained skeptical of Chambers. He seemed *too* knowledgeable about Hiss. How could a man speak so confidently of matters dating back more than ten years? Wasn't it possible Chambers had studied up on Hiss's life and then "concocted" an elaborate story around the details?

Even Nixon was beginning to have second thoughts. Rumors were rippling through Washington: Chambers was said to be mentally unstable, an alcoholic, a homosexual, or all three. These were familiar smears against ex-Communist witnesses. But given Chambers's general air of dishevelment—his seedy appearance and haunted manner, not to mention his unsavory history—the gossip could not be discounted, at least not by Nixon, uneasily conscious of having tethered his political future to a virtual stranger. Seized by an impulse to find out, "alone and informally," exactly what kind of man Chambers was, Nixon jumped into a car and drove to Westminster, following the back roads to Pipe Creek Farm.[22]

It was Monday evening, the beginning of the *Time* weekend. Chambers was at home. He betrayed no great surprise at seeing Nixon. He led the young congressman to the front porch, where rocking chairs overlooked the cropped meadows, a tired August green, and the fields swollen with the summer harvest. He also introduced Nixon to Esther, "a strikingly dark woman, who said very little but looked deeply sad and worried," Nixon later recalled.[23]

Nixon told Chambers of the proliferating rumors. There were many who believed the witness was driven by a "personal motive" to ruin Hiss. If so, said Chambers, then he had chosen a peculiar way to do it; his reputation too was being destroyed. The truth was, he bore Hiss no ill will. He was fond of him and of Priscilla Hiss and still considered them high-minded idealists who had embraced communism for the sincerest reasons. But Chambers too was acting on high principles. There was much more at stake than "a clash of personalities." The issue was not Hiss and Chambers. It was communism. "This is what you must get the country to realize," Chambers told Nixon, his voice filled with emotion.[24]

As the witness and the congressman talked, "the caricature drawn by the rumormongers" vanished. Nixon found himself responding to Chambers, to his air of quiet fatalism. "Like most men of quality, he made a deeper impression personally than he did in public," Nixon later said. He seemed a man of "extraordinary intelligence, speaking from a great depth of understanding; a sensitive, shy man," with an "almost absolute passion for personal privacy." In other words, Chambers reminded Nixon of himself. Indeed the similarities were striking. Nixon too was an introvert determined to play a role in history. Nixon too was painfully aware of the charm he lacked and diligently compensated for it by means of his "extraordinary intelligence." Nixon too harbored secret depths of loneliness and compassion. Nixon too was an unpacific Quaker who saw life in psychodramatic terms of struggle and conflict.[25]

Though cured of his doubts, Nixon wanted his judgment confirmed by others. Still keeping secret his private dialogue with Chambers, he showed the transcript of the August 7 hearing to two men well qualified to assess it. First, William P. Rogers, the counsel to the Ferguson Committee (the first to question Elizabeth Bentley) and an alumnus of the famous prosecutorial team Thomas Dewey had assembled as district attorney of New York County. After studying the transcript, Rogers agreed it was convincing. No one could fabricate so detailed a story without expecting to get caught. Chambers must have known Hiss.

That evening, over dinner, Nixon showed the transcript to a second trusted ally, Representative Charles Kersten, his colleague on the House Labor Committee. It was Kersten who had introduced Nixon to Father Cronin and also to Bishop Fulton J. Sheen, the confessor of the ex-Communist Louis Budenz. Nixon later credited Kersten with having "taught me most of what I know about Communism." Kersten went over Chambers's testimony and, like Rogers, was persuaded by it. He encouraged Nixon to pursue the inquiry.

Late that night Nixon heard distressing news. Members of the Carnegie board were pressuring John Foster Dulles to issue a statement in support of Hiss. If backed by Dulles, who had a seat warming in the Cabinet, Hiss was untouchable. Dewey and the Republican hierarchy would be obliged to protect him and call off the HUAC inquiry.

The next morning, after a Labor Committee hearing, Nixon explained his dilemma to Kersten in the caucus room, where Hiss had dazzled the crowd less than a week before. Kersten had a suggestion. Why not show the Chambers transcript to Dulles, a distinguished attorney? It might at least give him pause. Immediately Nixon phoned the Roosevelt Hotel in New York, headquarters of the Dewey campaign, and made an appointment to visit that evening. Kersten agreed to go too, for moral support.[26]

The congressmen rode up to New York on the train and were ushered into Dulles's suite. For Nixon this was an awesome moment. In 1937, with a degree from the Duke University Law School, he had gone to Wall Street and made the rounds of top firms. All had snubbed him. A shopkeeper's son from rural California, educated at tiny Whittier College, a Quaker school, Nixon had none of the polish required of a Wall Street lawyer. It had been Dulles's firm, Sullivan and Cromwell, that left the most vivid impression, the "thick, luxurious carpets and the fine oak paneling," the emblems of the East Coast patriciate, of its power, its wealth, its exclusivity.[27]

He had now to persuade a denizen of that plush and clubby world that another of its members, Alger Hiss, was not what he seemed. Dulles was not Nixon's only auditor this evening. The secretary designate's younger brother, Allen, a former OSS chief and future CIA director, was also present. So were two other eminences, House Republican Christian Herter and C. Douglas Dillon, Wall Street tycoon and later ambassador to France and undersecretary of state. All belonged to the Republican party's eastern wing, Dewey's wing, on the threshold of reclaiming the White House after sixteen years of uninterrupted Democratic rule. In the upper echelons of the Dewey campaign, then, the Chambers–Hiss controversy, barely a week old, was being taken very seriously.

Nixon explained his mission, raising the matter of Hiss's position at the Carnegie Endowment. In reply Dulles intimated that the organization was indeed contemplating a demonstration of "public support." He did not add that he had rapidly been putting distance between himself and Hiss, remembering very well the rumors that had trailed Hiss to the endowment. Dulles's doubts had been revived in March 1948, when Hiss was called to testify before the New York grand jury investigating communism. Then Chambers had come forward with his allegations. Dulles, advising Hiss before his answering testimony, had suggested Hiss more or less admit having "got mixed up with Communists" in the 1930s and then promise he would no longer "have anything to do with" them. This was the "invaluable" counsel Hiss had rejected, indeed been shocked by, since it amounted to a virtual confession. Even after Hiss's virtuoso performance, on August 5, Dulles remained wary. He had ignored the muted cry for support in Hiss's letter and had rejected a plea from Carnegie trustee Philip Jessup, a friend of Hiss's, that the board publicly back its beleaguered president. "It seems to me better to defer decision until after the present hearings have been concluded," Dulles had told Jessup. Since then the Dewey campaign already had heard, via William Rogers, about Chambers's secret testimony on August 7. And here was Nixon with a copy of the transcript. The Dulles brothers studied it closely while Nixon and Kersten sat by silently on a sofa.

Foster Dulles, ministerially somber, paced before the fireplace, hands clasped behind his back. At last he halted. "There's no question about it. It's almost impossible to believe, but Chambers knows Hiss."

Nixon cautiously asked the one man with the power to kill the inquiry if HUAC was "justified in going ahead with the investigation."

Dulles's endorsement sounded formal, as if spoken for the record. "In view of the facts Chambers has testified to, you'd be derelict in your duty as a Congressman if you did not see the case through to a conclusion."

Hiss had just lost his most powerful ally, and Nixon had kept the case—indubitably, now, *his* case—alive.[28]

Later that evening Nixon submitted the transcript to yet another discerning reader, the *Herald Tribune*'s Washington bureau chief, Bert Andrews. Ordinarily so important a figure would not come rushing over to the attic cubbyhole of a freshman congressman. But Andrews, a Californian, had early picked out Nixon from the herd of new faces in the class of '46, observing with others that the Orange County freshman, though the youngest HUAC member, was also the best—the shrewdest, the soundest, the least overt in his Red-baiting.

Nixon since had become a regular guest at the *Tribune*'s Washington bureau, the second largest in the capital (after *The New York Times*'s). Soon Andrews was boasting, "I can make that fellow President of the United States." He did not live to see it happen. A hard drinker and chain-smoker, Andrews was dead in five years, "a burned-out case at the age of fifty-two."

Nixon had solid reasons for singling out Andrews as his confidant. In May the reporter had won a Pulitzer Prize for a series of articles exposing inequities in Truman's loyalty program. The articles had since been published as a book, *Washington Witch Hunt,* widely praised for its defense of civil liberties, and Andrews had gained the reputation of being both an opponent of Red hunting and a liberal. In fact he was neither. He disliked the State Department and had no pressing interest in civil liberties. However, he had a superb instinct for the news and was ruthless in its pursuit. "He wouldn't commit murder for a good story, but would certainly consider it," remarked one of Andrews's rivals, the *Times*'s James Reston.[29]

Andrews read the transcript and reacted as the others had. It appeared "almost certain" Chambers had known Hiss. There were too many particulars. It made no sense that Chambers had researched or fabricated them. Nixon and Andrews struck a bargain. Andrews would offer his expertise, his "outside judgment on whether Chambers really knew Hiss as he claimed." In return Nixon would leak information to Andrews, as the case unfolded, "if it became possible to use it without injuring the investigation."

It was Nixon's canniest decision. Instead of relying on HUAC's spotty investigatory staff, he could turn for guidance to Andrews, with his nose for a story and his multiple contacts. More important, as long as Nixon remained in control of the case, its breaking developments would be published in the *Herald Tribune,* the nation's most reputable Republican daily, Tom Dewey's paper. And credit would go to Richard Nixon.

Andrews already had some advice. Nixon had better not rely on the transcript alone to expose Hiss. Chambers's uncorroborated memories counted for nothing.

That was a problem, Nixon admitted. HUAC investigators had so far established only two facts. Hiss had lived at one of the addresses Chambers remembered and had owned a dog. "That's about as far as we've gotten." He had interviewed Chambers, Nixon added, but he wanted another opinion. "Will you drive up to Chambers' farm with me?"[30]

They went three days later, on August 15. Chambers was home. Nixon had warned him he would be visiting with an unnamed newspaperman. When they arrived, Chambers, puffing his pipe, stared suspiciously at Andrews's hard features and cynical mouth. He knew about *Washington Witch Hunt.*

"I don't think I want to talk to you," Chambers said. "You don't approve of the committee or of anything it has done."

It was true, Andrews admitted. HUAC had "mishandled many matters," in his opinion. But he was far more critical of Truman's loyalty program. In his book Andrews had described the Kafkaesque ordeal of State Department officials forced out of their jobs without being told what the charges against them were and who had lodged them. Chambers too would be railroaded unless HUAC was able to substantiate his claim. If it came down to Chambers's word against Hiss's, Andrews pointed out, Hiss would prevail because his "record is so much better than yours."

Chambers, his pipe in his mouth, said nothing.

Nixon spoke up. "Andrews is absolutely right. I wish you'd let him ask you some questions."

There was a long silence, lasting half a minute or more. To Andrews it seemed Chambers had slipped into a trance. Finally the witness spoke. "Well, let him go ahead and ask them."

Andrews went directly to the rumors. Some said Chambers was a "chronic drunk." No, said Chambers. He disliked hard liquor; his colleagues at *Time* would testify to that. Had he ever been in a "mental institution or insane asylum?" No again. Chambers had "never been in any kind of sanitarium—period." What about the talk of "something strange" in Chambers's relationship with Hiss—that is, that one or both were homosexual? "I know all of those stories," Chambers said. "There is just nothing to them."

Nixon pulled out glossy eight-by-ten photographs of the houses Chambers had identified as being Hiss's during the time they were accomplices. On the back of each picture was a typewritten description of the house. Andrews asked Chambers to describe the dwellings. His memories tallied with the photos.

Had Chambers any evidence on Hiss? Andrews asked. What else had he, for instance, on Hiss's bird-watching? Chambers slipped into another reverie, this one lasting a full minute, and then removed two books on birds from his heavily loaded dining room bookshelves. "Alger Hiss gave me these." One, a costly volume with handsome color plates, had been distributed to members of the Agriculture Department in 1933–1934.

To Andrews it was odd that this evidence had to be extracted from the witness. Why did he never volunteer anything?

"I'm sorry but that's the way my mind runs," Chambers said. Again he offered to take a lie detector test. Hiss, he was sure, would refuse. "Ask him and see."

The interview lasted three hours. On the drive back to Washington Andrews lectured the young congressman. He stood on the verge of breaking a major case, but only if he handled it properly—that is, in a manner untypical of HUAC. The committee's low reputation was well deserved: the smears, the slapdash research. "I agree with everything you say," Nixon replied. "But where do we go from here?" First, with serious fact checking. For instance, on the Ford. "There must be a dozen places to check. Did someone own it before? What is Hiss's story of what became of it? Did Hiss trade it in when he got a new car? Most people do. Or did he sell it? At any rate, who got it? And why can't you trace the subsequent owner?" Hiss's residences also needed looking into: the dates, the leases. Sizable portions of Chambers's story could be, must be verified.

Giddy, Nixon said, "You've made up your mind, haven't you?"

"I've made up my mind on one thing," Andrews said. "I am positive Chambers and Hiss did know each other. No one could invent all the little items that Chambers has told. I don't believe, either, that anyone could learn them merely by studying a man's life. It just doesn't make sense."

But, Andrews added, HUAC must work harder to unearth the facts.[31]

Actually Nixon was not the naïf Andrews supposed. That very day he had placed the "first of 'numerous calls'" to the FBI, reporting the progress he was making on the case. The bureau was following the controversy closely and within days initiated a parallel investigation, with important details relayed to Nixon via Father Cronin. The priest's bureau contact "would call me every day," Cronin remembered, "and tell me what they had turned up; and I told Dick, who then knew just where to look for things, and what he would find."[32]

The day before he drove Andrews out to Westminster, Nixon had made another trip, this time with Robert Stripling. The investigator too was impressed. But he was troubled by Chambers's reticence. "He is holding something back," Stripling said on the drive home. "He is trying to protect somebody."[33]

# 20

# *A Man Named Crosley*

While Nixon had been probing deeper into Chambers's story, HUAC had been plodding through its list of the accused. Henry Collins, Charles Kramer, and Abraham George Silverman all declined to answer any questions. So did Abt, Pressman, and Witt. It was a milestone, the first concerted use of the Fifth Amendment defense by a group of HUAC witnesses.[1]

But the pattern was broken on August 13—Friday the thirteenth—when Lauchlin Currie, Harry Dexter White, and Donald Hiss all took the stand.[2] White's performance was gripping. Easily the most distinguished of all those under investigation, he was the architect of America's postwar monetary policy and a sometime executive with the International Monetary Fund, which he had helped create. A mild-looking man, short and bespectacled, White firmly stated that he "was not now a Communist and never had been, nor even close to becoming one. . . . I cannot recollect ever knowing either a Miss Bentley or a Mr. Whittaker Chambers, nor, judging from the pictures I have seen in the press, have I ever met them." Moreover, "the principles in which I believe, and by which I live, make it impossible for me to ever do a disloyal act or anything against the interests of our country." He then eloquently summarized the tenets of "my creed . . . the American creed." White stated his belief in "freedom of religion, freedom of speech, freedom of thought, freedom of criticism, and freedom of movement. I believe in the goal of equality of opportunity, and the right of each individual to follow the calling of his or her own choice, and the right of every indi-

vidual to an opportunity to develop his or her capacity to the fullest. . . .
Together those are the principles that I have been prepared in the past to
fight for, and am prepared to defend at any time with my life, if need
be." The applause was thunderous.

Turning to the specific charges, White characterized as "unqualifiedly
false" Bentley's assertion that he helped find government jobs for Communists. As for those officials whom Bentley identified as members of
the "Silvermaster Group," White knew them innocently as colleagues
and friends, with whom he had played weekend sports—softball, volley-
ball, and table tennis.

At the beginning of the hearing White had sent Parnell Thomas a
note explaining he had a heart condition and so would appreciate a rest
after each hour of testimony. With his signature vulgarity, Thomas read
the note aloud, commenting, "For a person who had a severe heart condition, you certainly can play a lot of sports."

White, blanching, said his days as a sportsman long predated his illness.
"I hope that clears that up, Mr. Chairman."

"Yes, sir," a chastened Thomas replied. The gallery burst into applause.

Lauchlin Currie was a New Deal hero, a senior government economist and special assistant to President Roosevelt in 1939–1945. He had
been FDR's personal representative to Chiang Kai-shek in 1942 and had
supervised China's lend-lease program. Currie reminded the committee
that Bentley's allegations against him were "hearsay three times removed." Then, in terms as forceful as White's, he denied all the charges
against him. (Chambers had told Adolf Berle that Currie was a fellow
traveler who "helped various Communists" but "never went the whole
way.")[3]

Last to appear was Donald Hiss, angry about Chambers's "personal attack on me; it has hurt my family, my mother who is 81 years old, and I
feel it very bitterly." Nixon, all but silent during White's and Currie's
testimony, asked Alger Hiss's brother if his memory had been jogged by
a "new development" reported in the press, bits of Chambers's executive testimony Nixon had fed Bert Andrews. Donald Hiss said the clues
meant nothing to him. He had not known Chambers as Carl or seen
him in Alger's apartment.

"If I am lying," said Donald Hiss, "I should go to jail and if Mr.
Chambers is lying he should go to jail."

They were the last words Donald Hiss said to the committee. Henceforth it would be Whittaker Chambers versus Alger Hiss, with the other figures relegated to the sidelines.

After his extraordinary week of preparation, Nixon was ready to take the next big step, a second interrogation of Hiss. At 2:00 P.M. on August 16 he convened a closed session in the small HUAC hearing room. Hiss came alone this time, with no attorney. The hearing lasted three and a half hours. Thomas, Hébert, and Nixon were present, along with Stripling and his staff.[4] Nixon again handled the questioning, leading Hiss over the ground Chambers had covered on August 7. Hiss stood by his earlier testimony. He had not known Chambers and could think of no one named Carl "remotely connected with the kind of testimony Mr. Chambers has given."

But when Nixon showed him two pictures of Chambers, Hiss wavered. "Actually the face has a certain familiarity." Hiss repeated his wish to see Chambers face-to-face. "I had hoped that would happen before. I still hope it will happen today."

Hiss went on to say he was wounded that the committee was treating him and Chambers as witnesses of equal credibility when Hiss had led a blameless public life, open to scrutiny, while his accuser, "a confessed former Communist," was incapable "of telling the truth or does not desire to." Furthermore, it was outrageous that Hiss should be expected to furnish "details of my personal life" that could then be used as fodder for Chambers's fantastic claims. "I have seen newspaper accounts, Mr. Nixon, that you spent the weekend—whether correct or not, I do not know—at Mr. Chambers' farm in New Jersey [*sic*]."

"I can say, as you did a moment ago, that I have never spent the night with Mr. Chambers," Nixon slyly replied.

Stripling spoke up, admonishing Hiss. There was no "prearrangement or anything else with Mr. Chambers. . . . He said he spent a week in your house and he just rattled off details like that. He has either made a study of your life in great detail or he knew you, one or the other, or he is incorrect."

Hiss protested. "The issue is not whether this man knew me and I don't remember him. The issue is whether he had a particular conversation that he has said he had with me"—the tearful parting of 1938—"and which I have denied and whether I am a member of the

Communist Party or ever was, which he has said and which I have denied."

Then Hiss suddenly reversed field. He announced he had written down the name of "a person whom I knew in 1933 and 1934 and who not only spent some time in my house but sublet my apartment. I do not recognize the photographs as possibly being this man." Hiss preferred not to divulge the name. It was not Carl and not Whittaker Chambers.

Where had Hiss been living at the time? asked Nixon.

Again Hiss preferred not to say. On the train down from New York he had jotted down a sequence of his addresses from June 1933 until September 1943. If he divulged them, the details might be published in the press, enabling Chambers to say, "I saw Hiss in such and such a house."

Hiss had a question of his own for HUAC. Was it not true that Chambers had testified privately in executive session before he made his public appearance?

Yes, said McDowell, but "the session lasted about two minutes." (Actually, about twenty.[5]) "It was a matter of getting his name and where he worked."

But, asked Hiss, did the committee know "he was going to testify about me?"

"No," said Stripling.

Hébert chimed in. "We did not know anything Mr. Chambers was going to say. I did not hear your name mentioned until it was mentioned in open hearing."

But of course Chambers had named Hiss along with the others. Moreover, before the executive session began, Stripling had studied Chambers's "dynamite" opening statement, which not only named Hiss but touched the high points of his career at State.

The falsehoods were multiplying on all sides. But only Hiss for the time being had been caught. It was his word against Chambers's.

"Whichever one of you is lying," Eddie Hébert declared, "is the greatest actor that America has ever produced." It made no sense, Hébert added, that Chambers would "pitch a $25,000 position as the respected senior editor of Time magazine out the window" simply for the satisfaction of smearing Hiss.

The questioning went forward. Hiss named housemaids he had employed in Washington and described the layout of an apartment on O Street, near Wardman Park, where he had lived in 1933–1934 (but not of the apartment on Twenty-eighth Street, where Chambers said he had stayed).

Then, again without prompting, he blurted out the name he had written on his pad, that of the mysterious boarder from the 1930s, "a man named George Crosley. I met him when I was working for the Nye Committee. He was a writer. He hoped to sell articles to magazines about the munitions industry." Next came a torrent of details. Crosley's hair was "rather blondish." His voice was soft, and he spoke "with a low and rather dramatic roundness." He was married with "one little baby, as I remember it." He had little money. One summer day, "in the course of casual conversation," Crosley said he would be staying in Washington for the season to complete his articles. He had no lodgings and wanted to bring his family down from New York.

At the time Hiss was moving his own family from P Street in George-town to a new apartment on Thirtieth Street. He offered Crosley the use of the vacant apartment. Several months remained on the lease. "The apartment wasn't very expensive, and I think I let him have it at exact cost." The Hisses had put the Crosleys up "two or three nights in a row" at their new place because the subletters' "furniture van was delayed."

So, Nixon said triumphantly, the Crosleys "did spend several nights in the house with you?"

"This man Crosley," said Hiss. "Yes."

"Can you describe his wife?" Nixon asked.

"Yes; she was a rather strikingly dark person, very strikingly dark. I don't know whether I would recognize her again because I didn't see much of her."

"How tall was this man, approximately?" asked Nixon.

"Shortish."

"Heavy?"

"Not noticeably. That is why I don't believe it has any direct, but it could have an indirect bearing."

"How about his teeth?"

"Very bad teeth. That is one of the things I particularly want to see Chambers about. This man had very bad teeth, did not take care of his teeth."

Stripling asked what kind of automobile Crosley had driven.

"No kind of automobile," Hiss replied. "I sold him an automobile. I had an old Ford that I threw in with the apartment and had been trying to trade it in and get rid of it. . . . It wasn't very fancy but it had a sassy little trunk on the back."

"You gave this Ford car to Crosley?" asked Nixon, not hiding his disbelief.

Yes, said Hiss. "Threw it in along with the apartment and charged the rent and threw in the car at the same time."

Hiss "added a little to the rent to cover the car?"

No. Hiss had rented out the apartment at cost and "threw the car in in addition."

"You just gave him the car?" Stripling repeated.

"I think I just simply turned it over to him." There was no transfer of documents as far as Hiss knew.

Did the Ford have windshield wipers?

Yes, hand-operated. "You had to work them yourself."

And what was the new car he had bought?

A Plymouth sedan.

Eventually Hiss came to regret his largess. "I finally decided it wasn't any use expecting to collect from him, that I had been a sucker and he was a sort of deadbeat; not a bad character, but I think he was just using me for a soft touch."

Crosley had promised to square his debts once he sold his articles. But as far as Hiss knew, he did not sell them and perhaps did not complete the assignments. "My recollection is he paid $15 or $20, and he gave me a rug, which I have still got."

Besides being a welsher, Crosley was a braggart. "He told various stories of his escapades. He purported to be a cross between Jim Tully, the author, and Jack London. He had been everywhere. I remember he told me he had personally participated in laying down the tracks of the street cars in Washington, D.C. He had done that for local color, or something. He had worked right with the road gang laying tracks."

In 1935 Hiss cut off the relationship and had since given no further thought to the man until this morning on the train, when it dawned on him that "Crosley is the only person I know who has been in my house who knows the lay-out of any house or apartment I lived in."

After evoking the mysterious freeloader in such plenteous detail—Hiss's evocation of Chambers in the 1930s is among the most penetrating on record—Hiss still could not say "positively" whether Crosley and Chambers were one and the same.

There was nothing left but for Hiss to implicate himself by supplying further facts.

What were the Hisses' nicknames?

Alger was Hill or Hilly, Priscilla Pross or Prossy. Timothy Hobson, Hiss's stepson, was Timmy and also Moby.

Where had the family vacationed in the 1930s?

On the Eastern Shore of Maryland.

Did they have any pets?

A brown cocker spaniel, Jenny.

Where did they board it on vacations?

"We had a very good vet out near Rock Creek Park."

What were Hiss's hobbies?

"Tennis and amateur ornithology." He also liked to swim and sail.

John McDowell had been silent for most of the inquiry. But HUAC staffers had prepped him to interject a question. Its moment had come. "Did you ever see a prothonotary warbler?" McDowell asked.

"I have right here on the Potomac," Hiss replied enthusiastically. "Do you know that place?"

"I saw one in Arlington," McDowell fibbed.

"They come back and nest in those swamps," said Hiss. "Beautiful yellow head, a gorgeous bird. Mr. Collins is an ornithologist, Henry Collins. He is a really good ornithologist, calling them by their Latin names."

Suppressing their excitement, Nixon and Stripling went on with their questioning, filling in more blanks. Chambers had made errors. Priscilla Hiss was called Prossy, but not Dilly. Hiss had actually moved his stepson to a costlier, not cheaper, private school. But Chambers was right about Hiss's boyhood occupation. At age twelve or so Hiss used to fetch spring water from Druid Hill Park, ten or fifteen blocks from his house. "I have always been very proud of that."

Chambers had remembered a drive from Washington to New York in Hiss's car, with a detour through Pennsylvania. Hiss thought he might have taken Crosley on such a drive.

Chambers, said Nixon, had agreed to a polygraph. The committee had contacted Leonardo Keeler, "probably the outstanding man in the country," the inventor of a widely used machine.

Hiss wanted time to think it over. "I have talked to people who have seen, I think, Dr. Keeler's own test and [say] that the importance of a question registers more emotion than anything else." And Hiss "was perfectly willing and prepared to say that I am not lacking in emotion about this business."

The committee, after adjourning to confer in camera, told Hiss there would be a public hearing nine days hence, on August 25, at 10:30 A.M. in the House caucus room. Hiss and Chambers both would testify.

"I will be very glad of the chance to confront Mr. Chambers," said Hiss.

Did he prefer a public hearing or a private one?

It made no difference. "My desire is to see him face to face."

Stripling feared a public hearing would "be ballyhooed into a circus." The matter could be handled better in private, with counsel present if the witnesses liked.

"As far as consideration to me after what has been done to my feelings and my reputation, I think it would be like sinking the Swiss Navy," Hiss said bitterly. "No public show could embarrass me now. I am asking to see this man. I think I prefer a public session." He asked if after today's hearing there would be leaks like those following Chambers's executive appearance.

Thomas promised there would be none. Everyone had sworn an oath of silence. "Thank you for coming," he said in conclusion. "We will see you August 25th."

At 5:30 P.M. Hiss stalked out of the hearing room. Reporters were waiting. Hiss refused to talk. "Any statement at this point will have to come from the committee."

What about a lie detector? he was asked.

He shrugged and walked on.[6]

That night Nixon and Stripling talked late in Nixon's office. Hiss was beginning to buckle. His deft disclaimers had given way to twisting evasions, and he had confirmed the accuracy of Chambers's reminiscences—not of all of them, but a very high percentage, even down to the prothonotary warbler. All that remained was to bring the two witnesses together in the same room. As far as Nixon was concerned, "the case had been broken."[7]

The next morning Chambers traveled to Washington, at the behest of HUAC, though he was not told why he was needed. It was early afternoon when he reached the Old House Building. He was stealing toward a side entrance when a contingent of HUAC staff fell upon him. They were headed for Union Station and a train to New York. He must come too. Nixon and McDowell were waiting in a car. Chambers was pushed into the vehicle, and someone thrust an afternoon paper at him. The headline was a shocker. Harry Dexter White was dead of a heart attack. The economist had been stricken mere hours after returning to his New Hampshire summer home from his HUAC appearance. He died at 5:45 P.M. on August 16, fifteen minutes after Hiss's closed interrogation had come to an end.

The memory of White's exchange with Thomas was fresh in everyone's mind. It had been an ugly moment and could easily pivot opinion against the committee and jeopardize the case against Hiss. HUAC was not directly responsible for White's heart attack, *The New York Times* editorialized. But the committee stood guilty of "ignoring the Bill of Rights and outraging our American sense of justice."[8]

At Penn Station, New York, the travelers took a page from the underground, waiting until the train emptied before getting up from their seats. Congressmen and staff swiftly departed the terminal, leaving Chambers behind to escape by another exit with junior investigator Donald Appell, a baby-faced ex-marine. They climbed into a taxi and rode a short distance to the Commodore, the two-thousand-room hotel where Chambers had met Lincoln Steffens in 1933.

Appell led Chambers through the ramp entrance and into the elevator up to Suite 1400 and left him in the bedroom under the watchful eye of Steve Bermingham, the federal marshal who had served Chambers with the subpoena that had begun this improbable story. Bermingham fixed the witness with a stare, growing alert when Chambers leaned out the open window to gulp a mouthful of fresh air.

Congressman McDowell came in and had a few calming words with the witness and then left, closing the door. All Chambers heard for the next ten or fifteen minutes was muffled angry voices.[9]

Earlier in the day Donald Appell had phoned Hiss at his uptown office, near Columbia University, and asked if the Carnegie president would be free to meet "for ten or fifteen minutes" that afternoon with Congressman McDowell. Hiss said he would be at the endowment's midtown office, at Fifth Avenue and Forty-fourth Street, in the afternoon, and McDowell could visit him there. Later McDowell wired to say he would stop by at five-thirty. A few minutes before the appointment, McDowell phoned, with a change of plan. Could Hiss come over to the Commodore, a few blocks away, and meet with McDowell, Nixon, and "one other"? Hiss, suspecting "something more than a casual conversation" was in store, asked his Carnegie colleague Charles Dollard to accompany him, as a precaution, lest the committee leak inaccurate reports of the session.[10]

When Hiss arrived at the hotel room, with Dollard in tow, he found Nixon and McDowell and staff. Stripling, Mandel, and Russell were present, along with Appell and another investigator, William Wheeler. A stenographer sat at her machine. Staff members were shifting furniture around.

Parnell Thomas had been detained, so McDowell acted as chairman. He seated himself in an upholstered chair, with a table lamp as his rostrum. Nixon sat beside him. This was to be conducted as a formal hearing.

It was Nixon's idea, his most ingenious yet. The previous night, after Stripling had gone home, Nixon had sat alone in his office for hours, almost till dawn, feverishly strategizing. The closed session with Hiss had been a triumph, but the August 25 date worried him. Nine days were a long delay—long enough for Hiss to fortify and fine-tune his story. The next morning Nixon had asked McDowell, the one HUAC member who knew Hiss, to arrange the impromptu meeting in New York.[11]

McDowell administered the oath to Hiss and told him, "You may smoke and be comfortable."[12]

Then Nixon turned to the witness, explaining the purpose of the hearing. Since Hiss had "raised the possibility of a third party"—George Crosley—it seemed a good idea to determine "at the earliest possible time" whether Crosley and Chambers were one and the same. Today, then, Hiss and Chambers would be brought face-to-face.

Hiss had walked into a trap. But he too could maneuver. "I would like the record to show," he began, "that on my way downtown from my uptown office, I learned from the press of the death of Harry White, which came as a great shock to me, and I am not sure that I feel in the best possible mood for testimony." That is, HUAC already had White's blood on its hands and had better be careful how it treated him.

There was something else. "I would like this record to show at this stage that the first thing I saw in the morning paper, the *Herald Tribune,* was a statement that the committee yesterday had asked me if I would submit to a lie detector test." That is, someone had leaked the contents of the hearing, in blatant violation of the committee's promise of secrecy.

The article had not appeared under Bert Andrews's byline, but under that of Carl Levin, of the *Tribune*'s Washington bureau. Andrews had put Levin on the story so as to buffer himself and Nixon, enabling Nixon to meet Hiss's charge with a tricky disclaimer: "I can assure you that no member of this committee or no member of the staff discussed the matter with Mr. Levin."

Hiss was not fooled. He had spent fourteen years in Washington and knew how the game worked. In fact he had played it himself. In his years at State he had been an energetic leaker.[13]

"Mr. Nixon, I didn't say anybody discussed it with Mr. Levin," said Hiss. "I said someone must have given information. How Mr. Levin got it, I do not know."

McDowell, for many years a newspaperman, added that he too was disturbed by the leaks. "In my own case, I very carefully guarded myself last night, saw and talked to no one except my wife in Pittsburgh. It is regrettable and unfortunate."

Nixon, uncomfortable with this subject, declared it was time for Chambers to be brought in from the other room.

The door opened, and Louis Russell entered, followed by Chambers, who circled in front of Hiss and was directed to sit alongside Mandel on a couch against the wall.

"Mr. Hiss," Nixon said, "the man standing here is Mr. Whittaker Chambers. I ask you now if you have ever known that man before."

Hiss had been sitting rigidly in an easy chair, facing the windows behind Nixon and McDowell. For the first time he cocked his head toward his accuser, "short, plump, perspiring, and very pale," his suit rumpled, his face a putty mask.[14]

Hiss got to his feet and studied Chambers detachedly, as if assessing a stage prop. To Nixon, Hiss said, "May I ask him to speak? Will you ask him to say something?"

"Mr. Chambers," asked Nixon, "will you tell us your name and business?"

The witness was also standing. "My name is Whittaker Chambers."

Hiss strode toward Chambers. An erect six feet (not the five-eight or -nine Chambers remembered), Hiss overtopped his accuser by nearly six inches. To Stripling, the exchange that followed seemed "something out of a dream."[15]

"Would you mind opening your mouth wider?" Hiss asked Chambers.

"My name is Whittaker Chambers."

"I said, would you open your mouth?" Hiss turned to Nixon. "You know what I am referring to." Again he addressed Chambers. "Will you go on talking?

Chambers had yet to look at Hiss. He stared fixedly ahead and then gazed up at the ceiling.[16] Tonelessly he said, "I am senior editor of Time magazine."

Hiss spoke. "May I ask whether his voice, when he testified before, was comparable to this?"

"His voice?" asked Nixon.

"Or did he talk a little more in a lower key?"

McDowell piped up. "I would say it is about the same now as we have heard."

Hiss wanted Chambers to speak further.

"Read something, Mr. Chambers," Nixon instructed. "I will let you read from—"

"I think he is George Crosley," Hiss said, "but I would like to hear him talk a little longer."

McDowell told Chambers he could be seated.

At last Hiss spoke directly to Chambers. "Are you George Crosley?"

"Not to my knowledge. You are Alger Hiss, I believe."

"I certainly am."

"That was my recollection."

"Just one moment," Nixon interjected. "Since some repartee goes on between these two people, I think Mr. Chambers should be sworn."

"That is a good idea," said Hiss. His tone was acid. He meant: Chambers should have been sworn in the moment he entered the room.

"Mr. Hiss, may I say something?" said Nixon after Chambers had taken the oath. "I suggested that he be sworn, and when I say something like that I want no interruptions from you."

"Mr. Nixon, in view of what happened yesterday," Hiss shot back, "I think there is no occasion for you to use that tone of voice in speaking to me, and I hope the record will show what I have just said."

The hatred between the two was now out in the open.

Chambers, handed a copy of *Newsweek,* read aloud a sentence at random about Truman's search for a new labor secretary.

"The voice," said Hiss, "sounds a little less resonant than the voice that I recall of the man I knew as George Crosley."

Hiss lowered his head to peer into Chambers's open mouth. "The teeth look to me as though either they have been improved upon or that there has been considerable dental work done since I knew George Crosley, which was some years ago."

Chambers described the work done on his teeth in 1944 by his Westminster dentist, "some extractions" and "a plate in place of some of the upper dentures."

Hearing this, Hiss was inclined to think Chambers was, after all, the same man who "represented himself to me in 1934 or 1935 or thereabouts as George Crosley, a freelance writer of articles for magazines."

However, Hiss first would like to consult Chambers's dentist. "One of my main recollections of Crosley was the poor condition of his teeth."

"Mr. Hiss," said Nixon, "do you feel that you would have to have the dentist tell you just what he did to the teeth before you could tell anything about this man?"

Hiss, ignoring Nixon's sarcasm, said he felt "very strongly" that Chambers was Crosley but still was unsure about differences in "girth and in other appearances—hair, forehead, and so on, particularly the jowls."

Nixon shifted to the relationship between Hiss and Crosley. He asked Hiss about the apartment. Hiss repeated his testimony of the previous day. Chambers had subleased the rooms for the entire summer of 1935. Hiss had tossed in the car, an early Model A. The Hisses had also left behind some sticks of furniture. When the Chamberses' household items were delayed, the Hisses had put the family up in their new place for several days, possibly as many as four. "I imagine my wife would testify it seemed even longer than that."

Though the Crosleys had been undesirable houseguests, Hiss later saw more of George Crosley, "several times in the fall of 1935"—even after the freelancer failed to pay "a single red cent in currency" for the owed rent, $225, no small sum in Depression dollars. Hiss repeated his testimony about the rug Chambers gave him, courtesy of a "wealthy patron."

Up to now Robert Stripling had been silent. But after absorbing this flood of detail, he turned to Hiss. "Now, here is a person that you knew for several months at least. You knew him so well that he was a guest in your home." Yet "when Mr. Chambers walked in and you examined him and asked him to open his mouth . . . you were basing your identification purely on what his upper teeth might have looked like." Was there nothing else in Chambers's appearance that might enable Hiss to say, "This is the man I knew as George Crosley"?

Hiss objected. From the beginning he had conceded "a certain familiarity in features" between Crosley and Chambers. But "I am not given on important occasions to snap judgments or simple, easy statements." He had known Crosley, whom "I would not call a guest in my house," at a time when "I was seeing hundreds of people." Since then Hiss had seen thousands more. Crosley had "meant nothing to me except as one I saw under the circumstances I have described." Had "this man said he was George Crosley in the first place," Hiss "would have no difficulty in identification." But Chambers had stood there and "denied it." Then, when Hiss had tried to put further questions to Chambers, Nixon had not allowed it. There were, besides, other possibilities to consider. What if Chambers had obtained information on Hiss from George Crosley? Also, "he may have had his face lifted."

Stripling and McDowell agreed to let Hiss question Chambers further.

"Do I have Mr. Nixon's permission?" Hiss asked icily.

"Mr. Chambers," said Nixon, "do you have any objections?"

"No," said Chambers, silent all this time.

Though not a litigator, Hiss was a skilled lawyer. His phrasings had a prosecutorial edge.

"Did you ever go under the name of George Crosley?" he began.

"Not to my knowledge," said Chambers.

"Did you ever sublet an apartment on Twenty-ninth Street?" (The address was actually Twenty-eighth Street, as Chambers had remembered.)

"No, I did not," Chambers replied.

"You did not?"

"No."

"Did you ever spend any time with your wife and child at an apartment on Twenty-ninth Street in Washington when I was not there because I and my family were living on P Street?"

"I most certainly did," said Chambers.

"You did or did not?"

"I did."

"Would you tell me how you reconcile your negative answers with this affirmative answer?"

"Very easily, Alger. I was a Communist and you were a Communist."

"Would you be responsive and continue with your answer?"

"I do not think it is needed."

"That is the answer." Hiss sounded disbelieving.

Nixon cut in. "I will help you with the answer, Mr. Hiss. The question, Mr. Chambers, is, as I understand it, that Mr. Hiss cannot understand how you would deny that you were George Crosley and yet admit that you spent some time in his apartment. Now would you explain the circumstances?" Cautiously Nixon added, "I don't want to put that until Mr. Hiss agrees that is one of his questions."

"You have the privilege of asking any questions you want," Hiss said tartly. "I think that is an accurate phrasing."

Nixon turned to Chambers. "Go ahead."

"As I have testified before," said Chambers, "I came to Washington as a Communist functionary, a functionary of the American Communist Party. I was connected with the underground group of which Mr. Hiss was a member. Mr. Hiss and I became friends. To the best of my knowledge, Mr. Hiss himself suggested that I go there [to his apartment], and I accepted gratefully."

Hiss had heard enough. He looked at McDowell. "Mr. Chairman—"

"Just a moment," said Nixon. He addressed Chambers: "How long did you stay there?"

"My recollection was about three weeks. It may have been longer. I brought no furniture, I might add."

Then came another of Hiss's sudden blurtings. He turned to McDowell. "Mr. Chairman, I don't need to ask Mr. Whittaker Chambers any more questions. I am now perfectly prepared to identify this man as George Crosley."

"Well," said McDowell, taken aback, "you positively identify—"

"Positively on the basis of his own statement that he was in my apartment at the time when I say he was there. I have no further questions at all. If he had lost both eyes and taken his nose off, I would be sure."

Stripling asked Hiss to produce three witnesses "who will testify they knew [Chambers] as Crosley."

Panic flitted across Hiss's face.[17] Then he bristled. "Why is that a question to ask me?" This was a matter dating back to 1935. Only Nye Committee staff were likely to remember Crosley, and Hiss had lost track of them.

So, then, asked McDowell, "Your identification is complete?"

McDowell turned to Chambers. Was this the Alger Hiss he had known?

"Positive identification," said Chambers serenely.

Hiss, fists clenched, strode toward the couch where Chambers sat. "I would like to invite Mr. Whittaker Chambers to make those same statements out of the presence of this committee without their being privileged for suit for libel. I challenge you to do it, and I hope you will do it damned quickly."

Hiss loomed over Chambers, his hand inches from Chambers's face. ("I wondered why Chambers didn't reach out and bite his finger," Nixon later said.[18]) Louis Russell reached for Hiss's arm. Hiss turned on him in fury, his voice rising. "I am not going to touch him. You are touching me."

"Please sit down, Mr. Hiss," urged Russell.

"I will sit down when the chairman asks me to sit down—"

"I want no disturbances," said Russell.

McDowell cut in. "Sit down, please."

"You know who started this," said Hiss.

It was nearing seven o'clock. Hiss, regaining his composure, said he had already missed one appointment and was in danger of missing another. He was willing to stay on but wanted the record to show that McDowell had not warned him Chambers would be present at this session.

Nixon asked Chambers if he had anything to say for the record.

"I don't think so."

"I am not surprised," said Hiss.

"I would be glad to answer any questions," Chambers said to Hiss.

"I suggest we adjourn," said Nixon.

Chambers and Hiss were told they would be brought together again as originally planned, on August 25, in the House caucus room. Stripling wrote out subpoenas. Hiss reminded the committee that his wife was traveling down from their summer place in Vermont for an interview Nixon had earlier requested. It would be best, said Hiss, if she could get it over with quickly, the following morning if possible. Their seven-year-old son was with a baby-sitter. Nixon agreed, sounding sympathetic.

"Am I dismissed?" asked Hiss.

"That is all," said Thomas, who had come in at the end of the session. "Thank you very much."

"I don't reciprocate," Hiss snapped.

"Italicize that in the record," Thomas instructed the stenographer.

"I wish you would," said Hiss. He and Charles Dollard left the hotel suite.

Stripling turned to Chambers and drawled, "Ha-ya, Mistah Crawz-li?"[19]


That night, at Hiss's invitation, reporters crammed into his apartment in Greenwich Village, a preemptive strike against the "tendentious leaks" sure to be published in the next day's *Herald Tribune*. Hiss described the Commodore hearing. When Chambers had been led into the room, Hiss said, he failed to recognize "a single feature in his appearance." Chambers's "perfect" teeth were nothing like the dental ruin that had been George Crosley's distinguishing feature.

Did *anything* about Chambers seem familiar? reporters asked.

Hiss shook his head vehemently. "No! He might as well have had his face lifted." Also, Crosley had spoken in low, rounded tones, but Chambers's voice was a high-pitched quaver. Hiss imitated it, squeaking, "My name is Whittaker Chambers."

Hiss said he objected to the surprise hearing. "It's not my idea of normal, carefully thought out procedure."

He was not a Communist, he added, and never had been. "I do not believe in Communism. I believe it is a menace to the United States."[20]

## 21

# "I Could Not Do Otherwise"

That night Richard Nixon, who had booked a room at the Commodore, was on the phone. First he leaked the highlights of the Chambers-Hiss confrontation to a *New York Times* reporter. Then he talked for three hours with Bert Andrews, who handsomely repaid his source on next morning's front page. Nixon alone, wrote Andrews, had "hammered away at this particular phase of the investigation after other committee members were inclined to give up" and in a two-week span had produced results "more tangible than the Federal Bureau of Investigation and the Federal grand jury in New York City had been able to show after long inquiries."[1]

The next morning, bleary from his late-night phone work, Nixon interviewed three more witnesses at the Commodore. Only Donald Appell was present from HUAC. Nixon first questioned Nelson Frank of the *World-Telegram,* coauthor of the Elizabeth Bentley exposé. An ex-Communist, Frank had met Chambers in 1928, had known him in the early 1930s, before Chambers went underground, and had renewed the acquaintance in the 1940s through the anti-Communist caucus of the Newspaper Guild, a group with which Chambers had been peripherally involved while at *Time.* Chambers had put on a lot of weight, Frank testified, but was instantly recognizable. "As soon as I looked at the face, I knew him."[2]

Next came Isaac Don Levine. Nixon had interviewed him on August 7, following Chambers's Foley Square session. Levine had shown Nixon the notes he had scribbled after the visit to Adolf Berle. Under oath,

Levine said Chambers had given a thorough rundown of the operation, "opening up the insides of the State Department and various other departments in Washington where he had underground contacts who supplied him with documentary and confidential information for transmission to the Soviet Government." It was the first direct allegation of espionage. Nixon did not pursue it.[3]*

Levine had brought along his nine-year-old notes. The name Alger Hiss appeared on them, in ink. Levine vouched for Chambers, "a crystal honest person, dependable, sound, patriotic, intelligent, without malice toward anyone, with a high sense of justice and fair play." Physically Chambers had changed little over the years. The various news photos were "fair to excellent" likenesses.

The third and final witness that day was Priscilla Hiss, accompanied by her husband and Charles Dollard. She had come down from Peacham, Vermont, the night before. She was on vacation from her job, teaching seventh and eighth graders at the Dalton School in Manhattan. She was slender with delicate features and faint gray streaks in her blond hair. In a soft voice Mrs. Hiss said she had known George Crosley in 1934–1937, but not well. He was a "business" acquaintance of her husband. She had a "very distinct memory of [the Crosleys] spending two or three days in our house before they moved into the sublet apartment," probably in the summer of 1935. "It all seems very long ago and vague," said Mrs. Hiss.[5] Her "very dim impression" was of a "small person, very smiling person—a little too smiley, perhaps. I don't recollect the face, but a short person." He was also a, well, the polite word for it was "sponger." He and his family were "unwelcomed guests, guests that weren't guests."

After only ten minutes Nixon let the witness go. Later he realized it was a mistake. "Chambers had described her as, if anything, a more fanatical Communist than Hiss."[6]

That day John Foster Dulles urged Alger Hiss to resign the Carnegie presidency "and relieve the Endowment of embarrassment." Hiss replied that he preferred to wait until the HUAC hearings were concluded. Dulles said that was acceptable. Hiss also wrote a letter to the committee

---

* In an article published in *Plain Talk* in December 1947, Levine had all but implicated Hiss as a Soviet spy without naming him. Hiss told the FBI he had been aware of Levine's allegations since the summer of 1945.[4]

declining to take a polygraph since the device did not measure truthful-
ness, only the respondent's emotions. The committee released the letter
to the press.[7]

The date was nearing for the much-anticipated public hearing, "Confrontation Day," as it was being billed.[8] After a combined seven hours of
testimony the two witnesses were now on record with two detailed and
contradictory stories. In the *Herald Tribune* Bert Andrews enumerated
"major points of conflict" between Chambers and Hiss. Hiss said he had
been introduced to Chambers at the Nye Committee offices in the winter of 1934–1935. Chambers said he had first met Hiss at a luncheon,
with J. Peters also present, in the summer of 1934. Hiss claimed he had
cut off the "deadbeat" Crosley in 1935. Chambers said he had last seen
Hiss in December 1938 at the time of their emotional farewell. Chambers said Hiss had known him as Carl, an underground Communist
functionary. Hiss remembered only George Crosley, the hapless freelance
writer. They differed as well on the disposition of the 1929 Ford; on the
money Hiss had given Chambers (loans, said Hiss; party dues, said
Chambers); on Chambers's use of the Twenty-eighth Street apartment (a
sublet, said Hiss; "informal headquarters" for apparatus work, said
Chambers). They agreed on only one point: They had known each other
for a period in the mid-1930s during which Chambers had stayed
overnight in Hiss's house and driven his car.[9]

It might be impossible to resolve all these contradictions. But perhaps
HUAC could determine whose story was the more credible.

The hearing began, as scheduled, at ten-thirty, on a day of "infernal
heat." The temperature was to soar to ninety-three, the first surge of a
heat wave that was rolling across the eastern two thirds of the nation.[10]

All of political Washington was keyed up. The special session of Congress had adjourned three weeks before, leaving a vacuum filled by
HUAC and the Chambers-Hiss controversy. Twelve hundred spectators
were admitted into the caucus room. Of the hundreds more turned
away, many remained in the corridor, listening in.[11]

Inside, the scene was a taut amalgam of white-knuckle quiet and
buzzing activity. Photographers threaded through the room in search of
dramatic setups. Radio announcers hunched whispering over their microphones. News reporters handed scribbled "takes" to copyboys, who

squeezed through the throng massed in the doorway. Behind the podium where the committee members sat, television cameras towered up atop tripods. Chambers and Hiss were about to become the first congressional witnesses to be televised live, ushering in a new age of political spectacle. After Hiss–Chambers would come the Army–McCarthy hearings, Watergate, Oliver North, Clarence Thomas–Anita Hill. There were only 325,000 television sets in the nation in 1948, and only one American in ten had ever watched a television program, but the power of the new medium was already large. In July some ten million Americans had tuned in to watch the Republicans nominate Thomas Dewey. Millions would watch on this day too. The event lasted, all told, nine and a half hours, and the testimony filled 131 pages of closely printed text.[12]

Chairman Thomas, back on his throne, reminded those assembled that these were solemn proceedings. At their conclusion, he promised, "one of these witnesses will be tried for perjury." All the spectators were "guests" and must "refrain from any demonstration whatsoever, including applause."[13]

The first highlight came fifteen minutes into the proceedings. Stripling, clad in a white summer suit, approached the witness chair, where Hiss was seated, and asked him to rise; then the stooped-shouldered chief investigator extended an arm toward a row where reporters were seated and bade Chambers also to rise. The two witnesses silently regarded each other from a distance of about twelve feet. It was the Commodore stare-down restaged for the watching world.

Hiss, lean, lithe, and impeccably tailored (light suit, striped tie), clasped his hands behind his back and wore an expression of mingled bemusement and disdain.[14]

Chambers stood rocklike, arms stiffly at his sides, his stubby fingers peeping out from his overlong jacket sleeves. His eyes were narrowed, and his lips clamped tight.

Pointing a finger at Chambers, Stripling addressed Hiss. "Have you ever seen this individual?"

"I have," Hiss replied. The man was George Crosley. Hiss "first knew him sometime in the winter of 1934 or 1935" and last saw him "sometime in 1935 . . . according to my best recollection, not having checked the records."

Stripling then faced Chambers, who identified his adversary as "Mr. Alger Hiss." Chambers had met him in "I think about 1934" and known him until "about 1938."

Both witnesses then sat down.

Chambers did not speak again that morning. The panel questioned only Hiss. He was accompanied by two lawyers, both new to the case. In place of William Marbury, who had gone to Geneva to help negotiate a trade agreement,[15] was Washington attorney John F. Davis, joined shortly by a second lawyer, Harold Rosenwald, another of Hiss's acquaintances from Harvard Law.

The delay so worrisome to Nixon had actually worked to HUAC's advantage. In the interim Stripling's staff had fitted in more witnesses and accumulated new evidence. There had been a breakthrough only two days before, when documents relating to Hiss's Ford at last turned up. HUAC had also probed the career of "George Crosley" and found records on the Twenty-eighth Street apartment, supposedly subleased by Chambers.

These last showed that Hiss had vacated the apartment on June 28, 1935, and no new tenant had arrived until August. The gas and electricity had been turned off for the whole of July. This indicated Chambers had not occupied the place in the summer, as Hiss had remembered.* However, records did show that Hiss had taken over a new lease, on the P Street apartment, on May 1, 1935, nearly two months before the prior lease expired. With time remaining on the Twenty-eighth Street flat, Chambers possibly had occupied it in May and June, a total of nearly two months, a length of time consonant with Hiss's recollection.

The records did not say, however, whether the apartment had been subleased to Chambers (as Hiss said) or loaned to him (as Chambers maintained). But what, Hiss impatiently asked, had "questions of leases" to do with the important issue "of whether I was a Communist"? The committee "should be getting after the question of my record and what did people who worked closely and intimately with me think of me."

The committee turned next to the mysterious George Crosley. They had checked on him. No one but Hiss seemed to remember the free-lance writer. Stripling read aloud a letter from former Senator Gerald P. Nye. "The name of Crosley does not enter my recollection in any way, shape, or manner," Nye had written. Nye's chief investigator, Steven Raushenbush, Hiss's supervisor, likewise had no memory of Crosley.

---

* See page 105 for the sequence of residences Chambers occupied in the spring and summer of 1935.

Hiss said he too had yet to find a witness who remembered Crosley. There had been an anonymous phone call "from someone, a woman, who said she had known George Crosley" in the relevant period but she "was fearful of getting her employer in Dutch or something by publicity. We were not able to trace the call. She may have been imagining."

Mundt asked if Hiss had checked with his brother, Donald, to see if he remembered Crosley. "I have and he has no recollection."

On to the Ford. Hiss had said he "threw it in" with the subleased apartment. Could he say whether Crosley kept the car, sold it, or returned it to Hiss?

"I frankly did not recall," Hiss said.

But hadn't Hiss said the Ford had great sentimental value, the first auto he and his wife had owned, a "collegiate model" with a "sassy little trunk"?

Yes, but the vehicle had been sitting around unused, "the tires going down," when he had let Crosley have it in 1935. Thereafter Hiss had paid the car no mind. It was possible Chambers used it. "It is even possible that he returned it to me after using it. I really would not be sure of the details. My impression and recollection was that I got rid of it by giving it to him, but if the records show that it bounced back to me from him, that would not surprise me either."

But why, asked Mundt, must Hiss consult "records"? A man might confuse the facts of a sublease, even of a man's name or profession. But he did not forget what happened to his car, certainly not a car he had owned in the Depression, when any vehicle was a luxury. It was inconceivable that Hiss should draw a complete blank. The witness, Mundt warned, was beginning to "stretch the credulity of this committee."

"I am not an expert on the credulity of this committee," Hiss snapped.

Hiss was briefly excused from the stand while Louis Russell testified about a document the committee had found two days before at the Department of Motor Vehicles. It was a certificate, a title transfer, signed by Hiss on July 23, 1936. Russell read aloud from a photostat. It recorded Hiss's sale of the Ford to the Cherner Motor Company, a large Washington dealership. The document also recorded the car's resale on that same day, to one William Rosen, for twenty-five dollars. Rosen's whereabouts were unknown, but Nixon had interviewed Joseph Cherner, the owner of the lot, along with two of his employees. None remembered the transaction, though Cherner Motors kept a full set of sequenced invoices dating back to 1936.[16] Somehow Hiss's car had slipped in and out of the lot in a matter of hours.

Hiss, then, had sold his car to Cherner Motors, seemingly by prearrangement, just as Chambers had remembered. And the transaction had occurred in 1936, not 1935, when Hiss said his relationship with Chambers had ended.

Russell was dismissed, and Hiss was recalled. Had he signed the transfer certificate?

It "certainly looks like my signature," Hiss replied. Might he see the original document?

It was at the Department of Motor Vehicles, Stripling explained.

Thomas interjected: Couldn't Hiss tell from the photostat whether the signature was his?

"It looks like my signature to me, Mr. Chairman," Hiss said.

"Well," Thomas replied, "if that were the original, would it look any more like your signature?" Laughter rang out.

There was more on the car. The previous day the committee had questioned W. Marvin Smith, a colleague of Hiss's during Hiss's year at the Justice Department. Smith had notarized the transfer certificate and said he would have done so only if Hiss himself were present.[17] Hiss agreed that had probably been the case.

"Then, as far as you are concerned, this is your signature?" asked Nixon.

"As far as I am concerned, with the evidence that has been shown to me, it is."

Representative Hébert spoke up. Since the witness's memory had been "refreshed," did he now "recall the transaction whereby you disposed of the Ford?"

Hiss was firm. "I have no present recollection of the disposition of the Ford."

"You are a remarkable and agile young man," said an exasperated Hébert.

It was one o'clock. The hearing was recessed for lunch.

When it resumed at two-thirty, the panel took up a new topic, the discrepancy between Hiss's first HUAC testimony, when he denied knowing Chambers, and his subsequent admissions he had known "Crosley-Chambers" (as Hiss now called him) very well. A look at the record, said Hiss, would show he initially said only that the *name* Whittaker Chambers meant nothing to him.

But had he not failed to identify a photo of Chambers?

No, he had said he could not be sure. More photos were now pulled out. Hiss got a laugh when he called one, a large *Life* image, "a moderately good likeness, slightly flattering, I would say."

Hiss also was handed two snapshots of Chambers from 1934. They showed a shirt-sleeved Chambers holding aloft the infant Ellen. Chambers was younger and fitter than the witness of 1948 but was clearly the same man. Why had Hiss—who at the Commodore had boasted of his "rather good visual memory"—failed to make the connection?

Because of Chambers's teeth. They were Hiss's "strongest recollection" of the man.

"My question may sound facetious," said Nixon, "but I am just wondering: Didn't you ever see Mr. Crosley with his mouth closed?"

There was loud laughter.

Hiss did not budge. "If the George Crosley of 1934 could somehow be materialized and walk into the room, particularly if he kept his mouth closed, Mr. Nixon, I am not sure that I would be able definitely to pick him out of a group of other people. I have no clear recollection."

"Without hesitancy," Hébert pointed out, "every individual has remarked about the similarity of the two men, which are naturally the same man. And yet you and you alone—you, and you alone—sit here today and stand out as a lone individual who hedges and resorts to technicalities."

"That was a very loaded statement," Hiss protested.

"I hope it was," Hébert replied, "because I want you to get the full impact of it."

There was applause.

Furthermore, said Hébert, "Either you or Mr. Chambers [is] the damndest liar that ever came on the American scene."

But Hiss was not done. Before the hearing he had circulated a prepared statement to the press. He now read it aloud, plowing through a roster of dignitaries, much expanded since August 5. It now included a total of thirty-four names, all "living personages of recognized stature." Hiss read off all the names, beginning with Senators Tom Connally and Arthur Vandenberg, proceeding through three secretaries of state, and concluding with Francis Sayre. (Felix Frankfurter was not on the list.)

Here, said Hiss, were the best witnesses to his career. "They saw my every gesture, my every movement, my every facial expression. They heard the tones in which I spoke, the words I uttered, the words spoken by others in my presence. They knew my every act relating to official business, both in public and in executive conference."

These were the witnesses HUAC should question as they were "best able to testify concerning the loyalty with which I performed the duties assigned me. All are persons of unimpeachable character, in a position to know my work from day to day and hour to hour through many years. Ask them if they ever found in me anything except the highest adherence to duty and honor."

At the same time HUAC should investigate Chambers, "a self-confessed liar, spy, and traitor," neither honorable nor reliable, "unbalanced or worse." "Is he a man of sanity? Getting the facts about Whittaker Chambers, if that is his name, will not be easy. My own counsel have made inquiries in the past few days and have learned that his career is not, like those of normal men, an open book. His operations have been furtive and concealed. Why? What does he have to hide?"

Hiss read off a list of questions he wanted put to Chambers. He demanded to know all the aliases Chambers had used, all the addresses where he had lived, and wanted a "complete bibliography of all his writings." Hiss wanted to know the facts of Chambers's marriage and family. Chambers should also say "whether he has ever been treated for a mental illness."

Nixon leaped at this. Had Hiss any evidence of this?

"I have had various reports made to me to the effect that he has been."

"What reports?" asked Nixon.

"Reports made by individuals."

"What individuals?"

"They are so far only hearsay. The reports that came to me were from individuals, individual members of the press, so far, that they had heard rumors to that effect."

Nixon insisted on a name. Hiss mentioned William Walton, a former *Time* writer now with *The New Republic*. He had clashed with Chambers in 1944–1945. (Walton, it turned out, had repeated a thirdhand rumor.)[18]

Finally, Hiss wondered if Chambers was willing to repeat his allegations outside the jurisdiction of the committee "so that I may test his veracity in a suit for slander or libel." This was the same challenge Hiss had made on August 17, to which Chambers had yet to respond.

It was almost six o'clock when Hiss left the stand. The hearing was nearly eight hours old. Thomas called a very short recess, only seven minutes.

Then Chambers took the stand. Throughout Hiss's testimony he had remained impassive, arms folded, eyes often trained on the ceiling. He moved to the witness chair heavily, drably dressed in charcoal suit and black tie. In press accounts Hiss, not quite forty-four years old, was universally described as a "young man." No one ever said that of the gray-haired Chambers, though he was only three and a half years older than Hiss.[19]

He was weary but also determined to see his job through. Later it was said, by Chambers and others, that he had never meant to expose Alger Hiss, that Hiss's name was simply one in a list. This was not true. In his prepared statement of August 3, Chambers had said only a word or two about most of the Ware cell members, briefly mentioning the government positions they had held in the 1930s. The exception had been Hiss. Chambers had lingered over his accomplishments in the 1940s—in fact had exaggerated Hiss's role at Dumbarton Oaks, Yalta, and San Francisco. Chambers was determined to expose Hiss and had told Ray Murphy in 1945 that if Hiss were named permanent secretary to the UN, Chambers would publicly denounce him.[20]

This was not the ideal forum, and yet as much as Chambers abhorred the HUAC spectacle, he secretly welcomed the opportunity to give witness, to speak out directly as an "I," explaining what he had done and seen, after so many years of concealment. It is hardly a coincidence that the cadences of Chambers's HUAC testimony should anticipate the prose of *Witness*. The House Committee on Un-American Activities had given him his true voice, more perhaps than had *Time* and its obscuring screen of "group journalism."

Chambers leaned toward the microphone, sometimes clutching its base. In staccato sentences he reiterated, a touch hoarsely, the story he had been telling since August 3. He and Hiss had been secret Communists together. Hiss deemed it "a privilege to have a superior in the Communist organization at his home." Chambers had stayed at Hiss's apartment, as Hiss had testified, though "not longer than six weeks. I would think that was on the outside."

"Could it have been less?" Nixon asked.

"It could have been less."

"Could it have been more?"

"It could have been possibly more."

Nixon then led Chambers through a reprise of his Hotel Commodore testimony. "You are sure you did not bring any furniture?"

"Absolutely sure," said Chambers.

"You are sure there was no agreement for rental?"

"There was no agreement for rental."

"Why would Mr. Hiss let you go in there for nothing?"

"Because Mr. Hiss and I were Communists, and that was a comradely way of treating one another. There is nothing unusual in such a procedure among Communists."

Had Hiss sold Chambers an automobile?

"No, he did not."

"Did he loan you an automobile for the period that you were in the apartment?"

"No, he did not."

"Did he at any time sell you an automobile?"

"He never sold me an automobile."

What *was* the story of the car?

The same one Chambers had told on August 7. Hiss, "a devoted and at that time a rather romantic Communist," had insisted the Ford be given to the open Party. Chambers was not involved in the transaction.

They proceeded to the questions Hiss had raised about Chambers. He answered them all, balking at only one. He preferred not to divulge his home address for fear of inviting assassination.

Nixon asked Chambers about his visit to Hiss in December 1938. Had he gone to see all the members of the Washington ring?

No, only a few.

Why Hiss?

Because Chambers was "very fond of him." Hiss was "perhaps my closest friend."

"Mr. Hiss was your closest friend?" Nixon repeated, letting the words sink in.

"Mr. Hiss was certainly the closest friend I ever had in the Communist Party."

Then Nixon asked a question on many people's minds. "Mr. Chambers, can you search your memory now to see what motive you can have for accusing Mr. Hiss of being a Communist at the present time?"

"What motive can I have?"

"Yes, I mean, do you—is there any grudge that you have against Mr. Hiss over anything that he has done to you?"

As Chambers formed his reply, his voice "slowed close to choking." He seemed on the verge of tears.[21] "The story has spread that in testifying against Mr. Hiss I am working out some old grudge, or motives of revenge or hatred. I do not hate Mr. Hiss. We were close friends, but we are caught in a tragedy of history. Mr. Hiss represents the concealed enemy against which we are all fighting, and I am fighting. I have testified against him with remorse and pity, but in a moment of historic jeopardy in which this nation now stands, so help me God, I could not do otherwise." Chambers reached for a paper cup of water and sipped from it. Hiss, two rows back among a group of reporters, taking notes, looked up and shook his head.[22]

When Chambers had recovered, Hébert complimented him on his rehabilitation. It was a great thing to have traveled the path from Communist "traitor" to friendly HUAC witness. (In the August 16 session with Hiss, Hébert had characterized Chambers as a "stool pigeon.") Was it not a fact, Hébert asked Chambers, "that there are many saints in Heaven today who were not always saints?"

"I am not a saint, indeed," said Chambers.

He was more at ease explaining the appeal communism had held for his generation, a question that genuinely interested him. In their youth, he explained, he and many others had been seeking "a moral solution in a world of moral confusion. Marxism-Leninism offers an oversimplified explanation of the causes and a program for action. The very vigor of the project particularly appeals to the more or less sheltered middle-class intellectuals, who feel that the whole context of their lives has kept them away from the world of reality. . . . They feel a very natural concern, one might almost say a Christian concern, for underprivileged people. They feel a great intellectual concern, at least, for recurring economic crises, the problem of war, which in our lifetime has assumed an atrocious proportion, and which always weights on them. What shall I do? At that crossroads the evil thing, Communism, lies in waiting."

The danger, he added, was that the believer, once within the fold, would commit any crime in its name, as Chambers had done. "Every Communist is a potential saboteur and a permanent enemy of this system of government."

It was 8:00 P.M. The committee adjourned. The vast crowd filed out of the caucus room. Television sets, up and down the eastern seaboard, flickered off.

Chambers left the hearing room with *Time*'s Washington bureau chief, Jim Shepley. In the marble corridor a teenager came up to them breathless. "Mr. Chambers, I want to thank you. That part about the tragedy of history—you don't know what it means to young people like me."

Chambers thanked him in return and walked on. It was small solace. He had, yet again, fetched his soiled bone.[23]

The next day HUAC members met to assess the case. Their job was finished, said the Democrat Eddie Hébert. They had identified Hiss as a perjurer and could turn over their findings to the Justice Department for "immediate prosecution." Nixon and Mundt disagreed. Why stop now? Stripling had located the purchaser of Hiss's Ford, William Rosen. And there were other witnesses to question. J. Peters, for one. Hébert angrily accused Nixon and Mundt of partisanship. They wanted to "drag" the hearings out through the election and punish Truman and the Democrats. (Hébert himself would not suffer. He was running on the segregationist Dixiecrat ticket, headed by South Carolina governor Strom Thurmond.[24]) Hébert had a point. HUAC Republicans were eager to turn the flame up under Truman, more vulnerable than ever. At the same time Republicans feared that Truman or Attorney General Clark would quash, rather than pursue, a perjury indictment.

Finally Nixon and Mundt prevailed, and the case went forward, with gathering speed. On August 26 William Rosen, testifying in secret session, pleaded the Fifth Amendment to all pertinent questions, refusing to say whether he had bought the used Ford car and whether he was a Communist.[25]

The next day *The New York Times* reported that Louis Budenz, sometime editor of the *Daily Worker* since turned informer and Fordham University professor, had told HUAC that in the 1940s he had often heard Hiss spoken of as being "under Communist discipline."[26]

After the public hearing Chambers accepted an invitation to be interviewed two days later (August 27) on the evening radio news program *Meet the Press*. He knew the program's host, Lawrence Spivak, the anti-Communist publisher of the *American Mercury*, the monthly to which

Chambers had contributed book reviews in 1944 as "John Land." The program aired live at 8:00 P.M.

But first Chambers had a stop to make. HUAC had called him in for an emergency session. There had been another lightning bolt. The evening edition of the *Baltimore News-Post,* a tabloid, had reported a new link between Chambers and Hiss. Edward Case, the Westminster Realtor who had sold Chambers the Shaw place in 1937, had letters and contracts showing Alger Hiss had originally negotiated to buy the property in 1936. "It was one of the oddest deals I ever had," Case told the *News-Post.* "The house was run down. It was five miles off a paved road. Yet here were two important men, both apparently anxious to buy it." At the time Case had not connected the two buyers. "But now, since reading about the hearings and the stuff about whether they knew each other—well, I'm not so sure."[27] The tabloid ran a large spread, featuring photos of the property and of letters both Chambers and Hiss had written to Case.

Nixon and Stripling questioned Chambers for an hour. Not long into their friendship, said Chambers, he and Hiss had discovered a common attraction to rural living. They had talked about getting land in the country. Hiss had seen Case's ad first and paid a small security on the property. Later Chambers accompanied Hiss to Westminster for another look. Eventually Hiss had backed out of the deal because Priscilla disliked the area. But Chambers had been taken by the setting, the house, and the unkempt acreage, and when he returned to Baltimore the following year, he had contacted Case and made a deposit, keeping the purchase secret from Hiss. "As far as I know he never knew I had that place, nor did I want him to." It all came down to conspiratorial practice. "I had two compartments, Whittaker Chambers on the one side, which is my more or less private compartment, and Carl in these groups here, and I did not want any bridge between them."[28]

Stripling was bothered. Why on earth was Chambers holding back on the committee at this late date? What was his real purpose? "Chambers is a peculiar individual," the investigator told the FBI. "He sits and lights his pipe, he is cold and calculating, and he knows exactly what he will do three weeks hence." Chambers was telling the truth, Stripling believed—but not all of it.[29]

After the hearing Chambers proceeded to the *Meet the Press* studio. The program was broadcast over 346 stations nationwide. It was later estimated that twelve million listeners tuned in that night. By now the world knew Hiss had dared Chambers to repeat his allegations outside the protective immunity of the hearing room.[30]

Chambers had hoped Spivak would assemble a balanced panel, with two of the four journalists not "actively hostile." It was not to be. The questioners were all pro-Hiss: Tom Reynolds of the Chicago *Sun-Times,* Nat Finney of the *Minneapolis Star and Tribune,* and Edward Folliard of *The Washington Post.* The moderator, James Reston of *The New York Times,* whose coverage of Dumbarton Oaks had won him a Pulitzer Prize, had recommended Hiss for the Carnegie presidency in 1946.[31]

Folliard asked the first question, going straight to the issue uppermost in many minds. "Are you willing," Folliard said, "to say now that Alger Hiss is or ever was a Communist?"[32]

"Alger Hiss was a Communist and may be now," Chambers replied.

Was Chambers prepared for a lawsuit?

"I do not think Mr. Hiss will sue me for slander or libel."

Tom Reynolds, the most belligerent questioner, asked Chambers if he was profiting from his role as an anti-Communist, a charge later repeated many times.

Chambers blandly replied that he had given no thought to money while a Communist and today had "no difficulty in making a living."

Reynolds brought up another point. It was well known that reporters had often gone to Hiss with questions in his days at State since he was considered a reliable and voluble source. Had Chambers, in his capacity as foreign news editor, ever used "material" supplied by Hiss?

"Not to my knowledge," said Chambers.

"Not to your knowledge?" Reynolds repeated incredulously. "How could you escape that knowledge if the memorandum came in marked 'from Alger Hiss'?"

"I recall no such memorandum," Chambers levelly replied.

Reynolds also probed into the ambiguous nature of Chambers's allegations. What exactly was he accusing Hiss of? "Did he do anything wrong? Did he commit any overt act? Has he been disloyal to his country?"

"I am only prepared at this time to say he was a Communist," said Chambers.

Could he point to a single disloyal act?

"I am not prepared legally to make that charge," Chambers carefully replied. "My whole interest in this business has been to show that Mr. Hiss was a Communist."

Not that the apparatus had been "playing around," he hastened to add. It had managed, after all, to penetrate the upper rungs of the State and Treasury departments. Chambers's contacts had influenced policy— "much more important than spying."

But had they done even this? asked Spivak. Could Chambers say whether Hiss "in any of the jobs he had, had any real influence on our policy?" At Yalta, for instance?

No, he could not.

"I was in Washington," said Reynolds, "at the time that the Soviet Union was recognized by the United States. Liberalism, so-called, was the fashion and the fad. Oliver Wendell Holmes was the god of such young people as Mr. Alger Hiss." Hiss's record was that of a "leftist in the Holmes pattern." Was *that* his crime?

"I am accusing him of membership in the Communist Party," said Chambers sharply. "I am not even accusing him of that. I am simply saying he *was* a member of the Party."

When it ended, Richard Nixon phoned the studio, fuming. The broadcast was "a damned outrage."[33] Chambers agreed. But there was more to the attack than simple animus. The panelists had drawn attention to an important fact. For all the furor it had caused, Chambers's testimony lacked substance. He had yet to say exactly what it was he and Alger Hiss had done as accomplices. Joining the Communist Party was a legal act in the mid-1930s. So were paying Party dues, meeting secretly with other Communists, giving a Communist the use of one's apartment, and turning over one's car to indigent Party "organizers" out West. It was not even against the law to lobby for the downfall of Chiang Kai-shek.

Elizabeth Bentley's allegations were another matter. She had spoken of spying. Chambers had not. There was a gaping hole at the center of his testimony.

Perhaps it would soon be filled. Chambers had met Hiss's dare. It was up to Hiss, once more, to decide what course the controversy took next.

# The Means of Justice

As if the discovered farm connection and Chambers's *Meet the Press* interview were not enough for one day, on August 27 HUAC released an "interim report" on the hearings. The committee, to no one's surprise, found that "the verifiable portions of Chambers's testimony have stood up strongly" while Hiss's "have been badly shaken." The burden of proof had "definitely shifted" from accuser to accused. The report also took aim at the executive branch. HUAC complained of being "hampered at every turn" by President Truman and the attorney general, whose "failure to enforce the laws as vigorously as he should has been in large part responsible for the growth and power of the Communist conspiracy."

Confident it had established "that a well-organized and dangerous espionage ring operated in the Government during the war," HUAC called for the New York grand jury to be reimpaneled and presented with the new testimony of Bentley and Chambers.[1]

Hiss volleyed back with an "open letter" to HUAC, fourteen pages long, in which he assailed his accuser as "a confessed traitor," psychologically unstable and "somewhat queer," who for thirteen years had wallowed "in the sewers, plotting against his native land. . . . No American is safe from the imagination of such a man, so long as [HUAC] uses the great powers and prestige of the United States Congress to help sworn traitors to besmirch any American they may pick upon."[2]

Hiss said nothing about a suit against Chambers. At first no one noticed. Too much else was happening in the case.

On August 30 Chambers appeared for another HUAC hearing, this time in New York, again at Foley Square. The star attraction was J. Peters, under custody since 1947 and now facing deportation. At age fifty-four the Hungarian still had a thick head of hair and wore his usual well-tailored suit. When Chambers rose to identify his former boss, whom he had not laid eyes on in ten years, Peters stared back stonily at the man he later referred to as a "police informer."

Under oath Peters gave his name ("Alexander Stevens") and address (Kew Gardens, Queens). He also said he had been a friend of Earl Browder, a sly admission since Browder had been read out of the movement in 1945, when Moscow shut down the Popular Front. For the rest Peters invoked the Fifth Amendment, as his superiors had instructed him to do.

After Peters had departed, Chambers took the stand and testified that Peters had been present at the first meeting of Chambers and Hiss, at a Washington restaurant, in 1934. Harold Ware may have been there too.[3]

Another important witness also testified on August 30: Adolf Berle. He had left the government in 1946, after losing out in a policy dispute. He was now practicing law in New York and teaching it at Columbia.

Berle's testimony was among the most curious and confusing HUAC was to hear. Disputing his own notes, Berle said Chambers had told him in 1939 of "a study group of some sort . . . formed of men who were interested in knowing something about Russia and Russian policy and the general Communist theory of life." The hope was that all these men "would go, as they called it, 'underground.' " But none, Berle was sure, was actually a Communist. Besides, "the idea that the two Hiss boys and Nat Witt were going to take over the United States Government didn't strike me as any immediate danger."

Yet, Berle went on to say, as a result of Chambers's allegations he had taken swift and decisive steps to overhaul the intelligence procedures he had been supervising. He built a pipeline through which information would be exchanged between the FBI and State's security division. He had also lobbied the Justice Department to draft the legislation that became the Foreign Agents Registration Act—that is, the Smith Act, passed by Congress in 1940, which had resulted in the grand jury indictments of July 1948. Together these measures, Berle said, "kept things pretty clear" in the department for several years.

Berle said not a word about the notes he had made in 1939 of a full-fledged underground conspiracy, vastly more developed than what Chambers had so far outlined to HUAC. His jottings included such notations as "Plans for two battleships—secured in 1937" and "Aerial bombsight Detectors." Why did Berle suppress this information? Because, in his opinion, the issue of Communist infiltration was best handled through surveillance rather than through open prosecution. Also, his Liberal party was backing President Truman in the election, and he did not want to harm the incumbent. His testimony was intended as a "sedative," which he hoped would inject "sanity into a supercharged atmosphere."

But Berle did drop one hint that something had been amiss. In 1944, when Soviet policy was being hammered out at State, "we were all trying not to tell anything that ought not be told." But "there were pretty consistent leaks whenever anything went through [Hiss's] office."[4]

On September 3, exactly one month after Chambers had first taken the stand, HUAC announced it was postponing further public hearings until September 15. The members dispersed to their home districts to campaign. President Truman, set to embark on his historic whistle-stop tour, once again dismissed the inquiry as a "red herring" and promised to prove as much by election day.[5]

But a new question was on everyone's mind, put most succinctly in the New York *Daily News*: "Well, Alger, where's that suit?" With William Marbury still out of the country, Hiss had been sifting through the conflicting advice of his supporters. Some were urging him to sue immediately. In Cambridge, where many were following the case intently, Harvard President James B. Conant, among others, feared that every day Hiss let slip by damaged his case and put other liberals at risk. But in New York Hiss was getting different advice. The attorney handling the suit in Marbury's absence, Hiss's Harvard classmate Edward McLean, a senior partner at the firm of Debevoise, Plimpton, & McLean, was urging caution. So were friendly members of the Carnegie board. John Foster Dulles, in touch with both Nixon and Hiss, was studiedly neutral. Hiss had yet to make up his mind in mid-September, when Marbury returned from Geneva and resumed control of the case.[6]

Marbury had been raised in the same Baltimore neighborhood as Hiss, Bolton Hill, and had preceded him to Harvard Law. He had later been chief legal adviser to the War Department, receiving the Presidential Medal for Merit, then the nation's highest civilian award. He was a superb legal technician and knew his way around slander cases.[7] Marbury advised Hiss that further delay could prove damaging. Hiss agreed.[8]

But Marbury spoke more confidently than he felt. While abroad he had read disturbing reports about Hiss's comportment during the HUAC hearings. And in conversation with General Lucius Clay, the military governor of Allied-occupied Germany, Marbury was taken aback when Clay told him that in his "own contacts with Hiss over Chinese matters, Hiss had consistently taken positions which were helpful to the Chinese Communists"—precisely the charge Karl Mundt had made.[9]*

On September 18 Richard Nixon took a break from his campaign to convene a hearing in Los Angeles with retired Admiral William H. Standley, a onetime chief of naval operations and FDR's Moscow envoy in 1942–1943. Standley had contacted Nixon after hearing of Berle's testimony about State Department leaks. The leaks Berle described were "common knowledge," said Standley. It was "also common gossip that the State Department codes were insecure"—the codes, he meant, in which diplomatic cables traveled between Washington and the Moscow embassy. President Roosevelt had switched to navy codes, fearing "disloyal personnel" at State had leaked messages to Moscow or that Soviet cryptanalysts had broken the code. The Hiss case might turn into a spy case after all.[11]

Hiss and Marbury, meanwhile, were moving closer to filing suit. In New York Marbury won the assurance of the Carnegie board that Hiss would be kept on as president until the trial was completed. Hiss's friend James Shotwell, a board member, would assume the day-to-day duties of the presidency, freeing Hiss to concentrate on the suit.

Marbury, meeting with Alger and Priscilla Hiss, counseled them of the dangers the suit posed. If either Alger or Priscilla had "any skeletons in the closet," Marbury warned, they were sure to come tumbling forth. Husband and wife assured him "there was no cause for worry." They had no secrets.

But Marbury had picked up hints of ambivalence from Priscilla Hiss. Drawing her aside, the attorney asked if she was holding something back. Mrs. Hiss said she was not. She "stoutly supported Alger's story of his association with 'George Crosley' and flatly denied that either she or Alger

---

* But according to Clay's biographer, in 1944 Hiss had favored granting a loan to Chiang Kai-shek and Clay had "bristled at the prospect."[10]

had ever been connected with a Communist party apparatus." Still, Marbury sensed she felt "responsible" for the fix her husband was in.

On September 22, at a conference in Marbury's Baltimore office, Hiss declared his readiness to proceed with the suit. The logical place to file was Baltimore. Hiss's reputation there was high, Marbury's practice was in that city, and Chambers was a Maryland resident.[12]

On the afternoon of Monday, September 27, a month to the day after Chambers's appearance on *Meet the Press,* Hiss filed suit for slander. The complaint (written by Ed McLean) said the "untrue, false and defamatory" charges made by Chambers had damaged Hiss's "professional reputation and office, brought him into public odium and contempt and caused him great pain and mental anguish." Hiss sought fifty thousand dollars in damages. In a press statement the plaintiff added, "I am glad that my case is now in the hands of the court."[13]

Chambers issued a terse reply from Westminster: "I welcome Mr. Hiss's daring suit. I do not minimize the audacity or ferocity of the forces which work through him. But I do not believe Mr. Hiss or anybody else can use the means of justice to defeat the ends of justice." Chambers's second sentence, implying Hiss was still a Communist, was "clearly libelous." Hiss retaliated by tacking on an additional twenty-five thousand dollars in damages.[14]

The next day, in a nationally broadcast address, President Truman said HUAC had "injured the reputations of innocent men" by spreading "wild and false accusations." The culprit was the Republican party, "the unwitting ally of the Communists in this country."[15]

Chambers's feeling of isolation, so powerful since August 3, had steadily increased. His career at *Time* was all but finished, even though he remained on the masthead, a formal declaration of Luce's own loyalty. Because of the distractions, he did not complete the *Life* essay on 1848 or attempt any further writing. Nor did he visit the Rockefeller Center offices, which divided over the case like the rest of America. Some staff members were convinced Chambers was telling the truth. Others were appalled at the spectacle of his paranoia being elevated into a national controversy. *Time's* National Affairs editor, Tom Griffith, found himself struggling to ensure reports on the case were not slanted *against* the senior editor.[16]

Chambers had not felt so powerless since 1938. And at times this experience seemed a reprise of his defection. Once more he feared assassination and found solace only in the company of a few trusted friends. Calvin Fixx's Queens apartment became a refuge. Seated in the living room, with a pot of tea at his elbow, Chambers talked with calm fatalism of Krivitsky, Poyntz, and Arnold Ikal. "His apprehension didn't show as fear," recalled Fixx's wife, Marlys, "but as intelligent understanding." At home he kept his gun within easy reach and placed bullets in every one of the thirteen rooms. He told staff at Ellen's and John's schools not to let the children leave the grounds and "to let no one take either child away on any pretext whatever."[17]

This seemed typical Chambers paranoia, and typically it was not without foundation. On October 20 Marvin Smith, the Justice Department official who had notarized the transfer document on Hiss's Ford, was found dead in a stairwell at the Justice Department building, evidently a suicide. There was no explanation for his death. Smith's widow was convinced he had been murdered.[18]

But in reality the time for an attempt on Chambers's life had long passed. On one point at least President Truman was right. Chambers's allegations, while by no means a red herring, were outdated. He described his purpose as "eradicating Communism in the United States,"[19] as though this were 1938, not 1948—a time when anticommunism had become the government's rallying cry via the loyalty program, the Marshall Plan, aid to Greece and Turkey, the Berlin airlift, the outrage over the Communist-backed coup in Czechoslovakia, hand-wringing over China, harsh words flying back and forth each day between Moscow and Washington. Chambers implied Hiss still posed a danger to national security when the man had been out of government since 1947. Like so many ex-Communists, Chambers was cocooned in a bygone period, that of his own underground exploits, the vanished era of 1936—of Spain, the show trials, the Popular Front, of Boris Bykov come to awaken *die Quellen* to their high revolutionary purpose.

But others too seemed to think the events of the 1930s demanded examination. Despite the passage of years, the transactions between Chambers and Hiss—whatever exactly they were—remained curiously freighted with implication. Was it possible Chambers and Hiss really had been friends? After all, no one was denying Chambers had been a Communist. If Hiss had consorted with such a man, did that mean the New Deal had a shadow side, secret alliances, sinister pairings, subversions? And might those subversions be the root cause of the current frustrations of the United States, helpless in the face of invisible enemies?

Back in August Richard Nixon had grasped how much rode on the question of a possible Chambers-Hiss friendship, if it could be established. Hiss too had known how damaging it could prove. No wonder he had initially denied ever having known Chambers when the wiser course—urged on him by Dulles, for one—would have been to own up to some reckless errors in the 1930s. Given the current political climate, he had no choice but to stand firm.

By now Chambers too realized Hiss would stick with his original story, admitting nothing and trying to discredit his accuser. And with a suit formally lodged, the rumors would spill out into the open, the whispers grow loud. It was the last thing Chambers needed. There were secrets deeply lodged in the multiple compartments of his life, not all of them well guarded.

Hiss's team of attorneys had already begun a thorough ransacking of Chambers's past. Investigators went to Lynbrook and interviewed neighbors who volubly related stories of "the French family" and its strange son. The Hiss team also searched for evidence Chambers had been institutionalized and was homosexual. Communist Party contacts, such as Lee Pressman and Henry Collins, turned up ex-comrades with much to say about the ménage on the Lower East Side with Mike Intrator and Grace Lumpkin. Hiss himself kept his lawyers supplied with useful tips on Chambers, many obtained through "anonymous" sources, presumably Hiss's own recollections.

Chambers's *Time* adversaries also offered help, repeating stories of his paranoia. Another helpful source was the journalist A. J. Liebling, *The New Yorker*'s press critic. In the fall of 1948 Liebling acquired a second role as clandestine operative for Alger Hiss. Conveniently exempting himself from the standards he applied to his fellow journalists, Liebling tricked Mark Van Doren into handing over his Chambers correspondence and then delivered the letters to Hiss's attorney Harold Rosenwald. Van Doren rued this deception. Liebling did not. In fact, with remarkable audacity, he continued to report on the case in his "Wayward Press" columns even as he tweaked the nation's dailies for their biased coverage.[20]

Luckily Time Inc. decided it too had a stake in the slander case—the credibility of a top editor had been challenged—and provided Chambers with a topflight attorney, Harold Medina, Jr., of the prestigious firm of Cravath, Swain. Chambers also retained counsel in Baltimore. After interviewing several candidates, he chose Richard Cleveland, the eldest son of Grover Cleveland. At one time the younger Cleveland had been mentioned as a possible Democratic vice president, until, disillusioned by the New Deal, he had opposed FDR's reelection, so ending his own political future. Since then Cleveland had built a solid corporate practice at the firm of Semmes, Bowen, & Semmes, specializing in bank mergers. Not a litigator, he brought his partner William Macmillan into the suit to assist with trial preparations.

In October Chambers drove daily from Westminster to Baltimore and the law offices of Semmes, Bowen, & Semmes, in the O'Sullivan Building, the city's tallest. Cleveland's twenty-first-floor office overlooked the expanse of Druid Hill Park, aburst in autumnal colors. Placid and thoughtful, like his presidential father, Cleveland gently led Chambers through a minute reconstruction of his past while Macmillan pressed for details—and more details.[21]

They tried but quickly abandoned the attempt to search for corroborating witnesses. Almost everyone in a position to help was loyal to Hiss and remained so for many years to come.

Chambers did have some allies, but they were not doing him much good, though at least one, Isaac Don Levine, strenuously tried to. As early as December 1947 Levine had written an article in *Plain Talk* in which he alleged "certain high and trusted officials in the State Department, including one who had played a leading role at Yalta and in organizing the United Nations, delivered confidential papers to Communist agents who microfilmed them for dispatch to Moscow." In his HUAC appearance on August 18 Levine had again raised the theme of spying. Nixon had let it pass. Possibly he doubted Levine's credibility. (He would not have been alone. The FBI also thought Levine an unreliable witness.) Perhaps too Nixon wished to downplay the conflict between Levine's testimony and Chambers's. No matter. Levine was used to solitary crusades. After Adolf Berle had testified Chambers had told him of an innocent Marxist "study group," Levine had indignantly summoned reporters to the Fifth Avenue offices of *Plain Talk* and showed them his notes with their references to spying.[22]

In the fall Levine struck again, with a two-part series in *Plain Talk* detailing Chambers's meetings with Berle and Walter Krivitsky. On the visit to Berle, wrote Levine, Chambers sketched in "the general picture of two Soviet undercover 'centers' or rings" that had operated in Washington. "Both groups were gathering and supplying confidential data to Moscow," via microfilm. Chambers had named six New Deal officials who had "knowingly furnished confidential data to Soviet undercover agents. Mr. Berle and I were shocked by the list, which included the Hiss brothers, then in inconspicuous positions." Levine was determined to link Chambers's allegations to Bentley's and to bring the spy ring to light, even if it meant contradicting Chambers's sworn testimony.[23]

Meanwhile the same New York grand jury that had indicted the Communist Party leaders in July was reconvened at Foley Square on October 14, with Chambers as its first witness. Not long into the session, a juror asked if Chambers could "give one name of anybody who, in your opinion, was positively guilty of espionage against the United States government."

"Let me think a moment," Chambers replied, "and I will try to answer that. I don't think so but I would like to have the opportunity to answer you tomorrow more definitely. Let me think it over overnight."

Chambers's indecision was pragmatic. With the election two weeks away, and President Truman's statements growing more combative, it looked as though the government had not "the slightest intention of proceeding against" the accused, including Hiss. Worse, it seemed the administration's "special wrath was reserved for anyone who might raise the issue of Communism in Government."

The next day, when Chambers returned for questioning, the juror repeated his question.

"I assume," Chambers cautiously replied, "espionage means in this case the turning over of secret or confidential documents."

Or "oral information," said the juror.

"I do not believe I do know such a name," said Chambers.[24]

On November 2, 1948, election day, Chambers sat by the radio listening to the returns. Truman defeated Dewey, confounding the experts. The Democrats also regained control of both houses of Congress. It was a stunning vindication, as Truman said, of the New Deal. The past had not been thoroughly repudiated as yet.

Richard Nixon, easily reelected—thanks in large part to his celebrated role in the Hiss case—visited Westminster and found Chambers "in a mood of deep depression." In rousing stump speeches Truman had promised to end the spy hearings and abolish HUAC. Chambers was certain the Justice Department would target him for retribution. Soon *The New York Times* would report HUAC was on the verge of extinction, and *The New Republic* would refer to it as a "lame duck" committee.[25]

On November 4 Chambers went to Baltimore for the first pretrial examination in the slander suit, held at Bill Marbury's office in the Maryland Trust Building. Chambers was accompanied by Cleveland and Macmillan. In addition to Marbury, Ed McLean and Harold Rosenwald were there for Hiss. Marbury did the questioning, methodically leading Chambers on a synoptic tour of the darkest passages of his history, beginning with the blasphemous "class prophecy" of 1919, proceeding through the months in the New Orleans flophouse, "The Play for Puppets" scandal at Columbia, and the book-thieving episode uncovered at the New York Public Library. Then it was on to Chambers's homosexual poetry, the long cohabitation with Ida Dailes, Richard Chambers's suicide, and Chambers's Communist career, open and underground. They had just reached the Ware Group when they adjourned, at four forty-five.

Resuming the next day, Chambers gave a vividly detailed account of his relationship with Hiss and for the first time hinted at the true dimension of the conspiracy. In 1934 or 1935, said Chambers, he had received State Department documents from Hiss, who had got access to them through his Nye Committee work. Later, when Hiss moved over to State, he "occasionally gave the Communist Party bits of information which he thought might be useful to them."

"You mean he handed you a document?" Marbury asked.

"I frequently read State Department documents in Mr. Hiss's house. Mr. Hiss very often brought a brief case with documents home, and I used to read those that were interesting."

Marbury, aware Chambers had expanded his claims, repeated an earlier demand that Chambers turn over "any correspondence, either typewritten or in handwriting . . . from any member of the Hiss family, letters from Mr. Alger Hiss, or Mrs. Hiss, or from Mr. Donald Hiss, or from Mrs. Donald Hiss." Cleveland asked for a postponement while Chambers searched for such evidence.[26]

Discussing the case privately, defendant and counsel agreed "the Hiss forces had turned the tables." Hiss's evasive HUAC testimony was no longer the issue. Nor did it matter if Hiss and Chambers had once been friends. The slander suit revolved on a single point: whether or not Hiss had been a Communist, the very issue Nixon had wisely skirted. Chambers's reminiscences, so persuasive during the HUAC hearings, would not stand up in court unsupported by hard facts or a second witness. As things stood, no jury would find in favor of Chambers.[27]

Finally Chambers said to his lawyer. "You feel, don't you, that there is something missing."

Yes, said Cleveland.

"There *is* something missing," Chambers admitted. "I am shielding Hiss." The attorney gazed over the rims of his half glasses while Chambers formed the word "Espionage."[28]

*Chambers at the time of the case in his habitual Quaker-gray. "Who would dress like that?" a* Time *colleague wondered. "A man on call as a pall-bearer? An enthusiast of a sternly cheerless sect?"*

*Hiss at the founding conference of the United Nations held in San Francisco in May 1945. Standing: U.S. Secretary of State Edward Stettinius. Seated next to Hiss: Soviet Foreign Secretary V.M. Molotov.*

*Father and son (age 12) doing the afternoon milking on New Year's Day 1949, shortly after Hiss was indicted for perjury. "Everyone seems to wonder how I am going to get along," Chambers told a reporter. "The milk from my cows grosses an average of about $500 a month."*

*Esther, Ellen (age 16) and John Chambers (age 12) at home in Westminster, Maryland, January 1949.*

*Juliette Poyntz, photo from Soviet archives. One of America's most accomplished women Communists — educated at Oxford and the London School of Economics, and a lecturer at Columbia University. She vanished mysteriously from her New York apartment in June 1937.*

*Ruth Robinson and Arnold Ikal. Their arrest on a visit to Moscow in November 1937 caused a diplomatic crisis and made front-page headlines. Soon it emerged that the couple had been travelling on two pairs of forged passports – normal practice for Soviet agents. (Photos from KGB archives.)*

*Walter Krivitsky, the defector from Soviet intelligence and confidant of Chambers, testifies to HUAC in 1939. Seated on his left: his interpreter, Menshevik writer Boris Shub. Krivitsky died under mysterious circumstances in 1941.*

*Esther Chambers (with her husband, in shadow) leaving the courthouse in an F.B.I. car after testifying at the first trial, in June 1949.*

*First-term Representative Richard Nixon (left), with Robert Stripling, HUAC's chief investigator (center), and John Townie, secretary of the Commerce Department's Loyalty Board, in 1948.*

*Hiss's first HUAC appearance, on August 5, 1948. "He absolutely took over that hearing," Robert Stripling later said.*

*The "freshman" makes good. Nixon after he seized command of the investigation, flanked by Stripling and Representative Edward Hébert.*

*Robert Stripling shows Alger Hiss a photograph of Chambers, who said he and Hiss had been close associates in the Communist underground during the 1930s. Hiss initially testified that he did not recognize Chambers from the photograph.*

*Nixon, Stripling, and HUAC chairman Parnell Thomas with typed testimony of the August 1948 hearings soon to be submitted to the Justice Department.*

*Chambers and Hiss brought together in public for the first time, on "Confrontation Day." HUAC members are seated in back, and television cameramen stand above.*

*The witness arrives at the U.S. Federal Courthouse on the morning of June 3, 1949, to face cross-examination in the first trial.*

*"Confrontation Day." Chambers testifies on August 25, 1948, a day of "infernal heat," in the House caucus room — the first televised congressional hearing in U.S. history.*

The jury in the first Hiss trial returns from a lunch break during their deliberations, which ended deadlocked in July 1949.

"Red Spy Queen" Elizabeth Bentley, the one-time Communist courier whose HUAC testimony in July 1948 led the committee to summon a corroborating witness – Chambers.

Nixon and Stripling meet the press in late August 1948, after "Confrontation Day" but before Chambers produced the documentary evidence that backed up his claims.

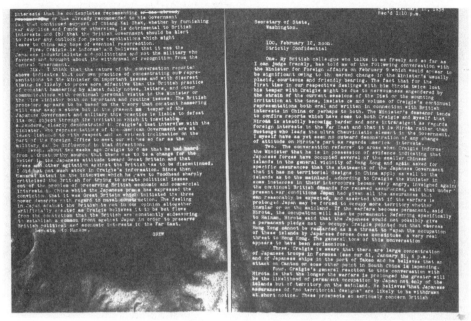

*The stolen documents. Some of the papers Chambers produced at his deposition in the slander trial in November 1948. Hard copies like this of messages normally transmitted by wire may have enabled Soviet intelligence to break U.S. diplomatic codes. As early as 1942 there was concern within the State Department that its cable traffic was being intercepted.*

*This hollowed-out pumpkin was just large enough to hold three metal microfilm canisters and two developed film strips wrapped in wax paper. Photograph taken on December 5, 1948, three days after Chambers turned the contents over to HUAC investigators.*

*Two very different HUAC witnesses: Elizabeth Bentley and Alger Hiss, in August 1948. Between them are (left) a Capitol Hill policeman and (next to Hiss) William Marbury, the former War Department official and member of the Harvard Corporation who volunteered to appear with Hiss after Hiss's first choice, Dean Acheson, declined.*

*The strawberry patch, overgrown with a pumpkin vine, where Chambers hid the microfilm he kept as a "life preserver" when he defected from the Soviet underground in 1938. The family's home is in back.*

*Nixon and Stripling with pumpkin microfilm. When a Kodak official first reported that the film stock appeared to have been manufactured in 1945 (eight years after Chambers had quit the Communst underground), Nixon was ready to abandon the case — and Chambers. It was soon established that the film came from stock made in 1937.*

*A newspaper photographer zeroes in on one of the "pumpkin papers," while Nixon stands by.*

*Reaping the rewards of the Hiss case: Karl Mundt, elected to the Senate in 1948, alongside Senator Joseph McCarthy, who sounded the theme of Communist subversion two weeks after Hiss's conviction.*

*McCarthy and Arkansas Senator John McClellan, his adversary on the Senate subcommittee dealing with the investigation. At left: "the goldbrick twins," David Schine (seated) and Roy Cohn (crouching).*

*McCarthy tells newsmen he will produce the names of 29 State Department officials under loyalty investigation.*

*"Nobody Loves Him But the People." McCarthy supporters gather in Washington to protest McCarthy's formal censure by his Senate colleagues in 1954.*

*Priscilla Hiss after her appearance before the federal grand jury, shortly before her husband's indictment in December 1948.*

*Alger and Priscilla Hiss leave the Federal Courthouse after Hiss concludes his testimony in the first trial in June 1949.*

*Chambers, at home, learning of the verdict in the second trial, in January 1950.*

One of the most famous photographs taken during the case: Hiss rides the subway home from Foley Square alongside a passenger who reads that day's report of the grand jury investigation.

One of the handwritten notes Hiss gave to Chambers when the two were collaborators in the Soviet underground.

Prosecutor Thomas Murphy and the Woodstock typewriter after Hiss's perjury conviction in January 1950. Chambers testified that many of the documents Hiss gave him had been typed on the Woodstock, probably by Priscilla Hiss. Forensic experts were able to match the documents entered into evidence with the typewriter.

Henry R. Luce, co-founder and editor of Time magazine, and the sponsor of Chambers's rise to the top rank of Time's writers and editors.

Literary man par excellence Lionel Trilling. He and Chambers met as undergraduates at Columbia in the 1920s, and Trilling later based a character on him in his novel "The Middle of the Journey."

Art historian Meyer Schapiro, who travelled to Europe with Chambers in 1923 and later purchased the Bokhara rugs Chambers gave as Christmas presents to his most productive government contacts.

*Anti-communist editor and writer Isaac Don Levine, who in 1939 arranged for Chambers to meet with a top security official in the Roosevelt administration.*

*T. S. Matthews, the patrician* Time *editor who hired Chambers in 1939 after being impressed by his proletarian fiction.*

*HUAC witness Julian Wadleigh, a former State Department official and confessed spy, examining a stolen document held by investigator Louis Russell in December 1948.*

*In 1975, not quite a year after Nixon resigned from the presidency in disgrace following the Watergate scandal, Hiss holds up a photo of Nixon examining the pumpkin microfilm.*

# 2 3

# *The Pumpkin Papers*

With Marbury's "order to produce," the Hiss case entered its most extraordinary phase, a month of dizzying surprises and reversals. Chambers's tactic—to expose and protect, divulge and withhold—had been disastrous. Soon he would be accused of having persistently lied about spying within the Washington apparatus. This was inaccurate. He had zigzagged. In his first executive HUAC appearance, on August 3, he had sidestepped Stripling's questions, only to admit in his prepared statement that "espionage was certainly one of [the Ware Group's] eventual objectives." This had opened up the possibility of further disclosures. But Chambers sealed it off, first on *Meet the Press* and then in his grand jury testimony. Under Marbury's questioning, he had reversed himself yet again and mentioned the "interesting" documents he had read at Hiss's house.

All this had subverted Chambers's intended effect. Those he had hoped to satisfy with generalities about Communist infiltration had instantly detected suspicious lacunae in his story. Hiss, whom Chambers had been trying to protect, had misread the signals altogether, concluding from Chambers's hedgings and denials that he lacked substantiating evidence.

A week after Marbury repeated his demand for documents, Chambers phoned Esther's nephew Nathan Levine and advised him he would soon be visiting him at Levine's Brooklyn apartment. He contacted Levine again the following Sunday, November 14, sending a message, via Western Union, from one "W. Simpson," of Greenmount, Maryland: "ARRIVING AROUND ONE. PLEASE HAVE MY THINGS READY. WHIT."[1]

Chambers had picked an awkward day to visit Levine, whom he had not seen in four years. The apartment was crowded with visiting family. Like much of America, they were intrigued by the case and brimmed with questions. Chambers managed polite answers and then pulled Levine aside and asked him if he still had the material.

Levine was confused. Did Chambers mean some pamphlets he had left at Levine's house in the 1930s?

No, the sealed envelope Chambers had given Levine at the time of his break from the underground.

Then Levine remembered. But he did not have the envelope. He had not removed it from his parents' house, where he had been living in 1938. The elder Levines were living there still. Nathan drove Chambers to the house, on Rochester Avenue. They climbed a flight of stairs to a bathroom. It had a dumbwaiter. Levine reached in and pulled out a bulky manila envelope wrapped with rubber bands. Ten years' accumulation of dust and cobwebs slid off. Levine cleaned up with a whisk broom and dustpan while Chambers took the package into the kitchen.

Some minutes later, when Levine came in, Chambers was standing with several pages in his hands and a stunned expression on his face. "Good Lord," he said. "I didn't think this still existed."[2]

It was midnight or later when he reached Baltimore. Esther was waiting at Penn Station. She had driven down from Westminster with Ellen and John, asleep in the backseat. They awoke and greeted their father drowsily. Chambers placed the package on the front seat between himself and his wife. He did not tell Esther what was in it. He himself did not exactly know. It had been ten years since he had assembled the materials, and he had not yet had a chance to study them. He did so early the next morning.[3]

His life preserver contained:

1 sheet of paper, roughly 3″ × 5″
4 small sheets of notepaper, neatly folded, with jottings
4 sheets of yellow legal paper covered with handwriting on both sides
65 typed sheets, 8½″ × 11″ and 8½″ × 10″
2 strips of developed microfilm, totaling 58 frames
3 metal cylinders of undeveloped microfilm, sealed with black adhesive tape

.　.　.

The next day, Monday, Chambers went to Cleveland's office and announced he had "found something." Cleveland suggested Chambers produce the papers at his next deposition, on Tuesday, November 16. But Chambers, suffering one last spasm of indecision, asked for time to think. Cleveland arranged for Esther to take Chambers's place on November 16.[4]

The morning of Esther's deposition had been like every other in recent years. She and Whittaker had arisen at dawn, to the first bite of winter, and gone to the barn. Their cow herd had grown to eighteen. When the milking was done, Whittaker stayed behind, hosing down the flanks of the cattle, while Esther returned to the house and made breakfast for the children before they left for school.[5]

By ten-thirty, when she sat in Marbury's office, Esther was tired. She was also nervous and frightened. She had been spared the spotlight up till now, not summoned by HUAC or hounded by the press. But with the slander suit her anonymity had ended. Her new task was to support her husband's story of a friendship with the Hisses.

Under Marbury's questioning, Esther described her relationship with Priscilla Hiss. The two women had more in common than was apparent. Both were attentive mothers. Both felt enormous compassion for the downtrodden. Both had an interest in the arts. (In 1934, when Esther remembered meeting the Hisses, Priscilla had completed a book on fine arts programs in American universities.) And both had been lonely. Whittaker's illegal work—the many changes of address, the aliases—had made it difficult for Esther to form friendships. Priscilla had been unhappy in her role as wife and hostess. Later Esther said Priscilla Hiss had been the only real friend she had had during the lonely underground years and Priscilla had confided similar thoughts to her.[6]

All this emerged haltingly. Timid to the point of self-abnegation, Esther lacked her husband's aplomb, his mental agility, his fluency. She wilted under Marbury's probing, his lawyer's purposeful impatience. She was in tears that afternoon when Chambers drove down to pick her up.[7]

She returned for more the next day. Marbury questioned her on the events of 1937–1938, the most anguished time the family had known. Esther described the months of hardship, many of their belongings in hock, the children harried from one hiding place to another. She had had to remove Ellen from school because "there was not gasoline for the car." Recalling this, Esther wept. When she had regained her compo-

sure, Marbury reiterated the demand he had made of her husband. Esther must produce "any letters or books or notes . . . papers of any kind"
given her by Priscilla Hiss. Esther remembered two books on child care,
gifts, she said, from Priscilla Hiss. Did either bear an inscription or other
identifying mark? Marbury asked. No, said Esther. Then Marbury did
not care to see them. The session broke off at lunchtime.[8]

That morning, as he delivered Esther into the hands of Hiss's attorneys,
Chambers told Cleveland he had reached a decision. He was ready to introduce the documents. After lunch, when the deposition resumed, it
was Chambers, not Esther, who entered the conference room, envelope
in hand.

He began with a brief statement. He said the envelope contained
"certain papers in Mr. Hiss's handwriting and certain other papers." He
had previously kept these secret because "I was particularly anxious, for
reasons of friendship, and because Mr. Hiss is one of the most brilliant
young men in the country, not to do injury more than necessary to Mr.
Hiss." Chambers did not mention his long-standing fear that he himself
would be prosecuted for espionage.

When he had retrieved the materials, he said, he had not known exactly what to expect. He remembered having "put by" the handwritten
notes but not the typed documents, which he had thought long destroyed. These indicated "a kind of activity, the revelation of which is
somewhat different from anything I have testified about before." The
wealth of evidence so surprised him that he had not known what to do.
"The result of my turmoil, which is merely the last act of the turmoil
that has been going on for a decade, was the decision to give you the
material." Then, with a flourish, Chambers placed his cache on the
table, the four notes plus the sixty-five typed pages.

Everyone at the table stared at the small stack of papers. Cleveland had
prepared photostats for Marbury's team. Harold Rosenwald, visibly
stunned, gathered them up and departed immediately for New York and
a conference with Alger Hiss.[9]

Macmillan then suggested the originals be numbered and inventoried.
He read aloud the first and last words of each document as it was marked.
Within moments it was clear these were typed copies of State Department papers. There were transcripts of memos and reports and of diplomatic cables, some marked "strictly confidential," sent to the secretary of

state (Cordell Hull) from the American ambassadors in Paris and Vienna and from the chargé d'affaires in London. In some instances the typist had copied or summarized a sequence of cables. The subjects ranged widely over political, economic, and military developments in Europe and the Far East.

The earliest date on any document was December 31, 1937. The rest dated from January and February 1938. All fell in the period when the world had been moving inescapably toward war. A hush fell over the room as Macmillan intoned the identifying phrases for marking: "Paris . . . [to the] Secretary of State . . . [from Ambassador] Bullitt; Berlin . . . February 17, 1938 . . . [to the] Secretary of State . . . Vienna . . . [to the] Secretary of State . . . Strictly confidential; Wiley . . . [from] Warsaw . . . in strictest confidence . . . Biddle; Bullitt cabled from Paris . . . complete understanding between Germany and Italy as to Austria. . . ."[10]

When Macmillan came to the handwritten notes, Marbury asked to see one. "I was shocked when I recognized what seemed to be Alger's handwriting."[11] The four notes were verbatim copies of cables. One read:

> M 28
> Tel from Mary Martin widow of Hugh Martin formerly employed for special work by Legation at Riga
> Remember well Rubens while working for Hugh, be strict if needed, Write Lib. Cong., Law Div.

These cryptic words had been cabled to Secretary Hull from Loy Henderson in Moscow ("M") on January 28, 1938, at the peak of the Robinson-Rubens controversy. Henderson was informing Hull that he had received a telegram from one Mary Martin, the widow of Hugh Martin, a member of the American legation in Riga in the 1920s, the period prior to American recognition of the Soviet Union, when Riga was the "United States' nearest and most important listening post for Soviet affairs." Mrs. Martin had worked in her husband's office and remembered Rubens as a Soviet agent. Thus Henderson should be "strict" in handling the case—that is, not interfere with Rubens's arrest and imprisonment. This was the cable Chambers had quoted in his unpublished article of 1938 and then described to Adolf Berle in 1939.[12]

It would be some time before State Department officers, consulting their files, were able to decipher the full meaning of this and Hiss's other jottings and of the typed documents. But even at first glance Marbury guessed the "devastating effect that these memoranda" would have on the slander suit. His client possibly faced "criminal prosecution."[13]

After half an hour the labeling was completed. Then the questioning began. Chambers discoursed freely on this new feature of his collaboration with Hiss. In early 1937, said Chambers, he had brought Alger Hiss together with a Soviet agent, Boris Bykov, for the purpose of asking Hiss to furnish State Department documents to the apparatus. Hiss agreed on the spot and soon "began a fairly consistent flow of such material as we have before us here." Chambers later estimated he procured documents from Hiss "at least fifty-two times." Bykov also wanted Donald Hiss to deliver documents, but Alger thought his brother not "sufficiently developed yet for that function."

Chambers acted as courier, receiving the documents from Hiss in Washington and then delivering them to Bykov in New York. They established a routine. Hiss brought home papers from his office, and Priscilla typed up copies. Every ten days or two weeks Chambers collected the typed material along with other, original documents. Sometimes, when Hiss was unable to remove documents from his desk, he jotted down "notations" such as appeared on the four handwritten scraps. In this way, Chambers said, Hiss had supplied him with documents for more than a year, until Chambers's break in April 1938. This material represented a fraction of the total volume.[14]

The terms of the case had changed dramatically. Chambers had introduced evidence backing up his charge against Hiss. But at the same time the documents established that Chambers had withheld vital facts about the Washington underground, first from HUAC and then from the grand jury. Worse, he was now definitively exposed as a former espionage agent guilty of crimes tantamount to treason. Under the statute of limitations, which placed a three-year limit on espionage, he could not be prosecuted as a spy. He could, however, be indicted for his false testimony to the grand jury (or to HUAC). So could Hiss, if the jurors believed Chambers's charges. For the time being, Chambers, the self-confessed perjuror, seemed the more obviously indictable of the two.

In any event, the documents took the case far beyond the reaches of a slander suit.[15]

In the meantime Rosenwald had shown Hiss the photostats—the typed documents plus the notes. Hiss said the typed pages were not familiar to him, though their contents resembled cables and memorandums he had routinely seen when he had been Francis Sayre's assistant in the Trade Agreements division of the State Department. However, the handwritten notes seemed to be in his own hand—except for the message on the Robinson-Rubens case. (Later Hiss conceded he had written this too.) All, in any case, were jottings Hiss had made "for his own use." He had no idea how Chambers had come into their possession. Perhaps the ex-spy or an accomplice had stolen them from Hiss's office. Hiss agreed the materials should be forwarded without delay to the Justice Department.

The head of the Justice Department's Criminal Division, Alexander Campbell, went to Baltimore and collected the photostats. All parties, including the presiding judge in the slander suit, W. Calvin Chesnut, agreed to suspend the suit for two weeks while the Justice Department analyzed the materials and decided whether to proceed against Chambers or Hiss.[16]

Chambers had not turned over everything. He was still keeping the microfilm secret. On a visit to New York on Thanksgiving weekend, he described his "clinching evidence" to two friends, Henry Zolan and Meyer Schapiro. He seemed "elated," Schapiro recalled, "like a kid planning something mischievous." The art historian urged his friend not to augment the spectacle of the case and do still graver injury to Hiss. He repeated this plea in a letter. Chambers did not reply.[17]

Richard Cleveland's office was in a state of "almost total confusion," the slander case having suddenly grown into a spy scandal. Justice Department officials were equally confused, as they weighed the competing perjuries of Chambers and Hiss. At the State Department officials were combing through ten-year-old records in an effort to authenticate the documents and assess their significance. At the FBI J. Edgar Hoover, suddenly shunted to the periphery of the case, impatiently awaited a transcript of Chambers's deposition and a look at the original documents.[18]

As yet the controversy remained squarely within the boundaries of the executive branch. Congress (and HUAC) knew nothing of the Baltimore documents. The press too was in the dark. In fact a United Press dispatch on December 1 reported a "dead end" in the Hiss-Chambers probe, adding that the Justice Department was "ready to drop its investigation" for lack of new evidence. The implication was clear: If the Justice Department could keep the case bottled up until January, when the

Democrats reclaimed control of Congress (and of HUAC), the inquiry would end and the controversy fade with minimal damage sustained by the administration.[19]

But there was a hint—one hint—that something was up. On the same day the UP article appeared, *Washington Post* columnist Jerry Kluttz, in his regular roundup of capital gossip, wrote that "some very startling information on who's a liar" had been uncovered in the Hiss case.[20]

Like many others, Bert Andrews had been waiting for some new word on the Hiss case. When he read the UP dispatch and then Kluttz's column, the two reports so obviously contradictory, he sensed a breaking story. The journalist phoned Alexander Campbell, who refused comment because the situation was "too hot." Those two words were enough. "Something big was in the offing." Andrews called Judge Chesnut, Marbury, Cleveland, and then Chambers. None would talk. From the beginning Andrews had suspected Chambers had been holding back. Now he was certain of it. That afternoon the journalist phoned Richard Nixon. "I think Chambers produced something important at the Baltimore hearing. He may have another ace in the hole. Why don't you try to find out?"

But Nixon seemed distracted. He was about to leave town with his wife, Pat, for a long-overdue vacation, a ten-day Caribbean cruise he had already canceled once before, much to her disappointment. They were taking the train to New York the next morning at eight and would board the ship the following day. This did not give him much time, Nixon said, but he would do what he could. He did not sound enthusiastic.[21]

Robert Stripling was in a funk. The Democrats' victory in November meant the Hiss case was dead and HUAC was "going down the drain." Calls for the committee's abolishment were growing louder. Stripling had already announced he was retiring at the end of the year and going home to Texas. It would be a sorry end to his decade on the committee.[22]

That same afternoon, December 1, a visitor came to Stripling's office, Nicholas Vazzana, a lawyer doing investigative work in Washington for Chambers's New York attorney, Harold Medina. Vazzana had grown friendly with Stripling, who had opened HUAC's files to him. Vazzana had also been at the Semmes, Bowen offices on November 17, the day Chambers produced his bombshell. Two weeks later he read the UP report indicating Justice Department officials were snuffing the inquiry. Vazzana was piqued. "I just didn't want the case to die," he later said.[23]

Seating himself across from the morose HUAC investigator, Vazzana said, "If I were Hiss . . ." He finished the sentence by drawing his finger across his throat.

"What?" Stripling asked.

Vazzana repeated the gesture.

Stripling demanded the lawyer explain himself.

"Can't talk," said Vazzana. "I might be held in contempt of court."[24]

Stripling marched Vazzana upstairs to Nixon's attic office. The congressman was seeing to some last details before he left for his cruise the next day.

At first Vazzana would say only that Jerry Kluttz was right. There *was* a new development in the Hiss-Chambers suit. It involved documents. Vazzana was "under an admonition from the Justice Department not to reveal their actual contents." But soon the whole story leaked out—as much as Vazzana knew of it.

"Do you think I should still go on vacation?" Nixon asked.

That was the congressman's decision, said Vazzana, who then departed.[25]

Stripling invited Nixon to lunch at Ted Lewis's restaurant, a popular place on the Hill. The investigator was in a "slight frenzy." He suspected Vazzana had been carrying a message, from Chambers or perhaps Richard Cleveland, that HUAC should resume control of the investigation.[26]

But Nixon seemed more disturbed than excited. Stripling was mystified. He did not realize Nixon was in shock. Time and again since August, when others—Stripling, Andrews, Mundt, Hébert, McDowell—had voiced doubts about Chambers's story, Nixon had risen to the informer's defense. Nixon had believed Chambers and believed *in* him. On August 7 Nixon had expressly asked Chambers to produce evidence Hiss had been a Communist. Chambers had said there was nothing. Again Nixon had believed him. His identification with Chambers was complete, in perfect counterpoise to his hatred of Hiss. Now he realized Chambers had been lying all along.

They must go to Westminster immediately, urged Stripling. Here was a chance to break the Hiss case and more: to expose a spy ring. He had "an overpowering feeling that I must see Chambers."

But Nixon was petulant. "I'm so goddamned sick and tired of this case. I don't want to hear any more about it and I'm going to Panama. And the hell with it, and you, and the whole damned business!"

In angry silence the two men strode back to their separate offices. Stripling ordered a car. He would make the drive alone. Before leaving, he phoned Nixon, asking him to reconsider. "Goddamn it, if it'll shut your mouth, I'll go," Nixon said.[27]

At 3:00 P.M. the two set off. Stripling drove—sped, rather, still in a frenzy. Nixon slouched sullenly beside him. The late-afternoon sun was sinking over the meadows when they reached the farm. Chambers was in the barn, milking his herd.[28]

They all trooped to the house and seated themselves in the living room, Chambers still wearing his earth-soiled farmer's togs. It was an awkward moment. Chambers and Stripling aimlessly discussed the election, Nixon so silent that in his later account of the meeting (in *Witness*) Chambers forgot he was there. Then Stripling unfolded a torn-out page of the *Post* with Kluttz's column. HUAC knew about the Baltimore depositions, Stripling said, and that Chambers had withheld evidence. It was true, Chambers admitted. He *had* withheld evidence. He was a Quaker and didn't "want to hurt anyone or ruin anyone's life." He was not at liberty now to discuss the new developments.[29]

But, as Stripling suspected, Chambers really wanted to talk. The silence imposed on him was by order of the Justice Department, and Chambers trusted the Justice Department no more than did Stripling and Nixon.

Yes, Chambers said, he had dropped a "bombshell." It was nothing compared with the second one waiting to fall.

So there *was* more evidence. Could Stripling see it? Chambers shook his head. He couldn't do that. But he had a question for Stripling. Did the investigator happen to know a "good photographic expert"?

Indeed Stripling did.

The man had to be good, Chambers repeated.[30]

"Well, what do you think he's got?" Nixon demanded as he and Stripling climbed back into the car.

"I don't know," Stripling said, "but whatever he has will blow the dome off the Capitol."

"I don't think he's got a thing," said Nixon, fed up with Chambers's mystifications.

Besides, nothing could deter the congressman from going on his cruise. He did not want to disappoint his wife.[31]

That evening Nixon, still brooding about Chambers's betrayal, phoned Bert Andrews. The reporter took a taxi to Nixon's office. Andrews had already filed a story saying Chambers had "added something new and important to his charges," though exactly what was as yet unknown. Nixon's account of the visit to Westminster whetted the reporter's appetite further. "You were too nice to Chambers," he said. "Did you slap a subpoena on him?"

No, Nixon admitted.

Well, he should have. "Before you leave town get hold of Bob Stripling. Tell him to serve a blanket subpoena on Chambers to produce *anything* and *everything* he still has in his possession."

"I'll think it over," Nixon said.[32]

Later that night Nixon phoned Louis Nichols of the FBI at his home "on a strictly personal and highly confidential basis." Chambers had produced "highly incriminating documentary evidence," said Nixon. There was more material besides. Nixon planned to subpoena it. When he returned from Panama, on December 15, he would reopen hearings. Nixon was letting the bureau know ahead of time as a courtesy. The congressman promised there would be "no criticism" of the FBI for its past failure to pursue Chambers's allegations.

In return Nixon asked a favor. Once Attorney General Clark learned of this new development, he would move quickly to procure the evidence and so thwart the committee. It would be a great help if Hoover did not alert Clark and also if the bureau left it to Nixon and company to locate the new materials. Nichols relayed the conversation to Hoover, who agreed to Nixon's plan.[33]

It was after 1:00 A.M. when, utterly transformed, Nixon left his office. House doorkeeper William ("Fishbait") Miller was putting in a late night readying offices for the new House members when he saw Nixon. The congressman seemed "very elated and keyed up, as if he were dancing on wires." Something important was in the offing, Nixon said. "I'm going to get on a steamship and you will be reading about me. I'm going out to sea and they are going to send for me."[34]

The next morning Nixon phoned Stripling at home and proposed a seven-thirty meeting, half an hour before Nixon's train departed for New

York. Stripling, caught in traffic, was late. When he reached his office, there was a note from Nixon, telling the investigator to serve a subpoena on Chambers "immediately, for everything he has." Stripling was writing out the order when Nixon phoned with one last instruction. The investigator should "sit tight" once he got the goods from Chambers.[35]

The next day, Thursday, Chambers had an appointment to testify at a loyalty hearing on State Department officer Richard Post, whom Chambers had named as a Communist as far back as 1939, in his interview with Adolf Berle.[36]

Before he left, Chambers got a call from Stripling asking the witness to stop by his office as soon as he reached Union Station. Chambers promised he would.

First he had to solve a problem. He had been moving the microfilm from one hiding place to another in his house, afraid the Hiss defense team or Communist agents might have the "happy inspiration" to "raid the house." What if they should come while he was in Washington? Suddenly every hiding place seemed too obvious. Then he thought of something. Just behind the house was a strawberry patch overgrown by a pumpkin vine. Chambers went in back, broke a gourd off the vine, and carried it into the kitchen. He placed it on a table, cut out the top and stem, as if to make a jack-o'-lantern, and then scooped out the pulp and seeds. The hollowed-out insides easily held the three metal cylinders plus the two developed strips of film, wrapped in wax paper. After fitting the items inside, he replaced the top and carried the pumpkin back to the vine, thereby making good on his ten-year-old promise to undo communism by "those arts which Communism had taught me."[37]

Chambers got to Washington at two o'clock and went directly to Stripling's office. Stripling rose from his desk and held out his hand. A subpoena duces tecum was in it.

Chambers shrugged. "All right," he said. "I'll turn the information over to you. It's at my home." He then departed for the loyalty hearing, promising to return afterward so they could drive together to Westminster.[38]

After the hearing Chambers briefly visited *Time*'s Washington bureau to chat with friends. It was about six-thirty when he reached Stripling's office. The investigator had left for the day, but his assistants Donald Appell and William Wheeler were waiting. The three had dinner at a Washington restaurant and then drove to Baltimore. Chambers picked up his car at Penn Station. Then they drove separately to Westminster and reached the farm at ten forty-five. The meadows were smothered in darkness. Chambers stepped inside the house and hunted for a flashlight. Unable to find one, he switched on the porch lights. They threw a faint yellow rinse on the backyard. He led the investigators to the pumpkin patch and, as the two HUAC men watched in amazement, fumbled among the pumpkins, hefting several before he found the right one. He yanked off the top. "Here is what you're looking for," he said.

"What is this, Dick Tracy?" asked Wheeler. He reached in and pulled out the wax paper and the metal canisters, icy to the touch. One tin was dented. Chambers replaced the pumpkin on the vine.

At a Westminster coffee shop, the American Café, Appell and Wheeler initialed and dated the five items. It was past midnight when they got back to Washington. Appell took the new evidence home and locked it in his bureau.[39]

The next morning, at nine-fifteen, Appell and Wheeler presented the labeled cylinders and the wax paper to Stripling. The investigator set up an enlarger in the men's room, the darkest place he could find, and fed in the developed strips. On the first frame he read the words *Strictly Confidential*. They were State Department documents, some originals, others typed copies of the kind Chambers had presented at the deposition.

That morning Wheeler had asked a Treasury Department photographer he knew to make two prints of each exposure on the developed strips, while Appell took the undeveloped rolls to a photographer at the Veterans Administration. The results were disappointing. The roll in the dented tin was light-struck, and portions of the other two printed badly; some frames were blank. Appell phoned Stripling, who decided they must settle for making whatever prints they could. Late that afternoon Appell returned with some developed frames, which Stripling then locked in HUAC's safe.[40]

Meanwhile Stripling was beginning to contact members of HUAC, widely dispersed since Congress was still in recess. Only John Rankin was in Washington. He came over for a look at the evidence and then ordered a twenty-four-hour police guard over the documents. Stripling also alerted Nixon's assistant Bill Arnold, and he in turn phoned Bert

Andrews, who rushed over to Nixon's office. Stripling and Andrews reached Karl Mundt, in South Dakota, and explained what had happened. In a statement issued through the committee, Mundt described the documents, which he had yet to see, as "the object of a ten-year search by agents of the United States government." They provided "definite proof of one of the most extensive espionage rings in the history of the United States." But of course, until two days before, no one but Chambers had known the films existed, and there was no evidence as yet of an "extensive espionage" ring. The facts, so extraordinary in themselves, seemed to invite exaggeration.

And not only on Mundt's part. That evening Stripling called a press conference. It seemed every reporter in Washington was present. With Congress adjourned there was little else going on in the capital. But this would have been a major story in any circumstances. Stripling, holding up a metal canister, said there were "many others" like it. (In fact there were two, one of them worthless.) The frames so far developed, said Stripling, "make a stack of letter-sized documents 3 or 4 feet high." (In fact the entire batch was less than an inch thick.)

Was Alger Hiss mentioned on any of the documents? reporters asked.

They were not all analyzed as yet.

Why had Chambers waited so long?

No comment.

What if the Justice Department claimed jurisdiction over the material?

That was a matter for the committee members to decide.

Had Stripling contacted the State Department?

No.

What evidence was there this material came from Hiss?

No comment, though Stripling promised an answer to that question soon, perhaps early next week, when HUAC renewed its hearings, with Chambers among the first witnesses.[41]

So much for Nixon's instructions to "sit tight." With the congressman gone, it was Stripling's show to run.

That afternoon Chambers got a call from Richard Cleveland, asking him to come to the Semmes, Bowen offices at five o'clock. FBI agents would be waiting. To Chambers it was a disturbing request. Normally the bureau contacted him directly. He feared the invisible hand of the Justice Department. He was right. Alexander Campbell, suspecting Chambers might have additional documents, had ordered the interview. Nonetheless, when the witness reached Cleveland's office, where the FBI men were waiting, he did not ask his attorney to accompany him to the bureau's Baltimore field office. When they got there, a federal marshal served Chambers with a summons commanding him to appear before the New York grand jury when it reconvened five days hence, on December 8.

Then the interrogation began. It lasted until midnight. Chambers said he had withheld the microfilm rolls because they were undeveloped and had withheld the developed strips because "I wanted to keep all the film together and possibly have the film developed and made readable at a later date." He also told the agents there was an additional document, some sheets of legal-size paper covered with writing, which at Richard Cleveland's recommendation he had suppressed because the handwriting clearly was not Hiss's. The author, Chambers now revealed, was Harry Dexter White. The pages outlined a monetary plan White had prepared for transmittal to the Soviets.

Turning to the microfilm, Chambers said "the bulk" of the copied documents came from Alger Hiss. Others possibly came from another State Department source, Julian Wadleigh. There were also, he believed, documents from the Bureau of Standards, though he did not name their source. The photographer for the operation was "an individual named Felix, whose last name I do not know." A second photographer, David Carpenter, also had done some microfilming. None of these names had previously surfaced. Chambers had named Wadleigh to Berle in 1939 but not since. He likewise had kept Carpenter and Felix Inslerman out of the inquiry. As an informer, Chambers explained, "I have had two purposes in mind. The first was to stop the Communist conspiracy. The second was to try to preserve the human elements involved. In this sense, I was shielding these people. For these reasons, I have not previously mentioned the procuring and passing of any documents."[42]

The Chambers-Hiss controversy, suddenly reborn as a spy case, was once again front-page news. The tension of the hearings paled beside the melodrama of this latest twist. Reporters and photographers swarmed to Westminster. Even staid dailies ran pictures with arrows indicating the pumpkin patch. And there was the microfilm. Its contents remained secret and under twenty-four-hour guard. Colonel Robert McCormick, publisher of the *Chicago Tribune*, offered Stripling ten thousand dollars for a copy of the papers and half that sum for a single frame. Stripling declined. However, he did let Bert Andrews read some of the documents. In the *Herald Tribune*, Andrews reported that the new evidence included a 1938 memo to the German ambassador from Undersecretary Sumner Welles, "the peacetime equivalent of top-secret stuff." Andrews quoted portions of another document, a telegram to the secretary of state sent from Paris on January 13, 1938. It bore a warning—"This telegram must be closely paraphrased before being communicated to anyone"—and, in capital letters, the legend "STRICTLY CONFIDENTIAL FOR THE SECRETARY."

Andrews's account carefully omitted his own actions and Stripling's but heaped plaudits on the absent Nixon. "Presumably acting on the theory that if Chambers had some undisclosed documents he might have others," the congressman had "issued a subpoena calling for anything and everything pertinent that Chambers had" and so had secured the prize, "a pumpkin and its contents." Once again Nixon had labored, virtually alone, to force "Hiss-Chambers facts into the open."[43]

By this time Andrews and Stripling both had sent radiograms to the steamer *Panama*, advising Nixon of the "new bombshell" and urging him to return posthaste. It was not only a question of sharing in the glory. A possible fight with the Justice Department was looming.[44]

Even as the FBI was questioning Chambers, the bureau also contacted Hiss, who took a midnight train to Baltimore and was interrogated the next day, with Marbury present. Within the space of two weeks Hiss had been dealt two tremendous blows. Chambers's revelations had brought a halt to the slander suit. Hiss was now the focus of a spy probe. Yet he maintained his composure, publicly offering "my full cooperation" to the Justice Department and promising to assist the grand jury "in a further investigation of this matter." With the FBI too Hiss adopted a tone of lofty detachment, sounding less like an accused spy than an outside consultant. On the basis of his "cursory examination," said Hiss, the sixty-five typewritten pages were "authentic copies of United States State Department documents or summaries of such documents." They did not, however, "appear to be documents of a very highly confidential nature and would not have been treated in the State Department with any special precautions at that time, according to security regulations in effect then." (This opinion was soon contradicted by State Department officials.)

More pertinently Hiss denied he was the source of the documents. He had removed no papers from his office at any time, had taken none home for his wife to copy, had passed no material to Chambers. Nor had he met or heard of "any Russian named Peter or Colonel Bykov." Chambers's story was "a complete fabrication." Hiss helpfully proposed a theory: Chambers was the thief. The Railroad Retirement Board, where Chambers had briefly been employed in 1937–1938, was in the vicinity of the State Department building. Chambers might have visited Hiss's office, familiarized himself with its layout, and then stolen the documents from Hiss's desk.

As for the typed copies, Hiss said he had owned a portable typewriter in the mid-1930s, a hand-me-down from Priscilla Hiss's father, "possibly an Underwood." Priscilla, an "amateur typist," had "typed a goodly portion of a book manuscript" on the machine. The couple had sold the typewriter to a secondhand shop "sometime after 1938." Hiss could not be sure of the "exact date or place" or say where the typewriter was now. Samples of Priscilla Hiss's typing might still exist. If any surfaced, Hiss would submit them to the FBI for laboratory analysis.

Off the record, Hiss urged his interrogators to dig deeper into Chambers's background. Hiss had conferred with psychiatric experts who suspected Chambers suffered from a condition known as psychopathic personality. It was not unusual for one so afflicted to exhibit "real affection and admiration for another person and still engage in actions" meant to injure him. Adducing *Class Reunion,* the Franz Werfel novel Chambers had translated in 1929, Hiss remarked the "striking" parallels between its plot and the present conflict. The novel described how one schoolmate had destroyed another, whom he envied, by planting false evidence on him.

Hiss also offered a second theory. The improbable story might have had its origins in the late 1930s, when Chambers, desperate to launch a career in journalism, had fobbed himself off as an inside authority on the Communist underground. Since the initial response had been lukewarm, he had spiced up his tales by fabricating charges against Hiss, a young public official on the rise. The ruse had fooled *Time* into giving Chambers a job, and for a decade had gone unchallenged—until Hiss called his bluff in the HUAC hearings. Forced to make good on his charges, Chambers had served up the stolen documents. The theory was clever, but it did not explain how Chambers had got the documents in the first place.[45]

. . .

With Nixon away, Stripling had assumed control of the case, bringing to it all his tactical savvy. But he could not continue much longer as the committee's public face. A congressman must take charge, preferably Nixon, universally credited with having broken the case and widely praised for his handling of it.

Soon a coast guard seaplane was hovering over Acklins Island, in the Bahamas, where Nixon, in life jacket and suit coat, sat hunched in a dinghy, as if posing for some future Herblock cartoon. He was flown to Biscayne Bay, in Miami, and then hustled aboard a crash boat. Reporters were waiting. As they sped to shore, cutting through the spray, Nixon promised new HUAC hearings of "top importance" that would "prove to the American people once and for all that where you have a communist you have an espionage agent."[46]

As yet Nixon knew the general outlines of the new events, but none of the details. He was asked to comment on the "pumpkin papers."

"What is this, a joke?" the bewildered congressman replied.

The journalists related the story of Chambers's theatrics at Westminster. On the flight to Washington, Nixon privately wondered "if we might really have a crazy man on our hands."[47]

With the New York grand jury about to reconvene, the legalities of the Hiss-Chambers case had grown more tangled than ever. The grand jury would almost certainly be asked to return a perjury indictment, whether against Chambers or Hiss no one knew. The U.S. attorney for the Southern District of New York would have to make up his mind quickly since the panel's eighteen-month term (dating back to June 1947) expired on December 15, less than two weeks away. And perjury was, in any case, merely a cover for the true crime, espionage.

At the same time Stripling was trying to slow down the U.S. attorney for the District of Columbia, George Morris Fay, who evidently was poised to indict Chambers for his HUAC perjuries. There was a tussle in Stripling's office when Fay demanded the original documents developed from the microfilm. Stripling surrendered only photostats. The prosecutor stormed off, threatening to name Stripling in the indictment.

Stripling then bounded off to Sumner Welles's five-hundred-acre estate in Oxon, Maryland, ten miles from the Potomac. Emerging from a meeting "cloaked in secrecy," Stripling solemnly told reporters the for-

mer undersecretary of state had cautioned against the release of the papers, lest national security be placed in "grave" danger.[48]

Nixon landed in Washington well past midnight on December 5 and was
met by Stripling. They drove straight to Nixon's office, stayed there
through the night studying the hot documents, and the next morning
called a press conference, at last ready to announce just what was contained in Chambers's pumpkin. A "record assembly of reporters," said
*The New York Times*—as many as three hundred—had jammed into the
HUAC suite. Before going downstairs to greet them, Nixon and Stripling
posed in Nixon's office for newsreel cameras and still photographers. The
investigator held up a strip of microfilm while Nixon feigned reading it
through a pocket-size magnifying glass. Then one of the photographers
casually asked, "What's the emulsion figure on those films?" He meant:
Had anyone verified the year of the film's manufacture?[49]

For a moment everyone froze: Nixon, Stripling, plus Bert Andrews
and Nicholas Vazzana, also present for the unveiling. There was a brief
delay while Stripling contacted Eastman Kodak's Washington office. Its
manager, Keith Lewis, hurried over and was handed a roll of microfilm
for dating. On the phone to Kodak's national headquarters, in
Rochester, New York, Lewis read off the emulsion numbers. There was
a short wait, and then Lewis turned to the HUAC men and said, "This
film was manufactured in 1945."

When Lewis left the room, Nixon erupted, "Oh my God, this is the
end of my political career!" He wheeled on Vazzana. "This is all your
fault! What are you going to do about it?"

"It's not my fault," Vazzana replied. "I didn't know there was any
microfilm there. It's your problem, not mine."

Nixon heatedly insisted Vazzana was to blame and had better "do
something."

Bitterly the congressman told Stripling to cancel the press conference
and send the reporters away.

"No, damn it, we won't," said Stripling. "We'll go down and face the
music. We'll tell them that we were sold a bill of goods."[50]

First Nixon phoned Chambers.

The grand jury had moved its first session up two days from Wednesday
(December 8) to Monday, to ensure the Justice Department had Chambers's testimony before HUAC got to him. He had already made his

first appearance and was on a break, in the downtown office of Harold Medina, Jr., when Nixon's call came.

Without bothering to say hello, Nixon, his voice raw with rage, demanded to know how documents photographed in 1938 had been put on film not manufactured until 1945.

"It cannot be true," Chambers said, "but I can't explain it. God must be against me."

"You better have a better answer than that," snapped the congressman.

Nixon told Chambers to be at the Hotel Commodore that evening at nine-thirty for questioning.

"I'll be there," Chambers promised.

"You'd better be," Nixon said. He slammed down the receiver.

Nixon and Stripling were set to face the assembled reporters and confess their colossal blunder when a call came from Keith Lewis. He had double-checked with Rochester. There had been a mistake. The film belonged to a series manufactured through 1938, discontinued during the war, and then resumed in 1945. Chambers's rolls dated from 1937.

Stripling, shouting with joy, then grabbed Nixon and waltzed him around the small office.

"Poor Chambers," Nixon said pensively. "Nobody ever believes him at first."

At the press conference a reinvigorated Nixon, back on the attack, scolded the Justice Department for "trying frantically to find a method which will place blame of possession of these documents on Mr. Chambers" when the real issue should be determining "who in the State Department furnished this material" to the informer.[51]

In fact, as Nixon knew, the "real issue" *was* being pursued—by the New York grand jury, which had outfoxed HUAC by summoning Chambers two days ahead of schedule. But Nixon and Stripling were not about to cede the spotlight. HUAC enjoyed one clear advantage. The grand jury was required to conduct its inquiry in secrecy. No such constraints bound HUAC. It could open its doors, invite in the press, and carry on in full public view. Nixon announced that hearings would be held the next day as promised, with Chambers as the first witness.

Justice officials promptly descended on HUAC and warned Nixon and Stripling not to disrupt the grand jury proceedings, either by stealing its witnesses or by releasing new evidence. Stripling and Nixon countered that they were heading to New York that day to question Chambers. When the delegation left, Nixon and Stripling hurried to Union Station, taking along John McDowell and some staff.

On the train to New York, Nixon contacted Bert Andrews by radiotelephone, a new technological marvel, and said he would demand the appointment of a special "blue-ribbon" panel to hear the new evidence, rather than let the biased Justice Department settle the indictment. Stripling, overhearing the phone call, was incensed. Nixon was planning "to take over the whole Hiss case." It was not a new complaint, and not Stripling's alone. Nixon's "lone wolfing" had become a serious irritant to his HUAC colleagues. They all knew it was Nixon who had leaked details of the secret hearings to Bert Andrews, snaring headlines for himself even as he made liars of the committee.

Stripling's anger was deeper and more personal. He had been HUAC's "brains" during the lean years, the years of ignominy and ridicule. At long last the chief investigator stood on the brink of silencing his many critics and of leaving Washington a hero. But Nixon was collecting all the accolades. "I don't think you realize that you're not in the bush league," Stripling angrily told the freshman congressman. "You're in the majors now. You can't undermine the committee and expect to be a member of Congress. This type of thing is not done."

But Nixon and Stripling soon were forced back in the trenches together. When the train pulled into Penn Station, U.S. Attorney John F. X. McGohey, plus staff, were waiting on the platform. They demanded the HUAC team hand over the microfilm and return to Washington. Nixon and Stripling refused. A shouting match ensued, and it continued all the way to the Commodore, with the press in pursuit. At the hotel reporters, packed in the corridor, heard the thump of fists on a table and the bellowed exchange of "scatological epithets." Stripling, flinging open a window, shouted, "We might as well let them hear about it on Fifth Avenue!"

At last the two sides reached an "armed truce." HUAC would furnish the U.S. attorney with full-size photostats of the "pumpkin papers" and Nixon's subcommittee would be allowed to question Chambers that night.[52]

To Chambers's symbolizing mind, always alert for portents, Kodak's initial error had come as a divine rebuke. He had strayed from his mission: to break the conspiracy but also spare those he named. Failing in this, he had become the "rejected instrument" of God's purpose, like the biblical figure he identified with most closely, the dishonored prophet Jonah.[53] Numbly Chambers had left Medina's plush office after the call from Nixon and wandered despondently in the narrow lanes of downtown Manhattan, his Nineveh. He had stopped in a gardening store and bought a tin of rat poison. At a second store he bought a second tin. Then he had returned to Medina's office and learned about Kodak's mixup. It had been a relief. But Chambers's spirits remained low. That evening, on the way to the Commodore, he had stashed the tins in a Penn Station locker.

It was not quite nine o'clock when Chambers reached the huge hotel. He was intercepted by Donald Appell, who steered him into a taxi. The short ride ended back at the Commodore, the ramp entrance, duplicating the journey of August 17. The two men slipped upstairs, pausing at the balcony to survey the lobby below, aswarm with reporters.

In HUAC's suite Chambers greeted Stripling with a lopsided grin. "You mistrusted me for a time today."

Chambers and Nixon scarcely exchanged a word. A wedge of distrust had opened up, and each had vividly glimpsed treacherous depths in the other.

Then the hearing began. Chambers was told the room had possibly been bugged by the U.S. attorney. The two-hour dialogue that followed had a "ghostly" quality, Chambers recalled, voices rising and falling unnaturally as the participants forgot and then remembered someone might be listening in.[54]

For the first time since August 3 Stripling handled the interrogation.* He began by asking the question uppermost in everyone's mind: Why had Chambers withheld the evidence so long?

There were two reasons, he said. First, the meeting with Adolf Berle in 1939. After giving Berle so many leads, he assumed "the espionage angle would certainly be developed." When it was not, Chambers had grown suspicious and thought it better to conceal his evidence. Second, he had hoped to protect his former accomplices, "men of high type, some of them widely recognized for intelligence and ability." Chambers "had been in their homes and knew their wives and children. . . . I de-

---

* All quoted testimony from this hearing comes from the HUAC transcript of the executive session, December 6, 1948, released by the U.S. House Committee on Internal Security in 1974 but never printed. It appears here for the first time.

sired to give these people an opportunity to make their own break damaged as little as possible by me."

But now, with the whole story out, Chambers did not hesitate to augment his list of underground operatives. He named the part-time photographer "Keith" (William Edward Crane). He identified his source at the Bureau of Standards, Ward Pigman, a chemist who had also supplied documents from the Navy Department. He added fresh details about Harry Dexter White. The economist had been more active than anyone had supposed. He had furnished intelligence reports—one contained "a list of Japanese agents" in Manchuria—and had passed along useful Treasury Department gossip, on one occasion relating to Chambers a discussion between Treasury Secretary Henry Morgenthau and the Soviet ambassador. Like Hiss, White had loaned his services to the apparatus "very eagerly." Both were dedicated and selfless.

In his spare time White had drawn up a rough plan for monetary and currency reform for the Soviet Union. Chambers had outlined its features to Bykov, who "suddenly became very excited," as well he might have—White was a world-class monetarist—and ordered Chambers to see White "at once and lose no time doing it." Chambers enlisted Hiss to make the drive with him to White's summer home in Peterborough, New Hampshire. Priscilla went too. They stopped overnight in Connecticut and reached White's house the next day. The Hisses waited in the car while Chambers went inside. That night Chambers and the Hisses had spent the night at a Peterborough inn.

It was Bykov who had decided Hiss should increase his output by typing nightly summaries of documents, which Chambers could add to the goods he collected on his visits every ten days or fortnight. Priscilla Hiss, who had "full knowledge of the operation," had done the typing, on a Woodstock, Chambers believed. Despite these efforts, Bykov had fumed at the "inferior" information he was getting, even from Hiss, whom he snidely referred to as "*Unser lieber Advokat* [our dear lawyer]."

The witness also indicated who among his Washington contacts had *not* spied for him: Donald Hiss, John Abt, Victor Perlo, Henry Collins, although Collins was a "candidate for the apparatus, pending his getting a job in the State Department," which he tried repeatedly to do.

As this information spilled forth, it was obvious Chambers had been suppressing more than the facts about Hiss. He had concealed the operations of a major spy ring. "You are by nature a witness who does not volunteer any information," said Stripling. "If there is anything in connection with this matter which we do not know, and which we should know, I ask you to speak up now."

Chambers assured him there was nothing. He could perhaps "develop more colorful details if I sat down and discussed the life" of the Washington apparatus, as he had done lavishly in the Baltimore depositions. But he assured his interrogators they now had "the full facts about the documents and the business of procuring, photographing and transmitting them." And no more evidence remained in his possession.

The hearing ended at 11:00 P.M. Chambers was dismissed. It had been an exhausting day, and the next morning he was scheduled to testify again to the grand jury. He went to Lynbrook for the night and put the tins of poison in his dresser.[55]

That night Nixon regaled the press with choice portions of the "secret" hearing, Chambers's account of the stealing, copying, and transmitting of State Department documents. The next day HUAC reconvened in open session, with Nixon and Stripling presiding. It was the committee's first extravaganza since August 25, held again in the caucus room, jammed with press and spectators. Never had HUAC's prestige been higher. The clowns and buffoons of yesterday were now authentic spy hunters.[56]

Stripling and William Wheeler led off by recounting their parts in the pumpkin drama. Keith Lewis of Kodak followed. He dated the microfilm to 1937. Then came Sumner Welles. The diplomat had been FDR's Groton schoolmate and then his closest aide at State until forced out in 1943 after a power struggle with Secretary Cordell Hull. He had since been living in patrician splendor on his Potomac estate, where he wrote *The Time for Decision* and other monitory tracts.

Welles took the stand wearing "the narrowest mustache we have ever seen, drawn geometrically across his upper lip like a pasted white thread," reported *The New Republic*'s TRB Richard Strout. That HUAC had dragged this establishment pillar out of storage—and as a friendly witness, not as a subject of attack or innuendo—indicated the widening seriousness of the Hiss case. First Welles was shown two of the microfilmed documents, both dating from 1938. The first was a cable, two pages long, sent from French Ambassador Bullitt to Secretary Hull. The second was a cable from Hull to the American Embassy in Vienna. At the time the dispatches were sent, said Welles, in a rumbling basso profundo, they would have been carefully guarded at the State Department, kept "under lock and key." Even in 1948 the documents, if published, would be "prejudicial to the nation's interest."

But, Welles went on, it was not the cables' content that had made them so valuable to the Soviets in 1938. It was, rather, the aid they would have given to foreign cryptanalysts trying to solve the State Department's diplomatic codes. Dispatches such as these would have provided code breakers with text that could be matched against intercepted telegrams.[57]

As sensational as Welles's testimony was—and it was splashed across the nation's papers that evening and the following morning—it came from someone five years out of government. But HUAC had summoned a second key witness, Assistant Secretary for Administration John Peurifoy, the officer who had assured Foster Dulles in 1947 that Hiss's dossier was clean.* Peurifoy too was handed the documents, though he was promptly whisked offstage to evaluate them privately. Nixon and Mundt then released a portion of his secret testimony. Like Welles, Peurifoy believed the stolen documents had enabled "foreign nations" to read secret diplomatic codes.[59]

HUAC had scheduled another hearing, for December 9. That morning, at ten-thirty, the president held a press conference. Since August he had not commented directly on the scandal, which was dominating the news as never before. To no one's surprise, the first question put to the president concerned the spy papers. Did Truman "know of any reason why those papers should not be made public?" No comment. It was in the hands of the attorney general and the courts. Did the president still think the "investigation has aspects of being a red herring?" The public thought so, and the president too. What about Nixon's charge that the Justice Department planned to indict Chambers as a means of quashing the investigation? That was a matter for the Justice Department to decide. The president himself had no intention of locking horns with a

---

* Peurifoy had since had a change of heart. On August 5, hours after Hiss's first HUAC appearance, Peurifoy had contacted Karl Mundt, a friend. "I don't know what to do," Mundt later remembered Peurifoy's saying. "I'm torn between loyalty and duty. . . . Frankly, all I am I owe, in this town, to Dean Acheson . . . and I don't want to do him a disservice. And still, I'm a good American. And I know what you are saying and insinuating about Alger Hiss is true." Peurifoy had then offered to show the congressman Hiss's security dossier, and the two had studied it together.[58]

"dead committee." Did this mean HUAC faced extinction? The new Congress would take up that issue in January.[60]

HUAC retaliated instantly, pushing up that day's hearing to eleven-thirty. The committee had a new witness, Julian Wadleigh.

He had been living in dread since July, when Elizabeth Bentley had testified. Wadleigh did not know her—he had quit spying in 1938, after Carl's defection—but it was obvious Bentley's ring had overlapped his own. Then Chambers had testified. The name meant nothing to Wadleigh, but he recognized the face at once. He was astonished when Chambers said nothing about espionage. Could it be the informer would spare his old accomplices? Then had come the pumpkin episode, "a most nauseating publicity stunt." Chambers should have turned the film over to the Justice Department, not the deplorable HUAC. The documents were of course "very bad news." Wadleigh consulted his attorney on the uses of the Fifth Amendment. Then he waited.

On December 6 the economist was at his office—he had a new job with the Italian Embassy—when a pair of FBI agents came calling. Lambert Zander and Maurice Taylor were both "courteous and businesslike" as they delivered the news Wadleigh had feared since the summer: Chambers had named him as a member of the underground. First Wadleigh denied it, denied everything. He had never met Chambers. He had not furnished documents to the defector or anyone else. The agents began to write all this down. Wadleigh sprang up from his chair. "I'm not going to sign that statement," he exclaimed. He wanted to make "a complete confession." At FBI headquarters Wadleigh unburdened himself while the agents made notes. His confession, typed up the next morning, filled four single-spaced pages. "I hope none of this information will go to that committee," Wadleigh said glumly.

The agents assured him the bureau's methods differed from HUAC's. "You don't often see the FBI giving out press releases, do you?"

The next morning a federal marshal served Wadleigh with a subpoena. He must testify before the grand jury. He took the night train up to New York, phoned from Grand Central for subway directions, and then testified on December 8, pleading the Fifth—a "fantastically absurd piece of mummery" since the jurors had already been shown his FBI confession.

Besides, Wadleigh had always prided himself on his candor. Even when he had been filching documents, he had made no secret of his political opinions—until Chambers and Bykov had warned him to be more discreet and he began to tuck a folded handkerchief in his pocket.

In the grand jury waiting room Wadleigh saw Chambers. "He looked so guilty! Like he wanted to drop through the shaft into the center of the earth."

Hiss, however, appeared serene and confident. Wadleigh marveled at "his control of his facial expression," like an actor's. Only once did the pressure show. Wadleigh happened to come into the room when Hiss was reading a newspaper spread out on a table. His face looked "gloomy and tired," his eyes "sunken, vacant." But instantly Hiss snapped back to his normal self and greeted Wadleigh courteously, "his affable smile only slightly faded."

Wadleigh had known Hiss at State, when both were in the Trade Agreements division. They had lunched together before Hiss began his sudden quick rise. Wadleigh sheepishly told Alger—and Donald Hiss, also present—that he had made a confession. "The FBI came to see me, and I got sort of panicky and told them that I had given some documents to Chambers." Wadleigh expected sympathy. He did not get it. The Hiss brothers stiffly warned him they were obligated to repeat his words to the grand jury.

"Couldn't you forget what I said?" Wadleigh pleaded.

No, they could not. Dejected, Wadleigh sagged back into his seat.[61]

While Wadleigh was in New York, HUAC investigators drove out to the economist's house, a half-finished cabin in Falls Church, Virginia, twelve miles from the capital. They had subpoenas. One of the investigators, Courtney Owens, left his number and said he had better hear from Wadleigh soon. If not, Mrs. Wadleigh would be subpoenaed and ordered to "produce" her husband.

Wadleigh returned that night after an exhausting day, the "mummery" at the grand jury followed by a second FBI interrogation. It was close to midnight when he phoned Owens and arranged an appointment for the next morning. Owens would meet him at the office of Wadleigh's lawyer, Herman Greenberg.

The next morning Greenberg cut his client loose. The case was "too much of a hot potato." Not one lawyer in Washington would dare represent Wadleigh. Unlike Chambers and Hiss, Wadleigh had no powerful institution behind him, no important friends, no fast-developing celebrity. The Italian Embassy had accepted his resignation on the spot, with no gallantries.

Having made a full confession to the FBI, Wadleigh was prepared to tell all to the grand jury. But not to HUAC. He hated the committee. Then Truman had given his press conference, and Wadleigh was fetched by Courtney Owens and led through a side entrance to HUAC's offices, avoiding reporters. In a preliminary interview Wadleigh pleaded the Fifth to every question. He was hauled into the caucus room, cleared of press and spectators, for a closed session. Again the witness gave no satisfaction. The committee declared the hearing open. Reporters and photographers rushed in. The sizzle of bulbs made Wadleigh blink behind his thick lenses. For the next hour and a half the witness chain-smoked, rubbed a sweat-soaked palm, and repeated his Fifth Amendment demurrals. No longer ashamed, Wadleigh inwardly "took a fiendish delight in every refusal to answer."

HUAC too relished the performance. Wadleigh's refusals were as good as admissions. He became, as planned, a plausible stand-in for Alger Hiss, a former State Department official found out as a spy. The next morning *The Washington Post,* flagrantly pro-Hiss in August, rebuked President Truman for his apparent "desire to suppress the whole business" and speculated that there might indeed be some basis to Nixon's charge of a Justice Department cover-up.[62]

# Indictment

Day after day Chambers was questioned by the grand jury—rather, by Tom Donegan, a former FBI man who had handled the bureau's Elizabeth Bentley investigation and been attached to the U.S. attorney's office. When the sessions ended Chambers rode the courthouse elevator up to the FBI field office, on the twenty-ninth floor, for further interrogation. He signed a statement implicating all those he had named in recent interviews: Pigman, Reno, Carpenter, "Keith" (William Edward Crane), and "Felix" (Inslerman).[1]*

Chambers also had been conferring with officials at Time Inc. Those at the top of the organization knew of his plans to retire on January 1. Until then Luce was sticking by him and said management must too. "Chambers is an honest man," John Shaw Billings noted in his diary, "and we must give him our faith."

Then the revelation of espionage had come, and Luce, in particular, took it as a "personal betrayal." Anyone could understand how Chambers had been drawn to communism and even into the underground. But a spy—in this case a spy who had pilfered state secrets in the tense period leading up to World War II—was something else. "He'll probably be indicted for perjury which will blacken us even more," Billings predicted. It was already getting embarrassing. The *Chicago Tribune,* editorial voice of the right, was demanding a public statement from Time

---

* Reno, Crane, and Inslerman eventually made full confessions. Only Reno was prosecuted. He received a three-year sentence for perjury.[2]

Inc. Columnist Walter Winchell, who nursed a long-standing grudge against Luce, had been crowing for days. "Gee Whittaker! Time Marxes on," the columnist had written when the documents surfaced. Just imagine, *Time* "was edited all these years by Whittaker Chambers, self-confessed Communist, accused perjurer, and Russian spy!" For months to come Winchell blasted *Time* for its Chambers connection, forty-seven salvos in one month alone from the most powerful daily journalist in America.[3]

*Time*'s readers were no more forgiving. Since August more than 250 letters had come in, all but a handful critical of both Chambers and the magazine. Of the 132 letters sent since the pumpkin papers were disclosed, 99 demanded Chambers's dismissal. "May I inquire," wrote one reader, "if you are still carrying the torch for your stalwart convert to Americanism—Comrade Chambers? Or is Time's face turning red?"[4]

On December 5 Chambers offered his resignation. "It's fallen through," he told a colleague. Roy Larsen, president of Time Inc., let Chambers choose the time and manner of his departure. On December 9 Chambers submitted a letter to the publisher, James A. Linen. All that day Billings, Larsen, Linen, Matthews, and the attorney Harold Medina huddled. That evening Billings wrote in his diary: "Should we accept? Much debate. Were we kicking an underdog and would we lose public sympathy? Was Hiss really a Communist—or was it two other fellows? Luce came down, tired and grey—and looking like a death's head. He liked the Chambers statement and did a little editing on it. He smacked down Larsen's notion that we should say Time was only interested in the ultimate truth, 'let the chips fall where they will.' "

The next day, at 11:00 A.M., Time Inc. released Chambers's statement. "When Time hired me in 1939," he had written, "its Editors knew that I was an ex-Communist; they did not know that espionage was involved." Since then Chambers's "mission" had been to articulate "the dangers of world-wide Communism" and "give expression to human values which I knew from my own experience Communism denies and destroys." But now, called upon "to expose the darkest and most dangerous side of Communism—espionage," Chambers must suffer the "indispensable ordeal" alone. James Linen added a terse statement for the company: "Against the admitted disservice to his country of a decade ago must be set the service we are convinced he is trying to perform for his country now."

To some, Time Inc.'s stance seemed disingenuous. "Maybe Henry Luce and T. S. Matthews were indeed shocked to find out Chambers's history in 1948," Murray Kempton later said, "but if they were, they were in a state of ignorance unique for their time and place." It was also true that *Time* had hired Chambers in the full knowledge he was a defector from the Communist underground. During the Chambers War angry colleagues had referred to Chambers, in memos Luce almost certainly read, as having been "second in command of the U.S. OGPU." It did not require a great stretch of the imagination to suppose such a man might also have been a spy.[5]

Chambers was at Foley Square when his resignation was accepted. That afternoon, at the end of a long day of testimony, Alger Hiss glimpsed Chambers "slipping out of the Grand Jury after the jurors had left. . . . He looked dejected and slipped unobtrusively through the stairway door in the corridor . . . apparently wishing to avoid the press by going to another floor to take the elevator. On other occasions this week he had always made a point of talking to the press when he left."[6]

Chambers's despair had been mounting since he turned over the documents in Baltimore. It was no longer possible to believe he was protecting Hiss even as he accused him. The nadir had come on December 6, when Nixon had bitterly accused him of handing over faked evidence. The error had been corrected, of course. But the incident had seemed premonitory. Since then Chambers had exposed the entire conspiracy, fetched bone upon bone, divulging more names. Then he had been set adrift by *Time,* left more alone than ever.

Chambers spent the night of December 10 at Lynbrook. After Laha had gone to bed, he retired upstairs to the room where he had stayed four nights out of seven for the better part of a decade. He wrote letters to his family and friends and then another, "To All." He had told the truth about Hiss, he explained, but it had not been his purpose to injure Hiss or anyone else. Perhaps by "removing myself as witness against them," he could put an end to the collective misery. The act would not be suicide but "self-execution."

His letters finished, Chambers removed the two containers of rat poison from his dresser and poured the toxic liquid into the cover of each tin. He contrived a "receptacle"—perhaps a carton he found in the house—and placed it over his head as he lay on his bed. He covered the opening with a damp towel, so the swarming fumes would be trapped.

He would inhale them and die painlessly. He dozed off immediately but at some point involuntarily dislodged the towel and came writhing to consciousness. The gas escaped, and so did Chambers, who was vomiting the next morning when Laha came to see what was the matter.

"Oh, how could you, how could you?" she cried. "The world hates a quitter." It was the credo of one who in a few days would turn seventy-seven and had lived for some twenty years with the ghosts of her husband and younger son. She fixed Chambers a pot of coffee. Then he made his way to Foley Square.

Later Chambers came to see the suicide attempt as "the high point of the case," a visible gleam of the inner light, the ultimate self-sacrifice, his long-deferred bid for a magnificent hara-kiri. But like so many of his grand acts, this one too had come to nothing. Burdened with a "saving fierceness," he lived on to do further injury to others and himself.[7]

On Saturday, December 11, HUAC fired its last round, releasing twelve of the stolen documents. They included verbatim transcripts of dispatches sent to the State Department from U.S. embassies in 1938, one of which described Japanese troop movements in China; typed digests of other cables; and one of the four handwritten notes, identified by an expert as being in Hiss's writing.[8]

In releasing the spy papers, HUAC had violated Nixon's promise to McGohey on December 6. Moreover, the committee had yet to supply the prosecutor with copies of all the documents. Pressed to justify this latest bid for publicity, Nixon solemnly vowed to make good on his deal with McGohey, saying he would himself hand-deliver the microfilm to the grand jury so the panel could include the evidence in its deliberations.

On Sunday night, December 12, Nixon ordered Stripling to unlock the safe and hand over the film. Stripling objected. "The minute you show this film to the grand jury it's going to become part of the evidence. And they will take physical control over it," the investigator warned.

There was no cause for worry, said Nixon. He would merely show the film to the jurors, without letting it out of his hands.

To Stripling the plan was obviously another of Nixon's "selfish capers." The congressman would make a dramatic entrance at Foley Square, snagging more headlines—at the expense of HUAC and its investigation. He reminded Nixon the film belonged to the House of Representatives and could be released only through a House resolution. A mere technicality, said Nixon. As a member of the committee he was authorized to receive the evidence. Stripling phoned John Rankin, HUAC's rules expert, who lived only two blocks away, and asked him to settle the issue.

When he came over, Rankin "nearly had a fit." The microfilm belonged to the House. Nixon had no authority to remove it. But Nixon stood his ground, and the elderly Rankin lacked the energy to contest him. Stripling had no choice but to submit. Nixon departed with the film.

The next morning, December 13, Stripling instructed his lieutenants Appell and Wheeler to trail the congressman to New York and wait outside the grand jury room "in case something happened."[9]

Nixon strode into the Foley Square courthouse at midmorning, carrying a brand-new calfskin briefcase with the evidence inside—the three canisters plus the two strips. Prosecutor Donegan, with some gamesmanship of his own, forced Nixon to sit for several hours in the witness room, under the watchful eye of an FBI agent, before allowing him in to make his presentation.[10]

As Stripling had warned, the grand jury instantly voted to subpoena the evidence. When Nixon balked, McGohey and Donegan hauled him into the chambers of the judge, John W. Clancy, who threatened Nixon with a contempt citation.

Chagrined, Nixon phoned Stripling for advice. Don Appell was waiting outside the judge's chambers, Stripling said. If the judge did not relent, Nixon should slip the microfilm to the HUAC investigator. Luckily for Nixon, McGohey accepted a compromise. Rather than surrender the film, Nixon would submit it to the FBI for authentication, a sound precaution in any case, since at this point there was only the word of HUAC (and its witness, Keith Lewis) that the 1937 date was accurate. Donegan would mark the film as evidence, and whenever the grand jury wished to examine it, Nixon would produce it. Until then HUAC could keep the film in Washington.

The next day, convening in executive session, HUAC voted its approval of the fait accompli, once again sanctioning Nixon's "lone wolfing."

The grand jury, however, was not impressed by Nixon's presentation. Undecided as yet whom to indict for perjury, the panel was thinking of issuing a "sharp report scolding the House Committee for getting in the way of the Justice Department."[11]

Two days after Hiss had promised to turn over specimens typed on his wife's Woodstock to the FBI, his attorneys had found papers typed by Priscilla in the 1930s. A documents analyst hired by Bill Marbury said Priscilla's specimens and the typed documents had "undoubtedly been written on the same typewriter." Hiss authorized his attorneys to give his wife's typing specimens—but not the analyst's findings—to the FBI.

At the same time the bureau had some 250 agents in forty-five cities conducting their own search for the Woodstock and for specimens. A break came when the headmaster of a private school Timmy Hobson had attended turned over pages from his files typed by Priscilla Hiss. The FBI lab tested them against the Baltimore documents and concluded all came from the same typewriter. These results went to the grand jury on December 13, less than forty-eight hours before the panel's term ended.[12]

The next day Alexander Campbell of the Justice Department talked privately with Hiss at the courthouse. "The FBI has cracked the case," said Campbell. "You are in it up to your eyes. Your wife's in it. Why don't you go out there and tell the truth?"

"I have continuously told the truth," said Hiss, "and will continue to do so."

"You are going to be indicted," Campbell warned. "I am not fooling. There are five witnesses against you."

"I am not fooling either," Hiss said.

"This is your government speaking," said Campbell. He added a threat. Unless Hiss confessed, Campbell would ask for a second indictment, against Priscilla. But Hiss, not intimidated, held fast "in an amazing manner."[13]

December 15. The grand jury's decision was due. The morning papers included sensational glints of Frank Reno's testimony: The Washington spy ring had penetrated the Aberdeen Proving Ground and secured data on the Norden bombsight.[14]

Chambers and Hiss both gave final testimony. Hiss was asked two questions that in varying form had been put to him many times in the course of the inquiry.

Q: At any time did you, or Mrs. Hiss in your presence, turn any documents of the State Department or any other Government organization,
or copies of any documents of the State Department or any other Government organization, over to Whittaker Chambers?

A: Never. Excepting, I assume, the title certificate to the Ford.

Q: Can you say definitely that you did not see him after January 1,
1937?

A: Yes, I think I can definitely say that.[15]

While the grand jury was deliberating, Chambers exited the waiting
room and slipped down a back stairway. A group of reporters ran down
a different stairway, hoping to intercept him. Moments later Hiss
emerged, refusing comment. Reporters followed him into the elevator.
It stopped at the eleventh floor. In walked Chambers. Accuser and accused rode down together in silence. Hiss was smiling. Chambers,
poker-faced, stared down at his shoes.[16]

That afternoon the grand jury voted to indict Alger Hiss. He had lied
in telling the grand jury he had not seen Chambers after January 1, 1937.
And—of much greater significance—he had lied in saying he had not
transmitted documents to the ex-Communist. Everyone understood the
technical charge of perjury masked the deeper allegation of espionage.

Some on the panel wanted to indict Chambers too, for perjuring himself in October, but were dissuaded when Donegan pointed out that if
Chambers were indicted, it "would substantially weaken the government's case against Hiss."[17]

Attorney General Clark was at the Waldorf, attending a dinner, when he
learned of the indictment from reporters. He said he was not surprised.
He expected the trial would commence in January.

Did he think President Truman would remain steadfast in his opinion
that HUAC had pursued a red herring?

"I don't think it will alter it."[18]

HUAC bestowed congratulations on the grand jury and hailed the indictment as a "vindication" of its own efforts. Karl Mundt voiced his
"hope that nobody will ever again refer to this case as a 'red herring.' "

"It is a justification of our many months of work," said Richard Nixon
of the proceedings he had done his best to undermine. "We started at the

beginning against overwhelming odds and we were opposed by the Administration and many commentators and news analysts."

The committee could boast—and did—that it had uncovered a spy ring. Even skeptics bowed before this accomplishment. "It is now apparent," said *The Nation,* "that this politics-ridden committee has broken one of the most sensational spy cases in American history," outdoing both the Justice Department and the FBI. Nixon, soaking up the praise, expansively conceded that HUAC's critics had often been right in the past about the committee's many unfair practices. He promised reforms, including a new "code of procedure" that would protect future witnesses against unfounded accusations. At the same time the attorney general announced plans to seek new legislation "to tighten up the country's espionage laws."[19]

On the evening of December 17, two days after Hiss's indictment, Chambers returned to Baltimore by train, expecting to be met at the station by Esther. She arrived more than an hour late, badly shaken. There had been an accident on the drive over. She had struck a pedestrian, an elderly woman now in the emergency room. The police had let Esther continue on to the depot. She and Whittaker hurried to the hospital but were not allowed to see the patient. Attending physicians sounded hopeful. The couple then drove to Westminster, Whittaker behind the wheel and Esther "convulsively shuddering" at the memory of the accident.

When they pulled into the driveway, a state trooper was waiting. The victim had died.

"Oh, God, why?" said Esther. Her knees buckled. Chambers and the trooper caught her as she sagged to the ground.

After a calming word with the children and a call to Richard Cleveland, the couple climbed into the trooper's car and headed back to the city. Neither spoke. The only sound was the dispatcher's staticky reports coming over the police radio.

At a precinct station Esther was charged with involuntary manslaughter. Cleveland was there to post bond, sparing Esther a night in jail. Five days later a magistrate dismissed the case. The seventy-year-old victim, totally deaf, had stepped headlong into Esther's path from between two parked cars. Her survivors filed a wrongful death suit, Chambers's third legal entanglement.

To Chambers the incident was "proof that there was no depth of the abyss that we were not to sound."[20] The "tragedy of history" had begun a downward spiral toward Grand Guignol.

To most observers the Hiss case was a matter involving two men, but to Chambers the issue had always been much larger. His mission was to expose the wider Communist conspiracy. Whenever possible, he broadened the terms of his witness. Thus even as he had concealed the facts of Hiss's (and his own) spying, in the slander depositions he had provided a minutely detailed account of the Washington underground and of Hiss's role in it.

According to Chambers, Hiss was an assiduous talent spotter, constantly on the lookout for recruits. He invited prospects to intimate dinner parties at which he steered the conversation to politics, gently eliciting his guests' views on the worldwide antifascist movement. It was a delicate business, and normally J. Peters would not have allowed it, but Hiss "knew very well what he was doing at all times" and so could be trusted.[21]

Two of those Hiss had "at various times worked on" were a pair of State Department officials, Noel Field and Laurence Duggan.

Field, born in 1904, had grown up in Zurich, the son of an expatriate Quaker scientist and his English wife. At the end of World War I Dr. Field had made a careful study of conditions in defeated Germany for an American peace commission. Noel, seventeen when his father died, inherited an ambition "to work for international peace" and "to help improve the social conditions of my fellow-beings."

Field joined the State Department in 1926 after an unhappy time at Harvard. Gangling, awkward, effusive, vaguely British in manner, and suspiciously Continental in taste, Field was miscast at State, rather as Julian Wadleigh was a decade later. Also like Wadleigh, Field had an undergraduate's intoxication with ideas and an ill-concealed disdain for convention. He loathed "the neat dark suits" of the State Department and "the neat Georgetown houses" where his colleagues lived. At his apartment he sometimes showed friends the issues of the *Daily Worker* he kept stacked in his closet.[22]

In 1934 or 1935 Field met Alger Hiss, through their mutual friend Laurence Duggan, a rising star in the State Department. "The three men were often together, a close and easy group with many common interests," says Field's biographer. "Alger was the quick, witty one who always landed on his feet, always seemed to feel at home. Larry Duggan was the lucid, reasoned one, practical and incisive. Noel was the sensitive one, learned but unsure of himself."[23]

In the spring of 1936 Field quit the State Department to work for the League of Nations in Geneva. Before he left, he met with his underground handler, Hede Massing, an Austrian Communist, who assured him further assignments awaited him in Europe. His new control would be Massing's European superior, "Ludwig"—Ignace Reiss, the *rezident* in Switzerland.[24]

Two years later Field was one of the first State Department officials accused of being a Communist. His accuser was Dies Committee investigator J. B. Matthews, who recalled a conversation in which Field had confessed his Party membership. In 1939 Walter Krivitsky told Don Levine that Field had done secret work. On a visit to the United States, Field, fearful of further allegations, made a brief detour to Washington and conferred with Hiss, who (Field later said) promised to send along a warning in the event Krivitsky expanded his allegations.[25]

Then the war had come, and Field was left unmolested. He remained in Geneva, on the payroll of the Unitarian Relief Fund, helping refugees, but was fired when his Communist associations became an embarrassment. He was still in Geneva in August 1948, when the Hiss case broke. Field obtained copies of the HUAC transcripts from friends. He knew he could not survive a similar grilling. "Alger defended himself with great intelligence," Field later said. "He had been trained as a lawyer and knew all the phrases and tricks. I, on the other hand, had no such experience. . . . I did not trust myself to stand before my accusers and shout 'innocent' in their faces. . . . I also understood the same from a short letter from Hiss, who obviously could not write openly." In May 1949 Noel Field slipped behind the Iron Curtain to Prague so as to escape extradition but was embroiled immediately in a fresh round of Stalinist purges and sent to a Budapest prison where he sat for five years.[26]

There remained the third member of the trio, Laurence Duggan. Chambers had been oddly silent on him. Days after Chambers's first HUAC appearance Herb Solow dropped in on Chambers and said, "How come you didn't mention Duggan?"

Chambers quickly closed the door. "Don't you forget anything?" he said. It was not a matter of remembering: Solow had kept his memo of his encounters with Chambers in 1938, when Duggan's name had made a deep impression on Sidney Hook.

Patiently Chambers explained the omission. He had not worked directly with Duggan, so his knowledge was secondhand. Also, Duggan was a devoted family man, "the father of four children, and I wouldn't want to do something irresponsible." Finally, Chambers suspected Duggan had been a fellow traveler, not a Communist. And "whatever Duggan's political sympathies might have been a few years ago, they might [since] have changed."[27]

On October 15, the same day Chambers lied to the grand jury about spying, the *New York Herald Tribune* published a front-page article summarizing the HUAC interim report. It included allegations against Field that Chambers had made during the hastily summoned session of August 27 before his *Meet the Press* interview. Shortly thereafter, in the November deposition, Chambers named Duggan, as Duggan undoubtedly learned from Hiss, who was studying transcripts as they became available.[28]

A month later the grand jury reconvened to weigh the new evidence Chambers had so dramatically presented, and the FBI interviewed Hede Massing, now an ex-Communist, who said she had tried to recruit Duggan for apparatus work in the 1930s. After a number of intense dialogues—one held over a weekend at Duggan's home—he had agreed to furnish information to the underground. He would not hand over documents, he told Massing, but would pass along "bits of news that came to his attention."[29]

On December 10, 1948, shortly after the grand jury was reconvened in New York, Larry Duggan was at his home in Scarsdale, recuperating from spinal disk surgery. The operation had left him with acute spasms and occasional "semi-fainting spells."[30]

Two visitors rang the bell. They were John Danahy and William McCarthy, agents with the FBI's major case squad in New York. Duggan's wife, Helen, surprised but not flustered, graciously fetched her husband, who came downstairs in a jacket and madras shirt. A fine-looking man, elegantly slim, he greeted the agents as if they were guests, not interrogators, and ushered them into his study.[31]

The agents repeated the allegations of Whittaker Chambers and Hede Massing. Speaking easily, Duggan said he was not a Communist and not a spy. He dimly recognized Hede Massing's photo. He had known her in the thirties as Hede Gumperz. They had met under "extremely hazy" circumstances, possibly through Noel Field. Massing had not tried to recruit him for espionage.

The FBI men also asked Duggan about an incident Massing dated to 1938, after her return from a seven-month stay in Moscow that had left her disenchanted with communism. Back in America, Massing had gone to Duggan's home in the hope of detaching him from the apparatus, in the event he had not already quit it. According to Massing, Larry had not been home, but Helen Duggan was in, hosting a children's party. She greeted Massing coolly and bade her to wait until Duggan came home. After an hour Massing gave up and left. But she was confident, because of Helen's manner, that Duggan had broken.

Duggan said he did not recall the incident. Perhaps the agents should question his wife. Helen Duggan came in and studied Massing's photo. She "faintly" remembered Massing's visit. Larry Duggan, unruffled to this point, blushed a deep crimson.

Then he made a startling confession. He told the agents he twice had been approached for apparatus work in the 1930s, not by Massing but by two other recruiters. One was Henry Collins, a social acquaintance. The other was Duggan's Harvard classmate Frederick Vanderbilt Field (no relation to Noel), an heir to the Vanderbilt fortune and a well-known Communist. Neither man, said Duggan, had asked him to steal documents, but both had urged him to assist the USSR or the Comintern—precisely which, Duggan could not recall. He had rejected both overtures.

As for Field and Hiss, both were friends, but neither, as far as Duggan knew, was a Communist.*

When the interview ended, Danahy gave his card to Duggan and told him to call if he wished to talk again. Duggan was noncommittal.

As soon as his visitors left, Duggan told his wife that Noel Field had been a Communist agent, and the FBI now knew it.[33]

At seven o'clock on the evening of Tuesday, December 20, ten days after his FBI interview, Laurence Duggan's body plummeted out of the executive offices of the Institute of International Education, in midtown

---

* In 1954 Noel Field told Communist interrogators in Budapest that Duggan, "my best, almost only friend," was "the first person at the State Department who knew my views. Later, Hiss joined [Duggan in this knowledge]."[32]

Manhattan, and struck a snowbank sixteen stories below. He was pronounced dead on arrival at Roosevelt Hospital. Police said he "either
jumped or fell." He was forty-three years of age.[34]

Within hours the whispers began. In Washington Karl Mundt phoned
the wire services and summoned reporters to HUAC's offices at midnight. Nixon and Stripling were also there. In his best elocutionary manner Mundt read aloud selected testimony Isaac Don Levine had given
secretly on December 8, a reprise of his *Plain Talk* allegations. According
to Levine, Duggan had been one of six State Department officials who
had provided "confidential information" to Soviet intelligence. Levine's
source was Chambers, who had named Duggan to Adolf Berle.

Who were the other five? reporters asked.

"We'll release the others," Mundt jauntily replied, "as they jump out
of windows."[35]

That morning Chambers had come up from Westminster to testify before the new grand jury. It had been only three days since the auto accident, and Esther still faced criminal charges. No one at HUAC had
bothered to contact him about Mundt's press conference. At Foley
Square he was mobbed by reporters. He professed bewilderment at
Duggan's "shocking" death and could suggest no motive for it. "From
all I knew of Mr. Duggan, he was a gentle and sensitive man, and was devoted to his family."

The reporters pressed for more. Were the allegations true? Had Larry
Duggan been one of six spies in the State Department? Chambers chose
his words carefully. "It would have been more proper to say I mentioned
six people." Duggan had been one of the six. But "I did not mention
Mr. Duggan as passing over papers to me." Nor had he accused Duggan
of being a Communist.[36]

The impact was tidal. One week after the triumph of Hiss's indictment HUAC was under the "worst cloud" in its ten-year history, buf-
feted from all sides—left, right, and center. The Americans for
Democratic Action (ADA), a distinguished organization of anti-
Communist liberals whose members included Reinhold Niebuhr and
Arthur Schlesinger, Jr., renewed their cry for the immediate termina-
tion of HUAC's "reckless career," calling on House Speaker Sam Rayburn to seek its abolishment on the opening day of the Eighty-first
Congress.

A "dead man's character is being destroyed," declared Edward R. Murrow, the great radio reporter, in his evening newscast. Who, asked Murrow, had accused Duggan of being a Communist? "Isaac Don Levine, who said he was quoting Whittaker Chambers. And who denies it? Whittaker Chambers."

Even the *Herald Tribune* was appalled. "At a stroke [HUAC] has undone months of genuine effort . . . to correct past excesses and bring its procedures within the limits of reason and fairness." The paper also published "Black Day," livid verses written by Archibald MacLeish, a friend of Duggan's:

> *God help that country where the informer's shame*
> *Outshouts the decent silence to defame*
> *The dead man's honor and defile his name!*[37]

At Duggan's funeral, attended by Sumner Welles and Adolf Berle, a statement was circulated likening HUAC's "unjust profaning" of Duggan's memory to tactics that flourished "under Stalin in Russia and Hitler in Germany."[38]

Most remarkable of all was the criticism the "committee of two" received from within HUAC's own ranks. In New Orleans Eddie Hébert—pushed beyond his limit by Nixon's lone wolfing and Mundt's partisan grandstanding—castigated his Republican colleagues ("the guilty ones") for conducting inquiries "with one eye on today's evidence and the other on tomorrow's headlines."[39]

But amid the outrage something was being missed, as Chambers quietly pointed out. "Too much emphasis has been placed on my statement that I personally never knew Laurence Duggan and that he never gave me documents," Chambers told reporters. The important fact was that "I found it necessary to give Duggan's name to Mr. Berle" in the first place.[40]

But this was no time for Chambersian nuance. The fury against HUAC, pent up these many months, burst forth with unstoppable energy. In Duggan many found the martyr they had been denied in Alger Hiss. The striking parallels between the two men were duly noted: the Ivy League backgrounds; the fine records in the State Department; the important work advancing international peace.[41]

On Christmas Eve Duggan received what seemed a full vindication when Attorney General Clark announced that the FBI had recently questioned Duggan and concluded he was "a loyal employee of the United States government," clear of any "connection with the Communist Party or with any espionage activity." In a follow-up television interview Clark commended Duggan for having provided the bureau with valuable leads (meaning Henry Collins and Fred Field) in its effort to root out Communist infiltration of the State Department.[42]

Duggan's death remained unsolved. It looked like suicide, but the evidence was inconclusive. Such clues as the police found were ambiguous. The victim had left no note. Also, he had been wearing one snow boot when he fell; the matching boot was near his desk. His tweed topcoat had been folded on a chair near the window; on the floor near his desk stood his briefcase with a plane ticket to Washington inside. The picture was that of a man getting ready to leave his office and go home for the evening.

On the other hand, as reports noted, the window in Duggan's office had been raised to a gaping height of twenty-eight inches—on a freezing December night. Since the window sat forty-four inches off the floor, the height of the opening was such that the five-ten Duggan could easily have stepped through it. On the ledge outside, the snow had been partly brushed away, indicating Duggan likely had sat there before leaping. A witness on the street said the falling body had been upright as it fell, the posture common in suicide leaps.[43]

Copies of a three-way correspondence among Duggan, Hiss, and Noel Field turned up. None of the letters was incriminating—they dealt with Field's plans for getting freelance writing assignments with American magazines—but it was clear Duggan had minimized his contacts with both Field and Hiss.[44]

But the most important evidence was in the FBI report of December 10, Duggan's voluntary admission that for more than ten years he had kept secret his knowledge of two men, one of them a government employee, who had tried to recruit State Department officials for underground work. Once this story emerged, HUAC would have forced Duggan to the stand. His career would have been finished, his reputation destroyed.

With Christmas and the New Year approaching, the new grand jury recessed for a week, and Chambers retreated to Westminster to observe the holidays. His gifts included a chain and bell (from Ellen) for his favorite cow, Minnie, a plump Guernsey. He proudly exhibited Minnie and her bell to a reporter from the *Baltimore Sun,* Patrick Skene Catling, who visited on December 27 for an interview.

It was a warm day, in the forties. Clad in denim trousers and bulky coat, Chambers led Catling over the grounds. The picturesque farmhouse, with its bowed lines and symmetrically sagging doorframes, seemed to the reporter something out of Thomas Hart Benton. Chambers looked comfortable in these rustic surroundings. "Everyone seems to wonder how I am going to get along," he said. "At the moment I have no pressing financial worries. I have some money. And the milk from my cows grosses an average of about $500 a month."

Later, seated in the living room and drinking hot chocolate, Chambers told Catling he had taken up Dostoevsky's *The Possessed* for "the sixth or seventh time" and also was reading W. H. Auden, whose latest volume, the Pulitzer Prize–winning *The Age of Anxiety,* explored themes much on Chambers's mind: post-atomic man's loss of faith, tradition, and sense of community.

"The world has always been in turmoil," the witness told Catling. "But the disturbances are getting considerably worse—and now are of seismic proportions. The vibrations are felt everywhere." He himself had been "hurled from comparative obscurity by a volcano."[45]

There were two other guests that day, Richard Nixon and Robert Stripling, determined to squeeze in one last session with Chambers before the committee issued its year-end report, due out January 3. Though Nixon and Stripling did not say so, they hoped for fresh allegations that would eclipse the Duggan fiasco. Chambers was willing to talk and welcomed the opportunity to get beyond the "personal controversy" of the Hiss case and explore "the dimension of the whole conspiracy." He agreed to a lengthy session the following afternoon at the farm.*

A five-man HUAC contingent, along with a stenographer, drove out, a "subcommittee of the subcommittee"—Nixon and Mundt plus

---

*All quoted testimony comes from the HUAC transcript of the executive session, December 28, 1948, released by the U.S. House Committee on Internal Security in 1974 but never printed. It appears here for the first time.

Stripling, Donald Appell, and William Wheeler. After a look at the fabled pumpkin patch the entourage settled into Chambers's living room, where a fire blazed in the hearth.

The witness, seated in his favorite rocker and gripping his pipe, "reminisced" for five hours. He began with the summons from Max Bedacht and worked forward to his defection. His testimony assumed the shape of a narrative; there were stretches when his interrogators simply listened. At one point Ellen and John quietly drifted into the room and seated themselves. These were matters they had never heard their father discuss.[46]

Chambers offered no startling revelations, though he did put a cap on the Duggan story. In 1937 Chambers had asked Frederick Vanderbilt Field, a contact of J. Peters's, to "go to Washington and sound out Laurence Duggan and see whether he would work with my apparatus." Field later returned with intriguing news: "Duggan was already connected with another apparatus."

In March 1996 decrypted cables released by the National Security Agency identified Duggan as having had contacts with Soviet intelligence as late as 1944.[47]

After the Westminster interview, a "jubilant" Mundt boasted that the witness had provided enough new leads to occupy the committee for at least six months and possibly a year.[48]

But no one was anticipating further spy probes just yet. Of the 101 new House Democrats, not one had requested a seat on the committee. In begging off, most said HUAC's obligations were too "time-consuming." The truth was, no freshman Democrat dared go near the committee President Truman wanted abolished.[49]

HUAC survived, thanks to the Hiss indictment, but the team had been broken up. Soon Nixon would move up to the Senate. Mundt was already poised to begin a mediocre Senate career as a pliable adjutant to Senator Joseph R. McCarthy. Parnell Thomas was soon to be indicted— and later convicted and jailed—for taking kickbacks. Hébert and Rankin retained their seats but in a few days were railroaded off HUAC by Speaker Rayburn. McDowell had lost his reelection bid.

The most costly loss was Stripling, bound for Texas and a profitable second career in oil speculation. All but invisible during the Duggan affair, the investigator departed Washington wreathed in glory. A lecture tour awaited him, plus a contract with the Hearst chain for a syndicated series.[50]

The old guard got in some last licks before the year ended, calling up a number of witnesses, but only after the grand jury was done with them. The Hiss case, out of the committee's hands, would be settled in the courts, where many thought it had belonged since August.[51]

# WITNESS II: THE TRIALS

## (January 1949–January 1950)

*Caught by a photographer in the subway beneath Foley Square. The book is probably* The Divine Comedy.
AP/WIDE WORLD PHOTOS

# 25

# *Preparations*

The new year brought no respite. Chambers was to remember 1949 as "a dead year"[1] lived humiliatingly in the public eye. His status had changed from friendly HUAC witness to defendant in a slander suit to key prosecution witness in the perjury trial of Alger Hiss.

First came the pretrial preparations. In order to prove perjury, the prosecution must have either testimony from two witnesses or one witness plus corroborative evidence. As things stood, Chambers was the sole witness, and his testimony was tainted by the many lies he had told. The government would seek to bolster its case with the Baltimore documents and the pumpkin microfilm. The defendant already conceded his authorship of three of the four notes, and analysts had linked the typed papers to Hiss. As yet the bureau had not located the Hiss Woodstock and was frantically trying to do so.

At the same time the FBI pursued its other leads. They were few in number. Chambers could blame himself. He had handled his various contacts too efficiently, making sure not one knew the full extent of the overall operation. Thus Julian Wadleigh had had no inkling Hiss, his colleague in the Trade Agreements division, might also be a Soviet agent. This compartmentalization held up and down the organization. Even so significant a player as William Edward Crane, questioned by the FBI in the winter of 1949, was unable to aid the prosecution. Out of the Party since 1940—he had started a freelance photography business in Long Beach, California—Crane freely discussed his collaboration with Chambers, recalling in particular a massive job in the spring of 1937, when

Chambers had delivered "briefcases full of Treasury and State Department documents." Crane also showed agents the Leica he had used. But he had never met Hiss or any other sources. They were simply names to him, jumbled loosely in his mind.[2]

Another disappointment was Felix Inslerman, who had photographed the pumpkin film. The FBI tracked him down in upstate New York. Now employed as an engineer with General Electric in Schenectady, he had left the underground years before. Still, he would not cooperate. The grand jury summoned him on seven occasions in the winter of 1949, with no luck. When reporters asked the cherubic witness if he was the same Felix who had filmed the spy papers, Inslerman, smiling enigmatically, said, "Let's put it down to coincidence." Not until 1954 did Inslerman divulge the facts of his underground career. Even then he could shed no light on Alger Hiss's role. The photographer had never met the man.[3]

The government had one potentially crucial witness, Hede Massing, who had told first the FBI and then the grand jury that in 1935 Hiss had tried to recruit her contact Noel Field into Hiss's own apparatus. According to Massing, she and Hiss had discussed their competition one night at Field's apartment. Hiss denied the incident had occurred, and Field fled to Prague in May 1949, weeks before the trial opened.[4] In any case, Massing might well be kept from taking the stand since her recollections, whether true or false, did not specifically address whether Hiss had handed State Department documents to Chambers.

Meanwhile the FBI put Chambers through an intensive regimen of interviews, from January through mid-April. The sessions were held in Foley Square, the trial's venue. (After some debate the bureau agreed to reimburse Chambers's travel expenses, a twenty-two-dollar round trip from Baltimore to Manhattan.) His chief interrogators were two of the bureau's best, agents Tom Spencer and Frank Plant of the major case squad in New York. The self-deprecating Spencer, who described himself as a graduate of "Marshall Law School over Webber's"—Webber's was a restaurant in Cleveland—had been the chief interrogator of Elizabeth Bentley and was a legend to his colleagues, "the best agent I ever saw," said one. Plant, like Spencer, had pursued Nazi agents during the war. He had also worked on the Gerhart Eisler deportation case and was "a walking archive of the identities, features and peculiarities of Soviet agents."[5]

Six days a week the three were closeted together through the morning and afternoon in sessions that lasted as long as seven hours, with a break at lunch, when they sent out for sandwiches and coffee. Spencer also accompanied Chambers on expeditions to Washington and Baltimore. Seated in the back of an FBI car, Chambers studied the rows of housefronts in an effort to retrieve the long-buried sensation of a staircase he had once mounted or a darkened doorway where he had stood. Handed the typescript of his testimony, some three hundred single-spaced pages, Chambers riffled through them, sighing, "We live in an age of paper."[6]

When Spencer asked if he had anything to add, Chambers took the agent's pen and scrawled "*E quindi uscimmo a riveder le stelle* [Where we came forth, and once more saw the stars]", the last line of the *Inferno*. The agents grew used to such flourishes. Chambers also wove philosophical and religious homilies into his reminiscences, always in a "natural, down-to-earth way," recalled Jack Danahy, who interviewed Chambers on some occasions. Danahy later remembered Chambers's explaining his prior withholdings by evoking the image of a "two-headed" God, one head representing mercy, the other justice. For himself, said Chambers, the God of mercy always took precedence.[7]

Henceforth Chambers would speak warmly of the FBI, forgiving past brushoffs. Plant, Spencer, and a few others filled the void once occupied by Chambers's younger colleagues at *Time*. The agents referred to Chambers, affectionately, as "Uncle Whit." His friendly relations with his interrogators lessened the ordeal, but not the shame, of giving out names, ruining lives, and making "what amounted to a total recall of my life" for the benefit of FBI dossiers.

When he repaired to Westminster for the occasional weekend reprieve, Chambers was "white with exhaustion," recalled Brad Darrach, a young *Time* writer staying rent-free with his wife in a house on Chambers's property.[8] But within hours, said Darrach, Chambers "would recuperate, and he had a lot of vitality." In fact his health was improving, owing to his more regular diet and the many hours he put in on the farm, as ever his great solace. "If you once ploughed a 30 acre field," he had told Herb Solow back in 1943, after his first heart scare, "you'd never want to do anything else in your life."[9]

The sleuthing was not limited to the prosecution. Hiss's legal team was also gathering evidence, of a different kind. The defense strategy, unchanged since August, was to establish Hiss's innocence by discrediting Chambers.

Since the trial would be in New York, Edward McLean and Harold Rosenwald supervised the preparations, aided by a professional investigator, Horace Schmahl.* The team turned up witnesses only too eager to discuss Chambers's abnormalities. One of his many Time Inc. adversaries, the former editor Leon Svirsky—he had since joined the staff of *Scientific American*—became an adjunct of the Hiss defense, canvassing employees past and present for damaging reminiscences.[11] But these revolved chiefly around Chambers's anticommunism, not a theme the Hiss defense could usefully exploit.

Taking a different approach, Harold Rosenwald followed up on a tip from the writer (and *Time* alumnus) Merle Miller[†] and interviewed Lionel Trilling, whose 1947 novel *The Middle of the Journey*—about fellow-traveling liberals in the 1930s—included a vivid portrait of Chambers. He appeared as Gifford Maxim, a "terribly committed" Soviet agent turned defector.[‡] Though Trilling had never much liked his Columbia schoolmate, he did not doubt the truth of Chambers's HUAC testimony and so refused to take the stand against him. "Whittaker Chambers is a man of honor," Trilling explained. The remark was met by an "outburst of contemptuous rage" from Rosenwald.[13]

Hiss's attorneys also looked for evidence that Chambers was homosexual. Again some were eager to talk, reviving gossip from the late 1920s and early 1930s. Grace Hutchins, the witness at Chambers's wedding, told Schmahl it was "common knowledge that Chambers had been a sex pervert when he was employed by the *Daily Worker*," though when pressed for specifics, she provided none. Another fount of rumor was Chambers's first Communist Party liaison, Sender Garlin. Steadfast in his communism—his faith had even withstood a stay in Moscow in 1936, at the height of the show trials—Garlin garrulously speculated about the Lower East Side ménage of 1931 and al-

---

* In the winter of 1949 Schmahl "defected" to the prosecution after he had become convinced of Hiss's guilt. Subsequently he figured in pro-Hiss conspiracy theories.[10]

† Miller reported on the second trial for the *The New Republic*.

‡ It puzzled Trilling for many years that his publisher, Viking, did not reissue the novel in 1948–1949. Since the book bore many intriguing parallels to the Hiss case, it was likely to excite fresh interest. Unbeknownst to Trilling, Viking's publisher, Ben Huebsch, was a Communist and had quietly offered his services to the Hiss defense.[12]

leged that Chambers, Esther, Grace Lumpkin, and Mike Intrator all had been homosexual.[14]

The defense team also questioned Lumpkin and Intrator on the same topic, and the pair alerted Chambers. He was not surprised. He had been expecting it for months. One day he had walked the quarter mile to Medfield and stunned Brad Darrach by telling him rumors would soon surface linking Chambers and his young tenant as lovers.

"I just blinked," Darrach later said. "I didn't know what that meant. I didn't know anything about the talk, the rumors. I sort of laughed at it." But then, not long afterward, "a young, Ivy League–looking man, rather heavyset, did come walking down the road and tried to question me about Whittaker. He was so clearly an emissary of Hiss that I said no, I didn't want to talk about it, and he went away. But it was obviously, as Whittaker foretold, some attempt to see what they could turn up in the neighborhood."[15]

When Chambers similarly warned Intrator, his old friend laughed it off. An incurable womanizer, he had never observed any homosexual "tendencies" in his good friend.[16]

The issue came to a head in February. Shortly after the indictment Hiss's attorneys had petitioned Judge Chesnut, the magistrate in the slander suit, to allow resumed depositions of Chambers, even though Hiss's suit was in abeyance pending the outcome of the perjury trial. The prosecution had strenuously argued that the depositions should not be allowed since they were simply a pretext for gathering additional ammunition for the upcoming trial. But Judge Chesnut ruled in favor of the defense because the ultimate objective of the two cases was identical: "to find the real and true relevant facts." After all, the judge pointed out, if not for the November depositions, the Baltimore documents and the microfilm might never have surfaced.[17]

Chambers, then, would have to sit once more for questioning in William Marbury's Baltimore office. The first session was scheduled for February 17. Before leaving for Maryland, on the fifteenth, Chambers put in another day in New York with his FBI interrogators. At its conclusion Chambers handed Tom Spencer a sealed envelope. The FBI man promised not to open it until Chambers had left the building.

With the Hiss team poised to disparage his character by any means, Chambers had written, the time at last had come when "I must testify to certain facts that should be told only to a priest." The letter set forth a "general statement" as the basis for "specific questions." After reading the letter, Spencer tried to reach Chambers at Lynbrook, but the witness had already left for Baltimore.[18]

On February 17 Chambers was grilled all day in Marbury's office. This time Edward McLean, Hiss's chief defense lawyer, handled the questioning. Homosexuality was not among the topics raised. Afterward Chambers proceeded to the Baltimore FBI office. He had asked that only one agent be present at the interview. The request was denied. He faced two confessors, not the trusted Plant and Spencer, but a local pair.

Chambers began by saying he was sure the defense would make much of his relationship twenty years earlier with Bub Bang, though it had been innocent, like that between "a father and son." Then he brought up something else. One evening in 1933 or 1934, when Chambers had been alone on the streets of Manhattan, he had been approached by a beggar. Chambers treated him to dinner, and his guest, a coal miner's son, "told a very interesting story of his life." The vagabond had no place to stay that night,

and since I was more or less "footloose and fancy free" I took him to a hotel, the name of which I cannot now recall. During the course of our stay at the hotel that night I had my first homosexual experience. It was a revelation to me. As a matter of fact it set off a chain reaction in me which was almost impossible to control. I do not know the identity of the young man I spoke of, nor does he know my true identity. I have never seen him since the first night I met him.

Since that time, and continuing up to the year 1938, I engaged in numerous homosexual activities both in New York and Washington, D.C. At first I would engage in these activities whenever by accident the opportunity presented itself.

However, after a while the desire became greater and I actively sought out the opportunities for homosexual relationships. I recall that incidents of this nature took place in the Hotel Annapolis and the Hotel Pennsylvania in Washington, D.C. I registered in these hotels under assumed names which I now cannot recall. I know that other incidents took place in hotels in New York City which I cannot now remember, but concerning which I might state that they were of the typical "flea bag" type of hotel one finds in certain parts of Manhattan.

I never had a prolonged affair with any one man and never visited any known places where these type of people were known to congregate. I generally went to parks or other parts of town where these people were likely to be found.

At the time Chambers broke with communism, he also "managed to break" himself of his homosexual "tendencies." Ten years later, though not "completely immune to such stimuli . . . my self-control is complete," and "I have lived a blameless and devoted life as husband and father." Chambers had mastered his desires at the same time he had rediscovered "religion and God."

To date Chambers had disclosed this, "my darkest personal secret," to no one, including his wife. "I tell it now only because, in this case, I stand for the truth. Having testified mercilessly against others, it has become my function to testify mercilessly against myself."[19]

It was the most humiliating moment of the case—and a wasted one, for the Hiss defense ultimately decided not to raise the homosexual issue, lest it rebound against their client, who was also the subject of sexual innuendo.[20]

Preparations dragged on. The trial date was postponed when the Hiss team brought in yet another attorney, Lloyd Paul Stryker, a renowned trial lawyer who normally commanded fees as high as seventy-five thousand dollars but agreed to represent Hiss for much less.[21]

There were further delays as both sides struggled to assemble evidence. As of April, the prosecutor, Assistant U.S. Attorney Thomas Murphy, had yet to interview Chambers, his chief witness, and the FBI had yet to locate the Woodstock typewriter.

Despite the postponements, public interest did not flag. Winter and spring brought numerous developments related to the Hiss case. There was a small furor in January 1949, when President Truman's nominee for secretary of state, Dean Acheson, told the Senate that Alger Hiss had been and remained his friend. Then, in March, a new spy case bloomed, involving Judith Coplon, a twenty-eight-year-old Justice Department official nabbed in New York by FBI agents who found in her purse extracts of FBI "data slips"—or memos, some relating to the Hiss investigation.[22]

In the spring two leaders of the Communist underground disappeared, days apart. First, J. Peters, who had been petitioning the Justice Department for permission to leave the country, was finally granted his request in April, and on May 8 he "deported himself" to Budapest, never to return, although he kept up with the Hiss case through contacts in the CPUSA.

A more spectacular incident occurred four days later, when Comintern representative Gerhart Eisler, awaiting trial in New York, jumped bail and stowed away on a liner sailing to Poland. He was apprehended in England and detained there while American and Polish authorities lodged competing claims for his extradition. On May 31—the same day the jury was selected in the Hiss case—a London magistrate voided the American warrant, and Eisler was flown to Prague, where Communist officials greeted him with a snifter of brandy.[23]

After the sixth and final delay—necessitated when prosecutor Murphy was stricken with appendicitis—a trial date for *U.S.* v. *Alger Hiss* was set for May 31, 1949, nearly six months after the indictment. The prosecution and the judge predicted the trial would last between two and three weeks. Indeed the first order of business, jury selection, went briskly, taking only two hours, even though thirty-one talesmen—half the total pool—had to be dismissed during the voir dire when they admitted to harboring prejudices against the testimony of the ex-Communist Chambers.

The foreman, erect white-haired Hubert E. James, was a minor executive at General Motors. His colleagues represented a cross section of middle-class America in 1949. All were white. All but one was employed. Their occupations ranged from credit analyst and direct-mail advertiser to dressmaker and secretary. There were ten men and two women, plus two women alternates.

After a final, routine plea by the defense to have the indictment dismissed,[24] the court was adjourned, and the next day the main event began.

# 26

# *"Unclean! Unclean!"*

The perjury trial of Alger Hiss began on Wednesday, June 1, 1949, a mild day in the seventies with a pleasant breeze gusting through the open spaces of Foley Square. Spectators had gathered by the hundreds. A line starting inside the marble lobby wound down the steep flight of steps outside. Early arrivals ate out of paper bags, waiting for the doors to open.[1]

The trial, everyone knew, would be a historic event. "The outcome will have major repercussions, whatever it may be," wrote *The Nation*'s Robert Bendiner:

> Acquittal should prove the undoing of the House Committee on Un-American Activities; that body would stand revealed as a collection of gulls who for two years had followed the lead of a man regarded by a jury of average Americans as a monumental liar or a mental case. Conviction, on the other hand, would show that Communist conspiracy has gone much farther in the United States than the run of liberals have thought possible, and that it has agents more devious, more highly placed, and more successful than any yet brought to book.[2]

The third-floor courtroom, more spacious than most, had eight rows of hard wooden benches on which more than 150 people could sit. But only a handful of ordinary spectators were admitted in. Most of the places were claimed by the press and by guests of the prosecution and the defense (selected guests were seated in a small VIP section facing the jury). Some fifty reporters had come from around the nation, plus a sampling of celebrity journalists. Edward R. Murrow was there, and *The New Yorker's* A. J. Liebling, as well as Westbrook Pegler and the Hearst columnist and radio voice Inez Robb. The *New York Post* had sent over its famous sportswriter Jimmy Cannon, whose atmospheric pieces were to adorn the tabloid's front page, amplifying the daily accounts of beat reporter Malcolm Logan and the cerebrations of columnist Max Lerner.[3]

Four of the journalists present would write books on the case: Bert Andrews, *Newsweek's* Ralph de Toledano (who had already interviewed Chambers in depth), Alistair Cooke of the *Manchester Guardian,* and John Chabot Smith, who was covering the trial for the *Herald Tribune.* Andrews and de Toledano were pro-Chambers. Smith would labor a quarter century on a sympathetic biography of Hiss. Only Cooke made a point of not speaking with any of the principals so as to produce a thoroughly impartial account.[4]

The most comprehensive coverage of all was not published. Harry Luce wanted a daily account of the proceedings, minutely detailed. The assignment went to *Time's* James Bell, "the only man in the Washington bureau who knew nothing about the HUAC hearings." In August Bell had been on the road, covering the Republican presidential campaign, and had completely missed the congressional spectacle. Summoned to Rockefeller Center, he was sternly warned to produce a nonpartisan record. Also, he was not to "fraternize" with the witness. This second injunction was difficult to obey since Bell liked Chambers and was indebted to him. Bell had rejoined *Time* after serving overseas in the war and had briefly served under Chambers, who had loyally defended Bell's work when some hinted it was not up to standard.

On the first day of the trial Bell awkwardly explained his orders to Chambers, who told him it was for the best. Thereafter the two *Time* men kept their distance, so scrupulously that other journalists assumed they disliked each other.

Each day of the trial Bell scribbled tirelessly, and each night he typed up his notes, in reports running to four thousand words, for Luce to study the next morning. The result was a nearly stenographic record of the testimony and arguments and of the shifting moods and forces of the courtroom and its clash of personalities.[5]

A murmur rose up over the hum of the air conditioner when a smiling Alger Hiss entered the courtroom with his wife, neat and demure, at his side. The two sat together in red leather chairs just inside the railing that ran along the courtroom well and marked it off from the first row of spectators.

At 11:30 A.M. Judge Samuel Kaufman bounded in and spryly mounted a tall-backed chair in green leather. A rookie appointee (of President Truman's), with only a month's experience on the bench, Judge Kaufman was plainly delighted to be presiding over so celebrated a trial. It did not happen by accident. The calendar judge in May, he had assigned himself the case.[6]

The judge looked down toward the table where the prosecution team sat: Tom Murphy and his assistants, who included Tom Donegan, prosecutor Clark Ryan, and FBI agent Jack Danahy, in charge of the government's 224 exhibits.

In a nearly inaudible voice Kaufman said, "Will you proceed, Mr. Murphy?"

The prosecutor, a hulking six feet four and 230 pounds, rose to his feet. His mountainous shoulders and back stretched the seams of his double-breasted chalk-striped suit. Murphy's physique, red cheeks, tanned blue-eyed face, and rusty walrus mustache gave him the appearance of a carnival strongman. In fact he was a devotee of the French novel with a particular fondness for Proust.

Murphy was a local product, born and raised in the Bronx. His grandfather was a New York City patrolman, and his father a city clerk. The family's most illustrious member was Tom Murphy's younger brother, "Fireman" Johnny Murphy, a top relief pitcher for the Yankees in the 1930s and 1940s. Tom Murphy, educated at Georgetown and then at Fordham Law School, had been in private practice a dozen years before joining the U.S. attorney's office in 1942, at age thirty-six. In seven years as a prosecutor—five as head of the office's criminal division—he had compiled a 99 percent conviction record.[7]

Rooting himself at a lectern in front of the jury box, his massive back to the spectators, Murphy adjusted a sheaf of notes and in low Bronx tones gave a straightforward explication of the case. The defendant Alger Hiss stood indicted of lying twice to a grand jury on December 15, 1948. "He lied the first time when he said he never gave any documents to Whittaker Chambers, State Department documents. He lied again when he said that he never saw Chambers after January 1, 1937."[8]

One witness alone, Whittaker Chambers, would testify, and "in the most explicit fashion," that he had received the State Department documents from Hiss "in wholesale fashion" and then had them photographed. Later, in an effort to increase the volume of material, Priscilla Hiss had joined the team, typing copies of documents her husband brought home nightly from his office. On visits occurring every ten days or two weeks, Chambers collected those copies along with original documents Alger had removed that day. The papers were photographed and then returned to Hiss that same night.

Alas, said Murphy, a key piece of evidence, Priscilla Hiss's Woodstock typewriter, was missing. The FBI had put on its trail two dozen agents, who "shook down the city of Washington to a fare-thee-well," with no success. However, the government had other "specimens of the typewriter," which experts would testify came from the same machine as the copied documents.

Those specimens and Chambers were the core of the government's case. The specimens were unassailable. But Chambers would come under heavy attack by the defense. All the better. The government "welcomes, actually welcomes a searching cross-examination of Chambers, because that is the way you are going to find out where the truth is." The jurors should study Chambers carefully. "Watch his conduct on the stand; watch the color of his face; watch the way his features move, because if you don't believe Chambers then we have no case under the Federal perjury rule." That was all. Murphy had spoken for twenty-three minutes, rigidly fixed at his lectern.

There was a five-minute recess. Reporters, exchanging notes in the corridor, were mystified. The prosecutor had left his chief witness open to withering assault but said not a word in defense of him, not a word to explain to the jurors why they should consider Chambers a credible witness despite a public record of untruthful testimony.

It was hardly an opportunity to be missed by Lloyd Stryker, who was to make the presentation for Hiss. Stryker brought more than a reputation to the courtroom. He was a consummate trial performer, possibly the greatest since Clarence Darrow.

At age sixty-three Stryker was thought by some to have passed his prime. But he was ruddy and robust and had the magnetizing presence of a born actor. Short and burly, he liked to pace swiftly along the jury box, lulling the jurors with his voice, a beautifully supple instrument he had trained in childhood by declaiming in a barn.

Stryker's supreme strength was his intuitive feel for the emotional wellsprings underlying celebrated trials. "A great case," he had written in 1947, "is made by the conflict of ideas passionately espoused or desperately opposed by the community or nation where the trial is held. It is this clash that lights the fires of interest and excitement. These, rather than the personality of the defendant or the nature of the crime charged, supply the elements of drama."[9]

What Murphy had presented in its literal dimension as a perjury case Stryker projected as something larger and more symbolic: a referendum on the political changes sweeping through the nation. Hiss was on trial, but so were the New Deal and Yalta, and so were Chambers and the feverish hunt for Reds. Stryker's job was to portray his client as a shining exemplar of the Roosevelt era and to demonize Chambers as a bleak representative of all who were seeking to defile that cherished legacy.

Stryker advanced toward the jury box, gripped the railing with his small neat hands, fastened his gaze on the jurors. His silver hair was close-cropped. A single forelock curled down over his noble brow. Comparisons would be made with Julius Caesar and Napoleon.[10] He began with an announcement. "The days of the Klieg lights, the television, and all the paraphernalia, the propaganda which surrounded the beginning of this story" were over. After months of brutal inquisition Alger Hiss, storm-tossed, had at last found safe haven in "the dignified, calm and quiet and fair court of justice."[11]

Stryker then leaped nimbly into the opening Murphy had so conveniently provided. The prosecutor was absolutely right, said Stryker, when he said the jury had to settle only one question, the question of Chambers's credibility. It was a matter of Chambers's word against Hiss's, the witness's character versus the defendant's. Stryker began with Hiss: the glittering résumé; the dizzying rise; the illustrious sponsors. "Alger Hiss was good enough for Oliver Wendell Holmes and of the many character witnesses I shall call if the case gets that far, I shall summon, with all due reverence, the shade of that great member of the Supreme Court."

Repeatedly in his career Hiss had been singled out for missions demanding the highest trust. The peak moment had come in 1945, when the defendant was made sole custodian of the United Nations Charter, a document likely someday to "be enshrined like our Constitution." He had been trusted too with the leadership of the Carnegie Endowment. Hiss had amply rewarded the many who had placed their faith in him,

and the jury would learn why, once they became acquainted with the to-
tality of the defendant's public life. "I will take Alger Hiss by the hand,
and I will lead him before you from the date of his birth down to this
hour. Even though I would go [through] the valley of the shadow of
death, I will fear no evil because there is no blot or blemish on him."

Judge Kaufman hopped out of his tall chair and planted himself in the
witness chair, for a better view.[12]

But now, said Stryker, Hiss was under siege, his brilliant record being
challenged. And by whom? A "furtive, secretive, deceptive man," a self-
admitted Communist who "believed wrong was right" and would
"commit any crime that would aid in the overthrow of this dear land of
ours." He was also a "confirmed liar." He had trafficked in falsehoods
long before he joined the Communist movement and had gone on lying
after he left it, right up to the present moment. With no fewer than sixteen opportunities to back his charges against Alger Hiss with concrete
evidence, Chambers had failed each time. At last, driven into a corner by
the slander suit, he had concocted the "fantasia" of espionage.

Through it all Hiss had been steady. With each new assault he had exhibited the quiet fortitude of an innocent man. When Chambers produced the Baltimore documents, Hiss had calmly insisted the papers be
turned over to the Justice Department for analysis. Was that the conduct of
a guilty man? When the FBI asked about a typewriter, Hiss "bent heaven
and earth" to locate the machine. And "let us see, what did Mr. Murphy
say they did, that they turned Washington upside down? . . . something
like that, wasn't it, Mr. Murphy?"

"Pretty close," Murphy muttered.

"Shook it down?" suggested Judge Kaufman.

Well, said Lloyd Stryker, the defense team lacked the "opportunities
for shaking anything down that Mr. Chambers had." But—Stryker's
gaze briefly left the jury and traveled a triumphant circuit of the courtroom as he formed the words that would dominate the next day's headlines—"We have the typewriter!"

Wheeling toward the prosecution table,[13] Stryker offered "to let these
FBI eyes who couldn't find [the Woodstock] come down and look at it
all they want."[14]

Stryker's announcement was not news to the prosecution. In May the
FBI had learned from Hiss's former household servant Clytie Catlett that
the defense had recovered the Woodstock—or at least claimed to have

done. The only verification came from the Hisses and their witnesses. Not that Murphy felt obligated to contest the machine's authenticity. His case rested on the FBI analysis of the two sets of typed documents—the Hiss specimens and the spy papers—and not on the identity of the typewriter.[15]

After savoring this climax, Stryker moved into his denouement. He depicted Hiss as the naïve victim of George Crosley, a "glib and interesting talker" and a "very able man . . . a dramatic writer. Alger Hiss was interested in what he thought was another Jack London. No one was there to warn him about this man as I am alerting you." Stryker had been bouncing along the jury box. He suddenly stopped. He had reached his peroration. "In the warm southern countries, you know, where they have leprosy, sometimes you will hear on the streets, perhaps among the lepers, a man crying down the street"—the roar became a wail—" 'Unclean, unclean,' at the approach of a leper. I say the same to you at the approach of this moral leper. Thank you."

Then Stryker spun on his heel and returned to the defense table. The effect was electric.[16] The judge recessed the court for lunch.

But the excitement subsided as Murphy presented the many pieces of the government's case, beginning with a laborious sequence of witnesses, six in all. Three were employees of the grand jury who testified about the events leading up to the indictment and clarified what was meant by it. They were followed to the stand by a trio of utility company employees who fixed the dates of Hiss's residence at various Washington addresses from 1933 to 1947. As each new witness emerged from a door behind the judge's bench, a collective sigh of disappointment surged through the courtroom. When would Chambers appear?

Finished with his technical witnesses, Murphy proceeded to the still more tedious business of entering exhibits into the record. Stryker, playing to the crowd, waved dismissively at a document Murphy presented for his inspection. At three thirty-five Murphy was at last done, and Kaufman called a brief recess. The spectators shuffled out into the corridor, some stifling yawns.

When they resumed twenty minutes later, Murphy called his next and seventh witness, who emerged from behind the judge's bench. He "paused a split second and took in the courtroom," wrote Jim Bell. "For

a moment he was not recognized. Then the room buzzed with excitement." Bailiffs quickly moved into the aisles shushing the spectators.

Stryker had keyed everyone up for "some sort of monster." Instead
they saw "a fat sad-looking man" shamble to the stand in an oversize
dark three-piece suit, white shirt, and black tie, as if in mourning.
Chambers's pale eyes betrayed no emotion as they searched out the
Hisses for a long moment.

The defendant, donning a pair of tortoiseshell eyeglasses, stared back,
arms folded, chin lifted. Then he removed an index card from his pocket
and jotted something on it with a stubby pencil. Chambers looked away.

Tom Murphy rose from his table and positioned himself at his lectern,
which he had moved to the deepest corner of the jury box, as if to appraise his witness from the same neutral distance as the jurors. Then, in
blunt, uninflected sentences, he led Chambers over the ground of his
personal and political history.

The witness placidly recited the facts he had been telling for months,
to HUAC, the grand jury, and the FBI. His hands were in his lap, thick
fingers interlaced. He made no eye contact with the jury or with Murphy but occasionally flicked a glance toward Hiss. For long periods his
gaze roamed over an imaginary field on the ceiling.[17]

Again, as in the HUAC hearings, he spoke almost in a whisper, swallowing the ends of his sentences. But he was voluble—too voluble. After
the long months of free-form testimony Chambers had developed the
habit of giving conversational and expansive replies, not always strictly
responsive. Time and again Stryker objected, each time slowing the
rhythm of question and reply.[18]

Murphy had reached Chambers's days in the open Party—the *Daily
Worker,* his desultory efforts at union organizing—when Stryker rose to
register a final objection.

It was now four twenty-five. The court was to adjourn in five minutes.
Judge Kaufman dismissed Chambers and the jury for the day and summoned Stryker and Murphy to the bench. They had reached "one of the
most important points in the case," said the judge. They must decide how
much Chambers should be allowed to say about his Communist career.
Kaufman invited the attorneys to speak. Stryker went first. The essential
facts had been amply established, he argued. No further elaboration was
needed or appropriate. Chambers's life as a Communist had no bearing
on the indictment, and his testimony would prejudice the jury.

Judge Kaufman turned to Murphy. Did the prosecutor intend to demonstrate that the witness's Communist activities had resulted in his having met Hiss?

"That is correct," said Murphy.

Then there was a problem, said the judge. Since Hiss was on trial only for perjury, Murphy could not bring in the irrelevant matter of his alleged membership in the Communist Party.

Murphy vehemently disagreed. The perjury question was inextricably bound up with Hiss's alleged communism. He was accused, after all, of handing over documents to a Communist agent. Justice Learned Hand himself had said that if other crimes are established in the course of proving "the ultimate crime, it is just unfortunate."

Only, countered Stryker, if the crimes were "closely connected in point of time and place," and in this instance they were not, the alleged espionage having occurred in 1937–1938 in Washington, the perjury ten years later in New York. Chambers's history as a Communist was inadmissible testimony even if "the Government thinks it is fun to put it in."

"I am not enjoying this half as much as Mr. Stryker is," said Murphy.

Kaufman gently admonished Stryker and cautioned him not to "indulge in any personalities."

Stryker took a few strutting steps toward the gallery. "I am sure I do not mean that he is having fun at all." There was laughter.

Judge Kaufman said he would rule the next day. Now they would adjourn.

First he called in the jury and put a request to them. The newsreel cameramen and press photographers wanted to take their pictures.[19]

The next morning the judge summoned counsel to chambers and ruled that the prosecutor would "not be permitted to build up this witness [Chambers] by a series of self-serving statements that the defendants [sic] have no possibility of checking or examining."

"Oh, quite on the contrary, your Honor," Murphy protested. "I daresay there has not been a witness that has ever appeared in any court, state or federal, who has been subject to such grueling cross-examination concerning the history of his life."

He meant the Baltimore depositions. Chambers's testimony filled nearly a thousand pages.

Kaufman relented. Murphy could "sketch" the outline of Chambers's Communist career, leading up to 1937, but not go into specifics.[20]

Shortly before noon Chambers remounted the stand. He testified that morning and afternoon, again over a continual din of objections from Stryker, most of them sustained. Kaufman warned the witness not to layer his answers with detail. At one point the judge took over the questioning himself.

But Murphy patiently extracted the major facts, carrying Chambers's biography forward through the Lovestone purge (which had estranged him from the Party), *The New Masses* editorship (which had recemented his allegiance), up to the posting to Washington, where he had been introduced to Alger Hiss. Murphy brought out the key revelations of the HUAC testimony: the Ford; the rugs; the stolen documents; the stealing and copying of documents; Chambers's defection (he was not allowed to explain his motives); the flight to Daytona Beach. Chambers also testified about his hiring by *Time,* his move to the farm, his Christian rebirth.

"At times, Chambers seemed almost bored with the whole proceedings," Edward R. Murrow told his listeners that evening. "He slouched to the right in his chair, looked up at the ceiling as if to meditate, heaved a sort of weary sigh, closed his eyes when counsel approached the bench."[21]

Through it all Hiss paid close attention, utterly expressionless, seeming more observer than defendant. "I think I have never seen anyone who had himself more completely under control, unless it was Whittaker Chambers," said Murrow.

It was after three o'clock when Murphy handed Chambers a stack of documents wrapped in cellophane. Chambers studied the pages one by one, a few seconds each, while Murphy stood by.

After some minutes Chambers returned them. "Yes, these are the documents."

Murphy next gave him two strips of microfilm. Chambers held them up to the light and said he would need a magnifying glass to identify them. Murphy had them marked as evidence anyway, "subject to connection."[22]

Then Murphy resumed his position, at a long distance from the witness, and put to him a final sequence of questions about his visit to Hiss's house in December 1938. Over objections from Stryker, Chambers summarized that last conversation, made famous in his first HUAC appearance, and added new details. He recalled that Hiss had said it was a pity Chambers had defected since "a new and more important post was to be given to me." There might still be time for Chambers to "make my peace with the Communist Party. All I had to do was acknowledge my error."

The Hisses also said "they now knew who I was"—had learned his real name.

Had they known him as Crosley?

"I can't recall the name Crosley, but it is quite possible that I used it."

As Chambers had prepared to leave the Georgetown house, thwarted in his mission, Hiss, with some of the old camaraderie, had asked him what sort of Christmas Chambers was expecting.

"Rather a bleak one," Chambers had replied.

Hiss had then handed him a present for Ellen, a tiny wooden rolling pin.

Murphy concluded by asking Chambers about the documents he had kept hidden through the first months of the HUAC hearings. Judge Kaufman interceded to ask if HUAC or the grand jury had instructed him to produce documents of this kind.

"No. If I was asked I would have said no."

Murphy reminded Chambers that Adolf Berle still maintained that in 1939 Chambers had told him only that Hiss had belonged to a Marxist "study group."

Chambers placidly disagreed. He had named Hiss "as a member of the Communist Party."[23]

"You may examine," Murphy said, turning the witness over to Stryker. It was three fifty-five. Precisely twenty-four hours had elapsed since Chambers had first taken the stand.

Lloyd Stryker leaped to his feet, a boxer answering the bell. He hitched up his trousers, tightened his belt, and strode to the jury box, where he paced the rail in his brisk gait. Only half an hour remained before the court adjourned, enough time to leave the jurors with something to think about overnight.[24]

"Mr. Chambers," Stryker barked, "do you know what an oath is?"

The witness cupped his chin in his hand.[25] "I suppose I do."

Could he define it?

Yes. "An oath is that declaration which a man makes when he promises to tell the truth."

"And in our courts and elsewhere," said Stryker, the witness "also calls on almighty God to witness the truth of what he says?"

"That is right."

Stryker showed Chambers a photostat of the oath of office Chambers had signed when he took the WPA job in 1937. Holding the document aloft with outstretched hands, Stryker read it aloud: "Jay Chambers" had sworn he would "support and defend the Constitution of the United States against all enemies, foreign and domestic" and bear "true faith and allegiance to the same."

When Stryker was finished, he said, "You took and subscribed to that oath, did you not?"

"Yes."

"And it was false from the beginning to the end, was it not, Mr. Chambers?"

"Of course."

"What?"

"Of course."

"And it was perjury, wasn't it?"

"If you like."

"And you did it in order to deceive the United States government?"

"That is correct."[26]

Stryker next brought out the familiar record of Chambers's misdeeds, ending with the many lies he had told when a Communist. In admitting so easily that he had defrauded his government, did Chambers mean to say "that you have no shame and your conscience didn't trouble you?"

"I meant to indicate that I was a Communist."

"The question of right or wrong as we ordinary Americans would see it was entirely out of your head then? You solved it along Communist lines?"

"That is right."

Stryker shook his head in mock dismay. It was four-thirty.[27] The court was adjourned.

In that half hour Stryker had established the pattern he was to follow for the next four days, as he used Chambers's confessions to demolish his character.

The next day Stryker resumed his assault. Wasn't it true, he asked Chambers, that each and every Communist must slavishly obey "orders in all the Party may tell him such as to change his job, his husband or wife as the case may be?" That the Party may order him to "lie, to steal, to rob, or to go out into the streets and fight?" Wasn't every Communist "a spy, a saboteur and an enemy of the government?" Wasn't "disloyalty a matter of principle" to the Communist?

Yes.

In the years when Chambers was a Communist, each Party member was "a traitor to his country, is that right?"

"That is right."

"And you were a traitor to your country?"

"That is right."[28]

In covering up the extent of the underground conspiracy, had Chambers made false statements to Adolf Berle, Ray Murphy, and HUAC?

Yes.[29]

What about Chambers's first appearance before the grand jury when he had testified that he had "no direct knowledge" of espionage? Had that answer been true or false?

False.

"Then you admit now that you testified falsely and committed perjury before the grand jury in this building, is that right?"

"That is right," Chambers said.[30]

At that Stryker buttoned his jacket and spun to face the clock at the rear of the courtroom. It read twelve fifty-eight. The session was to end in two minutes. In a muted voice, as if humbled by the confessional outpouring he had loosed, Stryker asked Kaufman for adjournment. Kaufman consented. They would reconvene on Monday, at ten-thirty. Stryker sank into a chair and mopped his brow while his colleagues converged to congratulate him.[31]

The weekend seemed to refresh the witness. On Monday he looked more relaxed and better composed. "He had picked up the knack of answering only what was asked," observed Alistair Cooke. "And he had gauged the harmless muzzle velocity of Mr. Stryker's professional anger."[32]

Chambers's bland replies now had bite, a touch of wit. His exchanges with Stryker sometimes turned into two-liners, with Chambers getting the better of it.

"You became quite a prominent personage?" Stryker asked acidly of the HUAC hearings. "You became quite a person."

Chambers sighed. "Unfortunately."

At another point Stryker tallied up the numerous perjuries the wit-ness had committed while "a God-fearing man." Chambers smiled. Stryker turned on him fiercely. "Are you smiling now at your admission of perjury?"

"Are you asking me that question?" said Chambers, sounding amused.

Judge Kaufman, softening toward Chambers, reproved Stryker for ar-guing with the witness.

For the first time the barrister seemed to be losing steam. More im-portant, he had as yet to suggest, much less establish, a motive for Cham-bers's perjuries against Hiss. But he was ready to do so.

All during the cross-examination, eyes had turned toward the first row of spectators just behind the defense table. There sat a professional-looking man, with a large, balding dome, spectacles, and a notepad, who studied Chambers intently, meditatively tapping his fingers, and some-times scribbled a note he passed over to the defense table. By now every-one knew he was a psychiatrist. Some newspapers began referring to him as "Dr. X." Murphy had objected to his presence, fearing the im-pression it would have on the jury. Even A. J. Liebling thought "it wasn't right for the Judge to allow that psychiatrist to sit there all the while that Mr. Chambers was on the stand." But Kaufman had allowed it. Soon it was reported that the mysterious observer was Dr. Carl Binger, a well-known New York psychiatrist.

A boyhood friend of the columnist Walter Lippmann, who had rec-ommended him to the defense,* Binger was the author of what the Hiss defense called the "theory of unconscious motivation." This held that Chambers's accusations were rooted in an obsession with Hiss that began in the mid-1930s, when the two men had briefly known each other. At that time Chambers had developed feelings of love and admiration for the charming New Dealer. But when Hiss had cut off the friendship, the obsession metamorphosed into its opposite, an irrational hatred and rage that had set Chambers upon his vengeful course, climaxing with the de-nunciations of August 1948.[34]

---

* Lippmann had further counsel: Since "the gravest charge against [Hiss] has to do with espionage . . . I am wondering whether as public evidence of his good faith, he ought not to . . . waive the statute of limitations so that the charge may be dealt with by due process of law." Hiss wisely rejected this punditry.[33]

For the first time, as he advanced this argument, Stryker seemed hesitant. He belonged to a generation for whom Freudian theory and its offshoots remained new and strange. There was also the danger that Hiss would be compromised if his relationship with Chambers were presented as abnormal. Pausing at times for whispered conferences with Dr. Binger, his Vergil in these arcane matters, Stryker gingerly introduced the theory of unconscious motivation.

He began with the Christmas gift from Hiss, the rolling pin. Did it have a "mystical connection" for Chambers?

The witness remembered none. The dime-store gift had been one of "mixed kindness."

Was it symbolic?

No. "It just hurt my feelings."

"Was it a curious combination in your mind?"

Chambers smiled. "Please don't try to read something into my mind."[35]

Stryker pulled out the transcript of the Baltimore deposition and in a dramatic whisper began to read a passage in which Chambers said he remembered keeping the present secret from Esther and Ellen and later burning it.

Murphy protested, "Will Mr. Stryker read this straight, Your Honor?"

"It is the subject matter that might spur me on, or stir me," Stryker explained. Then, his supple voice going rigid in parody of Chambers's affectless monotone, the lawyer quoted Chambers's remark that the rolling pin had seemed a gift "you would give to a child of a renegade."[36]

Stryker made much also of the pumpkin, picking up on a statement of William Wheeler's that the gourds on the vine had formed a V-shaped design, with the hollowed-out pumpkin at the vertex. Was this alignment staged?

Only by nature, said Chambers.

Stryker did better pursuing Chambers's defection. Had Chambers not testified that he had visited the Hisses' home despite his fear of being ambushed?

"I meant either kidnapping or assassination," said the witness.

By Mr. and Mrs. Hiss?

"No. Mr. Hiss and his comrades."

But hadn't Chambers said Hiss was "a man of great gentleness and simplicity of character?" And hadn't Chambers stayed to supper?

Both were true, the witness conceded.

What about Chambers's many trips to New York during the period he was supposedly in hiding. "Did you come with armored cars?"

"No, I did not come with armored cars."

"You are smiling," said Stryker.

"The facts that you are presenting are a little absurd."[37]

But the absurdity reflected on the witness as well as on Stryker.

Then Stryker returned to a favorite subject, Chambers's woeful family history, the fates met by Grandmother Whittaker (she "went insane," said Chambers), by Jay (Stryker flourished the death certificate), by Richard. Stryker read aloud death-haunted lines from Chambers's poem "September 21, 1926."[38]

Stryker also produced a copy of "Tandaradei." Disdaining to read it "in mixed company," he thrust it at Chambers. Obediently the witness began to read, but in a voice so muted Judge Kaufman handed the poem to the court reporter and instructed *him* to read it. Journalists scribbled furiously to get down all the homoerotic verses. Dr. Binger looked transfixed. The highly charged sexual language, when read in toneless Brooklynese, had some spectators smiling. At the words *Part Two,* there were titters. A sickly smile played on Chambers's normally impassive face. Judge Kaufman covered a smile with his hand.[39]

Stryker concluded with Chambers's breakdown of 1942, the long months in bed when he was forbidden even to raise his arms to shave. Had his physician noted Chambers's mouth was "filthy"?

Possibly, said the witness.

"What was wrong with your teeth?" Stryker demanded.

They were in "very poor condition."[40]

The next day, Tuesday, June 7, Stryker finished his cross-examination— "my public evisceration," Chambers later called it.[41]

Judge Kaufman, who had denied the defense unrestricted access to the grand jury minutes, as is customary, said he had examined the record himself for inconsistencies and found "very substantial discrepancies" in October 14–15, but no significant ones in December. Over Murphy's vigorous objections the judge showed Stryker all but five pages of the minutes from October 14 and 15 and let him read marked passages from the December record. Stryker then led the witness through a total of seven perjuries, all involving his denials of espionage. Stryker seemed untroubled by an obvious paradox: If Chambers had lied about espionage in October, then he had been telling the truth about it later.

Still searching to establish a motive, Stryker launched a second line of argument, the defense's theory of conscious motivation. According to it, Chambers's animus against Hiss was purely political and he had timed his HUAC appearances to coincide with the presidential election.

Stryker read aloud from two *Time* articles, both from 1945, on Hiss's role as secretary-general of the UN charter conference. Chambers admitted he was familiar with the articles. "I believe I wrote that," he said of the second, which extolled Hiss's performance in San Francisco. Stryker also introduced a third item, a *Life* "photo of the week" showing Hiss arriving at the Washington airport with the UN Charter in a briefcase.

Why, asked Stryker, did Chambers not "wire the Secretary of State, the President of the United States or the Department of Justice or the Attorney General and say, 'Watch out! This man should not be trusted with that important post'? He was in a conspiracy with me to get papers from the State Department and turn them over to some Russian fellow by the name of Bykov in Prospect Park. Did you communicate any such thing to your government then? Yes or no?" The attorney was shouting.

"I did not."

Didn't the witness think it important "to protect your government?"

"I didn't think it was possible to interest anyone in the subject," Chambers murmured.

Stryker finished up by exploiting minor discrepancies in Chambers's grand jury testimony. Then, shortly after 3:00 P.M., the attorney announced he had no further questions. Chambers left the stand exhibiting "unnatural calm," wrote one reporter. A psychiatrist—not Dr. Binger— said a "normal man" would have shown more signs of stress.[42]

In her column "My Day," Eleanor Roosevelt, an acquaintance of Hiss's, spoke for legions of his supporters: "Day by day as the defense attorney . . . brings out facts about Whittaker Chambers as a witness, one cannot help being mystified as to why the gentleman should be believed at all . . . he seems to have no hesitancy about telling various unsavory facts about his private life, which make him seem less and less valuable as a witness. One gets the feeling as one reads the newspaper accounts that Mr. Chambers is on trial and not Mr. Hiss."[43]

"The Hiss-Chambers case has undergone a remarkable transformation," wrote James Reston, the *Times*'s Washington analyst, after a day spent in the courtroom observing the talents of Lloyd Stryker. "There cannot have been many more brilliant performances in this theatrical city since Barrymore played Hamlet. . . . In Washington it was Mr. Hiss who could not talk back or explain things to the House committee; today it was Mr. Chambers."

Yet, Reston noted, something was missing. Stryker's presentation, purely a "defense by attack," skirted the question "still uppermost in many minds . . . not whether Mr. Hiss lied, but whether he spied."[44]

In his cross-examination Stryker had not once asked Chambers about the stolen documents: about their contents; about the methods by which they were stolen, copied, and filmed. Even as he characterized the story as fiction, Stryker made no attempt to show how it failed to meet the requirements of fact.

# Rich Finds

Chambers, released from the stand, gratefully retreated to Westminster while the prosecution resumed the effort of building the case against Hiss.

With the help of Tom Donegan, who handled some of the questioning, Murphy summoned in quick succession more than twenty witnesses who each added another piece to the government's case.

These included, among others, Donald Appell on the pumpkin; Nathan Levine on Chambers's "life preserver"; Meyer Schapiro on the purchase of the Bokhara rugs (he had a canceled check); rug dealer Edward Touloukian (he had the bill of sale); an FBI agent who had driven Chambers through Georgetown while the witness pointed out four homes where the Hisses had lived; a clerk at the Columbia School of Journalism who confirmed that Priscilla Hiss had passed a typing test (with the grade of B); a State Department employee who said personnel records indicated Hiss had been on vacation August 2–14, 1937, the period when the visit to Harry Dexter White in Peterborough, New Hampshire, had occurred; the managing director of the Peterboro Players, who testified that the company had staged *She Stoops to Conquer* on the day when Chambers remembered attending a performance with the Hisses.

Then, on Friday, June 10, the government called its twenty-seventh witness, Esther Chambers. She wore a blue-black felt hat, a gray wool suit, a plain white blouse, and flat-heeled shoes. Her warm eyes all but disappeared behind the thick lenses of her severe spectacles. Without makeup her complexion looked sallow. She wore no lipstick. But what drew stares were her hands—red, thick-knuckled, coarsened by farm work. "I milk eighteen cows," Esther Chambers told the jury, "and take care of some forty head of cattle, dairy cattle, and take care also of some six beef cattle, plus some chickens. I guess that's all." She glanced over at the Hisses, with a smile of sympathy. They stared back impassively. There was no support from her husband. He was barred from the courtroom while Esther testified.[1]

At his most abject, Chambers remained superbly articulate. Esther seemed to teeter on the verge of panic. But she had one distinct strength as a witness: her memory. It was at least as good as her husband's. Chambers had the writer's ability to recollect conversations, tics of behavior, turns of speech. Esther had the eidetic memory of the visual artist. She summoned up a wealth of domestic details that supported the prosecution's contention that the Chamberses and the Hisses had been close friends.

She remembered how Ellen, as an infant, had wet the floor of the Hisses' apartment, and "Priscilla gave me a lovely old linen towel to use as a diaper"; she described the secondhand furniture the Hisses had given them (a patched rug, a dining room table, a table in need of refinishing). She remembered a visit Esther and Priscilla had made to Timmy Hobson's pediatrician, a Dr. Nicholson, and the time the Hisses had driven up from Washington to New York to deliver Ellen's crib to Meyer Schapiro's house, where the Chamberses had briefly stayed in the summer of 1935. She remembered Priscilla coming up from Washington and meeting Esther in Mount Vernon Square and how the two had shared a soda at the "fountain shop" at Hutzler's, a Baltimore department store, when Priscilla was in town to register for a nursing course. She recalled Priscilla coming to the Twenty-eighth Street apartment, when the Chamberses were staying there. Julia, the Chamberses' maid, had served them both punch.

Esther also described the Hisses' homes. First, "the little white house" on Thirtieth Street, where the Hisses had lived in 1936–1937. It had a long pink living room lined with books. A ginkgo stood outside the window. The terrace had Spanish tiles. Next, the Volta Place house. Her memories of it were crucial since the Hisses had moved into residence in late December 1937, long after the two couples had last seen each other by the defense's account. The house had a stoned-in porch. The dining room, downstairs, had faded plum-patterned wallpaper and plum-colored chintz drapes and Hitchcock chairs with gilt stencil. The living room had "a box piano" and "one of those spindle-backed porch settees." The master bedroom had a bedspread, from Hutzler's, with a floral pattern. Esther remembered this because she had considered purchasing the item herself. "Mrs. Chambers, like Shakespeare's Mistress Quickly, had the gift of total recall," concluded *The Reporter.*[2]

At the end of the session—a short one since it was Friday—Murphy turned the witness over for cross-examination.

Stryker showed Esther a letter she had written to the Park School in October 1937 before the family had moved to Old Court Road. Had Chambers been in the underground when she wrote the letter?

"I believe so."

"As his wife, wouldn't you know when he was an underground Communist?" Stryker roared.

"I don't have a very good head for figures or dates." Her gaze slid up to the ceiling.[3]

"Look at the jury or me," Stryker snapped. "Please don't look up."

Murphy objected. "I submit that she can look anywhere she wants."

Kaufman admonished both lawyers.

Stryker returned to his point. When had Whittaker Chambers broken with communism?

Esther licked her dry lips. "I don't know why you're trying to stump me on dates."

Judge Kaufman rebuked her. "Nobody here is attempting to stump anybody. The court will not permit anybody to be stumped. We are attempting to get the facts . . . and it comes with very bad grace for you to indicate that anyone is attempting to stump you."[4]

This was merely the prelude to what the *Times* described as Monday's "harrowing" cross-examination. Esther was on the stand all day as Stryker exploited her confusion about dates. Although visibly calmer than on Friday—she had brought a handkerchief and touched it to her parched lips—she remained inarticulate, her sentences trailing off in a mist of disconnected phrases as she stared searchingly at the ceiling, blinking hard behind her lenses.[5] At one point she was so flustered the judge called a five-minute recess while she gathered her thoughts.[6]

Through it all, Stryker portrayed the witness as her husband's criminal accomplice. Had she not lied to the authorities of the Park School when she identified her husband as a freelance writer? Did she not suffer "pangs of conscience" in lying and deceiving the school officials about her husband, a criminal conspirator?

Esther sat smoldering. At last she replied, "It didn't seem to me very pertinent, important . . ." She trailed off. "If I were asked point blank, I probably would have told the whole truth, if it were permitted, if it were possible."

"In other words, you didn't think it was very much of a misrepresentation to present your husband to this school as a decent citizen whereas he was a—"

Esther stiffened. "I resent that! My husband is a decent citizen, a great man!" Her voice was still a whisper.

"Mrs. Chambers," Kaufman reproved. "It is your province to answer questions."

But Stryker happily closed in. "Was he a great, decent citizen in October 1937?"

Esther struggled.

"I just asked a simple question." Stryker taunted. "Was he a great and decent citizen in October 1937. Yes or no?"

"Yes! And always!"

"It is your idea that a man who is plotting and conspiring by any and all means to overthrow the government of his country, and who had been sneaking around for twelve years under false names, that is your conception of the great, decent citizen, is that right?"

"No," said Esther. "But if he then believed that is the right thing to do at the moment, I believe that he is a great man, who lives up to his beliefs. His beliefs may change, as they did!"

It was shortly after four o'clock when Stryker said, "That is all."[7] The trial was ten days old.

The strength of the prosecution's case had never been Whittaker and Esther Chambers. It was the spy papers. Seven months had elapsed since Chambers had first retrieved them from the Brooklyn dumbwaiter. But except for the dozen documents HUAC had released, their contents remained a mystery. Now the four handwritten notes plus almost all of the sixty-five typed pages were read into the record.

Walter Anderson, a white-haired supervisor in the State Department's records branch, took the stand. He held a file containing the original cables, reports, and memorandums from which the copies had been typed. One by one Anderson handed the pages to Murphy, who read aloud extensive portions and then read the corresponding Woodstocked passages, exhibited to the jury as poster-size blowups. Two assistants stood at easels, flipping the pages as Murphy read.[8]

The highlight of the presentation was the cables. Murphy led Anderson through an explanation of the coding system used in the late 1930s. Some of the copied documents had been sent in either of two low-grade color codes, "gray" and "green." Others had been sent in "confidential" letter codes, A through D. A few had been sent in D, the highest grade of secrecy—for instance, a report (dated January 5, 1938) to Secretary Hull from Ambassador Bullitt, recording French opinion on possible U.S. involvement in a Far East war.

When hidden from the public for "security reasons," the documents had been titillating. But when entered, laboriously, into evidence, they lost their allure. The minutes dragged, and then the hours, filled only by Murphy's flat, unhurried drone and Anderson's matter-of-fact replies. For the first time the courtroom gaped with empty seats as spectators drifted out. At one point Lloyd Stryker was seen glowering in the corridor, a wet stogie clamped between his forefinger and thumb. Murphy didn't care. He was thinking only of the jury and the impact the documents would have on them. "I'm going to pile it up," he grimly told reporters. "If I bore them, they will remember how much there was during this part of the case." The marathon lasted two full days.[9]

Then it was the defense's turn. The cross-examiner was Edward McLean. Stryker had been brought into the case to handle the theatrics, the building up of Hiss and the tearing down of Chambers. The technical matters were left to McLean.

As mild in manner as Stryker was flamboyant, the tall, gentlemanly McLean questioned Anderson, eliciting an account of State Department security practices in 1937–1938. These had been disturbingly lax. Documents of all kinds wound lazily through the bureaucratic maze in multiple copies, said Anderson; as many as fifty duplicates might be made of a "strictly confidential" cable. Extras sat unguarded in a code room locked only at night and to which a hundred staff members had access.[10]

Murphy challenged this picture of dishevelment by summoning Eunice Lincoln, Francis Sayre's private secretary in 1937–1938. Prim, precise, the model of secretarial efficiency, Lincoln had spent more than

twenty years at State. She crisply described the layout of the offices occupied by Sayre and his small staff on the second floor of the old State,
War, and Navy Building near the White House. She also summarized
the daily routine, the flow of incoming and outgoing messages, their
sorting into different piles according to their urgency.

In cross-examination McLean asked if Lincoln had ever seen Julian
Wadleigh on the premises.

Yes. Wadleigh occasionally had business there.

Could he ever simply have wandered in?

No one wandered in. Even high officials sat in the reception room before being admitted. Within the office, however, staff moved about
freely. Sayre and Hiss regularly conferred during the course of the day.
Sayre kept his door closed; Hiss kept his open. Both men saw all documents that came to the office and often took work home in briefcases,
especially when "the mail was running pretty heavy." Documents Lincoln "had given to them during the day would be missing from their
desks when I cleaned them off before going home. These documents
would always be back in the morning."

Was it Miss Lincoln's recollection that Hiss would "frequently make
handwritten memorandums of cabled messages?"

"It was not."[11]

The government's case was nearly completed, and the courtroom was
sunk in apathy, when two new witnesses reinvigorated the proceedings.
First, FBI laboratory expert Ramos Feehan took the stand to explain the
basis for the government's claim that the stolen documents had been
typed on the Hiss Woodstock. The veteran of many trials, Feehan had
learned the trick of making technical arcana vivid to the uninitiated. He
turned to an easel on which twin enlargements stood side by side: the
Hiss "standards of comparison" and the typed documents. Wielding a
pointer, Feehan indicated matching idiosyncrasies, ten in all, linking
both sets of papers to a single machine. Next, he compared original State
Department documents with typed copies included in the pumpkin papers and explained the probable sequence in which batches had been
photographed. Remarkably there was no cross-examination of Feehan.
The defense conceded the entire testimony.[12]

Then, at two-twenty on Thursday, June 16—the thirteenth day of the
trial, its precise midpoint—another witness stepped out from the witness

room, gaunt in a rumpled suit and wrinkled shirt, his tie knotted clumsily, his "garterless stockings . . . at half mast." It was Julian Wadleigh. "Jerking his head around to get his bearings," his mouth ajar, he looked as if he had wandered in from the weakly lighted stacks of a graduate library.[13]

But a change overtook him as soon as he was seated and sworn in. No longer the panicked and hostile HUAC witness of December, he leaned back importantly and then, strikingly articulate, testified that for two years he had removed papers from the State Department—roughly four hundred documents, by his own estimate—and delivered them to his Communist contacts, "mostly to the man who has been identified to me recently as [David] Carpenter" but also "on some occasions" to Whittaker Chambers, whom Wadleigh had known as Carl Carlsen.[14]

In an accent bearing the light impress of Oxford, Wadleigh outlined his mode of operation: "[I] selected from the documents that came to my desk the ones I understood would be of interest" to the Soviet Union and then "about once a week I would take those documents, put them in a briefcase, meet Carpenter at some street corner, pre-arranged, give him the briefcase. I would meet him at another corner the following morning on the way to work and he would hand me back the briefcase with the documents in it, and I would bring them back to the office." Wadleigh had followed the same procedure with Chambers.

Had he ever "typed any documents for anybody?"

"No."

Did he ever write out "any summary of documents" by hand?

Not "without comments of my own" on the paper.

Murphy handed Wadleigh the Baltimore exhibits. Had the witness possibly been their source? Wadleigh bent his bushy head over the stack with a scholar's absorption. "Now here is some material that might conceivably have gotten in [to Trade Agreements] in the [described] form, possibly," he said at last. "If I may read a sentence to illustrate what I mean—"

"I think we have enough, Mr. Wadleigh," murmured Kaufman.[15]

Wadleigh hunched over the pages again, reading silently for some moments. Then, looking up, he said he had not, after all, seen the document in question. Its first section had "no material" for Trade Agreements. As for the second, had Wadleigh ever read it, he would remember it vividly. It was "unusually interesting . . . a sufficiently rich find." The phrase, a spy's calm assessment, hung in the quiet air.[16]

After Murphy had finished his direct examination, there was a short recess. Stryker, who normally chatted up journalists during breaks, stayed behind at the defense table, huddled with assistants.

"For the first time in three days, the bailiffs didn't have to call 'all in' when the recess was over," Jim Bell reported that night. By now it was evident the defense would try to pin all the stolen documents on Wadleigh, who looked custom-ordered for Strykerian demolition: the reedy physique, the fussy diction, the accent.

As Stryker advanced toward the witness chair, Wadleigh nervously crossed and recrossed his legs and rubbed his knuckles.[17]

Had he ever removed documents from the desk of a colleague? Stryker asked.

No. "I never did anything so foolish." All the material came from his own desk; that was the "standard operating procedure."[18]

Stryker shifted into a discussion of Wadleigh's political views. The witness had said that while he had never joined the Party, he sympathized with the "general tenets" of communism.

Was lying a tenet of communism? (Stryker pronounced the word "tee-nate.")[19]

"I would hardly call that a tenet," said Wadleigh. "I would call it a procedure."

All right, said Stryker sarcastically, so Wadleigh was an Oxford man. But surely the witness "would not have had the slightest conscientious scruple . . . in pilfering documents from other desks, would he?"

"One gets conscientious scruples when one contemplates doing something, when the question arises, but the question never arose in my mind and therefore I can have no recollection of having had any conscientious scruples against doing it. In other words, your question is a hypothetical one."

The reply, precise and professorial, drew laughter. Even Judge Kaufman lifted a hand to his mouth, shielding a broad grin.[20]

Journalists "could hardly believe their ears" when, after a mere twenty-one minutes, Stryker ended his cross-examination and let Wadleigh go.[21]

But the attorney had seen the danger of keeping Wadleigh on the stand. With each well-turned phrase, Wadleigh made the impossible seem thinkable, even natural. If this Oxford-educated liberal and minister's son had been a spy, then why not Alger Hiss?

That day the government rested its case.

# The Woodstock

On Monday, June 20, the last day of spring, the defense began its presentation. Once again long lines snaked down the courthouse steps. Hiss's attorneys had promised their defendant would take the stand to answer all the charges, and Hiss said he was eager to state his innocence under oath.

But first the groundwork must be laid. Several witnesses were called to dispute the Chamberses' recollections of a close friendship with the Hisses. Geoffrey May, the Hisses' next-door neighbor in 1936–1937, testified that he had not once seen Chambers at the Thirtieth Street house. Joseph Boucot, the Chamberses' landlord in Smithton, Pennsylvania, said he did not remember a ten-day visit by Priscilla Hiss, in July 1935, which Esther had recalled in her testimony. (Boucot had told a different story to the FBI and to the defense team in pretrial interviews, as Murphy later got him to concede.)[1]*

Two witnesses also disputed Chambers's account of the car trip he and the Hisses had made in early August 1937 to visit Harry Dexter White in New Hampshire. One, Lucy Elliott Davis, the proprietress of the Peterborough guesthouse where Chambers remembered staying overnight with the Hisses, had no recollection of the three travelers and said they

---

* The best witness to the Smithton visit, Maxim Lieber, declined to appear for the defense, though he sympathized with Hiss. Of Chambers, Lieber later said, "That man ruined my life." This was no exaggeration. Many of Lieber's clients deserted him after the trials, as did many of his publishing contacts. In 1951 he closed his agency and moved to Mexico and later Poland. In the 1970s Lieber returned to the United States—and to FBI harassment.[2]

had not signed her guest register. (Later she said not all guests had signed the book.)[3]

J. Kellogg Smith, who ran a summer camp in Chestertown, Maryland, which Timothy Hobson had attended in 1937, said the Hisses had been on the premises "every day during the first two weeks" of August, when Timmy had broken his leg. Under cross-examination Smith admitted he was relying on dates supplied to him before the trial by the defendant.[4]

More important testimony came from State Department officials, past and present. Several were called to build the defense's case against Julian Wadleigh. Charles Darlington, Wadleigh's supervisor in Trade Agreements, characterized the economist as "a quite peculiar and odd individual" with "a well-developed curiosity. . . . [T]here were occasions when I would come back to my room after lunch and Mr. Wadleigh would be there reading a [department] paper." According to Darlington, Eunice Lincoln, Francis Sayre's secretary, had been a less vigilant gatekeeper than she had claimed. More than once Darlington had walked into Hiss's empty office without being stopped. Another witness, former Trade Agreements chief Harry Hawkins, said he had done so too.[5]

A third State Department employee, communications officer Frank Duvall, expanded on Walter Anderson's testimony about lax security practices. A hundred copies of a cable might sit unguarded where even "charwomen" and "messengers" could get at them. But all this proved only that any spy—not just the "peculiar" Wadleigh—could have operated without fear of being detected.[6]

The defense also summoned an impressive roster of character witnesses. A total of fifteen distinguished Americans vouched for Hiss, either in person or by deposition. These included Illinois Governor Adlai Stevenson, Hiss's colleague first in the AAA and then at UN conferences; President Truman's newly appointed ambassador at large, Philip Jessup, a Carnegie board member; and John W. Davis, Democratic presidential nominee in 1924, also on the Carnegie board. Justice Felix Frankfurter testified too, Hiss having concluded that his association with the Supreme Court justice would be received better in the courtroom than on Capitol Hill.*

---

* Former Secretary of State Edward R. Stettinius, Hiss's supervisor at Dumbarton Oaks, Yalta, and San Francisco, and the author of a recent memoir on Yalta lavish in its praise of Hiss, was too ill to take the stand. He died in the fall of 1949. The sitting secretary, Dean Acheson, who had called Hiss his friend, declined to testify, citing "my public responsibilities and duty."[7]

There was no precedent for Frankfurter's appearance, a member of the nation's highest tribunal taking the stand in a criminal trial. The occasion called for special tact, which Judge Kaufman did not exhibit when he bounded from his seat to pump the great jurist's tiny hand. Frankfurter, in summer suit and bow tie, beamed. "I will rely on Your Honor to keep me within bounds."

"Of course, sir!" the judge replied.[8]

Murphy punctured the air of ceremony by questioning Frankfurter about the AAA purge and the subsequent falling-out between Hiss and Jerome Frank when Frank learned Hiss had maneuvered to succeed his fired boss.

"I think Judge Jerome Frank had differences of opinion with Mr. Hiss," said Frankfurter. The disagreement "did not bear on questions of loyalty or integrity."

"It didn't, Judge?" Murphy asked. "But you remember talking to Judge Frank about it?"

"No, I remember his talking to me."

"Then I assume you talked to him when he talked to you?"

Frankfurter was annoyed. "Well, let us not fence. All I meant to say was—"

"Well, you were the one that started fencing with me, weren't you, Judge? I asked you whether you talked to Judge Frank and you said that Judge Frank talked with you. Am I accurate?"[9]

Frankfurter repeated that loyalty "to this country" had not been an issue.

But what about Hiss's loyalty—or lack of it—to his superior, Jerome Frank?

"I wouldn't know a thing about that."*

Murphy concluded by asking, gently, if the Supreme Court had adjourned for the summer.

Frankfurter owned it had not.

"Thank you. No further questions," Murphy said, having implied that Frankfurter had sacrificed his high civic duty in order to help Alger Hiss out of a scrape.

"But it is not in session today," Frankfurter quickly added.[11]

---

* In his HUAC testimony Hiss had cited Frank among the many "personages" who could vouch for his integrity. In fact Frank thought Hiss lacking in character, on the basis of his conduct during the AAA purge, and declined to testify on his behalf.[10]

. . .

The most important defense witnesses were brought forth from the opposite end of the social spectrum to testify on a crucial piece of evidence, the Woodstock typewriter. The defense had not challenged the prosecution's argument that the documents had been typed on the same machine as the Hiss "standards of comparison," the most damaging evidence on record.* But there was room to maneuver. The FBI expert Ramos Feehan had said the *typeface* on the "standards" was identical to that on the spy documents. He had not ventured to identify a single *typist* for both sets of papers. This left open the possibility that someone else had copied the stolen documents on the Hiss machine—either Chambers or an accomplice. The defense did not have to produce the culprit as long as it could show that the Hisses had disposed of the Woodstock sometime before the first of the State Department documents had been typed.

In fact the Hisses *had* gotten rid of the typewriter. Exactly when, however, remained open to question. They had given it to their maid Claudia ("Clytie") Catlett, who worked for the Hisses for three years in the 1930s, and to her sons, Raymond Sylvester ("Mike") Catlett and Perry ("Pat"). The testimony of the Catletts would thus prove critical.

Since the first weeks of the case, back in August, Hiss had been aware the Catletts would figure in it importantly and so had taken preemptive steps to keep them out of the inquiry. At his executive HUAC hearing of August 16, when Hiss had been questioned about his household servants in the 1930s, he had not mentioned Mrs. Catlett at all, deflecting the committee toward another housemaid, Martha Pope, who had worked for the Hisses in 1934. Priscilla Hiss had mentioned both women in her grand jury testimony but said Mrs. Catlett "is now dead."[12] The FBI had soon learned otherwise and in May had interviewed Clytie and her sons about the Hisses and the Woodstock.

There was an added complication for the defense. In their separate FBI and grand jury statements Alger and Priscilla had each situated the Woodstock in their Volta Place home, where they had moved on December 28, 1937, a few days before the first documents had been typed. Both Hisses further remembered having possession of the typewriter in 1938.[†13]

---

* Even more damaging than the handwritten notes. While Hiss admitted to being their author, it did not necessarily follow—nor could the government prove—that Hiss had given them to Chambers, who might have procured them without Hiss's knowledge.

† See p. 306 for Alger's FBI statement.

It was up to the Catletts, then, to supply an earlier date, correcting the testimony of their employers. Clytie Catlett took the stand first, a stout black woman of forty-seven in dark glasses and a flowered dress. In relaxed southern tones she testified first about her recollections of Alger Hiss's strange acquaintance George Crosley—or "Crosby," as she called him. A shabby-looking man, Crosley had visited the Hisses on one occasion, and she had served him tea. Since then she had not seen Crosley again until 1949 at a pretrial meeting arranged by the FBI when he had tested out his memories as to the Hisses' successive homes.

Mrs. Catlett next itemized useful hand-me-downs the Hisses had passed on over the years: a chair, a Victrola, some clothes, and "an old typewriter."

McLean asked about this last, a gift to her sons. Mrs. Catlett could confirm no details, including the make. In fact "I don't remember no typewriters at all."[14]

In cross-examination Murphy questioned the witness on her memory of names. She admitted it was poor. "I am good on faces but not on names."

"Do you remember mine?"

She could not.

Yet, said Murphy, after a single encounter with George Crosley in the early 1930s, Mrs. Catlett remembered his name ("Crosby"), all these years later. Could she say why that was?

It was an easy name, the witness replied.

Did she remember the names of any other guests at the Hiss home?

No.

Murphy then read aloud some sentences from Clytie's signed FBI statement. She had told the bureau she had recognized Chambers on sight but could not recall his name. Perhaps, said Murphy, the name Crosley had been suggested to her by the Hiss defense.

The witness denied it.

The prosecutor quoted from another of her FBI statements, dated May 15, only two weeks before the trial began. In this one Clytie said Hiss's lawyers had asked her if Chambers, on his visits in the 1930s, had used "the name Crosby."

Did Mrs. Catlett remember saying that?

There was a long silence. Murphy repeated the question.

The witness sighed mournfully. "There were so many times they asked me so many questions."

Murphy read on. " 'It has been a long time and I'm not really sure he said his name was Crosby. He could have said his name was Carl or some other name.' " The prosecutor lingered on *Carl*.

The witness did not remember that particular interview.

Murphy asked her about the Woodstock. The record showed that after the typewriter had been recovered, Ed McLean had asked Clytie if she recognized it. The witness said she hadn't been sure. "It was just like a piece of junk to me and I didn't pay attention."

Yet, Murphy reminded her, Clytie had volunteered to the FBI that the furnishings in her own home had included a typewriter, a gift from the Hisses. Murphy read aloud more of Clytie's FBI testimony. According to it, she had seen the Woodstock at several of the Hiss houses, including Volta Place. This meant the gift had dated no earlier than 1938.

So "the deadly, tedious game went on," as Murphy patiently guided the witness deeper into the contradictions of her testimony.[15]

Clytie was followed to the stand by her son Mike, a twenty-seven-year-old handyman and World War II veteran. He mumbled behind his lifted hand and was hard to understand. But his memories of the Woodstock were well calculated to aid the Hisses. He had come into possession of the machine, he told McLean, at the time of the Hisses' move to Volta Place. It had been in disrepair. "The keys would jam up on you and it would not work good. You couldn't do any typing hardly with it." Also, the wheel and the ribbon stuck.

McLean went over to the defense table. On the floor below sat a big cardboard box. After a struggle the defense team got it open and removed a large black office machine, Woodstock 230009, the totem made visible at last—defense exhibit UUU. McLean lugged it to the witness stand. "I show you this typewriter and ask you if that is the one the Hisses gave you."

Catlett pecked three keys, examined the roller, and—catching the drama—cried, "This is it!"

The witness then explained the path the Woodstock had traveled over the years. His sister-in-law had owned it briefly and then his sister and finally a junk dealer. Mike Catlett had helped the Hiss defense track it down.

Murphy rose to cross-examine. He did not challenge the authenticity of the typewriter. Instead he chipped away at Mike Catlett's testimony that the Woodstock had been defective. After three hours the witness at last conceded the machine had been in good enough working order in 1937–1938. Indeed the Catlett brothers had held on to it for years and loaned it to their sister for school assignments. Murphy also led the witness over the complicated route he and the Hiss defense, principally Donald Hiss, had traced in the winter of 1949, when they located the Woodstock after a two-month search.[16]

Mike Catlett was followed to the stand by his brother Pat, a year younger and nearly deaf; questions had to be shouted at him. He too identified the Woodstock by its defective parts. He said the Hisses had given the brothers the typewriter at the time of the move to Volta Place. Pat had subsequently taken it to a repair shop, where he was told new parts were no longer available for so old a machine.

In cross-examination Murphy read the witness his FBI statement. Pat Catlett had said it was possible the Hisses had been living on Volta Place "for several months before they gave [the Woodstock] to me." He had placed the time only by his memory that the weather had been warm when he had taken the typewriter to a repair shop to be fixed.

Was that truthful testimony? Murphy asked.

The witness hedged. The question was read aloud again. Pat Catlett conceded the statement might be true.

Murphy turned to the repair shop. The witness had told McLean it was on K Street and Connecticut Avenue. Why had Pat carted the heavy machine all that distance? Why not take it to a place nearer to his home?

It was the nearest place he knew of, the witness replied. Also, he had not been able to find a ribbon at a nearby stationer's.

A ribbon for a defective machine?

Well, maybe the keys did work after all.

"I want you to listen very carefully to this," Murphy roared. "Was the reason you took it to that repair shop [on K Street] because that was a Woodstock repair shop?" And "supposing I tell you that the Woodstock repair shop at Connecticut and K did not come into existence until September of 1938? Would that cause you to fix the time after September when you took it there?"[17]

One question went unasked: Why had Hiss given the typewriter to the Catletts at all? Had he sufficient foresight to know that discarding it altogether would look suspicious in the event he was questioned later? Or had Hiss's sense of justice, and of thrift, rebelled at disposing of the Woodstock when it could benefit the deserving Catletts, as his used Ford could benefit "some poor organizer" in the open Party?

By week's end Alger Hiss was ready to take the stand. Before he did so, Lloyd Stryker called the trial's "first honest-to-goodness 'surprise' witness," Malcolm Cowley. The defense had found him through the efforts of A. J. Liebling, who had learned of Cowley's meeting with Chambers in 1940. The FBI had questioned Cowley also. He had given them a photostat of his journal entry of December 1940, recording his one and only conversation with Chambers.

Cowley sympathized with Hiss and had ample reason to loathe Chambers. But he had no wish to testify. His political past had recently risen up to bite him once again. In the spring there had been a furor when he was appointed to a visiting professorship at the University of Washington and a regent had denounced Cowley's fellow traveling of the 1930s. But he agreed to take the stand.[18]

Speaking in a low, rich voice, Cowley avenged himself against the man who had excoriated him in the pages of *Time*. Recalling the 1940 meeting, Cowley said Chambers had "looked as if he had slept on a park bench the night before. His clothes were old, unpressed, and rather dirty. His linen was not clean." One of his teeth "was nothing but a piece of metal, evidently a bridge from which the enamel had been chipped."

Cowley also described Chambers's paranoia. "He would never look me in the eyes but kept glancing suspiciously around the restaurant. . . . [Chambers said] we were surrounded by spies, traitors and conspiracies." He had spoken darkly of sinister forces in Washington, naming names. Some meant nothing to Cowley; others registered dimly.

But one name had "shocked" Cowley. Chambers had said Francis B. Sayre was a member of the Communist apparatus.

The courtroom erupted.

"Just a moment!" Stryker exclaimed. "I should like at this point, if your Honor please, as an officer of this court, to state in the most emphatic way within my power that we completely repudiate this idea that the statement regarding Mr. Sayre is true, that we strongly and sincerely understand and believe that Mr. Sayre was a loyal member of the government at all times."

Cowley then recalled his astonishment. "Not Woodrow Wilson's son-in-law, the high commissioner of the Philippines?"

None other than he, Cowley remembered the defector saying. Sayre was "the head of a Communist apparatus in the State Department."

Once this had sunk in, Stryker read aloud from Cowley's journal account of the lunch, titled "Counter Revolutionary." Chambers had told Cowley he did not regret his years in the Party. "He learned the technique of the movement," Cowley had written, "and now he is going to apply that technique to destroy it."

When Murphy's turn came, he contented himself with a perfunctory run-through of Cowley's Communist ties in the 1930s and then let him go.

That night reporters phoned Chambers at Westminster. As far as Chambers knew, Francis Sayre "never had any connection of any kind with Communist activity, except inadvertently, in the case of Alger Hiss." Cowley's testimony was "patently absurd."[19]*

Then, at 3:08 P.M., on Thursday, June 23, Lloyd Stryker stood up and said, "Mr. Alger Hiss."[21]

---

* Chambers's executive testimony of December 6, 1948, included the following exchange:
  Stripling: Did you ever hear that Sayre might himself be a Communist?
  Chambers: I heard nothing to that effect; quite the contrary.[20]

# 29

# *Alger and Priscilla*

First there was a five-minute recess. "I feel fine," Hiss told a newspaperman in the corridor. "I've been waiting for this a long time." He was not the only one. The line had been especially long that morning, and the celebrity journalists were back. "The working stiffs had a hard time making notes with famous elbows in their ribs and famous voices asking stupid questions," Jim Bell groused that evening.

Hiss was already in the courtroom when the break ended. Jurors and spectators, filing in, saw the defendant huddling with a tiny, wizened man in a clerical collar, a retired Episcopal minister who had been Hiss's boyhood pastor in Baltimore.[1]

At 3:21 P.M. Hiss was sworn in, and so began, in the words of *The Washington Post*'s Murrey Marder, "the climactic moment to the months of worldwide headlines."[2]

It was Hiss's first public testimony in the ten months since HUAC's "Confrontation Day" and his first opportunity since August 5 to answer the charges in anything like a friendly setting. He took the stand in a cream-colored summer suit and white shirt. His quiet gray tie, patterned with tiny brown checks, was secured by a gold collar pin. His brown shoes were buffed to a high sheen. Despite all the hours spent in the courtroom, his skin glowed with a healthy tan, thanks to weekends in Vermont. A few minutes into his testimony the air conditioning suddenly failed. Others wilted. Not Hiss. Later, when asked about the suit he was wearing, Hiss flashed the label: Irish linen.[3]

He composed himself easily in the witness chair, a graceful man with a fine economy of movement. For all he had been through, he still looked younger than his years. The contrast with Chambers was extraordinary—the physical differences, of course, but also the difference in moral attitude. While Chambers radiated stoic guilt—"the remote and vaguely hostile loneliness of agonized reflection," in Jimmy Cannon's phrase—Hiss maintained a calm detachment. In the first weeks of the trial he had observed the proceedings with scholarly interest, making notes on index cards. (After the first day he had shed his eyeglasses, perhaps because they detracted from his youthful appearance.) During recesses he roamed the corridor, smiling at supporters, chatting with friendly journalists. "It might be someone else who was on trial," marveled the *St. Louis Post-Dispatch*'s Marquis Childs, one of the many distinguished journalists whose sympathies were with the defendant.* The only hint of strain was in Hiss's eyes, sunk deep in his face.[5]

Hiss's aura of sunny upper-caste privilege was perhaps the case's most intriguing irony, for he was no more an upper-class product than his accuser and came like him from a family enmeshed in "the crisis of the middle class." In 1907, when Alger was two and a half, his father, Charles, a partner in a Baltimore importing firm, brutally killed himself, slashing his throat with a razor and then bleeding to death on his bed. Alger was ten before he learned how his father died. "I overheard the remark of a neighbor sitting on her front steps. . . . 'Those are the children of the suicide.' "[6]

There was a second suicide in the Hiss family. In May 1929, Alger's older sister Mary Ann, unhappily married to a Boston banker ruined in the postwar slump of 1919–1920, had killed herself by swallowing a bottle of "caustic household cleanser."[7]

But the family tragedy that affected Alger most profoundly was the death of his older brother, Bosley, Alger's protector and guide. A heavy drinker of lethal Prohibition alcohol, Bosley died of a kidney ailment in 1926, at age twenty-five, at the outset of a promising career as a reporter for the *Baltimore Sun*. Alger, four years younger, had nursed Bosley in his last days, before going off to Harvard Law. "I now think that I uncon-

---

* Indeed the four most influential liberal columnists of the day—Walter Lippmann, James Reston, Joseph Alsop, and Childs—all were pro-Hiss. It was their sympathies, plus the disdainful commentary on Chambers and HUAC published in *The New Yorker* and *The New Republic,* that underlay Richard Nixon's bitter assertion, four decades later, that the "prestige media" were "shockingly biased" toward Hiss. The daily press coverage was divided more or less evenly between the prosecution and the defense, with two major syndicates, Hearst and Scripps-Howard, vehemently pro-prosecution.[4]

sciously identified Chambers with my brother Bosley," Alger reflected four decades after the trial. "They were born in the same year." (Actually Bosley was born in 1900.) "Both were aspiring writers, making do temporarily as journalists. Both regarded unskilled labor as a way of seeing life in the raw." (Bosley had worked briefly as an itinerant farmhand.) "Both were bookish—indeed, thought of themselves as men of letters."[8]

These terrible deaths had bracketed Hiss's sparkling career at Harvard. He had grieved mightily but privately and without once deviating from his upward trajectory of success. What had drawn Chambers to Hiss—and drew him still—was his powerful resolve combined with a tragic view of life. It was the ideal makeup for a Bolshevik. To Chambers, Hiss was the supreme *ernste Mensch,* possibly surpassing himself. "No other Communist but Alger Hiss," Chambers later wrote, "understood so quietly, or accepted with so little fuss or question the fact that the revolutionist cannot change the course of history without taking upon himself the crimes of history."[9]

Comfortably settled, Hiss looked expectantly at Lloyd Stryker. The attorney began with an ironic echo of the HUAC sessions of August.

"Are you now or have you ever been a member of the Communist Party?"

The witness folded his arms. "I am not and have never been."

"Or a fellow traveler or Communist sympathizer?"

"No, Mr. Stryker. I have never."

The attorney held the four handwritten notes. Were they in Hiss's hand?

"Yes, Mr. Stryker, they all are."

Did he "ever furnish, transmit or deliver" them to Whittaker Chambers?

"I did not."

Stryker showed Hiss the Baltimore papers. Had the defendant given them to Chambers?

"I did not."

"Did you in your lifetime ever furnish, transmit, and deliver any restricted, secret, or confidential documents of the State Department to Whittaker Chambers or any other authorized person?"

Hiss grinned. "I think you meant 'unauthorized.' "

Stryker corrected himself.

"As amended," said Hiss, "the answer is I did not."

Had his answers to the grand jury been truthful?

"They were and they are."[10]

For the next three days the attorney delivered on his promise, made in his opening argument, to take his client "by the hand" and lead him "from the date of his birth down to this hour." The itinerary led swiftly to the State Department and the defendant's most notable accomplishments, at Dumbarton Oaks, Yalta, and San Francisco.

Recent though the record was, it belonged to what seemed an ancient past, to the waning days of the Grand Alliance, the summits, the accords, the comity of 1944–1945, when a world war was all but won and the future seemed a blank slate on which optimistic visions could be inscribed. Hiss's part had been small but meaningful, that of the junior technician who had stood at the side of the great elders, effectuating their noble designs. "If a listener closed his eyes," wrote one courtroom observer, "the Hiss narrative sounded like a college classroom lecture—something in modern history. Important names fell every few seconds—Stalin, Churchill, Roosevelt, the King of Egypt, Haile Selassie—and the flow turned hypnotic."[11]

The meetings at Dumbarton Oaks, said Hiss, had been "extremely secret. For example, if the conversations had failed, certainly knowledge of that would have given aid and comfort to the enemy." The conference "was held at an estate in Georgetown with garden walls." Assisted by the War Department, "I set up a security system. We had a platoon of soldiers camped on the grounds. We had guards at all the gates. We issued passes and no one was permitted inside without passes. It was not open to the public or to the press."

"What was your relationship to the system?" asked Stryker.

"I was in charge of it, sir." By appointment of the secretary of state.

At Yalta Hiss had dealt personally with FDR "and participated in a very small way in trying to arrange the President's personal management" and his "itinerary."

Hiss's crowning achievement was the San Francisco Conference. Again he had made the security arrangements. The logistics had been staggering. He had flown in translators from all over the world on army transport vehicles and then put them on special trains, the first ever to travel nonstop from New York to San Francisco. During the summit the State Department was responsible for safeguarding the activities of fifty delegations, representing fifty nations. Hiss had engineered this massive task too, supervising a staff of some two to three thousand, including army and navy personnel. He had not worked alone, however. "The number two man of the FBI was in charge of that collaboration with me."

Stryker feigned astonishment. "You say the FBI was then collaborating with you?"—meaning, in saner times those now persecuting Hiss had been his colleagues.

"Yes," said Hiss. There was laughter. Jurors joined in.[12]

Unlike Chambers, who never looked over at the jury, Hiss often took in all twelve, plus the alternates, with a sweeping glance. He also had a way of catching their attention. Whenever he crossed his legs, he would reach down to grasp his calf and then, with the jurors' eyes upon him, he would flash his boyish grin in their direction.[13]

On Hiss's second day of testimony Stryker turned to the perjury charges. One by one he sent up Chambers's allegations and Hiss shot them down with staccato denials.

"Did you personally type a single word of the documents, 5 to 47, here in evidence?"

"I did not."

"Did you ever ask your wife to do so?"

"Certainly not."

"Did she ever do so, Mr. Hiss, in your presence or to your knowledge?"

"No, sir."

It was the most emphatic Hiss had sounded since his first HUAC appearance. Stryker pointedly contrasted Hiss's demeanor on the stand with that of the Communist Party leaders on trial in the same courthouse. They were staging a spectacle, making a mockery of the proceedings. But not Hiss. He respected the dignity of the courtroom and of the American judicial process.

"Did you at any time claim your constitutional privilege" not to answer questions put to him by HUAC?

"I certainly did not."

And before the grand jury?

No.

Had he cooperated fully with the FBI?

Hiss leaned forward. "I was as interested in trying to find out the real facts in this matter as much as they [the FBI] could possibly be."

Had he also provided the bureau with typing samples and ordered his attorneys to search for the Woodstock?

Yes.

Then "you instructed me at the opening of this case to state that it had been found and to offer [the typewriter] to the government for their inspection?"

"I did."[14]

On to the documents. Hiss explained how he had come to make the jottings Chambers had produced in Baltimore. It was simple. Copious reading matter poured into Francis Sayre's office each day. Hiss's job was to digest it. If a document was too lengthy for Sayre to study it whole, Hiss wrote down the relevant portion in a memo.

How had the notes gotten into Chambers's hands?

Thievery, perhaps. "At that time there were no restrictions as to visitors entering the building." Anyone could easily walk in. Once Hiss had found a total stranger, "a rather elderly, pleasant-looking gentleman," standing in front of the fireplace. The man's father had worked in the office many years ago, and the son had come to soak up the ambient memories. More pertinently, Hiss had come upon Julian Wadleigh in his own office and Sayre's "several times."[15]

Hiss reviewed his relationship with Chambers. He had terminated it in the "late spring" of 1936 and had not seen the man again until August 17, 1948, when they were brought together at the Hotel Commodore.

Stryker finished up on Monday, June 27, Hiss's third day on the stand. Hiss described the injustice of the HUAC hearings, especially the "Confrontation Day" spectacle under the glare of the television and newsreel lights and on a sweltering August afternoon, with no recesses afforded the witness save for a lunch break, the questions flung at him by six congressmen, with no one (in Stryker's words) "similar to a judge of a court, to hold the case to an issue and to see that order and fairness and decorum were enforced."

Finally Stryker faced his client and said, "Mr. Hiss, you have entered your formal and solemn plea of not guilty to the charges here against you, have you not?"

"I have."

"And in truth and in fact you are not guilty?"

Hiss answered slowly and evenly, pausing for emphasis after each word, "I am not guilty."[16]

It was shortly after eleven o'clock when Murphy rose and rooted himself at his lectern.

"Mr. Witness," he began, "do you want to amplify or change any of your testimony that you have given so far the last three days?"

"No, Mr. Murphy."

For the next two days, in testimony lasting a total of seven and a half hours, Murphy brought out the numerous inconsistencies in Hiss's statements to HUAC, the FBI, the grand jury, and in this courtroom. He reviewed the disposition of the Woodstock (had Hiss given it to the Catletts in 1937 or in 1938?); Hiss's retouched testimony about the 1929 Ford; his shifting recollections of the name Whittaker Chambers; his careful downplaying of his association with the Communist Lee Pressman.

Prepared for the onslaught, Hiss seized upon each question "in a sharp, professorial way which at times bordered on cockiness," observed Murrey Marder. He even corrected Murphy's English usage. Didn't he mean "inferred" and not "implied"? By "writing" (on the Woodstock) did Murphy mean "typing"?[17]

Each time the prosecutor bristled, and more than once was drawn into trivial debates. When questioning Hiss on Chambers's stay at P Street, Murphy asked Hiss if Chambers, as sublessee, had paid for utilities.

No, said Hiss. He himself had covered all those expenses.

The telephone too?

Yes.

Plus toll charges?

"If he had had a long-distance phone call of any size I certainly would have taken that up with him."

"You would have ran after that one?"

Hiss paused. "Excuse me?"

"You would have ran after him for that?"

Hiss smiled. "I would have *run* after him."[18]

Murphy froze amid barks of courtroom laughter. "You didn't mean to correct me that way, did you?" the prosecutor asked.

Hiss answered evenly. "I was merely giving my testimony."

"Just merely giving your testimony?"

"Yes. You asked me the question."

"You had no intention there of being sarcastic?"

"No, Mr. Murphy."

"It was merely your desire to use whatever correct grammar came to your mind?"

"It was merely that I was testifying in my normal speech."

Hiss's agile replies did not necessarily endear him to the jury, but they rattled Murphy and sidetracked his cross-examination, for instance when the prosecutor questioned Hiss about the Bokhara rug. Hiss was sticking broadly to the version he had given HUAC in August. One evening in the spring of 1936 George Crosley appeared at Hiss's door. He was alone and bearing the carpet, ostensibly a gift from a "wealthy patron."

"Do you know whether [Chambers] got out of a car?" Murphy asked.

The witness wasn't sure. "He simply came to the door and rang the bell." Hiss was not even certain "I went to the door."

Murphy pounced. "I thought you said he came to the door."

Hiss smiled forbearingly. "That is the way he entered the house." There was raucous laughter.

Murphy appealed to Judge Kaufman. "Your Honor, will you ask some of the clowns to stop laughing?"

The judge reproved him. The laughter was innocent, a "spontaneous outburst."[19]

Murphy grimly returned to his questioning, but obviously shaken, he failed to confront Hiss with the testimony of Meyer Schapiro and the rug dealer Edward Toulakian, who dated the purchase of the rug to December 1936, at least six months after Hiss claimed to have terminated his relationship with Chambers. The contradiction was safely in the record, but Murphy missed an opportunity to make Hiss explain it.

Even on the Woodstock, Hiss was impossible to pin down. Murphy read aloud portions of grand jury and FBI testimony in which Hiss said the Woodstock had been in his possession at Volta Place sometime after 1938. How did this square with his current claim that he had given the Woodstock to the Catletts in December 1937?

Hiss refused to acknowledge any discrepancy. His initial testimony had been his honest best "impression" at the time.

His recollection had since been "refreshed"?

No. He now spoke from the superior "knowledge of an independent fact," gleaned from the Catletts' testimony.[20]

In the HUAC hearings such haggling had cost Hiss dearly. But now it was obvious he had been preparing all along for his day in court. The evasions so exasperating to Karl Mundt and Edward Hébert had enabled Hiss to avoid making any assertions that could later prove perjurious. There would be no eight-column headlines that shouted HISS ADMITS

LYING, the sort of headline that had filled the papers when Chambers was cross-examined.[21]

Murphy never looked clumsier than when stalking Hiss. He lumbered from point to point, topic to topic, trying to wear Hiss down, wear down a man who had not cracked under HUAC's assault, even under the blaze of klieg lights. In Hiss, Murphy faced a witness whose mind was quicker than his own and whose legal skills were at least as finely honed. It was Harvard Law vs. Fordham, the protégé of Frankfurter and Holmes vs. the sturdy product of the U.S. attorney's office.

At one point Murphy questioned Hiss about the car trip he and Chambers had made to New York. Chambers told HUAC Priscilla had gone with them. Hiss had confirmed it. But in direct examination he had reversed himself. Murphy read aloud Hiss's statement to the grand jury: "Whether my wife was present or not I am not sure. I rather think she may have been."

Stryker and McLean both objected. Murphy had omitted a key sentence. Hiss had said, "I would have to ask her and I haven't asked her."

Murphy then rephrased his question. "It was your recollection then at the time you testified that your wife accompanied you and Mr. Chambers, is that correct?"

"Mr. Murphy," said Hiss indulgently, "you are characterizing what you have just read, why don't you just read it again?"

Murphy bellowed in rage. "Now, Your Honor, would you instruct this"—he searched for a word—"*character* to refrain from making remarks to me?"

Stryker leaped in indignantly. The remark was "offensive and improper, and were it not for the fact that I do not want a mistrial, I would move for it."

"The incident," Kaufman ruled, "is closed for the moment."

Murphy was not powerless. He had ammunition and used it. He patiently dredged up Hiss's worst moments in the HUAC hearings, reading aloud almost the entire transcript of the Commodore showdown.[22] The testimony was potentially as damaging as any on record. Stryker would have milked it expertly. He would have inhabited each role, bringing all the players to life and making the jury see that here was the moment, preserved in type, when Hiss's façade had been shattered. But Murphy overdid it, layering the account with heavy sarcasm, and the moment was lost.

By now it was plain to all that Lloyd Stryker could not match Murphy on the facts. He had not even tried. He was content instead to tell a story, leading the jury on a back-alley tour of Chambers's secret life. It was false. It was meretricious. But it was something for the jury to seize hold of, and it shifted the emphasis from defendant to accuser.

Murphy, on the other hand, stuck resolutely to the facts. He had harvested a large fund. But he had failed as yet to fit them into a theme. It was not all his fault. Some areas of inquiry were closed to him. He was not allowed, for instance, to quiz Hiss about his family horrors, as Stryker had done so effectively with Chambers. On the other hand, Murphy had missed the opportunity, in his opening argument, to plant doubts about what kind of man Alger Hiss might actually be. He had told the jury Hiss had lied, that the evidence against him was strong, and he had emphasized the legal dimensions of perjury. But he had not made the larger point: Hiss, if guilty, had painstakingly constructed a secret life and kept it an airtight compartment, just as his accuser had done.

Stryker had shown the jury how different Hiss and Chambers seemed as men in 1949. Murphy's task was to show how they had been united as accomplices in 1938, when the actual crime, espionage, had been committed, and then to draw out the implications of Hiss's subsequent lies over the years. He had also to evoke the climate of an era already passed into history: the age of antifascism and the Popular Front, when bright young men had flocked to New Deal Washington to seize the levers of power. All this needed to be explained, made intelligible to the jury, particularly with the defendant sitting calmly in court, looking guiltless and serene and eerily younger than his years. When Murphy halted his cross-examination, Hiss left the stand bruised but intact, his story unshaken.[23]

To courtroom observers, studying the couple daily for four weeks, Alger and Priscilla Hiss seemed more like brother and sister than husband and wife. It was as if the affection between them were rooted in long familiarity rather than in conjugal passion.[24]

Each morning the couple entered the courtroom together and sat side by side. During recesses they stood together, smoking. At the end of the day Hiss grasped his wife by the elbow and steered her gently toward the exit. She moved stiffly, as if in a trance.

The case had already cost her much. While her husband immured himself in legal minutiae, Priscilla had alternated between numbness and

panic. She had always worried about money, even when Alger had occupied the Carnegie presidency, with its twenty-thousand-dollar salary
and its many perks. Now she talked obsessively of their imminent financial ruin. They would be bankrupted by attorney fees. Priscilla would
lose her teaching job. They would have to pull Tony, aged seven, out of
private school.

Then there was the publicity. The New York tabloids were running
two and three stories a day. Priscilla saw her name and photo mixed in
with the scandalous divorces, the pinups, the adulterous murders. The
Hisses' phone, though unlisted, rang constantly and at all hours. Often it
was a reporter, working on a last-minute story. Other times it was harass-
ing strangers. In the morning, when the couple left their Village apartment for Foley Square, photographers, lying in ambush, trailed them to
the subway and even into the car, shutters snapping. Alger bore it all
equably, even jauntily. But Priscilla seemed to be coming unhinged. Defense attorneys feared she would collapse on the stand.[25]*

Knowing how fragile Priscilla was, Alger had shielded her from his
own attorneys. Ed McLean's associate Harold Shapero, assigned to re-
hearse Priscilla for her testimony, later could not remember having performed this vital task. Alger had not allowed it. Not that it would have
made much difference. The defense team found Priscilla "impossible to
deal with."[27]

She would have to testify, of course. She stood accused, if not indicted, as the Woodstock typist. She had to deny that and also put the lie
to the plenitude of domestic detail Esther Chambers had served up.

For months there had been rumors Priscilla was really the guilty one.
The suggestion came up often in courthouse speculation and elsewhere
too. In his Senate hearings Dean Acheson had been asked if Hiss might
be shielding his wife. "That theory has been expressed," he had tersely
replied, doing nothing to discourage a theory many found attractive
since it lent gallantry to Hiss's denials and also satisfied the ritual craving
for a guilty woman—in this case a woman warmly disliked by many of
her husband's friends, who had long thought her a femme fatale.[28] But
as an explanation it was nonsensical. For who had given Priscilla the
documents to type if not her husband? Or was he supposed to have

---

* Long afterward she spoke bitterly of her husband's willingness "to sacrifice other people, including me," on the altar of his vindication.[26]

brought them home guilelessly and then been deaf to the clacking of the Woodstock as she typed into the night? Both Hisses were innocent or both were guilty. Priscilla's testimony would go far toward determining which it was.

She followed her husband to the stand on Tuesday afternoon, June 28. If the Hisses seemed like siblings, then Priscilla was cast as the elder, with her gray-streaked hair and drawn features. In fact she was born only thirteen months before her husband. But Alger's invincible youth made the difference seem greater. When the oath was administered, Priscilla, a Quaker, "affirmed" in a tiny, timid voice.

Lloyd Stryker asked if she was the wife of Alger Hiss.

"I am," said Priscilla, gazing out with fierce pride.

The lifted chin and straight-backed posture told much. So did the background facts the witness murmuringly supplied: born in Evanston, Illinois; raised on the Philadelphia Main Line; educated at Bryn Mawr and Yale. It all accentuated the implied social distance between herself and Esther Chambers. Esther had taken the stand wearing gloomy and unseasonal gray. Priscilla was clad in muted summer white. Her dress, a white-and-black print, had large, solemn black buttons down the front with a round piqué collar and matching white cuffs. Her white straw hat trailed a black tendril of ribbon tied at the end in a bow. The one touch of color was the green leather handbag she clutched in her small white-gloved hands.[29] There would be no unsightly red knuckles on display when Priscilla Hiss testified. This witness was a lady.

But she too had a history, which she dreaded having to relate. Though often portrayed in later accounts as the classic thirties fellow traveler, a "Red Hot," Priscilla was in reality a casualty of the reckless twenties. Her first marriage, to publisher Thayer Hobson, a wealthy playboy out of F. Scott Fitzgerald, had ended humiliatingly, with Hobson obtaining a Mexican divorce over Priscilla's desperate pleas. Then, before Hiss rescued her in 1929, she had had a painful romance followed by an abortion, the great shame of her life.[30]

Stryker's direct examination was brief, only twenty-three minutes. He guided the witness toward the controversies of the case gently, as if showing off a piece of fine crystal by his delicate handling of it. Priscilla seemed to relax when recalling domestic life in Washington. Her high, small voice grew calmer as she echoed her husband's version of the couple's awkward dealings with their shabby tenants, the Crosleys. The apartment had been a furnished sublet. Priscilla had left behind "everything but linens, silver, pots and pans and Timmy's bed, and our clothes, and lamps, I think, we took too."

The Hisses had certainly not socialized with the Chamberses. Priscilla never visited Mr. and Mrs. Chambers at any of their Baltimore homes; never drove from Washington to sit with Mrs. Chambers and the baby in Mount Vernon Square; did not help the family move their belongings to New York in the summer of 1935.

Had she ever loaned Esther Chambers a "lovely old linen towel" to use as a diaper?

"No, nothing of the kind happened."

Esther's account was erroneous in many respects, said Priscilla. The families' dealings had ended in 1936. The two couples had not observed celebrations together. Esther's description of the Volta Place house was inaccurate: The dining room and kitchen were in the front, not the back, and there was no paneling in the dining room. Priscilla had not registered for a nursing course in Baltimore in 1937.

And the espionage?

She "certainly did not" provide documents to Chambers. (No one said she had, Murphy objected. Kaufman let the question stand.) Nor had Priscilla typed copies of the stolen papers. She had owned a typewriter, a big office machine, at one time her father's. Yes, the one sitting on the defense table, where it had been placed after the Catletts' testimony.

She had indeed told the grand jury she had donated the Woodstock to the Salvation Army or sold it to a junk dealer. But after hearing the Catletts, Priscilla realized she had been confusing the Woodstock with a second typewriter, a portable, which she had disposed of in the remembered way.

In a new piece of testimony Chambers had said the Hisses loaned him four hundred dollars in 1937, a sum Esther had used in December 1937 to buy the getaway car that took the family to Florida. The FBI had found the Hisses had withdrawn that amount from an account at the Riggs Savings Bank on November 19, 1937. Alger had testified the withdrawal was for furnishings at Volta Place, much larger than the Thirtieth Street place, with more and bigger rooms. Priscilla confirmed this, itemizing various purchases: a metal bed and mattress, bureau, and workbench, all for Timmy, plus a wing chair, a mirror, night table, lamps, rug, curtains, and more.

Had this exhausted the entire sum?

"I'm afraid it did," the witness said with a demure laugh.[31]

Stryker had saved one question for last. Had there been an occasion, at Volta Place, when Priscilla's pocketbook was missing?

"Yes, there was."

With a house key and car key inside?

"There was."

Did it later turn up?

No. She had new keys made.[32]

On that note—and to excited murmurs—Stryker ended his direct examination, having raised the tantalizing possibility that Chambers (or someone) had stolen the Hisses' house key and then slipped into their house to remove—or type—the incriminating documents.

Then it was Murphy's turn. He too showed the witness the utmost respect. He stood diffidently at his lectern, placed in the deepest corner of the jury box, as if to spare Mrs. Hiss the frightening image of his hulking figure.

In three and a half hours of cross-examination the prosecutor did not once raise his voice, in sharp contrast with Stryker's questioning of Esther Chambers.[33]

But the effect was equally brutal. Reviewing the witness's biography, Murphy lingered on Priscilla's unhappy first marriage and then on the assorted jobs she had held, including several at *Time,* in the 1920s. Priscilla had begun as a researcher, then become office manager, and finally was assistant to Harry Luce, a Yale friend of Thayer Hobson's. In Washington Priscilla had worked briefly at the Library of Congress and had taught at a private school. None of this was damaging, but it implied she was not the passive well-bred junior matron presented by Stryker. Murphy brought out Priscilla's restlessness, her incipient feminism, and her political history. When he reached the Hisses' move to Manhattan in 1930, the prosecutor asked, "And during that time you were a member of the Socialist Party?"

Priscilla paled. "I don't think so."

Did she register to vote as a Socialist?

"I don't think so," though she had voted for Norman Thomas, the Socialist candidate. Her voice had dropped to a whisper.

"Maybe I can refresh your recollection," said Murphy. He advanced toward the witness chair, holding a large photostat. It was of two pages of the 1932 voter registration book for New York City. The name Priscilla Hiss was listed along with address, date of birth, and the letters *soc.*

"It is my signature," the witness whispered. But, she said, she had signed only to indicate her intention to vote for Thomas.

"Mrs. Hiss," Murphy asked, "don't you know that the records of the Socialist Party, Morningside Branch, list you as a member?"

"I certainly do not know that."

Murphy moved on to the main issue, Priscilla's alleged role in her husband's spying. Was she a good typist? Did she use the touch system?

"I guess it's my own system." She had to look at the keyboard to find "a lot of the letters." She believed she "started trying to type" in the summer of 1926.[34]

What about the typing test she passed at Columbia?

"I don't think I was ever given a test."

Murphy showed her a transcript noting Priscilla's B.

He also produced a letter from the University of Maryland. Priscilla had enrolled in a medical technology course, not far from the "nursing" class Esther remembered. The letter was dated May 25, 1937, a year after the Hisses, by their testimony, had stopped seeing the Chamberses.

Murphy's randomly sequenced questions, so deftly parried by Alger Hiss, seemed to unnerve Priscilla and leave her permanently tensed for assault. With each question she drooped a little more. After an hour her face was drained of all color, her eyes "dead as raisins in a circle of dough."

She struggled to remain composed. She pressed her lips together tightly, touched a gloved hand to her nose, straightened her back, adjusted the angle of her hat—each gesture an effort to dam up the hysteria building within. She also glanced over at her husband, who gave her a small smile of encouragement, and at the defense table. Tom Donegan, studying her from the prosecution table, told reporters (though not for attribution) that Ed McLean and Mrs. Hiss "had the damndest system of signals going you ever saw."

Stepping down for a recess, the witness rejoined her husband. "We won't talk now," he said softly, handing her a cigarette. Her hands shook as she smoked it in the corridor.[35]

When the cross-examination resumed, Murphy questioned the witness closely about the Woodstock. What condition had the machine been in? Did Priscilla remember any defects?

Yes, the ribbon "puckered like a fold of cloth" and did not wind properly. Some keys jammed when struck, "like a hammer on a piano."

Murphy read aloud Priscilla's grand jury testimony in which she remembered no balky ribbon or jammed keys.

Did she type the Baltimore documents?

"Certainly not."

"You did not type those?"

"I have already said I did not type them, Mr. Murphy. I repeat I did not type them."

"But you would rather I wouldn't ask you any more about them?"

"No. You may ask me whatever you wish." Her voice was nearly inaudible.[36]

Next Murphy read aloud portions of Priscilla's grand jury testimony that flatly contradicted her courtroom statements. Priscilla had told the grand jury she remembered Chambers visiting, as a houseguest, "two or three times" before coming over to inspect the apartment. This conflicted with Priscilla's claim that she had met him only as a subletter.[37]

Murphy asked the witness to describe the clothes Esther Chambers had worn during her stay with the Hisses at P Street. The two women jurors leaned forward in their seats.

During their brief acquaintance, Priscilla remembered, Esther had been clothed "simply, informally, without much attention, I will say, to dress." On one occasion "a friend was coming to call, when Mrs. Chambers and I were at P Street. Her baby's things were strewn rather messily" in the garden behind the house, and "Mrs. Crosley was not very presentable." Priscilla retained a vivid image of "the contrast between [her] friend and Mrs. Crosley."[38] Here, at last, was a glimpse of the distant world of the 1930s, when two women as different as Esther Chambers and Priscilla Hiss might have been thrown together. By the time Murphy was done with Mrs. Hiss, she had skirted the abyss. But the ordeal had been excruciating, even for observers.

# Lucifer vs. the Serpent

The testimony was nearly complete. The defense had only a few remaining witnesses to call. On June 30, "Dr. X," psychiatrist Carl Binger, missing since Chambers had left the stand, was back in the courthouse. Scenting a new development, reporters surrounded him in the corridor. The gregarious Binger relished the attention, slapping journalists on the back.

"What do you think of Whittaker Chambers' personality?" he asked one.

"I'm not qualified to say, sir."

"You're qualified to have your leg pulled, aren't you?"[1]

Dr. Binger's task was to spell out the clinical case against Chambers and give full explication to the theory of unconscious motivation. Murphy was determined to prevent Binger from testifying. Kaufman too had reservations but, after hearing arguments from both sides, agreed to let Binger take the stand since "the tendency of the law is that this type of testimony be admitted." Still leery, the judge devised a curious halfway solution. Stryker would be allowed to pose questions to Binger, and then Kaufman would rule on whether the psychoanalyst could answer them.

Carl Binger was sworn in and took the stand, a large, impressive man with powerful hands he formed in a steeple and held ruminatively under his chin.

At Stryker's prompting, Binger reviewed his considerable medical accomplishments in a booming, genial voice and then assured the prosecutor he had observed Chambers on the witness stand and so, presumably, was competent to evaluate him.

"Now, doctor, I ask you to assume that the following facts are true," Stryker began, and then, confirming Murphy's worst fears, gave Binger—and the jury—a neatly wrapped résumé of Chambers's aberrant history, part fact, part invention. Stryker read from a prepared text, pausing at intervals to sip water, like a filibustering senator. The "question" lasted forty-five minutes.

Finished at last, Stryker faced Binger, who wore a glazed expression under his shiny dome. "Have you, as a psychiatrist, an opinion within the bounds of reasonable certainty as to the mental condition of Whittaker Chambers?"[2]

Murphy sprang up to object and was sustained. Judge Kaufman decided to exclude Dr. Binger's testimony. "The record is sufficiently clear for the jury, using its experience in life, to appraise the testimony of all of the witnesses who have appeared in this courtroom."[3] Stryker hardly minded. His "question" was safely entered into the record despite Murphy's protest that it should be stricken.

A disappointed Binger was excused. He had been only a prop.

Stryker summoned one last witness, the FBI agent who had interviewed—intimidated, said Stryker—the Catlett brothers ("just ignorant, uneducated colored boys"). Then, after a recess, the lawyer announced, "The defendant rests!"

The prosecution too had been saving some final thrusts, in the form of rebuttal witnesses. The most important was Hede Massing, lurking on the margins of the case since December. Murphy had set the stage for her eventual testimony in his cross-examination of Hiss, at one point asking whether he and Massing had bantered about Noel Field. "No such conversation ever occurred," said Hiss. Since then Murphy had been telling the press he would put Massing on the stand.[4]

The defense, of course, wanted her kept off, arguing that her testimony was prejudicial to Hiss and besides had nothing to do with the question of when Hiss had last seen Chambers and whether he had given him stolen documents. Murphy proposed a compromise similar to the one reached on Dr. Binger. Massing should be allowed to testify, and then the judge, if he wished, could exclude her remarks. But even this would be inflammatory, said Kaufman. He ruled Massing's testimony inadmissible. It was a crippling blow to the prosecution. Without Massing there was no one to corroborate Chambers's allegation that Hiss had been an underground Communist.

On July 6, after a three-day recess for the Fourth of July weekend and on the twenty-fifth day of the trial, Lloyd Stryker began his closing argument.

The attorney arrived for the event in a blue-gray suit and pink-and-white-checked bow tie. He had caught a summer cold, but as soon as he turned to the jury—"citizen-judges of the facts," "soldiers of justice"[5]—the great vocal instrument sounded woodwind-clear.

Pacing along the box in his graceful swinging stride, Stryker centered his attack on Chambers, "a recognized and accomplished perjuror, a liar by habit, by teaching, by training, by inclination, and by preference," and worse:

> [Chambers was] an enemy of the republic, a blasphemer of Christ, a disbeliever in God, with no respect either for matrimony or motherhood . . . he believes in nothing . . . and there is not one decent thing that I can think of that Whittaker Chambers has not shown himself against. . . . Roguery, deception and criminality have marked this man Chambers as if with a hot iron. He shows the pattern of an unusual personality, and his life is filled with strange incidents. He began as a petty larceny thief, and was dismissed from his library job for stealing books from Columbia University. He believed as a Communist Party member in lying, stealing and fighting as tenets of that party. . . . He had no doubt hoped to be a commissar in the Communist Party where he could run us all out to City Hall and where he could pick such of those as he chose to bring down there to apply the lash . . . [or] pull our fingernails out by the roots, or whatever the Russian plan is.[6]

Ordinarily, said Stryker, the ravings of such a man would not attract serious attention. But Chambers possessed great cunning. He had patiently stalked Hiss, waiting for the ideal moment, the middle "of a great presidential campaign," and then selected the ideal theater in HUAC, the latter-day edition of "the French Revolutionary tribunal in 1793."[7]

Stryker spent a total of only eleven minutes on the hard evidence, dismissing it all. The jottings in Hiss's hand were "trivia"; the microfilm was an unintelligible mess. Stryker opened a canister, letting the black coils bounce to the floor, and then tossed the heap at Murphy, saying, "You straighten it out." Murphy laughed heartily.[8]

The real spy was Chambers's "fellow thief and confederate in crime," Julian Wadleigh, "such an abysmal, abject specimen of mankind" that Stryker "just did not have the heart to really do a job cross-examining him."[9]

Stryker also brushed aside the collateral evidence. The Woodstock? The Hisses had disposed of it before the documents were typed. (The early statements by the Catletts, implying otherwise, had been wrung out of them by FBI bullies.)

The intimacy between the Hisses and Chamberses? Incredible. Take the visit to Harry Dexter White's summer home. "They motor four hundred miles from Washington to Peterborough, New Hampshire, so they can sit in the car while Whittaker Chambers goes down and talks to a dead man, a man now dead, and they cannot refute him, and then go to see 'She Stoops to Conquer.' If a man ever stooped to conquer, [Chambers] has."[10]

Esther Chambers's recollections? "Perjury, clear, simple, and mathematical."[11]

Stryker had spoken for three hours but was not finished when Kaufman adjourned the court, granting the defense a final hour the next morning, July 7. With Kaufman prodding him along, Stryker lamented the "hundreds of points" still left unsaid and then ambled back to the only point he had ever really made, that Chambers was a demented liar, a "coiled serpent" intent on Hiss's destruction. "This is not a case!" Stryker shouted. "It is an outrage!"

Stryker concluded by beseeching the jury to forgive him his excesses. "With all my faults if I have done anything that you don't like, if I have offended any one of you in any way, hold it against me, not Alger Hiss."

Then, eyes red, his voice a throb, he turned toward the defendant. "Alger Hiss, this long nightmare is drawing to a close. Rest well. Your case, your life, your liberty are in good hands. Thank you, ladies and gentlemen." Stryker bowed to the jury and then, thoroughly spent, sank into his seat.[12]

It was eleven o'clock. Judge Kaufman nodded toward Tom Murphy. But the prosecutor said he preferred to begin after lunch. He was not about to let his summation be interrupted—and his momentum stopped—by a lengthy recess.

At twelve-twenty, with everyone sluggish from an early lunch, Murphy presented the government's case. His lectern had been brought around from its deep corner to the middle of the box, so he could face the jurors squarely. At last spectators were afforded a direct view of the prosecutor, not merely of his vast back. Even so, it was hard to get a read on him. The walrus mustache hid his mouth, and his small blue eyes all but disappeared in the tanned hearty face.

Murphy's summation was nothing like his opening. He did not repeat the error of inviting close scrutiny of his chief witness. Instead he plunged straight into the evidence, the three "immutable witnesses"—the Woodstock, the original State Department documents, and the typed copies—and he reminded the jury of "some facts here that are uncontradicted."

First, "Mr. Chambers had in his possession, and they are now in this courtroom, documents which are undoubtedly copies, in some cases verbatim copies, of original, secret, confidential State Department documents. . . . What is the next uncontradicted fact? The documents themselves are all dated in the first three months of 1938. No dispute about that. The next is that they were all copies" and typed on the Hiss typewriter, just as the other pieces of evidence, the jotted notes, all were in Hiss's hand. These were the facts.[13]

Of course no fewer than fifteen eminences had vouched for Hiss's character, "from all walks of life, two from our highest court." Stryker had even summoned forth the shade of Oliver Wendell Holmes. Murphy suggested that Hiss had rather more in common with two other figures. "One man's name was Judas Iscariot and the other Major General Benedict Arnold." Judas had "a fairly good reputation. He was one of the Twelve. He was next to God, and we know what he did." And Benedict Arnold? He "led the siege against Quebec, got wounded, made a brigadier general." Later of course he "sold out West Point. He wasn't caught. But if he had been caught, don't you think he could have called George Washington as a reputation witness?"

Stryker said Chambers was a "coiled serpent." Then Hiss was the devil, "Lucifer himself . . . one of the fallen angels." He "traveled within the sight of God. Now he had a reputation, I daresay, and what happened to him?"[14]

Stryker had called Chambers a moral leper. But Chambers was the "bosom pal" of the defendant. What did that make Hiss? "What is the name for an employee of this government who takes government papers and gives them to a Communist espionage agent? What is the name for such a person? A brilliant man like this one, who betrays his trust, stinks. Inside of that smiling face that heart is black and cancerous. He is a traitor."[15]

This was not to gainsay Hiss's abilities. They were formidable, as he had proved on the stand. The defendant was a master of evasion and of the self-exonerating half-truth. Consider the car. First Hiss said he had given it to Chambers, thrown it in with the rent. Then, when the title transfer showed otherwise, he had neatly adjusted his story, saying he had given Chambers "the use" of the Ford. "That is Mr. Hiss's forte. He is able to distinguish, to combine truth with half-truth, a little bit to color it, a little bit more to testify, and then, if placed in a corner, to rely upon the truthful part, and you have to be pretty good to do that, and he *is* pretty good."[16]

Hiss had entered the trial holding the upper hand. "Wasn't it obvious to you," Murphy asked the jurors, "that there was not a blessed thing that the defense did not know before this trial commenced? They had examined Mr. and Mrs. Chambers under oath in Baltimore for some 1,300 pages." What a boon for the defense, "the opportunity of cross-examining, without restriction, without objection, the government witness before the trial."[17]

The one time the defense had been caught unaware—on the four-hundred-dollar loan—"they fumbled; they dropped the ball." Chambers had testified that Hiss gave him $400, and indeed that precise sum had been withdrawn from the Hiss account in 1937. How had Chambers known about that withdrawal? Either the man was "psychic" or he had told the truth. The Hisses feebly explained the $400 had financed a shopping spree. Turning to the two female jurors, Murphy asked, "Is that the way you do it when you have a checking account and a charge account, and you have not moved in? Do you take the $400 out in one lump? Do you go around and buy curtains and items for the house to be delivered later and pay for them in cash? . . . [Y]ou might as well pay by check. Is that $400 explanation reasonable to you or is it just another lie?"[18]

The loan aside, there had been no surprises for the defense. "They knew everything. They even had the typewriter." Yet, "armed with all that," what kind of defense had the Hiss team made? One that met and refuted Chambers's allegations point by point? On the contrary. The defense was "conceived to avoid the facts."

Stryker had utterly failed to discredit Esther Chambers's testimony. She had demonstrated intimate knowledge of the Hisses from a period postdating the time of their supposed friendship. She also had known

Mrs. Hiss had planned in 1937 to study nursing at Baltimore's Mercy
Hospital. How had Esther known that? Was she "psychic" too? No, "she
was chumming with Mrs. Hiss."[19]

The Bokhara rug was also telling. There the facts were all in place,
with corroborating evidence: Meyer Schapiro's canceled checks; the recollections of the rug dealer. Schapiro had bought four rugs, with a check
plus two hundred dollars in cash, and then shipped them to Washington.
Hiss admitted he had received one and still owned it.

Then the Woodstock. As soon as the documents were produced, Hiss
knew he was in trouble. He was the boy caught "with jam on his face."
His choices were either to confess or to try to brazen it out. He tried the
latter. He feigned an attitude of helpfulness. He wanted to "run in
there . . . be the first to yell 'Cop!' "[20] And he executed the charade
faultlessly. He hurried to Baltimore, in the dead of night—"Yes sir, he
wanted to help"—and told the FBI about an old typewriter he and his
wife had disposed of in 1938 "to a second-hand dealer in Georgetown."
Very helpful. It got the bureau off the scent, chasing a false lead. But then
the FBI had turned up the typing specimens that tied the Hisses to the
documents, and the defense had not even challenged the prosecution's
testimony. Of course Hiss had known all along where the Woodstock
was. The Catletts had it. No wonder Mrs. Hiss told the grand jury Clytie
Catlett was dead. "You could just eliminate her from the list of people to
see." Meanwhile, Mike Catlett had warned Donald Hiss the FBI was
snooping, and soon the defense had launched its own hunt, one that
took Harold Rosenwald all the way to Detroit.[21]

Murphy turned to the handwritten notes. He picked one up and read
it. Was it really meant for Francis Sayre? "Look at the phrasing there.
There is the summary on the top, '30 Potez-63, latest French type, a
light bomber-pursuit.' And then to make it clear for the photographer,
it is all written out." A summary? No, "a copy verbatim." Another
thing. "Notice the way it is creased. That is a paper that was thrown in a
wastepaper basket? With those creases? You know how that got out of
the office?" Murphy silently demonstrated. He placed a scrap of paper
on the rail of the jury box and folded the page along its creases into a tiny
square. Then he tucked it deep into his breast pocket.[22]

Murphy downplayed his two chief witnesses, the Chamberses. But he
did not ignore them or sidestep Stryker's contrast gainer theme. Alger
Hiss "is a clean-cut, handsome, intelligent, American–born male of

some forty-four years." Whittaker Chambers was "short and fat and he had bad teeth. . . . Mrs. Chambers is plain and severe. Mrs. Hiss is demure and attractive, and intelligent to boot. Very intelligent." All this was true. So what? They were "emotional facts." They did not speak to the issues before the jury, whose obligation was to examine "side by side the testimony of the Hisses and the Chamberses."

Take the two houses, on Thirtieth Street and Volta Place. The Hisses said the Chamberses had not visited them. Yet the witnesses had served up a staggering quantity of remembered detail. Priscilla Hiss had pointed out a few lapses in Esther's memory but had left the bulk unchallenged. "Is it possible in the nature of things for two people to describe two houses in such detail and not to have been there? It it humanly possible? Consider that when you ask yourself who is lying."[23]

Stryker imputed a political motive to Chambers. But "what was the senior editor of *Time* going to get as a result of injecting himself in a political campaign?" Certainly not a cushy appointment in Washington. Cabinet members earned less than the salary Chambers had been making. Political influence? "[T]here is no testimony that the man ever concerned himself with politics after 1938. He was intensely interested in politics prior to 1938. He was interested in Communist politics, with his friend Alger Hiss."[24]

Before this day Murphy's performance in the trial had been ordinary. "But his summation was a great one, a fact freely admitted by the most partisan Hiss fans in the press and conceded by some members of the defense staff," noted Jim Bell. *The Reporter* judged it "a masterpiece," pointing out Murphy had out-Strykered Stryker. "He pretended to offer a rational alternative to Stryker's spellbinding, but what he really did was to gather up all the emotional forces that Stryker had set in motion and turn them against the defendant."[25] No one had come further in the six weeks of the case than Murphy. He was like an actor who stumbles through rehearsals but on opening night comes into full possession of his role. For he had, at last, found the theme of the Hiss case, its story. It was not about perjury, not about what Hiss had said to a grand jury in 1948. It was about what Chambers and Hiss had both done in the distant days of the 1930s, when both had belonged to the Communist underground.

When Murphy finished, after not quite three hours, Judge Kaufman made his charge to the jury. He reviewed the indictment and the factors the jurors should weigh and finally asked them to work harmoniously and to hear one another out. Then, at 4:20 P.M., Judge Kaufman dismissed the two alternates, and the ten men and two women of the jury climbed out of the box and retired across the hall to begin their deliberations behind a closed door. They had heard a total of seventy-three witnesses (forty-three for the prosecution, thirty for the defense) give 570,000 words of testimony filling 2,851 pages of transcript. They had been shown 257 exhibits (224 by the prosecution).[26] Now came the wait.

# 31

# *Verdict*

At moments during Murphy's summation Alger Hiss had been "gray and shaking with rage." He soon recovered. When the jury retired, he sat in the courtroom, calmly reading *Geographical Review,* and now and again stepped into the corridor for a cigarette or slipped into the defense rooms, behind the courtroom, where his attorneys were huddled.

Hiss declined to predict an outcome. The defense team promised a "mass interview" as soon as the verdict came down. Hiss's immediate plans were to spend the weekend recuperating in New York and then head up to Vermont with his wife and son. Over the summer he was to begin teaching courses at a Quaker school.[1]

The day the jury retired, Chambers had arisen at his normal hour, between 4:30 and 5:00 A.M., and gone to the barn. When he emerged, reporters, photographers, and cameramen were waiting. He walked past them and attended to his chores, polite, friendly, but taciturn. One reporter parked himself in the house. "My city editor seems to think that you are going to skip to Canada tonight," he explained to the puzzled witness.[2]

This distrust typified the attitude of many reporters. But not all. One, Nicholas Blatchford of the *Washington Daily News,* traveled to Westminster with a photographer to get a better sense of Chambers the man. Esther fetched her husband from the barn, where he had been pitching hay. Seated in the living room in baggy trousers and a blue work shirt, sleeves rolled up, Chambers talked to Blatchford expansively, glad for a chance to unburden himself. It was the most revealing interview he had given during the eleven excruciating months of the case.[3]

Blatchford began with a simple question: "What do you think you're doing?"

The witness drew deeply on his pipe, his pale blue gaze fastened on the farmland, where mist, rising from the valley, clung to the hilltops. In August, when asked the same question by Nixon, Chambers had said, in a doleful echo of Martin Luther, "So help me God, I could not do otherwise." But the long months had worked a profound change in Chambers. The many humiliations of the case—the rumors, the smears, the disdainful looks—had reawakened his sense of mission and also his Bolshevik pride. Like so many of his pronouncements, the words that followed sounded scripted yet came only with prompting. "I am a man who is very reluctantly and grudgingly, step by step, destroying myself so that this nation and the faith by which it lives may continue to exist. It is not a role I would have chosen for myself. I am merely doing the job as I see it. Someone, some way, had to come along and lift off the lid. Someone had to say, 'This is what's inside.' The man who lifts the lid has to testify just as much against himself as against anyone else. I just seem to be able to stand the ordeal."

To some, Chambers added, the case seemed tragic because "two able men are destroying each other." But there was more involved. "We are all in this historical dilemma—all of us. But no one has gotten to the roots of the question. A religious age would have no difficulty at all in understanding this story. The story is how—why—men become Communists, why they continue to be Communists and why some break and some go on."

And if Hiss was acquitted?

Chambers shrugged. "I can't say where it will end. I have no plans other than to go on living. I'm running a dairy farm here. The rest is in the hands of the gods."

Then the witness excused himself. There was more hay to take in, and he had to look after the livestock.[4]

At five o'clock the first stirrings came from the jury. They requested a copy of the indictment, the documents, the Woodstock, and the typing specimens. At five forty-five they broke for dinner and then resumed deliberations at seven-ten.

Two hours later Hiss, who had been in the defense room, scanning bulldog editions of the *Times* and the *Herald Tribune,* came out and told reporters, "I expect the jury to be out all night. This is a very complicated case."

Downstairs in the lobby newsreel and television cameramen were setting up. Two men from a New York radio station were apprehended trying to sneak a wireless recorder into the courtroom. Everyone settled in for the siege. Many were predicting a hung jury. There was good-natured betting and also heated debate. "The place was beginning to take on the appearance of an election night," Jim Bell observed.[5]

At 10:30 P.M. Judge Kaufman entered the courtroom and called in the jury. "We don't want you to tell us where you stand," the judge advised the foreman, Hubert James. "We just wonder if you believe you can reach a verdict in a reasonable time, or if you'd rather go to a hotel for the night."

"I see no immediate verdict," said James. The panel looked reasonably composed.

In the custody of four marshals the jurors piled into an airport bus and were driven to the Knickerbocker Hotel, on West Forty-fifth Street.[6] The first night's vigil had ended.

The next morning at nine-thirty the jury resumed its deliberations. After two hours a knock came from inside the locked jury room. The marshal opened the door and received a sealed envelope from the foreman. Reporters wearily crammed into the courtroom. Alger Hiss was there, looking tense and drawn. He seemed to have gone without sleep. Judge Kaufman, not wearing his robe, came in. There was no verdict yet. The jury simply wanted portions of his charge read aloud. The jurors trooped in, the judge read the passages, and at twelve-ten the twelve retired again. They too looked tired.

In the corridor Priscilla Hiss, flushed and smiling tautly, chain-smoked with friends. Alger had switched to a pipe. A moody Lloyd Stryker refused to speak with reporters.

When the jurors broke again for lunch, the Hisses left too. They were met on the courthouse steps by a "score of photographers, newsreel men, and amateur camera fans," the *Daily Mirror* reported. Picketers protesting the trial of Communist Party leaders applauded as the couple passed by. Back from lunch Mrs. Hiss declared herself glad to discuss "anything but the trial."[7]

Chambers, meanwhile, had been up at dawn to see to his farm chores. The press contingent made itself at home, gathering on lawn chairs behind the house under leafy trees. Esther and Ellen served lunch and dinner and coffee and iced tea. "Anything yet?" Chambers called on his way to the barn for the afternoon milking. Some of the press were listening to portable radios. He himself would not stay up late listening for a verdict. He had to be up at dawn to milk his cows.[8]

At 3:15 P.M. the jury sent another note to the judge, who descended from his chambers to the courtroom. Murphy shuffled in with U.S. Attorney McGohey. The Hisses came in too and sank into their leather chairs. Alger rubbed a hand over his eyes, red from lack of sleep. He and Priscilla scanned the faces of the jurors as they filed in.

An exhausted Judge Kaufman read the note aloud. "The jury feels that it cannot arrive at a verdict." Reporters dashed out to the hall telephones. Hiss sagged and stroked his eyes. Priscilla flushed. She had removed her white gloves and now squeezed them tightly. Tom Murphy's mouth went slack. He wiped his brow.[9]

Judge Kaufman told the jury they must try again. At 3:29, looking "beaten and glum,"[10] the twelve retreated across the hall and returned to their task.

An hour later they were back. Coming through the doorway, a pair of jurors jostled, trading words. Others glared back and forth. It had been twenty-four hours. Again Kaufman sent them back. Thirteen minutes later he got another note, identical to the first.

Kaufman turned inquiringly to Murphy.

"I would suggest you take the jury at its word and discharge," the prosecutor said. "If I move to dismiss the jury, it might raise some questions of double jeopardy."

Stryker too wanted the judge to rule. At four-fifty the jurors staggered in yet again.

"It's possible to make another effort, Your Honor," said Foreman James.

"Next time I will take you at your word," Kaufman promised.

At six thirty-five the judge called in the jurors and asked if they wished to break for dinner. Several shook their heads no.

"Is the jury deadlocked?" asked the judge.

"Yes, sir, it is," said James.

Some jurors spoke up. "No, no."

James apologized. Just as they had been filing in, a juror had asked for more time.[11]

Again they withdrew across the hall, this time for more than two hours. Still, they could not reach a verdict.

Finally, at 9:01 P.M. on Friday, July 8, after twenty-eight hours and forty minutes—nearly fifteen of those hours spent in deliberation—a hung jury was announced.

The Hiss team sat motionless. Then Ed McLean walked over to the jury box and asked what the final vote had been. "Eight to four, for conviction," a juror replied.

Murphy moved immediately to have the Woodstock impounded. Stryker did not protest.

Alger Hiss, white-faced, sat rigidly in his leather seat. Priscilla seemed on the brink of tears. Defense attorneys came over and urged the defendant to his feet. This time it was he who needed a hand on his arm, Priscilla's, as they waded through the throng. "Please," he said to reporters blocking his way. He and his wife each managed a brief smile before leaving the courthouse. They got into a waiting car, a red Chevrolet. Photographers crowded at the windows. Hiss lifted up a magazine and covered his face.

Attorney General Clark said the case would go back to court as soon as possible, but not before October, since the docket was full. U.S. Attorney McGohey designated Murphy, his "fullback," to carry the ball again.

Murphy sounded optimistic, even pleased. "By the way the jury split, righteousness appears to have been on the side of the government by two to one."[12]

Then came the postmortems. There was widespread criticism of Judge Kaufman. The Hearst columnists Westbrook Pegler and George Sokolsky had been reviling him even before the jury retired—for his apparent bias toward the defendant and also for his New Deal and Tammany Hall connections. A new HUAC voice, Republican Harold Velde of Illinois, announced he had found six "flagrant examples" of judicial misconduct.[13]

The loudest howls came from Richard Nixon. He had not set foot in the courtroom but had been forwarding advice to Tom Murphy via Victor Lasky of the *World-Telegram* and receiving firsthand reports from a trio of Washington newspapermen, Bert Andrews, Willard Edwards, and Edwin Lahey, who had gone up to New York and were sharing rooms at the Gramercy Park Hotel. Nixon often stopped by for an update and to sound the familiar refrain: "What will happen to me if [Hiss is] found innocent? My career will be ruined."[14]

Publicly Nixon joined the chorus denouncing Judge Kaufman and demanded an investigation to "determine the fitness of Judge Kaufman to sit on the bench."[15]*

On Bert Andrews's radio program Nixon enumerated Kaufman's sins. The judge had let Stryker question Chambers about the death of Richard Chambers but kept Murphy from posing similar questions to Hiss. He had not allowed Hede Massing to take the stand. Of course there were legal grounds for these actions, Nixon conceded, but "I think the average American wanted all technicalities waived in this case." These were disturbing words, especially from a licensed attorney. Nixon seemed to think, as *The New Republic* observed, "that any man accused of Communism in these hysterical times is not quite entitled to the full protection of the law." Andrews, playing it straight, asked Nixon if there was any way the testimony of Massing could somehow be put on the record.

Yes, indeed, said Nixon. A new HUAC hearing was the answer, with Hede Massing as the first witness. She could explain "what she would have sworn to" in the trial. Thus enlightened, the American people could "form their own opinion as to what effect her testimony might have had on the jury." This proposed violation of due process was too much even for HUAC. Chairman John Wood ruled out new hearings as an "interference with Justice Department prosecution of the case."[17]

But one important player in the case was pleased by the outcome. Whittaker Chambers had expected an acquittal, a hung jury at best. He refused to comment on the 8–4 vote but declared himself ready for a second trial. Photos of Chambers, togged out in his farmer's work clothes, hoisting a bale of hay, showed him wearing a broad grin[18]—for one of the few times since the case had begun.

---

* Much was made of the prosecution's discovery, at the outset of the case, that the foreman, Hubert James, had privately vowed to see Hiss acquitted. However, Murphy, when discussing the matter with Stryker and Judge Kaufman, shared their view that James had seemed an exemplary candidate during the voir dire. Jurors who voted to convict told the FBI the foreman had conducted the deliberations fairly.[16]

# 32

# *The American Jitters*

Through the summer and most of the fall Chambers was in Westminster, farming, waiting. He was spared the round-the-clock preparations that had preceded the first trial, though there were interviews with Tom Murphy and with the FBI.

During the trial Chambers had had his doubts about Murphy. These were now erased. Though not in the courtroom for Murphy's summation, Chambers had read excerpts published in the August *Plain Talk* and been much impressed. As they discussed the second trial, the giant prosecutor seemed "almost another man. His grasp of the intricacies was now firm and supple. . . . He understood [the case] in its fullest religious, moral, human and historical meaning."[1]

The FBI too threw its ample resources into the new trial. Agents found (in St. Louis) the lessor of the Volta Place house, Gladys Tally, who had placed a rental ad in *The Washington Post* on December 5, 1937, and had discussed the house with Priscilla Hiss "a few days" later—or roughly three weeks after the four hundred dollars had been withdrawn from the Hisses' account. The lease showed that the Hisses' term of occupancy had begun on January 1, 1938. So much for their contention that the money had been used to furnish the Volta Place home. Mrs. Tally also remembered plum-colored drapes in the living room at Volta Place and wallpaper with a mulberry pattern, just as Esther had said.[2]

The bureau's chief task was to find a witness who could corroborate Chambers's testimony about Hiss. Hede Massing remained in the wings, but there was no guarantee she would be permitted to testify.

Chambers suggested other candidates. John Sherman, for one. Not long after the move to Baltimore, Sherman had come down from New York and met the Hisses, Chambers recalled. Getting the prickly Sherman to talk would not be easy. Twice he had rebuffed the bureau in interviews predating the case. Agents in California now put a cover on Sherman's mail. His main correspondents were his wife and daughter, whom he had left behind on a dirt farm in Buena Vista while he began a new job as humanities instructor at the Los Angeles University of Applied Education. In late September agents knocked on the door of Sherman's "office," a rented hotel room in La Habra. Combative and bitter, Sherman demanded the agents produce a warrant and then launched into an oration on the evils of capitalism. He would not be testifying at the trial.[3]

Chambers also suggested Josephine Herbst, a literary acquaintance from 1934. In the first trial she had held off the FBI and sent a warning to her ex-husband, Hal Ware's onetime assistant John Herrmann, then living in Mexico, that an investigation was under way. The Hiss defense had also questioned Herbst, who was ardently pro-Hiss. But her memories of the Ware Group were nearly identical to Chambers's, even down to the circumstances of "Carl's" first encounter with Hiss. Since then Chambers had heard, mistakenly, that Herbst had changed sympathies. He hoped she would recall an Easter visit he and Hiss had made to see Herbst at her country home in Erwinna, Pennsylvania, not far from Maxim Lieber's place. But Herbst, still pro-Hiss, told the FBI she remembered no such visit.[4]

One other potential witness remained. Chambers and Esther both recalled that a maid they had employed in Baltimore had met one or both of the Hisses. If she could be found, then an important piece of Chambers's story would be corroborated. For months the FBI had been looking for the woman, but their leads were few. The Chamberses remembered her first name, Edith, but not her surname. Agents had canvassed employment agencies in Baltimore and talked to residents in the African-American neighborhood where the Chamberses thought Edith might have lived.

Through the first trial and into the summer the search continued. Then, one day, while FBI agents were at Westminster, digging for fresh leads, Esther suddenly remembered a portrait she had once painted of Edith. She had given it to the maid—or had she kept it? Esther and the FBI men went up to the attic and rummaged among a pile of unfinished canvases. Esther fished out a portrait in oils. "That's Edith," she exclaimed.

The portrait was a "fair likeness" in the artist's assessment, so the bureau made pocket-size reproductions and circulated them throughout Baltimore. One who saw it was the janitor at the Eutaw Place residence. When interviewed earlier, he had remembered the tenants named Cantwell but not their maid. The picture jogged his memory, and when he happened to see Edith on a streetcar, he got her name and address, Edith Murray of Bloom Street.

One Sunday evening in early November an FBI agent knocked on Edith Murray's door and identified himself as someone "working for Mr. Cantwell." He showed Mrs. Murray the photograph. "Do you know who this is?"

"Oh yes, that's me," said Mrs. Murray. "Is Mr. Cantwell back in Baltimore? Are they looking for me to work for them?"

She had been out of domestic service, she explained, since 1942, when she had suffered a nervous breakdown. She instantly recognized a photograph of Chambers. "Looked just like him, only he was a little older."

She had known him as her sometime employer Lloyd Cantwell, a "traveling salesman" home only weekends. She was pleased to hear again from the Cantwells, "very nice people to work for." She had been especially fond of Ellen and had nicknamed her Peachie, which later evolved into Puggsy, the nickname the family still used.

FBI agents drove Mrs. Murray out to Westminster. After a happy reunion Esther led her former maid through the house. Edith noted familiar furnishings. But did Edith Murray remember the Hisses? She studied photos. Priscilla made the stronger impression. "I know I had seen her but I didn't know where at the time."

Upon further FBI questioning, she placed the Hisses at Eutaw Place. Priscilla had visited as many as four times, on one occasion coming over to help care for Ellen while Esther, pregnant with John, was seeing her obstetrician in New York. She remembered Alger visiting just once.

Just to be sure, the FBI arranged for Edith Murray to identify the Hisses in person prior to taking the stand, lest she draw an embarrassing blank. On the morning of November 17, the first day of the second trial, Edith Murray took the train up from Baltimore and was met at Penn Station by FBI agent Jack Danahy, who escorted the witness to Foley

Square. They stood outside the courtroom while Edith inspected the large crowd milling in the corridor—sixty prospective jurors plus journalists and spectators. None looked familiar. Edith "stood there and stood there." Then the elevator opened, and another group emerged. Edith instantly pointed out "the lady from Washington" and "that nice man"—Priscilla and Alger Hiss.[5]

Meanwhile there emerged a bizarre plan—partly devised by Chambers himself—that nearly led to a mistrial. In late September or early October Ralph de Toledano, finishing up his book on the case, invited Chambers to appear as a guest on *Newsweek*'s television program *Newsweek Views the News*. De Toledano promised. He would be Chambers's sole interviewer, making for a more congenial atmosphere than the *Meet the Press* fiasco.[6]

Chambers promptly accepted the offer. In his many talks with de Toledano, he had developed complete trust in the journalist. Chambers had a suggestion. Why not make the interview a public test of his veracity by hooking him up to a lie detector? A polygraph expert in the studio could then measure Chambers's responses as he made them. The proposal was greeted excitedly. It would be a television landmark, not to mention a chance for *Newsweek* to tweak its senior rival, *Time,* with the help of an ex-*Time*man.

As a courtesy Chambers alerted the FBI to the plan. The bureau urged him to drop it. The publicity could taint the jury pool and prejudice the trial. Stubbornly Chambers insisted on going forward. If the program served to "arouse public sentiment against Hiss," so much the better. The prosecution could get into the act too, he added, by screening de Toledano's questions. If that was unacceptable, Murphy and company could ignore the event altogether. Finally, Murphy himself intervened and had a long talk with Chambers, who reluctantly agreed to cancel the interview.[7]

The government was aided by something else, a dramatic change in the nation's political climate. By this time only a minority doubted there had been a Communist conspiracy of some kind. In late July, only a few weeks after the first trial ended, President Truman signed the NATO treaty, and Secretary of State Acheson called for $1.5 billion in aid for the democracies of Western Europe, threatened doubly by Soviet aggression and an "internal Communist" threat. A week later, in a thousand-page white paper, the State Department formally announced China had fallen to communism and no more U.S. aid would be forthcoming. There were angry denunciations by the China Lobby and charges that State Department Communists, including Alger Hiss, had "lost" China. The nation's new dictator, Mao Zedong, soon to establish a "people's government" in Beijing, declared his solidarity with Moscow. (Mao and Stalin had their first meeting in December 1949.)[8]

Then, in September, came the biggest shock of all when the Soviets exploded their first atomic bomb. No one had expected America's nuclear monopoly to last forever, but Western scientists had predicted it was secure for at least several years more, the years needed to fortify European defenses and to build up a long-range arsenal that would frighten off the Soviets with the threat of a massive atomic retaliation.

How, everyone wanted to know, had the Soviets got the bomb? Igor Gouzenko had spoken of an atomic conspiracy as early as 1945. Three weeks into the second Hiss trial HUAC was entertaining witnesses who accused distinguished New Dealers such as Harry Hopkins and Henry Wallace of having "expedited" atomic information to the Soviets during the war. Then shortly after a verdict was reached, the German-born physicist Klaus Fuchs confessed his role as an atomic spy to British intelligence authorities.

It all made for a national case of "the jitters," said *The New York Times*. *The New Republic* deplored the growing mood of "hysteria and demoralization." But the naming of maladies could not alone cure them. The collective memory of the last war and of the appeasements that had made it possible was too recent, vivid, and unsettling to be brushed aside.[9]

The impact of all this on the second trial of Alger Hiss is impossible to measure. But a striking fact emerged during the voir dire. This time only one of sixty potential jurors said he was inclined to disbelieve the testimony of ex–Communists.[10]

# 33

# *Blind Analysis*

On November 17, 1949, a year to the day after Chambers had produced the documents that transformed a slander suit into a spy scandal, the second perjury trial of Alger Hiss began. The defendant resumed his familiar place, impeccably dressed but a shade thinner, his summer tan faded. Priscilla, again at his side, appeared even tenser than before. To Alistair Cooke, resuming his post for the *Manchester Guardian*, it "looked the same old trial seen in a glass grayly."[1]

These forebodings soon were allayed. The second trial was an altogether different spectacle from the first. For one thing, Lloyd Paul Stryker was gone. He had been let go over the summer when the defendant had plotted a change of venue to Vermont. Hiss sensed Stryker, the slick "big-city boy," would not go over well on the rustic stage. The attorney had gallantly stepped aside, promising to remain on call should the change of venue be denied. It *was* denied but Hiss did not ask Stryker back. Never comfortable with the attorney's posturing and purple oratory, Hiss preferred an understated approach, befitting his persona. Also, Stryker's stamina had seemed to ebb in the final days of the first trial. Hiss feared the attorney, "slightly apoplectic" to begin with, was not up to the strain of a repeat performance.[2]

Something else also weighted Hiss against Stryker. Bluster aside, Stryker was a shrewd assessor of percentages. He had early calculated the chances of an acquittal, and concluded they were minute. He had gone instead for a hung jury. This reasoning underlay the relentless attack on Whittaker and Esther Chambers and the blithe dismissal of the documents. Some jurors, Stryker knew, would be repelled by his tactics. But others would respond to their theme: that it was unjust for a man with a spotless public record to be convicted on the word of a confessed perjuror, no matter how strong the supporting evidence. The result would be exactly what Stryker got, a split jury. "You've got to make up your mind whether you're really going for unanimity or trying to be divisive and get some of the jurors on your side," he later explained. "I could have kept trying that case until hell froze over and they could never get twelve jurors to convict."[3]

But Hiss was determined to have a clear-cut verdict, even if it meant his total ruin. He had already risked much. Why back down now? Maintaining the boldness he had demonstrated since August 1948, he revamped his defense, supplementing the demolition of Chambers's credibility with a frontal attack on the evidence. The attorney Hiss chose to succeed Stryker, Boston corporate lawyer Claude B. Cross, was meticulous in his use of documents, a "demon for detail,"[4] like Hiss himself. He would take the trouble to master the spy papers—their contents, their dating and sequence—and to learn State Department routing procedures. If there were flaws in the documentary evidence, Cross would find them.

But Cross was not the only new player in this second courtroom drama. Samuel Kaufman was also among the missing, displaced by Judge Henry W. Goddard, an appointee of Warren G. Harding's and, in the distant past, a director of the National Republican Club.

At age seventy-three Goddard was among the most senior federal judges on the New York bench. Bald, with a fine aquiline profile, he exuded a calm sagacity that reined in the excesses of both sides. When objections were raised, Goddard soberly considered them; when tempers flared, he soothed them. It made for a more tranquil courtroom.[5]

Judge Goddard decided early on to give greater latitude to both sides in the presentation of evidence than had Kaufman. Both the prosecution and the defense took advantage of this, and both profited from it.

For Murphy the ruling meant he could put Hede Massing on the stand. Many found her testimony the high point of the trial. Massing had been an actress on the Vienna stage in the 1920s. At forty-five, she retained a theatrical air and expertly played the role of "the woman with a past," as *Time* put it. Speaking in a soft accent, Massing evocatively summarized her Communist career, going back to her days in Vienna and Berlin, just after World War I, when she had met and married Gerhart

Eisler, now East Germany's propaganda chief. Her underground re-
cruiter, she told the jury, was Ignace Reiss ("a very noble and fine
man"), murdered by NKVD assassins in 1937. She recounted her own
trip to Moscow that year.

For the first time the jury heard a witness other than Chambers speak
familiarly of the Communist underground. In the 1930s, said Massing,
"I belonged to an apparatus. It is an organization connected with the
Communist Party," really a "Russian apparatus." In that capacity she had
met Noel Field, an officer in the Western European division of the State
Department, and had got to know him and his wife, Herta, "very intimately." (Field's defection behind the Iron Curtain in May 1949 had
been reported over the summer.)

In 1935—"late summer or early fall"—Massing had attended a small
dinner party at the Fields' home in Washington. There was a second
guest, Alger Hiss. Massing had spoken with him privately. She repeated
the conversation for the jury's benefit. "I said to Mr. Hiss, 'I understand that you are trying to get Noel Field away from my organization
into yours,' and he said, 'So you are this famous girl that is trying to get
Noel Field away from me,' and I said, 'Yes.' And he said, as far as I remember, 'Well, we will see who is going to win,' at which point I said,
'Well, Mr. Hiss'—I did not say 'Mr. Hiss'—'Well, you realize that you
are competing with a woman,' at which either he or I said, the gist of
the sentence was, 'Whoever is going to win we are working for the
same boss.' "[6]

Murphy also introduced new documentary evidence, Adolf Berle's
notes of his 1939 conversation with Chambers and Ray Murphy's two
memos from 1945–1946. Each demonstrated that Chambers's charges
against Hiss had come in the context of much wider disclosures. The
names in Berle's notes included Julian Wadleigh, Noel Field, and Laurence Duggan. Last had come the Hiss brothers:

*Donald Hiss*
(Philippine Adviser)
Member of C.P. with Pressman & Witt—
Labor Dep't—Ass't to Frances Perkins—
Party wanted him there—to send him
as arbitrator in Bridges trial—
Brought along by brother—

*Alger Hiss*
Ass't to Sayre—CP—1937
Member of the Underground Com.—Active
Baltimore boys—
Wife—Priscilla—Socialist
Early days of New Deal

The conspiratorial theme also threaded through State Department official Ray Murphy's memos, hastily composed, sloppily typed, vibrant with their author's excitement. "The persons listed below are said to have disclosed much confidential matter and to have arranged among themselves a program committing this government to a policy in keeping with the desires of the Communist Party," Murphy had recorded on March 20, 1945. He also listed the "top leaders of the underground . . . in the order of their importance." They were "1. Harold Ware. 2. Lee Pressman. 3. Alger Hiss." Chambers "dealt with these people from 1934 to the end of 1937 when he broke with the Party and attempted to persuade various of these contacts to break too." He tried hardest with Hiss in "several conversations in the early part of 1938." At their last meeting Hiss "refused with tears in his eyes and said he would be loyal to the Party." Hiss, Chambers had told Murphy, was "absolutely sincere in his convictions and motivated by the idea that he was on the right track."[7]

In keeping with its strategy of challenging the documentary evidence, the defense also outlined a conspiracy. It began with Claude Cross's contention that Chambers's cache of documents was culled from several different State Department offices. Wadleigh had supplied the Trade Agreements papers. A second and perhaps third accomplice had given Chambers a "pipeline" to papers from the Far East division.

The handwritten notes each contained information meant for Francis Sayre, as Hiss had said. True, they had ended up in Chambers's possession, but it did not necessarily follow that Hiss had handed them over. In fact the papers seemed not the harvest of a spy carefully sifting through the mounds on his desk but rather the "grab of some thief" who had sneaked into Hiss's office and hurriedly snatched whatever he found.[8]

Cross's strategy required a close cross-examination of Julian Wadleigh, a less dangerous proposition than in the first trial since Wadleigh was no longer an unknown quantity. On the contrary, he had become something of a public joke, thanks to a lurid serial he had written, "Why I Spied for the Communists," which had begun appearing in the *New York Post* two days after the hung jury had been announced. It was all there: Wadleigh's dawning realization that his Soviet masters were interested in documents, not in his economic forecasts; his grievances against the snobbish "bureaucrats" at State; the handkerchief he had tucked in his pocket as a badge of martyrdom.

Cross lingered on Wadleigh's description in the *Post* of his single meeting with Bykov—"Sasha." The *rezident's* right sleeve, Wadleigh had written, "was hanging loose. Sasha had no right arm." Chambers, of course, remembered no such defect. (Nor did Nadya Ulanovskaya or William Edward Crane, who both had known the Russian.)

But on the key issue Wadleigh remained unshakable. Though he conceded it was "remotely possible" he had "turned over" some of the documents, they would have been different copies, not these. He was certain too he had never removed any papers from Hiss's desk. And whatever doubts Cross raised did not explain how documents from Trade Agreements dated after March 11, 1938, when Wadleigh had departed Washington for an assignment in Turkey, had found their way into Chambers's hands.[9]

Once again the defense would have to discredit Chambers. He was on the stand seven days, ruddy and refreshed after four months of outdoor farm work and steeled for the rigors of cross-examination. He easily parried Claude Cross's thrusts, which in any case lacked the Strykerian bite. Civil and detached, Cross rarely overstepped his bounds and when he did met with mild reproof from the grandfatherly Judge Goddard. "Mr. Cross, I think you have done pretty well," the judge placidly observed at one point, "but let us have a clean score. . . . The witness does not have the same advantage you have."[10]

In substance the cross-examination replayed Stryker's, with an added twist. The defense had obtained a copy of Chambers's 1935 passport application under the name David Breen. Cross luxuriated in the fresh meadow of Chambersian perjuries, the many false answers he had supplied on the application, and made much of Chambers's "ghoulish" borrowing of a dead man's name and family history. As before, the witness readily, even cheerfully, owned up to his tainted past.

The most intriguing feature of the passport application was its accompanying photo. David Breen was pictured with a mustache. A mustache had never come up previously, not even during the first HUAC hearings, when Chambers's physical appearance had been a matter of significant dispute. Cross spent more than an hour questioning Chambers about the photo, at one point astonishing the witness and amusing the spectators by asking if the whiskers had been false.[11] Chambers bore it all equably.

Esther too was better composed than in the first trial. When Cross gently brought out inconsistencies in her testimony, she calmly explained that her confusion was the result of "fourteen years of not trying to remember this."

She also seemed physically transformed. The timid country mouse of the first trial now exuded a quiet radiance. Alistair Cooke noted with surprise "the revelation of fine feature and warmth in the eyes." Indeed on closer inspection this severe-seeming farm wife with the cracked red knuckles was "a very handsome woman."[12]

The defense had more damage to undo than in the first trial. Once again "reputation witnesses" ornamented the courtroom. Justices Frankfurter and Reed did not appear. But there were new dignitaries. One, Francis Sayre, extolled Hiss—"an outstanding man"—but disputed the defendant's explanation of the four handwritten notes, "not comments on memoranda nor personal advice in any way," Sayre testified, but "rather digests of copies of incoming cables."[13]

Hiss's second boss at State, Stanley Hornbeck, detected a similarity between the notes and "chits" he had received from Hiss, though the chits had always been initialed and had never consisted of verbatim jottings of cables. Hornbeck did the defendant no good by coughing up the name of a "friend," William C. Bullitt, who in 1939 had warned him Hiss was a rumored fellow traveler.[14*]

By the time Hiss mounted the stand, on December 19, he had sat in the courtroom some fifty days (dating back to the first trial), the principal figure in what had become, said *Time,* "a kind of mechanical, well-mannered nightmare." As ever his self-control commanded respect, even awe. Like his summer suits, his winter suits "were in impeccable taste," reported Merle Miller in *The New Republic,* and so was "everything else about him—the shirts with the French cuffs always discreetly hidden, the soft, becoming ties, the smartly shined black shoes." He arrived each morning at ten-fifteen, *Time* reported, "carrying a rolled-up umbrella,

---

* Bullitt later said his information came via French intelligence reports.[15]

wearing rubbers if there is a hint of rain." In the eye of the storm he seemed eerily detached. Even when reporters discussed the proceedings within earshot—in the elevator, in the corridor, at Andre's, the Foley Square restaurant where Hiss dined each day—the defendant betrayed no emotion.[16]

This time Tom Murphy was a better match for Hiss. He abandoned the labored sarcasm of "Mr. Witness" for the more temperate "Mr. Hiss." He also held his anger in check, seeming finally to realize Hiss was simply too deft to be rattled or to make a self-incriminating misstep. Instead he stuck to the evidence: the apartment; the Ford; the rug; the trips to New York with Chambers. And with his firmer grip on the case's political context, Murphy quizzed Hiss about his Communist associations, especially his friendship with Noel Field. Hiss admitted he had recommended Field in 1939 as an assistant to Francis Sayre in the Philippines, even though Field by then had been publicly accused of being a Communist.

When Hiss stepped down on December 29, the twenty-fifth day of the trial, he had sustained no new damage. Neither had he strengthened the case for his acquittal.

Then it was his wife's turn. Like her husband, Priscilla Hiss repeated the denials of the first trial—or most of them. Under cross-examination, she admitted she had made "small contributions" to the Socialist Party, had "served coffee and sandwiches" to the unemployed, and had stayed on to attend meetings.

Murphy also pursued the four-hundred-dollar withdrawal and the items Mrs. Hiss said she had purchased for the Volta Place home in the course of a month. Murphy showed the witness a dozen check stubs for the same period recording payments of ten and fifteen dollars and in one instance sixty dollars. "Do you tell this court and jury that you cashed all of those small checks between the dates that I have described when you had this cash [four hundred dollars] in your purse?" She did, but wearily.

Priscilla's testimony, interrupted by the new year, concluded on January 5, 1950.[17]

To the surprise of many, Judge Goddard, the elderly, conservative Republican, daringly ruled the defense could summon the psychiatric expert barred from testifying by Judge Kaufman. Since "the outcome of this trial is dependent to a great extent upon the testimony of one man—

Whittaker Chambers," the judge explained, the defense had the right to use psychiatric testimony "to impeach" his credibility. This set a precedent. Goddard had not found a single federal case in which such testimony had been permitted against a prosecution witness.[18]

Once more Dr. Binger took the stand and listened patiently as Cross read a new version of the "question" Lloyd Stryker had posed, now lengthened to more than an hour. Bidden at last to expound his views of Chambers's sanity, the psychiatrist offered his diagnosis of "psychopathic personality." Chambers was not psychotic or insane, said Binger. But his conduct often had "an amoral or an asocial and delinquent nature."

Dr. Binger itemized Chambers's symptoms: lying (the many perjuries); "withholding of truths" (from Adolf Berle, Ray Murphy, HUAC, the grand jury in October 1948, though again this implied his revised allegations were true); stealing (books from Columbia, the State Department documents); insensitivity "to the feelings of others" ("A Play for Puppets," which had offended Columbia faculty and undergraduates); "playing a part as if it were true, assuming a role" (the many aliases—before, during, and after his Communist days); "bizarre behavior" (the pumpkin); vagabondage (the "wretched dive" in New Orleans); "unstable attachments" (in and out of Columbia, of the Communist Party, of Christian sects); panhandling (the unpaid loans from Hiss and Wadleigh); "abnormal emotionality" (his immobility after his brother's suicide); "paranoid thinking" (fear of NKVD assassins); false accusations (against Francis Sayre and Laurence Duggan).

This diagnosis, achieved without the analyst's ever having spoken with the subject, rested on Binger's reading of the Baltimore depositions and other testimony, on his examination of selected writings by Chambers, and on the days he had spent studying Chambers's behavior on the witness stand, six in all, five during the first trial, one during the second.

Binger made much of Chambers's courtroom demeanor. As a witness Chambers "apparently had very little relationship with the inquirer" and often looked up at the ceiling as if trying to recall something he had previously said. In addition, said Binger, "he had an extraordinary lack of precision about events. In the first trial his mode of reply was usually 'It must have been—it would have been,' or 'It should have been thus and so.' . . . On the other hand he very often had an accurate memory for episodes that were somehow connected with his own imagination. He remembered, for example, a policeman carrying an Easter lily on a trip that he took to Erwinna, Pennsylvania. He did not remember the date of his marriage."

Dr. Binger also analyzed Chambers's writing. The elegiac stanzas of Chambers's poem to his brother conveyed an "abnormal emotion." So did Chambers's prose, at least the limited samples Binger had read: "The Damn Fool," *Class Reunion* (Binger allowed no distinction between original and translated work), and a fanciful *Life* essay, "The Devil," which depicted the "Prince of Evil" in modern dress, declaring "Hell is a conspiracy." Binger quoted liberally from this last, which he interpreted as a self-portrait. When Chambers's Satan said, "If I succeed in making man destroy himself I will destroy myself with him, having destroyed my function," the statement presaged Chambers's "I am a man who is . . . destroying myself so that this nation and the faith by which it lives may continue to exist."

Tom Murphy's cross-examination of Dr. Binger was a high point of the trial. The prosecutor began by asking Binger what he made of a passage from a recent psychiatry textbook. Murphy read it aloud: "The term 'psychopathic personality,' as commonly understood, is useless in psychiatric research . . . a scrap-basket to which is relegated a group of otherwise unclassified personality disorders and problems."

Binger, inexplicably, found these remarks "excellent" and agreed "with every word."

Murphy next raked over the specifics of Binger's diagnosis. Binger had made much of Chambers's having "lied quite simply" in 1924, when he told Dean Hawkes he wished to become a history teacher. But Chambers had confessed the lie "within a short time" to Mark Van Doren, "his faculty adviser, a man associated in . . . academic circles with the Dean." Had Binger properly weighed that factor when he included the letter to Van Doren as "evidence of a psychopathic personality?"

"I do not base my diagnoses on one lie," Binger explained.

On to Chambers's passport application. Had Binger taken into account the circumstances under which Chambers had made the false statements: "that he obtained this passport in the name of Breen for the purpose of going to England to set up a Communist apparatus over there?"

It made no difference, said Binger. Chambers had lied.

What about the WPA application? Did it matter that had Chambers answered the questions truthfully he would have been rejected for a job—and at a desperate time in his life?

"Well, I am not attempting to pass on the nature of his lies," said Binger. "I am stating that he has told many lies, that repeated lying is one of the evidences of psychopathic personality."

But "can't we agree," asked Murphy, "that lies are not ipso facto evidence of psychopathic personality?"

Yes, "lies by themselves are not evidence."

Binger had accused Chambers of "insensitivity." What did the doctor make of Chambers's HUAC statement about the tragedy of history? Was it the utterance of a man "insensitive to the feelings of others?"

"If that were a sincere statement I would say no."

Had Dr. Binger any evidence it was insincere?

No.

Binger's most embarrassing moments came when Murphy quizzed him on Chambers's conduct as a witness. For instance, Chambers's habitual use of the phrases *must have been, should have been, would have been.* Murphy had combed through the whole of Chambers's testimony and found a total of ten such usages. Did Binger know how many times Alger Hiss had used "similar phrases"?

"I haven't any idea; I didn't hear him testify."

"My computation, Doctor, is in 590 pages Mr. Hiss used a phrase like that or similar 158 times. Now, do you form any conclusions, Doctor, by the use of phrases?"

"No."

Murphy reminded Binger of his observation that Chambers often glanced up at the ceiling rather than met his questioner's eyes. "Now, Doctor," said Murphy, "we made a count this morning of the number of times you looked at the ceiling, and during the first ten minutes you looked at the ceiling 19 times; the next 15 minutes 20 times; and the next 15 minutes 10 times; and the following 10 minutes 10 times, making a total in 50 minutes of 59 times, and I was wondering, Doctor, whether that had any symptoms of psychopathic personality?"

Binger, shifting uneasily in his seat, gave Murphy an icy smile. "Not alone."

Murphy turned to Chambers's alleged panhandling. Did the doctor wish to "withdraw that now before I question you on it?"

"I would be glad to have you question me on it."

All right, then, wasn't panhandling "just an ordinary term we all know?"

Yes, a "lay term . . . used in the literature on this subject."

"And it means accosting strangers on the street?"

"I should think that was right, yes."

"And you tell this court and jury with all the seriousness that you can command as an experienced doctor that Mr. Chambers is guilty of panhandling?"

"I tell you that he on two occasions to my knowledge . . . borrowed money from friends and made no attempt to pay it back. I call that panhandling. If you want me to withdraw the name and call it something else, I will."

"Now, Doctor, do you say now that when a person borrows $20 from a man that he has been friendly with for a period of a few years, like Mr. Chambers was with Mr. Wadleigh, and did not pay it back, that that to a trained psychiatrist is evidence of panhandling?"

"No. I think you win on that."

Finally, Murphy turned to Chambers's supposed inability to form stable attachments. What about his eighteen-year marriage to Esther, the mother of his two children?

"If you ask me to assume that it is a good marriage and that he has stuck to this one woman as you describe, of course that is evidence of a stable attachment."

"Doctor," said Murphy, "assume that Mr. Chambers went with Time Magazine in 1939 as a book reviewer and over a period of almost ten years rose in that organization until he became one of six senior editors, at a salary of $30,000 a year, and during that time worked hard for that magazine, wouldn't that also be very cogent evidence of a real honest-to-goodness stable attachment?"

"In that particular instance, yes."[19]

Wisely Claude Cross had enlisted a backup expert, Henry A. Murray, one of the nation's leading psychologists, best known for having devised the Thematic Apperception Test (TAT), cousin to the Rorschach exam. A longtime director of the Harvard Psychological Clinic, Murray had screened wartime recruits for the OSS and had prepared an acute psychological profile of Adolf Hitler. Working only from public documents, including Hitler's speeches, Murray had impressively predicted the Führer's suicide. He was also a gifted interpreter of literary texts and had devoted twenty-five years to analyzing the work of Herman Melville.

His diagnosis of Chambers was formed more hastily. Cross had contacted the psychologist several days into the trial, leaving him only a month to prepare his testimony. With the help of students in his Harvard graduate seminar, Murray had embarked on a crash tutorial in Chambers's writings. In addition, Cross "coached him carefully, paying special attention to the traps that had brought poor Binger down."[20]

Like Binger, Murray did not interview Chambers. He had not even observed him in the courtroom. His was, by his own admission, a "blind" analysis, based primarily on Chambers's prose, whose morbid imagery, said Murray, indicated "a pathological preoccupation with the processes of tearing down and destruction and decay and death." Murray found a higher proportion of such images in Chambers's writings "than in any [others] I have examined."

But Murray had read very selectively. He had read none of Chambers's early lyric verse and nothing at all from the twenty-two-year interval between "Tandaradei" (1926) and his last *Life* pieces—not *The New Masses* fiction and poetry, not the cover stories on Toynbee, Einstein, Niebuhr, Marian Anderson, not the hundreds of articles on world politics, religion, books, film.[21]

Superficiality was only one of Murray's offenses. Worse, he had entered the case with his mind already made up. And Tom Murphy knew it. Two weeks before taking the stand, the eminent psychologist had gone to New York to interview *Time* staffers. James Agee had learned of this and sent an alert to Murphy. "He is a scientist hunting facts to fit a theory," Agee warned, "and he seems relatively uninterested in justice. He is no doubt honestly convinced that Hiss is innocent—and very 'emotionally' convinced."

"Now, Doctor," the prosecutor asked in his cross-examination, "have you done a little investigation yourself in this case?"

Yes.

"Have you talked with someone about Mr. Chambers?"

Yes, with a man who had worked under Chambers "eight or nine years ago" and said Chambers was the only editor at *Time* who kept his door shut. Murray remembered nothing else the man had said. It had not, in any case, indicated a side of Chambers "contrary to the hypothesis [already] forming" in Murray's mind. In fact, as the FBI had learned, Murray had testily accused the unnamed *Time* employee of "whitewashing" Chambers when he failed to produce damaging revelations about him.

Murray left the stand having done little harm to Chambers but having tarnished the discipline he so eminently represented. Psychologists interviewed at the time disapproved of Binger's and Murray's testimony. It dealt "a serious setback to the prestige of the profession," in the opinion of one. Another found it "deplorable."

But Henry Murray had no regrets. "The whole thing was very enjoyable," he later said.[22]

The prosecution brought out two important witnesses at the rebuttal stage. One was Air Force Sergeant George Roulhac, who had cohabited with Clytie Catlett in 1938. He remembered seeing a typewriter at the house. Murphy pointed to the Woodstock. Was it similar to that?

"I never noticed the exact make," said Roulhac, "but that is the same design."[23] The typewriter had first appeared on the premises in mid-April 1938, after the last of the documents had been typed and at just the moment when Hiss would have learned of Chambers's defection.

Then, on the thirty-seventh day of the trial and the last day of testimony, Edith Murray took the stand and described her period of service for the "Cantwells" (the Chamberses) and also the visits of "Miss Priscilla" to Eutaw Place. "When she would come there Mrs. Cantwell was always there to see her, and she seemed to be glad to see her and the baby, and she was very nice."

The visits were memorable because the Cantwells "never had no company at all, only those two." And Alger Hiss was the last friend she would have envisaged for Mr. Cantwell. "When I see him [Hiss], I seen the difference in the two of them, and naturally I noticed."

In his cross-examination Cross implied the witness had been coached. Edith Murray denied it. She also said she was not aware the Cantwells and their "friends" were the principals in the most publicized court case of the day.

Had she not seen a single newspaper article on the case?

No. She had stopped reading the papers in 1942 because of her "nervous condition." Nor had she seen any newsreel pictures. "I never go out except maybe to the movies once a week, and just listen to the radio." She had once heard "something about some filling was found in a pumpkin on a farm in Westminster, but I still didn't pay any attention to that."

Cross showed her a photograph of Chambers. Was it the one the FBI had first shown her?

No. "It was a better looking picture than that."

Could she describe Mr. Cantwell?

"Well, he is blond and short and stout."

Anything more?

"A nice man."

About his looks, Cross meant.

"Well, I mean about his looks. I thought he was nice-looking."

It was the first kind word said about him, Chambers later remarked, in either trial.[24]

On Friday, January 20, at 3:10 P.M., the jury—eight women and four men—retired to begin deliberations. The trial had lasted nearly twice as long as the first, with almost double the testimony, more than one million words. They were still reviewing the testimony at ten forty-five, when Judge Goddard ordered them to a hotel for the night. It looked like another stalemate.

Chambers again paid little attention. He went about his chores on the farm, as before, and ignored the reporters camped outside his house.[25]

The following day, at 2:48 P.M., the jurors filed into the courtroom. Reporters, lounging in the corridor, did not expect a verdict—until they saw the looks on the jurors' faces. "There could be no mistaking the gravity of the moment," the *Times* reported.

The forewoman, Bronx widow Ada Condell, her voice almost a whisper, pronounced the defendant guilty on both charges. Alger Hiss had lied twice to the grand jury, first in saying he had not seen Chambers after January 1, 1937, second in saying he had not transmitted the spy papers to Chambers.

As the verdict was pronounced, Alger Hiss turned ashen. Then the color came back to his face, and the boyish smile, almost a grin, returned. Priscilla Hiss stared blankly ahead, her hands crossed in her lap. "Her only sign of emotion was a tiny convulsion at the throat," observed Thomas O'Neill of the *Baltimore Sun*.

Judge Goddard told the jurors they had rendered a just verdict and suggested they spare themselves "considerable embarrassment" by refusing to comment on the case, advice they all followed. Then he dismissed them.[26]

When the jury had left, Alger Hiss took his wife's hand. The couple then rose and exited the courtroom.

. . .

Chambers received the news by phone. Reporters watched him take the call. Clad in dungarees and khaki shirt, he delivered a brief statement, speaking without emotion. "I hope that the American people realize the debt of gratitude they owe to this jury, to Mr. Murphy, and to the tireless and splendid efforts of the FBI." They should also not overlook the efforts of "Congressman Nixon, who almost singlehanded forced the House Un-American Activities Committee to pursue the Hiss investigation." There had been, he added, "two points at issue: whether or not the scope of the Communist conspiracy could be revealed and made clear to the American people; whether or not the conspirators would manage to use the due process of law to defeat the attack on the conspiracy." This was "a tremendous victory for the democratic process and [a] correspondingly great setback for Communism."

Did Chambers have any comment on the testimony of Dr. Binger?

It spoke for itself. "The American people have enjoyed the fun."

What were his plans?

"I intend to stay right here doing general farming."

Would he testify in other cases?

No comment.

Would he speculate on the possible repercussions of the case?

No.

Reporters trailed him to the barn. Seating himself on a milking stool, Chambers summed up: "My work is finished."[27]

In personal terms Chambers judged the case a calamity and a waste. Nothing had been gained.[28]

This misery was duly noted in the press, which brooded on "the pathos and tragedy" of Hiss's downfall and on the "sorry picture" of "fine talents perverted, of promising careers wrecked, of prolonged mental suffering." The outcome was especially hurtful to Baltimoreans, mourned the *Sun*. The entire community was united in grief at the ruin of a native son "of such distinguished attainments and of such high promise."[29]

Chambers, who had ended a self-imposed news blackout with a binge of editorial reading, was appalled at the tone of the postmortems. He could understand the sympathy for the Hisses. He himself had been shaken by a news photograph of the defeated couple, and he lamented the bleak future awaiting eight-year-old Tony Hiss.[30]

But the editorial writers did not simply pity Hiss. They seemed to identify with him and to despise Chambers. "If you are a witness for the government, you are, of course, exempt from punishment," Eleanor Roosevelt wrote scornfully in her column. "If you had a bad conscience and wanted to be sure you would be safe, this seems to me an eminently wise way to gain security and peace of mind for the future."

"What were Mr. Chambers's motives?" wondered *The Christian Science Monitor*. "Why did he lie even to the grand jury that indicted Mr. Hiss?"[31]—this, after Chambers's motives had been made abundantly clear, stated time and again, in words no one could mistake.

No one seemed to acknowledge that he too was a casualty of the case, with an "incurable wound." Scarcely a word was written about Chambers's tribulations—the career he had lost; the manifold indignities he had withstood, the gossip, the strenuous defamations; the pain to his family. Instead he remained for many the monster conjured up by Lloyd Paul Stryker, "bland, dumpy, and devious," in one assessment.[32] In *Witness* Chambers wrote famously:

> No feature of the Hiss Case is more obvious, or more troubling as history, than the jagged fissure, which it did not so much open as reveal, between the plain men and women of the nation, and those who affected to act, think and speak for them. It was, not invariably, but in general, the "best people" who were for Alger Hiss and who were prepared to go to any length for him. It was the enlightened and the powerful, the clamorous proponents of the open mind and the common man, who snapped their minds shut in a pro-Hiss psychosis, of a kind which, in an individual patient, means the simple failure of the ability to distinguish between reality and unreality, and, in a nation, is a warning of the end.[33]

A curious disjunction still ruled the minds of America's liberal community. By and large its members now acknowledged the totalitarian reality of Stalin's Russia, supported the Marshall Plan, the Berlin airlift, the North Atlantic Pact—all the measures by which the United States, for better or worse, defined its opposition to an expansionist Soviet Union. Yet Hiss's sympathizers failed to grasp what had been occurring before their eyes.

This failure, suggested one shrewd analyst, the literary critic Leslie Fiedler, grew out of "the implicit dogma of American liberalism," which inflexibly assumed that in any political drama "the liberal *per se* is the hero." For Hiss's supporters to admit his guilt also meant admitting "that mere liberal principle is not in itself a guarantee against evil; that the wrongdoer is not always the other—'they' and not 'us'; that there is no magic in the words 'left' or 'progressive' or 'socialist' that can prevent deceit and abuse of power." The *Partisan Review*'s Philip Rahv, writing in 1952, interpreted this sentiment as "a symptom of the anguish of the Popular Front mind and its unreasoning anger at being made to confront the facts of political life." When faced with "the disorder and evil of history," the pro-Hiss faction "fought to save Hiss in order to safeguard its own illusions."[34]

Nothing, perhaps, captured the willed innocence of Hiss's defenders more succinctly than the testimony of Drs. Binger and Murray, emissaries from the hallowed realm of psychoanalysis, emerging in the postwar years as the new dogma of America's educated classes, replacing the Marxian myth embraced in the 1930s. The theory of unconscious motive registered this change. It debased legal, ethical, and political questions into purely psychological ones and redefined intended acts as irrepressible urges and aspects of personality.

There were many of course who simply thought the case against Hiss had not been clinched and for whom important evidentiary questions remained unanswered. But given the ten-year interval between the commission of the crime (the actual crime, espionage) and its investigation, a great quantity of evidence had been brought to bear. Every major question was met and answered. What sets the Hiss case apart, then and now, was not its mystery but the passionate belief of so many that Hiss must be innocent no matter what the evidence.

# 34

# *Eleven Words*

On January 25 Hiss returned to Foley Square for sentencing. Flanked by a pair of deputy marshals, Hiss reiterated his innocence. "I am confident that in the future the full facts of how Whittaker Chambers was able to carry out forgery by typewriter will be disclosed," he added cryptically.[1*]

Judge Goddard gave Hiss the maximum sentence, five years in a federal penitentiary for each of the two perjury counts, the two sentences to run concurrently. Hiss did not flinch. Priscilla too was calm, though in each eye a tear glistened.[3]

After the formalities of Hiss's bail had been worked out (the amount had been doubled to ten thousand dollars), the convicted perjuror—and de facto spy—left the courtroom with his wife. As many as a thousand onlookers had gathered at Foley Square. Hundreds stood on a traffic island, and hundreds more pressed against wooden police barriers that ran down the courthouse steps, forming a narrow defile. When the couple appeared at the top of the steps, a cry went up: "Here they come!" The Hisses descended between the barriers, heads held high, smiling.

At the sidewalk they met a mass of spectators, solid and unyielding. There was a pause, and then Priscilla pushed through. Alger followed, and the crowd fell back on either side. A lone voice muttered, "Hang the traitor." No one answered or took up the call. The only sounds were the clicking of heels on pavement and the clumsy jostling of photographers

---

* This statement became the basis of Hiss's appeal, filed in 1952, and was picked up by conspiracy theorists who argued that Hiss was the victim of a frame-up.[2] See p. 516ff.

as they scrambled ahead of the couple, snapping pictures. The Hisses briskly traversed the small park at Foley Square, past nude branches and desolate benches, everything gray, though palely lit by the winter sun, risen to its noon height. Onlookers, more curious than menacing, closed in behind as the couple quickened their pace and then ran toward a taxi stopped at the curb. The crowd surged forward, but not aggressively. A pedestrian walking past said, "Boo." Hiss ducked his head into the cab and slammed the door. The vehicle pulled away, melting into the stream of uptown traffic.[4]

That day Secretary of State Dean Acheson held his weekly press conference, his first since the verdict. Already congressional Republicans had taunted Acheson with the remarks he had made at his confirmation hearing, in January 1949, when he had said Hiss was his friend and "my friendship is not given lightly." Richard Nixon, back on the radio, with Bert Andrews again playing straight man, had offered some "advice" to Secretary Acheson: "He ought to be sure that he is not giving his friendship to our enemies." Others on the Hill demanded the secretary's resignation.[5]

All of political Washington awaited Acheson's reaction. "What would he say?" wondered *The New Republic*'s TRB, "the suave, elegant, fastidious Secretary with the Hiss millstone tied around his neck?" The spacious State Department auditorium normally reserved for press conferences was not available, so as many as two hundred reporters crowded into a small fifth-floor room. Acheson entered, an imposing six-footer with a bristling royal guardsman's mustache and luxurious brows. But beneath his Olympian reserve he looked tense. Uneasy themselves, the journalists lobbed a few routine questions before Homer Bigart, veteran reporter for the *Herald Tribune*, asked, "Have you any comment on the case of Alger Hiss?"

Acheson edged forward in his chair, straightening his back. He seemed to count silently to ten before he said, "I think it would be highly improper for me to discuss the legal aspects or the evidence or anything to do with the case." There was a pause. Then in the familiar, dryly ironic tone he added, "I take it the purpose of your question was to bring something other than that out of me." There was laughter.

But emotion flooded into his voice as he spoke the next words. "I should like to make it clear to you that whatever the outcome of any appeal which Mr. Hiss or his lawyer may make in this case, I do not intend to turn my back on Alger Hiss. I think every person who has known Alger Hiss or has served with him at any time has upon his conscience the very serious task of deciding what his attitude is and what his conduct should be. That must be done by each person in the light of his own standards and his own principles." For Acheson himself, the standards and principles were clear. They had been enunciated by Christ in the Sermon on the Mount. He then directed the reporters to "the 25th chapter of the Gospel according to St. Matthew beginning at verse 34."

There was dead silence; then the questions turned again to foreign policy. Later someone asked if Acheson could be quoted directly, waiving the normal rule, which permitted only paraphrases.

"As you choose," said Acheson, sounding weary.[6]

When the conference ended, there was a scramble to see the copy of the King James Bible held by a press aide, who later provided mimeographs. The marked passage read, in part, "For I was an hungred, and ye gave me meat: I was thirsty, and ye gave me drink: I was a stranger, and ye took me in: Naked, and ye clothed me; I was sick, and ye visited me; I was in prison, and ye came unto me."

Reporters phoned Acheson's remarks to Capitol Hill. Karl Mundt was holding the Senate floor, expostulating on Hiss's "impact and influence" on foreign policy, when he was interrupted by Joseph McCarthy of Wisconsin, an obscure junior legislator and one of those crying for Acheson's head. Brandishing a copy of Acheson's "most fantastic statement," McCarthy read it aloud. Did the secretary mean he would "not turn his back on other Communists who were associated with Hiss?" McCarthy asked. The American people "ought to begin to wonder what's going on." Indiana's Homer Capehart then stood up and declared himself "prouder than ever" of having opposed Acheson's nomination the year before. It all went to show, said Mundt, reclaiming the floor, that Hiss had a "peculiar capacity" for winning the trust of high officials. "There are still some who say that Hiss is a nice young man with a Harvard accent and a neat crease in the front of his pants," said Mundt. Now, however, the time had come for Congress "to measure up to our dimension as men."

"Before we appropriate money to the State Department," added New Hampshire's Styles Bridges, "we should see just how deep Mr. Hiss's influence ran—and if connections are still there."[7]

There was tumult as well in the House. Richard Nixon found Acheson's remarks "disgusting, and I believe the American people will think so too." Like so many others, Nixon conveniently ignored that Acheson had not disputed the jury's verdict. Eleven words—"I do not intend to turn my back on Alger Hiss" ("that awful phrase," in Acheson's later assessment)—had drowned out his moving expression of Christian sympathy. Acheson promptly went to the White House and offered his resignation. Truman would not hear of it. He was by now convinced Hiss, "the s.o.b. . . . is guilty as hell." But himself a loyalist, Truman esteemed loyalty in others.[8]

A month later, when passions had cooled, Acheson gave the Senate a full explanation of his statement. He had had no choice, he said, but to speak as he had done. He could not let "timidity and cowardice" dictate his actions. It was a question of "peace of mind" and "a matter of integrity of character."[9]

What he did not say was that for a year and a half he had been agonizing over the case, torn between his affection for Hiss and suspicions of his guilt. It had been on his mind "incessantly." Thus his actions had been marked by indecision and ambiguity. He had helped Hiss prepare his first HUAC statement but declined to appear as his attorney. He had called Hiss his friend but then refused to offer "an unqualified endorsement" of his character. He had quietly asked Attorney General Clark to be lenient with Hiss but had refused to testify at either trial. He had assured President Truman that Hiss was innocent but had discouraged the Alsops from campaigning for Hiss in their column.

Acheson's torment resembled Chambers's own. Like Chambers, he had been Hiss's friend and was pained by the spectacle of his ruin. Like Chambers, he had been guided by the God of mercy, rather than of retribution. Like Chambers, Acheson saw the case as "stark tragedy, whatever the reasonably probable facts may be."[10]

In his interview with Bert Andrews, Nixon had promised to release information implicating "certain high officials in two administrations" in a "deliberate effort . . . to keep the public from knowing the facts" about Hiss.[11]

On January 26, the day after Acheson's comments, Nixon made good on his promise—on the floor of Congress. In a four-hour oration entitled "The Hiss Case—A Lesson for the American People," he presented an array of evidence, including nuggets from documents the FBI had been feeding him since the beginning of the case. These featured a memo from the secret files of J. Edgar Hoover, which recorded that Igor Gouzenko had implicated Hiss as a Soviet agent as early as September 1945 and, further, that Hoover had passed this information on to Acheson.

President Truman had also seen the memo, in November 1945. "What was done," Nixon asked, "when this shocking information came to the officials of our State Department and the President of the United States? Mr. Hiss continued to serve in high places in the State Department." Then, when the truth came out, Truman "threw the great power and prestige of his office against the Hiss investigation." If not for the pumpkin microfilm, Hiss would have gone unpunished. Nixon then produced the eight-page memorandum, never before made public, that Harry Dexter White had given Chambers in 1938 for transmittal to Boris Bykov.

It was a powerful presentation. Once again Nixon had the goods: The FBI reports on Gouzenko were authentic, and handwriting experts had confirmed the memo was in White's hand. Nixon stopped short of accusing the administration of complicity in a Kremlin plot or of saying Hiss's treasons of a dozen years before were being perpetuated in 1950. But he left room for others to draw that inference. And they did. Long Island Republican W. Kingsland Macy, taking the floor after Nixon, declared that "Hiss lied, not to protect himself, but to protect others . . . still active in Russian espionage."[12]

But it was another Republican who seized upon the controversy in its full ripeness. On February 9, fifteen days after Hiss was sentenced and Acheson had uttered his "awful phrase," Joseph McCarthy, addressing the Ohio County Women's Republican Club of Wheeling, West Virginia, declared that as many as 205 known Communists "are still working and shaping the policy of the State Department."[13]

So began the most destructive chapter in modern American political life.

# EXILE

## *(1950–1961)*

*On the farm. Chambers's livestock included dairy cattle, beef cattle, and sheep.*

# 35

# *Public Recluse*

Though not yet fifty, Chambers suspected he had not many years remaining to him. The case had left him and Esther both feeling old. As he surveyed his shortened span, he found himself brooding on a pair of epitaphs Lord Byron, another exile, had copied in an Italian graveyard: *Implora eterna pace, implora eterna quiete.*[1] Peace and calm. His had been a life short on both.

These intimations of mortality were heightened by practical worries. His savings had dwindled, drained by the farm and by the wrongful death suit against Esther, settled out of court at a cost of several thousand dollars. He and Esther would come through it all intact. But what of Ellen and John? Born the children of an outlaw, they had become, in adolescence, the children of an outcast. They would be tainted forever by the Hiss case.

Like so many unconventional men, Chambers had conventional plans for his children, plans rather like Laha's for him so many years before. His daughter and son both must be groomed at elite, socially approved colleges. Ellen must marry well, John find a white-collar career, ideally at Time Inc. And their father's last atonement must be to make all this possible. He could manage it only by reclaiming his place in the greater world. It was 1938 all over again, without the desperation and with the difference that the nameless defector had since become one of the most famous men in America.[2]

He began to plot his return to the world of salaried journalism, the only profession he knew (outside revolutionary communism). Reclaim-

ing a place at *Time* looked out of the question, even with Hiss's conviction. But there were other options. In late January Chambers asked
Ralph de Toledano to "take some quick soundings" at *Newsweek*. He
was eyeing the foreign news editorship, though he expected *Newsweek*
would be "as frightened of me at this point as [is] *Time.*" He was right.
De Toledano's inquiries elicited more suspicion than interest.[3]

Then Chambers received an overture from an unexpected quarter.
Pierrepont Prentice, editor and publisher of *Architectural Forum,* a Time
Inc. stepchild, had strongly supported Chambers during the case. After
Hiss's conviction Prentice offered Chambers a position as either a full-
time editor or a part-time contributor, at a salary "somewhere between
$10,000 and $12,000 a year."

Writing "informative and somewhat practical reviews of new books
in the building and architectural field" was hardly Chambers's idea of a
triumphant return to journalism. But the regular salary—even if a sharp
decline from his *Time* income—was tempting. Also, Chambers reasoned
the offer could not have been made without Harry Luce's express approval.[4] Might Luce himself be planning to slip Chambers back into the
fortress through a side entrance?

Harry, as it happened, did want Chambers back on *Time* or *Life,* if not
as "an operational editor," then as a "special writer," occupying the position he had held when the case broke. Fully recovered from the shock
of Chambers's past sins, Luce now believed Chambers had "done more
for the country than anybody else in five years." In addition, Luce had
lost none of his admiration for Chambers's "poetry," and ideologically
the pair were more in step than ever. Luce's recent public pronouncements had acquired a distinctly Chambersian ring. "We are in very great
trouble today," he said in a speech at this time, "we and the whole of
mankind. The organized form of that trouble is easy to name. It is Soviet
Communism."[5]

The signs all pointed toward the exile's return. Luce tested the idea on
Matthews, recently elevated to the editorship of *Time* (Luce had kept the
sovereign title of editor in chief). Matthews was enthusiastic and in early
February traveled to Westminster to deliver the good news. Chambers was
elated. He and Matthews "worked out . . . in detail the nature of my new
employment," with Chambers set to go to New York to clinch the deal.[6]

But one detail had been left for last. Chambers could not simply be
deposited back on the twenty-ninth floor—appear one day at his desk,

in the familiar drab uniform, and start scratching out copy. His future colleagues must agree to have him back. Yet, even as Chambers made an appointment to seal the terms of his reemployment, Luce had kept the plan secret from company executives and senior staff. Only Matthews knew about it.

Finally, with Chambers's return unscheduled but imminent, Luce hastily conducted a poll. Emmet Hughes, a Luce favorite and the articles editor at *Life,* was among those summoned to the penthouse and asked, "How'd you like to have Whit Chambers back as a senior editor?" A moderate Republican, soon to write speeches for Dwight Eisenhower, Hughes was not an entrenched opponent of Chambers. But Luce's question stunned him. "It came right out of left field," Hughes later recalled. "It was quite a dreadful idea. Chambers had been dismissed from *Time,* perhaps wrongly, because he had . . . not been totally honest with the company. . . . No matter how the Hiss case was resolved, you'd have a terrible time explaining why you'd taken him back."[7]

Luce got the same answer from others. In fact the proposal met with "almost unanimous resistance." The trouble was not the Hiss verdict. By this time most were persuaded that Hiss "was guilty as hell," as one editor put it. But many still felt betrayed by Chambers's long-suppressed secrets. Hiss's conviction had changed none of that. Hundreds of readers had canceled subscriptions during the case. If Luce rehired Chambers, the penalty would be severe: a possible staff mutiny; merciless attacks from outside.[8]

Not a word was said to Chambers, who on the appointed day rode the train up to New York to meet with Luce. Hours before Chambers was due to arrive, the editor in chief decided to retract the offer, dumping the task on an "appalled" Matthews. When Chambers taxied up from Penn Station, Matthews intercepted him and delivered the news. "I did *not* go into the various reasons; it wasn't necessary," Matthews reported to Luce. "I also took the liberty of apologizing to him, in both our names."[9]

Chambers was crushed. Luce had lifted his hopes, only to dash them. On February 21 he at last heard directly from the editor in chief. Though he offered neither apology nor excuse, Luce hinted the matter was not yet settled. "I will not be satisfied that a right decision is made unless I have an opportunity to talk with you myself," Luce said—this after having ducked just such an opportunity. Nor was he in any hurry to seize it now. Luce's letter was sent as he prepared to board a train to the South for a monthlong vacation.[10]

Chambers waited until Luce returned before writing to him. A meeting with his former boss, Chambers explained, would only "turn the knife in the wound." He remained grateful to Luce but vowed never to see him again.[11]

It was just as well. Chambers had outgrown *Time*. He had made too much history to melt back into the ranks of its anonymous recorders. There was an opportunity for him, greater than any presented hitherto, to address the public in his own voice. He had been approached more than once by book and magazine editors: Richard Crossman, *Partisan Review*'s William Phillips, and a new editor at Random House, David McDowell, who with his friend Jim Agee had been encouraging Chambers to write a memoir.[12]

One wintry day in late March, Chambers sat down to write the first pages of a book. He envisioned a compact volume, combining memoir and polemic. It would seek to answer the question dramatized by the Hiss case: why "men become Communists, why they continue to be Communists and why some break and some go on." If he succeeded, he could perhaps help illuminate "the tragedy of man in the 20th century."[13]

In April Chambers delivered two chapters of a manuscript to Carl and Carol Brandt, literary agents in midtown Manhattan. The couple, divided over the case—Carl was pro-Chambers, Carol pro-Hiss—"fought fairly fiercely about whether the office should represent him."[14] Carl Brandt prevailed, and a third agent at the firm, Bernice Baumgarten, the wife of novelist James Gould Cozzens, began negotiations with publishers.

Chambers preferred a major house, preferably one with a liberal reputation, to a conservative publisher, such as Henry Regnery Co., Devin-Adair, or Duell, Sloan, and Pearce. He did not want his book ghettoized. Baumgarten showed the chapters first to Ken McCormick, the highly respected editor in chief of Doubleday. McCormick recognized the submission was a "honey," a guaranteed best-seller. But he was also pro-Hiss and convinced Chambers was "on the wrong side, a bad guy." He turned the book down.[15]

But David McDowell of Random House, a conservative, had no such qualms. And the pages he read impressed him enormously. The only obstacle was Random House's publisher, Bennett Cerf. As far as Cerf was concerned, "Hiss was still the hero and Chambers the villain." Rather than try to argue Chambers's case, McDowell surprised the publisher one day by inviting Chambers to Random House's offices. While Chambers sat in the anteroom, McDowell casually informed Cerf that the villain was waiting outside "to talk about a book."

"Get him out of here," said Cerf.

A fine liberal Cerf was, McDowell countered, if he closed his mind to a writer just because he disliked him. Ashamed, Cerf invited Chambers in to talk. Within minutes the two Columbia men (Cerf was class of 1919) were chatting about friends they had in common, such as Clifton Fadiman, Hearst columnist George Sokolsky, and the anti-Communist screenwriter Morrie Ryskind. Though "still a little hostile," Cerf took Chambers's two chapters home to read and was as impressed as McDowell. Before making up his mind, however, the publisher consulted three writers he respected, all prominent liberals: Robert Sherwood, Moss Hart, and Laura Hobson (recently divorced from Thayer Hobson, Priscilla Hiss's first husband). "Every one of them said it was so well written that I had to publish it and let readers judge for themselves," Cerf later said. Random House would publish the book.[16]

In April Baumgarten negotiated a contract, with an advance of fifteen thousand dollars, half payable upon signing. It was a large figure, generous enough to ease Chambers's immediate financial worries. The firm anticipated a best-seller. *Seeds of Treason,* Ralph de Toledano's account of the case (co-written with Victor Lasky), was one of the hits of the spring, going into a third printing within two weeks of its release in late March. And Alistair Cooke's *Generation on Trial,* based on his brilliant *Manchester Guardian* columns, was due out soon. Cerf's partner, Donald Klopfer, initially proposed a deadline of July 1, giving Chambers less than three months to complete a manuscript of eighty-five thousand words, roughly 340 pages. Baumgarten, more realistic, amended the date to September 1, still quick work for a writer as deliberate as Chambers.[17]

At the same time Carl Brandt showed Chambers's completed chapters to *Life* for possible serialization. The text editor, Emmet Hughes, disliked the pages, which described the first days of the Hiss case, but others were excited, especially Luce, who suggested "the logical place" to publish an excerpt was not *Life* but *Time.* It was a bold idea. No book excerpt had ever been serialized in the newsmagazine. Chambers, though intrigued, was still smarting from the rejection Luce had dealt him only two months before. Also, he had heard through the grapevine that Emmet Hughes had found his manuscript "too messianic."[18]

Meanwhile Luce had overshot the deadline set by Brandt, and the agent had already shown the pages to *The Saturday Evening Post,* which promptly made a large bid. *Time* too declared its interest. With two large magazines vying for the manuscript, Brandt held an auction. Chambers traveled to the Brandts' Park Avenue office the day the bids were due, in May. Carl Brandt fielded the calls. James Linen phoned in *Time*'s offer, a substantial thirty thousand dollars. Chambers rejected it. Luce, his competitive instincts aroused, huddled with Linen, Roy Larsen, and Tom Matthews. After an hour Linen phoned Brandt, doubling the initial offer. Matthews asked to speak with Chambers directly but was deflected by Brandt's secretary, who said Chambers had already left the office.

Three hours went by before Brandt passed along a final rejection, adding that Chambers—he had been on the premises the entire time— had called off the bidding. *The Saturday Evening Post* had won. Had money been the deciding issue? Linen asked Brandt. "No," the agent tersely replied. He would not elaborate. Luce and Matthews tried one last time to speak with Chambers, but this time he really had left, to catch an afternoon train to Baltimore.[19]

Luce was puzzled and hurt. Others at Time Inc. were not. "He'd done a cruel and insensitive thing to Whit Chambers," Hughes later said, "and he couldn't understand that Chambers was giving it back." But as Luce pardoned himself, so he pardoned others. Shortly after losing the bid, Luce praised Chambers glowingly in a speech to Time Inc. executives at the Waldorf. Learning of the remarks, Chambers was moved to break his silence, sending Luce a letter. "If you really wanted my book, I am sorry that you did not get it." It had been Chambers's impression, he added, that Luce alone had been eager to serialize his manuscript.

Luce assured Chambers he had misread the situation. Five of six *Time* executives had favored the serialization. "Never in my recollection did such a radical idea get such a large measure of instant approval." But there were no hard feelings. The incident "is quite happily closed for me," said Luce. "I believe, as we all hope, that your book will be a great success and a source of enlightenment to many."[20]

If Chambers regretted his decision, he never said so. Besides, he had not acted solely out of pride. *The Saturday Evening Post*'s bid was a staggering seventy-five thousand dollars.[21]

.   .   .

Cheered by his windfall, Chambers wrote diligently. His daily schedule, and his family's, were as arduous as ever. He and Esther awoke each morning before dawn and went to the barn for the first milking. Chambers hefted the milk cans—when filled, each weighed one hundred pounds—into a cooler and then drove them out to the road for the morning pickup. Back at the house Ellen and John fixed their own breakfasts, packed lunches, and then walked down the road to await the school bus. By this time Esther and Whittaker, finished in the barn, sat down to their morning meal. Shortly before eight o'clock Chambers traipsed the quarter mile to his second farmhouse, Medfield, where Esther had set up a writing room, in the basement. Lighting an oil heater for warmth, he sat down to work. He wrote steadily and without interruption, breaking for lunch, and then returned to his desk for an afternoon session. At 4:00 P.M. Esther or Ellen picked him up in the car and drove him back to the house. He and the children then saw to the afternoon milking while Esther cooked supper. After the meal, if Ellen and John did not have 4-H meetings, the family might gather around the phonograph for an hour or two of music, Beethoven or Mahler. Many evenings they all were too fatigued and, after rising from the table and stacking the dishes, stumbled upstairs and to bed.[22]

The chastening asceticism of this routine appealed to Chambers. He began to think of himself as a latter-day monk and developed a fascination with the roots of Western monasticism. His only regret was that for the second consecutive year he had missed out on his favorite farm chore, sowing the spring crops. He contented himself with the vicarious pleasure of hearing John ride by on the tractor to join Stanley Pennington in the fields for his first planting.[23]

Solitary as his routine was, Chambers made time for guests—Richard Nixon, Ralph de Toledano, Tom Matthews, Sam Welles, Fred Gruin, Craig Thompson—and often saw Time Inc. chums living in the area. Duncan Norton-Taylor, a National Affairs writer who had moved over to *Fortune,* had a home on Maryland's Eastern Shore. And Tom Hyland, who had written Religion under Chambers, had quit the magazine and bought a house not far from Chambers's. Hyland had begun an entrepreneurial career that soon made him a millionaire several times over.

Chambers preferred seeing friends singly, so he could give more of his attention to each and also slip into deep and comfortable conversation. He and his guest sat in the living room before a fire or, weather permitting, retired to the porch, with its sweeping views. Chambers did not drink but kept a supply on hand for those who did. "Whenever I came there was always a bottle of whiskey for me," Tom Matthews recalled. "Esther was a good cook, and those farm meals were feasts. In his own house, Chambers was not the sardonic, warily silent character he seemed outside, but hospitable, relaxed, almost talkative. He and I would settle ourselves in a quiet room for a lengthy discussion that might start with the situation at *Time* but always ended with the situation of the world and the human condition."

Still convinced he had left the winning side for the losing one, Chambers foretold a global Communist victory. Gloomy as his predictions sounded, he was not devoid of hope. The West was honor-bound, he believed, to meet the Soviet challenge, which he saw as primarily moral and religious, rather than military, though he favored the emerging foreign policy of halting Communist expansion wherever it occurred. "He somehow didn't get me *down*," said Matthews of his talks with Chambers. "I invariably went away from these occasions with head and heart high, like a true believer after a brisk rubdown with a hellfire-and-damnation sermon who walks out of church feeling fighting fit and ready for Monday."[24]

Chambers missed the company of other friends. Jim Agee had left *Time* to begin a new career as an "alcoholic screenwriter" in California. He reported his adventures in long, lyric letters. Bob Cantwell had also disappeared from the scene. At his wife's insistence, he had undergone psychiatric treatment and had emerged "better adjusted"—that is, unwilling to socialize with his former friends. Even sadder, in March 1950, while on assignment in Atlantic City, Calvin Fixx suffered a second heart attack. This one was fatal. Fixx was only forty-three. The loss to Chambers was great. Fixx, both soul mate and confidant, had traveled a path similar to Chambers's own, from radicalism to conservative Christianity. Chambers took John with him to the funeral in New York.[25]

By the end of May a third of Chambers's manuscript, titled *Witness,* had been written. Klopfer, still avid for an early publication date, suggested the pages be fed to the typesetter as they came in—if Chambers could promise the manuscript would be completed by July 1.[26]

Chambers had not ruled out a July deadline,[27] but he made no strenuous effort to meet it. Instead he awarded himself a short break in late June and invited the de Toledano family—Ralph, his wife, Nora, and their two small sons—to spend a couple of weeks on the farm.

Both husband and wife had been mainstays during the trials. Ralph was in the courthouse each day for *Newsweek*. Nora had reported on the trial for the *New Leader*. After hard days on the witness stand Chambers had repaired to the couple's Central Park West apartment for a meal and conversation. He found common ground with Ralph, who was something of an outsider himself—an American born in Tangier, the son of a foreign correspondent, and raised on tales of his Sephardic ancestors and their heroic exploits. A student socialist at Columbia, in the 1930s, de Toledano had studied with Mark Van Doren as well as with Lionel Trilling and Jacques Barzun. His undergraduate friends had included Thomas Merton, the Trappist monk whose spiritual autobiography, *The Seven Storey Mountain,* published in 1948, was similar in some respects to the manuscript Chambers was writing. Before joining *Newsweek,* de Toledano, fiercely anti-Communist after the 1939 pact, had been on the staff of the *New Leader* and then *Plain Talk*. During the Hiss case he severed his remaining ties to the left, quitting the New York State Liberal Party in disgust at the uncandid testimony of Adolf Berle. De Toledano was among the first of a younger generation of intellectuals who saw Chambers as a towering moral figure.

The discussions between the two had formed the foundation of *Seeds of Treason,* an unashamedly partisan account of the case. Chambers did not read past the eight-page preface but was delighted by the impact the book was having, as measured by its strong sales and by the reactions of the "plain people" he talked to in Westminster and neighboring towns.[28]

At Pipe Creek Farm the de Toledanos stayed at the back farm, a mile from the main house, under primitive conditions. "The pigs were kept near the house, and when the wind shifted, we got the full aroma," Ralph later recalled. "The road to the house could be all mud, and our rented car stuck." Wasps flew through gaping holes in the kitchen wall.[29]

Chambers, on holiday from his manuscript, threw himself into farm chores and invited de Toledano to help. Working alongside his host, pitching bales of hay into a truck, the thirty-four-year-old de Toledano felt his "muscles and back at the breaking point," while Chambers, aged fifty and immensely overweight, "moved effortlessly and serenely in the boiling afternoon sun," easily hoisting the heavy bales. In the barn Chambers positioned de Toledano in the hayloft and had him stack the bales as Chambers tossed them up. "When I lagged behind I got a fore-shortened view of him down below, patiently holding up a bale of hay at the end of a pitchfork with one powerful arm while I struggled to catch up." When the cows entered the barn for milking, Chambers greeted each by name and gave it an affectionate swat on the rump.[30]

The most rewarding moments came in the evening, when Chambers invited de Toledano to join him on the porch to talk. In the growing darkness, to the background music of birdsong, Chambers ranged expansively over the themes of *Witness,* lingering on historical touchstones: Cromwell; the French Revolution; Kronshtadt; the atrocities committed in "the cellars of the Lubyanka." He evoked these events as if they were current events, segments in a continuous unspooling newsreel. To de Toledano, Chambers "*was* history."[31]

It was a good time for perspectivizing. History in its present tense seemed to be moving once more toward a climax. On June 25 the Communist army of North Korea crossed the thirty-eighth-parallel divide and invaded South Korea, weakly governed by Syngman Rhee, a corrupt American client. President Truman and Dean Acheson accurately glimpsed Stalin's hand in the invasion and detected an "extensive Soviet-Sino thrust" to come. They instantly authorized shipments of aid to South Korea and then cleared the way, through the United Nations, for General Douglas MacArthur to lead American forces into battle. Truman also stationed the Seventh Fleet at the Strait of Formosa, lest Mao Zedong attempt his long-planned assault on Chiang's exiled dictatorship in Taiwan. To Chambers, as to many others, the Korean campaign was the first in "the final struggle" against world communism.[32]

In early July Chambers returned to his manuscript. The book had changed. It was becoming a full-scale autobiography, long and complex. A compulsive rewriter, Chambers struggled to extract the full range of meaning from every incident he set down, even as he labored to give the book the simplicity of a parable in the hope "anybody at all could understand it, from beginning to end."

For inspiration Chambers turned to the masters of autobiography: St. Augustine, Rousseau, Henry Adams. *Witness* was to owe something to each, as well as to other giants. From Dante, Chambers borrowed the narrative theme of hellish descent: the moral chaos of 228 Earle Avenue, followed by the free fall down the tiered walls of communism, modernity's hell. From Dostoevsky, whom he was reading "constantly"—especially *The Possessed* and the fictionalized prison memoir *The House of the*

*Dead*—Chambers derived the guiding doctrine he had first expounded at *Time*—namely, that the "conflict which has taken form in this age [is] the struggle between Christianity and Communism." September 1 came and passed, with the manuscript still far from completed and Random House resigned to a long wait.[33]

Chambers was also performing, again, the role of ex–Communist informer. Along with Elizabeth Bentley and Louis Budenz, he had become one of the government's "kept witnesses," as the journalist Richard Rovere called them. In the spring and summer of 1950 the FBI questioned Chambers about atomic spy suspects Harry Gold and Julius Rosenberg. Chambers had not known either man. His days in the underground predated the atomic era.[34]

Chambers also lent his expertise to congressional investigations, joining the long list of veteran anti-Communists who advised Senator Joseph R. McCarthy during the first years of his clamorous crusade against the "egg-sucking phony liberals," the "Communists and queers" who in "twenty years of treason" had sold out America to the Kremlin.[35]

Chambers and McCarthy first met in January 1950, through Richard Nixon. But a relationship did not develop until the spring, when the theme of Communists in government emerged as one likely to dominate the November off-year elections. In an effort to minimize the damage, Senate Democrats formed a committee, chaired by Maryland's Millard Tydings, to investigate McCarthy's allegations of ongoing disloyalty in the State Department. The minority counsel was Robert Morris, a former navy intelligence officer who had interviewed Chambers repeatedly during the war. Morris's first step was to visit Westminster to confer with Chambers.

At the outset Tydings dared McCarthy to produce evidence supporting his scattershot accusations. McCarthy replied by raising the stakes, denouncing China expert Owen Lattimore, a journalist and Johns Hopkins professor, as "the top Russian espionage agent in the United States, the boss of Alger Hiss."[36] It was a wild charge, like so many others to come, and McCarthy was forced to retract it.

Up to that point there had been nothing exceptional about McCarthy. He had seemed simply the hardest-edged and most aggressive of the many Republicans crying treason in the aftermath of the Hiss case. But the Lattimore episode indicated a new recklessness, at least to some, such as Herb Solow, who early warned Chambers against joining the McCarthy crusade.

Chambers scoffed. Everyone named by McCarthy was working for the Communists, as far as he was concerned. And who were McCarthy's critics? The same crowd who "wept" at Hiss's conviction. As for Lattimore, he might not be a spy or even a Communist, but his record was suspect. He had been prominently involved with the Institute of Pacific Relations (IPR), which published *Amerasia* (in whose pages Lattimore condoned the Moscow trials). He also boasted friendships with the Communist Frederick Vanderbilt Field and Chambers's *Time* adversary Richard Lauterbach. In sum, Lattimore appeared to be an "agent" in spirit if not in fact. Chambers was pleased when the informer Louis Budenz, onetime editor of the *Daily Worker,* came forward to say Lattimore had belonged to a Party cell. Budenz was unable to back the claim. But Chambers didn't care. Budenz had set the anti-McCarthy forces on their heels.[37]

Chambers was agreeable when Robert Morris asked if he could take McCarthy up to Westminster for a talk. The visit was a success. McCarthy was not yet the morose figure he was to become. At age forty-one, bluff and burly—he had been a college boxer—McCarthy had an open, engaging manner and a raffish charm. He made no secret of his awe for Chambers, and Chambers was always available for adulation. Soon McCarthy and his assistant Jean Kerr (later his wife) were making unescorted pilgrimages. Chambers delivered his standard, if dated, lectures on the Communist apparatus while McCarthy listened "in awe" and Kerr took notes.[38]

These were not edifying tutorials from any perspective. McCarthy had little in common with Chambers's first congressional pupil, Richard Nixon. Nixon had really tried to educate himself in the subject. In his first days in Congress he and Charles Kersten had made a laborious circuit of the embassies of the Soviet Union and its satellites, "asking officials whether there was a free press, or free speech, in each country." A voracious reader, Nixon asked Chambers to recommend books to him—not only on communism but on history at large—and soon was speaking confidently of "the Bakunist-Nechaevist theory of revolution" and "a Messianic *mystique* [found] in the novels of Dostoevsky."[39] But McCarthy moved in a world of blissful ignorance. He knew nothing about communism as an ideology, a movement, or a party.

Nor was Chambers the ideal preceptor. He had no concrete knowledge of State Department Communists in 1950—or of any untoward activities postdating 1938. But then, neither did anyone else. McCarthy's five-year rampage failed to produce a single certifiable Red. To the senator—and many of his followers—it scarcely mattered, as long as there remained a sufficient supply of liberals to smear. That was all right with Chambers too. Soon he was holding up McCarthy as an example to the more cautious Nixon of a fearless anti-Communist fighter unafraid to "go forward" and state the anti-Communist case in the bold terms the issue required.[40]

Chambers was not alone in his early enthusiasm for McCarthy. After the Wheeling speech many veteran anti-Communists flocked to Joe's cause, volunteering leads, advice, strategy, encouragement. It was the same group that had backed Chambers during the Hiss case: Willard Edwards and Walter Trohan of the *Chicago Tribune;* the Hearst cadre of George Sokolsky, Westbrook Pegler, Howard Rushmore, and J. B. Matthews; the *New York World-Telegram's* Frederick Woltman; Ed Nellor, who had moved to the *Washington Times-Herald.* They were joined by Charles Kersten, Nixon's onetime adviser, ejected from his House seat by Wisconsin voters, and by China Lobbyist and *Plain Talk* publisher Alfred Kohlberg. And as late as 1952, such distinguished intellectuals as Lionel Trilling, Daniel Bell, and Irving Kristol—leading members of the American Committee for Cultural Freedom (ACCF), an organization of liberal anti-Communists— declined to issue a "general condemnation" of McCarthy, preferring instead to challenge him on specific cases, such as McCarthy's attack on Edmund Wilson's "pro-Communist" *Memoirs of Hecate County.*[41]

Never a camp follower, Chambers did not publicly align himself with McCarthy. But he kept private company with the senator and occasionally joined McCarthyites in public demonstrations of support. In September 1950 Chambers shared a podium with Kohlberg at the Statler Hilton, in Washington, D.C., and lashed out at "the big people, the nice people," who had run "hysterically" to Hiss's side during the case and were clinging to him still. These enemies were "neither all Democrats nor all Republicans," said Chambers, in a show of nonpartisanship. Rather they "formed an exclusive party—the party of betrayal. In the future they will be the party of appeasement."[42]

But Chambers did have a partisan rooting interest and was delighted with the election results in November. The Republicans gained seats in both houses, shaving the Democratic majority in the Senate from twelve to two and in the House from seventeen to twelve. A conspicuous winner was Richard Nixon, elected to the Senate by a large margin after an ugly Red-baiting campaign against Congresswoman Helen Gahagan Douglas. Chambers sent his friend a congratulatory letter. It was a great day for Nixon and "for the nation."[43]

The Hiss case had contributed to the Republican gains. So did McCarthy. Democrats had hoped he would be quieted, if not silenced, by Truman's strong actions in Korea. But the opposite had happened. McCarthy branded the war a "death trap" into which the United States had been lured by the Kremlin's State Department agents, who had prepared the way by first handing China over to the Communists, thus leaving all Asia exposed, just as Chiang Kai-shek had warned. The charge of treason resonated powerfully for a public frightened by world communism but reluctant to wage war or even disburse large sums in foreign aid. McCarthy's promise of a housecleaning at the State Department seemed a painless cure.

The election also showed how potent a force McCarthy himself had become. He engineered the defeat of his archenemy Millard Tydings, barnstorming Maryland on behalf of Tydings's Republican opponent, John Marshall Butler. McCarthy's tactics included distributing a faked composite photograph of Tydings, a war hero and anti-Communist, and Earl Browder.[44]

If Chambers was disturbed by these tactics, he did not say so. Close himself to the anti-Tydings forces, he subleased one of his properties to the local organizer of "Democrats for Butler," who planned to use the house "as an atomb bomb refuge for his seven granddaughters."[45] Publicly Chambers remained silent on McCarthy but continued to advise him. When the Senate launched an inquiry into McCarthy's role in the Tydings campaign, Chambers was worried.[46] He did his part to keep the crusade alive by testifying before the Senate Subcommittee on Internal Security (SSIS), which, under its McCarthyite chairman, Democrat Pat McCarran of Nevada, had rehabilitated the investigation of the Lattimore case and the IPR's role in "losing" China. In a secret hearing, at which Elizabeth Bentley and Paul Massing, Hede's husband, also appeared, Chambers named Joseph Barnes, a prominent journalist and an official with the Office of War Information (OWI), as an underground Communist, reviving a charge he had made as early as 1940, in an interview with the Civil Service Commission, and then had repeated to the FBI in 1942. But Chambers had never made the allegation publicly—for the sound reason that he had not worked with Barnes or even met the man. In an open session of the McCarran Committee, Chambers was asked to explain how he knew Barnes was a Communist. He could only reply: "J. Peters told me." This left him vulnerable to Barnes's prompt retort that Chambers was simply another of the "disreputable Communists and former Communists" whose pleasure it was to purvey "slanderous hearsay."[47]

In its final report the McCarran Committee rehabilitated McCarthy's charge of State Department treason and characterized Lattimore, in particular, as "a conscious, articulate instrument of the Soviet conspiracy." And McCarthy, unpunished for his role in the Tydings campaign, soon was back on the warpath, repeatedly invoking Joseph Barnes as one of the subversives who plotted with Owen Lattimore to hand China over to Moscow.[48]

At the same time Chambers was involved in an even more dubious Red-hunting spectacle, this time at his own instigation. The target was Asia expert O. Edmund Clubb, who had been placed in charge of the State Department's China desk in July 1950. A career Foreign Service officer, Clubb had been the last American diplomat stationed in China. When Chiang fell, Clubb had closed the Beijing consulate and evacuated its personnel.[49]

In the spring of 1950, shortly after Clubb's return from China, Chambers had come across the diplomat's name in the *Hanover* (Pennsylvania) *Sun,* the local paper he read, and had promptly contacted the FBI, telling the bureau he had encountered Clubb at *The New Masses'* office in 1932, just before Chambers had gone underground. One day, Chambers related, while on temporary leave from China, Clubb—or "Chubb," as Chambers remembered his name—had come to the office and "delivered a message to me, in the form of a letter" addressed to Grace Hutchins. To Chambers, reflecting on the incident twenty years later, it was obvious Clubb had been using the future underground recruit as a letter drop. This explained Clubb's "nervousness" upon finding Chambers, a stranger, in place of Chambers's predecessor, Walt Carmon. It was Chambers's only meeting with Clubb. "However," he told the FBI, "that incident made a lasting impression on me as it was my first real contact with the Communist underground."[50]

On the basis of Chambers's report, Clubb was suspended from the China desk while a security probe began. It lasted two years. During that time Clubb was grilled by a loyalty board, the FBI, and HUAC. In early interviews the diplomat failed to remember the incident Chambers described. But then British authorities found Clubb's diary in Beijing and passed along a summary of its contents to American security officers. An entry dated July 9, 1932, described the visit to *The New Masses* and Clubb's conversation with Chambers.[51]

Soon made public, it indicated nothing sinister in the meeting between Chambers and Clubb. The Asia hand had gone to *The New Masses'* offices to discuss China with Walt Carmon and been surprised to find Chambers there instead. The "sealed envelope" was an innocent letter of introduction, provided by Agnes Smedley, the Communist journalist. Smedley, as it happened, had done underground work. But there was no evidence Clubb knew anything about it.

While at the magazine's offices, Clubb had spoken with a few staff members, including "the successor to Walt Carmon, one Whittaker-Chambers [*sic*], a shifty-eyed unkempt creature who nevertheless showed considerable force and direction in asking me about the Red movement in China. In turn, I asked him of conditions in the United States, but we didn't talk smoothly. I was, after all, out of my bailiwick, masquerading under somewhat false pretenses, so that I felt too much like a stranger to show the proper 'revolutionary enthusiasm.' "[52]

Had Clubb tried to conceal this meeting, or had he simply forgotten about it after nineteen years? In a HUAC appearance Clubb pointed out no true Communist would have put quotes around the phrase *revolutionary enthusiasm*. Chambers, testifying before SSIS shortly before Clubb's diary surfaced, had already slid away from his emphatic FBI statement, saying it had been his "impression" that Clubb had been an underground messenger in 1932. Pressed to offer further details, Chambers declined, explaining "there are areas in my experiences, where I can no longer distinguish between what I once knew and what I learned in testimony."[53]

Yet this was enough for Clubb to be branded a security risk. He appealed the verdict, was upheld, and returned in February 1952 to State, where he was transferred to a research desk but given no specific assignment. Five days later he quit, finished as a diplomat.[54] Such was the cost of having once discussed Chinese Communists with *The New Masses'* editor Whittaker Chambers.

# 36

# Witness

In the spring of 1951, a year into *Witness,* Chambers intensified his writing schedule. He sat down to his task at 8:00 A.M., as before, but wrote as many as twelve hours a day, breaking only for lunch and skipping the afternoon barn work. He entertained fewer visitors and was slow to reply to letters.[1]

For the first time it was disadvantageous to be working in the monastic solitude of Westminster. He had begun his account of the Hiss case and had no documents at hand. Help came from loyal *Time* researchers, who sent along material from their capacious files. Ralph de Toledano provided a similar service at *Newsweek,* stealing many hours from his own work. And Nora de Toledano ransacked bookstores and libraries in search of obscure Latin tags and other arcana.[2]

Chambers's immediate goal was to complete his revisions of the early sections and show them to his primary readers, Tom Matthews and Ralph de Toledano. On May 1 Matthews was to depart for five weeks in England, and Chambers wanted his reaction before he left. In mid-April, when de Toledano made a brief detour to Westminster while on business in Washington, Chambers entrusted him with a large portion of manuscript.

Reading the pages on the train to New York, de Toledano wept over Chambers's foreword, "A Letter to My Children," which included Chambers's apology for writing so personal a testament:

My children, as long as you live, the shadow of the Hiss Case will brush you. In every pair of eyes that rests on you, you will see pass, like a cloud passing behind a woods in winter, the memory of your father—dissembled in friendly eyes, lurking in unfriendly ones. Sometimes you will wonder which is harder to bear: friendly forgiveness or forthright hate. In time, therefore, when the sum of your experience of life gives you authority, you will ask yourselves the question: What was my father?

Matthews too found the foreword "very moving." The entire manuscript was "excellently well written, and I could hope for at least as much again as I've seen." The editor passed along chapter 19, on *Time*—"very generous, Whit!"—to Luce.[3]

By June 15 Chambers had completed ten of the book's twelve sections, was partway through the eleventh, and hoped to be finished in two months, barring major distractions.[4]

But again he was ready for a break. After eighteen months he was beginning to loathe his manuscript, and was pleased when he received a surprising offer, in late July, from Matthews, asking Chambers to write a cover story for *Time* on Graham Greene, "pegged on" Greene's latest novel, *The End of the Affair.* It was a shrewd choice of assignment. Chambers's last *Time* piece, published in August 1948, had been on Greene's *The Heart of the Matter.* "I nearly forgot," Matthews added in a postscript. "There'd be some pay involved—$2,000." It was a titanic fee, enough to cover tuition and expenses at Smith, which had accepted Ellen for the fall.[5]

Chambers quickly agreed to the project. He had until October to complete it. But after a few weeks he realized he had made a mistake. Sick as he was of *Witness,* its claim on his attention was complete. After a month Chambers sheepishly told Matthews it wasn't going to work. Not to worry, said Matthews. They could find someone else to do the piece, if not so well. "I certainly never intended to get in the way of your completing your book."[6]

With the end in sight, Chambers began pushing harder. Taking off a weekend to drive Ellen up to college, in Northampton, Massachusetts, Chambers made the return trip with hardly a break and when he reached Westminster, at 4:00 A.M., he went straight to his desk, rather than to bed, and wrote the entire day, although cramped and aching from the drive.[7]

In October Chambers sent most of the manuscript to Random House. David McDowell was ecstatic. "It *is* really a wonderful book," he told the author, "even better than I had ever expected. I am also quite convinced that it will do well"—commercially, he meant. McDowell, who doubled as Random House's publicity director, promised a strenuous campaign "to see that [*Witness*] gets the hearing it deserves."[8]

In November, "under great editorial pressure," Chambers completed *Witness*. It had taken him twenty months, sixteen more than planned. And the manuscript was four times its original projected size—some 340,000 words, nearly fourteen hundred pages in typescript.[9]

Random House scheduled a spring release. The first omen of success was *Witness*'s purchase by the Book-of-the-Month Club as the main selection for June 1952.* This guaranteed substantial sales—and profits. Esther was thrilled. John sternly reminded them they were all still farmers with a flock of sheep to tend. Whittaker agreed. But he went to Baltimore and bought a new suit.[11]

Soon the euphoria subsided, as Chambers steeled himself for "the active struggle which my book must precipitate on all sides." The first test would be the serialization in *The Saturday Evening Post,* the most important series the *Post* "has carried in my ten years," said the magazine's editor, Ben Hibbs, who had taken out full-page advertisements in daily newspapers. In February, Chambers went to Manhattan to correct proofs and make promotional appearances. He stayed a month, booking a room at the Berkshire Hotel, across the street from Random House's Madison Avenue offices, so he could read galleys and micromanage his book's "editorial presentation." He wanted to avoid the fate met by Elizabeth Bentley, whose ghostwritten memoirs, disastrously titled *Out of Bondage,* had met with derision when excerpted in *McCall's*. The author was still serving penance for the epithet "beautiful blond spy queen" inflicted on her by the *World-Telegram*. Chambers sympathized, though "I don't see quite why she had to cooperate by way of obliging photos." For his own part, Chambers wielded his many journalistic contacts in the hope of getting friendly reviewers assigned to *Witness*.[12]

On February 9, 1952, the first installment of Chambers's book appeared in the *Post,* under the title "I Was the Witness." For the first time in its fifty-three-year history, the *Post* dispensed with a cover illustration

---

* The BOMC editorial board included Clifton Fadiman. The other judges were Henry Seidel Canby (chairman), Amy Loveman, John P. Marquand (who wrote the "Report" for readers), and Christopher Morley.[10]

(postponing a Norman Rockwell illustration of leaping cheerleaders) and ran instead a stark announcement, in red and black type: "One of the Great Books of our Time: Whittaker Chambers' own story of the Hiss Case." An extra hundred thousand copies of the magazine were printed and sent to newsstands a day early. The ten installments, totaling forty thousand words—more than 20 percent of *Witness*'s text—were more than the *Post* had ever previously run.[13]

On Sunday evening, February 10, Chambers went to the NBC radio studio at Rockefeller Center and read for twenty minutes over a nationwide hookup. The performance aired at nine-thirty. He repeated the performance the following night on television. His text was his foreword. "Beloved Children," he began, in the familiar flat voice,

> I am sitting in the kitchen of the little house at Medfield, our second farm which is cut off by the ridge and a quarter-mile across the fields from our home place, where you are. I am writing a book. In it, I am speaking to you. But I am also speaking to the world. To both of you I owe an accounting.
>
> My accounting is a terrible book which I am writing for the American people. It is terrible in what it tells about men. If anything, it is more terrible in what it tells about the world in which you live. It is about what the world calls the Hiss-Chambers Case, or even more simply, the Hiss Case. It is about a spy case.[14]

The cadences were as simple as those in a children's book. But they grew more complex as Chambers introduced his theme, the "turning point in history" that now faced the United States, leader of the West, encumbered with the task of determining "whether all mankind is to become communist, whether the whole world is to become free, or whether, in the struggle, civilization, as we know it, is to be completely destroyed or completely changed."

This call, not merely to arms but to Armageddon, accurately summarized the mood of many in 1952, with physicists fine-tuning the hydrogen bomb and a quarter million Chinese troops in Korea harrying American forces back to the thirty-eighth parallel. One finds a similar tone of foreboding in works contemporary with *Witness,* such as Arthur Schlesinger, Jr.'s *The Vital Center* and Hannah Arendt's *The Origins of Totalitarianism.* But apocalyptic diction and dark historicism had long been Chambers's specialty. At Foreign News he had warned that the future lay "between Russia and the United States," the "only two giants" left standing "in the world's arena."[15] He had spoken then with borrowed authority—*Time*'s, Harry Luce's. Now he spoke with his own authority, that of the witness who had helped usher in the new age of anxiety.

*Witness* was published on May 21, 1952, in an edition of one hundred thousand copies. Random House promised the "biggest and most ambitious campaign" in the firm's history. It was hardly necessary. *Witness* was already the "most eagerly anticipated book of the year," awaited by "all America," noted the *Times*'s Orville Prescott. The *Post* excerpts had done even better than predicted, drawing half a million new readers to the magazine, making for the largest audience in its history. Hollywood gossip columnist Louella Parsons reported that "I Was the Witness" had "more studios making offers than for any property since 'Gone with the Wind,' " with every major producer putting in a bid. The mogul Walter Wanger wanted Chambers himself on-screen, reading aloud the "Letter to My Children." No movie was made, however.

Within three weeks of its release *Witness* had climbed to number two on *The New York Times*'s nonfiction list, and on June 22 it reached number one, where it remained the entire summer before slipping back to second place on September 28. *Witness* finished the year as the ninth–best-selling book of 1952.[16]

And as the most heatedly debated. "I don't think any book in recent history has gotten the critical attention accorded *Witness*," said Bennett Cerf, in a letter to Chambers. Many of the nation's most formidable literary intellectuals—including Hannah Arendt, *The Reporter*'s Max Ascoli, John Chamberlain, John Dos Passos, Granville Hicks, Irving Howe, Sidney Hook, Philip Rahv, and Arthur Schlesinger, Jr.—wrote reviews. So did prominent Britons, such as Richard Crossman, John Strachey, and Rebecca West. There were cover stories in the book review pages of every major newspaper (the *Herald Tribune* additionally published a five-part series by Bert Andrews on his role in the Hiss case), plus lengthy features in the *Baltimore Sun, St. Louis Post-Dispatch, Kansas City Star*. The *Saturday Review* devoted nine pages to the book, with commentary by five reviewers. *Time* came through with a four-page spread.[17]

The author's celebrity guaranteed *Witness* would receive a great deal of attention, even had it been an undistinguished book. Reviewers agreed it was far from that. "It is not among the hundred great books," judged Sidney Hook on the front page of *The New York Times Book*

*Review.* "Yet it throws more light on the conspiratorial and religious character of modern communism, on the tangled complex of motives which led men and women of good will to immolate themselves on a fancied historical necessity, than all of the hundred great books of the past combined."[18]

Few had thought Chambers capable of such a feat. On the stand he had been laconic to the point of reticence. At *Time* he had written well, but as a journalist. *Witness* belonged to an altogether different order of literature. It was the work of a mature artist at the height of his powers. With its "penetrating and terrible insights," said Arthur Schlesinger, Jr. (in the *Saturday Review*), *Witness* had the stature of a "counter-statement to that book so influential twenty years ago, the 'Autobiography of Lincoln Steffens.' " Others drew comparisons with Augustine's and Rousseau's confessions, with George Fox's Journal, with *Pilgrim's Progress,* with Poe.[19]

Chambers's story begins with these highly allusive but simply written sentences:

> In 1937, I began, like Lazarus, the impossible return. I began to break away from Communism and to climb from deep within its underground, where for six years I had been buried, back into the world of free men. "When we dead awaken . . ." I used sometimes to say in those days to my wife, who, though never a Communist, had shared my revolutionary hopes and was now to share my ordeals: "When we dead awaken. . . ." For this title of an Ibsen play I have never read somehow caught and summed up for me feelings that I could not find other words to express—fears, uncertainties, self-doubts, cowardices, flinchings of the will—natural to any man who undertakes to reverse in midcourse the journey of his life. At the same time, I felt a surging release and a sense of freedom, like a man who bursts at last gasp out of a drowning sea.

The references to Lazarus and to Ibsen's late play, combined with unmistakable allusions to Dante (the life journey reversed in midcourse) and Jonah (the man who bursts out of the sea), all declare that the narrative of *Witness* will unfold as a parable of death and resurrection, although in the twentieth century the conditions of nonbeing and being are ironically transposed. "By any hard-headed estimate, the world I was leaving," Chambers says of his break from the underground, "looked like the world of life and the future. The world I was returning to seemed, by contrast, a graveyard." The book's wisdom is of the type William James identified as belonging uniquely to the religious convert, the "twice-born" soul who emerges from his harrowing experience proclaiming a message of "real wrongness in this world, which is neither to be ignored nor evaded, but which must be squarely met and overcome by an appeal to the soul's heroic resources, and neutralized and cleansed away by suffering."[20]

Chambers had seen himself in convert's terms as far back as 1922, in "The Damn Fool," whose sickly protagonist is transformed into a courageous, if deluded, martyr of Cromwellian dimension. The twice-born theme also infuses *The New Masses* stories, with their humble Communists who awaken to the glories of the revolution and then fling themselves sacrificially on its altar. It is the theme too of *Les Misérables,* the novel so important to Chambers as a boy.

It is appropriate that the book that first moved Chambers in childhood should haunt him as he sat down to tell the story of his life, for *Witness* is a triumph of memory, the hard-won profit of the many interrogations Chambers had withstood, the eviscerations, public and private. "Perhaps the greatest of all the surprises disclosed by the Hiss case," wrote Rebecca West in *The Atlantic,* "[is] that Whittaker Chambers should be capable of writing an autobiography so just and so massive in its resuscitation of the past." Nothing in the book is more powerful than its pages on its author's early life. Readers still squirm at the section titled, ironically, "The Story of a Middle-Class Family," wherein Chambers records, with nightmare clarity, the bleak family romance of Earle Avenue: Grandmother Whittaker waiting at the door to taunt Jay with his "depravity"; Jay sobbing with impotent rage as he pummels his second son, an alcoholic at age twenty-one; Laha picking up the ringing phone to learn Richard is dead. Each episode, terrible in itself, occurs within a sequence of mounting crises. And the whole unfolds as poeticized drama, telling more than it states, communicating *Witness*'s submerged but chilling message: that the most famous ex-Bolshevik in America, for all his strangeness, is no immigrant or exile from blood-soaked Europe, with its long centuries of caste and religious warfare, its ancient hatreds, its tyrannies, but rather a son of the Anglo-Saxon middle class, raised in a pretty coastal town on America's "front porch."

Reviewers in 1952 noticed an irony missed by so many later readers: that *Witness,* lavishly praised on the right as a Bible of patriotic anticommunism, itself stands far outside the normative tradition of American classics. Its influences are almost all European. Philip Rahv registered Chambers's large debt to Dostoevsky, whose presence "is literally everywhere in the book, in the action as in the moral import, in the plot no less than in the ideology." And Chambers's prose, as Arthur Schlesinger pointed out, had an "un-American . . . or at least un-Anglo-Saxon intensity."

Extraordinary in its self-revelation, *Witness* is also a work of extraordinary self-delusion. Chambers seems not to realize how committed a Bolshevik he remains—not in his objectives, of course, but in his habit of mind. In his account, political men and women are never more than the blind servants of ideology, motivated by "a soldier's faith." Thus Chambers portrays Alger Hiss's self-serving actions in the "Great Case" as those of a principled revolutionary, nearly heroic in his dedication to the great cause, when the salient fact of Hiss's career was not self-sacrifice but opportunism. Chambers, though he describes Hiss as his political twin, fails to see what was obvious to courtroom observers: that Hiss's desperate measures—the evasions, the lies, the acting, the smears—had the mundane purpose of preserving an endangered reputation.[21]

More broadly, Chambers champions American democracy but seems wholly inured to its practical operations—the give-and-take, the bargaining, the pragmatic adjustments, the constant dialogue. He deplores the materialism and ultrarationalism of Marxism and of modern man in general, yet his own political analysis is rigidly mechanistic.

Still, his political commentary contains a spark of intuitive insight. For instance, describing the New Deal, he writes, "I saw that the New Deal was only superficially a reform movement. I had to acknowledge the truth of what its more forthright protagonists, sometimes unwarily, sometimes defiantly, averred: the New Deal was a genuine revolution, whose deepest purpose was not simply reform within existing traditions, but a basic change in the social, and, above all, the power relationships within the nation. It was not a revolution by violence. It was a revolution by bookkeeping and lawmaking."[22] These sentences were much criticized in their day. Yet there is more truth in them than Chambers's critics could see in 1952, when the dominant interpretation of the New Deal was the one expounded by Richard Hofstadter in *The American Political Tradition,* published in 1948. Hofstadter characterized Roosevelt as a supreme pragmatist, untethered to ideology, making things up as he went along, his program "a series of improvisations" dictated by the requirements of the moment. But a later generation of New Deal historians, such as Jordan Schwarz and Alan Brinkley, would detect a more consistent pattern to the New Deal's innovations. To them the Roosevelt years ushered in a new era of "state capitalism," a "massive governmental recapitalization for purposes of economic development." Its architects (Adolf Berle, Jerome Frank, and others) were not only problem solvers but political intellectuals united by a "common vision."[23]

But if Chambers correctly grasps this truth, he vitiates it by his conspiratorial rhetoric. The "deeper purpose" he invokes hints of a sinister plot, with FDR himself the unwitting tool of secret masters. In the manner of so many who grasp ideas in their simple rather than complex forms, Chambers assigns them an influence verging on the mystical. To him ideas are stencils, giving infallible shape to history. Mediating events recede into the background.

Even his discussion of communism seems curiously off kilter. He "splendidly conveys what Communism meant to those who received its message during the first half of the twentieth century," said John Strachey, whose *The Coming Struggle for Power* was a seminal Marxist tract of the 1930s. But what Chambers thrilled to in 1925 (and again, nostalgically, in 1952) is the destructive potential of communism, its promise to obliterate the horrific present and so salve the psychological injuries of an alienated middle class. There is strangely little in *Witness* on the particulars of the Marxist-Leninist program, its plan for redressing economic injustice. Stranger still, there is not a word in *Witness*'s 799 pages on the movement's galvanizing causes during the time Chambers was a Communist: the Palmer raids, although Chambers worked beside some of its targets, laying track in Washington; Sacco and Vanzetti, though their martyrdom helped radicalize a generation of intellectuals; the Scottsboro Boys, the movement's rallying cry in the 1930s. "One doubts that he has ever been really at home in politics, if we take politics to be a delimited form of social thought and action," remarked a puzzled Philip Rahv. The critic Harold Rosenberg put it more bluntly: "This man is not interested in politics."[24]

It was true. Chambers was interested in religion—more precisely, in the convergence of religion and politics. "At every point," he writes, "religion and politics interlace, and must do so more acutely as the conflict between the two great camps of men—those who reject and those who worship God—becomes irrepressible."[25] This argument, with its conscious echo of Civil War rhetoric, is what makes *Witness,* for all its morbid imagery and Slavic passions, a uniquely American book, for only in America do religious and political ideals become interchangeable, even indistinguishable. *Witness*'s lineage traces back to the fire-and-brimstone prophecies of John Winthrop and Cotton Mather and the abolitionist manifestos of John Brown and William Lloyd Garrison. And the book's arguments extend those Chambers had developed thirty years earlier. "He was a Puritan, perhaps," the narrator says of Everett Holmes, "The Damn Fool." "That is radical, of course." The author of *Witness* is also a puritan. Like the dissenters who first came from Europe to the shores of North America, he emphasizes "the union of saint and society" and does not differentiate between "the spiritual and historical errand," to borrow terms used by Sacvan Bercovitch in *The American Jeremiad. Witness,* like the texts Bercovitch discusses, is best read as a political sermon proffered by an Everyman pilgrim, one of us, only more so, because he has gone further than we ever dared. "Out of my weakness and folly (but also out of my strength), I committed the characteristic crimes of my century."[26]

Chambers had undergone many revisions in his thinking over the years, but in every phase he demanded the "clash of swords." In *Witness* too he declares that anything less than total commitment, than moral absolutism, is a failure of nerve, of imagination, of historical grasp. Echoing his prior self, *The New Masses* editorialist of 1932, Chambers lauds communism not as a system of ideas but as a "great faith" towering out of the rubble of modern atheism. Its "simple vision" of "Man without God" rivals Christianity's vision "of God and man's relationship to God."[27]

In Chambers's world, only the Communist and the ex-Communist speak with full authority, and no one else can be taken seriously. Chambers's greatest contempt is reserved—as always—for liberalism, whose evils, he says, trace back to the Renaissance and the Age of Enlightenment, when an "intensely practical vision" was born, epitomized by the scientific method, which "challenges man to prove by his acts that he is the masterwork of the Creation—by making thought and act one. It challenges him to prove it by using the force of his rational mind to end the bloody meaninglessness of man's history—by giving it purpose and a plan. It challenges him to prove it by reducing the meaningless chaos of nature, by imposing his rational will to order, abundance, security, peace. It is the vision of materialism."[28]

This was not a new argument. Its premises had been stated by antirationalists going back to Joseph de Maistre. And it was forcefully restated, long after *Witness* was published, by Aleksandr Solzhenitsyn, in language eerily similar to Chambers's own.* Solzhenitsyn too would be misunderstood, his asperities interpreted as militant fanaticism.

"The *Daily Worker* itself would blush" at some of Chambers's fervid remarks about the splendors of communism, remarked I. F. Stone, one of the book's angriest critics. Chambers's scornful commentary on liberalism, Stone added, could be inserted in the Party press without a single word being changed.[30] Others too objected to Chambers's extreme formulations. "He recklessly lumps Socialists, progressives, liberals and men of good will together with the Communists," complained Sidney Hook. "All are bound according to him by the same faith; but only the Communists have the gumption and guts to live by it and pay the price. The others are the unwitting accomplices of communism precisely because they have put their trust in intelligence, not God. Only theists, not humanists, can resist communism, and in the end, save man."

Stung by the tone of these remarks and others, Chambers assumed they were punishment for his role in the Hiss case.[31] In some instances he was right. An intense personal animus seethed below the surface of some critics' reasoned arguments. Hannah Arendt, writing in *Commonweal,* was not content to meet Chambers on his own ground. Crudely caricaturing his role in the Hiss case, Arendt suggested he properly belonged "in a police state where people have been organized and split into two ever-changing categories: those who have the privilege to be informers and those who are dominated by the fear of being informed upon." Others went further, likening *Witness* to *Mein Kampf.* For this reason John Dos Passos (in the

---

* "The mistake must be at the root, at the very foundation of thought in modern times. I refer to the prevailing Western view of the world which was born in the Renaissance and has found political expression since the Age of Enlightenment. It became the basis for political and social doctrine and could be called rationalistic humanism or humanistic autonomy. . . . The West has finally achieved the rights of man, and even to excess, but man's sense of responsibility to God and society has grown dimmer." (Aleksandr I. Solzhenitsyn, *A World Split Apart* [Harper & Row, 1978], pp. 47–50.)[29]

*Saturday Review*) was moved to denounce the "moral lynching of Whittaker Chambers by the right-minded people of this country."*

At least some intellectuals recognized in Chambers's experience ordeals parallel to their own. One such was the émigré Polish poet Czeslaw Milosz, soon to suffer similar ostracism after the publication of *The Captive Mind,* his classic analysis of the plight of Central European intellectuals under communism. To Milosz, Chambers's odyssey composed an important chapter in American intellectual history, and it was disturbing to see Chambers "excluded from the circle of people worthy of having their hands shaken."[33]

But Chambers was not surprised. Temperamentally he was more at home among European than American intellectuals.[34] And the judgment of one, in particular, outweighed all others. In 1940, while reviewing books at *Time,* Chambers had come upon Arthur Koestler's *Darkness at Noon,* a fictional imagining of the Moscow trials. Chambers had since reread the novel many times and had urged it on others struggling to break with communism. He closely read Koestler's subsequent work too, though he had been disappointed by a piece Koestler wrote in *The New York Times Magazine* that defended Chambers's part in the Hiss case, but in tepid terms, likening the witness to a "defrocked priest." In the summer of 1952 the two ex-Communists met in New York and made a dinner appointment for further discussion. At the last minute Chambers canceled, thinking the time not right. Weeks later, when Koestler had returned to his home in England, Chambers sent off a copy of *Witness* with trepidation. He was afraid Koestler, who had not traveled as far to the right as he had, "would not like what I was doing."[35]

He did not hear from Koestler for eight months. Then a letter came. Having spent about a month in reading very slowly through *Witness,* Koestler wrote in April 1953:

> I felt so close that I don't feel the need to apologize for my not having answered your letter.

---

* "[*Witness*] can't be treated simply as a book," Mary McCarthy advised Hannah Arendt before Arendt wrote her review for *Commonweal.* "The great effort of this new Right is to get itself accepted as *normal,* and its publications as a *normal* part of publishing . . . and this, it seems to me, must be scotched, if it's not already too late. What do you think? I know you agree about the fact, the question is how it's to be done."[32]

There are trends of thought in "Witness," both explicit and implicit, which I am unable to follow. *Ceci dit,* it is a great book in the old, simple sense of greatness.

Independently from that, it is also a great chronicle. There are books which, if they had remained unwritten, would leave a hole in the world.[36]

# *Close Calls*

On November 4, 1952, after casting his ballot for the Republican ticket of Dwight Eisenhower and Richard Nixon, Chambers collapsed on the steps of the Westminster polling station. His local physician, Dr. Wilkins, gave him a hypodermic needle and got him home. That afternoon, while listening to the election returns on the radio, Chambers suddenly flopped onto his back, struggling for air. He was rushed to St. Agnes Hospital in Baltimore and placed in intensive care. The diagnosis was grave: anterior coronary thrombosis complicated by viral pneumonia.[1]

It was long overdue. Chambers had never seriously followed the regimen prescribed after his first breakdown in 1942. And he had been most neglectful during his periods of greatest stress: the year at Foreign News; the seventeen months of the Hiss case; the last stretch of writing *Witness*. Since then he had alternated periods of sedentary desk work with bursts of hard physical labor. Not really up to the farm chores he insisted on performing, he was often sore and stiff. He had also put on a great deal of weight. Self-denying in many respects, Chambers loved food and ate heartily. Observers at his 1951 Senate appearances noticed he was much heavier than during the trials and his breath came in gasps. In August 1952 Chambers had felt warning symptoms: sudden tiredness; sharp twinges in his shoulder.[2]

Chambers's physician, Dr. A. P. Alagia, a heart specialist, cautioned Esther to expect a four-month hospital stay. Ever devoted, she was at her husband's side each day and was his conduit to the outside world. She read him his mail (first censoring it) and counseled Ralph de Toledano, who was handling editorial negotiations for two foreign editions of *Witness,* in Britain and France.* He was permitted no visitors save Esther and the children; Ellen had hurried down from Northampton. It amused Chambers that a pair of government security officers had slipped past the desk guard and were keeping vigil.[4]

After six weeks the patient was permitted to sit up in bed and dangle his feet over the edge for ten minutes each day. It would be another two months, said Dr. Alagia, before he could give an accurate prognosis. Chambers seemed to be doing "as well as could be expected," given his age, obesity, and overall poor health. On the day before Christmas Chambers was allowed to go home, by ambulance, under orders to stay flat on his back for at least another month, after which he might possibly begin limited exercise and eventually resume "a more normal life."[5]

In February Chambers was still in bed—and not minding it. He was grateful to be back home, amid the surroundings he loved,[6] deluged by visitors. These included Norton-Taylor, Frank McNaughton, Tom Hyland, the de Toledanos (Nora carried on a successful one-woman campaign to discredit *The Strange Case of Alger Hiss,* a sloppily researched pro-Hiss account by the English jurist Lord Jowitt), Richard Nixon, Carl Brandt, Bennett Cerf, the English ex-Communist Douglas Hyde (whose memoir *I Believed* was a kind of small-bore *Witness*), plus a number of Catholic clergymen (the Catholic press had been especially admiring of *Witness*). Even Madame Chiang Kai-shek was contemplating a visit—so Harry Luce reported to Chambers. In all, so many people came that Chambers had to turn down Joe McCarthy when Jean Kerr asked for an appointment.[7]

But none could cure his despair. He was prey to black, death-seeking moods. More than once he professed not to care, "not the slightest little bit," whether he ever got out of bed again or even survived another day. Good health, he knew, would never return. As long as he lived, he would feel constriction in his chest, constant pain in his shoulder, sudden flare-ups of sickness. In jottings to himself he extrapolated luxuriantly from his gloom. "The sheer mass and complexity of historical error

---

* The British edition was published (by Andre Deutsch) in 1953, to mixed reviews. The French edition never appeared, owing to editorial differences between de Toledano and the publisher.[3]

is [*sic*] now too great to be coped with," he wrote on March 1. "The only possible solutions will be made by the Bombs."[8]

In April, just after turning fifty-two, Chambers was at last allowed to get out of bed and "totter around the house."[9] He had been bedridden a total of five months. He was greatly weakened and had lost many pounds. The round face now was thin and drawn. His hair had turned almost completely gray. Unable to manage the quarter-mile uphill hike to Medfield, he moved his study to the basement in the main house. He wrote there for the remainder of his life.

Alas, his days as a working farmer had ended. He had hoped to transform the farm into a business that would pay for itself and no longer deplete his savings. Along with a second major book, it was to have been his last life's project. Now it was out of the question.

In July 1953 Ellen Chambers married Henry Into, son of a wealthy gun manufacturer from Lake Forest, Illinois. A Yale undergraduate, Into had suspended his studies while he served an army hitch. The ceremony was at the Ascension Episcopal Church in Westminster. The press descended en masse. Chambers gave away the bride, radiant, slim, and graceful, overtopping her father by several inches. The guests included Bennett and Phyllis Cerf, who stayed over on the farm.[10]

The Episcopal service was only partly a concession to the groom. There was a second reason: Chambers had grown embittered with the Friends. During the case the Quakers had been disturbingly silent. Even members of the Pipe Creek Meeting had kept their distance, some of them solidly with Hiss. Then, in the spring of 1951, Ellen's application to Swarthmore, the elite coeducational Quaker college, had been summarily rejected despite her exemplary scholastic record. Chambers, suspecting she had been blackballed by pro-Hiss administrators and faculty, consulted his friend Henry C. Patterson, a well-known civil rights advocate and member of the Swarthmore Meeting. After making some inquiries, Patterson reported back that Chambers's suspicions might indeed be justified. Chambers was aghast. He vowed "to remain a Quaker" but before long he began to withdraw and, said his friend Tom Hyland, "lost all enthusiasm for Quakerism."[11]

In August Chambers suffered a second heart episode, milder than the first. He calmly noted the familiar symptoms: "the dragging fatigue, that drained-out feeling, and that uncomfortable inflated feeling . . . as if the heart were being steadily blown up." Also, "the never-failing pains in the left shoulder—sometimes quite difficult to bear." Dr. Alagia called it a "warning" and told Chambers he must reduce his stress. He was also given two new medications. At the hospital the X ray showed his scar was healing, and there was no new clot. But his heart had enlarged.[12]

By mid-September he was on his feet again and able to assist in the dreaded task of auctioning off his beloved Guernseys—"on the slave block," he mourned. Ellen came down for the sale. Chambers found her "weeping in the pen with the old brood cow."

His wedding gift to Ellen had been her choice of one of the two outer farms. She chose Medfield, the smaller property, but dear to her. Whittaker was confident she would return to the land someday. He was less sure about John, who turned seventeen in August. Though raised a farmer—he first drove a tractor at age nine—and deeply attached to the soil, John too would leave soon for the greater world, and young men were not easily lured back to the quiet life of farming. Chambers held on to the sheep and beef cattle "against the time when the children may be drawn back. But there really are no more beginnings left in me."[13]

With Eisenhower's election, most Republicans were ready to set aside the Communists in government issue. It had done its work, helping drive the Democrats out. But Joe McCarthy and his allies took a different view. For them, Red-hunting season was still on. Within weeks of Eisenhower's inauguration, McCarthy was grumbling over presidential appointments, though he was reined in by Robert Taft, the new Senate majority leader.

Then, in February, Ike announced his candidate to fill the post of ambassador to Russia, vacant since October, when Truman's last ambassador, George F. Kennan, had been ejected by the Soviets. With Stalin dead and relations entering a period of uncertainty, Eisenhower wanted someone on the spot whose judgment he trusted. His choice, Charles E. ("Chip") Bohlen, was startling to many. Not because of Bohlen's credentials. They were exemplary. A Harvard graduate and Russian specialist, Bohlen had been in the Foreign Service since 1929 and was familiar with Kremlin officials from his two Soviet tours. But he was also closely tied to the previous two administrations. He had been FDR's Russian translator at Yalta and so a witness to Roosevelt's secret tête-à-têtes with

Stalin in which (as many Republicans believed) an enfeebled FDR had bent pliantly to the dictator's ferocious will. In the Truman years Bohlen had drafted the outline of the Marshall Plan and been one of Dean Acheson's top two Russian advisers (the other was George Kennan). Bohlen's assessments had informed Acheson's early decisions on Korea. In sum, as *Time* objected, Bohlen was "part & parcel of the Roosevelt-Truman-Acheson foreign policy"—the policy the Republicans, and in particular John Foster Dulles, had sworn to dismantle.[14]

When Bohlen defended the Yalta accords in his confirmation hearings, Senate hard-liners—McCarthy, McCarran, Styles Bridges, William Knowland, and others—sprang to the attack. But with Taft keeping the troops in line, and the Democrats pragmatically keeping silent, the nomination looked secure. On March 18 the Senate committee approved Bohlen 15–0, with the full Senate vote scheduled the following Monday, March 23. This time, however, McCarthy promised to take his fight to the Senate floor, heralding, some said, "the beginning of an all-out fight between McCarthy and Eisenhower."

It soon turned ugly. The State Department's rabid new security chief, Scott McLeod, an ex-FBI man close to McCarthy and company—and chosen by Dulles to placate them—had leaked the results of Bohlen's FBI security dossier to the hostile senators. The file included foggy allegations that the nominee had "used bad judgment in associating with homosexuals." Since a new Eisenhower directive had broadened the scope of inquiries, from "loyalty" to the catchall term "security," Bohlen was now a fair target.[15]

Amid the controversy McCarthy had arranged to visit Westminster, presumably for consultation, but at the last minute Jean Kerr called ahead to cancel, saying McCarthy's car had been in a wreck. The excuse sounded contrived, but Chambers gave it little thought since Kerr said they would come on Saturday, March 21—two days before the Senate debate began.

This time McCarthy made it, arriving just before dinner. He went upstairs to talk to Chambers, still bedridden, while downstairs Esther prepared a meal. They discussed Bohlen. Chambers asked what was in the diplomat's security file. McCarthy was "pretty vague." It seemed Bohlen had associated with homosexuals and also with leftists. Was that all? Chambers asked. If so, it meant nothing. McCarthy protested there was more. "I didn't believe him," Chambers reported to Duncan Norton-

Taylor. McCarthy was distraught, it seemed to Chambers, "precisely because there wasn't more."

McCarthy said he was planning to ask Bohlen to submit to a polygraph. It was a bad idea, in Chambers's view. Even if Bohlen passed, he
would be stigmatized and thus weakened in his ambassadorial role. Besides, the fight was lost. The Senate was certain to approve the nomination. Rather than smear Bohlen, McCarthy should register a symbolic
protest, opposing the nominee purely on the basis of Yalta, and so ele-
vate the debate to the realm of "statesmanship."

But McCarthy barely listened. Throughout the two-hour visit his behavior was odd, at once defensive and distracted, as though he were con-
cealing something. It was curious too that the instant McCarthy had
walked through the door, a call had come for him from *The Washington
Post,* obviously alerted to the visit.

Late Monday morning, with the floor debate on Bohlen getting
under way, a *Baltimore Sun* reporter came to Pipe Creek Farm with a list
of questions. Esther took them up to Chambers. They were all about the
Bohlen nomination. Chambers realized what had happened. After his
brief visit to the farm, McCarthy had ostentatiously dropped out of sight
for the remainder of the weekend, encouraging speculation that he had
been in Westminster the whole time, fattening his dossier on Bohlen. He
had assumed Chambers would go along with the ruse. He was mistaken.
Chambers instead told the *Sun* he had no information whatever im-
pugning the nominee's loyalty. As expected, the nomination sailed
through. The final tally was 74–13.[16]

McCarthy's stunt had been an ordinary political maneuver, benign by
his usual standards, but Chambers was appalled. He had assumed all
along that McCarthy, his many defects aside, was at least sincere. Now he
saw otherwise. It was a sobering discovery. The senator's recklessness
threatened less harm to communism than to its enemies. But what
should Chambers do? In the minds of millions McCarthy had become
synonymous with anticommunism. To denounce him could weaken the
entire position and give comfort to "anti-anti-Communists," who depicted anticommunism as a greater menace than communism. For one
of the few times in his life Chambers felt forced into a neutral position.
He was neither for McCarthy nor against him. In the spring, when *Look*
magazine asked him to write an article on the McCarthy phenomenon,
Chambers begged off, though he knew "it could be a decisive piece."[17]

He did mention McCarthy, glancingly, in an essay for *Life* published in June, "Is Academic Freedom in Danger?," a defense of congressional Red hunting. After taunting "doom-haunted" liberals who exaggerated McCarthy's influence, Chambers reversed himself, conceding that McCarthy, though probably simply "an instinctive politician of a kind fairly common in our history," might actually represent a force "wholly new in our history."[18] Just what was "wholly new" about him, however, Chambers was not yet prepared to say.

Chambers still agreed with McCarthy's basic premise—that the government needed further housecleaning—if not with his rhetoric and his showmanship. Though few remembered it, *Witness* virtually accused Felix Frankfurter* and Dean Acheson of running interference for the Communist underground and included hyperbolic remarks on the intrigues of the anti-Chiang "cell" and on how it had "decisively changed the history of Asia, of the United States, and therefore, of the world."[20] It was not a great leap from these overripe musings to McCarthy's obscene charge that General George Marshall had treasonously delivered China to the Communists. The awful fact, which Chambers could not admit—and never did—was that his own worldview, stripped of its lyrical refinements and humanist vibrato, had helped bring McCarthyism into existence.

Thus even at this late date he found it impossible to disown McCarthy. Still clinging to the hope the senator could be enlightened, reformed, or tamed, he continued to meet with McCarthy, trying to exert a moderating influence. It didn't work. Soon McCarthy was off on another binge, threatening the CIA with an investigation and renewing his harassment of the State Department, which he accused of spreading pro-Communist propaganda through its overseas libraries. Cowering under the assault, State authorized the removal of some forty books from shelves around the world. In Tokyo books were actually burned. One of the banned titles, the press reported, savoring the irony, was *Witness*.[21] And why not? Hadn't Chambers labeled communism a "great faith"? McCarthyism was turning into Comstockery, with over-

---

* In 1952 Chambers had urged Ralph de Toledano to write a study of Frankfurter that would expose him as the Rasputin of the New Deal. Chambers also discussed the project with the publisher Henry Regnery.[19]

tones of Orwell's *1984*.* Yet the senator's popularity was soaring—
from a 34 percent favorable rating in the summer of 1953 to 50 percent
in December.[23]

By autumn Eisenhower's advisers had decided they could head
McCarthy off only by producing Red scalps of their own. The trouble
was, subversives were hard to find. The "conspiracy on a scale so immense as to dwarf any previous such venture in the history of man"—in
McCarthy's words—had indeed been formidable. But the most important agents had been flushed out years before. Critics still harped on Truman's "red herring" statement. They ignored the thrust of his remarks:
The FBI had already been on the case two years; only a handful of the
accused remained on the federal payroll, and those few were in innocuous positions. So things had stood in 1948. Five years later the pickings
were even slimmer, as almost everyone knew but was afraid to say, for
fear of inciting McCarthy, whose grip had become paralyzing.

In October the administration announced the triumphant results of its
own investigations. Since January more than fourteen hundred "subversives" had been dropped from the federal payroll, according to Eisenhower's press secretary, James Hagerty. When asked how many were
spies or even Party members, Hagerty acknowledged the number was
few. But all were "security risks," a term by now transparently devoid of
meaning.[24] No one was impressed.

Eisenhower's Justice Department now had to produce something big,
must "out-McCarthy McCarthy,"[25] preferably with a sensational case.
When in doubt, rustle the dossiers of the previous administration. In
November Eisenhower's attorney general, Herbert Brownell, addressing
a gathering of business executives in Chicago, dredged up the half-
forgotten name of Harry Dexter White.

Death had spared White in 1948. Had he lived even a few months
longer he would have been engulfed in scandal after Chambers produced
the first spy papers, which had included the lengthy memo written in
White's hand. Chambers had subsequently followed up with detailed
testimony on his dealings with White. But Red hunters and the public

---

* McCarthy was quick to denounce *Witness*'s inclusion among the proscribed books.
"Someone has tried to sabotage efforts to clean up the libraries," he declared, and "is trying to make the State Department look silly. . . . [I]t shows the need to speed up a housecleaning there."[22]

were not much interested in deceased agents. Even when Nixon had produced White's memo on the floor of Congress—in his speech of January 1950, following Hiss's conviction—scarcely anyone noticed.

Reviving the case almost four years later, Brownell made an issue not of White but rather of President Truman, who in 1945 had ignored FBI warnings (via Elizabeth Bentley) that White was a Soviet agent. "Incredible though it may seem," said Brownell, Truman ignored the FBI and nominated White, then assistant secretary of the treasury, "for an even more important position as executive director for the United States in the International Monetary Fund."

Brownell's allegation hit Washington "harder than any loyalty charge since the Hiss case," reported James Reston on the *Times*'s front page. By this time few questioned that White had been a Communist. Even his former Treasury colleagues were not shocked by the charge. But Brownell's allegation of a cover-up rekindled—on all sides—the partisan conflagration of the Hiss case.

Once again Harry Truman entered the fray, calling the whole story a lie and saying he had read no FBI report on White in 1945. Then came embarrassing testimony by Truman's first secretary of state, James Byrnes, now governor of South Carolina. Byrnes told a Senate committee *he* had read the 1945 FBI report, and so had Truman. What was more, said Byrnes, the report plainly stated White "was known to be engaged in espionage activity." Byrnes said he had been alarmed, but Truman had pushed through White's IMF nomination anyway. Cornered, Truman went on national television in Kansas City and castigated the Republicans. Brownell was guilty of "shameful demagoguery" and Eisenhower of having "fully embraced, for political advantage, McCarthyism . . . this evil at every level of our national life."[26]

Chambers, meanwhile, had been working on an essay for *Look,* published in December as "The Herring and the Thing." It was his most widely read prose since *Witness*. Its subject was Harry Dexter White, whose "role as a Soviet agent was second in importance only to that of Alger Hiss—if, indeed, it was second," Chambers wrote. "The pluperfect bureaucrat," White had quietly risen to a position where he was able "to shape U.S. Government policy in the Soviet government's interest." This overstated the case, but not by much. Far more influential than Hiss had ever been, White had been a leading formulator of postwar economic policy. He had been the architect of the IMF and the author of the Morgenthau Plan, conceived at war's end to "smash" the German economy, though abandoned in the face of Allied protests that Germany would be so weakened by the plan as to invite a Soviet takeover.[27]

In Chambers's analysis, the Ur-culprit was not White or even Truman, but FDR, whose program of "concealed socialism" had all but invited Communist infiltration. Eventually Roosevelt found Communists a liability but when under attack had protected them, lest the New Deal's true nature be exposed at its source. Thus in 1939 FDR had airily dismissed Chambers's allegations, setting the precedent for Truman's grave error of 1945. Chambers pointed out that White was not the only senior official named in the FBI report Truman had ignored. Hiss was named in it too, "three years before President Truman said 'red herring.' " Thus was the White case legitimated—sacralized—by its link with Hiss.

Chambers's piece does not once mention McCarthy. The bumptious senator would not befoul this exercise in nostalgia. But McCarthy barged in anyway. A week after Truman's attack on the "evil" of McCarthyism the senator too went on the air. Most assumed he would answer Truman's attack. They were wrong. McCarthy wasted little time on Truman—just another "defeated politician." He lunged after bigger targets, Eisenhower and John Foster Dulles, guilty alike, said McCarthy, of perpetuating the "whining, whimpering appeasement" of the Truman regime. Despite McCarthy's own best efforts, the new administration was rife with holdovers from the "old Acheson-Lattimore-White-Hiss group." Much as McCarthy hated to say it, Communists were still being sheltered in government, and, the senator promised, this "raw, harsh, unpleasant fact" would be a key issue in the 1954 election.

The White House interpreted this as "a declaration of war"[28] but was, as always, slow to retaliate. Eisenhower had no stomach for a gutter fight with McCarthy.

But Chambers had had his fill. McCarthy's recklessness was threatening the Republicans. Still reluctant to denounce him publicly, Chambers began to make his case behind the scenes, to fellow men of the right.

In December book publisher Henry Regnery, a friend of Chambers's since 1952, sent Chambers an advance copy of *McCarthy and His Enemies,* a ringing defense of McCarthy written by William F. Buckley, Jr., and L. Brent Bozell, two young Yale-educated McCarthyites. Regnery wanted to know, particularly, what Chambers made of the book's "pro-logue," written by Chambers's onetime Time Inc. ally Willi Schlamm, who extolled McCarthy as a heroic anti-Communist gladiator and "one of the few contemporary politicians who earnestly believe in the efficacy of ideas."[29]

This was absurd, in Chambers's view. It bothered him too that Schlamm scoffed at analogies some had drawn between McCarthy and Hitler. To Chambers the analogy *was* valid and "cannot be whisked away by a scratch of the pen."[30] The "wholly new" politics McCarthy repre-sented was, then, fascism. This was extreme. McCarthy was not the ti-tanic force many feared. He had no independent organization and was building no grassroots campaign. He had not even talked of a third party. His strength, in fact, came from the rank and file of the Republican Party with whom he was to remain popular even after his downfall. Chambers had been closer to the mark when he described McCarthy as "an instinctive politician of a kind fairly common in our history." What set him apart was his demagogic skills and the overheated climate in which he flourished. But Chambers's new interpretation was one shared by many whose political outlook was formed by European models and who translated all populist movements into the terms of the totalitarian extremes of fascism and communism.[31]

By now Chambers was sure McCarthy would impair, perhaps even destroy, a serious anti-Communist movement in the United States. In a letter to Buckley, explaining why he could not endorse his book or allow his name to be associated with it, Chambers spelled out his forebodings about McCarthy: "His flair for the sensational, his inaccuracies and dis-tortions, his tendency to sacrifice the greater objectivity for the momen-tary effect, will lead him and us into trouble. . . . Senator McCarthy will one day make some irreparable blunder which will play directly into the hands of our common enemy and discredit the whole anti-Communist effort for a long while to come."[32]

These words were as prophetic as any Chambers ever wrote. Two months later the Army-McCarthy hearings began, and with them McCarthy's downfall. In September a Senate committee recommended McCarthy be disciplined for a long string of abuses, including his illegal recruitment of federal employees to steal files for him—his own brand of subversion. McCarthy was finished, though his memory plagued the right for decades to come. Chambers never spoke out publicly against him. The time for that had already passed. He had been one of a handful of Americans who could have challenged McCarthy at his zenith and perhaps restored prestige to anticommunism. But for once in his life Chambers lacked the passion for a fight.

And lacked the strength. Just before Christmas 1953 he suffered another heart attack and was warned the next might be his last. Then, in February, came four separate cardiac episodes, two of them serious, a sequence of shocks "rather like a little earthquake." It was his worst scare since the thrombosis. He was ordered back to bed for at least two months. "Two requiems," he dryly observed when Esther unwrapped some recordings, a gift from Ralph de Toledano. "One would have done me."[33]

# *The Last Path*

In May 1954 Chambers became a grandfather when Ellen gave birth to her first child, christened John Norman Into. The young family was living in Augusta, Georgia, where Henry Into was finishing up his military service before resuming his studies at Yale. Esther traveled to Augusta to help Ellen.[1]

In August John Chambers turned eighteen and drove into town to register for the draft. Whittaker felt a "simple pang" as he watched his son, crew-cutted and broad-shouldered, several inches taller than his father, walk the brick path, shaded by locusts and English walnuts, to the barn where the cars were kept and then drive up the slope and out of view. Three weeks later John loaded up his car and set off for Gambier, Ohio, to begin his freshman year at Kenyon College. Raised on the farm, John would have preferred to stay there. But his parents wanted him out in the world. "I was sent to college," John later said. "I mean *sent*."[2]

With both Ellen and John out of the house, its thirteen rooms echoed loudly with the silence. The opening line in *Prometheus Unbound,* a play he had first read in Europe, came back to haunt Chambers: "We have come to the last path of the earth, in the Scythian country, in the untrodden wilderness." Chambers changed the last word to "solitude."[3]

He desperately missed his son. David McDowell, whose contacts at Kenyon had smoothed John's acceptance there, offered to join Chambers on a visit to the campus in October. Chambers couldn't wait that long. On "sudden impulse," he and Esther jumped into their big

Buick—purchased with the royalties from *Witness*—and drove out to Gambier. In a conference with the dean of students, Whittaker was relieved to learn that his son was "running with the very best men on campus."[4]

Before long Chambers's feeling of isolation was eased by a new friendship, the most important of his last years. After receiving an apologetic letter from Chambers, explaining why he could not endorse *McCarthy and His Enemies*, William Buckley had replied with a letter equally cordial, assuring Chambers he had not taken offense. Not only that: "It has long been the irrevocable consensus in my numerous family (ten brothers and sisters), that your courage, your skills, and your faith are the brightest beacon of the free world. I am sure thousands, if not millions of people agree with us, and I hope that a knowledge of this leavens the aching loneliness so evidenced in all your writings."[5]

Buckley asked in his letter if he might pay a call on Chambers. "By all means come," Chambers replied. "Come anytime of the day." The letter enclosed road directions and a taste of Chambers's signature gloom: "The total situation is hopeless, past repair, organically irremediable."[6]

The young visitor, coming up to Westminster from Washington, where he had business, half expected to find a scene of biblical desolation, "Jeremiah lying alongside a beckoning tomb." Indeed Chambers was supine, under doctor's orders not even to raise his head, when Buckley arrived. But once the patient began to talk, the heaviness lifted.

The young man of the right and the aging one settled into easy conversation. They spoke of McCarthy; of the perilous state of conservatism, with Robert Taft dead and the moderate President Eisenhower perpetuating New Deal heresies; of the pressing need for a meeting of conservative minds. They would have gone on longer had a worried Esther not shooed Buckley out the door.[7]

"He is something special," Chambers told his wife after the young visitor left. "He was born, not made, and not many like that are born in any time."[8]

At twenty-eight, a shade over six feet, handsome and blue-eyed, Bill Buckley brought to the American right qualities no one could remember its ever having possessed: glamour and style, the heedless joy of privileged youth. He was already a celebrity who had catapulted himself toward controversy, blazing out of the consensus fifties as an authentic radical, a firebrand at war with the prevailing orthodoxies of his day, orthodoxies that happened to be liberal.

He achieved notoriety at age twenty-five with *God and Man at Yale,* perhaps the single most influential book to come out of the postwar conservative movement. "Yale derives its moral and financial support from Christian individualists," Buckley wrote of his alma mater, "and then addresses itself to the task of persuading the sons of these supporters to be atheistic socialists." Presaging the attacks on "elites" that would become a staple of right-wing ideology, he called for Yale's alumni to rise up and seize the helm of their university, guiding it toward the paradisal shores of Christianity, "individualism," and capitalism.[9]

Almost alone among right-wing intellectuals of his era Buckley had no radical past to live down. He had not been a Stalinist, Trotskyist, socialist, or even a liberal. He had acquired his conservatism at Great Elm, his family's forty-seven-acre estate in Sharon, Connecticut, where he had also learned to play Bach on the piano, to ski, to sail. "Bill's to the manor born," his great friend Murray Kempton later said, "and he has no political past he feels guilty about."[10]

For some years Buckley had wanted to start up a new conservative magazine. Bankrolled by his father, Will Buckley, a transplanted Texas oil millionaire, he had already put in bids for two existing publications, first the right-wing weekly broadsheet *Human Events,* and then *The Freeman,* the iconoclastic journal founded by one of Buckley's heroes, the Tory anarchist Albert Jay Nock. Buckley failed in both attempts but in the second had found a partner, and foil, in Chambers's Time Inc. acquaintance Willi Schlamm. A Galician Jew, born in 1904, Schlamm was one of European communism's most formidable apostates. In the 1930s he had edited the socialist *Die Weltbühne* and written a penetrating anti-Stalinist tract, *The Dictatorship of the Lie,* whose admirers included Edmund Wilson. Since immigrating to the United States in the late 1930s, Schlamm had been taken up by John Chamberlain, who helped him get on the staff first of the *New Leader* and then of *Fortune.* Small, clever, with a nimble gift for English idioms and a courtier's sly irony, Schlamm had become a top adviser to Luce, part of the right-wing coterie that in the war years had included Chamberlain and of course Chambers. For years Schlamm had been after Luce to publish a new magazine, a first-class intellectual journal, conservatism's answer to *Partisan Review,* with W. H. Auden, T. S. Eliot, Arthur Koestler, George Orwell, and Lionel

Trilling among the projected (or wished-for) contributors. Luce had at last agreed, and Schlamm left Time Inc. to found *Measure*. But at the last minute, frightened off by a dip in the economy, Luce had changed his mind, and Schlamm had been left adrift—until Buckley came along.[11]

The historic partnership of the lanky, articulate Buckley and the slick, voluble Schlamm—Skull and Bones meets the Vienna Kaffeehaus—signaled a sea change in American conservatism. Before the war the movement had been marred by strong strains of isolationism, nativism, and anti-Semitism. Buckley and Schlamm wanted to purge the right of all that and reshape it along more humanistic and cosmopolitan lines, with global anticommunism its holy crusade.

The weekly magazine they planned to publish—as early, they hoped, as the spring of 1955—would be the voice of this revitalized conservatism, edited by Buckley with Schlamm in the background role of éminence grise. Ex-radical luminaries such as John Chamberlain and James Burnham had already agreed to join the staff, and Max Eastman had joined its editorial board. In the summer Buckley gingerly sounded Chambers out for a position as senior editor, and "to my overwhelming surprise, the answer was, Yes."[12]

But first, Chambers warned, he must be sure just what Buckley and Schlamm had in mind. He would attach his name to *National Review* only if its political outlook coincided with his own. His experience with McCarthy had left him suspicious of the right, of its "crackpotism," while Buckley and Schlamm, as he knew, remained pro-McCarthy. In addition, they deplored Eisenhower's centrism. Buckley had privately vowed "to read Dwight Eisenhower out of the conservative movement" in one of the new magazine's first issues. Buckley and Schlamm also distrusted Chambers's favorite politician, Richard Nixon. The vice president boasted the impeccable Hiss credential but otherwise was poised ambiguously between the two poles of the Republican Party, its eastern moderates and its old guard, the archconservatives of the Midwest and the Far West. Also, Nixon had distanced himself from McCarthy during the 1952 election, angering many on the right—who had supported the ticket only because the Red-hunting Nixon was on it—and then had been a backstage player in Joe's demise.

Chambers, on the other hand, was moving further away from the radical right and toward the center. He saw Eisenhower as the most plausible Republican leader—there was no other electable candidate in

sight—and he was fiercely loyal to Nixon, who (thanks to Ike) stood on
the brink of the presidency. Indeed, if Eisenhower were serious about retiring in 1956, after a single term—as he had hinted—the path would be
clear for Nixon to succeed him.[13]

Beyond these considerations there was the all-important matter of
defining the conservative position. Chambers had begun, yet again, to
rethink his politics, this time softening his counterrevolutionary line.
The passions of the Hiss case behind him, he had grown convinced that
the social upheavals of the twentieth century could not be revoked—and
perhaps shouldn't be. Marx and Lenin remained towering figures, masters of reality who had firmly grasped the nature of the modern crisis,
political and economic, and had devised workable solutions. The right
must do the same. It could not simply "preach reaction" and dream of an
irrecoverable past. "A conservatism that cannot face the facts of the machine and mass production, and its consequences in government and
politics, is foredoomed to futility and petulance." For "the machine"—
capitalism—"has made the economy socialistic."

There could be, Chambers meant, no rolling back of the New Deal.
It was an astonishing admission. Chambers still equated the New Deal
with revolution. But at the same time he recognized that Americans had
embraced the Rooseveltian vision. One need only look at Chambers's
typical neighbor, the yeoman farmer of Westminster, who "has sold off
his horses and rides his tractors, and sends soil samples to the state college to learn how to up his yields." What better proof that the revolution had become permanent, in Trotsky's phrase?

Chambers feared conservatives were missing the drift of history, always for him the unforgivable sin. He did not renounce in 1954 what he
had written in *The New Masses* in 1932: "In history, defeat is the penalty
of blindness or apathy—and sometimes annihilation." A conservatism
blind to changed political realities, he now believed, "is not a political
force, or even a twitch; it has become a literary whimsy."[14]

Schlamm was indignant. Chambers talked as if the fight were over
and the right must acquiesce in "the socialist needs and hopes of the
masses," when the purpose of *National Review* was to make the opposition case. Conservatives too were permitted to "cast a vote in this continuous ballot."[15]

Buckley sided with Schlamm but was reluctant to antagonize Chambers, whom he held in awe—as ideologue, as writer, as hero of the Hiss

case. Also, Buckley did not want his venture to founder on the shoals of "sectarianism," the right's long-standing curse.[16]

So he kept the conversation alive, less by his arguments than by the gift of his friendship. With John Chambers away at Kenyon, the vibrant young Buckley filled the chasm in Chambers's life. Despite a hectic schedule—which now included transcontinental travel in search of sponsors—Buckley stayed constantly in touch with Chambers, by phone or letter, and went to the farm whenever he could for visits that were highlights of Chambers's last years. A few hours with his young friend lifted his gloom, the heavy compound of physical discomfort, mental exhaustion, and moral despair. "I am delighted by the thought that you may, one of these days, visit us." Chambers wrote. "Come to us when you can." "Come down, . . . when you will and can."[17]

In November 1954 Buckley convened a meeting in New York with Chambers and Schlamm, hoping their major differences could be ironed out. First, Chambers spent the night at Buckley's house in Stamford, Connecticut, eleven spacious rooms perched above Long Island Sound. Buckley, who had seen Chambers's cramped writing quarters, was a little embarrassed when he showed Chambers his own study, which massively occupied a converted garage. But Chambers pronounced it beautiful, as he did the house and grounds. Chambers also was charmed by Buckley's wife, Pat, a Vancouver heiress as tall and striking as her husband, with a dry, sparkling wit.[18]

The next day Chambers and Buckley met Schlamm in Manhattan, at the Barclay Hotel. The off-year elections had just concluded, a disaster for the Republicans. They had lost control of both the Senate and the House. Nixon had absorbed blame from all sides. Moderates objected to his low-road attacks on the Democrats while old guard Republicans remained bitter at Nixon's abandonment of McCarthy. At the Barclay, Buckley and Schlamm spoke approvingly of William Knowland, Taft's successor as Senate majority leader, then making noises about succeeding Eisenhower in 1956—or challenging him if Ike decided after all to seek a second term.[19]

Chambers came away from the meeting afraid Buckley and Schlamm might be drumming up a third-party ticket, a pairing of Knowland and McCarthy, with *National Review* as its vehicle. Not long after this he heard Buckley on the radio extolling Knowland. It was too much. "I am, of this moment, so firmly opposed to a third party, that I cannot permit my name to be used in any way that might imply that I support or abet it or anything connected with it," Chambers declared. Buckley and Schlamm hastily assured him he was overreacting. They liked Knowland but would not encourage him to bolt the Republican Party.[20]

At the same time Chambers harped on his ideological disagreements with Buckley. "What is it that you want to hear from me?" Buckley pleaded, his frustration at last showing. "I doubt very much if it is at war with anything I actually want to say." Buckley volunteered to step down as editor of the magazine.[21] It was an extraordinary concession, but not what Chambers was looking for. He craved assurances that *National Review* would show forbearance toward the current administration and "maneuver" within the terms of existing political reality. No such guarantee was forthcoming. Chambers did not break off negotiations, but his doubts were growing.

On November 27, 1954, a few weeks after the meeting at the Barclay and two days after Thanksgiving, Alger Hiss was released from the Lewisburg penitentiary, in Pennsylvania, having served forty-four months of his five-year term. He had been a model prisoner, and a popular one, "Al" to his fellow inmates. "Three years in jail is a good corrective to three years at Harvard," he later said. He worked in the prison library and was a generous fount of free legal advice. Inmates, pressing against their barred windows, shouted encouragement to him as he left the compound. He was met by Priscilla and Tony Hiss and by his appeals attorney, Chester Lane, who had driven up in a new convertible, bright red in mockery of the charges against Hiss.

Back in New York, Hiss faced an uncertain future. His license to practice law had been revoked, and no job offers awaited him. However, he had publishers' advances totaling ten thousand dollars for a book that would assert his innocence. Priscilla earned a small income working at the Doubleday bookstore.[22]

The United Press asked Chambers to write an article on Hiss's release. He refused, in a brief statement. "Alger Hiss will be passing from the ordeal of prison to the ordeal of daily living, which may well prove more trying. . . . [C]ommon decency dictates for me just one course: to be, as little as possible, seen or heard. In particular, any suggestion that I am making copy out of this business must offend many humane minds, as it does mine." He quoted a couplet from Andrew Marvell's ode to

Cromwell: "He nothing common did or mean/Upon that memorable scene."[23]

Hiss's reemergence worried Chambers less than did another event long on his mind. In 1952 Willy Pogany, a New York art designer, had sued Chambers and Random House for libel because *Witness* had erroneously identified him as the brother of Joseph Pogany, a Hungarian Comintern official. Pogany asked for one million dollars in damages. Chambers was convinced Communists or fellow travelers had pressured Pogany into filing suit, perhaps by threatening to expose some dark secret in his past. Chambers, then, must uncover that secret and threaten Pogany in turn. He enlisted as many allies as he could—including the de Toledanos and Arthur Koestler—to make inquiries about Pogany. But he learned nothing,* and the suit moved forward inexorably and in October 1954 went at last to trial. Five days into the proceedings the judge threw out Pogany's claim. Since the plaintiff Pogany was not himself characterized in *Witness* "as a Communist or a Communist sympathizer," said the judge, no libel had occurred. Chambers was relieved, but the episode fed his growing sense of futility. He was still convinced Pogany had been manipulated by Communists or defenders of Alger Hiss. Was there to be no escape from the Hiss case?[25]

Even Christmas, the family's great holiday, was less joyous than usual. Ellen was unable to make the trip. Her husband, due to be discharged from the army in thirty days, had been denied a furlough. Once more the big house felt empty. When the snows came, sealing Whittaker and Esther indoors, they felt like "two old birds . . . who have outstayed the season." The couple talked idly of traveling, perhaps to the warmth of the Iberian coast. Esther had never been abroad.[26]

Meanwhile *National Review* was scheduled to go to press with its first issue in April 1955. There was a delay when Bill Buckley's father suffered a stroke, and Bill rushed to his bedside. Also fund-raising was going slowly. Schlamm, however, was pushing hard to get the magazine out,

---

* Although he found out from Theodore Draper, then at work on *The Roots of American Communism,* that *American Labor's Who's Who,* a compendium published in the 1920s, included a lengthy entry on Willy Pogany, who had painted murals in the old Communist Party headquarters on Union Square. Chambers gratefully borrowed Draper's copy of the book.[24]

even if it was underfunded. They revised the target date to November 1955, in time for the 1956 Republican campaign season.[27]

In the interim Chambers had yet to receive satisfactory answers to the Nixon question. Almost everyone involved with the journal either supported McCarthy or was at least an "anti-anti-McCarthyite," in the words of James Burnham. Buckley's *McCarthy and His Enemies* coauthor, Brent Bozell, slated to serve as *NR*'s Capitol Hill columnist, had even been writing speeches for McCarthy. Not that anyone was listening to them. McCarthy now orated to empty galleries. Buckley and company were already looking to new anti-Communist heralds, such as William Knowland. But they loyally spoke up for McCarthy, to Chambers's exasperation. "For the Right to tie itself in any way to Senator McCarthy is suicide," he warned. "He is a raven of disaster."[28]

In July Chambers agreed to go to New York for a discussion with Buckley and Schlamm, a last-ditch effort to work out terms of collaboration. He had to cancel when he suffered more chest pains. The meeting was postponed to September, when Buckley and Schlamm drove down to Westminster. By this time Chambers had made up his mind. He greeted his visitors cordially but said he could not join their venture. Buckley tried to bring him around. Chambers heard him out and finally said, "No." For Buckley it was "an awesome moment . . . a climaxing disappointment."[29]

The first issue of *National Review* appeared on November 19, 1955, a few days before Buckley turned thirty, without Whittaker Chambers on its masthead. Buckley indicated no readiness, at the moment, to maneuver within the necessities of a socialized America. In a publisher's statement he wrote that *National Review* "stands athwart history, yelling Stop, at a time when no one is inclined to do so, or to have much patience with those who do."[30]

Even had Chambers resolved his differences with *National Review,* he could not have contributed to its first issues. On October 20 he had suffered another heart attack and was stricken with a kidney hemorrhage. Five weeks later, when a dinner invitation came from Richard Nixon, Chambers was still laid up. Esther wrote Nixon explaining a visit was out of the question, unless Chambers came by ambulance.[31] In January Chambers still could not turn over onto his left side without feeling a twinge, even through the cushion of drugs. "I have a small toe in eternity," he told David McDowell. But the rest of him was not yet ready to submit.

In February Chambers received a jolt of fresh energy when reports were published of Nikita Khrushchev's extraordinary address to a closed session of the Twentieth Congress of the Communist Party. In ringing tones the Soviet premier declared an end to the "personality cult" surrounding Joseph Stalin, whom Khrushchev characterized as a blunderer, murderer, and tyrant.[32]

More remarkably, thousands of Stalin's victims, wasting away in the gulag, found their sentences abruptly commuted. Chambers, following this development with wonder and awe, hoped the Ulanovskys might be among the liberated. In fact they were. Later both became influential dissidents, active in samizdat. After Aleksandr's death, in the late 1960s, Nadya immigrated to Israel, with her American-born daughter, Maya.[33]

In the West Khrushchev's revelations had a tidal impact. The CPUSA all but dissolved overnight, its few thousand diehards reeling toward the exits as they learned that the counterrevolutionary fictions invented by Trotsky and then perpetuated by renegades like Chambers had been true after all. More widely, the speech was seen as a turning point in the cold war. A historic change was occurring inside Russia. But what underlay it? A genuine revision in Communist thinking? An internal power struggle?

To Chambers it seemed the real meaning was being missed. He promptly sat down to write an explanatory essay. More inspired than at any time since writing *Witness,* he worked steadily, but very slowly, able to type only half a page before he began "to wobble on the chair." After six weeks he had completed a manuscript that *Life* bought for five thousand dollars and then edited down to a skeletal version, published on April 30. It was Chambers's first byline in more than two years.[34]

Like almost everyone else, Chambers saw the "reverse purge" as a pivotal event and hailed Khrushchev for his boldness in "smashing . . . the Stalinist big lie." But in Chambers's view, Khrushchev's speech did not portend the end of communism. On the contrary, by discrediting Stalin, Khrushchev meant to revitalize the true spirit of the revolution and also rehabilitate the movement internationally. "What the 20th Congress meant to do, and may well succeed in doing, was to make Communism radioactive again." The Soviets were as determined as ever "to take over the rest of the world." The challenge now was the West's. It would have to "match that resonance from some depths within itself. Therein lies the threat to it of the great turn, the drama, now playing out among its inveterate enemies." This judgment seemed to find corroboration in the fall, when Soviet tanks rolled into Budapest and brutally suppressed an uprising there.

Chambers's thoughts turned now toward writing another book. Actually he had been struggling to write one for years but had been unable to settle on a topic. First he had considered an ambitious study of Christianity, two volumes on its rise and fall. Then he had worked for many months on an extended essay, despairingly titled *The Losing Side* and intended as "conservatism's moral apologetic." He had shown pages to Bennett Cerf in late 1954. The publisher was deeply impressed, but Chambers had grown discouraged and finally burned a large portion of the manuscript.[35]

Khrushchev's historic speech had made him see he had something left to say. The theme of the *Life* article was really the theme that had eluded him in *The Losing Side* and that he had tried to elucidate to Buckley and Schlamm—namely, that Communism retained the capacity for swift and sure political maneuver and the West had better catch up.

Chambers wrote to Bernice Baumgarten and David McDowell outlining a new plan for *The Losing Side.* He now had in mind two volumes. The first, *The Third Rome,* a medieval epithet for "the universal Muscovite empire," would expand on the *Life* article, exploring the Communist worldview. The companion volume—titled *Cold Friday,* after the northernmost field on Chambers's property—would discuss "the real revolution of our time . . . a psychological revolution." This was an idea rooted in Marx, who had written powerfully on the alienating dislocations wrought by the Industrial Revolution. *Cold Friday* would also include an account of Chambers's intellectual development and that of his generation at large, magnetized by the promise of social revolution. It was a subject he had originally included in *Witness* but had eliminated for reasons of space and narrative momentum. The two books would form a triad with *Witness.*[36]

But while Chambers had solved the conceptual puzzle of his last work, he faced still the difficulties of getting the books written. He wanted to create a myth of the universe, as Marx, Spengler, and Toynbee had done. Like them, Chambers had an authentic feel for history as poetic drama. But he lacked the intellectual requirements of a system builder. For all his immense reading and his considerable mental strength, Chambers was neither a scholar nor a systematic thinker. Working out an argument, presenting a case from many sides, contesting his opponent's strongest rather than weakest premises: All these were alien to his temperament. His intellectual style was a hybrid of the auto-didact's and the educated publicist's. He was a forager of texts, who read widely and collected memorable tag lines he employed as a form of il-lustrative shorthand, filling out his intuitions and adding them to the ac-cumulated wisdom of his own experience. Much as he deplored "attempts to explain the Communist experience primarily in personal, psychological terms,"[37] it was the one thing he really knew how to do. And he had already done it, in *Witness*.

The new year found the Chamberses hard up. Since the windfalls of 1952 money had been scarce. *Witness*'s sales had dwindled after the first months of publication.* By Christmas of 1954 the family's savings were so low Esther had to postdate a check to David McDowell, who had purchased her Christmas present to Whittaker, an edition of the *Ency-clopaedia Britannica*. Since then Chambers's only income derived from the few articles he had sold, and that amounted to very little, while the farm, far from turning a profit, remained a sinkhole, "the shortest cut to bankruptcy"—this while his medical expenses were high and he had to meet John's tuition payments at Kenyon. At one point, when Chambers was especially strapped, Buckley gave him three thousand dollars—"a call loan," Chambers insisted, which he would repay at the normal 5 percent interest.[39]

Though cash-poor, Chambers was land-rich. The time had come to sell off portions of his property. He put Pipe Creek Farm on the market. The thirteen rooms were vastly more than he and Esther needed. He found a buyer for the house plus thirty-five acres, and at a handsome price. "What really swung the house deal was the pumpkin patch—the bubbly idea of owning Whittaker Chambers's calabash-bed. Wonder-fully queer world!" Chambers reported gleefully to Buckley.

---

* As of 1964, Random House reported that 95,583 copies had been sold, exclusive of Book-of-the-Month Club sales.[38]

On March 1 Whittaker and Esther planned to move into the house on Creek Farm, the property deeded to John. Esther had been renovating the house, much smaller than the Pipe Creek homestead but of "beautifully toned brick" from the clay bank of the Big Pipe Creek. The property too was lovely, ringed on all sides by wooded hills and with a small pond in back.[40]

In mid-January, six weeks before he and Esther were to move out of the big house and the new buyer was to take it over, the place caught fire, owing to a defect in the chimney. The flames were soon brought under control, but the smoke and water damage was substantial. Neighbors rescued household items and hauled them over to Creek Farm. Whittaker and Esther moved in ahead of schedule, billeted amid unpapered walls and "collapsing tunnels of stacked books."

Luckily Chambers's buyer did not back out. With remarkable foresight, he had taken out an insurance policy worth forty-five thousand dollars. This sum, when added to Chambers's fifty-five-hundred-dollar policy, covered the costs of rebuilding. Workmen started in immediately. The new owner's move-in date was July 1.[41]

In May Alger Hiss's book *In the Court of Public Opinion* was published. It was an extended legal brief, four hundred–plus pages, in which Hiss reviewed all the arguments he had made during the case and in his appeal, with the same unconvincing result. He portrayed Chambers as a psychopath and downplayed the wealth of corroborative evidence. He also restated his argument that the true target of the assault had been the New Deal. "One misses the passionate protest and burning sense of outrage usually found in the writings of those who consider themselves victimized," wrote Sidney Hook in *The New York Times Book Review*. "Nor is there the icy logic of unassailable argument which sometimes conveys the same feeling." Author Hiss was as coldly aloof as defendant Hiss. "There is not a paragraph or even a line about the man Alger Hiss or his wife Priscilla," Richard Crossman complained in the *New Statesman,* "how they lived, what they believed in, and how well they knew the [others] whom Chambers named."[42]

Hook suggested to editors at *Life* that Chambers be assigned to review the book. Chambers offered instead to write a larger essay on the case. The proposal was rejected. His written commentary was limited to a statement for AP and UPI. For the first time he publicly exhibited anger at Hiss,

. . . one of the remarkable figures of our time. For almost nine years, he has put on an act for which I know no precedent. Twisting, turning, dodging, though trapped at last by the weight of evidence, which was thoroughly ventilated in the course of exhaustive public hearings and in two prolonged court trials, he nevertheless persists impenitently in claiming that he is innocent. If he could succeed in confusing the public mind on this point, he would succeed in poisoning the truth at its source, and the effect on justice would be not much different from the fall-out of a hydrogen bomb.[43]

Chambers did not want to be available when the book was released. He and Esther escaped to New York, first spending a day with the Buckleys in Stamford. While there, they learned Joe McCarthy had died that day, May 2, in Bethesda Naval Hospital, his liver ruined. Back in Westminster—Chambers missed, by an hour, an AP reporter who had come with questions about Hiss's book—he luxuriated in the arrival, long delayed, of spring. "The apples were in bloom and so were 30 or more dogwoods, self-seeded on the hills. Senator McCarthy was much on my mind; and it seemed to me the strangest chance that I should be seeing these things, and that he could not; that I had survived *him*. It is incongruous."

He tried to write about McCarthy, for a memorial issue of *National Review*, but couldn't bring himself to do it. "I could not follow him living; I could only pity him. Pity of that kind is condemnation of the dead; and silence is more fitting."

Some months later Henry Zolan came to Westminster for his first visit to the farm. The old friends were seated in the living room, in rocking chairs, before the hearth. Zolan had been one of those disappointed at Chambers's failure to denounce McCarthy.

"Tell me, Whit," Zolan asked, "why was it that McCarthy never found a single Communist, not one?"

Smiling enigmatically, Chambers said, "The last time I saw McCarthy, he sat in that chair where you are now and cried."[44]

Though neither a critical nor a commercial success, *In the Court of Public Opinion* succeeded in reviving the Hiss case controversy. Duncan Norton-Taylor, who had been at a seminar attended by several prominent intellectuals, was dismayed to hear Harvard historian Arthur Schlesinger, Sr., a loyal champion of Sacco and Vanzetti, say that while he remained convinced of Hiss's guilt, he now suspected the trial had not been fair. "I can see this myth persisting for years," Norton-Taylor predicted.[45]

He had a solution, which Chambers eagerly took up: the publication, in book form, of Jim Bell's voluminous trial reportage. But neither Time Inc., which owned the copyright, nor David McDowell (the potential editor) showed much interest. Chambers saw they were right. The public at large was not deluded by Hiss.[46]

But some of Chambers's supporters were intent on making a public statement and thought they had found a useful vehicle, a dramatization of the Hiss case. The playwright was Sol Stein, a book publisher and the executive director of the American Committee on Cultural Freedom (which Chambers had joined in December 1954). Stein's play, drawing equally on the case and on *Witness,* was highly sympathetic to Chambers. In December 1955 Stein had shown an early draft, titled *A Shadow of My Enemy,* to Chambers, who was not impressed. Stein failed to grasp the issues of the case and had no true feel for its players. And the writing was poor. Chambers cringed at its many "blaring false note[s]."[47]

But Chambers did not want to disappoint Stein, who meant well and had worked hard. Also, the de Toledanos, Stein's go-betweens, were all for the project, which had at least the merit of stating Chambers's side of the issue. A number of readers, including Thornton Wilder and Lionel Trilling, predicted success.[48]

Unwilling to obstruct Stein or the de Toledanos, now helping with rewrites, Chambers left the decision to Bernice Baumgarten. He trusted her judgment. To his dismay, the agent encouraged Stein and the de Toledanos to proceed, and Chambers dutifully studied revisions as they came in, pastiches of *Witness* that unerringly captured all the book's excesses and none of its poetry. But with the publication of Hiss's book, and the resultant publicity, *A Shadow of My Enemy* seemed fated for a Broadway production, to Chambers's dread. However much revamped, the play could only "add to the racket, and thereby play the game of the [Hiss] book and its author and partisans." It opened anyway, at the ANTA Theater, on December 11, 1957. The cast featured Ed Begley as Augustus Randall (the Chambers character) and Gene Raymond as Horace Smith (Hiss). The director was Daniel Petrie. The reviews were tepid. The play "restates the obvious without adding anything to it of much significance," wrote the *Times*'s theater critic, Brooks Atkinson, echoing Chambers's own opinion. The production closed, mercifully, after a week. There was no stronger ally, at times, than an indifferent public.[49]

.   .   .

With Ike and Nixon securely returned to the White House, Chambers began to rethink his decision on *National Review*. In its first year of existence—in which it changed from a weekly to a fortnightly—the magazine had found a small but loyal readership (of about eighteen thousand) and had established itself as a provocative and articulate, if not yet indispensable, organ of the right.

Chambers remained on close terms with Buckley and played, as promised, the role of sideline adviser, deluging Buckley with suggestions and criticisms. Why not commission Cyril Connolly to write a piece on the defectors Burgess and Maclean? What about a regular "Where Are They Now?" feature reporting the current doings of such villains as Eleanor Roosevelt, Owen Lattimore, O. Edmund Clubb, John Hersey, and Teddy White?[50]

He also was stimulated by a prolonged debate Willi Schlamm and James Burnham were holding in *NR* on the changing Soviet situation. Schlamm was convinced Khrushchev's tightening of the noose in Eastern Europe signaled great danger, while Burnham oppositely maintained the moves were defensive, a sign of incipient weakness, not growing strength. Chambers sided with Schlamm's conclusions but admired Burnham's logical mind.[51]

Chambers was impressed as well by the ex-Communist Frank Meyer, *NR*'s book review editor, with whom he had been in touch since 1953, through their common friend Ralph de Toledano. Chambers had been dazzled by a proposal Meyer had written for a book (eventually published as *The Moulding of Communists*). Meyer was also engaged, less fitfully than Chambers, in the effort of shaping a coherent conservative doctrine, and he was formidably erudite. He introduced Chambers to *Les Temps modernes,* Jean-Paul Sartre's left-wing magazine, among the most brilliant publications of the era, and he delighted Chambers by applying on his behalf for a card at the Boston Athenaeum, which mailed books to subscribers.[52]

But much in *NR* troubled Chambers. The magazine had yet to divorce itself from the "crackpot" right. During the 1956 election only Burnham endorsed the Republican ticket. At the same time the editors remained loyal to McCarthy, forming a cult around him. After his death *NR* eulogized McCarthy in two consecutive issues, with Brent Bozell extolling Joe's "vivid moral sense," Bill Buckley deriding the "superstitions . . . brewed by liberal intellectuals," and Willi Schlamm fervently rededicating himself to McCarthy, whom he depicted as a heroic young god punished for having dared to grapple with "the gargoyles of Anti-Christ."[53]

At the same time Chambers deplored *NR*'s superficial treatment of major figures on the left, such as Sartre, George Orwell, and Milovan Djilas. Chambers would have preferred salvos fired in the direction of the Austrian economist Ludwig von Mises, who had gained renown for arguing that anticapitalist sentiments were rooted in "envy," the resentment of have-nots. To Chambers this "shocking" thesis epitomized "know-nothing conservatism" at its "know-nothingest." In his own years as a Communist, Chambers stiffly said, *he* had not envied capitalists in the least.[54]

Above all, Chambers hesitated for fear he had lost the energy, physical and moral, to rejoin the political fray. It all came down to a simple question: "What can be done with a shattered life at the age of 56; or is it worth trying to do anything with it?"[55]

After promising, in July, to make up his mind in thirty days, Chambers wrote to Buckley the next month saying he was ready to join the staff of *National Review*. Scheduled to travel to Europe the following day, Buckley chartered a one-engine plane and flew to Westminster's small airstrip. Chambers met him and drove him to the farm. He complimented Buckley on his instinct for the grand gesture. Only Harry Luce had demonstrated equivalent flair, flying up once from Washington. The difference, Chambers pointed out, as they jounced along the pitted dirt road, was that Harry had had a limousine waiting at the airstrip.

At the farm they discussed the terms of Chambers's employment. He would draw a salary of $125 a week and write at home, submitting copy for each issue, if possible. He was still spending much of the day in bed and could manage at most three hours' work, in the morning.[56]

Buckley was ecstatic. Apart from the prestige Chambers would bring to the magazine, he was writing now as well as ever. His letters, miniature surrogates for the book Chambers would never complete, were vibrant, allusive, and—with their quick flashes of wry wit—closer to Chambers's conversation than the studied stately rhythms of *Witness*. In 1969, eight years after Chambers's death, Buckley published the correspondence in book form. Today *Odyssey of a Friend* stands beside *Witness* as Chambers's finest prose and as a breviary of his evolving humanism.

Buckley's main concern was Chambers's perfectionism. Buckley knew Chambers's habits all too well, knew about the burned letters and manuscripts, about the book Random House would never see. "Let us judge whether what you write is publishable," the young editor pleaded. "You have no judgment on such matters."[57] Chambers assured him there was no cause for concern. If anything, he would be sending in too much copy.

On September 4 Chambers mailed in his first contribution, the first half of a two-part review of *The New Class,* Milovan Djilas's landmark analysis of the Stalinist bureaucracy. Buckley judged the piece "superb." But it was all he saw. Chambers did not finish the second part and would not allow Buckley to print the manuscript he had.[58]

But soon the pieces started coming in, ruminations on the Soviet Union and world communism, each headlined "Letter from Westminster." Like his private correspondence, these public letters set forth the basis of Chambers's opposition to a rigid and unrealistic conservatism. Having allied himself to the right, he seemed bent on challenging, rebuking, and even outraging its axioms.

His most important article was among his first, a savage review of Ayn Rand's novel *Atlas Shrugged,* a follow-up to the author's best-selling *The Fountainhead* and, like it, a declaration of the author's philosophy of objectivism, much in vogue among conservative libertarians. Chambers was appalled. "The book's dictatorial tone is much its most striking feature," he wrote. "Out of a lifetime of reading, I can recall no other book in which a tone of overriding arrogance was so implacably sustained. Its shrillness is without reprieve. Its dogmatism is without appeal. . . . From almost any page of *Atlas Shrugged,* a voice can be heard, from painful necessity, commanding: 'To a gas chamber—go!' "

Rand did not read the review but was furious. So were many readers. "Chambers the Christian communist," wrote one, "is far more dangerous than Chambers the Russian spy."[59]

Less than a month after he began writing for *National Review,* Chambers felt completely renewed. "It has given me a new lease on life."[60]

In the summer of 1957 Laha Chambers began to slow down, taking to her bed for long stretches. In February she went to Westminster and stayed there through April. She returned to Lynbrook still weakened. Her ailments included myocarditis, arteriosclerosis, and nephritis. Mary

Zolan, Henry's wife, came out from Brooklyn and nursed her for a week, until Laha's physician ordered Laha to the hospital, in East Meadow. Esther, "my Jewish daughter-in-law," as Laha called her, came up to help. After a day in the hospital, Laha died, on June 5, 1958. She was eighty-six. One last time Chambers supervised funeral rites in Lynbrook.[61]

Until the end Laha had been the resourceful "daughter of the Northwest." She kept up her busy social routine, "the usual luncheons—dinners—outings—clubs." She had enjoyed a flurry of celebrity during the Hiss case when journalists (and Hiss operatives) came out to record her story and were impressed by her clever wit and sharp tongue. Laha led them through the house, introduced them to her cat, displayed her "antiques." In her eighties she learned how to use a typewriter, enrolled in French lessons, and planted a new flower garden. Theatrical as ever, she bore a resemblance to Maria Ouspenskaya, the tiny, wizened Russian actress.

Like her elder son, Laha had come to religion in her last years, deciding it "is only in complete surrender that one reaches perfect stature."[62]

In 1958 Chambers decided to make a trip to Europe in August. Esther had never been abroad. Their pretext was the Brussels World's Fair, which Chambers was to cover for *National Review*. After a few days in Brussels they would travel for several weeks in France and Italy. He also wanted to see friends and soul mates: Arthur Koestler, Tom Matthews (now living in England), the ex-Communist novelist Manès Sperber, and, if possible, André Malraux,[63] who had written kindly to Chambers after *Witness* (at Koestler's prompting)* and was now an official in Charles de Gaulle's cabinet. Soon Chambers had lengthened his itinerary to two months. He asked the FBI to find him an apartment in Paris.

But a week before they were to leave, Esther, fearful of the cost the trip would incur, suffered a "heart spell." She said nothing to Chambers

---

* "My dear Malraux," Koestler wrote on April 28, 1953, "I don't know how much you know about Chambers' Odyssey and personality. If you have any faith in my judgment—he is one of the most outstanding, most maligned and most sincere characters whom I have met, and his story is a bizarre and symbolic twentieth-century martyrdom. . . . He lives in terrible physical and spiritual loneliness, and a line from you will mean very much to him." In a letter Malraux told Chambers, "You are one of those who did not return from Hell with empty hands."[64]

but confided in John, home from Kenyon awaiting the draft. John told his father, and Whittaker immediately canceled their plans.[65]

But he remained determined to end his isolation. In August he notified Buckley he wanted to make regular trips to *National Review*'s offices in New York and become a visible presence on the magazine.[66]

It had been ten years since the Hiss case broke, eight years since his exile had begun. That was long enough.

# "The Witness Is Gone"

In the late summer of 1958 Chambers began to commute to Manhattan. He came in on alternate Tuesdays, sweating in his business suit, just in time for the fortnightly editorial lunch of senior staff held at the Catawba Corporation, the business headquarters of William F. Buckley, Sr., a few blocks east of Penn Station. Then he accompanied his new colleagues to *National Review*'s editorial offices on East Thirty-fifth Street.

The quarters, small and grimy, more nearly resembled those of *The New Masses* than the plushly appointed tower of Time Inc. But Chambers settled in happily, nesting his bulk in a tiny, windowless cubicle which he filled with pipe exhalations as he scribbled in pencil, covering yellow second sheets with spidery corrections. He did his own typing, laboriously tapping out draft upon draft, his final copy letter-perfect.

The senior staff worked till eight o'clock, then broke for dinner. After spending Tuesday night at a hotel or at Buckley's house in Stamford, Chambers was at his desk the next morning by eight, helping see the magazine to press. He and Buckley had a sandwich for lunch, and Chambers caught the five o'clock train back to Baltimore.

The years of exile had not diluted Chambers's fame. But they had changed it. The instrument of history had become its relic. On the street and in restaurants New Yorkers turned to stare at the grayer version of the image familiar from newspapers, magazine covers, newsreels, and television. Though only in his mid-fifties, he looked much older, and he carried himself with an ill man's gingerly care.[1]

To his new colleagues, Chambers's arrival was a momentous event. He was a giant, the patron saint of the anti-Communist faith they all shared. But they had no idea what to expect. Some envisioned a walking edition of *Witness,* a fount of apocalyptic utterances. Even Buckley was nervous. At Chambers's first editorial meeting the editor, finishing a convoluted sentence, turned to Chambers deferentially, and asked, "Don't you agree, Whittaker?"

"Up to a point, Lord," Chambers replied, dryly quoting William Boot, the hapless journalist in Evelyn Waugh's *Scoop.*

The room erupted. "I damn near fell on the floor laughing," recalled Jim McFadden, *NR*'s associate publisher. "I hadn't realized that he had such a tremendous sense of humor."[2]

Others too were caught off guard by the "wit and constant laughter" that emanated from Chambers, "this great corpulent ho–ho sort of guy."[3] He scarcely resembled the man who had stalked the corridors at Time Inc., avoiding the gaze of colleagues. The histrionic silences and sly, secret smiles, the intellectual hauteur: They all had vanished.

Gradually Chambers's new colleagues realized this proudly isolated figure was in fact terribly lonely. At editorial lunches Chambers talked as "hungrily" as he ate, Buckley later recalled, and on a limitless range of subjects, "swooping in to make a quick point, withdrawing, relaxing, laughing, listening—he listened superbly, though even as a listener he was always a potent force."[4]

After ten long years it was exhilarating for Chambers to be once again a professional journalist, working alongside talented men on a mission both ideological and literary. *NR*'s contributors were a gathering of the best that postwar conservatism had to offer. James Burnham, Yale political scientist Willmoore Kendall, Frank Meyer: These were men like himself, deeply cultured, multilingual ex-radicals, as skeptical as any on the left of the numbing embourgeoisement of America in the 1950s. They made *National Review*'s offices a stimulating place. So did Buckley, the most charismatic figure in American conservatism, with his ecumenical friendships, his nonideological passion for good prose, his humor, his warmth.

Chambers especially enjoyed the company of much younger writers, staff and contributors, and they in turn were taken with him. At their first meeting Chambers engaged John Leonard, thirty-five years his junior, in a spirited discussion of the beat writers, singling out for praise Jack Kerouac and Allen Ginsberg, Columbia dropouts and bohemians, as Chambers had been twenty years before. "The man knocked me out," recalled Leonard, recruited for *NR* from the pages of the *Harvard Crim-*

*son.* "He was a slovenly toadlike person more interesting than most of the people I ever met, more interesting than Arthur Schlesinger, Jr., or Henry Kissinger"—both stars of the Harvard faculty in the 1950s. *NR's* prodigy, Garry Wills, who poured forth voluminous copy while doing graduate work in classics at Yale, remembered Chambers participating in an excited discussion of a new literary sensation, Vladimir Nabokov's *Lolita.* "I was pushing the Poe references, Jim Burnham the *Grand Guignol,*" Wills recalled, while Chambers insisted, "It's just a funny book."[5]

It was marvelous while it lasted—roughly three months. In mid-November Chambers suffered a heart attack and was ordered to bed for two months. He got up after one month and was plotting a return to the office when Esther put a stop to it. He settled instead for thinking up new articles to write. Maybe something on Pasternak or a postmortem on the 1958 elections, another Republican loss—attributable, said Chambers, to the party's failure to "get some grip on the actual world we live in."[6]

His closer involvement with *National Review* had reinforced Chambers's conviction that the right in general was still avoiding "hard facts." Many at *NR* had been startled by *Sputnik* and insisted it must be a hoax; how could the primitive Soviets have outpaced the United States? To the Russophile Chambers this was preposterous. What was not possible in the country of Tolstoy and Dostoevsky, of Lenin and Trotsky?[7]

There were other differences too. *NR* officially championed the free market economics of von Mises and F. A. Hayek. Chambers was stimulated by the Keynesian heresies of John Kenneth Galbraith's *The Affluent Society.* "There will be no peace for the islands of relative plenty," Chambers wrote in *NR,* "until the continents of proliferating poverty have been lifted to something like the general material level of the islanders."[8] This, though Chambers did not say it, had been the summary objective of the New Deal.

But the most surprising of Chambers's departures from conservative orthodoxy came on the subject of internal security. A new controversy arose in June 1958, when the Supreme Court ruled it unconstitutional for the State Department to deny a passport to any citizen on the basis of his political beliefs. The department protested, pleading the need for tighter restrictions to keep home "known Communists who are going abroad for the purpose of assisting and supporting the international Communist conspiracy." John Foster Dulles sought legislative redress but was rebuffed by a Democratic Congress. The debate climaxed in the spring of 1959, when a passport was issued to Alger Hiss. To reporters, who had phoned for comment, Chambers blandly said, "Alger Hiss is an American citizen. He has every right to apply for and receive a passport."

No, Chambers told the perplexed readers of *National Review.* He had not been misquoted. He had said those words and meant them. "I am a bug on the question of unrestricted travel, as I am against the obscenities of wire-tapping, mail tampering, and related mischiefs that, in the name of good intention, are helping to pave the road that leads to 1984." Was this the same Chambers who in 1952 had advocated expanded powers to an FBI already engaged in wiretapping, mail tampering, and related mischiefs? Times had changed, and so had America's responsibilities in the world. "The spectacle of an artist like Paul Robeson, denied a passport by his own government, makes us traduced of other nations," wrote Chambers. "A little shift in the political weather, and it may be the spokesmen of the Right whose freedom of travel is restricted. . . . The precedent will be almost unassailable. Anti-Communists will have promoted it." The right must catch up with reality and "examine and define with a special scrupulousness the civil liberties field." Why should "the Liberals, by default, preempt the humane and intellectually sound positions?"

Chambers was sounding precariously like a liberal. So be it. He had wearied of ideological battles. "I have scarcely an interest in invective tags." His prevailing interest was simply to "grope for reality." He quoted Trotsky ("one of my great contemporaries"): "Anybody looking for a quiet life has picked the wrong century to be born in."[9]

In the spring of 1959 Esther was ready to travel abroad. Her health was declining, and it was her dream to see Europe, especially France, before she died. The expense of traveling was no longer a worry. Chambers had enjoyed a good run on the stock market, his newest hobby.[10]

In June they would fly to Amsterdam and then proceed directly to Paris. From Paris they would go to Austria for several days with Koestler, then to Italy for a tour lasting some weeks. They would conclude with a few days in West Berlin and then rest up in Greece, where friends, the Norton-Taylors, were vacationing.[11]

They spent the morning of June 9 with the Buckleys, who drove them to Idewild Airport that evening. Chambers and Esther easily weathered their first transatlantic flight, "some 8 or more hours of wholly supportable discomfort."

Amsterdam, glimpsed fleetingly, was "jolly." Paris was "cold, dirty, vast, engulfing, but, above all, cold." They disliked their hotel, the Palais d'Orsay, despite a balcony overlooking the Seine and the Tuileries. But they were pleased to discover a Westminster friend, publisher John W. Eckenrode, staying there also. Eckenrode, who had brought along a station wagon and driver, invited the couple along for a tour of the city.[12]

The high point in Paris was meeting the novelist Manès Sperber, one of the great survivors of Europe's terrible recent decades. His travail had taken him from a tiny Jewish village in Galicia to secret Comintern work in the 1920s, to arrest and solitary confinement in a Nazi prison cell after the Reichstag fire of 1933, thence to Paris. In his thousand-page trilogy *Like a Tear in the Ocean,* written during the occupation, Sperber memorialized torments endured, not imagined. He was now as dogmatically anti-Communist as Chambers.

The appointment was arranged by Koestler. He revered Sperber, whom "he considered his master and the most competent psychologist of our time," noted Simone de Beauvoir. At the same time, Koestler warned Chambers, Sperber could be a depressing companion. But Chambers found him exhilarating. Sperber, who wore a gentle mystic's look of radiant suffering, told Chambers about the moment, at the outbreak of World War II, when he realized Europe was worth saving. He had been penniless and living in a windowed garret. Staring out it at Notre Dame one day, he thought, "Just those stones are still worth killing for and dying for." Chambers had had a similar thought, about Chartres, while he was at *Time.* Sperber counseled Chambers that finding the truth did not matter, but seeking it did. The two tentatively agreed to meet again in Provence.[13]

The Chamberses had been in Paris only a few days when they heard from Koestler, who had already booked rooms for them at the Boeglerhoff, his hotel in the Alpine village of Alpbach. The couple flew to Innsbruck at once. At the hotel Chambers tried to phone Koestler, but the line was tied up. They were awakened late that night by the ringing phone. It was Koestler, explaining that a landslide, the worst in half a century, had wiped out portions of the mountain road. "Nevertheless, we got through," Chambers wrote to Buckley, "by jeep, on a road just wide enough for a jeep, and not always quite that. On my side, without leaning out at all, I could see straight down several hundred feet. Happily, the Austrian army was at the wheel of the jeep." Koestler was waiting at the point where the trail emerged. He regaled Chambers with imaginary newspaper headlines: WHITTAKER CHAMBERS CRASHES OVER ALPINE TRAIL ON SECRET VISIT TO ARTHUR KOESTLER/BRITISH INTELLIGENCE QUESTIONS SURVIVING WRITER.[14]

For Chambers this reunion was a culminating moment. Koestler was the contemporary he esteemed above all others. No intellectual of the era had peered so deeply into the abyss and felt so bleakly its hard return stare. Imprisoned by the Falangists during the Spanish Civil War, he had been placed in solitary confinement for three months. One night "the inmates of cells 39, 41, and 42 on my left and right were all marched off, with only my cell No. 40 spared, after the warder had put his key, no doubt, by mistake, into my own lock, and then withdrawn it." Koestler kept sane by deriving geometrical formulas (mathematics was a long-standing hobby) and by writing a journal. "My predicament," he decided, "was merely an extreme form of the predicament inherent in the human condition." This discovery explained the curious exaltation of *Darkness at Noon*.[15]

There was no awkwardness between the two ex-revolutionists. In letters they had cemented the bond formed instantly in New York. Koestler thought Chambers "one of the most outstanding, most maligned, and most sincere" of men.[16] With his secretary (and future wife), Cynthia Jeffries, Koestler led the Chamberses on a tour of the house they were building in Alpbach. But mainly they talked, switching from English to German and back. (Esther, with her Yiddish, followed German fairly easily.)

Koestler wanted Chambers to meet Margarete Buber-Neumann, who was staying in Arlberg. Scarcely anyone alive had a richer pedigree than Grete Buber-Neumann. She was the wife of "the fabulous Heinz Neumann who had engineered the Communist revolt in Canton in 1929," the daughter-in-law of philosopher Martin Buber, the sister-in-law of Willi Münzenberg (the Comintern's most brilliant propagandist). Grete had endured sentences first in Soviet and then Nazi prison camps. In Alpbach, Buber-Neumann recounted her experiences in the Nazi death camp at Ravensbrück, where she had helped organize a group of Polish women who stole into the commandant's office and effaced the lists of those scheduled for the gas chamber. Her closest friend at Ravensbrück was the Czech journalist Milena Jesenská, the recipient of Kafka's last impassioned letters.

"So there we sat and talked," Chambers told Buckley. "Then, we realized that, of our particular breed, the old activists, we are almost the only survivors—the old activists who were articulate, consequent revolutionists, and not merely agents." To be accepted—embraced—by these "great spirits" was balm for one still despised by many of his countrymen.[17]

After a week in Alpbach the travelers flew to Italy, via Zurich, amid a rainstorm. The clouds parted once, briefly, to reveal "the raw Alps below." When they touched down at Milan's Malpensa ("never was an airport so happily named)," the sky was refulgent with lightning. Their landing cleared the way for a TWA plane to take off. While ascending, it crashed. The victims included Enrico Fermi's sister. The Chamberses, wading through customs, had no idea what had happened until Whittaker saw the headlines in the next morning's *Corriere della Sera*.

It was on to Venice, by train. Chambers fell in love with the city, the world's "last polis." The walls were crumbling, the water flowed brackishly through the canals, but the city "has the cleanest human climate of any I have known." He envisioned living out his remaining days there. But they had only a week.[18]

From Venice they traveled south to Rome, their arrival unfortunately timed with the onset of the blistering July heat. Their lodgings were at the Hotel Metropole, on the via Principe Amedeo. Chambers deplored Rome's "proliferant vulgarity," the "miles of second and third rate this and that." But then all of Europe, risen from the ashes, seemed reborn as a tourist arcade. Even after a side trip to Florence, a "wonder city," where Esther lost herself amid the masterpieces, Whittaker rued the many changes since 1923, when the Continent, pregnant with disaster, had yet seemed "full of hope and tremendously exciting."[19]

It was not Europe's fault alone. The pace of travel was catching up with Chambers. The strain on his heart was too much. In Rome he delved into his supply of nitroglycerin tablets and for the next ten days was "living on the stuff," though it left him in a "rancid mental state." A return to Venice helped. His chest pains ebbed, and he cut back on nitroglycerin. Entranced once again, he idly dreamed of renting a house or apartment there.[20]

Recovered, he prepared for a visit to Germany, his first in thirty-six years. He had made tentative plans to meet Willi Schlamm, who had quit *National Review* in a huff in 1957 and later persuaded himself that Chambers had orchestrated his departure. In fact Schlamm had been intriguing to take over the magazine, and Buckley had eased him out. In Germany Schlamm had become an anti-Communist sage, celebrated for his advocacy of a holy nuclear showdown with the Soviets, and had since "forgiven" Chambers the imagined perfidy. The two, eager to reunite, had twice failed to meet in Zurich. Chambers also wanted to see Hede Massing, a friend since shortly after the Hiss case, who was traveling in Germany.[21]

The Chamberses made it to Berlin and Munich, and then, thoroughly exhausted, canceled their plans to relax in Greece. They were back in Westminster in early August, a month ahead of schedule. Chambers's doctor "put me to bed, shot me full of morphine and much else besides, and told me to stay there for a month."[22]

Chambers came home resolved to complete some unfinished business. In September he enrolled at the local college, Western Maryland. He hoped to earn his B.A. by the end of the summer and then begin work on his master's, in Romance languages. He also registered for ancient Greek. (He had already been studying Russian via a televised lecture series offered at George Washington University.)

First he sat for an interview with the dean of students at the small, neat campus, overlooking Westminster and the surrounding farms. When asked what he planned to do with his M.A., the fifty-eight-year-old applicant admitted he had no idea, though he expected "I shall be different from what I am at this moment."

The dean nodded understandingly. He was the same age as Chambers.[23]

Over the next two years—the last of his life—Chambers was a full-time student. To his language courses he added others in economics and biology, the latter at the urging of Koestler, the author of books on the history of science. He had told Chambers, "You cannot understand what is going on in the world unless you understand science." Chambers, "born a perpetual student," joyously attacked his studies. Each morning he was in his basement office at dawn, preparing for class, and on weekends he studied all day long. For the first time he excelled in the classroom. "Straight A's," he bragged to Koestler in June 1960, after completing his first year. He was delighted when his lab partner, a girl almost forty years his junior, taught him the lyrics to a pop hit, "Itsy Bitsy Teenie Weenie Yellow Polka Dot Bikini." The learning never stopped.

He was disheartened, however, by his classmates' curious lack of political passion. In his own day it had been so different, debating with the
*ernste Menschen* over creeds and books. Why, Chambers wondered, was
there so little radicalism among the young? He hoped it wasn't because
they were young conservatives, "a contradiction in terms." The very
phrase *young conservatives* "has always 'stuck in my throat like a dead
rat,' " he said, quoting a favorite expression of Khrushchev's.[24]

In the fall of 1959 Chambers stopped writing for *National Review*. The
stated reason was lack of time, owing to his studies. The unstated reason
was his differences with the magazine. These had become irreconcilable
in September, when Khrushchev made a historic ten-day visit to the
United States, at Eisenhower's invitation. *NR* judged this the latest in
Yalta-like appeasements. Bill Buckley formed a Committee Against
Summit Entanglements (CASE) and at Carnegie Hall brought a delighted audience of twenty-five hundred to its feet when he castigated
Eisenhower for welcoming the Soviet premier to the White House after
having barred Joe McCarthy.

Chambers, who favored the goodwill visit, countered wearily that
Khrushchev was not a monster "in the sense that Stalin *was* a monster;
and it does much disservice to say he is. It blurs where we need win-
dowpanes." Chambers was certain "Khrush really wants disarmament,
because he really needs it." And what was the preferable alternative,
World War III? That seemed to be *NR*'s true position—one "popular, I
am told, with the SAC [Strategic Air Command], though I doubt it
would be so with wider circles." Since 1958 Chambers had opposed
even the existing arms race. "The West keeps piling up weapons sys-
tems," he complained, "which lead of course to two bad alternatives: (1)
to retreat wherever there is any danger of using the weapons; (2) the
temptation to use them, which is catastrophic."[25]

In November Chambers resigned from *NR*. "I have never taken any
real part in editing the magazine, have contributed only some random
and infrequent writing," he told Buckley. "It is now clear that, for some
time, I shall be unable to do even that. So I must go."

Buckley felt the loss keenly. Chambers remained a lodestar to the
right, even if the right was slow to follow sometimes, and he "never
wrote a piece for us . . . that was out of harmony with the thrust of *National Review*'s position." Buckley and Chambers remained close friends

and each week talked on the phone, except one day when the phone company cut off Chambers's service because he refused to let them trim one of his favorite trees.[26]

In the summer of 1960 Chambers and Esther discussed a second European trip, for the fall, but neither had the strength. The following spring they canceled a drive to the South with Buckley. Chambers apologized for botching up the plans. "Weariness, Bill—you cannot yet know literally what it means." He felt the end approaching and was ready. Once, when Henry Zolan came to visit, he scolded Chambers for having put on so much weight. It was bad for his health.

"I don't care," Chambers said. "I feel better this way."[27]

In June 1961 John Chambers married. The ceremony was in Washington, where John had begun the journalistic career his father had long wanted for him. Mindful of the press clamor at Ellen's wedding, Chambers kept the event secret, inviting only a handful of friends to the ceremony, held at the same Georgetown church where the infant John F. Kennedy, Jr., the new president's son, had been baptized months before.

Afterward the party dined at the Statler Hilton. It had been nine years since Chambers had shared a podium there with Alfred Kohlberg and decried "the big people, the nice people" who had run "hysterically" to the side of Alger Hiss.

He made no speeches on this occasion. "Whittaker was quiet, but I think he was very happy," Buckley remembered. He even sipped champagne. At age sixty he had met the last of his paternal duties.[28]

A month later, on the night of July 8, a Saturday, Chambers felt sharp chest pains. At midnight he phoned Dr. Wilkens but discouraged the physician, elderly herself, from coming over. Esther stayed up with him. In the early morning she dozed off. When she awoke, at about seven, her husband lay motionless on the floor. He had rolled off the bed. Esther phoned Dr. Wilkens, who came over and pronounced him dead, of coronary occlusion.

John and Esther told Dr. Wilkens they wanted Chambers's death kept secret, lest reporters descend on them. On Sunday morning the body was cremated in Washington. Only John was present. Ellen couldn't get away in time. Esther had been rushed to a Gettysburg hospital, comatose, after swallowing an overdose of barbiturates. She regained consciousness on Friday, July 14, and was released several days later. She lived until 1986, staying at Creek Farm, which she converted into a shrine to her husband, its walls covered with her portraits of him. Copies of *Witness* and of his *Cold Friday,* the posthumous work Esther edited with the help of Duncan Norton-Taylor, were displayed in a bookcase, but visitors were discouraged from touching them.[29]

On July 11 the news of Chambers's death was made public. Arthur Koestler sent a telegram to *National Review,* for a memorial issue: "I always felt that Whittaker was the most misunderstood person of our time. When he testified he knowingly committed moral suicide to atone for the guilt of our generation. . . . The witness is gone, the testimony will stand."[30]

To many Chambers remained a puzzle. He had offered himself to the nation as both sinner and savior. Some saw him as an exemplar of humble martyrdom, others as a monstrous egotist. His moral attitude at times recalled the stoic resignation of the ancient tragedians, at times the antiheroism of Sartre or Beckett, at times the torment of the twice-born soul.

"You never changed, Whit," Henry Zolan told him near the end, "you just changed sides."[31]

It was true. Each side, in the instant he joined it, seemed outnumbered, but he chose it anyway. This was his secret pride. Since early childhood, when he first awoke to the doom of Earle Avenue and resolved in his mind to escape it, Chambers had known he could never really be free. The instrument of history was also its captive. "I was about 23," he reflected, "when I discovered, rather by chance, that Oedipus went on to Colonus."[32] In the tragedy of history there is always another act, always another penalty. And there can be no justice, only pity, for those still standing when the curtain falls.

# Appendix:
## Sifting the Evidence

To this day the Hiss case remains one of the great controversies of the postwar era, especially as new evidence, real and alleged, has surfaced.

The first strong challenge to the guilty verdict came in Hiss's motion for a new trial, filed on January 24, 1952, and denied (by Judge Goddard) six months later. The motion rested on two major contentions.

The defense argued that Chambers had testified falsely at the trial (and earlier) about the date of his defection from the underground. Chambers had initially said he broke "in late 1937 or very early 1938." But after producing the spy papers, some of which dated from April 1938, he pushed the date back to April 15, about the time he had begun work on the *Dunant* translation for Oxford University Press.

But the defense, in its motion, cited as evidence correspondence from Oxford's files that indicated Chambers had been in touch with Oxford in March 1938. How, then, to explain documents in Chambers's possession dating several weeks later?[1]

The confusion was easily solved when FBI agents questioned Chambers on the events leading up to and culminating in his break. Rethinking the sequence of moves he had made in those weeks of high anxiety, Chambers realized the defense was partly right. He had received the manuscript from Paul Willert in March 1938 and promptly translated some chapters. Then he had set the job aside while he saw to the next, definitive stage of his defection, his physical separation from the underground and his flight to Daytona Beach. It was there, in mid- to late April, that he seriously began work on the translation, racing to meet

Oxford's May 1 deadline. This chronology was borne out by his correspondence with Willert, by Esther's letters to the Park School, and by the timing of the flight to Florida and back.[2]

The centerpiece of the defense's appeal was a charge of conspiracy, first broached by Hiss at his sentencing when he declared himself the victim of "forgery by typewriter." The 1952 motion theorized that Woodstock 230009, the machine produced so dramatically at the first trial by Lloyd Stryker, was a fake built by Chambers (and unnamed accomplices). To demonstrate the feasibility of the theory, Hiss hired a wizard of typewriter construction, Martin K. Tytell, who devised a typeface that closely duplicated Woodstock 230009. According to the defense's document expert, Elizabeth McCarthy, Tytell's copy was so good she herself would "find it difficult if not impossible" to tell apart samples typed on the two machines. Thus, the defense argued, a phony machine *could* have been built.[3]

The defense went on to challenge the authenticity of Woodstock 230009. Was it really the machine owned by the Hisses in the 1930s? There were reasons for suspicion. For one thing, Woodstock records were not clear on when exactly the original typewriter, a hand-me-down from Priscilla Hiss's father, Thomas Fansler, had been manufactured and sold. Defense experts also raised questions about possible tampering. The keys on the recovered machine had strange solderings, possibly "not done at the Woodstock plant or by a professional repair man."[4]

But if the Woodstock was a fake, who had manufactured it and how had he—or they—succeeded in planting it on the Hiss defense? Here the defense was hard put to supply plausible answers.

Martin Tytell's experiment seemed to establish the feat was possible. But he was an outstanding technician with years of experience customizing typewriters. Even so, he had struggled mightily to build a replica. His first effort, five months in the construction, was a failure that came nowhere near duplicating Woodstock 230009. Only when Elizabeth McCarthy joined in, checking weekly on Tytell's progress, did the results improve. The final product was the outcome of more than a year's careful labor, and kinks still remained. McCarthy noted imperfections. FBI analysts found more. It was hard to imagine how Chambers could have had produced a flawless copy in a far narrower period, the three-month interval between August 17, 1948 (when Hiss had first dared him to risk a slander suit), and November 17, 1948, when Chambers had walked into the Baltimore deposition with a sheaf of typed documents. As for his mechanical aptitude, it was best summed up by Laha, who, when told of the theory, laughed. "Why, Beadle couldn't even pound a nail in the wall," she said. "He was all thumbs."[5] What was more, he would have had to accomplish this feat at a time when his schedule was filled with interrogations and trial preparations.

The only answer, then, was that the FBI and possibly HUAC had been the true authors of a conspiracy to frame Hiss. The bureau, at least, had the technical wherewithal to build a typewriter. But even if this had happened—and not one document in the massive FBI archive suggests it did—how had the fraudulent Woodstock wound up in the hands of Hiss's attorneys, who were following their own leads? And what of the two dozen or more FBI agents who "shook the City of Washington down to a fare-thee-well" in a frantic search for the Woodstock? Had that been an act, a phony hunt complete with mountainous paperwork? Or had J. Edgar Hoover sent his foot soldiers in one direction while he subtly guided the Hiss team through the winding path of inquiry that eventually led them to a Washington junk dealer?

This theory also required a redefinition of Chambers's role. He was no longer the depraved mastermind of Hiss's ruin, driven by "motives of revenge or hatred," but, in the defense's new rendition, a pawn manipulated by the true conspirators, Hoover and possibly Nixon.[6]

Besides being improbable, the theory did not account for two important facts: (1) The government's case against Hiss had never rested on the authenticity of the recovered Woodstock, but on the similarity of the typeface on the two sets of documents, evidence not linked to any particular typewriter, and (2) Chambers had also been in possession of handwritten notes whose authorship Hiss acknowledged.

Meanwhile, even as the Hiss defense mounted its appeal, a new witness had come forward: Nathaniel Weyl, sometime AAA economist and Ware Group wunderkind. Weyl had quit the unit in July 1934, finding the pressure of secrecy intolerable. Had he lasted a few weeks longer, he would doubtless have been introduced to Carl, the courier from New York. As it was, the two did not meet, so Weyl could not testify to any relationship between Chambers and Hiss, although he could have said whether he remembered Hiss as a cell member.

But Weyl had been silent all during the case. More curious still, in *Treason,* a book he had written in 1949 on the Communist conspiracy, he had implied the charges against Hiss were false. "I had to write about the Hiss case," he later explained. "But the matter was still in court . . . the first trial was a hung jury. So as far as I was concerned the matter of espionage was still an open question." Besides, Weyl himself had not participated in espionage and knew nothing about it. As for the activities he did know about, "I was not going to reveal my involvement. . . . I did not desire any career as a former Communist. So I approached [the subject] as if I had no personal knowledge of Communist party membership."[7]

Finally, in the fall of 1950, ten months after Hiss's conviction, Weyl had gone to the FBI and confessed his membership in the Ware unit. He repeated his testimony before the McCarran Committee in February 1952, a month after Hiss had filed his appeal. As a charter member of the Ware Group, Weyl had attended "fifteen to twenty" unit meetings at Helen Ware's violin studio and was able to name his other accomplices. They included Alger Hiss, whom Weyl recalled as a dues-paying and doctrinaire Party member, "a true believer, a deeply committed Communist."[8]

One last fling at establishing Hiss's innocence came in 1992, when selected Moscow archives were unlocked and opened to researchers. At the request of Alger Hiss, then aged eighty-eight, General Dmitri A. Volkogonov, chairman of the Russian government's military intelligence archives, authorized a search of KGB files and then sent Hiss a letter exonerating him on the basis of available files, none of which indicated Hiss had ever spied for Soviet intelligence. Within weeks, however, Volkogonov sheepishly admitted his search had been cursory and many relevant files had been destroyed. He did not offer to check again. Other Russian researchers, diligently combing intelligence files, privately reported that after Volkogonov's blunder officials had scoured the archives and removed all files pertaining to Chambers and Hiss.[9]

But documentation on Hiss did turn up in a Communist archive. In 1993 Maria Schmidt, a Hungarian historian working in the files of the Interior Ministry, in Budapest, came upon the dossier of Noel Field, who had been imprisoned in Budapest in 1949 after his defection behind the Iron Curtain. Released in 1954, Field was debriefed by Communist police, to whom he gave a detailed accounting of his secret work in the United States and of his close friendship with Alger Hiss, a fellow agent. According to Field, Hiss had tried to recruit him into the underground in 1935—the same incident Hede Massing had recalled. "I knew from what Hiss told me that he was working for the Soviet secret service," said Field. Surprised by Hiss's overture, Field "carelessly told him I was already working for Soviet intelligence." When Field reported his blunder to Hede Massing, "I received a stern rebuke from her. . . . A little later she told me I had done greater damage than I would believe and that because of me the whole network had to be reorganized."[10]

Not long after this new revelations emerged from the U.S. government. First, in 1993 the State Department declassified documents relating to a security investigation in 1946 that disclosed Hiss had procured top secret reports he was not authorized to see—on atomic energy, China policy, and other matters relating to military intelligence. The investigation was concluded in late November 1946. Two weeks later Hiss notified John Foster Dulles he was available, after all, to head the Carnegie Endowment.[11]

Then, in the summer of 1995, the National Security Agency began to release the Venona traffic, a total of more than two thousand cables sent from U.S.-based Soviet agents to the home office in Moscow. The messages had been intercepted in the 1940s by American counterintelligence officers and in the next years were painstakingly decoded. The most important batch of cables, released on March 5, 1996, confirmed that there had been a large espionage network centered in the federal government. Among those implicated were Harry Dexter White, Victor Perlo, Laurence Duggan, and Alger Hiss, who was implicated in a single cable, dated March 30, 1945.

In the cable Anatoly Gromov, the NKVD *rezident* in Washington, reports on a conversation with another Soviet handler, Ishkak Akhmerov, "the leading NKVD illegal" in the United States. Akhmerov had recently interviewed a well-placed unnamed GRU agent within the State Department. The official told Akhmerov he had attended the Yalta Conference and then flown on to Moscow, where he was thanked by Soviet diplomat Andrey Vyshinsky for his devoted service.

The Yalta delegation included only four members of the State Department, all of whom flew on to Moscow. The four were Secretary of State Stettinius; his assistant, Wilder Foote; the director of the Office of European Affairs, H. Freeman Matthews; and the deputy director of the Office of Special Political Affairs, Alger Hiss. In Moscow the contingent met with Vyshinsky. Only Hiss was ever suspected of being a Communist.

The American agent further told Akhmerov he had been working for Soviet intelligence since 1935 and "for some years . . . has been the leader of a small group" of agents, "for the most part consisting of his [family] relations."

All this led American counterintelligence officers to conclude that the agent, identified only by his code name Ales, was "probably Alger Hiss."[12] Thus Hiss remained a Soviet agent long after Chambers's defection and possibly up until the moment he was forced out of the State Department. Chambers had made a thoughtful surmise, not a wild accusation, when, under threat of a lawsuit, he declared, "Alger Hiss was a Communist and may be [one] now."

# *Notes*

| NA | National Archives (Washington, D.C.) |
|---|---|
| RCP | Russian Center for the Preservation and Study of Documents Relating to Modern History (Moscow: Formerly Central Party Archives) |
| RDT | Ralph de Toledano Papers (Hoover Institution; Mugar Library, Boston University) |
| RMN | Richard M. Nixon Papers, Richard Nixon Library and Birthplace (Yorba Linda, Calif.) |
| SOLOW | Herbert Solow Collection (Hoover Institution Archives, copyright Stanford University) |
| TIME | Time Inc. Archives (New York City) |
| VENONA | Venona traffic (especially documents released by the National Security Agency on March 5, 1996, available on the World Wide Web at http://www.nsa.gov:8080) |
| ZELIGS | Meyer Zeligs Papers, Harvard Law School Library (Cambridge, Mass.) |
| WAR | William A. Reuben Papers, Labadie Collection, University of Michigan (Ann Arbor, Mich.) |
| WFB | William F. Buckley, Jr., Papers (Yale, *National Review,* plus papers in his own possession) |
| 1st Trial | Minutes of First Trial, United States of America vs. Alger Hiss. Microfilm (Scholarly Resources Inc., Wilmington, Del.) |
| 2d Trial | Transcript of Record, Second Trial, United States of America vs. Alger Hiss. Bound volumes. (U.S. Court of Appeals, 2d Circuit) |

All others are identified in the Notes.

## SELECTED NEWSPAPERS AND PERIODICALS

| BAS | *Baltimore Sun* |
|---|---|
| DW | *Daily Worker* |
| LD | *Labor Defender* |
| NM | *The New Masses* |
| NR | *National Review* |
| NYHT | *New York Herald Tribune* |
| NYT | *The New York Times* |
| SSO | *South Side Observer* (Long Island) |
| TNR | *The New Republic* |
| WP | *The Washington Post* |

All others are identified in the Notes.

## OUTCAST *(1901–1925)*

### Epigraph

1. W. H. Auden, *Selected Poems: New Edition,* ed. Edward Mendelson (Vintage, 1989).

### Chapter 1: Vivian

1. Whittaker Chambers, *Witness* (Random House, 1952), pp. 91–97 (hereafter WC and *W*).

2. Richard Godfrey Chambers, born September 26, 1903, copy of birth certificate (ZELIGS); "Personal History of Whittaker Chambers," FBI NY 65-14920, p. 151; Prospect Park address, New York City Directory, 1901–1903.

3. *W,* p. 96; Wilbur Macey Stone, "Jay Chambers, Artist," *Bulletin of the New York Public Library,* vol. 34 ( January 1930).

4. "Abstract of the Title" of property on 228 Earle Avenue (courtesy of Rodney Dawnkaski, current owner); Horace Schmahl, "Investigation of [WC] in Nassau County," Oct. 20, 1948 (WAR); Laha Chambers estate documents (WAR); *W,* p. 93.

5. For history of Lynbrook, see three unpublished mss.: Steven J. Willner, "Lynbrook Legacy," c. 1960, originally published in the *Town Leader;* "Lynbrook's 50th Anniversary"; and "Lynbrook, U.S.A." (all courtesy of Arthur S. Mattson). *W,* p. 102.

6. Charles Whittaker death certificate, in his Civil War pension file (NA); news clipping, "D. Whittaker Traveler, Dies," *Milwaukee Journal,* Oct. 1, 1928, at the State Historical Society of Wisconsin, at Madison. David Whittaker, Charles's older brother, was a "traveler, sportsman, and railroad builder," and a prominent figure in Milwaukee.

7. He was principal, in all, of four different schools, in 1867–1879. See *Our Roots Grow Deep* (2d ed., 1836–1967), publication of Milwaukee Public Schools.

8. "Registration of Marriages," Milwaukee Historical Society; Mary Whittaker death certificate (WAR). *W,* p. 128.

9. *Milwaukee Sentinel,* Jan. 26, 1871, Apr. 3, 1871, Nov. 11, 1871; also Frank Luther Mott, *A History of American Magazines: 1885–1905* (Harvard, 1957), pp. 55, 101. *Milwaukee Sentinel,* July 25, 1868, Dec. 7, 1868. See also Directory of U.S. Patent Office, Jan. 23, 1877, pp. 147, 221. CW's invention, for a hat rack attached to the underside of a theater seat, is accurately described in "Personal History," p. 153, and in *W,* p. 101.

10. See *Milwaukee Sentinel,* Dec. 25, 1872, on failure of Whittaker's magazine. See *Milwaukee Sentinel,* Feb. 21, 1876, for "fine gothic residence . . . on Farwell Avenue, near Royall Place, built at a cost of $6,500." In 1878 Whittaker sold his "stock" at a sheriff's sale and later declared bankruptcy. *Milwaukee Sentinel,* Feb. 28, May 3, May 6, 1878; Laha told her sons (*W,* p. 101) their grandfather had been the city's school superintendent. In fact he ran for the office in 1800 but was defeated in a bitter contest and later driven from his principalship and, in effect, from the city. He moved to Chicago in 1880: *Milwaukee Sentinel,* Apr. 7, Apr. 24, May 15, July 2, July 4, 1880.

11. See Eugene Leach, "Story of Later Private Schools in Racine," unpublished ms. at the Racine County Historical Society and Museum. In *W* (p. 101), WC mentions "the Horlicks" as one of the prosperous families who sent their daughters to the Home School. Alice Horlick and Laha Whittaker both appear on Leach's list (p. 5) of "well-known pupils of the school."

12. See Chicago Business Directory, 1886–1893, and also City Directory. In 1886 Whittaker is listed as president of the Charles Whittaker Manufacturing Company. He made and sold brass fixtures, including hot- and cold-water faucets of his own invention. See U.S. Patent Office, Nov. 1, 1881, p. 266; Nov. 21, 1882, pp. 1728–29; May 9, 1882, p. 1373; Aug. 15, 1882, p. 519. See also "Personal History," p. 153, and *W,* p. 101.

13. *W,* p. 101. On Mary Stuart McMurphy, the Home School's founding head-mistress, see *Woman's Who's Who of America,* editor in chief John William Leonard (American Common Wealth Company, 1915), p. 530. According to Leach, "Story" (p. 3), Home School graduates were "accepted by the leading colleges of the east."

14. See "Personal History," p. 154, and *W,* pp. 102, 124.

15. "Six or seven years": Oliver Pilat, "Report on Whittaker Chambers," *New York Post,* June 14, 1949 (first of two articles). Charles first taught (French) in the New York City public schools. See New York City Directory, 1897–1898; "Personal History," p. 154. The lunch counter opened c. 1898. See New York City Directory; "Personal History," p. 154.

16. On Charles's illness, death, and estate, see various documents in his Civil War pension file, at NA.

17. The couple had met by 1898. See *Jay Chambers, His Book-Plates,* a limited-edition volume (350 copies), published in 1902, with an introduction by Wilbur Macey Stone. A plate titled "Laha Whittaker" is dated 1898. (A copy is in the Print Collection of the New York Public Library.)

18. Jay's background: Stone, "Jay Chambers, Artist" and his introduction to Jay's *Book-Plates.* Jay's mentor at Drexel was Howard Pyle, the period's best-known book illustrator. See Edward D. McDonald and Edward M. Hinton, *Drexel Institute of Technology, 1891–1941: A Memorial History* (Drexel, 1942), pp. 130–31; Ann Barton Brown, *Howard Pyle, a Teacher: The Formal Years, 1894–1905,* published in conjunction with the exhibition "Howard Pyle, a Teacher" at Brandywine River Museum, Chadds Ford, Pennsylvania, May 31–Sept. 1, 1980. On Jay's boyishness, see Stone's introduction; also E. B. White, "Noontime of an Advertising Man," *The New Yorker* (June 6, 1949). White and Jay were friends at Frank Seaman Inc., an advertising agency, in 1924, just before White joined *The New Yorker.*

19. Both groom and bride gave false ages on their marriage application, presumably so as to narrow a disparity the couple found embarrassing. See marriage certificate, Jan. 23, 1900, NYC Municipal Archives. On Dora Chambers's disapproval of Laha, see "Personal History," p. 154, and *W,* p. 128.

20. "Breeding": *W,* p. 110. "In her heart of hearts, my mother always felt, or at least she made me feel, that she had married the cook." *W,* 102. Yet it was Laha who had cooked and waitressed—for Jay—at the lunch counter.

21. See Thomas Beer, *The Mauve Decade: American Life at the End of the Nineteenth Century* (Knopf, 1926), for a catalog of its tastes. See also Jay Chambers, "Anent Book-Plates, Being a Thumbnail History," *The Optimist* (January 1901); *W,* pp. 104–6;

22. *W,* pp. 103–4.

23. Laha's Mother's Club presidency: *SSO,* Apr. 26, June 7, June 21, 1912; May 16, May 22, 1914; *Rockville Centre Owl,* Oct. 16, 1914, and Jan. 7, 1915. Library: *SSO,* July 19, 1912, Nov. 21, 1913. Also, see clip from unidentified newspaper, dated March 12, 1929; "Lynbrook's 50th" (courtesy of Arthur S. Mattson). Friday Club: *SSO,* Jan. 24, Nov. 6, 1908, Jan. 13, 1911, March 13, 1914; also "Lynbrook's 50th Anniversary," p. 71.

24. See "History of the Case," forty-four-page FBI document on WC family and background, no serial number (in HISS). Also, "Background of Whittaker Chambers:

Former Classmates and Teachers," FBI 3059. Author interview with Roy Wiedersum, Nov. 16, 1991. WC's longtime friend Henry Zolan remembered Laha boasting she knew the Broadway producer and director John Daley (WAR). *W* (p. 102) refers to Isadora Duncan as "probably the most gifted of [Laha's] theatrical friends"; also "Personal History," p. 155.

25. "Personal History," p. 155; *W,* pp. 97–98, 119. In 1924 Jay and two colleagues privately published *The Triptych's Book of Penny Toys,* with fanciful drawings, mainly by Jay (copy at New York Public Library). An exhibition of his toy collection was a success at the St. Gabriel's branch of the NYPL. See "Display of 'Penny' Toys Draws Eager Pilgrims," *NYT,* July 26, 1925. The exhibit included some of Jay's matchbox houses; the article mentions his puppet theater. See also White, "Noontime." WC dislike: WC to Mrs. Charles S. Knapp, Dec. 28, 1950 (Brandeis University). WC, "Kedding Zee Kaiser," *The Breeze,* student publication of South Side High School (May 1918); courtesy of Margaret Hopkins.

26. *W,* p. 98.

27. "Personal History," p. 154. *W,* pp. 92–94, 103, 119; "marks" are in WC, "I Was the Witness," *The Saturday Evening Post* serialization of *W* (Feb. 16, 1952), p. 62.

28. *W,* p. 120; "Personal History," p. 155.

29. There is no definitive record of Jay's homosexuality, but there are numerous clues. See Meyer A. Zeligs, M.D., *Friendship and Fratricide: An Analysis of Whittaker Chambers and Alger Hiss* (Viking, 1967), p. 31 (hereafter *F&F*). Henry Zolan remembers Laha speaking of Jay's homosexuality: author interview, July 15, 1991. In the late 1940s Laha's bookshelves included many volumes on aberrant sexuality; she evidently read one, *The Third Sex,* with particular care: Schmahl, "Investigation of J. Whittaker Chambers," Oct. 20, 1948 (WAR). WC avoided commenting on the subject, either to the FBI or in *W,* but does remark on it obliquely in an early short story: "After the husband, you know that story. And what the revulsion must have been": "The Damn Fool," *The Morningside,* vol. 10, no. 4 (March 1922) (student publication of Columbia University, in Columbiana, COLUMBIA). "Separate compartments" is in WC to Knapp, Dec. 28, 1950. Ralph de Toledano said of WC, "He had a compartmentalized life": author interview, Oct. 25, 1990.

30. *W,* pp. 123–24; "Personal History," p. 154. Train line electrified: "Lynbrook, U.S.A."

31. *W,* pp. 124–26. "Lustrous" hair: Pilat, "Report."

32. *W,* pp. 121–22.

33. Ibid., pp. 122, 109.

34. Union Avenue school, see Willner, "Legacy." *W,* pp. 105, 109–15.

35. W. A. Swanberg, *Luce and His Empire* (Dell, 1973), p. 47.

36. *W,* p. 109. "Amusement," Henry Zolan, "The Case of Carl B———," unpublished ms., 1937–1938 (courtesy of Mr. Zolan). Honor roll: *SSO,* Feb. 13, May 15, 1914.

37. On baymen, *W,* p. 92; see also Robert A. Caro, *The Power Broker: Robert Moses and the Fall of New York* (Vintage, 1975), pp. 147–49. Student and teacher reminiscences of WC are in Pilat, "Report"; see also FBI, "Background."

Chapter 2: Distant Horizons

1. *W,* p. 140; see also WC to Mrs. Knapp, Dec. 28, 1950 (Brandeis University).

2. *W,* p. 143; on Jay and Laha's many cultural activities, see, e.g., *SSO,* Jan. 15, 1912; June 6, 1913; Jan. 23, Feb. 27, March 13, 1914; Jan. 22, May 28, Oct. 22, 1915; Feb. 18, March 31, June 30, 1916; also, *Rockville Centre News,* June 26, 1914.

3. *W,* p. 102. The New York State Education Department rated South Side among the top 3 percent of the more than nine hundred high schools in the state: *SSO,* Apr. 11, 1919. Its faculty included graduates of Princeton, Vassar, Barnard, and Cornell: *SSO,* Feb. 4, 1916. Also Frances Mullady, "The Phillips House Museum Recollections," *Long Island News and Owl,* Sept. 24, 1987.

4. "Criminal Record," in *The Breeze* (June 1919). *W,* p. 144.

5. "Stinky": Schmahl, "Investigation." "Chamber Pot," in Mullady, "Phillips House," Dec. 31, 1987. This adolescent witticism anticipates the commentary in William Gaddis's novel *The Recognitions* (1955), wherein (pp. 353, 616–17) WC appears as Mr. Pott, a "poor fellow who joined a notorious political group, behaved treasonably," and then, "after satisfying that peculiar accumulation of guilt which he called his conscience by betraying everyone in sight, joined a respectable remnant of the Protestant church," finally becoming the best-selling author of an "incredible book."

6. John Kenneth Galbraith, "A Revisionist View," *TNR* (March 28, 1970).

7. However, in his senior year he was listed among those with an average of 85 or better: *SSO,* Feb. 14, 1919.

8. "Personal History," p. 155; *W,* p. 133. For authors and volumes, see WC's application to Columbia, in 1920 (HISS).

9. *W,* pp. 133–37; Henry Roth, *Mercy of a Rude Stream* (St. Martin's, 1994), vol. 1: *A Star Shines Over Mt. Morris Park,* p. 149; André Malraux, *Anti-Memoirs,* trans. Terence Kilmartin (Holt, 1968), p. 131.

10. *W,* p. 145.

11. "Personal History," p. 156; Whittaker Chambers, *Cold Friday,* ed. and intro. Duncan Norton-Taylor (Random House, 1964), pp. 95–96 (hereafter *CF*); "arty": *W,* p. 107; *intellectual:* See Christopher Lasch, *The New Radicalism in America (1889–1963),* (Vintage, 1965), p. 174; "yearning": *W,* p. 144; lunches: *Odyssey of a Friend: Whittaker Chambers' Letters to William F. Buckley, Jr.,* ed. with notes William F. Buckley, Jr. (Putnam, 1969), p. 120 (hereafter *O*). WC remembered meeting Mrs. Ellen "quite by chance" at a public lecture, perhaps at Lynbrook High School ("Personal History," p. 16). But Clarence Ellen, Dorothea's widower, told the FBI his wife met WC through Laha and the Lynbrook library (FBI, "Background").

12. Columbia application (HISS).

13. "Personal History," p. 156.

14. *W,* p. 146. There was much patriotic fervor in Lynbrook and in neighboring towns. When Marshal Joffre, the hero of the Marne, dined at Henri's, a famous local restaurant, a school holiday was called and some twenty thousand Long Islanders turned out to greet him: Wilner, "Lynbrook Legacy," p. 8.

15. On fear of munitions explosions, see "Home Defense Co.," unpublished ms. on the local Lynbrook defense unit, esp. p. 2 (courtesy of Arthur S. Mattson); "Kedding Zee Kaiser." WC's sympathetic analysis of Schlange (the name means "snake in the grass") is considerably more nuanced than many accounts of Germans then appearing in the mainstream press.

16. Indeed Jay was terrified of him: "Personal History," p. 154.

17. See Fairfax Downey, *Richard Harding Davis and His Day* (Scribner's, 1933), pp. 32–36. Also see James Chambers obit, *Philadelphia Public Ledger,* Feb. 2, 1923. He was associated with the *Ledger* for twenty-one years.

18. *Philadelphia Public Ledger* obit.

19. *W,* pp. 130–33; *Philadelphia Public Ledger* obit; author interview with John Chambers, Oct. 24, 1990.

20. See, e.g., "In Memory of R. G.," in *The Morningside,* vol. 13, no. 2 (December 1924).

21. *W,* p. 146. "Undifferentiated savagery": *CF,* p. 104.

22. Class roll: *SSO,* June 27, 1919; prophecy incident: FBI, "Background"; Pilat, "Report," June 14, 1949; Zeligs, *F&F,* p. 48.

23. "Scions": *W,* p. 101; "Personal History," p. 157. "White-collar": *W,* p. 149. Bank job: Pilat, "Report," June 15, 1949 (second article).

24. "Personal History," p. 157. WC added (to the FBI) that he had helped Muller "run away to join" the army, though he did not specify how.

25. "Personal History," pp. 157–58.

26. Embarrassing: *W,* p. 92. Adams: 2d Trial, vol. 1, p. 375.

27. *W,* pp. 150–53.

28. Letters to classmates: FBI, "Background," p. 7; family contacts police: *W,* p. 157.

29. "Personal History," pp. 158–59; FBI report 74-1333-3013 (March 8, 1949); *W,* pp. 158–62.

30. "Personal History," p. 159; WC drew on his waterfront experiences in "The Damn Fool."

31. "The Damn Fool," p. 89; "Personal History," p. 159; 2d Trial, vol. 1, p. 376; *W,* p. 163.

32. *W,* p. 163.

33. Ibid.

34. A friend who saw Jay almost daily for many years did not even know Jay had a second son: Zeligs, *F&F,* p. 31. "He never talked about his family or his home life": White, "Noontime."

35. "Personal History," p. 159; *W,* p. 163.

36. "Personal History," p. 170; Stone, "Jay Chambers, Artist"; White, "Noontime"; WC to Knapp.

37. "Personal History," pp. 159–60.

38. Ibid. p. 160; Ralph de Toledano and Victor Lasky, *Seeds of Treason: The True Story of the Hiss-Chambers Tragedy* (Funk & Wagnalls, 1950), p. 6; Zeligs, *F&F,* pp. 56–67; 2d Trial, vol. 1, p. 377. After leaving Williams, WC sent several letters to his Williams roommate, Karl Helfrich, which included fanciful reports of his travels. "In one letter Chambers told of being in a mining camp and having seen 'murder at worst under my nose' ": Elinor Ferry memo of interview with Helfrich, July 12, 1955 (ZELIGS). 2d Trial, vol. 4, pp. 2278–80.

Chapter 3: A Serious Man

1. William Ernest Weld and Kathryn W. Sewny, *Herbert E. Hawkes, Dean of Columbia College, 1918–43* (Columbia, 1958), p. 78.

2. Columbia application (HISS).

3. *Columbia College Bulletin 1920–21.* Estimated expenses for "the first half year" were four hundred dollars.

4. *CF,* p. 124.

5. World War I was the first war to "invade" American campuses, hundreds of which became barracks and training grounds for the Students Army Training Corps (SATC). Some two thousand student soldiers were housed on Morningside Heights. WC belonged to the first postwar class. It included a handful of veterans. See *The Columbian*

(yearbook), 1920; Jacques Barzun, "As We Were," in *University on the Heights,* ed. Wesley First (Doubleday, 1969), esp. p. 91; "Class of 1924 . . . A Summary," by class president Beril Edelman, Nov. 10, 1989, and "Class of 1924, 65th Reunion," pamphlet published by Columbia College, 1989 (courtesy of Beril Edelman); author interview with Beril Edelman, Nov. 10, 1989.

6. The transformation began in 1897, when the campus moved uptown and large-scale building began: Weld and Sewny, *Hawkes,* p. 37.

7. Columbia originated the great books approach long standard in humanities curricula. See Barzun, "As We Were," p. 92; Barzun to author, Dec. 1, 1989; also Lionel Trilling, "The Uncertain Future of the Humanistic Educational Ideal," *American Scholar* (Winter 1974); Mortimer J. Adler, "Great Books, Democracy, and Truth," *Columbia College Today* (Spring–Summer 1989).

8. Helen Lefkowitz Horowitz, *Campus Life: Undergraduate Cultures from the End of the Eighteenth Century to the Present* (Knopf, 1987), p. 76. Columbia retained strong vestiges of anti-Semitism. See Diana Trilling, "Lionel Trilling: A Jew at Columbia," in Lionel Trilling, *Speaking of Literature and Society,* ed. Diana Trilling (Harcourt, 1980).

9. *CF,* pp. 125–32.

10. "Personal History," p. 165; FBI 3220, Summary Report on WC, May 11, 1949; *CF,* p. 126; author interview with Meyer Schapiro, Feb. 6, 1990.

11. See Trilling remarks quoted in Zeligs, *F&F,* p. 364 fn; author interview with Schapiro, Feb. 6, 1990. On teeth, see Trilling's introduction to reissue of *The Middle of the Journey* (Harcourt, 1975), p. xiv (hereafter *MOJ*).

12. Trilling, *MOJ,* pp. xiv–xv.

13. Zeligs, *F&F,* p. 66.

14. "Van Doren at 100: Remembering the Quintessential Great Teacher," *Columbia College Today* (Winter 1995). Like Chambers, MVD was ambivalent about an academic career. "Grub Street sounds better," he said when the Columbia appointment was offered: *Selected Letters of Mark Van Doren,* ed. and intro. George Hendrick, foreword Dorothy Van Doren (LSU, 1987), pp. 11–12. See also *The Autobiography of Mark Van Doren* (Harcourt, 1958), pp. 107–8. "Humility": Thomas Merton, *The Seven Storey Mountain* (Harcourt, 1948; reissue, 1978), p. 138. Merton (Columbia '38), a bohemian poet turned Trappist monk, was the MVD protégé most akin temperamentally to Chambers. See also Louis Simpson, "Ideas and Poetry," in *University on the Heights,* pp. 228–29.

15. *CF,* p. 115.

16. Mark Van Doren, "Jewish Students I Have Known," *Menorah Journal,* vol. 13, no. 3 (June 1927). The students are unnamed. But MVD identified them in his *Autobiography.*

17. *CF,* p. 114.

18. *The Dialogues of Archibald MacLeish and Mark Van Doren,* ed. Warren V. Bush (Dutton, 1964), p. 73; Van Doren, *Autobiography,* pp. 127–28.

19. "Personal History," p. 160.

20. *Dialogues of MacLeish and Van Doren;* Van Doren, *Autobiography,* pp. 127–28.

21. She held the job for twenty years, from Sept. 23, 1921, to Sept. 26, 1941, resigning because of ill health. Her initial salary was $1,380 per annum. Information provided to Maura S. Doherty, Nov. 13, 1992, by Department of Child Welfare Administration, NYC Human Resources.

22. *Columbia College Bulletin, 1920–21.*

23. FBI report 74-1333-3016, March 25, 1949, interview with Edward E. Lewis; "Personal History," pp. 163–64; *CF,* pp. 96–97. Schapiro and Trilling both later commented on WC's "maternal solicitude" toward his friends, younger men in particular. See Schapiro's notes on his conversation with Zeligs, Dec. 6, 1961 (AWP); and Trilling, *MOJ,* p. 68.

24. Author interview with Mortimer Adler, Feb. 2, 1990. Erskine also devised first Columbia's great books list. See Adler, "Great Books."

25. "The Damn Fool," pp. 81–101.

26. Three decades later, WC made this identical remark to his fellow ex-Communist informer, Hede Massing. See WC letter dated May 23, 1951, Hede Massing Papers (HOOVER).

27. Barzun to author, Dec. 1, 1989.

28. Trilling, *MOJ,* p. xv.

29. O. W. Holmes, "The Soldier's Faith," in *The Essential Holmes: Selections from the Letters, Speeches, Judicial Opinions, and Other Writings,* ed. and intro. Richard A. Posner (University of Chicago, 1992), pp. 87–93. For reactions of Roosevelt and Cleveland, see Sheldon M. Novick, *Honorable Justice: The Life of Oliver Wendell Holmes* (Little, Brown, 1989), p. 206. "Only the priest, the soldier and the poet have ever known reality," WC to William F. Buckley, Jr., June 1957, in paperback edition of *Odyssey* (Regnery, 1987), p. 178 (hereafter *O* [1987]). This second edition includes several letters not published in the first.

30. *Columbia College Bulletin, 1920–21.* Author interview with Beril Edelman, Nov. 10, 1989.

31. Charles A. Wagner, "With Whittaker Chambers at Columbia," p. 10, unpublished ms. in Columbiana (COLUMBIA).

32. Zeligs, *F&F,* p. 66.

33. Tutoring: Herbert E. Hawkes note, March 27, 1922 (HISS). Physical regimen: *O* (1987), p. 151; *CF,* p. 94; FBI report 74-1333-3016, March 25, 1949.

34. Hawkes to J. P. Gottlieb, Feb. 13, 1931 (HISS).

35. *CF,* pp. 107, 123.

36. Author interview with Henry Zolan, Jan. 12, 1991.

37. Zeligs, *F&F,* pp. 64–65.

38. *CF,* p. 94.

39. "Personal History," p. 164.

40. *The Morningside,* vol. 11, no. 1 (November 1922).

41. Zeligs, *F&F,* p. 67.

42. "A Play for Puppets," *The Morningside,* vol. 11, no. 1 (November 1922), pp. 3–6.

43. "Personal History," p. 165.

44. Van Doren, *Autobiography,* p. 128; *CF,* p. 122.

45. *New York Evening Post,* Nov. 7, 1922.

46. Charles Wagner, "Arts and the Columbia Man," *Columbia College Today* (January 1957).

47. Letter dated Oct. 27, 1922 (Rare Book and Manuscript Library, COLUMBIA).

48. *Post,* Nov. 7, 1922; *NYT,* Nov. 7, 1922; New York *Tribune,* Nov. 7, 1922. Only the *Tribune* commented on the literary quality of the play: "The sketch is written with a distinctly Wildean flavor and suggests similar ones which appeared in the 'Yellow Book,' and Oxford publications from 1890 to 1900."

49. "Personal History," p. 165.

50. WC, "Temperament," January 1923 (in Louis Zukofsky Papers, Humanities Research Center, University of Texas, Austin).

51. WC to Hawkes, Jan. 3, 1923 (HISS).

52. Hawkes to Van Doren, Jan. 5, 1923 (HISS).

53. Van Doren to Hawkes, Jan. 8, 1923 (HISS). See also Hawkes reply, Nov. 9, 1923: "I have no doubt that [WC] has done the wisest thing" in "withdrawing" (HISS).

54. "Personal History," p. 172; *W,* pp. 166–67.

55. "Personal History," p. 173. *Philadelphia Public Ledger,* Feb. 2, 1923, James Chambers obit.

56. "Personal History," p. 172; *W,* p. 167. "It was more likely that he was refused because of immaturity": Clarence Pickett, executive secretary of American Friends Service Committee, in *The Saturday Evening Post,* June 14, 1952, p. 32. But Pickett was a supporter of Alger Hiss's and intervened on his behalf during the case: See "Memorandum of Conversation with Clarence Pickett of AFSC," Sept. 17, 1948 (HISS); see also C. Marshall Taylor to Henry C. Patterson, July 26, 1951 (Henry C. Patterson Papers, Balch Institute, Philadelphia).

57. *W,* p. 170.

58. "Personal History," p. 172. "Petition for Administration," filed by WC at Nassau County Surrogates Court, July 1931 (WAR).

59. "Personal History," p. 165.

60. WC, "East Rockaway Harbor," dated June 12, 1923 (Zukofsky Papers).

61. "Personal History," p. 166. WC, untitled poem, dated June 29, 1923 (Zukofsky Papers).

Chapter 4: Signing On

1. "Personal History," p. 166. Author interviews with Schapiro, Feb. 6, 1990; Zolan, July 15, July 19, 1991.

2. Letter from Holland-America Line to Henry Zolinsky, Aug. 24, 1923 (courtesy of Mr. Zolan); Schapiro interview, Feb. 6, 1990.

3. WC poem, untitled, June 29, 1923; *O,* p. 156.

4. 2d Trial, vol. 6, p. 3343; Zeligs, *F&F,* p. 70. *CF,* p. 133.

5. WC, untitled, July 1, 1923. The diary (in Zukofsky Papers) is inscribed "Whittaker Chambers, 427 Hartley Hall, Columbia College, New York City."

6. *CF,* pp. 32, 133.

7. Joachim C. Fest, *Hitler,* trans. Richard and Clara Winston (Harcourt, 1974), p. 232.

8. "Epidemic": quoted in Anton Kaer, Martin Jay, Edward Olmendberg, *The Weimar Republic Source Book* (Univ. of California, 1994), p. 63. "Made-up boys": Stefan Zweig, quoted in Peter Gay, *Weimar Culture: The Outsider as Insider* (Harper and Row, 1968), pp. 128–29; *CF,* p. 135; *O,* p. 200.

9. *CF,* pp. 135–36. In July street fighting broke out between Nazis and Communists in Berlin. *Die Rote Fahne* "advocated killing every fifth Fascist": *Time Capsule/1923: A History of the Year Condensed from the Pages of Time* (Time Inc., 1967), p. 90.

10. *CF,* p. 140; Schapiro interview, Feb. 6, 1990.

11. "Personal History," p. 167. Holland-America to Zolinsky, Aug. 24, 1923; Schapiro interview; WC to MVD, Aug. 30, 1923 (HISS).

12. *Ghosts,* p. 54; *CF,* p. 240.

13. WC to Van Doren, Aug. 30, 1923 (HISS).

14. Holland-America to Zolinsky, Aug. 24, 1923. "Personal History," p. 167.

15. "Personal History," p. 167; for a full record of WC's job hours and wages, from Sept. 29, 1923, to Apr. 18, 1927, see NYPL to author, Jan. 18, 1990. WC's "appointment slip" is in 2d Trial, vol. 10, p. 3655.

16. "Personal History," pp. 167, 174; Henry R. Bang to William A. Reuben, Oct. 30, 1968 (WAR); FBI 74-1333-3059, interviews with Bang brothers, March 28, 1949.

17. "Personal History," p. 168; author interview with Zolan, July 19, 1991; "On the Beach," *Lavender,* vol. 3, no. 6 (January 1926). WC used the nom de plume Julian Fichtner.

18. *W,* p. 165. Also see Caro, *Power Broker,* pp. 154–58.

19. On Sorel's antiprogressivism, see T. E. Hulme, "Reflections on Violence," in *Speculations: Essays on Humanism and the Philosophy of Art* (Harcourt, 1924), pp. 250–51; on his praise of warfare, see Christopher Lasch, *The True and Only Heaven* (Norton, 1991), p. 310. In 1926, after he had joined the Communist Party, WC was still reading Sorel and projected several translations of his work. WC to Schapiro, Nov. 3, 1926, Dec. 16, 1926 (AWP). In his last years WC kept a copy of *Reflections on Violence* on his bookshelves: WC to James Rorty, July 1960 (AWP).

20. Bourget: Author interview with Zolan, June 25, 1991. On Tolstoy, "Personal History," p. 170. Leo Tolstoy, *The Kingdom of God Is Within You* (Scribner's, 1925), p. 335.

21. "Personal History," p. 174. WC to Schapiro, Aug. 23, 1924 (AWP).

22. WC to Hawkes, July 14, 1924; Hawkes to WC, Aug. 11, 1924 (both HISS).

23. WC to Van Doren, Sept. 15, 1924, 2d Trial, vol. 10, p. 3669.

24. See absent notice to Hawkes, Oct. 21, 1924 (HISS). No WC transcript appears for the fall term, 1924. See records on WC, Rare Book and Manuscript Library (COLUMBIA). However, he contributed fiction and poetry to *The Morningside.* See the issue of December 1924.

25. Author interview with Adler, Feb. 2, 1990. In 1928 Adler recruited WC to team-teach an evening great books seminar for adults, held at a Manhattan church. See also Adler, *Philosopher at Large* (Macmillan, 1977), p. 66.

26. Allen Weinstein, *Perjury: The Hiss-Chambers Case* (Knopf, 1978), p. 93; author interviews with Zolan, July 15, July 19, 1991.

27. Author interviews with Zolan, July 15, July 19, 1991.

28. FBI report 74-1333-2152, Feb. 18, 1949, p. 4. William A. Reuben interview with Frank Bang, Nov. 20, 1968 (WAR).

29. FBI report 74-1333-3059, interview with Frank Bang, March 28, 1949, p. 26. William A. Reuben interview with Bang, Nov. 20, 1968 (WAR).

30. Zeligs, *F&F,* p. 31.

31. WC, "In Memory of R. G.," pp. 34–40. This, WC's best early short story, is strikingly similar thematically to a classic written at almost the same moment, Ernest Hemingway's "Soldier's Home." In 1953 WC identified Hemingway as the one contemporary American writer he truly admired: WC to Arthur Koestler, Apr. 30, 1953 (KOESTLER).

32. WC, "Lothrop, Montana," *The Nation* (June 30, 1926).

33. WC, "Tandaradei," *Two Worlds* (June 1926). On Roth, see summary of "The Secret Life of Samuel Roth," remarks by Professor Leo Hamalian delivered at University Seminar in American Civilization, Columbia University, Oct. 17, 1968 (AWP); see also Richard Ellmann, *James Joyce,* new and rev. ed. (Oxford, 1982), pp. 585–87.

34. "Personal History," p. 171; *W,* pp. 168–71.

35. "Personal History," p. 170; *W,* pp. 172–73; Zolan, "The Case of Carl B." FBI report 74-1333-3016, interview with Edward E. Lewis, March 25, 1949; Zeligs, *F&F,* p. 66. Richard graduated from junior high school in June 1919 and entered South Side High in September: See transcript (WAR). According to records in the Colgate registrar's office, Richard Chambers lettered at South Side High in football, baseball, and track (Marcia Kurop interview with registrar's office, June 31, 1991).

36. "Personal History," p. 170; *W,* pp. 173–74.

37. 1st Trial minutes, p. 136; *W,* pp. 194–95.

38. Max Eastman, *Reflections on the Failure of Socialism* (Devin-Adair, 1955), p. 10.

39. These and subsequent quotations from Nikolai [*sic*] Lenin, *The Soviets at Work: The International Position of the Russian Soviet Republic and the Fundamental Problems of the Socialist Revolution* (Rand School of Social Science, 1918).

40. On Kropotkin, see James Joll, *The Anarchists,* 2d ed. (Harvard, 1980), pp. 164–67, 174. Rosa Luxemburg's "The Problem of Dictatorship" (1919) is in *Essential Works of Socialism,* ed. Irving Howe, 3d ed. (Yale, 1986), pp. 144–47. Emma Goldman, *My Disillusionment in Russia* (Doubleday, 1923).

41. *CF,* pp. 109, 189.

42. "Tiny image": *W,* p. 186; "brooding": "Personal History," p. 171.

43. *W,* p. 174.

44. "Personal History," p. 165; FBI 3220, May 11, 1949, p. 2. *W,* p. 196. Garlin, though an alumnus of the Young People's Socialist League, did not join the CP until February 1927. See RCP 495-261-1014 for his signed autobiographical statement, Feb. 8, 1936. Also on Garlin, see Albert Halper, *Good-bye, Union Square: A Writer's Memoir of the Thirties* (Quadrangle, 1970), p. 106ff. For changing names of CP, see Theodore Draper, *American Communism and Soviet Russia: The Formative Period* (Viking, 1960), p. 160.

45. On Krieger, see Weinstein, *Perjury,* p. 100. He used the alias Clarence Miller. A second Communist who used that same alias was implicated in a murder related to the Gastonia textile strike of 1929. In *W* (p. 202) WC confuses the two.

46. *W,* pp. 202–5. As of August 1925, less than a third of the total CP membership belonged to English-speaking organizations. See Nathan Glazer, *The Social Basis of American Communism* (Harcourt, 1961), p. 49.

47. WC took John Gassner to a CP meeting and proposed him for membership. He was rejected, with the remark "It seems to me that this branch is getting not the cream of the proletariat, but the scum of the bourgeoisie." FBI 3220, May 11, 1949, p. 3. Louis Zukofsky was likewise rejected. See Hugh Kenner, "Chambers's Music and Alger Hiss," *The American Spectator* (June 1979). Yet Gassner and Zukofsky both came from poor immigrant families.

48. WC to Van Doren, March 8, 1925, 2d Trial, vol. 10, p. 3671.

49. Miller was the organization secretary for the CP's New York district: Draper, *American Communism and Soviet Russia,* p. 412. Later, as an ex-Communist and under his given name, Ben Mandel, he was HUAC's research director. He held that position during the Hiss case.

50. *W,* pp. 206–7. Eve Davidson to author, Apr. 19, 1993.

51. Draper, *American Communism and Soviet Russia,* p. 162.

52. Ibid., p. 187. By late 1925, the number was reduced by half. See also Harvey Klehr, *The Heyday of American Communism: The Depression Decade* (Basic, 1984), p. 5. The

CP boasted of having as many as twenty thousand members. See Glazer, *Social Basis of American Communism,* p. 49.

## BOLSHEVIK (1925–1932)

### Chapter 5: His Brother's Keeper

1. Ignazio Silone, in *The God That Failed,* ed. and intro. Richard Crossman (Harper, 1949), p. 99.

2. *W,* pp. 209–11. The phrase *Jimmie Higgins*—"the socialists' archetypal factotum"— derives from the eponymous hero of Upton Sinclair's pacifist novel, published in 1919. See Stephen J. Whitfield, *Scott Nearing: Apostle of American Radicalism* (Columbia, 1974), p. 122.

3. Weinstein, *Perjury,* p. 100. See RCP 495-261-5900, for Krieger's signed autobiographical statement, Aug. 21, 1935. (The signature reads "Robert Kane." "Real name S. Krieger" is written below the signature, presumably by a Soviet official.) Permission to read the complete file was granted to the author by Sadie Krieger, who also authenticated the document (letters to the author—Sept. 30, 1992, Feb. 18, 1993). See also Sam Krieger, "An Historian's Falsehoods," *Rights* (September 1979); Jonah Raskin, "Sam Krieger— Odyssey of a Red," *The Nation* (May 23, 1981); plus Sadie Krieger reply, June 27, 1981.

4. *W,* pp. 211–13. "intellectual center": Theodore Draper, *The Roots of American Communism* (Viking, 1957), p. 141. "I guess all of us were 'smitten' with Nearing the man, the courageous thinker": Eve Davidson to author, Apr. 19, 1993. Mrs. Davidson (née Eve Dorf) and her husband, Ben Davidson, both attended the seminar with WC and later were driven out of the CP in the Lovestone purge of 1929. Ben later cofounded the New York State Liberal Party. (See *NYT,* Dec. 22, 1991.) For Nearing and Ware, see Nearing's *The Making of a Radical: A Political Autobiography* (Social Science Institute, 1972), p. 147.

5. "Personal History," pp. 169–70; *W,* pp. 214–17.

6. *The Law of Social Revolution: A Cooperative Study by the Labor Research Study Group* (Social Science Publishers) appeared in 1926, with chapters by Nearing, "Clarence Miller" (Sam Krieger), Eve Dorf (Benjamin), and "D. Benjamin" (Ben Davidson).

7. De Toledano and Lasky, *Seeds,* p. 14.

8. "Drill": *W,* p. 207; "mystification," Weinstein, *Perjury,* p. 99; Van Doren, *Autobiography,* p. 128. Trilling, *MOJ,* pp. xiii–iv.

9. "Curative": "Personal History," p. 172; "trinkets": "History of the Case"; "cat urine": author interview with John Chambers, June 12, 1990; pension checks, William A. Reuben interview with Zolan (WAR); "depraved face": *W,* p. 171.

10. "Personal History," p. 171; *W,* p. 169.

11. "Personal History," pp. 170–73; "vivid": *W,* pp. 179–80; Willner, "Lynbrook Legacy," p. 12.

12. "Personal History," p. 171; *W,* p. 175.

13. "Personal History," pp. 170–71; *W,* p. 175.

14. *W,* pp. 175–76.

15. Ibid., pp. 178–79. Henry Zolan, who sometimes accompanied the Chambers brothers on these prowls, recalled that WC would lose control after a single drink: Author interview, July 19, 1991.

16. *W,* p. 180.

17. "Personal History," p. 168; WC resigned his library job on July 15 but resumed it in January: NYPL to author, Jan. 18, 1990. *Anthology of Magazine Verse for 1925 and Year-book of American Poetry,* ed. William Stanley Braithwaite (Brimmer, 1925). See WC letter to Braithwaite, Sept. 21, 1925, granting permission to include the poem (Houghton Library, Harvard). See also *The Dialogues of MacLeish and Van Doren,* p. 74.

18. "Personal History," p. 173.

19. Marriage affidavits, certificate, and license for Richard Chambers and Dorothy Miller all are in WAR. Zolan, "The Case of Carl B"; "specimen": "Personal History," p. 173; *W,* p. 181.

20. NYPL to author, Jan. 18, 1990.

21. "Personal History," p. 176; FBI 74-1333-3059, interviews with Bang brothers.

22. "Personal History," pp. 174–75. Horseback riding, WC to Schapiro, Apr. 24, 1927 (AWP). NYPL to author, Jan. 18, 1990.

23. "Personal History," pp. 173–74; *W,* pp. 181–82; police report quoted in Horace Schmahl memo, October–November 1948 (WAR); *Nassau Daily Review,* Sept. 10, 1926. See also *The Long Island News and Owl,* Sept. 9, 1926; *The New Era,* Sept. 10, 1926 (Hofstra University).

24. "October 21st, 1926," in *Poetry: A Magazine of Verse,* vol. 37, no. 5, Feb. 1931 ed. Louis Zukofsky, pp. 258–59. The last stanza reads:

> You know it is the cessation of the motion in me I am
> waiting:
> And not lack of love, or love of the sun's generation,
> and the motion
> Of bodies, or their stasis, that keeps me—but my
> perfection for death I am waiting.

The poem was read aloud at Alger Hiss's first trial, in 1949.

For Zukofsky's elegy (written in 1928), see *"A" 1–12,* no. 3 (Doubleday, 1967; orig. pub., 1959), pp. 15–17. See also Kenner, "Chambers's Music and Alger Hiss."

25. "My brother's suicide set the seal on my being a Communist. I was a Communist before but I became a fanatical Communist afterwards": "Personal History," p. 174. See also 2d Trial, vol. 1, p. 424.

### Chapter 6: Upheavals

1. "Investigation of JWC," unsigned memo, dated Nov. 18, 1948, Edwin White Gaillard, special investigator, Circulation Department, NYPL, to Dr. C. C. Williamson, director, School of Library Service, Apr. 14, 1927 (all HISS); "librarian" to Herbert Hawkes, Apr. 19, 1927; Hawkes to Howson, n.d. (Rare Book and Manuscript Library, COLUMBIA). See also Keyes DeWitt Metcalf, *Random Reflections of an Anachronism or Seventy-five Years of Library Work* (Readex, 1980), pp. 157–58.

2. WC to Schapiro, Apr. 24, 1927 (AWP).

3. "Personal History," p. 177; Zukofsky interview, Sept. 18, 1967 (WAR). Author interview with Zolan, July 15, July 19, 1991.

4. Many of the *Review*'s contributors also appeared in the pages of the *Menorah Journal,* the precursor to *Commentary.* Trilling and Solow both were editors of the *Journal.*

Chambers was its German translator. See Alan M. Wald letter to Allen Weinstein, March 31, 1976 (AWP). For more on the *Menorah Journal,* see "A Novel of the Thirties," in *The Last Decade: Essays and Reviews, 1965–75* (Harcourt, 1979), ed. Diana Trilling; Alan M. Wald, *The New York Intellectuals: The Rise and Decline of the Anti-Stalinist Left from the 1930s to the 1980s* (North Carolina, 1987), pp. 27–50.

5. See *DW,* Jan. 22, 1927.

6. *W,* pp. 217–20, though WC confuses the chronology: "With my brother's death, I stopped writing for the *Worker.*" WC, "March for the Red Dead," *DW,* May 23, 1927; "Before the End," July 9, 1927.

7. Sandino: see *NYT,* May 14, July 16, July 17, 1927; *DW,* July 19, March 3, 1927, Sept. 2, Sept. 8, 1927; *NYT,* May 11, 1928. FBI 3220, May 5, 1949, p. 8.

8. FBI 3220, May 11, 1949, pp. 4–5. *W,* pp. 241–42.

9. WC's first translation for *LD* was of Arnold Kainer, "Hamburg: 1923," *LD* (October 28). WC's poem "Rail Road Yards (Long Island City)" was published in *NM* in May 1926, the magazine's inaugural issue. Another lyric, "In Spring (in the Century of the Great Social Wars)," was published in September 1926. See also *W,* p. 337.

10. *W,* pp. 221–24. On his Columbia application WC had listed "newspaper work" as one of three possible future careers, the others being "literature" and "advertising." Application (HISS). For new CP headquarters, see Benjamin Gitlow, *I Confess: The Truth About American Communism* (Dutton, 1939), p. 307.

11. *W,* p. 226. "There was not": *W,* p. 224. "Courageous and disciplined, the rank-and-filers of my days were ready to give up their lives for the Party": Gitlow, *I Confess,* p. 290.

12. Gitlow, *I Confess,* p. 307. Klehr, *Heyday,* p. 5.

13. Bertram D. Wolfe, *A Life in Two Centuries* (Stein and Day, 1981), p. 445.

14. Wolfe, *A Life,* pp. 403–4.

15. FBI 3320, May 11, 1949, p. 4.

16. On Burck's fondness for WC, see two ms. pages from "Jacob Burck memories of Whittaker Chambers, ca. 1931" (WAR). See *NYT,* Jan. 13, Feb. 10, 1935, on Burck's mural, "Five-Year Plan," designed for the Moscow office of Intourist Inc., the Soviet travel agency. Burck was staff cartoonist at the Chicago *Times* when he won the Pulitzer. See *NYT,* May 6, 1941. On his threatened deportation, see Richard Rovere, *The American Establishment and Other Reports, Opinions, and Speculations* (Harcourt, 1962), p. 125.

17. On Intrator, see FBI 74-1333-3059, interview with Intrator, March 16, 1949, pp. 39–42; Wolfe, *A Life,* pp. 403–4; "child of the slums" and further detail: *O,* pp. 179–82.

18. FBI 3220, May 11, 1949, pp. 4–5; *W,* 226–28; on Chicago, see, e.g., *DW,* Jan. 15, 1927. Both pieces edited by WC are in *DW,* Jan. 23, 1929.

19. WC's review of Maurice Parijanine, *The Krassin,* appeared in *NM* in April 1929. Joseph Freeman—Harry's older brother and an outstanding Communist writer in this period—was a founding editor of *NM.* See Daniel Aaron, *Writers on the Left* (Oxford, 1977), pp. 96–99.

20. Wolfe, *A Life,* p. 404.

21. Krieger, "An Historian's Falsehoods," p. 12. *W,* p. 236; WC course at Workers School: *DW,* Sept. 10, 1929.

22. "Inner life": Irving Howe and Lewis Coser, *The American Communist Party: A Critical History* (Praeger, 1962) p. 146. For Stalin's rise, see Dmitri Volkogonov, *Stalin: Triumph and Tragedy,* ed. and trans. Harold Shukman (Grove Weidenfeld, 1991), pp. 85–201. See also Walter Laqueur, *Stalin: The Glasnost Revelations* (Scribner's, 1990), p. 46.

23. Gitlow, *I Confess,* p. 491.

24. *W,* p. 238.

25. James P. Cannon, *Notebook of an Agitator,* 2d ed. (Pathfinder Press, 1973), p. 303. *W,* p. 28. Shachtman bore Chambers no ill will and spoke highly of him in his last years. Author interview with Yetta Shachtman, Nov. 5, 1991.

26. Earl Browder, CPUSA secretary-general from 1930 to 1945, later characterized Chambers as "a neurotic and an irresponsible Trotskyist": FBI teletype 2457-500, March 15, 1949. In the second Hiss trial WC did not deny having told his onetime accomplice Julian Wadleigh that Moscow "had accused [WC] of becoming converted to Trotsky-ism": 2d Trial, vol. 1, p. 411. In 1957 Browder said WC was caught out in "a number of Trotskyite tendencies and expressions" in the late 1920s: William A. Reuben interview with Browder, June 20, 1957 (WAR).

27. *W,* pp. 237–38. He later described himself, in retrospect, as being of the CP "Center with Left leanings"—with leanings, that is, in the direction of Trotsky: See *O,* p. 180.

28. "Personal History," p. 169. *W,* p. 182. Gitlow, *I Confess,* p. 316.

29. FBI 74-1333-3059, interview with Frank Bang, March 28, 1949; FBI teletype 74-1333-2746, March 28, 1949; FBI 74-1333-3051, interview with Kenneth Hutchinson, Apr. 14, 1949; "party marriage"/"intolerable": See FBI 74-1333-3059, interview with Ida Dailes, March 29, 1949.

30. For background, see FBI-Dailes. "Announcement of Courses," Workers School, spring term, 1929 (Tamiment Library, New York University). "Personal History," p. 177; "toilet": Sidney Hook, *Out of Step: An Unquiet Life in the 20th Century* (Harper & Row, 1987), p. 277.

31. "Personal History," p. 177; FBI-Dailes, p. 29; *W,* pp. 183–84; Jay's death certificate says "Nepatitis" [*sic*], meaning possibly nephritis or hepatitis (WAR). Stone, "Jay Chambers, Artist."

32. *W,* p. 184; "Personal History," p. 170; also WC to "Mrs. Knapp," Dec. 28, 1950.

33. Reuben interview with Henry Zolan, Nov. 3, 1968 (WAR).

34. "Personal History," p. 177; Elinor Ferry, "Memo of interview with sister of Ida Dailes," June 19, 1954 (ZELIGS); FBI-Dailes. Jay's estate, in WAR.

35. Author interview with Zolan, July 19, 1991.

36. FBI-Frank Bang; FBI-Dailes.

37. Magil remembered staying as long as ten days. Elinor Ferry interview with Magil, Oct. 8, 1952 (ZELIGS). FBI-Dailes. "Romeo": Halper, *Good-bye, Union Square,* p. 114ff.

38. Author interview with Zolan, July 19, 1991; also Reuben interview with Zolan (WAR); "shrieks": Ferry-Dailes interview.

39. See Laha to Veterans Administration, Feb. 7, 1932. She begged to be allowed to keep the last three checks for herself since "my mother owed me board for a period of ten years." The request was denied: VA to Laha, Jan. 27, 1932, all in Charles Whittaker Civil War pension file (NA).

40. FBI-Dailes. Author interview with Zolan, July 19, 1991.

41. "Personal History," p. 177. FBI-Dailes.

42. *W,* p. 231; U.S. District Court, Maryland, Civil No. 4176, Alger Hiss (Plaintiff) v. Whittaker Chambers (Defendant), deposition of Esther Chambers, Nov. 16, 1948, p. 470 (hereafter EC deposition).

43. EC background: EC deposition, Nov. 16, 1948, pp. 451–62; also FBI 3230-84, May 11, 1949, interview with EC, pp. 204–6; Art Students League: Rosina A. Florio letter to author, Nov. 19, 1991.

44. Lumpkin background: See Lumpkin letter to Alden Whitman, June 26, 1974 (HISS); Lumpkin letter to editors of *NR* (June 22, 1971), Grace Lumpkin Papers (South Caroliniana Library, University of South Carolina); also *Southern Writers: A Biographical*

*Dictionary,* ed. Robert Bain et al. (LSU, 1978), pp. 287–88; FBI 74-1333-359, interview with Grace Lumpkin, March 16, 18, 23, 1949.

45. "Warm": EC deposition, Nov. 16, 1948, p. 458; "the most admired": Lumpkin to *NR* (June 22, 1971).

46. Klehr, *Heyday,* p. 72. EC sold tickets for a John Reed Club dance and stood on the reviewing stand for a May Day rally. As a result, she was fired from a job with Amtorg, the Soviet trading corporation, which required employees to conceal their CP loyalties. See FBI 3230, May 11, 1949, p. 206. On JRC history, see Laurie Ann Alexandre, "The John Reed Clubs: A Historical Reclamation of the Role of Revolution," unpublished master's thesis, New York University, 1979 (Tamiment).

47. EC deposition, pp. 467–68; *O,* p. 182; Klehr, *Heyday,* p. 72.

48. FBI-Lumpkin, March 16, 18, 23, 1949.

49. FBI-Dailes; "Personal History," p. 177; Ferry-Dailes interview. The WC–Dailes relationship was well known. See Hook, *Out of Step,* pp. 277, 280.

50. Rebecca West to Reuben, June 12, 1969 (WAR).

51. Lumpkin to *NR,* June 23, 1971; EC deposition, Nov. 16, 1948, p. 475. "Personal History," p. 178; "Sea of shit": Weinstein, *Perjury,* p. 110. See Edward McLean, "Memorandum of Conference with Sender Garlin," Feb. 8, 1949 (HISS).

52. WC to WFB, May 19 [?], 1957, passage deleted from *O* (WFB).

53. Petition for Administration of Estate (WAR).

54. "The marriages were almost simultaneous": Elinor Ferry interview with Grace Hutchins, Oct. 20, 1951 or 1952 (ZELIGS). Marriage certificate, WC-EC. WC listed his occupation as "journalist," EC hers as "artist." Rochester gave generous loans to EC and Lumpkin. EC repaid hers (one thousand dollars) in weekly installments until the time of her marriage, when Rochester told her "to forget about the rest." Lumpkin regarded her loan (fifteen hundred dollars) as a gift and did not repay it. FBI-Lumpkin, March 16, 18, 23, 1949; Ferry-Hutchins.

55. Volkogonov, *Stalin,* pp. 174–79.

56. Draper, *American Communism and Soviet Russia,* pp. 422–29.

57. Klehr, *Heyday,* p. 9.

58. "Knife": de Toledano and Lasky, *Seeds,* p. 18. "Personal History," p. 178; FBI 3220, May 11, 1949, p. 11. *W,* pp. 250, 253.


## Chapter 7: The Hottest Literary Bolshevik

1. Louis Kronenberger, *No Whippings, No Gold Watches: The Saga of a Writer and His Jobs* (Little, Brown, 1970), p. 267.

2. FBI 74-1333-3059, interview with Clifton Fadiman, March 22, 1949.

3. Fadiman remembered the fee as $500: Harold Rosenwald, "Memorandum" of interview with Clifton Fadiman, Oct. 15, 1948; the publisher Richard Simon said it was $250; see Rosenwald, "Memorandum" of interview with Dick Simon, Nov. 10, 1948 (both HISS). Simon's statement would seem the more accurate since he could consult company files, but his recollections on related matters are dubious.

4. Felix Salten, *Bambi,* trans. Whittaker Chambers, foreword John Galsworthy (Simon and Schuster, 1929). It was published under an S&S imprint, the Inner Sanctum. For prepublication publicity, including announcement of BOMC main selection for July and initial print, see *NYT Book Review,* July 8, 1928, which also includes a glowing review of *Bambi* by John Chamberlain, later WC's friend at Time Inc.

5. WC's subsequent translations include:

Felix Salten, *Samson and Delilah* (S&S, 1930)
             *Fifteen Rabbits* (S&S, 1930)
             *The City Jungle* (S&S, 1932)
Heinrich Mann, *Mother Mary* (S&S, 1928)
Franz Werfel, *Class Reunion* (S&S, 1929)
Johannes Tralow, *Cards and Kings* (Ray Long & Richard Smith, 1931)
Kasimir Edschmid, *The Passionate Rebel: the Life of Lord Byron* (A. & C. Boni, 1930)
Anton Noder, *The Venetian Lover, the Romance of Georgino* (R. P. Smith, 1931).
Waldemar Bonsels, *Adventures of Mario* (A. & C. Boni, 1930)
Anna Elisabet Weirauch, *The Scorpion* (Greenberg, 1932)
Paul Gartner, *Mugel, the Giant* (Longmans, Green, 1930)
A. T'Serstevens, *Sentimental Vagabond* (Farrar & Rinehart, 1930).
Martin Gumpert, *Dunant: The Story of the Red Cross* (Oxford, 1938)
Gustav Regler, *The Great Crusade,* trans. WC and Barrows Mussey (Longmans, 1940).

6. On *Class Reunion,* "The translation by Whittaker Chambers is excellent": Joseph Wood Krutch, *The Nation* (July 31, 1929); "It is praise enough to say that one is not aware of it as translation": Edgar Johnson, *NYHT,* June 16, 1929; the *Times Literary Supplement* found WC's translation of *The Passionate Rebel* "excellent" (June 19, 1930).

7. Barrows Mussey, "What Makes Whittaker Chambers Tick Like a Bomb," unpublished ms., courtesy of Mrs. Barrows Mussey. The rate WC requested was what he had been paid by Boni for his translation of *Mario.* See undated letter to WC (probably summer 1930) confirming "verbal agreement" (HISS).

8. "Independent": *W,* p. 259; "better Communist": 2d Trial, vol. 1, p. 226.

9. EC at Art Students League: Rosina A. Florio to author, Nov. 19, 1991. EC's cartoon "Alookin' F'r a Home . . ." appeared in *NM* (May 1931). Bronx exhibit: Klehr, *Heyday,* p. 72.

10. Grace Lumpkin, *To Make My Bread* (Macaulay, 1932). For Gorky Award, see *NYT Book Review,* Jan. 15, 1933; see also "A Novel of the Southern Mills," review in *NYT Book Review,* Sept. 25, 1932. For fifteen-hundred-dollar subsidy see note 53, previous chapter. See also *Southern Writers,* p. 287; Lumpkin's subjects also included racial and economic injustice in the Deep South. She remains among the better-known proletarian writers, though she abandoned radicalism for Christianity in 1941, under the influence of WC. See Edward McLean, "Memorandum re Grace Lumpkin," Dec. 31, 1948, and "Interview with Grace Lumpkin," Jan. 5, 1949 (both HISS).

11. See "Rail Road Yards (Long Island City)," in *NM* (May 1926); "In Spring (in the Century of the Great Social Wars)," *NM* (September 1926); "Elm Grove, W. VA, 1925," *NM* (July 1931).

12. Poetry superior: author interview with Schapiro, Feb. 6, 1990; Malcolm Cowley letter to Reuben, July 10, 1969 (WAR). "[Clifton] Fadiman told me that [WC] had the makings of a truly great poet": Bennett Cerf, *At Random: The Reminiscences of Bennett Cerf* (Random House, 1977), p. 242; "métier": *W,* p. 166.

13. "500 Farmers Storm Arkansas Town Demanding Food for Their Children," AP, Jan. 3, 1931.

14. V. I. Lenin, *What Is to Be Done?: Burning Questions of Our Movement* (International Publishers, 1986), p. 30.

15. Whittaker Chambers, "Can You Make Out Their Voices?," *NM* (March 1932). Later published as *Can You Make Out Their Voices?*, International Pamphlet, No. 26, and included in the anthology *Ghosts on the Roof: Selected Journalism of Whittaker Chambers, 1931–59*, ed. and intro. Terry Teachout (Regnery, 1989). All quotations from this edition (hereafter *Ghosts*).

16. Norman Macleod to Reuben, March 28, 1969 (WAR).

17. *W*, p. 261.

18. Robert Cantwell, "The Chambers Story," *Newsweek* (May 26, 1952).

19. Granville Hicks, *A Part of the Truth* (Harcourt, 1965), p. 95. Halper, *Good-bye, Union Square*, p. 113. See also Aaron, *Writers on the Left*, p. 384. "Voices" was pointedly omitted—along with the rest of WC's proletarian writings—from *New Masses: An Anthology of the Rebel Thirties* (International Publishers, 1969). The editor, Joseph North, had been WC's close friend in the 1930s. For their friendship, see FBI 3220, May 11, 1949, p. 21; see also unsigned "Memorandum to Mr. McLean: Paraphrase of Interview with Miss Josephine Herbst," Jan. 8, 1949, p. 5, in which Herbst, leading writer on the left, recalls her reunion with WC at North's apartment in 1935 (HISS).

20. Letters: Frances Strauss, "Vassar College Presents a Play," *NM* (June 1931); "hottest": Joseph Freeman to Daniel Aaron, July 6, 1958 (courtesy of Professor Aaron).

21. Hallie Flanagan, *Dynamo* (Duell, 1943) pp. 106–7.

22. Ibid., p. 110; Joanne Bentley, *Hallie Flanagan: A Life in the American Theatre* (Knopf, 1988), p. 121. Yiddish version: See A. Elistratova, "New Masses," *International Literature*, no. 1 (January 1932), p. 110.

23. Elistratova, "New Masses," p. 110. (The critic confuses "Voices" with "Our Comrade Munn," a later story by WC, published in *NM* in October 1931.) See also Edwin Rolfe's review of the pamphlet edition, *Can You Make Out Their Voices? The Arkansas Farmers' Fight for Food*, in *NM* (September 1932): "It has been acclaimed both here and abroad as the most mature piece of working class fiction ever written in America."

24. All reprinted in *Ghosts*.

25. Dated June 18, 1933. In *The Letters of Lincoln Steffens*, vol. 2, ed. with intro. notes Ella Winter and Granville Hicks (Harcourt, 1938), p. 961.

26. "In This Issue," *NM* (July 1931).

27. "Purest": Murray Kempton, *Part of Our Time: Some Monuments and Ruins of the Thirties* (Delta, 1967), p. 132. "Prestige": See *Conversations with Malcolm Cowley*, ed. Thomas Daniel Young (Univ. Press of Mississippi, 1986), p. 70. *NM* (October 1931), p. 31; Harold Rosenwald memo of interview with Paul Peters, Nov. 19, 1948 (HISS); Arnold Rampersad, *The Life of Langston Hughes*, vol. I, *1902–41: I, Too, Sing America* (Oxford, 1986), pp. 315–16. WC and Hughes acquaintanceship: "Personal History," p. 163; Rampersad, *Langston Hughes*, p. 281.

28. As of October 1931. His article "But the Toilers of China Storm On" was published in *LD* in August 1931.

29. WC's collaborators included Joe Freeman and Joe North. *NM* asked readers to subsidize the project with weekly one-dollar donations. See Russell Campbell, *Cinema Strikes Back: Radical Filmmaking in the United States, 1930–1942* (UMI Research Press—University of Michigan, 1982), pp. 73–74.

30. Rampersad, *Langston Hughes*, p. 235.

31. Norman Macleod to Reuben, March 28, 1969; Harry Roskolenko to Reuben, Apr. 7, 1969 (both in WAR).

32. FBI 3220, May 11, 1949, pp. 23–24; "densely wooded": *W,* pp. 277–78; "enormous garden": EC deposition, Nov. 16, 1949, p. 501.

33. FBI 3220, May 11, 1949, pp. 19–20. Salary: EC deposition, p. 498. According to EC, the couple spent only five dollars a week, thanks to the vegetable garden.

34. "Voices" was the only story published in 1931 that addressed issues "set before the entire international revolutionary movement [by] Comrade Stalin's letter 'On Some Questions of the History of Bolshevism' ": Elistratova, "New Masses."

35. "Thank you very much for your prompt work . . . ": WC to Louis Lozowick on *NM* letterhead, March 29, 1932 (WAR).

36. "[WC] stated that he secured this position mainly because . . . [Carmon] . . . had not been going along smoothly with the Party": FBI report 100-25824-36, June 26, 1945. See also Norman Macleod to Reuben (WAR); Douglas Wixson, *Worker-Writer in America: Jack Conroy and the Tradition of Midwestern Literary Radicalism, 1898–1990* (University of Illinois), pp. 270–71.

37. FBI 3220, May 11, 1949, pp. 19–20; WC's board election: Oakley Johnson, "The John Reed Club Convention," *NM* (July 1932).

38. "Little dark": *W,* p. 268; Cantwell, "The Chambers Story." "I edited": *W,* p. 268. See also WC to Charles Yale Harrison, on *NM* letterhead, May 6, 1932 (WAR); WC to Nathan Adler, July [n.d.], 1932 (ZELIGS); "Bolshevik self-criticism": Wixson, *Worker-Writer,* pp. 270–71; WC to Jack Conroy, May 16, May 25, 1932, in Conroy Papers (Newberry Library, Chicago). Kempton, *Part of Our Time,* p. 131, describes how WC put novelist James T. Farrell in his place. Wixson surveys changes instituted under WC (pp. 270–72); Howe and Coser, *American Communist Party,* pp. 278–79, say the Stalinization of *NM* dates from 1928.

39. "To All Intellectuals," *NM* (May 1932), p. 1. The statement is signed "The Editors," but in 1951 WC confirmed his authorship, adding, "I would not change a word of what, having written it in 1932, I have so richly proved in 1948": WC letter to RDT, Aug. 17, 1951 (RDT).

40. Horace Gregory to Reuben, Sept. 11, 1968 (WAR). "Progress": "To All Intellectuals."


## *SPY (1932–1938)*

### Chapter 8: Going Underground

1. FBI 3220, May 11, 1949, p. 24. 2d Trial, vol. 1, p. 228–29; *W,* pp. 271, 275–76.

2. Draper, *American Communism and Soviet Russia,* pp. 420, 430–31.

3. WC later placed the meeting on Thirteenth Street. (See FBI 3220, May 11, 1949, p. 24; 2d Trial, vol. 1, p. 288; and *W,* p. 271.) But Bedacht, once forced out of the Party's top command, lost his office there and operated out of the Workers Center. See chapter 25, "The Witness," in Bedacht's memoirs, p. 322, unpublished ms. (Tamiment). On Bedacht's background and history, see Draper, *Roots of American Communism,* pp. 304–5; James P. Cannon, *The First Ten Years of American Communism: Report of a Participant* (Pathfinder Press, 1962), p. 115.

4. *W,* p. 275.

5. "Whittaker Chambers Meets the Press," *American Mercury* (February 1949), p. 156. (Transcript of radio interview, Aug. 27, 1948.)

6. Benjamin Gitlow, *The Whole of Their Lives: Communism in America—A Personal History and Intimate Portrayal of Its Leaders* (Scribner's, 1948), p. 146. Gitlow is possibly the "former high functionary of the Communist Party" who in a letter dated Feb. 13, 1938, referred to Bedacht as "the high contact man between the Politburo of the American CP and the 'center.' " Letter is in FBI report NY 100-59538, on Juliet S. Poyntz, p. 3. See also Harvey Klehr, John Earl Haynes, and Fridrikh Igorevich Firsov, *The Secret World of American Communism* (Yale, 1995), pp. 25–26. Bedacht denied any role in the Communist underground. In 1957 he recalled a conversation with WC in late 1932 but said it dealt only with IWO business: Elinor Ferry interview with Max Bedacht, May 14, 1957 (ZELIGS). See also Bedacht, "The Witness," pp. 319–29.

7. Robert Conquest, *Inside Stalin's Secret Police: NKVD Politics 1936–1939* (Hoover Institution, 1985), p. 1. On OGPU-GRU collaboration, see Christopher Andrew and Oleg Gordievsky, *KGB: The Inside Story of Its Foreign Operations from Lenin to Gorbachev* (HarperCollins, 1990), pp. 173–74.

8. Klehr et al., *Secret World,* pp. 20–21.

9. *W,* pp. 275–76.

10. FBI-Intrator, March 16, 1949.

11. EC deposition, p. 501. FBI 3220, May 11, 1949, p. 24; *W,* pp. 277–78.

12. FBI 3220, May 11, 1949, p. 24. *W,* p. 279. See also Felix Morrow letter to *Esquire* (November 1962): "Now that he [WC] knew too much, he was told he could not stay in America!" Morrow, a Communist, was WC's good friend through much of the 1930s.

13. WC also remembered Sherman's alias as Arthur: U.S. District Court, Maryland, Civil No. 4176, Alger Hiss (Plaintiff) v. Whittaker Chambers (Defendant), deposition of WC, Nov. 4, 1948, p. 144. *W,* pp. 279–80. WC suspected it was Sherman who first recommended him for secret work: FBI 3220, May 11, 1949, pp. 24–25. Reborn: *W,* p. 280.

14. HUAC EXEC, Dec. 28, 1948; FBI 3220, May 11, 1949, pp. 24–26; "commanding face": *W,* p. 281; "amber-colored": WC deposition, Nov. 4, 1948, p. 147. *CF,* p. 196.

15. HUAC, Dec. 28, 1948, p. 5; "ideological position": FBI 3220, May 11, 1949, p. 25. *W,* p. 281.

16. FBI 3220, May 11, 1949, p. 25. Salary and expenses: "Personal History," p. 180; 1st Trial minutes, pp. 290–91. Esther remembered the couple living on roughly thirty-five dollars a week. She added, "Whatever clothes we had was probably on our backs": EC deposition, Nov. 16, 1949, p. 503.

17. FBI 3220, May 11, 1949, p. 27.

18. WC to Nathan Adler, July [n.d.], 1932 (ZELIGS).

19. WC deposition, Nov. 4, 1948, p. 156; also FBI 3220, May 11, 1949, p. 27. "The use of German words in trade craft may have stemmed from the large number of Soviet intelligence officers who originated in the pre–World War I Austro-Hungarian Empire": Herbert Romerstein and Stanislav Levchenko, *The KGB Against the Main Enemy: How the Soviet Intelligence Service Operates Against the United States* (Lexington Books, 1989), p. 84.

20. Allen Weinstein, "Nadya—A Spy Story," *Encounter* (June 1977), p. 73.

21. FBI 3220, May 11, 1949, pp. 31–32; FBI report 65-57792-23, May 13, 1949, on "the gallery"; on Stern, see Romerstein and Levchenko, *KGB Against the Main Enemy,* pp. 14–17.

22. Within the first week of his underground activity, or so WC told HUAC on Dec. 28, 1949.

23. Ulrich also used the alias Walter: WC, HUAC, Dec. 28, 1948, p. 6; FBI 65-58428-3, report on Isador Miller et al. "Monkeylike": *W*, pp. 291–92; Stalin's coat, from summary of Ulanovsky's KGB file. See also Nadezhda Ulanovskaya and Maya Ulanovskaya, *Istoriia Odnoi Semyi* [The Story of One Family] (Chalidze, 1982), chapter 6. Early in her account of her American experiences Ulanovskaya writes, "To a great extent my narrative will resemble Whittaker Chambers's . . . in his book *Witness*. We met the same people he did. They are no longer alive. Thus I can confirm his testimony." This and subsequent translations (all from chapter 6) by Svetlana Rozovsky for the author.

24. Weinstein, "Nadya—A Spy Story," pp. 72–73; FBI 3220, May 11, 1949, p. 30.

25. Ulanovskaya, *Istoriia*.

26. Ulanovskaya, *Istoriia;* "very kind": Weinstein, *Perjury*, p. 124.

27. Ulanovskaya, *Istoriia*.

28. FBI 3220, May 11, 1949, pp. 35–36; "dark": *W*, p. 299.

29. FBI 3220, May 11, 1949, p. 37.

30. FBI 3220, May 11, 1949, pp. 35–40. *W*, pp. 299–306.

31. Stern's boast: Alan Cullison interview with Vladmar Stern, Moishe's son, Moscow, 1992. Moishe Stern became a hero of the Spanish Civil War under the alias "General Emilio Kleber" and then was executed by Stalin in 1937 along with many other Red Army commanders, including Jan Berzin, the GRU's top officer. See David J. Dallin, *Soviet Espionage* (Yale, 1955), p. 397; Robert Conquest, *The Great Terror: A Reassessment* (Oxford, 1990), p. 213.

32. FBI 3220, May 11, 1949, pp. 41–42.

33. New London: FBI 3220, May 11, 1949, pp. 45–48. Also FBI reports on Joseph Guilietti et al.: FBI 62-31468-19X3, Feb. 17, 1949; FBI 62-31468-23, Apr. 4, 1949; FBI 62-31468-26, Apr. 5, 1949; FBI 62-21468-39, Aug. 25, 1949; and FBI teletypes: FBI 1259, Jan. 24, 1949; FBI 2290, March 31, 1949; FBI 2817, Apr. 7, 1949; FBI 62-31468-27, Apr. 12, 1949. Picatinny: FBI 3220, May 11, 1949, pp. 44–45; FBI 65-58428-2, signed statement by Isador Miller, Feb. 2, 1949; FBI 65-58428-3, March 29, 1949.

34. FBI 3220, May 11, 1949, p. 43; Ulanovskaya, *Istoriia;* Weinstein, "Nadya—A Spy Story," p. 76; Romerstein and Levchenko, *KGB Against the Main Enemy*, pp. 16–17. On the Osman case, see also Louis Waldman, *Labor Lawyer* (Dutton, 1944), p. 221ff.

35. FBI 3220, May 11, 1949, p. 42.

36. From spring 1932 to fall 1933, WC's residences were: (1) the New Jersey farm; (2) West Eleventh Street; (3) McGuire Avenue, in Princess Bay, Staten Island; (4) The Castle, near Fort Lee, New Jersey; (5) the farm again; (6) Fort Lee again. See "Personal History," p. 180; also FBI teletypes: 2415, March 16, 1949; 2530, March 15, 1949; FBI teletype 2615, March 23, 1949.

37. *W*, p. 325.

38. Letter, Booth Memorial Hospital to Zeligs, Nov. 20, 1961 (ZELIGS).

39. Weinstein, *Perjury*, p. 115.

40. Bang: Interview with Frank Bang, Nov. 20, 1968 (WAR). Schapiro: Author interview and Herbert Solow memo, Nov. 20, 1938, p. 14. Solow: Solow memo, Nov. 12, 1938, p. 5 (both SOLOW); Zablodowsky: Interview with DZ, May 12, 1962 (ZELIGS); WC testimony before Senate Internal Security Subcommittee (SISS), transcript of Oct. 23, 1952, hearing, p. 300ff. Diana Trilling, *The Beginning of the Journey: The Marriage of Diana and Lionel Trilling* (Harcourt, 1993), pp. 216–17. Cantwell: Edward McLean, "Interview with Robert Cantwell," Nov. 2, 1948 (HISS); Solow memo, Nov. 20, 1938, p. 14; Goldwater: Diana Trilling interview with Goldwater No. 2, Jan. 11, 1979, pp. 75–83

(courtesy of Mrs. Trilling); also Samuel Lipman, "Walter Goldwater: A Memoir," *New Criterion* (January 1991), p. 16.

41. "Bore": Justin Kaplan, *Lincoln Steffens: A Biography* (Simon and Schuster, 1974), p. 314; "warm spot": *W,* p. 601. The fee offered was five thousand dollars. See Cantwell review of Kaplan, ms. pp. 15–16 (Robert Cantwell Papers, University of Oregon); Ulrich: Ulanovskaya, *Istoriia.*

42. Winter and WC: John Lowenthal report, "Interview of Ella Winter," Feb. 6, 1969 (ZELIGS); Reuben interview with Alger Hiss, Aug. 6, 1969 (WAR); Weinstein, *Perjury,* p. 124. EW was first approached in California by John Sherman, who used the alias Harry Phillips. WC took over this same alias when he approached EW in New York.

43. "He was probably the most gossiped-about secret agent in the long history of espionage": Malcolm Cowley to Benjamin DeMott, May 6, 1978 (Cowley Papers, Newberry Library). Lionel Trilling remarks the "comic absurdity . . . the aura of parodic melodrama" of WC's underground persona, in *MOJ,* p. xvii. On public knowledge of WC's secret work, see Kempton, *A Part of Our Time,* p. 132; Hicks, *Part of the Truth,* p. 95; Matthew Josephson, *Infidel in the Temple* (Knopf, 1967), p. 180; Harold Rosenwald memo of interview with Paul Peters, Nov. 19, 1948 (HISS); Cantwell, "The Chambers Story"; Reuben interview with Felix Morrow, Nov. 29, 1968 (WAR).

44. "I categorically state . . . that my only visit to Europe was in 1923": FBI 3220, May 11, 1949, p. 140. Also, FBI 105-51764-34, Dec. 13, 1956: WC "ridiculed the idea that he was ever in Moscow." Schapiro told the author about the woodcuts, Feb. 6, 1990. Weinstein, *Perjury,* pp. 115–16. Diana Trilling, "Remembering Whittaker Chambers," letter published in *Encounter* (May 1976). Mrs. Trilling confirmed her recollection in a letter to the author, March 5, 1993. Solow memo, Nov. 12, 1938, p. 4.

45. And possibly led to the Ulanovskys' being recalled to Moscow in 1934. Weinstein, "Nadya—A Spy Story," p. 76.

46. *W,* pp. 313–14.

47. HUAC EXEC, Dec. 28, 1948, p. 18.

48. *W,* pp. 313–18; FBI 3220, May 11, 1949, pp. 51–55.

49. *W,* 321; FBI 3220, May 11, 1949, p. 55. Royalties: Weinstein, "Nadya—A Spy Story," p. 73.

50. Ulanovskaya, *Istoriia.*

51. Weinstein, "Nadya—A Spy Story," p. 76.

52. Summary of Ulanovsky file (KGB).


Chapter 9: The Ware Cell


1. "Ham and eggs": *W,* p. 332; Ware background: Ella Reeve Bloor, *We Are Many, an Autobiography* (International Publishers, 1940), pp. 266–67; HW obit: *DW,* Aug. 16, 1935. "harvest": John Abt, *Advocate and Activist: Memoirs of an American Communist Lawyer* (University of Illinois, 1993), p. 39.

2. Bloor, *We Are Many,* pp. 270–71.

3. Hope Hale Davis, *Great Day Coming: A Memoir of the 1930s* (Steerforth Press, 1994), pp. 102–3.

4. Bloor, *We Are Many,* pp. 272–73.

5. John L. Shover, *Cornbelt Rebellion: The Farmers' Holiday Association* (University of Illinois, 1965), p. 67ff.

6. FBI teletype 3347, June 10, 1949.

7. "Left-wing": Robert Cruise McManus memo to Alger Hiss, Aug. 31, 1948 (AWP). Hiss quoted in Weinstein, *Perjury,* p. 14 fn.; see *Labor Fact Book III,* prepared by Labor Research Association (International Publishers, 1936), p. 121.

8. FBI 74-1333-4570, memo to director, on interview with Nathaniel Weyl, Nov. 27, 1950, p. 3. Also "I Was in a Communist Unit with Hiss" (interview with Nathaniel Weyl), *U.S. News & World Report* (Jan. 9, 1953).

9. Arthur Schlesinger, Jr., *The Coming of the New Deal* (Houghton Mifflin, 1959), p. 17; "common vision": Alan Brinkley, "The New Deal and the Idea of the State," in *The Rise and Fall of the New Deal Order, 1930–80,* ed. Steve Fraser and Gary Gerstle (Princeton, 1989), p. 92.

10. Laura Kalman, *Abe Fortas: A Biography* (Yale, 1990), p. 30.

11. See Schlesinger, *Coming,* p. 50; "The Agricultural Adjustment Administration," in *The Making of the New Deal: The Insiders Speak,* ed. Katie Louchheim (Harvard, 1983), p. 236ff. On Jerome Frank, see Robert Jerome Glennon, *The Iconoclast as Reformer: Jerome Frank's Impact on American Law* (Cornell, 1985).

12. See Glennon, *Iconoclast,* p. 75: "The New Deal used brilliant lawyers who, as generalists, were creative problem solvers. . . . At the end of the 1930s, legal positions began to be subject to civil service requirements." See also Felix Frankfurter, "The Young Men Go to Washington," in *Law and Politics: Occasional Papers of Felix Frankfurter, 1913–38,* ed. Archibald MacLeish (Harcourt, 1939), p. 247.

13. Arthur Schlesinger, Jr., "The First 100 Days," in *The Aspirin Age, 1919–1941,* ed. Isabel Leighton (Simon and Schuster, 1949), p. 287.

14. "No Final Answer to the Farm Problem" (interview with Henry A. Wallace), *U.S. News & World Report* (Jan. 18, 1954). Schlesinger, *Coming,* p. 55ff.

15. Abt, *Advocate,* p. 40.

16. "Young hotheads": Davis, *Great Day,* p. 46. "No Final Answer," p. 43.

17. *TNR* (Feb. 6, 1935).

18. Abt, *Advocate,* p. 40.

19. Davis, *Great Day,* pp. 101–2.

20. WC, FBI 3220, pp. 70–71. "Most of the men I had met in the Party at first were now unit leaders. Each unit represented five or six members": Davis, *Great Day,* pp. 123–24.

21. Schlesinger, *Coming,* p. 40.

22. Weyl, "I Was in a Communist Unit." See also Davis, *Great Day,* p. 123.

23. Weyl, "I Was in a Communist Unit."

24. Davis, *Great Day,* p. 71.

25. Ibid., p. 69.

26. Abt, *Advocate,* p. 41.

27. Klehr et al., *Secret World,* pp. 73–83. Also Maria Schmidt, "Behind the Scenes of the Show Trials of Central-Eastern Europe," unpublished ms., pp. 16–21. Mrs. Schmidt was the first scholar—and at this writing the only one—granted access to Peters's handwritten autobiography, in Budapest. See also Schmidt, "The Hiss Dossier," *TNR* (Nov. 8, 1993).

28. Broadway and Hollywood: Schmidt, "Behind the Scenes," p. 17; FBI infiltration: WC, FBI 3220, p. 58.

29. FBI 3220, p. 70.

30. WC deposition, Nov. 4, 1948, pp. 186–90; "unromantic": *W,* p. 336; "learn the setup": FBI 3220, pp. 70, 76. Hope Davis recalled a session in which Peters excoriated

her husband, Hermann Brunck, a New Deal economist, when he naïvely invoked the name of anti-Stalinist philosopher Sidney Hook: Davis, *Great Day*, p. 99.

31. This date is an approximation based on a memorandum to Edward McLean: "Paraphrase of Interview with Miss Josephine Herbst" and on EC's recollection that she and Ellen joined WC in Baltimore in August 1934: FBI 3230, interview with Esther Chambers, May 11, 1949, p. 209.

32. WC deposition, Nov. 4, 1948, pp. 188–99; FBI 3220, p. 70.

33. Davis, *Great Day*, p. 252.

34. Collins as treasurer: WC deposition, Nov. 4, 1948, p. 200; FBI 3220, p. 76; see also Davis, *Great Day*, p. 138, on HC as treasurer "of the whole group of units" and on his social clout. WC as dues courier: FBI 3220, pp. 77–78. He surmised the function was taken over (in 1935) by the roommate of one "Andre Embrey" (as the name was rendered by the FBI). The roommate, whom WC remembered as "Jewish and small and dark," remains unidentified. Embrey was Edith (Ondra) Emery, a prominent Communist and later the wife of Roy Hudson, a CP labor organizer. See Klehr et al., *Secret World*, pp. 319–20. See also FBI 74-94-2243, letter to director, Feb. 23, 1949; and FBI 74-94-2500, March 8, 1949.

35. FBI 74-1333-4570, Weyl interview, p. 5. See also Weyl, "I Was in a Communist Unit," p. 23.

36. "They were there because they believed in revolution. They thought the capitalist world was dying and would have to change over to a socialist form of government": Weyl, "I Was in a Communist Unit," p. 24; "levers": Abt, *Advocate*, p. 30.

37. Earl Browder, *What Is Communism?* (Workers Library, 1936), p. 188. See also Frank A. Warren, *Liberals and Communism: The "Red Decade" Revisited* (Columbia, 1966), pp. 105–7; Arthur M. Schlesinger, Jr., *The Politics of Upheaval* (Houghton Mifflin, 1960), p. 181ff.

38. Weyl, "I Was in a Communist Unit."

39. FBI 3220, May 11, 1949, p. 79; McLean, "Interview with Robert Cantwell," Nov. 2, 1948 (HISS); *W*, p. 357.

40. *W*, p. 60.

41. FBI teletype 5021, Feb. 16, 1952; FBI 3220, interview with EC, Feb. 10, 1949, p. 208; EC deposition, Nov. 16, 1948, p. 509.

42. HUAC EXEC, Dec. 28, 1948, p. 33; FBI 3220, May 11, 1949, p. 59; *W*, p. 354. WC was not sure whether Bill was Estonian or Finnish, but WC's future underground colleague Felix Inslerman, one of Bill's recruits, met him through a contact at the Estonian Workers Club in New York. FBI report of interview with Felix Inslerman, Feb. 18–19, Feb. 27–28, March 13–14, 1954, p. 7 (serial no. missing).

43. HUAC EXEC, Dec. 28, 1948, p. 34; FBI 3220, May 11, 1949, pp. 59–60.

44. WC, "The Faking of Americans," unpublished ms., in two parts, 1938 (SOLOW).

45. WC, "Faking," part II, "Welcome, Soviet Spies!"; "at least": "Faking," part I, "The Soviet Passport Racket," p. 4. The chief Soviet operative was the Latvian GRU agent Arnold Ikal (see chapter 11).

46. FBI 3220, May 11, 1949, p. 60. On Lieber, see Weinstein interview with Lieber, May 10, 1975 (AWP); Halper, *Good-bye, Union Square*, pp. 45–56; Dan B. Miller, *Erskine Caldwell: Journey from Tobacco Road* (Knopf, 1995), p. 143. WC met Herbst in Washington; her husband, John Herrmann, also a leftist writer, was Hal Ware's assistant in Washington. See Elinor Langer, *Josephine Herbst* (Atlantic Monthly Press, 1984), pp. 151–57; Langer, "The Secret Drawer," *The Nation* (May 30, 1994); "Paraphrase of Interview with

Miss Josephine Herbst"; Herbst to William A. Reuben, Nov. 6, 1968 (WAR); Slesinger was briefly married to Herbert Solow. On WC and Halper, see Halper, "Whittaker Chambers on 14th Street," in *Good-bye, Union Square,* pp. 110–13.

47. Lieber remembered seeing WC every two weeks or so in the period when WC was living in Washington: Chester T. Lane, "Memorandum of Conference with Maxim Lieber," Apr. 26, 1951 (HISS). Andrew, *KGB,* pp. 173–80, 264–65.

48. FBI 3220, May 11, 1949, pp. 61–63. "Chambers and Chase and I set up that syndicate": Weinstein interview with Lieber, May 10, 1975 (AWP). Copy of business certificate "of Maxim Lieber, Charles F. Chase, and Lloyd Cantwell," all operatives of American Feature Writers Syndicate, is in 2d Trial, vol. 6, p. 3239. See also FBI 65-53508-74, Feb. 17, 1949. Also FBI 65-59091-14, interview with Charlotte Bartels Smirnoff, Lieber's secretary in 1935, March 28, 1940. She knew WC as Bob and surmised he and ML were collaborating on "secret work for the Communist Party."

49. See Noda obit, *NYT,* Jan. 14, 1939; Bertram D. Wolfe, *The Fabulous Life of Diego Rivera* (Stein and Day, 1963), p. 323; Noda to Schapiro, May 12, 1934 (AWP).

50. FBI 3220, May 11, 1949, p. 62. A total of four articles appeared in the *Post,* under the byline of "C. F. Chase, writer and newspaperman. . . . for years a student of Japanese political and economic problems." The copyright was owned jointly by the *Post* and by AFWS. See *Post:* Jan. 21, Feb. 19, Feb. 21, Feb. 23, 1935.

51. FBI 3220, May 11, 1949, pp. 64–65; FBI 65-53508-95, report on interview with Crane, July 12, 1949. It also includes much detail on Sherman's activities in California. Also, FBI 65-59091-14, interview with Crane, March 28, 1950.

52. Weinstein interview with Lieber; FBI 3220, May 11, 1949, p. 63; *W,* p. 388.

53. FBI 3220, May 11, 1949, p. 64. Solow memo, supplement, Dec. 3, 1938 (SOLOW).

54. FBI 3220, May 11, 1949, p. 63. Solow memo, supplement, Dec. 3, 1938 (SOLOW).

55. FBI 3220, May 11, 1949, p. 64. Solow memo, supplement, Dec. 3, 1938 (SOLOW).

56. FBI 3220, May 11, 1949, p. 63; Weinstein, *Perjury,* p. 128; WC to Schapiro, n.d., probably January 1939 (AWP).

57. Noda obituary, *NYT,* Jan. 14, 1939; WC to Schapiro, n.d., 1939 (AWP).

58. FBI 3220, May 11, 1949, pp. 68–69. For copy of David Breen passport application, see 2d Trial, vol. 6, p. 3335. A copy in HISS includes WC's passport picture, with mustache. WC gives his mailing address as c/o "M. Lieber, 545 Fifth Avenue" (Lieber's office address). The original passport is in HISS.

59. EC did not apply for a passport as Edna Rogers. Nor was an application submitted for Ursula Breen. But her birth was indeed registered in Atlantic City: See copy of document in 2d Trial, vol. 6, p. 3333. WC and EC opened a joint bank account as David Breen and Edna Rogers: 2d Trial, vol. 6, p. 3337.

60. FBI 3220, May 11, 1949, p. 69. His recruit was Jerome Bartels, the brother of Max Lieber's secretary. She knew nothing of the arrangement. FBI 65-59091-14, interview with Charlotte and Jerome Bartels, March 28, 1940, pp. 22–24.


Chapter 10: Saving the World


1. Stealing documents: Langer, *Herbst,* p. 156. Interest to the CP: RCP 495-14-115. Leica: FBI 3220, May 11, 1949, p. 82. Collins's place: John Herrmann, letter to

Josephine Herbst, Dec. 12, 1934 (Herbst Papers, Beinecke Library, Yale). Davis, *Great Day* describes transmittal of documents (in 1935). See, e.g., pp. 66, 75.

2. On AAA "purge," see Schlesinger, *Coming,* p. 79; Theodore Saloutos, *The American Farmer and the New Deal* (Iowa State, 1982), pp. 117–23; Peter H. Irons, *The New Deal Lawyers* (Princeton, 1982), pp. 156–80. Abt, *Advocate,* pp. 36–37; "The Purge at the AAA," *The Nation* (Feb. 20, 1935); "The Week," *TNR* editorial (Feb. 20, 1935); "Washington Notes," *TNR* (Feb. 27, 1935). On Hiss's being spared, see Hiss, "Memorandum on Circumstances Attending the AAA 'Purge' " (HISS); McManus, "Agriculture Purge," undated memo (AWP); Zeligs interview with Gardner Jackson, May 6, 1963 (ZELIGS). According to Jackson, Hiss "was on list of purgees and wangled himself off." Also Davis, *Great Day,* pp. 77–78. "Timid liberal": Abt, *Advocate,* p. 17. On Davis's offer to AH, see Glennon, *Iconoclast,* p. 36.

3. Ware obit, *DW,* Aug. 16, 1935; Davis, *Great Day,* pp. 108–9, 111; also author interview with Hope Davis, Oct. 25, 1994.

4. FBI 3220, May 11, 1949, p. 65; *W,* p. 368.

5. WC in Washington, spring 1935: AH, HUAC I, Aug. 16, 1948, p. 956; WC deposition, Nov. 5, 1948, p. 287. EC deposition, Nov. 16, 1948, pp. 557–58; Smithton, August 1935: FBI 3230, interview with EC, May 11, 1949, pp. 209–10. Schapiro sublease: EC deposition, Nov. 16, 1948, pp. 563–64; FBI 3230, interview with EC, May 11, 1949, p. 210; "Personal History," p. 181; Harold Rosenwald interview with Meyer Schapiro, Nov. 22, 1948 (HISS); 2d Trial, vol. 2, p. 724 (Schapiro testimony). Smithton rental: EC deposition, Nov. 16, 1948, pp. 564–65; WC deposition, Nov. 5, 1948, p. 285. The period covered by the Smithton lease was "July and August, through Labor Day": testimony of landlord Joseph Boucot, 2d Trial, vol. 3, p. 1639. For Lieber connection, see WC deposition, Nov. 17, 1948, pp. 751–52; Chester T. Lane, "Memorandum of Conference with Maxim Lieber," Apr. 26, 1951 (HISS); also Harold Rosenwald, "Memorandum re Maxim Lieber," Nov. 12, 1948 (HISS). In Smithton WC used the alias David Breen.

6. Davis, *Great Day,* pp. 109–11; author interview with Hope Davis, Oct. 25, 1994.

7. "[Peters] took over responsibility for our group in Washington after Hal Ware was killed": Abt, *Advocate,* p. 178: See also FBI 65-58728-53, interview with Lee Pressman, March 8, 1951. Pressman denied most of WC's allegations about the Ware cell but eventually admitted he had himself belonged and had met both WC and Peters. On the latter, "Pressman identified a photograph of J. Peters as a man who on one and possibly two occasions after Ware's death, delivered Communist Party literature to the group." On Peters's authority over the Ware Group, see Davis, *Great Day,* pp. 98–99. "J. Peters was in and out of Washington all of the time that I was there": WC, FBI 3220, May 11, 1949, p. 75.

8. WC meets Carpenter: FBI 3220, May 11, 1949, p. 85. *W,* pp. 384–85. On Carpenter's background, see FBI summary (no serial no.) "David Vernon Zimmerman with Aliases: David Carpenter, Steve Potter, Harold Wilson," Feb. 17, 1949. On FAECT: See McLean, "Memorandum re William Ward Pigman," Dec. 21, 1948 (HISS); FBI 65-14920, interview with William Ward Pigman, Dec. 8, 1948. FAECT and espionage: Ronald Radosh, "The Venona Files," *TNR* (Aug. 7, 1995); see also FBI report 3326, interview with Dr. Herbert Insley, May 11, 1949, on " 'secret meetings' . . . primarily for Communist underground activity." Bodyguard: Julian Wadleigh, "Why I Spied for the Communists," *New York Post,* July 13, 1949. "Smoldering": Wadleigh, "Why I Spied," July 12, 1949. "Wield power": Wadleigh, "Why I Spied," July 13, 1949.

9. Wadleigh, "Why I Spied," July 13, 1949. FBI 419, report on Henry Julian Wadleigh, Dec. 7, 1948.

10. Wadleigh, "Why I Spied," July 13, 1949: "[Carpenter] was jealous of my other contact and resented having to introduce me to [WC]." See also WC, FBI 3220, March 11, 1949, pp. 85–86. "We disliked each other on sight": *W,* p. 384.

11. Wadleigh, "Why I Spied," July 14, July 20, 1949. See also 2d Trial, vol. 2, pp. 1111–42 (Wadleigh testimony); Zeligs interview with Wadleigh and others, May 5, 1963 (ZELIGS).

12. *W,* p. 395; FBI 65-2440, interview with Tom Marshall, n.d., pp. 13–14. Purchase of car: FBI 3320, May 1, 1949, p. 123; "Personal History," p. 181; "in *cash*" (italics in original): Kay Marshall letter to Bruce Craig, March 21, 1989 (courtesy of Mr. Craig). On WC's absences, Horace Schmahl, "Investigation of WC in Smithtown [*sic*], near Frenchtown, and New Hope, Pennsylvania," Nov. 16, 1948 (HISS). WC "put in very irregular appearances" and "received many long distance calls."

13. Schapiro rental: *W,* p. 396; John Chambers's birth: Letter, Booth Memorial Hospital to Zeligs, Nov. 20, 1961 (ZELIGS).

14. "We remained at the Marshall farm for approximately ten or eleven months": "Personal History," p. 182.

15. FBI 3220, March 11, 1949, p. 86; *W,* p. 401; "cadres": Conquest, *Inside Stalin's Secret Police,* p. 2; WC's future accomplice Felix Inslerman saw Bill in Moscow in late 1935. FBI-Inslerman, Feb. 18–19, Feb. 27–28, and March 13–14, 1954, pp. 14–15. But Bill seems to have returned to New York for several months. Another operative, William Edward Crane, said Bill remained the GRU *rezident* "at least until the winter of 1935–36": FBI-Crane "Supplemental [to] Summary Report" (no serial no. or date), p. 37.

16. FBI 3220, May 11, 1949, p. 89. W. G. Krivitsky, *In Stalin's Secret Service* (Harper, 1939), p. 272. The name, pronounced *boo-koff,* was probably an alias. There is a Bykov Street in Dostoevsky's *The Possessed,* trans. and intro. David Magarshack (Penguin, 1987), p. 98.

17. FBI 3220, May 11, 1949, p. 89; *W,* pp. 405–6. Nadezhda Ulanovskaya, who had known Bykov since 1919, also remembered him as "a little bit of a coward" (*Istoriia*).

18. *W,* p. 413. "Checking up was the way Boris Bykov worked": Ulanovskaya, *Istoriia.*

19. FBI 3220, May 11, 1949, pp. 109–10; *W,* pp. 408–11. When W. E. Crane left Baltimore for California in 1937, WC "warned him to stay away from Sherman," a "marked man": FBI-Crane 2236, Feb. 16, 1949; FBI-Crane 74-1333-213, Feb. 14, 1949.

20. "Foul": HUAC executive hearing, Dec. 28, 1948, p. 57. *W,* p. 414.

21. FBI 3220, May 11, 1949, pp. 91–92; WC, HUAC executive hearing, Dec. 6, 1948, pp. 23–24; HUAC executive hearing, Dec. 28, 1948, p. 51; "*Wer auszählt*": *W,* p. 414.

22. HUAC EXEC, Dec. 6, 1948, p. 25; FBI 74-1333-95, interview with Meyer Schapiro, Feb. 1, 1949, p. 15; FBI report 65-58226-6, on Henry Julian Wadleigh, Dec. 15, 1949, p. 18; 2d Trial, vol. 2, pp. 724–25 (Schapiro testimony); vol. 6, pp. 3359–63, copies of Schapiro's canceled check plus sales and delivery slips of Massachusetts Importing Company; "grateful": *W,* p. 416.

23. WC deposition, Nov. 17, 1948, pp. 740–41; FBI, signed statement by Henry Julian Wadleigh (no serial no.), Dec. 10, 1948, p. 4. FBI 3220, May 11, 1949, pp. 93–94; *W,* p. 418.

24. Wadleigh, "Why I Spied," July 14, 1949.

25. Ibid., July 15, 1949; HUAC EXEC, Dec. 6, 1948, pp. 16, 18, 25. 2d Trial, vol. 1, p. 256 (WC testimony).

26. HUAC EXEC, Dec. 6, 1948, pp. 5–8, 14–17; FBI 3220, May 11, 1949, pp. 97–100; 2d Trial, vol. 1, pp. 257–60 (WC testimony); also, vol. 2, pp. 1111–14 (Wadleigh testimony).

27. WC to Schapiro, "Sunday night," n.d., probably January 1937 (AWP).

28. J. W. Chambers to E. W. Case," Feb. 3, 1936, published in *Baltimore News-Post,* Aug. 28, 1948.

29. Details of the transaction are in *Baltimore News-Post,* Aug. 27, 1948; see also "three papers relating to purchase of Westminster farm," 2d Trial, vol. 10, p. 3717. WC testimony, Aug. 27, 1948, HUAC I, pp. 1255–56, 1259–60; EC deposition, Nov. 17, 1948, p. 700.

30. "Personal History," p. 182; FBI 3220, May 11, 1949, p. 127.

31. FBI-Inslerman, Feb. 18–19, Feb. 27–28, and March 13–14, 1954. WC may have supplied Inslerman with his forged passport: FBI-Inslerman, p. 24. For details on photographing procedure, see FBI-Inslerman, pp. 27–32.

32. HUAC EXEC, Dec. 6, 1948, p. 7.

33. Carpenter: FBI 3220, May 11, 1949, pp. 102–3. Carpenter photographed documents turned over by Julian Wadleigh and Ward Pigman, a chemist at the Bureau of Standards. FBI-Crane, 2236, Feb. 16, 1949; FBI-Crane, 74-1333-2706, March 4, 1949; FBI-Crane, 65-14920.

34. *W,* p. 426.

35. *W,* p. 426. "Abundantly": 2d Trial, vol. 2, p. 1254 (Wadleigh testimony). Wadleigh-Bykov encounter: Wadleigh, "Why I Spied," July 14–15, 1949. Also see Wadleigh's signed FBI statement, Dec. 10, 1948.

36. FBI-Crane, 74-1333-213, Feb. 14, 1949; FBI report 74-1333-947, on Morris Asimow, Jan. 7, 1949; on émigrés, see FBI teletype 3242, Apr. 20, 1949, interview with Vladimir de Sveshnikov; also 65-57899-31X, interview with Crane, May 3, 1949.

37. FBI interview with Franklin Victor Reno (no serial no.), Dec. 12, 1948; FBI-Reno 61-7728-10; Reno told the FBI the diagram of the Norden bombsight "represented my own conclusions of the operation and did not represent any actual bombsight." Reno signed FBI statement, Dec. 13, 1948 (no serial no.). "Intelligence": Reno signed FBI statement, Dec. 13, 1948.

38. Weinstein, "Nadya—A Spy Story," p. 75.

39. *W,* p. 427; FBI-Crane, 65-14920.

40. White's moods: *W,* pp. 49, 68. White, "essentially a timid man, . . . 'doesn't want his right hand to know what his left is doing' ": Elizabeth Bentley, *Out of Bondage* (Devin-Adair, 1951), p. 165. "He proposes occasional conversations lasting up to half an hour while driving in his automobile," White's Soviet handler reported to Moscow in 1944 in a cable describing the economist's anxieties about secret work: VENONA S/NBF/T244, Aug. 4–5, 1944. White's monetary report: HUAC, Dec. 6, 1948, p. 24.

41. *W,* pp. 427–28.

42. Intrator, e.g., knew WC was microfilming government documents. FBI-Intrator 3059, p. 40. FBI 3220, May 11, 1949, p. 142; *W,* p. 413.

43. See WC to Schapiro, "Sunday night," n.d., probably January 1937; also, Weinstein interview with Schapiro, Oct. 7, 1974; Schapiro letter to Weinstein, July 26, 1975; Schapiro letter to Alan Wald, Dec. 24, 1975 (all AWP). The Trotskyist Felix Morrow claimed he saw WC all through the 1930s: Reuben interview with Morrow, Nov. 29, 1968 (WAR).

44. John Costello and Oleg Tsarov, *Deadly Illusions* (Crown, 1993), pp. 285–86; Conquest, *Great Terror,* pp. 209, 213. Conquest also notes (p. 209) that Moishe Stern, the one-time GRU *rezident* in New York, was arrested, beaten with iron bars, and sentenced to twenty-five years in a labor camp, where he perished.

45. On WC and *Mar Cantabrico:* FBI 3220, May 11, 1949, pp. 142–43; FBI-Crane 74-1333-213, Feb. 14, 1949, p. 8; author interview with Zolan, June 25, 1991. On the ship's

voyage and capture, see *NYT,* Jan. 6–7, Feb. 20, March 9–10, 1937. Solow memo, Nov. 20, 1938, p. 15. In 1937 WC told Mike Intrator and Grace Lumpkin he had twice "managed to get out of" trips to Moscow: FBI-Lumpkin, March 16, 18, 23, 1949.

46. "Personal History," p. 182.


# DEFECTOR *(1938–1939)*

### Chapter 11: Disappearances

1. WC letter to Robert Cantwell, n.d. but evidently sent in 1938 (Cantwell Papers).

2. Krivitsky, *In Stalin's Secret Service,* pp. 254–63.

3. Ibid., pp. 256–72; Flora Lewis, "Who Killed Krivitsky?," *WP,* Feb. 13, 1966; Isaac Don Levine, *Eyewitness to History: Memoirs and Reflections of a Foreign Correspondent for Half a Century* (Hawthorn, 1973), pp. 184–85.

4. E.g., the cases of Nikolai Bukharin and Aleksandr Barmine. For WC and Bukharin, see *O,* pp. 163–64. Barmine, the Soviet chargé d'affaires in Athens, defected to Paris rather than return to Moscow. In an appeal to the League for the Rights of Man, Barmine named numerous victims of the purge, all diplomats. He followed up with a by-lined article, "Stalin a Betrayer," published on the front page of the *NYT,* Dec. 23, 1937. See also *NYT,* Dec. 4, 1937.

5. In 1940 WC told Felix Morrow he had had "scores of government functionaries at his disposal": Morrow, "Conversation with W: His Opinions," memo in Leon Trotsky Collection (HOOVER). Poisoned candies: Krivitsky, *In Stalin's Secret Service,* p. 262; "clan of enemies": Volkogonov, *Stalin,* pp. 141–42.

6. *W,* p. 40. Solow memo, Nov. 20, 1938; also supplement 3, Dec. 7, 1938.

7. *W,* p. 37.

8. Requisition for personnel, filed by A. G. Silverman (Sept. 30, 1937); personnel application, WPA, signed Jay V. David Chambers (Oct. 18, 1937); oath of office, sworn by JVDC (Oct. 18, 1937)—all in 2d Trial, vol. 10, p. 3663.

9. Jay and Esther Chambers to Scholarship Committee, Park School, Oct. 4, 1937, 2d Trial, vol. 10, p. 3769; application for admission (Ellen Chambers), Oct. 11, 1937 (HISS); see also EC deposition, Nov. 17, 1948, p. 669.

10. Maid: EC deposition, Nov. 16, 1948, p. 628.

11. FBI 3220, May 11, 1949, p. 125.

12. Ibid., p. 124; operator's license for EC, approved June 16, 1937 (HISS). Purchase of car: Page from record book, Schmidt Motor Car Company, 2d Trial, vol. 6, p. 3357.

13. For Mount Royal Terrace dates, see FBI trial exhibit BA-36, "Rent receipt to Mrs. Esther Chambers," from Andrew J. Ludwig, Dec. 25, 1937; FBI "Review of Testimony Concerning Withdrawal and $300.00 Loan from Riggs National Bank in January, 1937"; FBI 65-1642, "Itemized List of Receipts and Miscellaneous Papers Furnished 2/19/52 to S.A. Joseph C. Trainor by WC."

14. WC, "Faking," part I, pp. 11–23.

15. KGB interrogation of Arnold Ikal, Dec. 14, 1937, procured in Moscow for author by Alan Cullison, 1992 (KGB copy at HOOVER).

16. WC, "Faking," part I, p. 22; "I met a man called Peter. He had a trusted position in the American Communist Party": Ruth Norma Ikal, holograph questionnaire, in KGB (author; copy at HOOVER).

17. WC, "Faking," pp. 20, 26; *W,* p. 356.

18. Pads expense account: "Protocol Interrogation" of Ikal, Jan. 24, 1939 (KGB).

19. Ikal meets Ruth Boerger/naturalization: "Protocol Interrogation" of Ikal, Jan. 8, 1939 (KGB). Marriage date: *Foreign Relations of the United States, Diplomatic Papers: The Soviet Union, 1933–1939* (U.S. Government, 1952), p. 709 (hereafter *FRUS*). Ikal as publisher: Ruth Norma Ikal, KGB questionnaire, gives Gallian. WC, FBI 3220, May 11, 1949, pp. 136–37, said his Columbia friend David Zablodowsky assisted in this venture. See also Solow memo, Nov. 20, 1938, p. 10 (SOLOW); WC, "Faking," part I, p. 25; also Solow, "Stalin's American Passport Mill," *American Mercury* (July 1939). Ruth assists in passport work: "Protocol Interrogation" of Ikal, Jan. 8, 1939.

20. Tilton: KGB "Protocol Interrogation" of Ikal, Jan. 24, 1939. Carr: KGB interrogation, Dec. 14, 1938. 100 passports: WC, "Faking," part I, p. 23. "Two cars": Solow, "Passport Mill."

21. Spring 1936: Telegram, Moscow to Washington, Feb. 10, 1938 (AWP); WC, "Faking," part I, p. 29, places visited in "the fall of 1935, if memory serves."

22. "Old man": WC, "Faking," part I, pp. 32–33.

23. Ibid., p. 26.

24. *FRUS,* p. 708. "Unstable": WC, "Faking," part I, p. 33; stepdaughter: Ruth Ikal letter to "Comrade Yezhov" (KGB).

25. *FRUS,* pp. 497–98, 713.

26. Ibid., p. 498; *NYT,* Dec. 10–11, 1937.

27. Dewey: *NYT,* Dec. 17, 1937.

28. *FRUS,* pp. 499–500.

29. WC, "Faking," part I, pp. 8–9.

30. *FRUS,* p. 718; see also *NYT,* Feb. 11, 1938.

31. *NYT,* Feb. 1, Feb. 15, 1938.

32. "Incriminatory Conclusion," in case No. 18429, "the charge against Ruth-Norma Boerger-Rubens-Robinson," approved by Lavrenti Beria (People's Commissar for Home Affairs of the USSR), May n.d., 1939 (KGB). "Declaration" by Ruth Marie Boerger Rubens, declining "to engage an advocate for my defense," June 6, 1939 (KGB). Moscow telegram to secretary of state, Washington, Nov. 17, 1939 (AWP). Also see *FRUS,* pp. 906, 908–11.

33. Berta Adamovna Ikal execution notice, signed Jan. 25, 1938; carried out Feb. 3, 1938 (KGB). She had been arrested on June 12, 1937; see prisoner questionnaire (KGB).

34. Ikal interrogation, Dec. 24, 1937 (KGB). Later Ikal repudiated these confessions, saying "the testimony I [previously] gave was demanded of me." See interrogation of Jan. 24, 1939 (KGB).

35. Handwritten copy of cable, "M 28," 2d Trial, vol. 7, p. 3433.

36. Joseph E. Davies, *Mission to Moscow* (Simon and Schuster, 1941), p. 264 fn.

37. FBI 100-206603-4, summary report on Juliet Stuart Poyntz, Feb. 24, 1938, p. 4. *New York World-Telegram,* Dec. 18, 1937; *NYT,* Dec. 19, 1937.

38. *W,* p. 204; background: Dorothy Gallagher, "Disappeared," *Grand Street* (Winter 1990), p. 145. Workers School: Draper, *American Communism and Soviet Russia,* p. 88. Also, FBI 100-206603-4.

39. FBI 100-206603-4, p. 4.

40. Ibid., p. 6. The report cites information obtained from the ex-Communist Ludwig Lore. Also Herbert Solow, "Missing a Year!" *New Leader* (July 2, 1938).

41. Bentley, *Out of Bondage,* p. 45ff.

42. Solow, "Missing." "Inner workings": FBI 100-206603-4, p. 2.

43. *W,* p. 439. The novel was published in 1936.

44. Solow, "Missing." On Rubens: "Spy-Scares Serious Dangers to Peace," *New Leader* (Jan. 29, 1938). (Solow used the byline "W. C. Hambers.") Solow's four-part *Sun* series began appearing Feb. 8, 1938. For Tresca suspicions: "U.S. Jury Will Sift Poyntz Mystery," *NYT,* Feb. 8, 1938; also Solow, untitled ms., pp. 5–6 (SOLOW).

45. WC-HS quarrel, Solow memo, Nov. 12, 1938, p. 7; and Solow, untitled, pp. 4–5. See Walter Hambers, "New Indictments Prove Rubens Soviet Agent," *New Leader* (Apr. 9, 1938).

46. From the philosopher Sidney Hook, an organizer of the Dewey Commission of Inquiry. Hook had heard the rumors from Meyer Schapiro. See Hook, *Out of Step,* p. 281.

47. Solow, untitled, pp. 1, 6–9 (SOLOW).

48. FBI 3220, May 11, 1949, pp. 113–14; *W,* pp. 435–37; On Rosenbliett, see Ulanovskaya, *Istoriia;* also FBI 65-58428-3, signed statement of Isador Miller, Feb. 2, 1949.

49. Ulanovskaya, *Istoriia;* Ikal interrogation, Dec. 22, 1937 (KGB).

50. FBI 3220, May 11, 1949, pp. 113–14; Ulanovskaya, *Istoriia.*

51. Unsigned memo on Federal Works Agency files, Aug. 31, 1948 (HISS). Janet Wile (National Research Project), letter to Jay V. David Chambers, Feb. 24, 1938, 2d Trial, vol. 10, p. 3663.

52. Schapiro to Alan Wald, July 26, 1975; Weinstein interview with Schapiro, Oct. 7, 1974; WC to Schapiro, n.d.: "Briefly, I hope you find some translation I can do" (all AWP); WC deposition, Nov. 5, 1948, pp. 437–38.

53. FBI NY 65-14920, government Exhibit IV-B-8 (prepared for AH appeal to overturn perjury verdict, 1952): Letter from Oxford University Press, March 4, 1938, indicating forthcoming change of translators; see also FBI (no serial no.) signed statement of the dismissed translator, Rita Reil, Feb. 29, 1952; Exhibit IV-B-9: record of rush mailing of Gumpert ms. from OUP to "David Chambers," 2124 Mount Royal Terrace, March 18, 1938. Willert later said he was put in touch with WC by OUP editor Philip Vaudrin, a Columbia acquaintance of WC and Schapiro's and an ex-CP: PW to Arthur Koestler, Feb. 2, 1953 (KOESTLER); see also B. H. Haggin letter, *TNR* (Jan. 23, 1965). WC to Schapiro (probably March 1938); also FBI teletype 5076, Feb. 21, 1952, p. 8. Payment, due date: Willert to WC, Apr. 12, 1938, Exhibit IV-B-11a.

54. *BAS,* Feb. 27, 1938; FBI 65-1642, "Itemized list," Feb. 9, 1952: Receipts kept by WC indicate he made last utilities payment at Mount Royal Terrace at the end of March. According to a neighbor, WC vacated the apartment on Apr. 19, 1938: FBI report 5125, Feb. 2, 1952. Also on move: FBI teletype 4993, Feb. 1, 1952; EC deposition, Nov. 17, 1948, p. 688; FBI 3220, May 1, 1949, p. 128; 2d Trial, vol. I, p. 263 (WC testimony); also *W,* pp. 39–40. "Roamed": WC deposition, Nov. 5, 1948, p. 413.

55. FBI 74-1333-5009, Feb. 12, 1952, p. 8; FBI teletype 4993, Feb. 1, 1952.

56. FBI Exhibit BA-42, repair order of Schmidt Motor Co., Apr. 1, 1938; EC to Dr. Hans Froelicher, Apr. 2, 1938 (HISS).

57. *W,* p. 42; FBI 65-1642-1782, Feb. 21, 1952, interview with EC.

58. EC letter to Froelicher, Apr. 9, 1938, sent from Lynbrook (HISS); "floor": 2d Trial, vol. 2, p. 970 (EC testimony); WC deposition, Nov. 17, 1948, p. 783. April 11 meeting: EC letter to Froelicher, Apr. 9, 1938. April 12: FBI Exhibit IV-B-11 9, letter from Willert to WC, Apr. 12, 1938. Date approximated by WC: 2d Trial, vol. 1, p. 264.

The last of the documents he collected, State Department cables, were dated Apr. 1, 1938: 2d Trial, vol. 9, pp. 3629–30. The entire time WC was at Old Court Road he kept up the pretense of living at Mount Royal Terrace. Utilities were cut off there on Apr. 9, 1938, and new tenants did not move in until Apr. 27, 1938: FBI teletype 5038, Feb. 13, 1952.

59. FBI teletype 4917, Feb. 21, 1952; FBI teletype 4999, Feb. 7, 1952; FBI teletype (no serial no.), Feb. 15, 1952; FBI teletype 5029, Feb. 16, 1952; FBI 5113, Feb. 19, 1952; FBI teletype 5041, Feb. 18, 1952; FBI teletype 5081, Feb. 25, 1952. FBI 3220, May 11, 1949, pp. 128–29. EC kept a hatchet under her pillow: EC deposition, Nov. 17, 1948, p. 696.

## Chapter 12: "Whose Ghost Are You?"

1. "Tail": Weinstein interview with Maxim Lieber, May 13, 1975 (AWP). *W,* pp. 45–46.

2. "Addressee moved": FBI Exhibit IV-B-12. "Unavoidable": FBI Exhibit IV-B-13, WC to Paul Willert, May 1, 1938 (HISS).

3. Aware: Willert to Arthur Koestler, Feb. 2, 1953 (KOESTLER). "Remain": Willert to WC, May 4, 1938 (HISS).

4. FBI Exhibit IV-B-19: WC telegram to Willert, May 17, 1938; FBI Exhibit IV-B-20, May 18, 1938, Oxford University Press "receiving report" of "part translation"; FBI Exhibit IV-B-21, May 20, 1938, "receiving report"; FBI Exhibit IV-B-22, "receiving report/" "Excellent": FBI Exhibit IV-B-18: Willert to Martin Gumpert, May 4, 1938.

5. "Devil": Quoted in RDT and Lasky, *Seeds,* p. 71; shotgun: FBI 3220, May 11, 1949, p. 129; FBI 74-1333-5009, p. 4.

6. "Temporary tactic": *W,* p. 60; "establish ourselves": EC deposition, Nov. 17, 1948, p. 698.

7. EC deposition, Nov. 17, 1948, p. 698; *W,* pp. 60–61. Contract of sale for house at 2610 St. Paul Street, June 11, 1938; agreement: June 25, 1938 (both HISS).

8. See Hook, *Out of Step,* p. 281; also B. H. Haggin letter, *TNR* (Jan. 23, 1965); Willert to Arthur Koestler, Feb. 2, 1953. WC to Schapiro, n.d., marked "summer 1938" by Schapiro (AWP); Solow memo, Nov. 12, 1938, p. 10 (SOLOW).

9. Solow memo, Nov. 20, 1938, p. 10a (SOLOW). Also FBI 65-14920-2995, interview with Solow, March 10, 1949.

10. WC to Schapiro, n.d., probably mid-Dec. 1938 (AWP).

11. Weinstein interview with Schapiro, Oct. 7, 1974; WC to Schapiro, n.d., "March 1938"; WC to Schapiro, n.d., "July 1938" (all AWP).

12. Worry: WC to Schapiro, n.d., "July/August 1938"; "nightmare": WC to Schapiro, n.d., "summer 1938" (both AWP). EC deposition, Nov. 17, 1948, p. 705. WC "had indicated to me at times that [the Communists] were going to either assassinate him or hurt him or members of his family": Nathan Levine testimony, Dec. 10, 1948, HUAC II, p. 1452.

13. WC to Schapiro (probably mid-Dec. 1938) refers to one "political" WC feels he can trust, obviously Lieber. "Leave": Weinstein interview Lieber, May 13, 1975 (AWP); *W,* pp. 46–47.

14. Peters's demotion: Klehr et al., *Secret World,* p. 87. "Any day": Ulanovskaya, *Istoriia;* see also Weinstein, "Nadya—A Spy Story," p. 75; see ibid. for German agent.

15. Lore: Draper, *American Communism and Soviet Russia,* pp. 87–95, 106–7, 110–11. "The *Volkszeitung* . . . the best of the American Communist newspapers . . . helped swing me into Communism": *W,* pp. 201, 389. "Genial Stalin": *W,* p. 390. See also Lore obit, *NYT,* July 9, 1942. "Her daddy": Robert von Mehren, "Memo of Conversation with Mrs. Lore," Aug. 1, 1949 (HISS).

16. Solow memo, Nov. 20, 1938, p. 11.

17. Tresca and De Silver: Dorothy Gallagher, *All the Right Enemies: The Life and Murder of Carlo Tresca* (Rutgers, 1988), pp. 148, 168. Immunity: Solow memo, Nov. 20, 1938, p. 12 (SOLOW).

18. Solow memo, Nov. 20, 1938, p. 12 (SOLOW). "Social fascists . . . Buddha": Hook, *Out of Step,* p. 277. Solow's approach to Hook on WC's behalf: Ibid., pp. 278, 281; Solow memo, Nov. 12, 1938, p. 10 (SOLOW).

19. Solow memo, Nov. 20, 1938, p. 12 (SOLOW). Decorations: Diana Trilling, *Beginning,* p. 220. Anita Brenner to Reuben, Apr. 23, 1969 (WAR). "Whittaker": Hook, *Out of Step,* p. 286ff. "Libelous": Lionel Trilling, *MOJ,* p. xviii. "Whose ghost": Diana Trilling, *Beginning,* p. 220. "Fixed": Hook, *Out of Step,* p. 286.

20. Hook, *Out of Step,* p. 286.

21. Solow memo, Nov. 20, 1938, pp. 13–15 (SOLOW).

22. Some time after WC told Solow "Rubens is a Latvian and his true name is Ewald," Solow interviewed Walter Krivitsky and said, "Robinson's true name is Ewald." Krivitsky "almost jumped out of his seat. He said, 'My God, did they get him too?' ": Solow memo, "Interviews given to Dr. Zeligs," n.d. (ZELIGS).

23. WC to Solow, n.d., probably mid-Dec. 1938 (SOLOW)

24. WC to Schapiro, n.d., "February 1939." WC to Solow, probably Jan. 1939 (SOLOW). WC to Duncan Norton-Taylor, May 2, 1956 (AWP).

25. Wadleigh testimony, 2d Trial, vol. 1, p. 411. "Bourgeois": Wadleigh, "Why I Spied," July 17, 1948.

26. WC to Solow, n.d., probably Jan. 1939 (SOLOW); WC to Solow, n.d., probably Jan.–Feb. 1939. "More to fear": Hook, *Out of Step,* p. 287; see also p. 283.

27. Von Mehren, "Memo of Conversation with Mrs. Lore," Aug. 1, 1949 (HISS); FBI 2927, July 12, 1949, p. 13; Nathan Levine, HUAC II, p. 1452.

28. Harold Rosenwald, memo on WC translation, Dec. 2, 1948; Edward McLean, "Memorandum re Longmans Green," Dec. 10, Dec. 20, 1948; See also correspondence "David Chambers" to Mills, July 1938–June 1939 (all HISS); FBI 3220, interview with EC, Feb. 10, 1949, p. 220.

29. *W,* p. 62; EC deposition, Nov. 16, 1948, p. 698; two hundred dollars: WC to Solow, n.d., probably Nov. 1938 (SOLOW). Cantwell: FBI 65-14920, n.d., p. 4. Lumpkin: *W,* p. 61.

30. "Negative force": WC to Solow, n.d., probably Jan.–Feb. 1939 (SOLOW). "Contaminate": WC to Schapiro, probably mid-Dec. 1938 (AWP).

31. WC to Cantwell, n.d., 1938 (Cantwell Papers).

32. Wadleigh, "Why I Spied," July 18, 1948.

33. WC to Schapiro, "Summer 1938" (AWP). Fadiman loaned him fifty dollars, however. Harold Rosenwald, memo, Oct. 15, 1948 (HISS); "so mysterious": Van Doren, *Autobiography,* p. 219.

34. WC to Schapiro, "March 1938" (AWP). "Crude": Macdonald to William A. Reuben, Aug. 29, no year (WAR). Another of WC's stories was titled "The Doctor Is in the Cellar." See WC to Schapiro, probably Jan. 1939 (AWP). Neither story has survived.

35. WC to Cantwell, n.d., 1938 (Cantwell Papers); McLean memo of interview with Cantwell, Nov. 9, 1948 (HISS); *W,* pp. 85–86. FBI 2995, n.d., "Background Information on WC, re Robert Cantwell," p. 4. See also Cantwell to WC Aug. 18, 1950 (Cantwell Papers).

36. The title plays on Gertrude Stein's *The Making of Americans.* WC, "Faking." For full text of quoted cable, chapter 23; "Portable": WC deposition, Feb. 17, 1949, p. 1024.

37. "Rehash": Solow prefatory note to "Faking," July 27, 1961. Five thousand dollars: Lewis, "Who Killed Krivitsky?" Levine reaction: Solow, supplement to memo, Dec. 3, 1938 (SOLOW).

38. Aversion to Russians: *W,* p. 459. All quotes: Levine, *Eyewitness,* pp. 189–90. Levine also ghosted Jan Valtin's *Out of the Night* (Alliance, 1941), another influential memoir by an ex-Communist. WC later said he suspected Levine wanted to act as *his* ghostwriter: WC deposition, Nov. 17, 1948, p. 790; also author interview with RDT, Nov. 15, 1990.

39. "Urgent": Willert to WC, c/o Nathan Levine, Dec. 15, 1938 (HISS). "Ulrich": WC to Schapiro, probably Dec. 1938. Visit with Ellen: Solow supplement to memo, Dec. 17, 1938 (SOLOW).

40. Solow supplement to memo, Dec. 17, 1938 (SOLOW).

41. "Skip": ibid. Also, WC to Schapiro, probably mid-Dec. 1938 (AWP).

42. Once or twice a month: FBI, "History of the Case," pp. 41–42. "I used to see him when I worked . . . in the classic stacks at the Johns Hopkins": Murray Kempton letter to author, Feb. 19, 1995. Kempton was an undergraduate at the time. WC to Solow, probably Jan. 1939. Trudging: *Baltimore News-Post,* Aug. 27, 1948.

43. WC to Schapiro, Jan.–Feb. 1939 (AWP). "If you really": *NYT,* Feb. 21, 1954.

44. "Political": WC to Schapiro, Jan.–Feb. 1939 (AWP); "worried": *W,* p. 47. "Katz": FBI 3220, May 11, 1949, p. 131.

45. Katz, better known by his nom de plume André Simone, was executed in Prague in 1952, amid a fresh round of Stalinist purges. See Theodore Draper, "The Man Who Wanted to Hang," *The Reporter* (Jan. 6, 1953); also Babette Gross, *Willi Münzenberg: A Political Biography* (Michigan State, 1974), pp. 310–13. Willert twice confirmed WC's story. "At that time Otto Katz [was] staying with me. . . . It is possible [he] asked me to pass a message to Chambers": Willert to Arthur Koestler, Feb. 2, 1953 (KOESTLER). "Willert told me that the story about Ulrich visiting him . . . was true": Weinstein interview with Willert, March 17, 1975 (AWP). WC, confused by the Russian alias Ulrich, later guessed that the agent might be the author Vladimir Posner. FBI 3220, May 11, 1949, p. 131.

46. *W,* p. 47.

47. WC to Edward Mills, Dec. 28, 1938 (HISS).

48. WC to Schapiro, probably Feb. 1939. McLean memo of interview with Cantwell, Nov. 9, 1948 (HISS); Cantwell to Meyer Zeligs, March 30, 1963 (ZELIGS).

## CRUSADER *(1939–1948)*

### Chapter 13: The Clash of Swords

1. Robert T. Elson, *The World of Time Inc.: The Intimate History of a Publishing Enterprise,* vol. 2, *1941–1960* (Atheneum, 1968), p. xiv. W. A. Swanberg, *Luce and His Empire* (Dell, 1973), pp. 118–20.

2. Dormitory/"people": *Weldon Kees and the Midcentury Generation: Letters, 1935–1955,* ed. Robert E. Knoll (Nebraska, 1986), p. 80. "Cosmic": Swanberg, *Luce,* p. 110. On socializing, see John Kobler, *Luce: His Time, Life, and Fortune* (Doubleday, 1968), p. 139; also Laurence Bergreen, *James Agee: A Life* (Penguin, 1985), p. 119.

3. For background on Matthews, see his *Name and Address: An Autobiography* (Simon and Schuster, 1960). "Grammarian": Kobler, *Luce,* p. 134. On Matthews's improvements, see David Halberstam interview with John Hersey (David Halberstam Papers—Mugar Library, Boston University). Briton Hadden, the originator of Timestyle, "regarded *Time* readers . . . as members of a small and intimate circle of admirers": Noel F. Busch, *Briton Hadden: A Biography of the Co-Founder of Time* (Farrar, Straus, 1949), p. 114.

4. "Malraux"/"pipe": T. S. Matthews, *Angels Unaware: Twentieth-Century Portraits* (Ticknor & Fields, 1985), pp. 169–70; "There was such a suppressed air of melodrama about him that I should not have been greatly surprised if one day a Communist gunman shot him down in one of the office corridors": Matthews, *Angels,* p. 170; see also Cantwell to WC, Aug. 18, 1950; "first real job": *W,* p. 86; date/salary: WC's "personnel card," quoted in Edward McLean, "Memorandum re 'Time,' " Jan. 8, 1949 (HISS).

5. Initiation period: Kronenberger, *No Whippings,* p. 106; Kobler, *Luce,* pp. 135–36. Shaved pencils: Alfred Kazin, *New York Jew* (Vintage, 1979), p. 85. Staring out the window: *W,* p. 479. Clinching the job: *W,* p. 86. "One bomby": "Intelligence Report," *Time* (May 1, 1939) (also in *Ghosts,* p. 49).

6. "Night Thoughts," *Time* (May 8, 1939) (*Ghosts,* pp. 50–55). Matthews quotes: *Angels,* pp. 170–71. WC preferred his obituary on Joyce, "Silence, Exile & Death," in *Time* (Feb. 10, 1941) (*Ghosts,* p. 63). See *W,* p. 477.

7. Welles incident: Swanberg, *Luce,* pp. 279–80; see also Welles to Weinstein, Jan. 14, 1975 (AWP).

8. "Personal History," p. 184. Ellen briefly attended school in Lynbrook. See EC deposition, Nov. 17, 1949, p. 708. See also FBI report 65-6766, on WC, Oct. 2, 1941, pp. 8–9.

9. FBI 65-14920-2995, March 10, 1949, p. 14.

10. WC on Solow: "I would think he is not a very politically-minded person," WC deposition, Nov. 17, 1949, p. 787. This judgment alone shows how far WC had traveled from the world of the New York intellectuals, who considered Solow perhaps the most astute political mind in their group. See Sidney Hook letter to Alan Wald, Dec. 30, 1975 (Hook Papers, HOOVER). "[Solow] was meant to be a great political journalist": Lionel Trilling, "A Novel of the Thirties," in *The Last Decade,* p. 8. Levine testimony, Dec. 8, 1948, HUAC II, p. 1404; "antipathy": *W,* p. 459. Krivitsky's articles were the basis of his book *In Stalin's Secret Service.* On Krivitsky's doubts, see Levine, *Eyewitness,* p. 190.

11. Levine, *Eyewitness,* pp. 190–91. Victor Serge, *Memoirs of a Revolutionary, 1901–1941,* trans. Peter Sedgwick (Oxford, 1963), p. 343. "He could have been taken for a teacher or a poet": Levine, *Eyewitness,* p. 185; Soviets lobby/fear of assassins, *NYT* obit, Feb. 11, 1941.

12. *W,* pp. 459–60; Max Eastman, Boris Souvarine, and Dwight Macdonald all were shaken by Kronshtadt: See William L. O'Neill, *The Last Romantic: A Life of Max Eastman* (Oxford, 1978), p. 191. So was Victor Serge: *Memoirs,* p. xv. See also John P. Diggins, *Up from Communism* (Columbia, 1975), pp. 183–84. For Yeltsin, see *NYT,* Nov. 10, 1994. "Clash of swords": WC to Schapiro, probably Sept. 1938.

13. "Jigsaw puzzle": Levine, HUAC II, p. 1404.

14. *W,* pp. 462–63. Krivitsky, *Secret Service,* p. 272.

15. "Honeycombed"/"48 hours"/Kremlin-Comintern: Lewis, "Who Killed Krivitsky." See also Waldman, *Labor Lawyer,* p. 352. HUAC: Krivitsky obit, *NYT,* Feb. 11, 1941; see also Walter Goodman, *The Committee: The Extraordinary Career of the House Committee on Un-American Activities* (Farrar, Straus, 1968), pp. 67–68.

16. "Soviet Signs Pact Not to Join War on Nazis," *WP,* Aug. 24, 1939.

17. Conquest, *Great Terror,* p. 196.

18. "Lively exchanges": Fest, *Hitler,* p. 615. "Soviet Russia is Hitler's natural ally": WC, prefatory note to "Faking," part I. For Krivitsky, see *The Saturday Evening Post,* Apr. 29, 1939. See also *NYT* obit, Feb. 11, 1941.

19. Levine, HUAC I, p. 1405. WC quotes: Levine, *Eyewitness,* pp. 192–93.

20. *WP,* Aug. 24, 1939. Frank Freidel, *Franklin D. Roosevelt: A Rendezvous with Destiny* (Little, Brown, 1990), p. 318. "The stranger"/"Berle's word": Levine, *Eyewitness,* pp. 193–94.

21. "Hitler 'Ready for 10-Year War' ": *WP,* Sept. 2, 1939.

22. *W,* p. 463. "Civilization": "Is Neutrality Possible?" *WP,* Sept. 2, 1939.

23. On Woodley history, see N. Sturtevant, untitled ms., May 11, 1980; "New House Acquired by Secretary Stimson," *NYT,* June 29, 1929; "Some Folks Won't Take 'No' for Answer on Woodley," *Washington Daily News,* Nov. 1, 1950 (all on file at Maret School, Washington, D.C., occupant of the site since 1952).

24. Eight o'clock: Levine, *Eyewitness,* p. 194. On Berle, see Jordan A. Schwarz, *Liberal: Adolf A. Berle and the Vision of an American Era* (Free Press, 1989). See also *Navigating the Rapids, 1918–1971: From the Papers of Adolf A. Berle,* ed. Beatrice Bishop Berle and Travis Beal Jacobs, intro. Max Ascoli (Harcourt, 1973), pp. 249–50.

25. Levine, *Eyewitness,* p. 194. Description of dining room: from period photos at Maret School.

26. "Special information"/"extremely agitated/clean": *W,* p. 464.

27. "Manipulated": Berle, *Navigating,* p. 250.

28. *The Secret Diary of Harold Ickes: The Lowering Clouds, 1939–41* (Simon and Schuster, 1954), p. 620.

29. Names and "plans/aerial": Berle notes, "Underground Espionage Agent," 2d Trial, vol. 6, p. 3325. Jotted names: Levine testimony, Aug. 18, 1948, HUAC I, pp. 1007–8; see also Levine, "The Inside Story of Our Soviet Underworld," part II, *Plain Talk* (October 1948).

30. Berle, "Underground Espionage Agent."

31. "Utmost delicacy": Levine, HUAC II, p. 1408.

32. "Simple measures": Berle memo (diary), Sept. 4, 1939. "Under cross-examination, [WC] qualified everything to the point of substantial withdrawal": Berle, *Navigating,* p. 598. For full account of steps taken by Berle, see his testimony, Aug. 30, 1948, HUAC I, pp. 1294–95. "All-powerful": Berle, HUAC I, p. 1299.

Chapter 14: "God Bless You, Harry"

1. "The cause": Swanberg, *Luce,* p. 205; pockets: Hedley Donovan, *Right Places, Right Times: Forty Years in Journalism Not Counting My Paper Route* (Holt, 1989), p. 157; summoned: Kazin, *New York Jew,* p. 83; "chilled axe"/"dogs": John Hersey, "Henry Luce's China Dream," *TNR* (May 2, 1983).

2. "The Grapes of Wrath," Feb. 12, 1940 (*Ghosts,* pp. 58–59). A novel of similar theme much more to his liking was Ignazio Silone's *The Seed Beneath the Snow,* whose hero, WC noted approvingly, "thinks too well of the poor as they are, and too ill of the rest of the world, to be much interested in reducing poverty": See "Bomb or Pearl?" *Time* (Aug. 24, 1942).

3. Swanberg, *Luce,* p. 278. *W,* pp. 480–81.

4. Swanberg, *Luce,* p. 304.

5. On HRL's background, see ibid., pp. 31–70. "Goddam Republicans": Donovan, *Right Places,* p. 102.

6. WC's hatred of the New Deal: *W,* p. 472; on WC's baptism: *W,* p. 483; baptismal roll, Cathedral Church of St. John the Divine, New York, Sept. 26, 1940 (ZELIGS); William Dudley Foulke Hughes letter to Zeligs, Feb. 22, 1963 (ZELIGS); Sam Welles letter to WC, Nov. 26, 1949 (AWP); "pulverization": "Personal History," p. 160.

7. Best writer: Cerf, *At Random,* p. 242. "Flow": Author interview with Joseph Kastner, Dec. 21, 1989.

8. "Down the middle": Reuben interview with Manfried Gottfried, May 8, 1969 (WAR); Elson, *World of Time,* p. 104.

9. WC was not the only one disturbed by Cowley's politics. "What in God's name has happened to you? I was told . . . you were circulating a letter asking endorsements of the last batch of Moscow trials": Edmund Wilson to Cowley, March 20, 1938, in *Letters on Literature and Politics,* ed. Elena Wilson, intro. Daniel Aaron (Farrar, Straus, 1977), pp. 309–10. "Opportunist": Cowley, "Krivitsky," *TNR* (Jan. 22, 1940).

10. Cowley, "Counter Revolutionary," journal entry, Dec. 13, 1940, pp. 66–67 (in Cowley Papers, Newberry).

11. "The Revolt of the Intellectuals," *Time* (Jan. 6, 1941) (*Ghosts,* pp. 60–61). Curiously, WC later denied having written the article. See *New York World-Telegram,* June 24, 1949; *New York Sun,* June 24, 1949.

12. Trotsky assassination: Pavel Sudoplatov and Anatoli Sudoplatov with Jerrold L. and Leona P. Schecter, *Special Tasks: The Memoirs of an Unwanted Witness—A Soviet Spymaster* (Little, Brown, 1994), pp. 65–80. "Krivitsky": Morrow, "Conversation with W," p. 3 (HOOVER).

13. "kidnapping": *NYT,* Feb. 11, 1941. "One day": Waldman, *Labor Lawyer,* pp. 346–47.

14. Anthony Cave Brown, *Treason in the Blood: H. St. John Philby, Kim Philby, and the Spy Case of the Century* (Houghton Mifflin, 1994), pp. 219–21. According to Krivitsky, "Within twenty-four hours after any vital conference in London," Soviet authorities would have learned what secret decisions had been reached: Waldman, *Labor Lawyer,* p. 352.

15. Lewis, "Who Killed Krivitsky?" *The New Masses,* outraged by Krivitsky's early revelations of Soviet-Nazi collaboration, had taunted the defector with an anti-Semitic slur, referring to him as Shmelka Ginsberg (his birth name): Levine, *Eyewitness,* p. 186. Converting: *W,* p. 486; Reverend Hughes letter to Zeligs, Feb. 22, 1963 (ZELIGS).

16. *NYT,* Feb. 11, 1941; Waldman, *Labor Lawyer,* Lewis, "Who Killed Krivitsky?" Brown, *Treason,* pp. 222–23. Krivitsky and Ignace Reiss both were rehabilitated under glasnost: Laqueur, *Stalin,* p. 344.

17. "Killed": *Washington Times-Herald,* Dec. 20, 1948; *W,* p. 486.

18. Weinstein, *Perjury,* p. 331 fn.

19. FBI memos to director: (no serial no.), March 1, 1941; (no serial no.), March 3, 1941; FBI 1X3, March 18, 1941; FBI letter to director, Sept. 3, 1948. At the time Berle

wrote in his diary, "General Krivitzky [*sic*] was murdered in Washington today. This is an OGPU job. It means that the murder squad . . . is now operating in New York and Washington": Berle, *Navigating,* p. 231. "Mr. Berle is quoted as saying he was afraid that the Russian agencies were looking for [WC]": FBI (no serial no.) memo for the director, Sept. 1, 1948. "History, hypothesis": FBI 100-25824-22, letter from Assistant Director P. E. Foxworth to director, May 14, 1942. The bureau decided to interview WC after hearing about him from a number of journalists, including Ludwig Lore, *American Mercury* editor Eugene Lyons, Victor Riesel of the *New Leader,* and Will Allen of the *Washington Daily News.* See FBI teletype (no serial no.), March 30, 1941; FBI memo 62-62107, Aug. 1, 1941; FBI report 65-6766, Oct. 2, 1941; FBI 100-15826, letter [to director?], Jan. 22, 1942. Also author interview with Victor Riesel, Oct. 6, 1994. The FBI began a background check on WC on Aug. 18, 1941: Letters from FBI director: 100-62-62107, Aug. 18, 1941; also FBI 25824-15, Nov. 21, 1941.

20. *W,* pp. 486–87. For farm purchase, see FBI 65-1642-927, "memo for the files," March 17, 1949. WC's salary: *Time* "personnel card." See also WC to Grace Lumpkin, July 24, 1941 (Lumpkin Papers, University of South Carolina). At the time of the Hiss case WC owned a total of 314 acres: "Personal History," p. 184. According to WC's *Time* friend Tom Hyland, WC moved to the farm so as to elude assassins. He also kept his Lynbrook address more or less secret: Reuben interview with Hyland, June 23, 1969 (WAR).

21. Freeman to Daniel Aaron, July 6, 1958. See also FBI report 100-287275-30, interview with Freeman, Oct. 20, 1949, p. 28; Aaron, *Writers on the Left,* p. 384.

22. Kronenberger, *No Whippings,* p. 132.

23. *W,* pp. 483–84.

24. WC memo to Luce, May 6, 1942 (TIME).

25. Morrow, "Conversation with W," p. 4 (HOOVER).

26. FBI 65-1642-927, March 17, 1949.

27. Matthews, *Angels,* p. 172.

28. "Inopportune," *Time* (Feb. 16, 1942). MacLeish to Luce, Feb. 13, 1942 (TIME); see also Cowley, letter to the editors of *Time,* March 16, 1942; Cowley to MacLeish, Jan. 21, 1942 (Cowley Papers, Newberry); letter of resignation, March 12, 1942, and MacLeish acceptance, March 13, 1942 (WAR); *The Selected Correspondence of Kenneth Burke and Malcolm Cowley, 1915–1981,* ed. Paul Jay (Viking, 1988), pp. 250–51. "[WC's] story cost [Cowley] his job": Aaron, *Writers on the Left,* p. 383.

29. Author interviews with James Bell, Dec. 12, 1990, and Judith Friedberg, Jan. 3, 1990. Penn Kimball, *The File* (Harcourt, 1983), pp. 260–61; refused vacations: WC to David McDowell, Oct. 16, 1954 (WFB).

30. Elson, *World of Time,* p. 104. The other contributors were William Ernest Hocking, William Pepperell Montague, Jacques Maritain, Julian Huxley, Alfred Noyes, William A. Sperry, Robert M. Hutchins, Charles Morris, Charles W. Hendel, and Susanne K. Langer. See Luce memos to WC, May 6, May 7, 1942; Hocking to HRL, Dec. 10, 1948 (all TIME); "A Chambers Legacy," *Fortune* (September 1961); also Kazin, *New York Jew,* p. 83; *W,* p. 494.

31. Elson, *World of Time,* pp. 104–5. The only section WC did not edit was Business. "Personnel card": FBI 65-14920; *W,* p. 494; Swanberg, *Luce,* p. 305.

32. Author interview with Marlys Fuller Fixx, Aug. 21, 1995; Fixx obit in *FYI,* Time Inc. in-house publication, March 10, 1950 (courtesy of Mrs. Fixx); *W,* p. 494. Fixx's son Jim, who became a magazine editor, wrote the best-selling *The Complete Book of Running* (1977), which set off the national jogging craze in the 1980s. See *NYT* obit, July 22, 1984. Father and son both died young of heart attacks.

33. *W,* p. 494.

34. WC to Zolan, March 25, 1943 (courtesy of Mr. Zolan).

35. WC memo to HRL, Sept. 11, 1942 (TIME).

36. Author interview with Marlys Fixx; Margaret D. McConnell to Marlys Fixx, May 23, 1983 (courtesy of Mrs. Fixx); *FYI* obit.

37. HRL memo to "Writers in Mr. Chambers' Division," Nov. 24, 1942. WC letter to HRL, n.d., probably "early December 1942"; HRL to WC, Dec. 7, 1942 (both TIME); mortgage: WC to Zolan, March 25, 1943.

38. "Now tell": WC to Zolan, March 25, 1943.

39. Ibid., March 15, 1943; WC to Solow, n.d., spring 1943 (SOLOW). "A heifer slammed Esther into a fence . . . and hurt her shoulder pretty badly": WC to Grace Lumpkin, Nov. 14, 1943 (Lumpkin Papers, University of South Carolina).

40. WC to HRL, early 1943 (TIME). FBI 100-184255-67, report on Alexander Stevens (J. Peters), March 6, 1943; FBI 65-14920-2995, March 10, 1943, p. 7. *W,* pp. 495–96.

41. WC to Solow, spring 1943 (SOLOW). *W,* p. 495.

42. WC to Solow, spring 1943; WC to Zolan, March 25, 1943; WC to HRL, March 16, 1943 (TIME).

43. Medical report, Dr. E. W. Bridgman, Apr. 12, 1943 (ZELIGS).

44. "Writing book reviews for [WC] is a real pleasure, said Kees" But Kees was one of several young writers dismissed in a "purge" in September 1943. "I have watched [WC] . . . in operation," Kees later remarked, "and it is not a pretty sight": Kees, *Letters,* pp. 79–84. Moss, let go "in a very pleasant way," was astonished when WC, who barely knew him, offered to "get me a job in a defense plant near his Maryland farm" and also invited him to spend weekends at WC's farm, writing. Moss letter to Reuben, March 1, 1969 (WAR). WC made similar offers to other young writers, one of whom, Brad Darrach, took him up on it and lived on the farm for six months. Author interview with Darrach, Nov. 3, 1990.

The most illustrious writer fired by WC, Saul Bellow, lasted only a day under WC as a film reviewer in 1945. Bellow drew on the incident in his novel *The Victim* (Vanguard, 1947; Penguin reissue, 1988), pp. 36–40; also Martha Fay, "A Talk with Saul Bellow," *Book-of-the-Month-Club News,* August 1975; Ruth Miller, *Saul Bellow: A Biography of the Imagination* (St. Martin's, 1991), p. 15; James Atlas, "The Shadow in the Garden," *The New Yorker* (June 26 and July 3, 1995—double issue).

45. "Personnel card": July 1, 1944. The next year his salary climbed again, to $14,800. Senior Group: Matthews memo to Roy Larsen, Dec. 11, 1943 (TIME). Profit sharing: Robert E. Herzstein, *Henry R. Luce: A Political Portrait of the Man Who Created the American Century* (Scribner's, 1994), p. 349. Income: McLean memo, Nov. 10, 1949 (HISS).

Chapter 15: Ghost on the Roof

1. "John Chamberlain Tells of His Acquaintance with Whittaker Chambers," *New Leader* (Oct. 15, 1949).

2. WC to Ralph de Toledano, July 27, 1951; see, e.g., John Land, "The Future of American Foreign Policy," *American Mercury* (May 1944), pp. 428–32.

3. See, e.g., "For World War III," Foreign News, *Time* (June 5, 1944).

4. Sumner Welles, *The Time for Decision* (Harper, 1944), p. 327. Under WC, *Time* published a surprisingly friendly review of Welles's book (Sept. 24, 1944).

5. "Miracle in the East," *Time* (July 24, 1944). Romania: *Time* (July 17, 1944). Finland: *Time* (July 3, 1944). Lauterbach's optimism—or naïveté—reached fruition in his book *These Are the Russians* (Harper, 1945), which included two pages on "Stalin's humor" but not one word on the purges.

6. "Anti-Russian": Ronald Steel, *Walter Lippmann and the American Century* (Little, Brown, 1980), p. 410.

7. "Strong propaganda"/"smother": HRL memo to John Shaw Billings, Jan. 6, 1945 (TIME).

8. Elson, *World of Time*, p. 101. "Prejudice": Swanberg, *Luce*, p. 305.

9. "I believe he was crazy": Author interview with John Hersey, Sept. 25, 1990. "[WC] was regarded by many . . . as mysterious, and possibly sinister, brilliant but unbalanced": Thomas Griffith, *Harry and Teddy: The Turbulent Friendship of Press Lord Henry R. Luce and His Favorite Reporter, Theodore H. White* (Random House, 1995), p. 136; see also Reuben interview with Allen Grover, May 7, 1969 (WAR). "[WC was] known by some as the Resident Fascist": Swanberg, *Luce*, p. 386. See also John Osborne's review of John Chabot Smith, *Alger Hiss: The True Story* (Holt, 1976) in *TNR* (Apr. 17, 1976).

10. "Science": Herzstein, *Henry Luce*, p. 349. "Outlandish": Matthews, *Angels*, p. 172. See also David Halberstam, *The Powers That Be* (Knopf, 1979), p. 80. Luce's sister later said, "Harry admired [WC's] mind": See Griffith, *Harry and Teddy*, p. 122.

11. WC memo to HRL, Sept. 18, 1944 (TIME). *W*, p. 497.

12. "Dominate": "Why Not?," *Time* (Aug. 14, 1944); "blueprint": *Time* (Aug. 7, 1944); "Finland" (Aug. 14, 1944). "This was a gauntlet thrown down, in a spirit of malicious glee, before the Western powers. What it meant to imply was: 'We intend to have Poland, lock, stock, and barrel' ": George F. Kennan, *Memoirs, 1925–1950* (Little, Brown, 1967), p. 211. In Dec. 1944 FDR wrote to Stalin in protest of "Soviet determination to recognize the Lublin Committee as the provisional government of Poland": Martin J. Sherwin, *A World Destroyed: The Atomic Bomb and the Grand Alliance* (Vintage, 1977), p. 133.

13. Elson, *World of Time*, pp. 106–7; Swanberg, *Luce*, pp. 316–17. Author interview with Thomas Griffith, Feb. 3, 1990. Wertenbaker's novel *Death of Kings* (Random House, 1954) includes a character closely modeled on WC.

14. Calhoun quoted in Elson, *World of Time*, p. 107; Stephen Laird letter to Reuben, Apr. 22, 1969 (WAR); "no secret": Reuben interview with Tom Hyland, June 23, 1969; "Squib": Reuben interview with Walter Graebner, Apr. 22, 1969 (both WAR); author interview with Thomas Griffith, Feb. 3, 1990. See also Elson, *World of Time*, p. 106.

15. Herzstein, *Henry Luce*, p. 352.

16. "Transferred": Griffith, *Harry and Teddy*, p. 138. Fred Gruin letters to author, Oct. 13, Oct. 19, 1990; author interview with Marylois Purdy Vega, July 8, 1991; Elson, *World of Time*, pp. 105–6; Swanberg, *Luce*, p. 316; Herzstein, *Luce*, p. 352; See also various interviews with Time Inc. staff (WAR) and also in Dorothy Sterling Papers (University of Oregon).

17. WC's routine: Gruin to author, Oct. 13, 1990. Russian publications: Robert Fitzgerald letter to Reuben, Nov. 10, 1968 (WAR).

18. Gruin to author, Oct. 13, Oct. 19, 1990. "Finland: Night," *Time* (Nov. 20, 1944); "China: TV," *Time* (Dec. 18, 1944).

19. "Poland: *Vernichtungslager,*" *Time* (Aug. 21, 1944); Lauterbach, "Murder Inc.," *Time* (Sept. 11, 1944). "The correspondents generally agree that [WC] made pretty full use of all their 'color stuff' ": HRL to Billings, Jan. 6, 1945 (TIME).

20. "Awfully low": Reuben interview with Graebner (WAR).

21. WC memo to HRL, Sept. 18, 1944 (TIME); HRL, "The American Century," *Life* (Feb. 17, 1941). The image of the dynamo comes from Henry Adams, "The Dynamo and the Virgin," in *The Education of Henry Adams.*

22. "Best show": Dororthy Sterling interview with Richard Lauterbach, Feb. 17, 1950 (Sterling Papers, University of Oregon); Matthews to HRL, Sept. 28, 1944 (TIME); "Superb": Elson, *World of Time,* p. 105.

23. Theodore H. White, *In Search of History: A Personal Adventure* (Warner, 1978), p. 126.

24. WC, "You Have Seen the Heads," *NM* (April 1931) (*Ghosts,* pp. 22–29); WC, "But the Toilers of China Storm On," *LD* (August 1931). Since 1941: Herzstein, *Luce,* p. 349.

25. White and HRL: White, *Search;* Griffith, *Harry and Teddy;* Halberstam, *Powers,* pp. 69–84; Patricia Neils, *China Images: In the Life and Times of Henry Luce* (Rowman and Littlefield, 1990), pp. 98–104. Byline: White, "The Rape of Chin Valley," *Time* (Dec. 18, 1939) (also in *Theodore H. White at Large: The Best of His Magazine Writing, 1939–1986,* ed. and intro. Edward T. Thompson [Pantheon, 1992], pp. 3–7).

26. "Great intelligence": White, "*Life* Looks at China," *Life* (May 1, 1944) (*At Large,* pp. 96–110). Stilwell: White, *Search,* pp. 133, 176.

27. "Beyond": Quote in White, *Search,* p. 170. "Direct orders": Barbara Tuchman, *Stilwell and the American Experience in China, 1911–1945* (Macmillan, 1971), p. 501. Stilwell was informed on Oct. 19: See also Joseph W. Stilwell, *The Stilwell Papers,* ed. Theodore H. White (Sloane, 1948), pp. 344–46.

28. White, *Search,* p. 205.

29. Gruin letters, Oct. 19, Oct. 13, 1990. Chiang and Hitler: Tuchman, *Stilwell,* p. 320. "Crisis," *Time* (Nov. 13, 1944) (*Ghosts,* pp. 104–10).

30. White, *Search,* p. 210. See also Halberstam interviews with White and Annalee Jacoby (Halberstam Papers, Boston University).

31. Halberstam, *Powers,* p. 79. White, *Search,* p. 254. Jacoby later married Clifton Fadiman.

32. White, *Search,* p. 209. FBI 65-58367-82, interview with WC, Oct. 13, 1949, pp. 2–3. There was indeed a CP cell at Time Inc. It controlled the company's chapter of the Newspaper Guild and published an in-house gossip sheet, "High Time," whose contributors identified themselves as "the Communist Party Members at Time Inc.": See Elson, *World of Time,* p. 370; also John Chamberlain, *A Life with the Printed Word* (Regnery, 1982), pp. 97, 149; Robert Fitzgerald letter to Reuben, Nov. 10, 1968 (WAR).

White later conceded he had oversentimentalized Chinese Communists. See his introduction to reissue of *Thunder out of China* (Apollo, 1961), pp. xiii–iv. At least one contemporary China scholar says WC's analysis "was substantially supported by subsequent events. . . . Had other foreign editors [besides WC] pressed their 'captivated' correspondents to [see] the reality of the Chinese Communist party, reportage of the China situation would have dramatically improved": Steven W. Mosher, *China Misperceived: American Illusions and Chinese Reality* (Basic, 1990), p. 68.

33. "Office boys"/"Chambers War": Swanberg, *Luce,* pp. 315–16; "deliberately": Elson, *World of Time,* p. 106.

34. Gruin letter to author, Oct. 19, 1990. "Commie": Welles to Weinstein, Jan. 4, 1975 (AWP).

35. Author interviews with Brad Darrach, Nov. 3, 1990, Thomas Griffith, July 8, 1994; Graebner interview (WAR). "Superheated": Chamberlain, "Acquaintance with Whittaker Chambers."

36. "Subject": Elson, *World of Time,* p. 106. "Policymaker": Swanberg, *Luce,* p. 303. Previous squabbles: Laird letter to Reuben, Apr. 22, 1969 (WAR).

37. Grover to HRL, Nov. 29, 1944 (TIME); Matthews, *Angels,* p. 173.

38. "Monotone": Hersey, "Luce's China Dream." Hersey later calculated that of the 11,000 total words he cabled from Moscow, WC used 168: Kobler, *Luce,* p. 147.

39. "Excerpt from Billings' Monthly Editorial Report," Jan. 7, 1945 (TIME). Hersey, "Luce's China Dream"; Swanberg, *Luce,* p. 317. FBI 65-14920-2995, March 10, 1949; *W,* p. 498. HRL to John Shaw Billings, Jan. 6, 1945 (TIME).

40. "Interactions": HRL to John Shaw Billings, Jan. 6, 1945 (TIME). See also Griffith, *Harry and Teddy,* p. 144. "By far": HRL memo to WC, Jan. 17, 1945 (TIME).

41. James Burnham, "Lenin's Heir," *Partisan Review* (Winter 1945). Under WC, *Time* had praised Burnham's *The Managerial Revolution* (John Day, 1941), a landmark analysis of emerging bureaucratic tyrannies: See "Man and Managers," *Time* (May 19, 1941). The reviewer was probably Calvin Fixx. For a contemporaneous analysis of Stalinism in line with Burnham's and WC's, see Arthur Koestler, "The End of an Illusion," in *The Yogi and the Commissar and Other Essays* (Macmillan, 1945); "Historic Force," *Time* (Feb. 5, 1945).

42. Filmore Calhoun memo to Allen Grover, Feb. 6, 1945 (TIME).

43. "Hopeful": Quoted in Edward R. Stettinius, Jr., *Roosevelt and the Russians: The Yalta Conference* (Doubleday, 1949), p. 303.

44. Matthews, *Angels,* pp. 172–73. "Well-poisoner": author interview with Thomas Griffith, Feb. 3, 1990.

45. "The Ghosts on the Roof," *Time* (May 5, 1945) (*Ghosts,* pp. 111–15).

46. "Ten phone calls": Griffith, *Harry and Teddy,* p. 147. "Destroyed me": Halberstam interview with Hersey (Halberstam Papers, Boston University); also author interview with Hersey, Sept. 25, 1990.

47. Elson, *World of Time,* pp. 114–15. See also Chamberlain, *A Life,* p. 67.

48. Poland: Freidel, *Roosevelt,* p. 600. "Development": Arthur Schlesinger, Jr., *The Vital Center: The Politics of Freedom* (Houghton Mifflin, 1949), p. 95; "strong enough": David McCullough, *Truman* (Simon and Schuster, 1992), p. 372.

49. "U.S. leaders": Daniel Yergin, *Shattered Peace: The Origins of the Cold War and the National Security State* (Houghton Mifflin, 1977), p. 85. "World War III": Michael S. Sherry, *In the Shadow of War: The United States Since the 1930s* (Oxford, 1995), p. 124. "Iron Curtain": Quoted in McCullough, *Truman,* p. 489. Long telegram: Kennan, *Memoirs,* pp. 547–59.

50. "Scare": Calhoun memo, Nov. 14 [?], 1944 (TIME). McCullough, *Truman,* p. 534.

51. Matthews, *Angels,* p. 173. Allen Grover also conceded WC had been right to a large extent. See Grover to Reuben, Apr. 10, 1969 (WAR).


Chapter 16: Sorrow Songs

1. WC's relapse: Sterling interview with Lauterbach (Sterling Papers, University of Oregon). Chest pains: FBI memo to D. M. Ladd (no serial no.), Dec. 22, 1953. "Blacked out": *W,* p. 503.

2. Matthews letter to WC, Nov. 10, 1945 (TIME).

3. In a memo to WC and TSM, Osborne judged the piece "brilliant": Osborne, *TNR* (Apr. 17, 1976).

4. Ibid.; WC letter to HRL, Nov. 4, 1945; TSM to WC, Nov. 10, 1945 (TIME). According to Allen Grover, he and two other editors put an ultimatum to Luce in 1945—"Either Whit goes or we go"—and Luce fired WC that same day: Reuben interview with Grover, May 7, 1969 (WAR).

5. Matthews to WC, Nov. 10, 1945 (TIME); "Whole flight": *W,* p. 504.

6. "A Letter from the Publisher," *Time* (Feb. 10, 1947).

7. "Voluminous energy": Author interview with Darrach, Nov. 3, 1990. Also see Bergreen, *Agee; Remembering James Agee,* ed. David Madden (LSU, 1974), esp. essays by WC, Robert Fitzgerald, Louis Kronenberger, T. S. Matthews, Dwight Macdonald (WC's piece also appears in *CF,* pp. 268–71); Diana Trilling, "An Interview with Dwight Macdonald," *Partisan Review,* 50th anniversary issue, vol. lxi (1984), pp. 813–14; John Hersey, "A Critic at Large," *The New Yorker* (July 18, 1988). Mia Agee said WC was her husband's closest friend at Time Inc.: Reuben interview with Mia Agee, Sept. 13, 1969 (WAR).

8. "Best writers": Reuben interview with Ralph Thompson, Jan. 27, 1969 (WAR). "The most talented man on the staff, in everyone's opinion, was Agee. . . . But [WC] was regarded as maybe the second most talented": Author interview with Darrach, Nov. 3, 1990. "Company": author interview with James A. Bell, Dec. 12, 1990.

9. Quoted in Bergreen, *Agee,* pp. 295–96.

10. "In Egypt Land," *Time* (Dec. 30, 1946) (*Ghosts,* p. 138).

11. Quoted in Robert Fitzgerald, "A Memoir," in *Remembering,* p. 77. Agee on *W: Letters of James Agee to Father Flye* (Braziller, 1962), p. 201.

12. "Group journalism"/"finest statement"/Jesuit reprint/"Novelist Rawlings": All from "A Letter from the Publisher." In 1942 WC interviewed Rawlings for *Time* at her home in Florida: See Elizabeth Silverthorne, *Marjorie Kinnan Rawlings: Sojourner at Cross Creek* (Overlook, 1988), p. 296. "The mark of [WC's] writing and thought upon the [Luce] magazines . . . have enabled devotees to spot his authorship": Thomas Sancton, "The Case of Alger Hiss," *The Nation* (Sept. 4, 1948).

13. William H. McNeill, *Arnold J. Toynbee: A Life* (Oxford, 1989), pp. 184, 215–17. Says McNeill: "Thanks to *Time* and to Henry Luce, and literally overnight, Toynbee thus became famous in the United States." See also George F. Kennan, "The History of Arnold Toynbee," *The New York Review of Books* (June 1, 1989), p. 19.

14. "The Middle Ages," *Life* (Apr. 7, 1947). The other pieces are: "Medieval Life" (May 26, 1947); "The Glory of Venice" (Aug. 4, 1947); "The Age of Enlightenment" (Sept. 15, 1947); "The Edwardians" (Nov. 17, 1947); "Age of Exploration" (March 22, 1948); "The Protestant Revolution" (June 14, 1948)—all in *Ghosts.* The book is: *Picture History of Western Man* (Time and Simon and Schuster, 1951). The publisher "isn't advertising the fact that [WC] wrote 7 of the 8 pieces in it. Nor is anyone paying [WC] a penny," wrote Walter Winchell in his syndicated column, March 6, 1950.

15. "Faith for a Lenten Age," *Time* (March 8, 1948) (*Ghosts,* pp. 184–93). See *W,* pp. 505–7.

16. "Drumroll": In David Halberstam, *The Fifties* (Villard, 1993), p. 13. "I think [WC] never really liked leaving the winning side for ours, the crazy losers": Matthews letter to author, Oct. 24, 1990.

17. Crossman approach: *O* (1987), p. 192.

*WITNESS I: THE HEARINGS (AUGUST–DECEMBER 1948)*

Chapter 17: Fetching a Bone

1. Sam Welles, who left *Time* for the State Department in 1942, put Murphy in touch with WC. See Welles letter to WC, Nov. 26, 1949 (AWP). Murphy was among the first U.S. officials to interview Walter Krivitsky: Brown, *Treason*, p. 195. Two hours: 2d Trial, vol. 2, p. 680 (WC testimony). Ray Murphy, "Memorandum of Conversation, Tuesday, March 20, 1945, Westminster, MD": 2d Trial, vol. 6, p. 3323. Murphy "was very excited about the trip and what [WC] told him, and repeated it to me afterwards in great, enthusiastic detail": Welles to WC (AWP). Memo's wide circulation: FBI 65-56402-2962, memo to director, Oct. 10, 1947; FBI 65-56462-2941, memo to D. M. Ladd, Oct. 16, 1947—includes letter from Reverend John Cronin to Patrick Coyne (FBI), Oct. 14, 1947; FBI 65-56462-2942, memo to director, Oct. 18, 1947; FBI 65-56462-2943, memo to Ladd, Oct. 14, 1947; FBI 65-56462-2944, memo to Ladd, Oct. 13, 1947; FBI 65-56462-2945, memo to Ladd, Oct. 16, 1947. See also James Walter letter to Benjamin Mandel, Oct. 5, 1946 (courtesy of Herbert Romerstein).

2. The dates were May 10 and May 17: FBI report 100-25824-36, June 26, 1945; FBI memo (no serial no.), Dec. 22, 1953; FBI memo 74-1333-5594, Jan. 5, 1954. The FBI requested Berle's notes in "the first part of June 1943": FBI memo (no serial no.), July 8, 1943. Levine said Berle tried to inform FDR but received "the cold shoulder": *Eyewitness*, p. 197. Berle later said he had repeated WC's allegations not to FDR but to Marvin McIntyre: *NYT*, Aug. 31, 1948; Berle, *Navigating*, p. 598. The others approached by Levine included (then) Ambassador to France William C. Bullitt, State Department official Loy Henderson, union leader David Dubinsky, and HUAC chairman Martin Dies. See *Eyewitness*, pp. 198–99. For FDR and Winchell, see Winchell letter to Reuben, June 4, 1969 (WAR); Winchell, *Winchell Exclusive*, intro. Ernest Cuneo (Prentice-Hall, 1975), pp. 149–53.

3. The fullest glimpse of Soviet penetration came in March 1996, with the NSA's third release of Venona traffic, some five hundred decrypted cables from the World War II years. See VENONA; also *WP*, March 6, 1996, *BAS*, March 6, 1996. Including Truman: Joyce Milton, "The Old Left," *TNR* (Nov. 4, 1996).

4. Harvey Klehr and Ronald Radosh, *The Amerasia Spy Case: Prelude to McCarthyism* (North Carolina, 1996), p. 6.

5. WC to Solow, n.d. 1943 (SOLOW).

6. FBI (no serial no.), director memo to attorney general (Tom Clark). Dec. 13, 1946. See also Igor Gouzenko, *This Was My Choice* (Dutton, 1948); *NYT*, Dec. 26, 1948; J. W. Pickersgill and D. F. Forster, *The Mackenzie King Record*, vol. 3, *1945–1946* (University of Toronto, 1970), pp. 16–17, 40–41; James Barros, "Alger Hiss and Harry Dexter White: The Canadian Connection," *Orbis*, vol. 21, no. 3 (fall 1977), pp. 593–605.

7. James F. Byrnes, *All in One Lifetime* (Harper, 1958), p. 321. FBI surveillance: FBI 100-267360-113, Apr. 19, 1945; FBI 2058, memo to director from Ladd, Jan. 28, 1949, esp. p. 5.

8. Bentley, *Out of Bondage;* Robert J. Lamphere and Tom Shachtman, *The FBI-KGB War: A Special Agent's Story* (Berkley, 1987), pp. 36–42. See also FBI 3620X2, memo to the director, Aug. 24, 1948; FBI teletype 65-56402-172, Nov. 28, 1951. For the latest Bentley confirmation, see Klehr et al., *Secret World*, pp. 309–17; and VENONA (e.g., 3/NBF/T110).

9. FBI report, "Soviet Espionage in the United States," (no serial no.), Nov. 27, 1945. *W*, p. 530; also FBI memo 2058, Jan. 28, 1949.

10. "Every responsible": Goodman, *The Committee,* p. 197. Loyalty program: McCullough, *Truman,* pp. 550–52. Clark's list: Richard M. Freeland, *The Truman Doctrine and the Origins of McCarthyism* (New York University, 1985), p. 207ff.

11. Ray Murphy, "Memorandum of Conversation, August 28, 1946," 2d Trial, vol. 6, p. 3323. Five interviews: FBI 74-1333-5594. White: Stephen J. Spingarn, Oral History Interview No. 103, vol. 1, p. 934 (HST).

12. FBI memo "sec 33," Jan. 26, 1949.

13. Emmanuel S. Larsen, "The State Department Espionage Case," *Plain Talk* (October 1946). See also Klehr and Radosh, *Amerasia,* p. 147ff; Levine, *Eyewitness,* p. 202.

14. Arthur M. Schlesinger, Jr., "The U.S. Communist Party," *Life* (July 29, 1946). One of those WC named was Alger Hiss. Schlesinger had already heard Hiss was a Communist, probably from Gardner Jackson, Hiss's acquaintance in Cambridge in the 1920s and later his AAA colleague. Author interviews with Barbara Kerr (Time-Life researcher present at the WC interview), July 18, 1990; Arthur Schlesinger, Jr., Oct. 18, 1990.

15. "In view of the negative information supplied by [WC], [prosecutor] T. J. Donegan was of the opinion that [WC's] testimony before the Grand Jury would not be helpful": FBI 46, Aug. 2, 1948.

16. Levine, *Eyewitness,* p. 202. "Resigned": "Interviews given to Dr. Zeligs," n.d., p. 6 (ZELIGS).

17. *W,* p. 454.

18. *Washington Times-Herald,* Oct. 16–17, 1947; *New York Sun,* Oct. 16, 1947.

19. For Murphy's memo reaching the hands of Walter, Nellor, Cronin, Mandel, see note 1 (this chapter, above); for Mandel visit to WC, see 2d Trial, vol. 1, p. 281 (WC testimony); Robert E. Stripling, *The Red Plot Against America,* ed. Bob Considine (Arno Press, 1977), p. 96; Weinstein, *Perjury,* p. 5; *W,* p. 530.

20. WC memo to HRL, n.d. (TIME); Barzun letter to author, Oct. 24, 1994.

21. WC letter to HRL, July 31, 1948. Matthews letter to WC, July 19, 1948 (both TIME).

22. For Smith Act, see *Digest of the Public Record of Communism in the United States* (Fund for the Republic, 1955), p. 194ff. "Red Ring Bared by Blond Queen," *New York World-Telegram,* July 21, 1948; see also articles published July 22–23, Aug. 5, 1948; Bentley, *Bondage* (1951), pp. 308–9.

23. Edward Nellor, "Editor Supplies Red Spy Link," *New York Sun,* July 30, 1948. Chamberlain letter to Reuben, July 25, 1969 (WAR).

24. Elizabeth Bentley testimony, Aug. 31, 1948, HUAC I, pp. 503–62.

25. *W,* pp. 530–31.

26. Frank McNaughton letter to Reuben, May 12, 1969 (ZELIGS); *W,* pp. 529–30. It was HUAC Republican Karl Mundt who decided WC should be subpoenaed. See Karl Mundt, "What the Hiss Trial Actually Means," Senate speech, Jan. 25, 1950 (U.S. Government), p. 10; Weinstein interview with Robert Stripling, Apr. 28, 1975 (AWP).

Chapter 18: Pure Dynamite

1. *W,* p. 531.

2. Hearst: FBI 74-1333-4598, *W* ms. chapter 1. WC sent the bureau the entire unedited ms. Only the first chapter has survived. It corresponds, with changes, to the opening pages of chapter 11, "The Hiss Case," in the published book.

3. *NYHT,* Aug. 3, 1948.

4. McNaughton to Reuben, May 12, 1969 (ZELIGS).

5. "Idealists," in Goodman, *The Committee,* p. 53. See also pp. 210–20, 501. For public reaction, see Kempton, *Part of Our Time,* p. 205.

6. "Poker": author interview with Samuel McNaughton, Aug. 8, 1996; see McNaughton's *Time* dispatches, in McNaughton Papers (HST). Frank McNaughton and Walter Hehmeyer, *Harry Truman—President* (McGraw-Hill, 1948); "shrewd": *W,* p. 532.

7. "Slipshod": FBI *W,* chapter 1. WC deleted this phrase from the published version, evidently finding it too critical. See *W,* p. 536, for WC's charitable view on HUAC.

8. McNaughton to Reuben, May 12, 1969 (ZELIGS).

9. *WP,* Aug. 3–4, 1948.

10. *W,* p. 535.

11. "Unique"/"from the hip": *WP,* quoted in Robert K. Carr, *The House Committee on Un-American Activities, 1945–50* (Cornell, 1952), p. 265. Stripling background, see Carr, pp. 263–67. Also, Stripling, *Red Plot,* p. 46ff. "Always alert": *NYT,* Aug. 15, 1948, cited in Alger Hiss, *In the Court of Public Opinion* (Knopf, 1957), p. 6.

12. Stripling interview (AWP).

13. Bentley testimony, Aug. 31, 1948, HUAC I, p. 557.

14. On Rankin, see Goodman, *The Committee,* p. 167. Thomas's illness: See J. Parnell Thomas to Karl Mundt, July 26, July 27, 1948 (copies in AWP); also *NYT,* Dec. 23, 1948.

15. Stripling, *Red Plot,* p. 97; Stripling interview (AWP).

16. "Buzzing"/"circus": *W,* pp. 538–39; "sit": McNaughton to Reuben, May 12, 1969 (ZELIGS).

17. Mundt background: *NYT,* Aug. 17, 1974; inaudible/sound system down: Frank McNaughton dispatch, Aug. 7, 1948 (HST); Richard M. Nixon, *Six Crises* (Simon and Schuster, 1990; orig. 1962), pp. 2–3. "I will": open session, WC testimony, Aug. 3, 1948, HUAC I, p. 564.

18. RMN, *Six,* p. 3.

19. *WP,* Aug. 4, 1948.

20. Alistair Cooke, *A Generation on Trial: U.S.A. v. Alger Hiss* (Knopf, 1950), p. 57.

21. Quoted in Marvin N. Olasky, "Liberal Boosterism and Conservative Distancing: Newspaper Coverage of the Chambers-Hiss Affair, 1948–1950," *Continuity,* no. 15 (Fall–Winter 1991), p. 34. See also *Washington Times-Herald,* Aug. 4, 1948.

22. McNaughton, Aug. 7, 1948 (HST).

23. "Toilet": Not in HUAC but in FBI 100-25824-36, June 26, 1948. *W,* p. 546.

24. McNaughton to Reuben, May 12, 1969 (ZELIGS); *W,* p. 545.

25. *W,* p. 548.

26. Ibid., p. 549.

27. *NYT,* Aug. 4, 1948. Abt later admitted he had belonged to the Ware Group. See *Advocate and Activist,* pp. 39–41. Pressman statement: FBI report 1001-11820-433, Feb. 2, 1949. In 1950 Pressman told both HUAC and the FBI that he, Abt, Witt, and Kramer all had been recruited: HUAC testimony, Aug. 28, 1950; FBI report 4651, Oct. 2, 1950; see also Abt, *Advocate,* p. 173.

28. *NYT,* Aug. 4, 1948.

29. "I don't": *WP,* Aug. 4, 1948; "so far": *NYT,* Aug. 4, 1948; advice: Hiss, *Court,* p. 5; telegram: Aug. 4, 1948, HUAC I, pp. 585–86.

30. "Smear": cited in Roger Morris, *Richard Milhous Nixon: The Rise of an American Politician* (Holt, 1990), p. 398.

31. "Slowly": *WP,* Aug. 6, 1948; Testimony: Aug. 5, 1948, HUAC I, p. 643. Acheson declined: Zeligs memo of interview with Marbury (henceforth WLM), May 6, 1964 (ZELIGS): Marbury, Johnston, Acheson assistance: AH letter to John Foster Dulles, Aug. 5, 1948 (HISS).

32. For AH background, see Alger Hiss, *Recollections of a Life* (Arcade, 1988). Dean Rusk, *As I Saw It,* ed. Daniel S. Papp (Penguin, 1990), p. 135. *Time* (May 28, 1945). Vice-chairman: *NYHT,* Aug. 4, 1948.

33. Titters: *WP,* Aug. 6, 1948; "vivid": *WP,* Aug. 4, 1948; laughter: *WP,* Aug. 6, 1948.

34. "Arguments": See Charles E. Bohlen, *Witness to History, 1929–1969* (Norton, 1973), p. 194. Eventually AH's role at Yalta would be much exaggerated by his enemies, but in the early phase of the case AH himself played up his part. "The day the hearings opened, Charles E. 'Chip' Bohlen and I . . . saw a summary of Alger's testimony relating to the 1945 Yalta Conference between Roosevelt, Stalin, and Churchill. Chip said, 'What Hiss said about Yalta isn't the way it happened. I know. I was Roosevelt's interpreter. I don't know why Hiss is doing so, but he is lying' ": Paul Nitze, *From Hiroshima to Glasnost: At the Center of Decision, a Memoir* (Grove Weidenfeld, 1989), p. 20.

35. "quick": Cooke, *Generation,* p. 63. Procession: Joseph F. Johnston to John Foster Dulles, Aug. 10, 1948 (HISS). "absolutely": Stripling interview (AWP).

36. *NYT,* Aug. 6, 1948; *WP,* Aug. 6, 1948; McCullough, *Truman,* p. 652; "political dynamite": McNaughton dispatch, Aug. 7, 1948 (HST).

37. "shock"/"ruined"/"mess"/"collateral": RMN, *Six,* pp. 10–11, RMN, "Memorandum on the Hiss-Chambers Case," Feb. 1, 1949 (RDT-HOOVER); *NYHT,* Aug. 6, 1948; *Chicago Tribune,* Aug. 6, 1948.

38. RMN, *Six,* pp. 9, 15. "Pedestrian": In Olasky, "Newspaper Coverage," p. 35.

39. AH to Dulles, May 5, 1948 (HISS).

40. *W,* pp. 549–50; *WP,* Aug. 6, 1948.

Chapter 19: "I Can Make That Fellow President"

1. RMN, *Six,* pp. 10–11; RMN memo, Feb. 1, 1949 (RDT-HOOVER); "vaguely": Stripling, *Red Plot,* p. 116.

2. See McManus, "Agriculture Purge" (AWP); FBI 101-606 report on AH, Feb. 18, 1942; FBI 3860 letter to director; State Department memo, Bannerman to Russell, March 22, 1946 (FBI); FBI report, "Re Interview with Former Associate Justice James Byrnes" Sept. 15, 1949; Stripling interview (AWP).

3. "Resignation of Hiss Bares Key U.N. Role," *Christian Science Monitor,* Dec. 14, 1946. See also "Memorandum of the Press and Radio News Conference" of the secretary of state, July 12, 1946 in RG 59 General Records of State Department, vol. 17 (NA); J. C. Ross letter to AH, July 27, 1946 (HISS). China Lobby: See Alfred Kohlberg letter to Foster Dulles, Dec. 31, 1946 (HISS); Aug. 5, 1948, HUAC I, pp. 648–49 (AH testimony).

4. Stripling interview (AWP).

5. RMN, *Six,* p. 4. "Alger Hiss was first mentioned to Nixon in February, 1947": Earl Mazo, *Richard Nixon: A Political and Personal Portrait* (Harper, 1959), p. 51. Reverend John Cronin, SS, "The Problem of American Communism in 1945: Facts and Recommendations: A Confidential Study for Private Circulation," pp. 49, 37 (Notre Dame). See also Garry Wills, *Nixon Agonistes: The Crisis of the Self-Made Man* (New American Library, 1971), pp. 35–37; Allen Weinstein, "Nixon vs. Hiss," *Esquire* (November 1975), p. 76.

6. FBI surveillance: FBI 100-267360-113, Apr. 19, 1945; FBI 2058, memo to director from Ladd, Jan. 28, 1949.

7. Ronald W. Pruessen, *John Foster Dulles: The Road to Power* (Free Press, 1982), p. 371.

8. Aug. 5, 1948, HUAC I, p. 647; "mouthy," *W*, p. 555.

9. Aug. 5, 1948, HUAC I, p. 644.

10. "Hot dogs": *The Supreme Court of the United States: Hearings and Reports on Successful and Unsuccessful Nominations of Supreme Court Justices by the Senate Judiciary Committee, 1916–1975*, comp. Roy M. Mersky and J. Myron Jacobstein (William S. Hein, 1977), vol. 4, p. 67. "Angling": Stripling interview (AWP).

11. FBI 3243, letter to director, June 3, 1949. "Following": RMN memo, Feb. 1, 1949 (RDT-HOOVER).

12. Crimson: Bert Andrews and Peter Andrews, *A Tragedy of History: A Journalist's Confidential Role in the Hiss-Chambers Case* (R. B. Luce, 1962), p. 51; "ass": Stripling interview (AWP).

13. "condescending": RMN, *Six*, p. 6; "insolent": Andrews, *Tragedy*, p. 52; "insulting": RMN memo quoted in Mazo, *Nixon*, p. 60; turned his back: RMN, *Six*, p. 7. "Personal"/"billy goat": Weinstein, "Nixon vs. Hiss," p. 76. RMN's later comments: See Garry Wills, "The Hiss Connection Through Nixon's Life," *NYT Magazine*, Aug. 25, 1974; H. R. Haldeman, *The Haldeman Diaries: Inside the Nixon White House*, intro. Stephen Ambrose (Putnam, 1994), pp. 280, 303, 623.

14. RMN on Eisler: Stephen E. Ambrose, *Nixon: The Education of a Politician, 1913–1962* (Simon and Schuster, 1987), pp. 146–47; Taft-Hartley: Ibid., pp. 152–54; anti-CP bill: Ibid., p. 160ff. Mandel: *W*, p. 558. Late night: RMN, *Six*, p. 15; Morris, *Nixon*, p. 404.

15. *W*, p. 558; testimony, July 8, 1948, HUAC I, pp. 661–72.

16. FBI 2058, Jan. 28, 1949, p. 6. WC was asked for evidence on March 28, 1946.

17. Hiss, *Recollections*, p. 140.

18. "I should appreciate it . . . if you could arrange matters in your Department so that Mr. Hiss could be assigned to the [Bridges] case again": Labor Secretary Frances Perkins letter to Francis Sayre, Apr. 11, 1938, quoted in William A. Rusher, *Special Counsel* (Arlington House, 1968), p. 264. On Bridges's CP membership, see Harvey Klehr and John Haynes, "The Comintern's Open Secrets," *The American Spectator* (December 1992), p. 34.

19. Puzzled: Stripling, *Red Plot*, p. 119.

20. Ibid.

21. Testimony, Aug. 9, 1948, HUAC I, pp. 673–713. In 1944 Perlo's ex-wife, Katherine, sent a letter to the FBI "setting forth a partial list of members of an underground Communist group in Washington, DC." The names included were Perlo, Nathan Witt, Henry Collins, Charles Kramer, John Abt, Abraham George Silverman: FBI 65-14920-2633, March 7, 1949. See VENONA 3713–3715 for minute documentation of Perlo's espionage.

22. Skepticism/"concocted"/rumors: Mazo, *Nixon*, p. 56. Stripling had heard some of these smears on Aug. 5, 1948, "before and during" AH's HUAC appearance: RMN, *Six*, p. 11; "alone": Ibid., p. 21.

23. Richard Nixon, *RN: The Memoirs of Richard Nixon* (Simon and Schuster, 1978; reissue, 1990), p. 56.

24. RMN, *Six*, p. 22. "[WC] personally thought an awful lot about [AH] and considered him an intelligent and decent young man": FBI 100-25824-36, June 26, 1945.

25. "Caricature"/"quality"/"intelligence": RMN, *Six,* p. 22.

26. Rogers: Morris, *Nixon,* p. 412; Kersten: Wills, *Nixon,* p. 35; RMN, *Six,* pp. 20–21; Foster Dulles: Mazo, *Nixon,* p. 58.

27. "Thick": Mazo, *Nixon,* p. 26.

28. Campaign had already heard: Morris, *Nixon,* p. 413; "public support": Morris, p. 415; "mixed up": Smith, *Alger Hiss,* pp. 160–61. RMN knew Herter well and had met Allen Dulles in Europe: See Morris, *Nixon,* p. 365; "defer": Pruessen, *Dulles,* p. 372; "no question"/"justified"/"derelict": RMN, *Six,* p. 21. "The meeting with Nixon was the turning point in Dulles's relationship with Alger Hiss": Pruessen, *Dulles,* p. 372.

29. "Make that fellow": Halberstam, *Powers,* p. 260; "burned-out": Richard Kluger, *The Paper: The Life and Death of the New York Herald Tribune* (Knopf, 1986), p. 410; *NYT,* June 4, 1948; *Washington Witch Hunt* (Random House, 1948); the book was published in late June 1948. "Andrews . . . has written a heart-warming book for liberals," judged *TNR,* in a review that extolled his courage in doing "battle for the preservation of civil liberties, even at the cost of being called a fellow-traveler" (Amos S. Basel, "Star Chamber," *TNR* [Sept. 6, 1948]); Andrews disliked the State Department: See Halberstam interviews with Robert Donovan, John Chabot Smith. Andrews's opinion of AH is unclear. According to Tony Hiss, AH once upbraided Andrews for publishing a leak about Yalta and the journalist took offense: Tony Hiss, *Laughing Last* (Houghton Mifflin, 1977), p. 166. But in 1946, when Foster Dulles asked Andrews to rate AH as a possible Carnegie head, Andrews gave him high marks: Bert Andrews, "How Alger Hiss Was Brought to Trial," *NYHT,* June 3, 1952; "commit murder": James Reston, *Deadline: A Memoir* (Random House, 1991), p. 207.

30. "Outside judgment"/"without injuring"/"almost certain"/"as far": Andrews, *Tragedy,* pp. 72–73.

31. Andrews, "How Alger Hiss Was Brought to Trial," *NYHT,* June 3, 1952. See also Andrews, *Tragedy,* pp. 73–77.

32. "The first": Morris, *Nixon,* p. 419; "would call": Wills, *Nixon,* p. 37.

33. RMN, *Six,* p. 23.


### Chapter 20: A Man Named Crosley

1. Testimony of Abt, Pressman, Witt—Aug. 20, 1948; Collins—Aug. 11, 1948; Perlo—Aug. 9, 1948; Kramer—Aug. 12, 1948, all HUAC I, pp. 1015–33. Goodman, *The Committee,* p. 250.

2. Testimony of White, Currie, and Donald Hiss: Aug. 13, 1948, HUAC I, pp. 851–933.

3. Berle, "Underground Espionage Agent." White was implicated in the Venona release of March 5, 1996; see, e.g., S/NBF/T244, Aug. 4–5, 1944 (VENONA).

4. AH testimony, Aug. 16, 1948, HUAC I, pp. 935–74.

5. WC was in the HUAC offices a total of thirty minutes: McNaughton dispatch, Aug. 17, 1948 (HST).

6. *BAS,* Aug. 17, 1948.

7. RMN memo, Feb. 1, 1949 (RDT-HOOVER).

8. WC to DC: *W,* p. 600; for afternoon reports of White's death, see AH, *Court,* pp. 81–82; RMN, *Six,* p. 31; *NYT,* Aug. 18, 1948. "We consider this committee the real cause of the death of Harry White": *TNR* (Dec. 6, 1948).

9. Trip to NYC/Commodore: *W,* pp. 601–2.

10. AH, *Court,* pp. 80–82.

11. RMN, *Six,* pp. 30–31.

12. Testimony, Aug. 17, 1948, HUAC I, pp. 975–1001.

13. "The correspondents for foreign news around the State Department had as one of their better sources Alger Hiss": remark by the *Chicago Sun-Times*'s Tom Reynolds, who questioned WC on *Meet the Press* on Aug. 27, 1948. See transcript, "Whittaker Chambers Meets the Press."

14. WC entrance and seating: Stripling, *Red Plot,* p. 128; Smith, *Hiss,* p. 216; "short": AH, *Court,* p. 85.

15. Stripling, *Red Plot,* p. 129.

16. AH, *Court,* p. 85.

17. Panic: *W,* p. 615.

18. RMN memo quoted in Mazo, *Nixon,* p. 60.

19. "Hi-ya": *W,* p. 615.

20. "Tendentious": AH, *Court,* p. 82; press conference quotes: *NYHT,* Aug. 18, 1948.


Chapter 21: "I Could Not Do Otherwise"


1. Weinstein, *Perjury,* p. 39; "hammered": *NYHT,* Aug. 18, 1948.

2. Frank testimony, Aug. 18, 1948, HUAC I, pp. 1003–5. WC had joined the anti-CP faction of the guild: Chamberlain, *A Life,* p. 149; author interview with Victor Riesel, Oct. 16, 1994; Kempton to author, Feb. 19, 1995.

3. August 7: Morris, *Nixon,* p. 416; Levine testimony, Aug. 18, 1948, HUAC I, pp. 1005–9.

4. Isaac Don Levine, "Stalin's Spy Ring in the U.S.A.," *Plain Talk* (December 1947). "According to [AH], . . . Levine had written an article claiming that at the Yalta conference, Hiss had persuaded [FDR] to agree to the admission of the Ukraine and Bye-olorussia to the United Nations": FBI 3243, letter to director, June 3, 1949.

5. Priscilla Hiss testimony, Aug. 18, 1948, HUAC I, pp. 1011–13.

6. RMN, *Six,* p. 38. "[WC] pointed out [that] in his opinion one of the strongest reasons for [AH's] maintaining contact with the CP was the fanatical loyalty to the CP on the part of his wife": FBI report 100-25824-36, June 26, 1945.

7. Pruessen, *Dulles,* p. 372; *NYT,* Aug. 20, 1948.

8. See, e.g., *NYT,* Aug. 17, 1948; *BAS,* Aug. 18, 1948.

9. *NYHT,* Aug. 19, 1948.

10. "Infernal": Cooke, *Generation,* p. 85.

11. *WP,* Aug. 26, 1948.

12. Caucus room scene: Sancton, "Case of Alger Hiss." TV numbers: Joseph Goulden, *The Best Years, 1945–1950* (Atheneum, 1976), pp. 174–78, 329.

13. HUAC I, pp. 1075–1206.

14. *NYHT,* Aug. 26, 1948; see photo in *Los Angeles Times,* Aug. 26, 1948.

15. William Marbury, *In the Catbird Seat* (Maryland Historical Society, 1988), p. 268.

16. See testimony of Joseph Cherner, Samuel A. Mensh, and Henry J. Gertler, Aug. 12, 1948, HUAC I, pp. 1052–70.

17. See testimony of W. Marvin Smith, Aug. 24, 1948; HUAC I, pp. 1071–74.

18. FBI, "History of the Case," p. 26.

19. See *NYT,* Aug. 26, 1948; *WP,* Aug. 26, 1948.

20. See Cronin, "Problem of American Communism," pp. 37, 49.

21. *WP,* Aug. 26, 1948.

22. HUAC I (p. 1191) and *W* (p. 695) both have "in a moment of history in which this nation now stands." But contemporary news accounts have "historic jeopardy" or "jeopardy": See *NYT,* Aug. 26, 1948; *WP,* Aug. 26, 1948; *BAS,* Aug. 26, 1948.

23. *W,* p. 695.

24. Edward F. Hébert, *"Last of the Titans": The Life and Times of Congressman F. Edward Hébert of Louisiana* (Southwestern Louisiana), p. 312.

25. Testimony, Aug. 28, 1948, HUAC I, pp. 1207–22.

26. *NYT,* Aug. 27, 1948; see Budenz testimony, Aug. 24, 1948, HUAC I, pp. 1037–40.

27. *Baltimore News-Post,* Aug. 27, 1948.

28. Testimony, Aug. 27, 1948, HUAC I, pp. 1255–66.

29. FBI 458, memo to Tolson, Dec. 20, 1948.

30. Audience: In AH slander complaint. See *NYT,* Sept. 28, 1948.

31. *W,* pp. 705, 710; Reston and Carnegie: *W,* p. 648. AH and Reston had come to know each other during Dumbarton Oaks. Reston's coverage won a Pulitzer Prize.

32. "[WC] Meets the Press."

33. *W,* p. 712.


Chapter 22: The Means of Justice


1. "Interim Report on Hearings Regarding Communist Espionage in the United States Government," Aug. 27, 1948, HUAC I, pp. 1347–57.

2. Weinstein, *Perjury,* pp. 68–69.

3. Custody/deportation: *NYT,* Oct. 10, 1947; *Washington Times-Herald,* Oct. 10, 1947; *NYT,* May 6, 1949; "police informer"/Peters's instructions: Schmidt, "Behind the Scenes," pp. 19–21; John Herrmann may also have been present at the luncheon. See Langer, *Herbst,* p. 269.

4. Berle testimony, Aug. 30, 1948, HUAC I, pp. 1291–1300. "My private opinion is that Hiss was pretty deep in something or other in the early days; nevertheless I am not prepared to think that he maintained these obligations after he got into a position of in-fluence": Berle, *Navigating,* p. 584. "Sedative"/"sanity": Schwarz, *Liberal,* pp. 298–303.

5. *NYT,* Sept. 4, 1948.

6. "Well, Alger": Quoted in Morton Levitt and Michael Levitt, *A Tissue of Lies, Nixon vs. Hiss* (McGraw-Hill, 1979), p. 68. Boston vs. New York, see Marbury, *Catbird,* p. 273. McLean's caution: Marbury, pp. 275–76; John Foster Dulles in touch with both: see RMN letter to JFD, Sept. 7, 1948 (AWP); Weinstein, *Perjury,* p. 164. "On September 15th [AH] had not yet made up his mind to sue": WLM letter to John Chabot Smith, March 2, 1976 (John Chabot Smith Papers, part of HISS collection at Harvard).

7. On Marbury's background, see *Catbird; BAS* obit, March 7, 1988; on his experi-ence with libel cases, WLM to Smith, March 2, 1976 (Smith Papers, Harvard).

8. Marbury, *Catbird,* pp. 275–76.

9. Ibid., p. 272.

10. Jean Edward Smith, *Lucius D. Clay: An American Life* (Holt, 1990), p. 176.

11. *NYT,* Aug. 19, 1948.

12. Marbury, *Catbird,* pp. 275–77. Shotwell: Pruessen, *Dulles,* p. 372.

13. *NYT,* Sept. 28, 1948.

14. Ibid.; "clearly libelous": Marbury, *Catbird,* p. 277.

15. *NYT,* Sept. 30, 1948.

16. *W,* p. 600; Luce's loyalty: "Memorandum of Conversation with Clarence Pickett of American Friends Service Committee," Sept. 21, 1948 (HISS); uncompleted essay: HRL memo to Thorndike, Oct. 29, 1948 (TIME); slanted: author interview with Tom Griffith, July 8, 1994.

17. Author interviews with Brad Darrach, Nov. 3, 1990, Marlys Fuller Fixx, Aug. 21, 1995; bullets/"let no one": *W,* p. 721.

18. Baltimore *News-Post,* Dec. 23, 1948.

19. "[WC] Meets the Press."

20. See, e.g., Harold Rosenwald, "Information Received from Mr. Leon Sversky" (a *Time* adversary of WC's), Sept. 8, 1948; HR memos on WC's application for life insurance via *Time,* Oct. 13, Oct. 19, 1948; Schmahl, "Investigation of WC," Oct. 10, 1948; unsigned memo, "Investigation of JWC," Nov. 18, 1948; HR memo on interview with Paul Peters, Nov. 19, 1948; AH memo re conversation with Henry Collins, Dec. 8, 1948; AH memo re conversation with Mrs. Alexander Hawes, Dec. 8, 1948 (all HISS); unsigned memo on interviews with Grace Hutchins, A. B. Magill, Paul Peters, Jan. 27, 1949 (ZELIGS); unsigned memo on "progress report" provided by Lee Pressman, Feb. 7, 1949; unsigned memo on interview with Sender Garlin, Feb. 9, 1949 (HISS).

See A. J. Liebling's various "Wayward Press" articles, in *The New Yorker,* including "All About Inside-Policy Data" (Aug. 28, 1948); "At the Sign of the Red Herring" (Sept. 4, 1948); "Spotlight on the Jury" (July 23, 1949); also A. J. Liebling, *The Press* (Ballantine, 1961), pp. 141–62; unpublished Liebling ms., "The Titus Oates Case . . . and Its Present Day Parallel" (HISS). On AJL's handling of WC letters to MVD, see unsigned memo, Oct. 7, 1948 (HISS); Liebling was friendly with the Hisses and with Harold Rosenwald. See AJL letter to HR, Dec. 31, 1949 (HISS); *W,* pp. 546–47. In 1996 AH had Liebling's complete works in his home: *BAS,* March 9, 1996. At the time of the first trial Mark Van Doren said, "I did not know it would be put to such use. I am uncomfortable over this": *Newsweek* (June 13, 1949). See also Van Doren, *Autobiography,* p. 307; there he states his belief that WC lied about AH. For a full account of Liebling's actions, see Raymond Sokolov, *Wayward Reporter:* The Life of A. J. Liebling (Harper & Row, 1980), pp. 201–9.

The primary source of rumors regarding WC's mental illness was another journalist turned clandestine Hiss operative, William Walton, a former *Time* hand who in 1948 headed the Washington bureau of *TNR:* See Walton letter to Dr. Carl Binger, Jan. 25, 1949; Lawrence S. Kubie, M.D., to Gordon S. Reid, Jan. 26, 1949; Reid letter to Dr. Lawrence S. Kubie, Jan. 27, 1949 (all ZELIGS). *TNR* was openly hostile to WC during the case (see, e.g., "Washington Wire," *TNR* [Dec. 6, 1948]). Yet the magazine's editor, Michael Straight, who himself had spied for the Soviets in the 1930s while attached to the State Department, suspected AH was guilty. See Michael Straight, *After Long Silence* (Norton, 1983), pp. 144, 231–32.

21. *W,* pp. 727–29; On Cleveland, see *Baltimore Sun* obit, Jan. 11, 1974.

22. Levine, "Stalin's Spy Ring"; *NYT,* Sept. 1, 1948. "Levine likes to give the impression that he is knowledgeable and intimate about things and situations [about] which he is not": FBI memo (serial no. illegible), Dec. 21, 1948.

23. Isaac Don Levine, "The Inside Story of the Soviet Underworld," *Plain Talk* (September 1948); part II (October 1948).

24. WC testimony quoted in AH, *Court,* pp. 170–71. "Intention"/"wrath": *W,* pp. 725–26.

25. Election returns: *W,* p. 750; "mood": RMN, *Six,* p. 46; *NYT,* Nov. 14, 1948; see also Nov. 11, 1948; *TNR,* Dec. 20, 1948.

26. WC deposition, Nov. 4–5, 1948. See p. 208.

27. "Turned the tables": *W,* p. 734; Marbury, *Catbird,* p. 279.

28. *W,* p. 730.


### Chapter 23: The Pumpkin Papers

1. Nathan Levine testimony, Dec. 10, 1948, HUAC I, p. 1454; "arriving": Weinstein, *Perjury,* p. 172. Greenmount was an avenue in Baltimore.

2. Levine testimony, Dec. 10, 1948, HUAC I, pp. 1453–54. "Good Lord": HUAC EXEC, Dec. 28, 1948. Levine remembered WC's saying "holy cow or some exclamation."

3. *W,* p. 737.

4. Ibid., p. 738.

5. Dawn: EC deposition, Nov. 16, 1948, p. 528; 18 cows: 1st Trial, EC testimony, p. 844; family's morning routine, Craig Thompson, "The Whittaker Chambers I Know," *The Saturday Evening Post* (Nov. 5, 1952); Alice Leone Moats, "She Lives with Fear," *American Weekly* (Nov. 23, 1952); also *W,* pp. 514–16.

6. Moats, "She Lives"; FBI 3230-84, May 11, 1949, p. 208.

7. *W,* p. 748.

8. "Not gasoline": EC deposition, Nov. 17, 1948, p. 698.

9. "Put by"/"kind"/"result": WC deposition, Nov. 17, 1948, pp. 717–18; HR, *W,* p. 747; flourish/departed: Marbury, *Catbird,* pp. 279–80.

10. See 2d Trial, vol. 7, "Government's Baltimore Exhibits," pp. 3433–533.

11. Marbury, *Catbird,* p. 280.

12. For explanation of cable, see 2d Trial, vol. 4, pp. 2163–75; "listening post": Weinstein, *Perjury,* p. 246.

13. Marbury, *Catbird,* p. 280.

14. WC deposition, Nov. 17, 1948, pp. 738–44; "fifty-two": HUAC EXEC, Dec. 28, 1948, p. 64.

15. Marbury, *Catbird,* pp. 280–81.

16. "Own use": Ibid., p. 281. "The memorandum from Mr. Campbell requested an immediate investigation to determine whether [WC] had committed perjury": FBI 5600, memo from Ladd to Belmont, Nov. 14, 1953.

17. "Elated": Weinstein, *Perjury,* p. 193; Reuben interview with Zolan, Nov. 3, 1968 (WAR).

18. "Total confusion": Weinstein, "Nixon vs. Hiss," p. 147; Hoover: FBI 5600, memo from Ladd to Belmont, Nov. 14, 1953.

19. "Dead end"/"ready": quoted in "Soviet Espionage Within the U.S. Government," second HUAC report, Dec. 31, 1948, p. 4.

20. *WP,* Dec. 1, 1948.

21. Andrews, *Tragedy,* pp. 174–75.

22. Stripling interview (AWP); retirement/abolishment: *NYT,* Nov. 23, 1948.

23. Weinstein, "Nixon vs. Hiss," p. 147. See also Stripling, *Red Plot,* pp. 141–43.

24. "If I"/"what"/"contempt": Stripling interview (AWP).

25. "Do you": Weinstein, "Nixon vs. Hiss," p. 147.

26. "Frenzy": Stripling, *Red Plot,* p. 143.

27. "Overpowering": ibid.; "goddamned": Weinstein, "Nixon vs. Hiss," p. 147.

28. WC in barn: McNaughton dispatch, Dec. 4, 1948 (HST); *W,* p. 751.

29. WC later forgot: *W,* p. 751; "want to hurt": McNaughton dispatch, Dec. 4, 1948 (HST).

30. "Photographic": Stripling interview (AWP).

31. "Bombshell": Stripling, *Red Plot,* p. 143; "he's got"/"blow the dome"/"got a thing": Weinstein, "Nixon vs. Hiss," p. 147; disappoint his wife: RMN, *Six,* p. 48.

32. Andrews story: *NYHT* and *WP,* Dec. 3, 1948; "too nice"/"subpoena"/"think": Andrews, *Tragedy,* pp. 175–76.

33. "Strictly"/"incriminating"/"no criticism"/favor: FBI (no serial no.), Nichols memo to Tolson, Dec. 2, 1948.

34. RMN-Miller exchange quoted in Morris, *Nixon,* p. 465.

35. Stripling, *Red Plot,* pp. 144–45.

36. *W,* p. 752; Post: WC, HUAC EXEC, Dec. 28, 1948, p. 98. Berle notes, "Underground Espionage."

37. Moving the film/"raid the house": HUAC EXEC, Dec. 28, 1948; "happy inspiration": HUAC EXEC, Dec. 6, 1948; *W,* p. 751; also Donald Appell testimony, 2d Trial, vol. 2, p. 712; wax paper: William Wheeler testimony, Dec. 7, 1948, HUAC II, p. 1383; "those arts": *W,* p. 753.

38. "All right": Stripling, *Red Plot,* p. 145.

39. WC testimony, 2d Trial, vol. 1, p. 294; Donald Appell testimony, 2d Trial, vol. 2, p. 708; William Wheeler testimony, Dec. 7, 1948, HUAC II, pp. 1381–86. Stripling, *Red Plot,* p. 146; FBI 3038, report on interview with Stripling, Apr. 28, 1949.

40. Wheeler-Stripling testimony, Dec. 7, 1948, HUAC II, pp. 1383–84; FBI 3038; Stripling, *Red Plot,* p. 147.

41. FBI 3038; Andrews, *Tragedy,* p. 177; Stripling interview (AWP) "the object"/press conference: *WP,* Dec. 4, 1948.

42. *W,* pp. 755–57; FBI 5600, memo Belmont to Ladd, Nov. 14, 1953; all quotations: FBI 74-1333-106, WC signed statement, Dec. 3, 1948, testimony; for more on HDW's memo, see unpublished HUAC EXEC, Dec. 6, 1948.

43. *NYT,* Dec. 4, 1948; McCormick: Weinstein, "Nixon vs. Hiss," p. 151; *NYHT,* Dec. 4, 1948.

44. Stripling, *Red Plot,* p. 147; Andrews, *Tragedy,* pp. 178–79.

45. Marbury, *Catbird,* p. 283; "cooperation"/"further": *WP,* Dec. 4, 1948; FBI (no serial no.), AH signed statement, Dec. 4, 1948; also FBI (no serial no.), "Details of Interview with AH not included in signed statement," n.d., pp. 28–29; also FBI NY 65-14920, n.d., pp. 101–2.

46. Stripling, *Red Plot,* pp. 147–48; "top importance"/"prove": *NYT,* Dec. 5, 1948; Morris, *Nixon,* pp. 471–72.

47. "Joke"/"crazy": RMN, *Six,* p. 49.

48. Stripling and Fay: FBI (no serial no.), interview with Stripling, n.d., p. 12; Stripling interview (AWP). Andrews, *Tragedy,* pp. 183–84; "cloaked"/"grave": *NYT,* Dec. 6, 1948.

49. Stripling interview (AWP); *NYT,* Dec. 6, 1948; "emulsion": Stripling, *Red Plot,* p. 148.

50. RMN and Vazzana: Weinstein, "Nixon vs. Hiss," p. 151; "the music": Stripling, *Red Plot,* p. 149.

51. *W,* pp. 768–69. Andrews, *Tragedy,* pp. 188–89; "better answer": RMN, *Six,* p. 55; testimony of Keith B. Lewis, Dec. 7, 1948, HUAC II, pp. 1385–86; "poor WC": Stripling, *Red Plot,* p. 150; "frantically": *NYT,* Dec. 7, 1948.

52. *NYT,* Dec. 7, 1948; *NYHT,* Dec. 7–8, 1948; Morris, *Nixon,* pp. 477–78; "lone wolfing"/"bush league": Stripling interview (AWP). "scatological": *Newsweek* (Dec. 20, 1948); "armed": *NYHT,* Dec. 11, 1948.

53. "Rejected instrument": *W,* p. 770; for more on WC and Jonah, see *CF,* pp. 265–68; *O,* p. 61.

54. Levine, *Eyewitness,* p. 208; lopsided: Stripling interview (AWP); "mistrusted": Stripling, *Red Plot,* p. 151. "ghostly": *W,* p. 772.

55. Lynbrook/dresser: *W,* pp. 772–73.

56. *NYHT,* Dec. 7, 1948.

57. Stripling testimony, pp. 1380–81; William Wheeler, pp. 1381–85; Lewis, pp. 1385–86; Welles, pp. 1386–91; all Dec. 7, 1948, HUAC II; Groton: Joseph W. Alsop, *"I've Seen the Best of It": Memoirs* (Norton, 1992), p. 138; "closest aide": Robert Dallek, *Franklin D. Roosevelt and American Foreign Policy, 1932–1945* (Oxford, 1979), p. 421; "mustache": TRB, "Washington Wire," *TNR* (Dec. 27, 1948).

58. Weinstein, *Perjury,* pp. 21–22. Of Peurifoy's reversal, Roger Morris writes, "It was, altogether and typically, an example of the craven, *sauve qui peut* mentality that now seized many in government" (*Nixon,* p. 414). But Peurifoy was not intimidated so easily. In 1950, in a climate even more charged, Peurifoy, then deputy undersecretary of state, called a news conference to refute allegations of State Department subversion made by Senator Joseph McCarthy. See Thomas C. Reeves, *The Life and Times of Joe McCarthy* (Stein and Day, 1982), p. 231. A likelier explanation is that Peurifoy initially gave AH a clean rating so as to expedite his departure from State but with a public scandal breaking decided it was not worth protecting him any longer.

59. Peurifoy testimony, Dec. 7, 1948, HUAC II, pp. 1391–97; *NYT,* Dec. 8, 1948; *NYHT,* Dec. 8, 1948.

60. *NYHT,* Dec. 9–10, 1948.

61. FBI 419 report, Dec. 7, 1948, includes Wadleigh's signed statement of Dec. 6, 1948; also see FBI (no serial no.), signed statement of Dec. 10, 1948; "I hope"/"don't see"/"mummery"/"gloomy"/"control": Wadleigh, "Why I Spied," July 21, 1949; "so guilty": Zeligs interview with Wadleigh and others, May 5, 1963 (ZELIGS); "panicky"/"forget": AH memo, "Appearance Before the Grand Jury Today," Dec. 8, 1949 (HISS).

62. "Produce"/"hot potato": Wadleigh, "Why I Spied," July 22, 1949; Courtney E. Owens testimony, Dec. 9, 1948, HUAC II, pp. 1449–50; Wadleigh testimony, Dec. 12, 1948, HUAC II, pp. 1429–49; "fiendish": Wadleigh, "Why I Spied," July 22, 1949; Wadleigh demeanor: Ibid.; *NYT,* Dec. 10, 1948; "suppress": *WP,* Dec. 10, 1948.

### Chapter 24: Indictment

1. Donegan: See Gary May, *Un-American Activities: The Trials of William Remington* (Oxford, 1994), p. 87; see FBI 65-14920, WC signed statement, Dec. 8, 1948, pp. 31–32; FBI report (no serial no.), Dec. 12, 1948, on FVR.

2. Reno: FBI-FVR signed statement, Dec. 13, 1948; Crane: FBI 65-59508-05, July 12, 1949; FBI 65-59091-14, March 28, 1950; Inslerman: FBI (no serial no.), Feb. 18–19 and 27–28, and March 13–14, 1954. FVR indictment/conviction/sentence: *NYT,* Nov. 14, 1951, Feb. 28, 1952; *Denver Post,* Feb. 27, July 2, 1952.

3. Billings diary, Aug. 20, 1948, p. 298 (Billings Papers, Caroliniana Collection, University of South Carolina); "betrayal"/"indicted": ibid., Dec. 6, 1948, pp. 162, 167; *Tri-*

*bune:* Bernard Barnes memo to Roy Larsen, Dec. 6, 1948, Time Inc.; Winchell: Swanberg, *Luce,* pp. 404–5; Neil Gabler, *Winchell: Gossip, Power and the Culture of Celebrity* (Knopf, 1994), pp. 382–83. Winchell of course had long known of WC's allegations, via Isaac Don Levine.

4. Billings diary, Aug. 19, 1948, p. 299; "*Time* must get out from under now that [WC] has revealed himself as a Soviet spy.": Ibid., Dec. 8, 1948, p. 167 (Billings Papers, University of South Carolina); "torch": Quoted in Margaret McConnell memo to James A. Linen, Dec. 17, 1948; see also McConnell to Linen, Dec. 10, 1948 (both TIME).

5. "Fallen": Kobler, *Luce,* p. 148; *W,* p. 758; Billings diary, Dec. 9, 1948, p. 169. Resignation statement: WC letter to Linen, Dec. 9, 1948; "against": Time press release, Dec. 10, 1948 (both TIME); Kempton letter to author, Feb. 19, 1995; "second": Filmore Calhoun memo, Nov. 14 [?], 1944 (TIME).

6. AH, "Appearance Before the Grand Jury Today," Dec. 10, 1948 (HISS).

7. *W,* pp. 773–75; see also WC letter to RDT, Sept. 20, 1951 (HOOVER). WC had contemplated suicide earlier. See *W,* pp. 20–21. "High point": WC to Bertram D. Wolfe, June 7, 1957 (HOOVER); quote in Wolfe, *A Life,* p. 405; "fierceness": *W,* p. 185. The date of the suicide attempt is unknown. I have placed it on Dec. 10, 1948, on the basis of the formal announcement of WC's resignation and AH's remarks on WC's despondency.

8. Papers released: *NYT,* Dec. 12, 1948.

9. Hand-deliver: *NYT,* Dec. 12, 1948; "minute"/"capers"/"in case"/: Stripling interview (AWP); "fit"/Appell to NYC: FBI 2752, interview with Stripling, March 30, 1949; also Stephen W. Salant interview with Donald Appell, n.d. (HISS).

10. Calfskin: Andrews, *Tragedy,* p. 199. Gamesmanship: author interview with retired FBI agent John J. Danahy, Sept. 28, 1994.

11. Andrews, *Tragedy,* p. 199; Stripling interview (AWP); RMN, *Six,* p. 60; Weinstein, *Perjury,* p. 282; FBI 263, Dec. 14, 1948; "report": Andrews, *Tragedy,* p. 197.

12. "Undoubtedly": Marbury, *Catbird,* p. 284; 250 agents: Morris, *Nixon,* p. 483; headmaster/relayed: Weinstein, *Perjury,* pp. 295–96.

13. Exchange between Campbell and AH: AH, "Appearance Before the Grand Jury Today"; "amazing": Morris, *Nixon,* p. 483.

14. *NYT,* Dec. 15, 1948; *NYHT,* Dec. 16, 1948.

15. *NYT,* Dec. 16, 1948.

16. Ibid.

17. Not unanimous/"weaken": Rosenwald memo (of conversation with *New York Star* reporter John Weiss), Dec. 17, 1948 (HISS).

18. *NYT,* Dec. 16, 1948.

19. "Odds": *WP,* Dec. 16, 1948; "apparent": Thomas Sancton, "Hiss and Chambers: A Tangled Web," *The Nation* (Dec. 18, 1948); "code": *NYHT,* Dec. 28, 1948; "tighten" *NYT,* Dec. 18, 1948.

20. "Shuddering"/"why"/"proof": *W,* pp. 777–80; see also *NYT,* Dec. 22, 1948, Feb. 17, 1949.

21. WC deposition, Nov. 5, 1948, pp. 319–26; HUAC EXEC, Dec. 28, 1948.

22. See Flora Lewis, *Red Pawn: The Story of Noel Field* (Doubleday, 1965), pp. 25, 33, 43.

23. Ibid., p. 58; see also Edward McLean, "Memorandum re Laurence Duggan," Dec. 27, 1948 (HISS).

24. Hede Massing, *This Deception* (Duell, Sloan and Pearce, 1951; reissue, Ivy, 1987), pp. 176–78; Lewis, *Pawn,* pp. 91–92.

25. Matthews testimony, Nov. 7, 1938, HUAC, vol. 3 (1939), p. 2172; also Lewis, *Pawn,* pp. 92, 121; Karel Kaplan, "Triplo gioco per Stalin," *Panorama* (May 24, 1977); AH and Field: Schmidt, "Behind the Scenes," p. 25; Sam Tanenhaus, "Hiss Case 'Smoking Gun'?" *NYT,* Oct. 15, 1993.

26. Schmidt, "Behind the Scenes," pp. 29, 31; Tanenhaus, "Smoking Gun."

27. Herbert Solow, "Interviews given to Dr. Zeligs," May 10–11, no year (ZELIGS).

28. *NYHT,* Oct. 15, 1948.

29. "Bits": FBI (no serial no.), letter to the director, Feb. 9, 1949. FBI interview of Massing was done Dec. 7–8, 1949. See also Lamphere and Shachtman, *FBI-KGB War,* p. 102.

30. "Spells": Drew Pearson, *Diaries, 1949–1959,* ed. Tyler Abell (Holt, 1974), pp. 11–12; see also *NYT,* Dec. 22, 1948.

31. Details of the Duggan interrogation come from author interview with Danahy, Sept. 28, 1994; FBI 65-14920, "Re: Laurence Duggan," report filed by Danahy and McCarthy after Dec. 10, 1948, interview.

32. Schmidt, "Behind the Scenes," p. 12. AH told his attorneys, "Mr. Duggan I regard as a close personal friend for whom I have the highest admiration": AH, "Memorandum Relating to Noel Field," n.d. (HISS).

33. McLean, "Memorandum re Laurence Duggan."

34. *NYT,* Dec. 25, 1948.

35. McNaughton dispatch, Dec. 24, 1948 (HST).

36. *NYT,* Dec. 22, 1948.

37. "Worst": McNaughton, Dec. 24, 1948 (HST); "reckless": *NYT,* Dec. 23, 1948; "dead man's": Alexander Kendrick, *Prime Time: The Life of Edward R. Murrow* (Little, Brown, 1969), p. 45; "quoting": A. M. Sperber, *Murrow: His Life and Times* (Freundlich, 1986), p. 319; "undone"/"Black": *NYHT,* Dec. 25, 1948. "Black Day" was reprinted in *TNR* (Jan. 10, 1949).

38. "Profaning": *NYHT,* Dec. 24, 1948.

39. *NYHT,* Dec. 23, 1948.

40. *NYT,* Dec. 23, 1948.

41. Ibid.

42. *NYT,* Dec. 25, Dec. 27, 1948; *BAS,* Dec. 27, 1948.

43. FBI "Re: Laurence Duggan" (no serial no.), n.d.; *NYT,* Dec. 21, 1948; *WP,* Dec. 23, 1948; *Time* (Jan. 3, 1949); Isaac Don Levine, "The Strange Case of Laurence Duggan," *Plain Talk* (February 1949).

44. See Noel Field to Laurence Duggan, Apr. 19, 1948; Duggan to Field, Apr. 27, 1948; Duggan to AH, Apr. 27, 1948; AH to Field, May 7, 1948, HISS.

45. *BAS,* Dec. 28, 1948.

46. Living room scene: Ralph de Toledano, "The Hiss Case," in William F. Buckley, Jr., and the editors of *National Review, The Committee and Its Critics: A Calm Review of the House Committee on Un-American Activities* (Putnam, 1962), p. 174; *Newsweek* (Jan. 10, 1948).

47. See 3/NBF/T2178, Aug. 4, 1944 (VENONA).

48. "Jubilant": *Time* (Jan. 3, 1949).

49. *NYT,* Dec. 30, 1948.

50. See *TNR* (Dec. 27, 1948). Westbrook Pegler, "Robert Stripling Resigns on Note of Triumph," *Los Angeles Examiner,* Dec. 23, 1948. Stripling's series formed the basis of *Red Plot.*

51. *NYT,* Dec. 23, 1948.

## WITNESS II: THE TRIALS (JANUARY 1949–JANUARY 1950)

### Chapter 25: Preparations

1. "Dead": *W,* p. 787.

2. "Briefcases": FBI 65-14920, pp. 176–77; names: Weinstein, *Perjury,* p. 405 fn.

3. "Coincidence": *NYT,* Jan. 5, 1949; FBI-Inslerman (no serial no.), Feb. 18–19 and 27–28 and March 13–14, 1954; author interview with Danahy, Sept. 28, 1994; also *NYT,* Jan. 5, Jan. 14, 1949.

4. FBI 65-14920, pp. 16–17; Massing, *Deception,* pp. 173–75; McLean, "Interview with Hetty [*sic*] Massing," Dec. 10, 1948 (HISS).

5. "Webber's": Author interview with Danahy, Sept. 28, 1994; "best agent": Author interview with Robert Blount, Oct. 5, 1994; "archive": *W,* p. 787; see also Lamphere and Shachtman, *FBI-KGB War,* pp. 62, 64.

6. Six days/seven hours: FBI 65-14920-5480, p. 12. "Paper": Author interview with Danahy, Sept. 28, 1994.

7. Dante: *W,* p. 787; "two-headed": Author interview with Danahy, Sept. 28, 1994.

8. Uncle Whit: Author interview with Danahy, Sept. 28, 1994; "total recall": *W,* p. 878; "white": Author interview with Darrach, Nov. 3, 1990.

9. WC to Solow, n.d., spring 1943 (SOLOW).

10. See Weinstein, *Perjury,* pp. 584–85.

11. Harold Rosenwald, "Information Received from Mr. Leon Sversky," Sept. 8, 1948 (HISS).

12. On Trilling's puzzlement, see Diana Trilling, *Beginning,* pp. 389–90. "A Mr. Heubsch, owner of the Viking Press . . . is known to possess some detrimental information about [WC's] lawyer [Nathan] Levine": Unsigned memo, Jan. 27, 1949 (ZELIGS).

13. "Terribly"/"honor"/"outburst": Trilling, *MOJ,* pp. 255, xi.

14. "Sex": Weinstein, *Perjury,* p. 381; Garlin: McLean, "Memorandum of Conference with Sender Garlin," Feb. 8, 1949 (HISS); Garlin in Moscow: RCP 495-261-1014.

15. McLean, "Memorandum re Grace Lumpkin," Dec. 31, 1948; Intrator: Unsigned memo, Jan. 27, 1949; also FBI 74-1333-2152, Feb. 18, 1949; author interview with Darrach, Nov. 3, 1990. "Little could be learned about Darrach . . . although there are persistent rumors to the effect that [he] plays an intimate role in [WC's life]" (page from Hiss Defense Files in AWP).

16. Womanizer: WC to William F. Buckley, Jr., May 19 [?], 1957 (WFB); "tendencies": FBI 3059, interview with Intrator.

17. Suit suspended: *NYT,* Dec. 30, 1949; "relevant": *NYT,* Feb. 1, 1949.

18. "Priest"/"general"/"specific": FBI 74-1333-2237, Feb. 16, 1949; tried to reach: author interview with Danahy, Sept. 28, 1994.

19. Statement: FBI 74-1333-2152, Feb. 8, 1949; "only because": FBI 74-1333-2237, Feb. 16, 1949.

20. Hiss's stepson, Timothy Hobson, had been discharged from the navy because he was homosexual: See Smith, *Hiss,* pp. 151, 195. There were rumors WC had been involved either with Hobson or with AH. See McLean, "Memorandum re Laurence Duggan," Dec. 27, 1948, interview with Helen Duggan: "She does not know anyone . . . who actually knows anything about Timmy's possible relations with [WC]. . . . [Mrs. Duggan's] brother works on Time [and] has told her that Time regards this case as a 'battle between two queers' " (HISS).

21. Stryker fee: *Time* (July 18, 1949); also Smith, *Hiss,* p. 251. "The decision to hire [Stryker] 'was made by Alger's friends in Washington,' " among them "Acheson and Frankfurter": Weinstein, *Perjury,* p. 375.

22. Acheson: Testimony before U.S. Senate, Committee on Foreign Relations. *Executive Sessions . . .* (Historical Series), vol. 2, 81st Congress, 1st and 2d Sess., 1949–1950, Jan. 14, 1949, p. 3ff; Coplon: *WP,* July 1, 1949; Weinstein, *Perjury,* pp. 402–4. Coplon was convicted of conspiring to commit espionage, but the verdict was overturned because the FBI had obtained evidence illegally. On Coplon's spying, see VENONA, Jan. 8, 1945 (no ref. no.).

23. *NYT,* Apr. 9, 1948; also, Peters letter from Budapest to CPUSA, n.d., probably 1949 (courtesy of Herbert Romerstein); Eisler: *NYT,* June 1, 1949.

24. "The Trials of Alger Hiss, as Reported by James A. Bell, Time Inc." vol. 1, pp. 6–8 (James A. Bell Papers, Sterling Library, Yale—hereafter Bell); *NYT,* June 1, July 20, 1949.

## Chapter 26: "Unclean! Unclean!"

1. Robert K. Bingham and Max Ascoli, "The Case of Alger Hiss," *The Reporter* (Aug. 30, 1949).

2. Robert Bendiner, "The Trials of Alger Hiss," *The Nation* (June 11, 1949).

3. Cooke, *Generation,* p. 101 (hereafter Cooke); Bell, p. 8. See "Jimmy Cannon Covers Hiss Trial," June 2, 1949, "Portrait of Chambers—by Jimmy Cannon," June 3, 1949, "Chambers Struggles with His Conscience," June 8, 1949—all *New York Post.*

4. Alistair Cooke letter to author, Jan. 24, 1991.

5. Author interview with James A. Bell, Dec. 12, 1990. *Time*'s published reports on the trials were written from Bell's notes by one of WC's closest friends on the magazine, Duncan Norton-Taylor: Swanberg, *Luce,* p. 404. Thus the two major newsweeklies both favored WC, not AH. Other journalists' impressions: See Ralph de Toledano, *Lament for a Generation* (Farrar, Straus, 1960), p. 113.

6. AH entrance: Cooke, p. 107; on Kaufman's "self-appointment" to case, see *New York Journal-American,* July 10, 1949.

7. Murphy background/99 percent: *NYT* obit, Oct. 3, 1995; Proust: de Toledano, *Lament,* p. 110.

8. Murphy's opening: 1st Trial minutes, pp. 14–24.

9. Bell, p. 10; *Newsweek* (June 13, 1949). Murphy "seems inhibited by the very nature of his employment from making a real defense of his own witness": Bendiner, "The Trials." Darrow/barn: Lloyd P. Stryker obit, *NYT,* June 22, 1955; Stryker, *For the Defense: Thomas Erskine, The Most Enlightened Liberal of His Times, 1750–1823* (Doubleday, 1947), p. 210.

10. See Cooke, p. 105; Bell, p. 10; *NYT,* June 7, 1949.

11. Stryker opening, 1st Trial, pp. 25–52.

12. Bell, p. 11.

13. Stryker's gaze/wheeling: Cooke, p. 117.

14. See, e.g., the banner headline in the *WP,* June 2, 1949: HISS DEFENSE FIND MISSING TYPEWRITER.

15. See FBI 3172, interview with Claudia Catlett, May 16, 1949; also FBI 3173, May 15, 1949, p. 21ff. Prosecution strategy: See Herbert L. Packer, *Ex-Communist Witnesses: Four Studies in Fact Finding* (Stanford, 1952), p. 30.

16. Roar/wail: Cooke, p. 118; electric: Bell, p. 14.

17. Yawns/"paused"/"monster": Bell, pp. 14–15; "fat"/laced fingers: Cooke, pp. 121, 125. WC's gaze: Bell, p. 15; Edward R. Murrow, CBS radio broadcast, June 2, 1949 (at Museum of Television and Broadcasting, New York City).

18. *WP,* June 2, 1949; Bell, p. 19; Murrow, June 2, 1949; Cooke, p. 125.

19. 1st Trial, pp. 115–22.

20. Ibid., pp. 133–34.

21. Murrow, June 2, 1949.

22. 1st Trial, pp. 215–16.

23. Ibid., pp. 219–27.

24. Bell, p. 27; Cooke, p. 131; Murrow, June 2, 1949.

25. Bell, p. 27.

26. 1st Trial, pp. 228–32.

27. Bell, p. 30.

28. 1st Trial, p. 259.

29. Ibid., pp. 296–98.

30. Ibid., p. 301.

31. Cooke, p. 136; Bell, p. 38.

32. Cooke, p. 136.

33. Walter Lippmann to Binger, Dec. 24, 1948 (Walter Lippmann Papers, Manuscripts, and Archive, Yale University Library).

34. "Dr. X": *BAS,* June 3, 1949; Weinstein, *Perjury,* p. 418. Liebling, *The Press,* p. 151; boyhood: Steel, *Lippmann,* p. 6; Binger identified: *New York World-Telegram,* June 3, 1949; see Lippmann letter to Binger, Dec. 24, 1948; "unconscious motivation": See Rosenwald, "Memorandum of [WC's] Motivation," March 15, 1949 (HISS).

35. 1st Trial, p. 372.

36. Ibid., p. 374.

37. Ibid., pp. 401–3, 409.

38. Ibid., p. 440.

39. *BAS,* June 7, 1949; Bell, pp. 49–50.

40. 1st Trial, p. 442.

41. *W,* p. 728.

42. *BAS,* June 14, 1949.

43. Eleanor Roosevelt, "Who Is on Trial—Chambers or Hiss?," *New York World-Telegram,* June 8, 1949. AH and ER had met aboard the *Queen Elizabeth* while en route to London for a UN conference. Much later AH wrote: "She had long been a favorite of young New Dealers. We regarded her as President Roosevelt's conscience": AH, *Recollections,* p. 139.

44. *NYT,* June 7, 1949.

Chapter 27: Rich Finds

1. 1st Trial, p. 844; Cooke, pp. 151–52; EC's hands: *WP,* June 11, 1949; also Moats, "She Lives with Fear."

2. 1st Trial, pp. 873; 877–78; *NYT,* June 11, 1949; Cooke, p. 154. Bingham and Ascoli, "The Case."

3. 1st Trial, p. 902.

4. Ibid., p. 904. Dry lips: Cooke, p. 155.

5. Bell, p. 103; Cooke, pp. 157–58.

6. *NYT,* June 14, 1949.

7. 1st Trial, pp. 934–35.

8. Bell, pp. 119–20; *WP,* June 15, 1949.

9. Bell, pp. 125, 119.

10. 1st Trial, pp. 1208, 1213, 1227.

11. Ibid., pp. 1251, 1256, 1266, 1286.

12. Ibid., pp. 1297, 1317.

13. "Garterless": Bell, p. 142; "jerking": Cooke, p. 170.

14. 1st Trial, pp. 1336–37.

15. Ibid., pp. 1336–39, 1346.

16. Ibid., p. 1347; courtroom reaction: Author interview with Murrey Marder, Jan. 30, 1995.

17. Bell, pp. 144, 146; Cooke, p. 171.

18. 1st Trial, p. 1354.

19. Bell, p. 147.

20. 1st Trial, p. 1361; Cooke, pp. 172–73.

21. Bell, p. 150.

## Chapter 28: The Woodstock

1. AH: *NYT,* June 24, 1949; 1st Trial, p. 1782.

2. See Miller, *Caldwell,* p. 350; Weinstein, p. 525. "Ruined": Reuben interview with Lieber, June 9, 1969 (WAR).

3. 1st Trial, p. 1459.

4. Ibid., pp. 1468, 1473.

5. Ibid., pp. 1434, 1446–48.

6. Ibid., pp. 1526–29.

7. "[AH] performed brilliantly. . . . I always had reason to believe that [he] acted honorably and patriotically in the performance of his duties": Stettinius, *Roosevelt and the Russians,* p. 31; Acheson to Stryker, n.d., probably early April 1949 (HISS).

8. Cooke, p. 180: Bell, p. 168.

9. 1st Trial, p. 1557.

10. AH testimony, Aug. 25, 1948, HUAC II, p. 1163; Glennon, *Iconoclast,* p. 36.

11. 1st Trial, pp. 1580–81.

12. AH testimony, Aug. 16, 1948, HUAC II, pp. 954–55; "They asked me what maid we had and I said we had Clydie [*sic*] who is now dead": PH, "Mrs. Hiss's appearance before the Grand Jury," Dec. 10, 1948 (HISS).

13. For PH, see "Mrs. Hiss's appearance before the Grand Jury": "I had a feeling we had it [the Woodstock] on Volta Place in 1938" (HISS).

14. 1st Trial, pp. 1707, 1622, 1642–45, 1609.

15. Ibid., pp. 1619, 1623, 1653–54, 1633–34, 1660; "deadly": Bell, p. 180.

16. 1st Trial, pp. 1685, 1741–58.

17. Ibid., pp. 1761–62, 1767, 1777–79, 1785–86, 1788.

18. "Surprise": Bell, p. 192; see Rosenwald, "Memorandum re Malcolm Cowley," Oct. 29, 1948 (HISS); FBI report 1793, Feb. 1, 1949. See "Cowley Amazed by Controversy," *Seattle Post-Intelligencer,* Jan. 2, 1948 (Cowley Papers).

19. 1st Trial, pp. 1821–22, 1818–19; "Patently": *New York World-Telegram,* June 24, 1949.

20. HUAC EXEC, Dec. 6, 1948.

21. 1st Trial, p. 1838.

Chapter 29: Alger and Priscilla

1. *NYT,* June 9, 1949. Bell, pp. 192, 197.

2. *WP,* June 24, 1949.

3. *NYT,* June 24, 1949; Bell, pp. 197–200.

4. RMN to author, Jan. 9, 1993. Lippmann aided the defense (or tried to), but did not comment on the case. Alsop offered but was restrained by Dean Acheson (Weinstein, *Perjury,* p. 385 fn). Reston and Childs were mildly skeptical. Pro-prosecution columnists, such as Westbrook Pegler and George Sokolsky, were openly vituperative. See, e.g., Pegler's column "Judge Samuel Kaufman and the Alger Hiss Trial," *New York Journal-American,* June 30, 1949.

5. "Remote": Jimmy Cannon, "Chambers Struggles"; "Someone else": Marquis Childs, "Hiss on Trial," *WP,* June 25, 1949; eyes: Gertrude Samuels, "The Trial: Tension in the Courtroom," *NYT,* June 12, 1949.

6. AH, *Recollections,* p. 2.

7. Smith, *Hiss,* p. 65.

8. AH, *Recollections,* p. 208.

9. *W,* p. 361.

10. 1st Trial, pp. 1837–40.

11. Meyer Berger, "Hiss Takes Stand; No Red, He Insists," *NYT,* June 24, 1949.

12. 1st Trial, pp. 1860, 1865, 1868–70; *NYT,* June 24, 1949.

13. *NYT,* June 28, 1949; AH trick: FBI 3887, "Re Hiss Jury Reaction, Comments and Bases for Decisions"—posttrial interview with jurors, July 13, 1949.

14. 1st Trial, pp. 1906–43; AH leaned: *WP,* June 25, 1949.

15. 1st Trial, pp. 1900–1.

16. Ibid., pp. 1971–72.

17. Ibid., pp. 1972, 1996, 2018; "professorial": *WP,* June 28, 1949.

18. 1st Trial, p. 2035.

19. *WP,* June 28, 1949.

20. 1st Trial, pp. 2063–64.

21. See, e.g., "Chambers Admits He Lied to Congress," *WP,* June 7, 1949; "Lied for Hiss, Chambers Says," *WP,* June 8, 1949; "Chambers Admits He Lied to Hiss Grand Jury," *BAS,* June 4, 1949; "Chambers Admits Lying . . . Before [HUAC]," *New York World-Telegram,* June 6, 1949.

22. Cooke, p. 213; *WP,* June 29, 1949.

23. 1st Trial, pp. 2195–96, 2197; author interview with Murrey Marder, Jan. 30, 1995.

24. See, e.g., Samuels, "The Trial."

25. Tony Hiss, *Laughing Last,* p. 137; Zeligs interview with Anne Winslow, May 8, 1963 (ZELIGS); Smith, *Hiss,* pp. 289–90; see also Smith interviews with AH, n.d. (Smith Papers, Harvard).

26. John Chabot Smith to Thomas C. Wallace, June 1, 1975 (Smith Papers, Harvard).

27. "Deal with": Smith, *Hiss,* p. 288.

28. Smith, *Hiss,* p. 289; author interview with Danahy, Sept. 28, 1994; Acheson Senate testimony, Jan. 14, 1949. Weinstein, *Perjury,* p. 96; Zeligs interview with William Marbury, May 6, 1974 (ZELIGS).

29. *NYT,* June 29, 1949; *WP,* June 29, 1949. Bell, pp. 247–48.

30. Smith, *Hiss,* pp. 66–67, 289.

31. 1st Trial, pp. 2260; 2267, 2267–73, 2274–85, 2902–92; Bell, p. 254.

32. 1st Trial, p. 2293.

33. *WP,* June 30, 1949; Bell, p. 253.

34. 1st Trial, pp. 2320–21.

35. "System": Bell, p. 255; "raisins": Cooke, p. 221; "talk": *WP,* June 30, 1949; hands: Bell, p. 264.

36. 1st Trial, p. 2336.

37. Ibid., pp. 2377–79.

38. *NYT,* June 30, 1949; 1st Trial, pp. 2396–96a.

Chapter 30: Lucifer vs. the Serpent

1. Bell, p. 274.

2. 1st Trial, pp. 2450–73; *WP,* July 1, 1949.

3. 1st Trial, p. 2475.

4. *WP,* June 29, 1949.

5. 1st Trial, p. 2813.

6. Ibid., pp. 2745–56.

7. Ibid., pp. 2758, 2740.

8. Ibid., p. 2757; Bell, pp. 304–7.

9. 1st Trial, p. 2778.

10. Ibid., p. 2790.

11. Ibid., p. 2824.

12. Ibid., p. 2843; Cooke, p. 255; Bell, p. 314.

13. 1st Trial, p. 2847.

14. Ibid., pp. 2853–54.

15. Ibid., p. 2857.

16. Ibid., p. 2880; "*is*": Cooke, p. 260, for emphasis.

17. 1st Trial, pp. 2865–66.

18. 1st Trial, pp. 2867–71, 2899.

19. Ibid., p. 2901.

20. Ibid., pp. 2883–84.

21. Ibid., pp. 2885–86.

22. Ibid., p. 2907; tucked: Cooke, pp. 264–65.

23. 1st Trial, p. 2873.

24. Ibid., p. 2862.

25. Bell, p. 315. Bingham and Ascoli, "The Case."

26. A. J. Liebling, "Spotlight on the Jury," *The New Yorker* (July 23, 1949); *NYT,* July 8, 1949.

Chapter 31: Verdict

1. "Gray": *BAS,* July 7, 1949; "mass": Bell, p. 320; *Geographical:* Bell, p. 337; outcome/Vermont: *New York World-Telegram,* July 9, 1949; *NYT,* July 9, 1949; *Time* (July 18, 1949).

2. *W,* p. 715.

3. Nicholas Blatchford to Reuben, July 14, 1969 (WAR).

4. *Washington Times-Herald,* July 9, 1949. *W,* pp. 714–15. In a rare bow to a rival, the *Times-Herald* picked up the story from the *Daily News* and ran it on the front page.

5. "I expect": *NYT,* July 8, 1949; "election": Bell, p. 337.

6. "Wonder": Bell, p. 337; Knickerbocker: *New York Journal-American,* July 9, 1949.

7. *WP,* July 9, 1949; Bell, p. 338. AH/PH: *New York Daily Mirror,* July 9, 1949.

8. *WP,* July 9, 1949.

9. *NYT,* July 10, 1949.

10. Bell, p. 339.

11. Ibid.

12. *NYT,* July 9, 1949; *Time* (July 18, 1949); Bell, p. 341.

13. *New York Journal-American,* June 30, 1949; Liebling, "Spotlight on the Jury," *The New Yorker* (July 23, 1949); *New York World-Telegram,* July 8, 1949.

14. David Halberstam interview with Willard Edwards (Halberstam Papers, Boston University).

15. *New York World-Telegram,* July 9, 1949.

16. See FBI 3887, July 13, 1949. It was another juror, Arthur Pawlinger, who informed his fellow panelists he would never accept the testimony of an ex-Communist and "immediately tried to usurp the powers of Foreman James."

17. *NYHT,* July 10, 1949; *TNR* (July 18, 1949); "interference": *NYT,* July 10, 1949.

18. WC prediction: Blatchford to Reuben, July 14, 1969; photo: *NYT,* July 10, 1949.

Chapter 32: The American Jitters

1. "Summation to the Jury," *Plain Talk* (August 1949); *W,* p. 791.

2. 2d Trial, vol. 5, p. 3061, vol. 6, p. 2512.

3. WC deposition, March 25, 1949, p. 1299; FBI 65-1573-2328, Jan. 28, 1949; FBI 74-1333-3677, July 17, 1949; FBI 65-53508-96, Aug. 13, 1949; FBI 74-1333-3755, letter to director, Aug. 16, 1949; FBI NY 65-14920, pp. 312–13; FBI 3855, letter to director, Sept. 2, 1949; FBI teletype 74-1333-3862, Sept. 22, 1949. In March 1950, shortly after the second AH trial concluded, Sherman was summoned by HUAC but declined to answer any questions. He protested he was the victim of a "frame-up" produced by a "disordered mind" (presumably WC's). Sherman added, "I would regard it as a privilege to have the acquaintance of Alger Hiss, but I am convinced that he would not know me from Adam": *NYT,* March 2, 1950. WC later said he had introduced AH to Sherman under the alias Adam: *W,* p. 367.

4. FBI 4239, Nov. 18, 1949; Herbst letter to John Herrmann, Feb. 2, 1949 (Josephine Herbst Papers—Beinecke Library, Yale). Harold Rosenwald, "Paraphrase of Interview with Miss Josephine Herbst," Jan. 8, 1949; DDW (probably Daniel West), "Interview with Miss Josephine Herbst," Nov. 25, 1949 (both HISS); Herbst letter to Reuben, Nov. 6, 1968 (WAR).

5. Win Brooks, "How the FBI Trapped Hiss," *American Weekly* (Aug. 6, 1950); John J. Danahy, "Re: Alger Hiss," unpublished ms. (courtesy of Mr. Danahy); author interview with Danahy, Sept. 28, 1994; 2d Trial, vol. 5, pp. 3025–26, 3023–33, 3042, 3050–53; *W,* p. 394.

6. RDT to WC, Oct. 7, 1949 (this and all WC-RDT correspondence cited in Notes are at HOOVER).

7. FBI 65-14920-4613, Oct. 11, 1949; FBI 14920-4658, Oct. 18, 1949; Victor Lasky, "Chambers Lie Test on TV Canceled by 2nd Hiss Trial," *New York World-Telegram,* Oct. 21, 1949; Levitt, *Tissue,* pp. 151–52. Bert Andrews proposed WC sit for a polygraph after the verdict, but again Murphy ruled it out, this time because AH's appeal was pending: FBI 65-14920-5447, Jan. 31, 1950.

8. *TNR* (July 18, 1949); I. F. Stone, "From Butter to Guns," July 31, 1949, in *New York Star* (reprinted in Stone, *The Truman Era, 1945–1952: A Nonconformist History of Our Times* [Little, Brown, 1972], pp. 74–77); TRB, "Acheson," *TNR* (Aug. 8, 1949) (reprinted in Richard Strout, *TRB: Views and Perspectives on the Presidency* ([Macmillan, 1979], pp. 82–83); first meeting: Tim Weiner, "Stalin-Mao Alliance was Uneasy, Newly Released Papers Show," *NYT,* Dec. 10, 1995.

9. See "Ex-Major Says Hopkins Sped Uranium to Soviet in 1943," *NYT,* Dec. 6, 1949; "Un-American Hunt Goes On," *NYT,* Dec. 11, 1949; "Wallace Denies He Helped Reds Get Uranium or Gave Them Data," *NYHT,* Jan. 27, 1950; *TNR* (Oct. 3, 1949).

10. Cooke, p. 284.


Chapter 33: Blind Analysis

1. Cooke, p. 284.

2. "Big-city": John Chabot Smith interview with AH, n.d. (Smith Papers, Harvard); Smith, *Hiss,* p. 399; "apoplectic": Levitt, *Tissue,* p. 152.

3. Smith, *Hiss,* p. 399.

4. Ibid., p. 400.

5. Goddard's background: *NYT,* Nov. 18, 1949.

6. *Time* (Dec. 13, 1949); *NYT,* Dec. 10, 1948; 2d Trial, vol. 2, pp. 1299–1300, 1262–66.

7. Berle, "Underground Espionage Agent," 2d Trial, vol. 6, p. 3325; Murphy, "Memorandum," March 20, 1945, 2d Trial, vol. 6, p. 3323.

8. 2d Trial, vol. 5, p. 3153.

9. *NYT,* Dec. 9, 1949; Wadleigh, "Why I Spied," July 15, 1949; 2d Trial, vol. 2, p. 1108.

10. 2d Trial, vol. 1, p. 441.

11. Merle Miller, "The Second Hiss Trial," *TNR* (Feb. 4, 1950); *NYT,* Nov. 24, 1949. Miller assisted the Hiss defense in the first trial but by the second was persuaded of AH's guilt.

12. Cooke, p. 295.

13. 2d Trial, vol. 3, p. 1505.

14. Ibid., pp. 1360, 1375.

15. FBI 4224, letter to Ladd, Apr. 9, 1952.

16. "Nightmare"/"umbrella": *Time* (Jan. 9, 1950); "impeccable": *TNR* (Feb. 6, 1950).

17. 2d Trial, vol. 4, pp. 2369–71, 2387–94, 2362.

18. 2d Trial, vol. 4, pp. 2517–18.

19. Ibid., pp. 2550–52, 2562, 2572–77; vol. 5, pp. 2623, 2664, 2683, 2719, 2760–62, 2765; also *NYT,* Jan. 6, Jan. 11, 1950.

20. "Coached": Forrest G. Robinson, *Love's Story Told: A Life of Henry A. Murray* (Harvard, 1992), p. 334.

21. 2d Trial, vol. 5, pp. 2825–26, 2863–67.

22. FBI (no serial no.), Jan. 4, 1950, Agee letter to Murphy, Nov. 29, 1949; 2d Trial, vol. 5, pp. 2941, 2949; "serious"/"deplorable": Robert Bendiner, "The Ordeal of Alger Hiss," *The Nation* (Feb. 11, 1950). Bendiner's coverage of both trials was subtle and scrupulous. In the future *The Nation* became a pro-Hiss redoubt. "Enjoyable": Robinson, *Murray,* p. 334.

23. 2d Trial, vol. 5, p. 2967.

24. Ibid., pp. 3025–27, 3031, 3057, 3037, 3023; WC to Hede Massing, May 23, 1951 (Massing Papers, HOOVER).

25. *NYT,* Jan. 22, 1950.

26. Ibid., *BAS,* Jan. 22, 1950.

27. *Washington Times-Herald,* Jan. 22, 1950; *NYT,* Jan. 22, 1950; *BAS,* Jan. 22, 1950; *Time* (Jan. 30, 1950).

28. WC to RDT, Jan. 26, 1950.

29. *NYT,* Jan. 22, 1950; *NYHT,* Jan. 23, 1950; *BAS,* Jan. 22, 1950.

30. WC to RDT, Feb. 1, 1950.

31. Eleanor Roosevelt, "Save the Soil and the Trees," Jan. 26, 1950; *The Christian Science Monitor,* Jan. 23, 1950. Mrs. Roosevelt thought AH "might be guilty of perjury, but not of espionage": *NYT,* Jan. 23, 1950.

32. "Wound": WC to RDT, May 20, 1950; "bland": Thomas O'Neill, review of *Witness,* in *BAS,* May 22, 1952.

33. *W,* p. 793.

34. Leslie Fiedler, "Hiss, Chambers, and the Age of Innocence," *Commentary* (August 1951) (reprinted in Fiedler, *An End to Innocence: Essays on Culture and Politics* [Beacon, 1962], pp. 9, 8, 24); Philip Rahv, "The Sense and Nonsense of Whittaker Chambers," *Partisan Review* (Autumn 1952) (reprinted in Rahv, *Essays on Literature and Politics* ed. Arabel J. Porter and Andrew J. Drosin [Houghton-Mifflin, 1978], pp. 317–27).


Chapter 34: Eleven Words


1. *BAS,* Jan. 26, 1950.

2. See Fred Cook, *The Unfinished Story of Alger Hiss* (Morrow, 1958), p. 136ff.

3. *NYT,* Jan. 26, 1950.

4. *BAS,* Jan. 26, 1950; *NYT,* Jan. 26, 1950; *WP,* Jan. 26, 1950.

5. *BAS,* Jan. 22, 1950; *Chicago Sun-Times,* Jan. 26, 1950.

6. *TNR* (Feb. 6, 1950); *NYT,* Jan. 26, 1950; *BAS,* Jan. 26, 1950; *WP,* Jan. 26, 1950.

7. *Washington Times-Herald,* Jan. 26, 1950; *NYHT,* Jan. 26, 1950; *BAS,* Jan. 26, 1950; *NYT,* Jan. 30, 1950; *WP,* Jan. 26, 1950; McCullough, *Truman,* p. 760.

8. *NYHT,* Jan. 26, 1950; "awful": Walter Isaacson and Evan Thomas, *The Wise Men: Six Friends and the World They Made, Acheson, Bohlen, Harriman, Kennan, Lovett, McCloy* (Simon and Schuster, 1986) p. 491; "s.o.b.": Robert J. Donovan, *The Tumultuous Years: The Presidency of Harry S Truman, 1949–1953* (Norton, 1982), p. 133; McCullough, *Truman,* p. 760.

9. *NYT,* March 1, 1950.

10. "Incessantly"/"stark": Quoted in Dean Acheson, *Present at the Creation: My Years in the State Department* (Norton, 1969), p. 359; AH letter to John Foster Dulles, Aug. 4, 1948; Acheson to Lloyd P. Stryker, early April 1949 (both HISS); Zeligs memo of inter-

view with William L. Marbury, May 6, 1954 (ZELIGS); Acheson and Donald Hiss spoke with Clark together: Oral History No. 240, Interview with Tom C. Clark, p. 191 (HST); "unqualified": Acheson Senate testimony, Jan. 14, 1949; assured Truman: Donovan, *The Tumultuous Years,* p. 133; Alsops: Weinstein, *Perjury,* p. 385 fn.

11. *WP,* Jan. 22, 1950.

12. Morris, *Nixon,* p. 500; *NYHT,* Jan. 27, 1950; *Washington Times-Herald,* Jan. 27, 1950.

13. David M. Oshinsky, *A Conspiracy So Immense: The World of Joe McCarthy* (Free Press, 1983), p. 109.


## *EXILE (1950–1961)*

### Chapter 35: Public Recluse

1. *W,* p. 798; *implora:* WC to RDT, Jan. 26, 1950. For original quote, see *Lord Byron: Selected Letters and Journals,* ed. Leslie A. Marchand (Harvard, 1982) pp. 201–2.

2. On WC's children: WC to Solow, May 4, 1956 (SOLOW); WC to Buckley, Oct. 12, 1956 (WFB); also WC to Duncan Norton-Taylor, March 30, 1953 (AWP). "Whittaker was very bourgeois": Author interview with WFB, July 3, 1991.

3. "Frightened": WC to RDT, Jan. 28, 1950; suspicion: RDT to WC, Feb. 15, 1950.

4. Prentice memo to Luce, Jan. 25, 1950; HRL memo to Prentice, Jan. 25, 1950; "informative"/"$12,000": Prentice to WC, Jan. 27, 1950 (all TIME); WC to RDT, Jan. 28, 1950.

5. "Operational": HRL to William L. White, Feb. 1, 1950; "done more": quoted in WC to HRL, March 25, 1950 (both TIME); "trouble": Swanberg, *Luce,* p. 408; "poetry," HRL letter to Edward K. Thompson, Apr. 10, 1956 (TIME).

6. Matthews's promotion: *NYT,* Dec. 22, 1949; his enthusiasm: Elson, *World of Time,* p. 242; HRL to Reverend John F. Cronin, Jan. 30, 1950 (TIME); "detail": WC to RDT, Feb. 11, 1950.

7. Halberstam interview with Hughes (Halberstam Papers, Boston University).

8. "Unanimous": Griffith, *Harry and Teddy,* p. 179; "guilty": author interview with Griffith, Sept. 8, 1994.

9. "Appalled": Halberstam interview with Hughes (Halberstam Papers, Boston University); taxied: Elson, *World of Time,* p. 243; "apologizing": Matthews to HRL, n.d. (TIME).

10. "Knife": quoted in WC to HRL, March 25, 1950; "opportunity"/vacation: HRL to WC, Feb. 21, 1950 (TIME).

11. WC to HRL, March 25, 1950 (TIME).

12. William Phillips to WC, Dec. 16, 1948 (courtesy of Mr. Phillips); David McDowell to WC, Oct. 4, 1951 (special ms. collection, Random House, COLUMBIA).

13. Wintry/"tragedy": WC letter to Carroll County Historical Society, n.d., but enclosed with presentation copy of *Witness* in 1952 (ms. collection of Historical Society); "why men": *Washington Times-Herald,* July 9, 1949.

14. Two chapters: Cerf, *At Random,* p. 242; "fought": Carl D. Brandt to author, Nov. 8, 1989.

15. Author interview with Ken McCormick, Apr. 15, 1991.

16. Cerf, *At Random,* pp. 242, 13.

17. See correspondence of Bernice Baumgarten and Donald Klopfer: May 4, May 9, May 18, May 19, May 22, 1950 (all WAR); third printing: RDT to WC, Apr. 12, 1950; eighty-five thousand: John K. Hutchins, "On the Books, on an Author," interview with WC, *NYHT Book Review,* May 25, 1952.

18. Disliked: Halberstam interview with Hughes (Halberstam Papers, Boston University); "logical": James A. Linen memo, Apr. 26, 1950 (TIME); no excerpt: Elson, *World of Time,* p. 243; "messianic": WC to HRL, May 12, 1950 (TIME).

19. Linen memo, Apr. 26, 1950 (TIME).

20. Halberstam interview with Hughes (Halberstam Papers, Boston University); WC to HRL, May 12, 1950; HRL to WC, May 16, 1950 (both TIME).

21. *Newsweek* (Feb. 11, 1952).

22. Writing room/"out of sight": WC to RDT, Feb. 1, 1950; work/family schedule: Thompson, "The Whittaker Chambers I Know."

23. Monasticism: See WC, "The Sanity of Benedict," *Commonweal* (Sept. 19, 1952) (*Ghosts,* pp. 157–264); also WC to RDT, Dec. 11, 1951; WC to HRL, March 21, 1952 (TIME); Hutchins interview, *NYHT;* John Barkham, "Whittaker Chambers in 'Witness' Bares a Scarred, Tortured Soul," interview with WC, *Hartford Times,* May 31, 1952; regret: WC to RDT, Apr. 19, 1951; pleasure: WC to RDT, May 10, 1950.

24. Matthews, *Angels,* pp. 178–79.

25. "Alcoholic": Bergreen, *Agee,* p. 356; Agee letters: WC letter to TSM, March 19, 1951 (TIME); Fixx death: author interview with Marlys Fixx, Aug. 21, 1995; "so intensely"/funeral: WC to RDT, March 3, 1950.

26. Klopfer to Baumgarten, May 19, 1950 (WAR).

27. Baumgarten to Klopfer, May 22, 1950 (WAR).

28. Author interview with RDT, Oct. 25, 1990; also de Toledano, *Lament,* pp. 4–7, 11, 125–29; George H. Nash, *The Conservative Intellectual Movement in America Since 1945* (Basic, 1976), pp. 101–3. RDT remembers a correspondence between WC and Merton, but no records of it exist: Letter from International Thomas Merton Society to author, Oct. 11, 1991; preface reactions: WC to RDT, Apr. 5, 1950; "plain people": WC to RDT, Apr. 20, May 10, 1950.

29. "Pigs": RDT to Robert Doriss, Nov. 17, 1992 (courtesy of Mr. Doriss).

30. "Muscles"/"boiling"/"lagged": de Toledano, *Lament,* pp. 130–31; rump: RDT to Robert Doriss, Nov. 17, 1992.

31. "Cellars": RDT, "Whittaker Chambers Remembered: The Imperatives of the Heart," *NR* (Aug. 1, 1986); "*was*": Thomas Vinciguerra, "Neither Lost Nor Beat," interview with RDT, *Columbia College Today* (Winter 1990).

32. "Extensive": Walter LaFeber, *America, Russia, and the Cold War, 1945–1971,* 2d ed. (Wiley, 1972), p. 104; "final struggle": "Stopped Big Plot, Says Chambers," *Washington Times-Herald,* Sept. 5, 1950.

33. Parable: WC to Mother Mary Judge, Apr. n.d., 1950 (TIME); "anybody"/"constantly": Hutchins interview, May 25, 1952. In October WC told the FBI he was now working without a deadline: FBI 4646, memo to the director, Oct. 11, 1950.

34. FBI 65-57449-90, May 24, 1950; FBI 65-59181-34, June 2, 1950; FBI 65-59095-209, June 22, 1950. WC evidently was shown the same film footage of Gold, shot in Philadelphia, that had been the basis of Klaus Fuchs's identification of him: FBI 65-59181-183, July 6, 1950; see also Lamphere and Shachtman, *FBI-KGB War,* pp. 149, 156; "kept": Richard Rovere, "The Kept Witnesses," *Harper's* (May 1955).

35. Oshinsky, *Conspiracy,* p. 157.

36. WC meets McC: Reeves, *McCarthy*, p. 712; author interview with Robert Morris, Oct. 1, 1991; see also Morris, *No Wonder We Are Losing* (University of Plano Press, 1953), pp. 13, 21, 98–100; "top": Robert K. Newman, *Owen Lattimore and the "Loss" of China* (University of California, 1992), p. 215.

37. WC to Solow, March 22, 1950 (SOLOW); Lattimore and Lauterbach: Newman, *Lattimore*, p. 189; for F. V. Field, p. 23; Budenz: WC to RDT, Apr. 20, 1950.

38. Author interview with Robert Morris, Oct. 9, 1991; "awe": Reeves, *McCarthy*, p. 249.

39. "Asking": Wills, *Nixon*, p. 35; WC recommends books: RMN to WC, Apr. 30, 1956 (RMN); "Bakuninist"/"Messianic": RMN, foreword to de Toledano, *Lament*, p. xii.

40. WC to RMN, Jan. 20, 1951 (RMN).

41. McC's followers: Oshinsky, *Conspiracy*, p. 119; Reeves, *McCarthy*, pp. 247–49; ACCF: Wald, *New York Intellectuals*, p. 273.

42. "Stopped Big Plot," *Washington Times-Herald*, Sept. 5, 1950.

43. WC to RMN, Nov. 9, 1950 (RMN).

44. Oshinsky, *Conspiracy*, pp. 175–76; McCullough, *Truman*, p. 814.

45. "Atom": WC to RDT, Apr. 19, 1951.

46. WC to RDT, Aug. 9, 1951.

47. WC and Barnes: Harry B. Mitchell (chairman, U.S. Civil Service Commission) to John F. Davis, Oct. 28, 1949 (HISS); FBI 77-13677-190, Aug. 16, 1951; "Peters"/ "disreputable"/"slanderous": Murrey Marder, "Barnes Listed as Red, Chambers Was Told," *WP*, Aug. 17, 1951. Barnes did not file suit against WC.

48. Oshinsky, pp. 215–17; *McCarthyism, The Fight for America: Documented Answers to Questions Asked by Friend and Foe by Senator Joe McCarthy* (Devin-Adair, 1952), pp. 36, 59, 60, 86, 88.

49. O. Edmund Clubb, *The Witness and I* (Columbia, 1974), pp. 25–26; also *NYT* obit, May 11, 1989.

50. FBI 121-22998-1X4, signed statement by WC, May 22, 1950; also *W*, pp. 270–71.

51. WC to RDT, Aug. 9, 1951.

52. "The successor": Murrey Marder, "Clubb's Diary Shows He Met Whittaker Chambers in 1932," *WP*, Aug. 21, 1951.

53. "Areas": Marder, "Barnes Listed as Red."

54. *NYT*, May 11, 1989. WC at least had grounds for suspecting Barnes and Clubb. It is more difficult to justify his secret assessment, in this same period, of a *Time* researcher who had applied for a government job. When questioned by the FBI, WC vouched for her "reputation and character" but urged she not be hired, giving the reason that the applicant, a European, had immigrated to the United States "late in life," and in WC's view, "such people come to this country with the minds fully molded to the way of life in their native lands" and so "never become real Americans": FBI 124-4757-9, June 5, 1950.

Chapter 36: *Witness*

1. WC to Matthews, March 19, 1951 (TIME).

2. Author interview with John Chambers, Oct. 24, 1990; see Nora de Toledano to WC, Oct. 2, 1951; RDT to WC, Oct. 9, 1951; NDT to WC, Oct. 25, Nov. 1, 1951 (NDT correspondence included with RDT correspondence at HOOVER).

3. Matthews to England: Matthews to WC, March 25, 1951; ms. to RDT: WC to Matthews, Apr. 21, 1951 (both TIME); RDT cries: Author interview, Oct. 25, 1990; "My children": *W,* p. 5; "moving"/"excellently"/"generous": Matthews to WC, Apr. 30, 1951 (TIME).

4. FBI 4761, memo to director, June 23, 1951.

5. "Wretched": WC to RDT, Aug. 9, 1951; "pegged"/"forgot": Matthews to WC, July 23, 1951 (TIME); *Time* (Aug. 9, 1948); tuition: WC to RDT, July 27, 1951.

6. Won't work: WC telegram to Matthews, Sept. 4, 1951; "never": Matthews to WC, Sept. 7, 1951 (both TIME).

7. "Peace"/drive: WC to RDT, Sept. 25, 1951.

8. "Wonderful"/"deserves": McDowell to WC, Oct. 4, 1951 (Random House Collection, COLUMBIA).

9. "Pressure": WC letter to Carroll County Historical Society; 340,000 words: Hutchins interview, *NYHT Book Review,* May 25, 1952.

10. *Book-of-the-Month Club News,* May 1952.

11. "Change"/"stay"/suit: WC to RDT, Dec. 11, 1951.

12. "Hard": WC to RDT, Jan. 22, 1952; "most important": *Book-of-the-Month Club News,* May 1952. WC to Berkshire: FBI teletype 4923, Feb. 21, 1952; FBI teletype 5144, March 4, 1952; "editorial"/"obliging": WC to NDT, June 12, 1951; friendly: See WC to RDT, Apr. 6, 1952.

13. *Post* facts: "Chambers the Witness," *Newsweek* (Feb. 11, 1952).

14. WC readings: I. F. Stone, "The 'Martyrdom' of Chambers," *Daily Compass,* Feb. 12, 1952 (reprinted in Stone, *Truman Era,* pp. 182–85); "beloved": Audiocassette of reading (courtesy of WFB); *W,* p. 3.

15. "Five Years of War," *Time* (Sept. 4, 1944).

16. Hundred thousand copies: *Publishers Weekly* (May 21, 1952); biggest: "Bookstall Gossip," *Boston Post,* May 25, 1952; "anticipated"/"all": Orville Prescott, "Of the Year's Books, These Have Impressed Me Most," *NYT Book Review,* June 8, 1952; half million/movie studios: Louella Parsons, "Hollywood Highlights," *New York Journal-American,* Apr. 2, 1952; largest: Thompson, "The Whittaker Chambers I Know"; Wanger: RDT to WC, May 27, 1952. See best-seller list, *NYT Book Review;* ninth: Stephen J. Whitfield, *The Culture of the Cold War* (Johns Hopkins, 1991), p. 18.

17. Cerf to WC, June 10, 1952 (Random House, COLUMBIA); Hannah Arendt, "The Ex-Communists," *Commonweal* (March 20, 1953); Max Ascoli, "Lives and Deaths of Whittaker Chambers," *The Reporter* (Sept. 8, 1952); John Chamberlain, "Whittaker Chambers: Witness," *The Freeman* (June 2, 1952); John Dos Passos, "Mr. Chambers's Descent into Hell," *Saturday Review* (May 24, 1952); Granville Hicks, "Whittaker Chambers's Testament," *New Leader* (May 26, 1952); Sidney Hook, "The Faiths of Whittaker Chambers," *NYT Book Review,* May 25, 1952; Irving Howe, "God, Man and Stalin," *The Nation* (May 24, 1952); Rahv, "The Sense and Nonsense of Whittaker Chambers"; Arthur Schlesinger, Jr., "Whittaker Chambers and His 'Witness,' " *Saturday Review* (May 24, 1952) (reprinted in Schlesinger, *The Politics of Hope* [Houghton Mifflin, 1962], pp. 183–95); R. H. S. Crossman, "The Hiss Case," *Political Quarterly,* vol. 24, no. 4, Oct.–Dec. 1953; John Strachey, *The Strangled Cry and Other Unparliamentary Papers* (Sloane, 1962), pp. 32–44; Rebecca West, "Whittaker Chambers," *Atlantic Monthly* (June 1952); "Publican & Pharisee," *Time* (May 26, 1952). "In 'Witness,' Chambers Sums Up the Case Against Communism," *Kansas City Star,* May 1, 1952; Marcus Duffield, "Amazing Autobiography of a Famous Ex-Communist," *NYHT,* May 25,

1952 (also Hutchins interview, same issue); Bert Andrews, "How Alger Hiss Was Brought to Trial," *NYHT,* June 1–5, 1952; *Saturday Review* published a lead review by Schlesinger, plus shorter notes by Dos Passos, Richard B. Morris, Richard Nixon, and Charles Alan Wright; Thomas O'Neill, "Reporter at Both Alger Hiss Trials Reviews Whittaker Chambers Book," *BAS,* May 22, 1952; Thomas P. Sherman, "The Confessions of Whittaker Chambers: And Their Political Significance," *St. Louis Post-Dispatch,* May 18, 1952.

18. Hook, "Faiths."

19. Augustine/Rousseau: Hicks; Fox, *Pilgrim*'s: Dos Passos, "Mr. Chambers's Descent"; Poe: Crossman "Hiss Case."

20. William James, *The Varieties of Religious Experience: A Study in Human Nature* (New American Library, 1958), pp. 140–41, 281.

21. "Dare": "Whittaker Chambers's Comments," *NYHT,* Feb. 1, 1950 (partial transcript of WC radio interview with Bert Andrews); courtroom observers: author interview with Murrey Marder, Jan. 30, 1995.

22. *W,* p. 472.

23. Richard Hofstadter, *The American Political Tradition and the Men Who Made It* (Knopf, 1948), p. 327; "state"/"massive": Jordan A. Schwarz, *The New Dealers: Power Politics in the Age of Roosevelt* (Vintage, 1994), p. xi; "common vision": Brinkley, "The New Deal and the Idea of the State," in Fraser and Gerstle, *Rise and Fall,* p. 92.

24. Strachey's *Coming Struggle* was "the most influential book [in England] of the thirties": Stuart Samuels, "The Left Book Club," in *The Left Wing Intellectuals Between the Wars, 1919–1939,* ed. Walter Laqueur (Harper, 1966), p. 70. "Not interested": Quoted in Kazin, *New York Jew,* p. 260.

25. *W,* p. 449.

26. WC, "The Damn Fool"; "union": Sacvan Bercovitch, *The American Jeremiad* (University of Wisconsin, 1978), p. 11. *W,* p. 449.

27. *W,* p. 9.

28. Ibid., p. 10.

29. For another view strikingly similar to WC's and Solzhenitsyn's, see Václav Havel, "The End of the Modern Era," *NYT,* March 1, 1992. For Havel, communism heralds the end of "the modern age" and its belief "that the world . . . is a wholly knowable system governed by a finite number of universal laws that man can grasp and rationally direct for his own benefit."

30. Stone, " 'Martyrdom.' "

31. See WC to RDT, June 25, 1952. He was pleased by some reviews, especially Granville Hicks's in the *New Leader.* See WC to Hicks, Aug. 12, 1952 (Hicks Collection, Syracuse University).

32. McCarthy to Arendt, in *Between Friends: The Correspondence of Hannah Arendt and Mary McCarthy, 1949–1975,* ed. and intro. Carol Brightman (Harcourt, 1995), pp. 11–12 (italics in original).

33. "Police State": Arendt, "Ex-Communists." "Where else has an unknown man risen from the depths to denounce liberalism as part of the Communist disease and to call his countrymen to destroy both, root and branch? Where else have the repressions of childhood without love and the resentments of an unappreciated lonely adolescence been rationalised into a volcanic *Weltanschauung?* Where else has a conspiracy against Christian civilization been presented as a valiant defence of it? Yes! The prophet of the Third Reich might well have called his book *Witness,* just as WC could have renamed

his—*My Struggle*": Crossman, "Hiss Case," p. 403; Dwight Macdonald thought *Witness* "an exercise in sincere-phony paranoia, v. interesting politically, like *Mein Kampf*": Macdonald to Reuben, Aug. 29, no year (WAR). In a review of *CF,* David Cort found *W* "comparable to, but funnier than, *Mein Kampf*": "Blind Man's Bluff," *The Nation* (Nov. 2, 1964). Czeslaw Milosz, "A Year of the Hunter," *Partisan Review,* vol. LXI, no. 3, 1994, pp. 479–80. "[I] have always felt great sympathy for [WC] and thought about his tragic life. He suffered much": Milosz to author, Jan. 18, 1991.

34. "All my life I have felt weighed down by the burden of communication [but] I rarely have that problem with Europeans (we speak within the same frame of reference)": WC to RDT, Apr. 19, 1951.

35. WC discovers *Darkness:* WC to Arthur Koestler, Sept. 27, 1959; Oct. 22, 1953 (all WC-AK correspondence cited in Notes is in KOESTLER); among those WC urged the novel on was Grace Lumpkin: See FBI-Lumpkin 74-1333-215, Feb. 18, 1949; Arthur Koestler, "The Complex Issue of the Ex-Communists," *NYT Magazine,* Feb. 19, 1950, WC thought the piece "poorly written and scarcely thought out at all. Almost a slap in the face": WC to RDT, March 3, 1950; WC cancels dinner: WC to AK, n.d.—June–July 1952; "not like": WC to AK, Aug. 12, 1952.

36. AK to WC, Apr. 15, 1953.


### Chapter 37: Close Calls


1. Zeligs, "Memorandum of a Conversation with Dr. Elizabeth Reese Wilkens," May 8, 1962 (ZELIGS); FBI 74-1333 (no last digits), Dec. 22, 1952; FBI 74-1333-5438, Dec. 22, 1952; EC to HRL, Nov. 11, 1952 (TIME); WC to RDT, May 29, 1953; *CF,* p. 10.

2. Strain of farm chores: WC to RDT, July 6, 1950; weight gain: Murrey Marder, "Barnes Listed as Red"; gasps: author interview with Robert Morris, Oct. 9, 1991; warnings: *CF,* p. 29.

3. The English edition included numerous deletions subject to approval by RDT: See correspondence between Nicholas Bentley (of Andre Deutsch), RDT, and Bernice Baumgarten, Oct. 28, 1952–May 11, 1953 (all RDT, Boston University); also EC to RDT, Nov. 14, 1952 (RDT); WC to RDT, Feb. 4, 1953; RDT to WC, Feb. 6, 1953; NDT to WC, Feb. 18, 1953. For various reviews, see Harvey Breit, "In and Out of Books," *NYT Book Review,* Aug. 9, 1953. French edition: See correspondence between RDT, Clifford Forster, and General Pierre de Bénouville (Éditions Gallimard and Éditions de l'Atlantique), Jan. 26, 1953–Feb. 23, 1953 (all RDT, Boston University); also RDT to author, Aug. 3, 1991. WC, incapacitated during the negotiations, wanted RDT to keep the royalties, but he refused: WC to RDT, May 29, 1953; author interview with RDT, July 11, 1991.

4. No visitors: FBI 74-1333-5438, Dec. 22, 1952; EC: *CF,* p. 9; also EC to Henry Regnery, Nov. 10, Dec. 7, 1952 (in Mr. Regnery's possession).

5. "As well"/"normal": FBI 74-1333 (no last digits), Dec. 22, 1952; vigil: *CF,* p. 8.

6. "Loved": RC to RDT, Feb. 4, 1953; WC to RDT, March 19, 1953.

7. WC to RDT, Feb. 13, May 29, 1953; HRL to EC, Nov. 14, 1952 (TIME); Reuben interview with Tom Hyland (WAR); William Allen Jowitt, first earl, *The Strange Case of Alger Hiss* (Doubleday, 1953). See WC to RDT, Feb. 16, 1953; NDT to WC, Feb. 18, March 22, 1953; WC to RDT, March 11, 1953; WC to RDT, March 19, 1953;

WC to NDT, March 19, May 8, May 16, 1953; see also "Book on Hiss Postponed. . . . 5,000 copies . . . Are Recalled," *NYT,* May 9, 1953; Nora de Toledano, "The Strange Case of Lord Jowitt," *American Mercury* reprint (courtesy of RDT); turns down McC: WC to Norton-Taylor, March 23, 1953 (AWP); Catholic support: See WC to Henry Carter Patterson, July 28, 1951 (Henry C. Patterson Papers, Balch Institute, Philadelphia); Catholic press: See, e.g., Reverend James M. Gillis, CSP, "Whittaker Chambers' 'Witnesses,' " *Catholic Monthly Review* (May 1952); Gerald Flynn, untitled review in *American Benedictine Review* (n.d.); Reverend Richard Ginder, " 'Witness' Shows Anti-Communist Fight to Be Essentially Religious," *Our Sunday Visitor,* July 27, 1952; Robert E. Burns, "The Enemy We Face!" *Voice of St. Jude* (July 1952). "[*W*] was the only secular work read aloud during meals in our novitiate refectory": Garry Wills, *Confessions of a Conservative* (Doubleday, 1979), p. 5. Shortly after *W* was published, WC received an honorary degree from Mount Mary College in Milwaukee. See Henry Regnery, *Memoirs of a Dissident Publisher* (Harcourt, 1979), p. 156. After WC resigned from *Time,* his Westminster neighbor John William Eckenrode, publisher of the Newman Press, a Catholic firm, offered him an "excellent editorial job": *W,* p. 760.

    8. "Slightest": WC to RDT, March 19, 1953; "sheer": *CF,* p. 27.

    9. WC to Koestler, Apr. 20, 1953.

    10. *NYT,* July 5, 1953; WC to Cerf, July 8, 1953 (Random House, COLUMBIA).

    11. See "Memo of Conversation with Clarence Pickett" (HISS); for Ellen's record, see Karl E. Mundt Senate remarks, Feb. 27, 1956, in *Congressional Record,* Appendix (1956); "slanders"/"suspect": WC to Patterson, July 28, 1951; "Of course the whole AFSC crowd are dead against [WC], following in [AFCS leader] Clarence [Pickett's] footsteps, gooselike": C. Marshall Taylor to Patterson (both in Henry C. Patterson Papers, Balch Institute); "enthusiasm": Hyland interview (WAR).

    12. "Dragging"/"pains": *CF,* p. 29; scar/enlarged: WC to RDT, Sept. 5, 1953.

    13. "Slave"/"weeping"/"beginnings": WC to RDT, Sept. 17, 1953.

    14. "Part": "The Bohlen Case," *Time* (March 30, 1953). Dulles: See David Fromkin, *In the Time of the Americans: FDR, Truman, Eisenhower, Marshall, MacArthur—The Generation That Changed America's Role in the World* (Knopf, 1995), p. 522.

    15. "All-out": *Time* (March 30, 1953); "judgment": Curt Gentry, *J. Edgar Hoover: The Man and the Secrets* (Norton, 1991), p. 436; "loyalty"/"security": Oshinsky, *Conspiracy,* p. 355.

    16. All WC quotes: WC to Norton-Taylor, March 23, 1953; see also WC to RDT, Apr. 6, 1953; *O,* p. 52; vote: Oshinsky, *Conspiracy,* pp. 290–91.

    17. WC to RDT, June 24, 1953.

    18. WC, "Is Academic Freedom in Danger?," *Life* (June 22, 1953) (*Ghosts,* pp. 265–78).

    19. RDT to WC, June 21, 1952; Regnery to WC, June 6, 1952 (Regnery).

    20. Accused/"changed": *W,* pp. 741, 331.

    21. CIA: Oshinsky, *Conspiracy,* p. 356; book banning/*W*: *NYT,* June 22, 1953.

    22. "Sabotage": *NYT,* June 24, 1953. In February 1953 a book reviewer at the Voice of America told McCarthy's committee she had been fired from the agency the day after she favorably reviewed *W* in a French broadcast: *NYT,* Feb. 21, 1953. In reply the reviewer's superior said, "I, too, considered 'Witness' a great book. The question was whether it contained the most effective material for broadcast to a foreign audience." In June 1952 Pennsylvania jurist Michael Musmanno publicly denounced WC for "propagandizing in behalf of Communism" and showing "studied disrespect to Washington, Lincoln and other immortal patriots of America": *Tampa* (Florida) *Tribune,* June 20,

1952; see also Justice Michael A. Musmanno, "That Man Chambers," *V.F.W. Magazine* (December 1952).

23. Poll: Michael Paul Rogin, *The Intellectuals and McCarthy: The Radical Specter* (MIT, 1967), p. 232.

24. "Immense"/"security": Reeves, *McCarthy*, pp. 372, 527.

25. "Out-McC": Oshinsky, *Conspiracy*, p. 356; "important": *NYT*, Nov. 7, 1953.

26. *NYT*, Nov. 9, 1953; treasury colleagues: See Henry Morgenthau III, *Mostly Morgenthaus: A Family History* (Ticknor & Fields), pp. 313–14; for Byrnes and HST, see *NYT*, Nov. 8–10, 1953; see also "The Strange Case of Harry Dexter White," *Time* cover story (Nov. 23, 1953); Stephen Ambrose, *Eisenhower*, vol. 2, *The President* (Simon and Schuster, 1984), p. 138.

27. WC, "The Herring and the Thing," *Look* (Dec. 29, 1953); see also "Chambers Implies a New Spy Figure," *NYT*, Dec. 13, 1953; "smash": Morgenthau, *Mostly Morgenthaus*, p. 362.

28. "Whining"/"raw"/"old Acheson": *Joseph R. McCarthy*, ed. Allen J. Matusow (Prentice-Hall, 1970), p. 79; "war": Oshinsky, *Conspiracy*, pp. 349–50.

29. WC and Regnery: Regnery, *Memoirs*, p. 156; author interview with Henry Regnery, May 16, 1990; "earnestly": Willi Schlamm, prologue to William F. Buckley, Jr., and L. Brent Bozell, *McCarthy and His Enemies: The Record and Its Meaning* (Regnery, 1954).

30. WC to Regnery, Dec. 28, 1953 (italics in original—Regnery).

31. For an incisive analysis of the McC phenomenon, see Will Herberg, "McCarthy and Hitler: A Delusive Parallel," *TNR* (Aug. 23, 1954) (reprinted Matusow, *McCarthy*, pp. 120–25); McC's Republican support: Rogin, *Intellectuals*, p. 247; European models: see Kennan, *Memoirs, 1950–1963*, vol. 2 (Little, Brown, 1972), p. 220.

32. WC, *O*, p. 52.

33. FBI 5608, Feb. 10, 1954; FBI 5611, Feb. 11, 1954; FBI 62-66329-22, March 11, 1954; two months: WC to David McDowell (WFB); "earthquake"/"requiems": author interview, RDT, Oct. 25, 1990; WC to RDT, March 15, 1954.

## Chapter 38: The Last Path

1. WC to Regnery, "May something or other," 1954 (Regnery).

2. "Pang": *CF*, p. 251; "*sent*": Author interview with John Chambers, Oct. 24, 1990.

3. "Solitude": *O*, pp. 121–22.

4. McDowell offer: WC to McDowell, Sept. 2, 1954; "Impulse"/"running": WC to McDowell, Oct. 16, 1954 (both WFB). Buick: Reuben interview with Tom Hyland (WAR).

5. WFB to WC, Feb. 20, 1954 (WFB).

6. *O*, pp. 53–54.

7. Visit: William F. Buckley, Jr., "The End of Whittaker Chambers," *Esquire* (September 1962).

8. *O*, p. 95.

9. William F. Buckley, Jr., *God and Man at Yale: The Superstitions of "Academic Freedom,"* intro. John Chamberlain (Regnery, 1951).

10. WFB background: John B. Judis, *William F. Buckley, Jr.: Patron Saint of the Conservatives* (Simon and Schuster, 1988; paperback, 1990); "manor": Kempton quoted in Dan Wakefield, *New York in the Fifties* (Houghton Mifflin, 1992), p. 262.

11. WFB's magazine plans/partnership with Schlamm: Judis, *Buckley*, pp. 114–16; Wills, *Confessions*, pp. 31–32. Schlamm was "more attentive to little American details than any other refugee intellectual I met [in the 1940s]": Kazin, *New York Jew*, p. 91. On *Dictatorship:* See Edmund Wilson, "Stalin, Trotsky, and Willi Schlamm," *The Nation* (Dec. 11, 1937) (reprinted in *From the Uncollected Papers of Edmund Wilson*, intro. Janet Goth and David Castronovo [Ohio University Press, 1995], pp. 217–27); also, Daniel Bell, "Interpretations of American Politics," in *The Radical Right: The New American Right,* expanded and updated (Anchor, 1964), p. 64. Schlamm appears in *W* (pp. 616–17) as Smetana. On *Measure,* see Dwight Macdonald, "Memo to Mr. Luce," in Macdonald, *Politics Past: Essays in Political Criticism* (Viking, 1957), pp. 254–61; Swanberg, *Luce,* pp. 304, 345.

12. WFB, "The End."

13. WC's doubts: *O,* pp. 70–74; "crackpotism": *CF,* p. 238. "Read out": Diggins, *Up from Communism,* p. 343. RMN and McC: See RDT to WC, Sept. 10, 1952. Eisenhower's electability was of paramount concern to WC, who feared retribution from the Democrats (for the Hiss case) should they regain the White House: See, e.g., WC to McDowell, Aug. 7[?], 1955.

14. "Position"/"preach"/"machine": *O,* pp. 79–83. "Given the automobile, the New Deal follows": WC to McDowell, July 23[?], 1955.

15. Judis, *Buckley,* p. 126.

16. John Judis transcript, interview with WFB; author interview with WFB, July 3, 1991.

17. *O,* pp. 92, 94, 99.

18. Ibid., p. 88; author interview with WFB, July 3, 1991.

19. Ambrose, *Nixon,* p. 357; *O,* pp. 98, 95.

20. "Opposed"/assured: *O,* pp. 89–90 fn.

21. "Doubt"/step down: Judis, *Buckley,* p. 127.

22. "Corrective": Tony Hiss, "My Father's Honor," *The New Yorker* (Nov. 16, 1992); Smith, *Hiss,* pp. 432–33; *Recollections,* pp. 184–86.

23. *WP,* Nov. 24, 1954.

24. Theodore Draper letter to author, Aug. 1, 1991.

25. WC to Koestler, Apr. 10, 1954; WC to RDT, Jan. 17, Jan. 31, 1954; NDT to WC, Jan. 25, 1954; WC to NDT, Feb. 3, Feb. 9, 1954, NDT to WC, Feb. 16, 1954; WC to McDowell, Apr. 20, 1954; *O,* p. 84; "as a": *NYT,* Oct. 6, 1954.

26. Christmas: EC to McDowell, Jan. 11, 1954 (WFB); "birds": *CF,* p. 56; *O,* p. 97; WC to Koestler, Apr. 10, 1954.

27. Judis, *Buckley,* pp. 121, 127.

28. Bozell's speeches: Richard Rovere, *Senator Joe McCarthy* (Harper, 1973), p. 225; "raven": *O,* p. 102.

29. "Awesome": WFB, "The End."

30. *NR* (Nov. 19, 1955).

31. FBI 74-1333-5660, Oct. 25, 1954; *O,* p. 119; EC to RMN, Nov. 30, 1955 (RMN); WC to RDT, Jan. 5, 1956; WC to McDowell, Jan. 19, 1956 (WFB).

32. Khrushchev: Volkogonov, *Stalin,* pp. 577–79.

33. WC hoped: WC to Norton-Taylor, May 2, 1956 (AWP); they were: Ulanovskaya, *Istoriia;* Weinstein, "Nadya—A Spy Story."

34. "Wobble": WC to McDowell, Jan. 19[?], 1956; six weeks: FBI 74-1333-5663, letter to director, March 30, 1956; five thousand dollars: Carl Brandt to A. B. C. Whipple

(*Life*), Oct. 8, 1956 (TIME). WC, "The End of a Dark Age Ushers in New Dangers," *Life* (Apr. 30, 1956) (*Ghosts,* pp. 279–90).

35. "Apologetic"/burned: *O,* pp. 86, 112; impressed: Cerf to WC, Dec. 27, 1954 (Random House—COLUMBIA).

36. Book plan/"human"/"so little": WC to McDowell: May 5, 1956; see also *O,* p. 121; for title, see *CF,* pp. 39, 163; deleted material: WC letter to Carroll County Historical Society; see also *O,* p. 76.

37. "Attempts": *CF,* p. 207.

38. "News from Random House, Inc.," June 19, 1964 (press release for *CF*—WFB).

39. *Britannica:* EC to McDowell, Jan. 11, 1955; "shortest": WC to Koestler, May 11, 1959; "call loan": *O,* pp. 146–47.

40. *O,* pp. 145–46.

41. Fire: FBI teletype 72, Jan. 16, 1957; *O,* pp. 151–52, 157.

42. Sidney Hook, "A Fateful Chapter of Our Times," *NYT Book Review,* May 2, 1957; R. H. S. Crossman, "The Case for Hiss," *New Statesman and Nation* (June 1, 1957). However, Crossman was impressed by AH's argument that he was the victim of an FBI-WC frame-up.

43. Hook to *Life,* Jan. 30, 1957; WC proposal: Feb. 2, 1957 (both TIME). WC statement: FBI 74-1333-5674, Apr. 18, 1957.

44. *O,* pp. 149, 176–77; "tell me"/"cried": author interview with Zolan, Nov. 13, 1994.

45. WC to Norton-Taylor, May 28, 1957 (AWP).

46. Norton-Taylor to WC, May 19, May 28, 1957 (both AWP); WC to Norton-Taylor, May 21, 1957; deluded: WC to Norton-Taylor, June 2–4[?], 1957 (AWP).

47. WC and ACCF: Solow to WC, Dec. 30, 1954 (SOLOW); "doesn't": WC to NDT, Dec. 27, 1955; "blaring": WC to RDT, Dec. 31, 1955.

48. RDT to WC, Dec. 15, 1955.

49. "Racket": *O,* p. 149; Brooks Atkinson, "Theatre: Drama Based on Hiss Trial," *NYT,* Dec. 12, 1957.

50. See WC to WFB, Jan. 3, 1956 (WFB); the letter appears in *O,* pp. 116–17, but with names deleted.

51. *O,* pp. 136, 152, 154, 167.

52. Meyer and WC: See RDT to WC, Feb. 22, 1953; Meyer's proposal: WC to McDowell, Sept. 2, 1954; Sartre/Athenaeum: Meyer to WC, May 5, 1958; WC to Meyer, June 2–3[?], 1957, Aug. 21, 1956 (all courtesy of Eugene Meyer).

53. *NR* (May 18, 1957); see also Judis, *Buckley,* p. 138.

54. *O,* pp. 141–42, 169, 220–21.

55. Ibid., p. 191.

56. Thirty days: *O,* p. 191; WFB visit: WFB, "The End"; salary: Judis, *Buckley,* p. 159.

57. "Let us": WFB, "The End."

58. "Superb": WFB telegram to WC, Sept. 5, 1957 (WFB); mailed/not allow: *O,* p. 198.

59. WC, "Big Sister Is Watching You," *NR* (Dec. 28, 1957) (*Ghosts,* pp. 313–18); "I have not read [WC's review], on principle; those who have read it, told me that this former Communist spy claimed that my book advocates dictatorship": *Letters of Ayn Rand,* ed. Michael Berliner (Dutton, 1995), p. 527; "dangerous": Terry Teachout, intro. to *Ghosts,* p. xxvii; see also Nash, *Conservative Tradition,* pp. 157–58. Apparently, WC was impressed by the first hundred pages of the novel. See Barbara Branden, *The Passion of Ayn Rand* (Doubleday, 1986), pp. 297–98.

60. *O,* p. 203.

61. Laha: FBI 5697, Apr. 30, 1958; "Jewish": author interview with Mrs. Harold Saperstein, July 8, 1991.

62. "Luncheon": Laha to Grace Lumpkin, June 21, 1953; "perfect": Laha to Lumpkin, Oct. 6, 1954 (both Lumpkin Papers, University of South Carolina); journalists: Pilat, "Report on Whittaker Chambers"; Ouspenskaya: author interview with Saperstein.

63. Travel plans/"last look": WC to Koestler: July 24, 1958; also WC to John O. Montgomery: FBI 65-1642-2347, July 24[?], 1958.

64. Koestler to Malraux, Apr. 28, 1953; Malraux to Koestler, May 5, 1953; Malraux to WC: *O,* p. 78.

65. FBI memo (no serial no.), March 7, 1958; EC's fears: *O,* p. 211; also WC to Koestler, Oct. 3, 1958.

66. WC to New York: *O,* p. 214.

## Chapter 39: "The Witness Is Gone"

1. WC to New York: WFB, "The End."

2. Judis transcript, interview with McFadden.

3. "Wit": Wills, *Confessions,* p. 50; "corpulent": William Rusher, quoted in Judis, *Buckley,* p. 159.

4. WFB, "The End."

5. "Knocked": Judis transcript, interview with John Leonard; "pushing": author interview with Garry Wills, July 23, 1992.

6. Heart attack: FBI 74-1333-5702, Nov. 20, 1958; two months/Pasternak/"grip": *O,* pp. 232, 214–18.

7. Hoax: Judis transcript, interview with John Leonard; see also *O,* p. 220, re Soviet "atomic plane."

8. WC, "Foot in the Door," *NR* (June 20, 1959) (*Ghosts,* pp. 345–50).

9. "Citizen": *Newsweek* (Apr. 20, 1958); "bug"/"shift"/"invective"/Trotsky: WC, "The Hissiad: A Correction," *NR* (May 9, 1959) (*Ghosts,* pp. 340–44); for WC on the FBI in 1952, see FBI memo (no serial no.), June 19, 1952, summarizing WC's appearance on the television program *Youth Wants to Know.* In response to a question from the studio audience of teenagers, Chambers urged "larger arrest power" for the bureau and "pointed out that at the present time the FBI must have a warrant to arrest people"; "spectacle"/"examine"/"preempt": *O,* pp. 240–43.

10. EC's dream/: WC to Koestler, May 11, 1959; EC's health: *O,* p. 268; stock market: WC's millionaire friend Tom Hyland first urged him to play the market: Reuben interview with Hyland (WAR); also, *O,* pp. 155, 158.

11. WC to TSM, July 7, 1949 (WFB); WC to Koestler, May 11, 1959.

12. WFB, "The End"; "supportable"/"jolly"/"cold": *O,* p. 248. Eckenrode: WC to Koestler, Aug. 11, 1959; Eckinrode to Reuben, June 2, 1969 (WAR); WC to Hede Massing, July 4, 1959 (Massing Papers—HOOVER).

13. Sperber's background: See John Hunt, "Manès Sperber: Comrade of Choice," *Bostonia* (Summer 1992); Simone de Beauvoir, *Force of Circumstance,* trans. Richard Howard (Putnam, 1965), p. 110; "stones": *O,* p. 251; Chartres: Craig Thompson, "The Whittaker Chambers I Know"; Provence: WC to Hede Massing, July 4, 1959 (Massing —HOOVER).

14. *O,* p. 249.

15. Arthur Koestler, *The Invisible Writing* (Beacon, 1955), pp. 422, 345–47, 347, 364, 420.

16. Koestler letter to Malraux, April 28, 1953 (KOESTLER).

17. "Fabulous": Koestler, *Invisible,* p. 273; "So there"/"great spirits": *O,* pp. 250–51; WC also recounted the meeting to Matthews in letter, July 7, 1959 (WFB).

18. "Raw"/Fermi's sister/*Corriere*/"polis"/"climate": WC to Koestler, Aug. 11, 1959; *O,* p. 253.

19. "Proliferant"/"hope": WC to TSM, July 7, 1959 (WFB); "wonder": WC to Koestler, Aug. 11, 1959.

20. "Stuff"/"rancid"/living in Venice: *O,* pp. 253–54.

21. Orchestrated/forgives: WC to Massing May 5[?], 1958; intriguing: Judis, *Buckley,* pp. 155–57; sage: *O,* p. 262; Zurich/also wanted: WC to Massing, July 4, 1959 (Massing —HOOVER).

WC had originally kept his distance from Massing because Krivitsky had warned him she had taken hush money from the Party after her defection: HUAC EXEC, Dec. 28, 1948. His mind was changed after he read Massing's memoir, *This Deception:* See WC to Massing, May 23, 1951 (Massing—HOOVER).

22. WC telegram to Massing, July 23, 1959 (Massing—HOOVER); home early: WC to WFB, July 22, 1959 (WFB); "put me": WC to Koestler, Aug. 11, 1959.

23. WC at college/conversation with dean: WC to Koestler, Sept. 27, 1959; televised: WC, "Foot in the Door," *NR* (June 20, 1959) (in *Ghosts,* pp. 345–50).

24. "Cannot"/attacked/"dawn"/"Itsy": WFB, "The End"; "perpetual"/"A's": WC to Koestler, June 17, 1960; "contradiction": *O,* p. 263.

25. Carnegie: Judis, *Buckley,* pp. 175–76; see also Matthews, *Angels,* p. 179; "monster": *O,* p. 261: "really wants": WC to Koestler, Sept. 27, 1959; World War III/ "popular": *O,* p. 265; "piling": *O,* p. 213.

26. "Real part": *O,* p. 273; "harmony": William F. Buckley, Jr., "Notes Toward an Empirical Definition of Conservatism," in Buckley, *The Jeweler's Eye* (Berkley, 1969), p. 12; phone/trim: WFB, "The End."

27. "Weariness": *O,* p. 291; "don't care": author interview with Zolan, Nov. 13, 1994.

28. "Quiet": WFB, "The End."

29. WC's death: Zeligs interviews with Dr. Wilkens, John E. Meyers (undertaker), both May 8, 1962 (ZELIGS). Bookcase: author interview with Robert Doriss, Nov. 26, 1991; portraits: James Burnham to Koestler, July 23, 1965 (KOESTLER).

30. Made public: See, e.g., *NYT* obit, July 12, 1961; "misunderstood": "On Whittaker Chambers," remarks by Duncan Norton-Taylor, Ralph de Toledano, and Arthur Koestler, *NR* (July 29, 1961).

31. "Sides": Zolan letter to Weinstein, Dec. 2, 1978 (AWP).

32. "Discovered": *O,* p. 292.

Appendix: Sifting the Evidence

1. See U.S. Court of Appeals, 2d Circuit, No. 22478. U.S.A. v. Alger Hiss, Appellant's brief (on Appeal from Order Denying Motion for New Trial), November 1952, pp. 43–44; also, AH, *Court,* p. 398ff.

2. See pp. 552–53, Notes 53–59.

3. "Expert": Appellant's brief, p. 11; "difficult": quoted in Cook, *Unfinished,* p. 146.

4. Doubts: See ibid., pp. 147–52; Weinstein, *Perjury,* p. 578; also John Lowenthal, "What the FBI Knew and Hid," *The Nation* (June 26, 1976); "not done": Quoted in Cook, *Unfinished,* p. 156.

5. Tytell's efforts: Weinstein, *Perjury,* pp. 571–73; "Beadle": Reuben interview with Henry Zolan, Apr. 17, 1971 (WAR).

6. AH has advocated this new interpretation in recent years. In *Recollections* (p. 202) he presents himself as the victim of an "unholy trinity" composed of "Richard Nixon, the power-hungry politician; J. Edgar Hoover, the ultimate bureaucrat; and Whittaker Chambers, the perfect pawn." The theory received unwitting support from Nixon, who in the first edition of *Six Crises* (p. 60) wrote that the FBI (rather than the defense) had found the Woodstock. Later, amid the wreckage of Watergate, RMN bragged of having "built" a Woodstock that framed Hiss: See Weinstein, *Perjury,* p. 579.

7. Alan Cullison interview with Nathaniel Weyl, Dec. 8, 1992.

8. FBI 74-1333-4670, interview with Nathaniel Weyl, Nov. 27, 1950; "true believer": Cullison interview with Weyl, Dec. 8, 1992.

9. AH cleared: see *NYT,* Oct. 29, 1992; Tanenhaus, "The Hiss Case Isn't Over Yet," *NYT,* Oct. 31, 1992; Volkogonov retraction: *NYT,* Dec. 17, 1992; researchers: Sergei Zhuravlev letter to Alan Cullison, n.d., c. January 1993 (in author's possession).

10. See Schmidt, "Behind the Scenes," p. 26. The Budapest archive also casts new light on Field's letter to AH, sent on July 21, 1957, in which Field offered to sign an affidavit challenging Hede Massing's testimony at the second trial—"false testimony by a perjured witness," in Field's words. Mrs. Schmidt found successive drafts of this letter in the Hiss dossier, which implies it had been screened by Communists. She comments: "It is clear from the Field file . . . that [his] every letter, statement, etc., was thoroughly reconstructed before [being] permitted to be sent out" (p. 28).

11. See memo on "SPA Survey," Sept. 25, 1946; "SPA Security Survey," Oct. 2, 1946; J. Anthony Panuch memo to AH et al., Oct. 2, 1946; Klaus memo of conversation with AH, Oct. 4, 1946; various memos "for the Files," Nov. 26, Nov. 27, Dec. 9, 1946; memo, Feb. 11, Feb. 24, 1947; undated, unsigned memo to the attorney general (probably March 1947); Charles M. Hulton letter to John Peurifoy, March 18, 1947. All documents are in Record Group 059 Lot 64D551, Box 103, Office Files of Samuel Klaus (NA); for a summary of the investigation, see Sam Tanenhaus, "New Reasons to Doubt Hiss," *The Wall Street Journal,* Nov. 18, 1993.

12. VENONA (no reference no.), March 30, 1945; for Yalta-Moscow, see Stettinius, *Roosevelt and the Russians,* pp. 30, 284–88; Weinstein, *Perjury,* p. 354; "leading": Andrew, *KGB,* pp. 286. Andrew (p. 287) identifies Akhmerov as AH's wartime handler.


## Interviews

Daniel Aaron, Mortimer J. Adler, James A. Bell, Pearl Bell, Robert Blount, Pat Buckley, William F. Buckley, Jr., John Chamberlain, John Chambers, John J. Danahy, Brad Darrach, Hope Hale Davis, Rodney Dawnkaski, Ralph de Toledano, Robert Doriss, Beril Edelman, Eva Eliel, Marlys Fuller Fixx, Clifford Forster, Judith Friedberg, Tom Griffith, John Hersey, John B. Judis, Joseph Kastner, Barbara Kerr, Hilton Kramer, Carol Levine, Ken McCormick, Samuel McNaughton, Murrey Marder, Robert Morris, Norman Podhoretz, Alfred Regnery, Henry Regnery, William A. Reuben, Victor Riesel,

Rabbi and Mrs. Harold Saperstein, Yetta Shachtman, Meyer Schapiro, Arthur Schlesinger, Jr., Maria Schmidt, Joseph Spieselman, Sol Stein, Vladmar Stern, Marylois Vega, Nathaniel Weyl, Roy Wiedersum, Garry Wills, and Henry Zolan.

I have not here included those—identified in the Notes and Acknowledgments—who provided information only by letter.

# Select Bibliography

PRINCIPAL PUBLISHED SOURCES QUOTED OR CITED

Chambers, Whittaker. *Cold Friday,* ed. and intro. Duncan Norton-Taylor. New York: Random House, 1964.

———. *Witness.* New York: Random House, 1952.

*Ghosts on the Roof: Selected Journalism of Whittaker Chambers, 1931–1959,* ed. Terry Teachout. Washington, D.C.: Regnery, 1989.

*Odyssey of a Friend: Whittaker Chambers' Letters to William F. Buckley, Jr., 1954–1961,* ed. William F. Buckley, Jr. New York: Putnam, 1969.

Aaron, Daniel. *Writers on the Left.* New York: Oxford University Press, 1977.

Abt, John. *Advocate and Activist: Memoirs of an American Communist Lawyer.* Urbana: University of Illinois Press, 1993.

Ambrose, Stephen E. *Nixon: The Education of a Politician, 1913–1962.* New York: Simon and Schuster, 1987.

Andrew, Christopher, and Oleg Gordievsky. *KGB: The Inside Story of Its Foreign Operations from Lenin to Gorbachev.* New York: HarperCollins, 1990.

Andrews, Bert, and Peter Andrews, *A Tragedy of History: A Journalist's Confidential Role in the Hiss-Chambers Case.* Washington, D.C.: R. B. Luce, 1962.

Bendiner, Robert. "The Trials of Alger Hiss." *The Nation* (June 11, 1949).

Bercovitch, Sacvan. *The American Jeremiad.* Madison: University of Wisconsin Press, 1978.

Bergreen, Laurence. *James Agee: A Life.* New York: Penguin, 1985.

Berle, Beatrice Bishop, and Travis Beal Jacobs, eds. *Navigating the Rapids, 1918–1971: From the Papers of Adolf A. Berle.* New York: Harcourt, 1973.

Bloor, Ella Reeve. *We Are Many, an Autobiography.* New York: International Publishers, 1940.

Buckley, William F., Jr. "The End of Whittaker Chambers." *Esquire* (September 1962).

Cannon, James P. *Notebook of an Agitator,* 2d ed. New York: Pathfinder, 1973.

Chamberlain, John. *A Life with the Printed Word*. Chicago: Regnery, 1982.

Cerf, Bennett. *At Random: The Reminiscences of Bennett Cerf*. New York: Random House, 1977.

Cook, Fred J. *The Unfinished Story of Alger Hiss*. New York: Morrow, 1958.

Cooke, Alistair. *A Generation on Trial: U.S.A. v. Alger Hiss*. New York: Knopf, 1950.

Davis, Hope Hale. *Great Day Coming: A Memoir of the 1930s*. South Royalton, Vt.: Steerforth Press, 1994.

De Toledano, Ralph. *Lament for a Generation*. New York: Farrar, Straus, 1960.

————, and Victor Lasky. *Seeds of Treason: The True Story of the Hiss-Chambers Tragedy*. New York: Funk & Wagnalls, 1950.

Donovan, Robert J. *The Tumultuous Years: The Presidency of Harry S Truman, 1949–1953*. New York: Norton, 1982.

Draper, Theodore. *American Communism and Soviet Russia: The Formative Period*. New York: Viking, 1960.

————. *The Roots of American Communism*. New York: Viking, 1957.

Elistratova, A. "The New Masses." *International Literature*, no. 1 (January 1932).

Elson, Robert T. *The World of Time Inc.: The Intimate History of a Publishing Enterprise, vol. 2, 1941–1960*. New York: Atheneum, 1968.

Fiedler, Leslie. A. *An End to Innocence: Essays on Culture and Politics*. Boston: Beacon Press, 1962.

First, Wesley, ed. *University on the Heights*. New York: Doubleday, 1969.

Fraser, Steve, and Gary Gerstle, eds. *The Rise and Fall of the New Deal Order, 1930–1980*. Princeton: Princeton University Press, 1989.

Gitlow, Benjamin. *I Confess: The Truth About American Communism*. New York: Dutton, 1939.

Goodman, Walter. *The Committee: The Extraordinary Career of the House Committee on Un-American Activities*. New York: Farrar, Straus, 1968.

Griffith, Thomas. *Harry and Teddy: The Turbulent Friendship of Press Lord Henry R. Luce and His Favorite Reporter, Theodore H. White*. New York: Random House, 1995.

Halper, Albert. *Good-bye, Union Square: A Writer's Memoir of the Thirties*. Chicago: Quadrangle, 1970.

Hersey, John. "Henry Luce's China Dream." *The New Republic* (May, 2, 1983).

Herzstein, Robert E. *Henry R. Luce: A Political Portrait of the Man Who Created the American Century*. New York: Scribner's, 1994.

Hiss, Alger. *In the Court of Public Opinion*. New York: Knopf, 1957.

————. *Recollections of a Life*. New York: Arcade, 1988.

Holmes, O. W., "The Soldier's Faith," *The Essential Holmes: Selections from the Letters, Speeches, Judicial Opinions, and Other Writings*, ed. and intro. Richard A. Posner. Chicago: University of Chicago Press, 1992.

Hook, Sidney. *Out of Step: An Unquiet Life in the 20th Century*. New York: Harper and Row, 1987.

"I Was In a Communist Unit with Hiss (interview with Nathaniel Weyl)." *U.S. News & World Report* (Jan. 9, 1953).

James, William. *The Varieties of Religious Experience*. New York: New American Library, 1958.

Judis, John B. *William F. Buckley, Jr.: Patron Saint of the Conservatives*. New York: Touchstone, 1990.

Kazin, Alfred. *New York Jew*. New York: Vintage, 1979.

Kempton, Murray. *Part of Our Time: Some Monuments and Ruins of the Thirties.* New York: Dell, 1967.

Klehr, Harvey. *The Heyday of American Communism: The Depression Decade.* New York: Basic Books, 1984.

————, John Earl Haynes, and Fridrikh Igorevich Firsov. *The Secret World of American Communism.* New Haven: Yale University Press, 1995.

Koestler, Arthur. *The Invisible Writing.* Boston: Beacon Press, 1955.

Krivitsky, W. G. *In Stalin's Secret Service.* New York: Harper, 1939.

Lamphere, Robert J., and Tom Shachtman. *The FBI-KGB War: A Special Agent's Story.* New York: Berkley, 1987.

Lasch, Christopher. *The True and Only Heaven.* New York: Norton, 1991.

Lenin, Nikolai [sic]. *The Soviets at Work: The International Position of the Russian Soviet Republic and the Fundamental Problems of the Socialist Revolution,* trans. Alexander Trachtenberg. New York: The Rand School of Social Science, 1918.

Lenin, V. I. *What Is to Be Done?: Burning Questions of Our Movement.* New York: International Publishers, 1986.

Levine, Isaac Don. *Eyewitness to History: Memoirs and Reflections of a Foreign Correspondent for Half a Century.* New York: Hawthorn, 1973.

Lewis, Flora. *Red Pawn: The Story of Noel Field.* New York: Doubleday, 1965.

Liebling, A. J. *The Press.* New York: Ballantine, 1961.

Marbury, William. *In the Catbird Seat.* Baltimore: Maryland Historical Society, 1988.

Massing, Hede. *This Deception.* New York: Duell, Sloan, and Pearce, 1951.

Matthews, T. S. *Angels Unaware: Twentieth Century Portraits.* Boston: Ticknor & Fields, 1985.

————. *Name and Address: An Autobiography.* New York: Simon and Schuster, 1960.

Mazo, Earl. *Richard Nixon: A Political and Personal Portrait.* New York: Harper, 1959.

Morris, Roger. *Richard Milhous Nixon: The Rise of an American Politician.* New York: Holt, 1990.

Nash, George H. *The Conservative Intellectual Movement in America Since 1945.* New York: Basic Books, 1976.

Nixon, Richard. *Six Crises.* New York: Simon and Schuster, 1990.

Oshinsky, David M. *A Conspiracy So Immense: The World of Joe McCarthy.* New York: Free Press, 1983.

Pilat, Oliver. "Report on Whittaker Chambers." *New York Post,* June 14–15, 1969.

Pruessen, Ronald W. *John Foster Dulles: The Road to Power.* New York: Free Press, 1982.

Reeves, Thomas C. *The Life and Times of Joe McCarthy.* New York: Stein and Day, 1982.

Sancton, Thomas. "The Case of Alger Hiss." *The Nation* (September 4, 1948).

Schlesinger, Arthur M., Jr. *The Coming of the New Deal.* Boston: Houghton Mifflin, 1959.

Schwarz, Jordan A. *Liberal: Adolf A. Berle and the Vision of an American Era.* New York: Free Press, 1989.

Smith, John Chabot. *Alger Hiss: The True Story.* New York: Holt, 1976.

Stettinius, Edward R. *Roosevelt and the Russians: The Yalta Conference,* ed. Walter Johnson. Garden City, N.Y.: Doubleday, 1949.

Stone, I. F. *The Truman Era, 1945–1952: A Nonconformist History of Our Times.* Boston: Little, Brown, 1972.

Stripling, Robert E. *The Red Plot Against America,* ed. Bob Considine. New York: Arno Press, 1977.

Swanberg, W. A. *Luce and His Empire.* New York: Dell, 1973.

Trilling, Diana. *The Beginning of the Journey.* New York: Harcourt, 1993.

Trilling, Lionel. *The Middle of the Journey.* New York: Harcourt, 1975.

Ulanovskaya, Nadezhda, and Maya Ulanovskaya, *Istoriia Odnoi Semyi* (The Story of One Family). Benson, Vt.: Chalidze, 1982.

Van Doren, Mark. *The Autobiography of Mark Van Doren.* New York: Harcourt, 1958.

Volkogonov, Dmitri. *Stalin: Triumph and Tragedy,* ed. and trans. Harold Shukman. New York: Grove Weidenfeld, 1991.

Wadleigh, Julian. "Why I Spied for the Communists," *New York Post,* July 11–24, 1949.

Waldman, Louis. *Labor Lawyer.* New York: Dutton, 1944.

Weinstein, Allen. "Nadya—A Spy Story." *Encounter* (June 1977).

———. "Nixon vs. Hiss." *Esquire* (November 1975).

———. *Perjury: The Hiss-Chambers Case.* New York: Knopf, 1978.

White, E. B. "Noontime of an Advertising Man." *The New Yorker* (June 6, 1949).

White, Theodore H. *In Search of History: A Personal Adventure.* New York: Warner, 1978.

Wills, Garry. *Confessions of a Conservative.* New York: Doubleday, 1979.

———. *Nixon Agonistes: The Crisis of the Self-Made Man.* New York: New American Library, 1971.

Wolfe, Bertram D. *A Life in Two Centuries.* New York: Stein and Day, 1981.

Zeligs, Meyer A., M.D. *Friendship and Fratricide: An Analysis of Whittaker Chambers and Alger Hiss.* New York: Viking, 1967.

## Acknowledgments

I owe thanks to many who offered invaluable assistance in the writing of this book. Three researchers supplied me with materials and at times initiated their own investigations. Alan Cullison, now of the Associated Press, spent six months in Moscow in 1992–1993, prying secret documents out of the KGB and gathering additional material from the Russian Center for the Preservation and Study of Documents Relating to Modern History (formerly the Central Party Archives). Maura Doherty diligently ran down leads on books and articles and thoroughly researched Laha Whittaker's theatrical career. Marcia Kurop located many useful documents, particularly on the early history of the Chambers and Whittaker families.

I'm grateful also to those scholars and writers who generously shared their research with me or otherwise loaned their expertise to the project: Daniel Aaron, James Atlas, Bruce Craig, John Fox, David Halberstam, Edward Jones, John B. Judis, Harvey Klehr, Stephen Koch, Patricia Neils, William A. Reuben, Herbert Romerstein, Michael Scammell, Scott Stanfield, Maria Schmidt, David Tanenhaus, Terry Teachout, Alan Wald, Allen Weinstein, and Douglas Wixson.

I thank too friends of Chambers's who loaned me materials from their own collections: William F. Buckley, Jr., Ralph de Toledano, Fred Gruin, Eugene Meyer, the late Henry Regnery, the late Meyer Schapiro, and Henry Zolan.

And thanks to others who provided information or made it available to me: Timothy Anderson, Martin Baldessari (photos), Lawrence Campbell, Robert Cowley, Rodney and Diane Dawnkaski, Robert Doriss, Lizzie Edgeworth, Vincent Fitzpatrick, Marlys Fuller Fixx, Dana Gioia, the late Harold Harris, Margaret Hopkins, John Hunt, Tony Judt, Hugh Kenner, Hilton Kramer, Sadie Krieger, Elinor Langer, Samuel McNaughton, Robert L. Morris, Sen. Daniel Patrick Moynihan, Arthur Mattson, Mrs. Barrows Mussey, William Phillips, Svetlana Rozovsky, Dorothy Sterling, the late Diana Trilling, Charles Van Doren, Alan Wald, Dorothy Zaiser, Sergei Zhuravlev, and the late Paul Zukofsky.

A list of those interviewed for this book appears at the end of the Notes.

I am grateful as well to those who answered questions by letter: Jacques Barzun, Carl D. Brandt, Alistair Cooke, Theodore Draper, Robert Doriss, Eve Davidson, Rosina Florio, John Scott Fones, Fred Gruin, Fay Jacoby, Sidney James, Oleg Kalugin, Murray Kempton, Robert Lamphere, Czeslaw Milosz, Frances Mullady, the late T. S. Matthews, the late Richard Nixon, the late Diana Trilling, Douglas Wixson, and Ella (Mrs. Bertram) Wolfe.

I was assisted by staff at the following institutions and sites: Emily Balch Collection (Philadelphia); Boston University (Mugar Library); Brandeis University; Carroll County (Maryland) Historical Association; City College of New York Library; Columbia University (Columbiana Collection; Rare Book and Manuscript Collection); Drexel University (Philadelphia); Edinburgh University Library; Federal Bureau of Investigation (Freedom Of Information Act Reading Room, in Washington, D.C.); Harvard University (Houghton Library; Law School Library); Hoover Institution on War, Revolution, and Peace; Humanities Research Center (Austin, Texas); Hofstra University (Long Island Historical Society); Lynbrook (Long Island) Historical Society; Maret School (Washington, D.C.); University of Michigan, Ann Arbor (Labadie Collection); Milwaukee County Historical Society; Milwaukee Public Library; *National Review;* Museum of Television and Radio (New York City); Newberry Library (Chicago); New York Public Library (Special Collections); Richard Nixon Library and Birthplace (Yorba Linda, California); New York University (Tamiment Collection); Notre Dame University (Hesburgh Library); Racine (Wisconsin) Historical Society; National Archives (Washington, D.C.); University of Oregon (Knight Library); Philadelphia Research Library; Franklin D. Roosevelt Library; University of South Carolina (South Caroliniana Library); South Side High School (Rockville Centre, Long Island); Syracuse University; Time Inc. Archives; Harry S Truman Library; Wisconsin Historical Society (Madison); Yale University (Beinecke Library; Sterling Library).

I record a special debt to David de Lorenzo (Curator of Manuscripts and Archives at the Harvard Law School Library); Hollee Haswell (head of the Columbiana Room); and the efficient and indulgent staff of the Warner Library in Tarrytown, New York.

I thank Paula Edelson, Thomas Hinds, Abigail Meisel, and Robert Salter—all friends who pitched in when the need arose. Family members—especially Pat Bonomi, Jack Bonomi, John Bonomi, Gussie Tanenhaus, and Bill Winsten—also provided help.

I am indebted to Greg Tobin for encouraging me to write a proposal for a Chambers biography and then finding me an agent, Jane Cushman, who remained an abundant source of wit and good humor even as the project dragged into its seventh year. My editor at Random House, Bob Loomis, steered the project through with calm mastery. His associate Barbé Hammer solved many problems along the way.

I could not have seen this job through without the assistance of a number of organizations that provided needed funds at critical moments. I thank Lynne Cheney and George Lucas, both formerly of the National Endowment for the Humanities; James Piereson of the John M. Olin Foundation (and the late Samuel Lipman, one of its advisers); Antony Sullivan of the Earhart Foundation; Dino Pionzi of the Historical Research Foundation; and Thomas Bolan of the Educational Reviewer.

Not one of these individuals or their colleagues ever asked to see the manuscript in progress or sought to influence the course my research followed or the conclusions I reached.

Special thanks are owed to William F. Buckley, Jr., who came to my aid more often than I can possibly remember but always maintained a tactful distance from my work. My thanks as well to John Chambers, my subject's son, who generously sat for interviews. Scott Stanfield gave the final manuscript an exacting read.

My deepest gratitude goes to the three people to whom this book is dedicated: my late father, who died long before I undertook this project but was its first inspiration; my wife, Kathy Bonomi, who solved research puzzles, read the manuscript with penetrating insight, and served throughout as my sounding board and conscience; and our daughter Lydia, whose young life began in the middle of this journey and has enriched it beyond description.

My deepest thanks also to Old Street for publishing this new and more complete edition of the book. Elena Lappin, my editor at Old Street, shepherded the introduction through its various drafts and also had the good idea to add many more photographs, which Jeff Roth, my colleague at the New York Times, located in the newspaper's remarkable morgue.

# Index

reputation of, 213, 214, 228, 245, 254, 283, 330–31, 400; targets of, 213, 214; Thomas as chairman of, 206; and Truman, 213–14, 227–28, 275, 279, 283, 287, 315, 324, 334; and typewriter, 376; and verdict in first perjury trial, 412; and White's (Harry Dexter) death, 254, 255. *See also specific witness or committee member*
Howe, Irving, 463
Huebsch, Ben, 342*n*
Hughes, Emmet, 445, 447, 448
Hughes, Langston, 73–74, 75, 99
Hugo, Victor, 11–12, 18, 465
Hull, Cordell, 129, 294, 313, 369
humanism: and Chambers as humanist, 500; and humanist revolutionaries, 44; rationalistic, 469*n*
Hungary, 50, 95, 190, 191, 518–19
Hutchins, Grace, 66, 342, 457
Hutchinson, Gertrude, 61
Hyde, Douglas, 473
Hyland, Tom, 449, 473, 474

Ickes, Harold, 162
Ikal, Arnold, 107, 122, 126–31, 134, 139, 142, 146, 158, 284, 294, 296
Ikal, Ruth Braman, 127, 128, 129–30, 162
*In the Court of Public Opinion* (Hiss), 496–97, 498
"In Egypt Land" (Chambers), 196–97
"In Memory of R.G." (Chambers), 41
industrial espionage, 115. *See also* GRU
Industrial Workers of the World ("Wobblies"), 49, 53
informant, Chambers as: and Bentley testimonies, 206, 210, 212, 217, 218, 220, 221; and Chambers's lies, 207, 216; and Chambers's motives, 284, 304; Chambers's views about, 204, 206–8, 210, 212, 214; and Chambers's writings, 207; and collaboration of Chambers's allegations, 204, 206, 218, 220, 221; and FBI interviews, 203, 206–7, 222; fears of, 212, 214, 283–84; and McCarran Committee, 456–57; and McCarthy, 453–55; and Murphy interviews, 203, 206, 208; and Nazi-Soviet Pact, 220; and Schlesinger interview, 207. *See also* Berle, Adolf A., Jr.: Chambers's meetings with; House Un-American Activities Committee

Inslerman, Felix, 112–13, 136, 148, 304, 318, 318*n*, 340
Institute of Pacific Relations (IPR), 454, 456
intellectuals: Chambers's writings about, 166–67; as dilettantes, 167; as liberals, 166–67; and McCarthy, 455; and New Deal, 97, 467; in 1930s, 73–74, 167; and Sacco and Vanzetti, 467; and *Witness*, 463, 470. *See also specific person*
International Labor Defense, 57
International Ladies Garment Workers Union, 65
International Workers Order, 79, 127
Into, Henry, 474, 484, 491
Intrator, Michael "Mike," 63, 285; and Chambers as agent, 80; and Chambers's defection, 132–33; and Chambers's doubts about communism, 117; Chambers meets, 59; at *Daily Worker,* 59; and first perjury trial, 343; as homosexual, 342–43; and Lumpkin, 65, 66, 66*n;* marriage of, 66; purge of, 67; and Solow-Chambers relationship, 132–33
"Is Academic Freedom in Danger" (Chambers), 478
Italy, 111, 510

Jacoby, Annalee, 185
James, Hubert E., 346, 409, 410, 411, 412*n*
Japan, 100–102, 102*n*, 111
Jeffries, Cynthia, 509
Jessup, Philip, 242, 374
Jews, 19, 22–23, 42, 51, 213
John Reed Club, 65, 69, 73, 75, 99, 141
Johnston, Joseph, 225
Jones, Hugh. *See* Chambers, Whittaker: names of
Joyce, James, 30, 42, 155–56
Justice Department, U.S.: and Baltimore Papers, 296, 298, 299, 352; and Berle's HUAC testimony, 280; Chambers's views about, 287–88; dropping of inquiry by, 296–97; and HUAC, 275, 305, 308–10, 317, 321–22, 412; and McCarthy, 479; and Pumpkin Papers, 303, 305, 310, 321–22. *See also* first perjury trial; New York grand jury; second perjury trial; *specific person*

*About the Author*

SAM TANENHAUS is the author of *Literature Unbound: A Guide for the Common Reader.* His articles and essays have appeared in *The New York Times, The Wall Street Journal, The American Scholar, Commentary,* and other publications. During the writing of this book he received a three-year grant from the National Endowment for the Humanities. He lives in Tarrytown, New York, with his wife and daughter.

*About the Type*

This book was set in Bembo, a typeface based on an old-style Roman face that was used for Cardinal Bembo's tract *De Aetna* in 1495. Bembo was cut by Francisco Griffo in the early sixteenth century. The Lanston Monotype Machine Company of Philadelphia brought the well-proportioned letterforms of Bembo to the United States in the 1930s.